THE
PREACHER'S
OUTLINE & SERMON
BIBLE®

1 SAMUEL

THE PREACHER'S OUTLINE & SERMON BIBLE®

OLD TESTAMENT

KING JAMES VERSION

Leadership Ministries Worldwide
Chattanooga, TN

THE PREACHER'S OUTLINE & SERMON BIBLE® 1 SAMUEL

KING JAMES VERSION

Please address all requests for information or permission to:
Leadership Ministries Worldwide
Ph.# (800) 987-8790 E-Mail: info@lmw.org
Web: lmw.org

Library of Congress Catalog Card Number: 96-75921
ISBN Softbound Edition: 978-1-57407-162-7

Printed in the United States of America

DEDICATED

To all the men and women of the world who preach and teach the Gospel of our Lord Jesus Christ and to the Mercy and Grace of God

&

- Demonstrated to us in Christ Jesus our Lord.

  "In whom we have redemption through His blood, the forgiveness of sins, according to the riches of His grace." (Ep.1:7)

- Out of the mercy and grace of God, His Word has flowed. Let every person know that God will have mercy upon him, forgiving and using him to fulfill His glorious plan of salvation.

  "For God so loved the world, that he gave His only begotten Son, that whosoever believeth in Him should not perish, but have everlasting life. For God sent not his son into the world to condemn the world, but that the world through him might be saved." (Jn.3:16-17)

  "For this is good and acceptable in the sight of God our Saviour; who will have all men to be saved, and to come unto the knowledge of the truth." (1 Ti.2:3-4)

10/22

The Preacher's Outline & Sermon Bible®

is written for God's servants to use in their study, teaching, and preaching of God's Holy Word...

- to share the Word of God with the world.
- to help believers, both ministers and laypersons, in their understanding, preaching, and teaching of God's Word.
- to do everything we possibly can to lead men, women, boys, and girls to give their hearts and lives to Jesus Christ and to secure the eternal life that He offers.
- to do all we can to minister to the needy of the world.
- to give Jesus Christ His proper place, the place the Word gives Him. Therefore, no work of Leadership Ministries Worldwide will ever be personalized.

ACKNOWLEDGMENTS AND BIBLIOGRAPHY

Every child of God is precious to the Lord and deeply loved. And every child as a servant of the Lord touches the lives of those who come in contact with him or his ministry. The writing ministries of the following servants have touched this work, and we are grateful that God brought their writings our way. We hereby acknowledge their ministries to us, being fully aware that there are so many others down through the years whose writings have touched our lives and who deserve mention, but the weaknesses of our minds have caused them to fade from memory. May our wonderful Lord continue to bless the ministry of these dear servants, and the ministry of us all as we diligently labor to reach the world for Christ and to meet the desperate needs of those who suffer so much.

THE REFERENCE WORKS

Archer, Gleason L. Jr. *A Survey of Old Testament Introduction*. Chicago, IL: Moody Bible Institute of Chicago, 1974.

Atlas of the World. Hammond Concise Edition. Maplewood, NJ: Hammond Inc., 1993.

Baker's Dictionary of Theology. Everett F. Harrison, Editor-in-Chief. Grand Rapids, MI: Baker Book House, 1960.

Barker, William P. *Everyone in the Bible*. Westwood, NJ: Fleming H. Revell Co., 1966.

Brown, Francis. *The New Brown-Driver-Briggs-Gesenius Hebrew-English Lexicon*. Peabody, MA: Hendrickson Publishers, 1979.

Cruden's Complete Concordance of the Old & New Testament. Philadelphia, PA: The John C. Winston Co., 1930.

Dake, Finis Jennings. *Dake's Annotated Reference Bible, The Holy Bible*. Lawrenceville, GA: Dake Bible Sales, Inc., 1963.

Easton's 1897 Bible Dictionary. Database NavPress Software, 1996.

Enhanced Nave's Topics. Database NavPress Software, 1991, 1994.

Funk & Wagnalls Standard Desk Dictionary. Lippincott & Crowell, Publishers, 1980, Vol.2.

Geisler, Norman. *A Popular Survey of the Old Testament*. Grand Rapids, MI: Baker Book House, 1977.

Good News Bible. Old Testament: © American Bible Society, 1976. New Testament: © American Bible Society, 1966, 1971, 1976. Collins World.

Good News for Modern Man, the New Testament. New York, NY: American Bible Society, 1971.

Goodrick, Edward W. and John R. Kohlenberger, III. *The NIV Exhaustive Concordance*. Grand Rapids, MI: Zondervan Publishing House, 1990.

Harrison, Roland Kenneth. *Introduction to the Old Testament*. Grand Rapids, MI: Eerdmans Publishing Co., 1969.

Holman Bible Dictionary. Nashville, TN: Broadman & Holman Publishers, 1991. Database NavPress Software.

Josephus, Flavius. *Complete Works*. Grand Rapids, MI: Kregel Publications, 1981.

Kipfer, Barbara Ann, Ph.D. *Roget's 21st Century Thesaurus*. New York, NY: Dell Publishing, 1992.

Kohlenberger, John R. III. *The Interlinear NIV Hebrew-English Old Testament*. Grand Rapids, MI: Zondervan Publishing House, 1987.

Kouffman, Donald T. *The Dictionary of Religious Terms*. Westwood, NJ: Fleming H. Revell Co., 1967.

Life Application® Bible. Wheaton, IL: Tyndale House Publishers, Inc., 1991.

Life Application® Study Bible. New International Version. Tyndale House Publishers, Inc.: Wheaton, IL 1991, and Zondervan Publishing House: Grand Rapids, MI, 1984.

Lindsell, Harold and Woodbridge, Charles J. *A Handbook of Christian Truth*. Westwood, NJ: Fleming H. Revell Company, A Division of Baker Book House, 1953.

Living Quotations For Christians. Edited by Sherwood Eliot Wirt and Kersten Beckstrom. New York, NY: Harper & Row, Publishers, 1974.

Lockyer, Herbert. *All the Books and Chapters of the Bible*. Grand Rapids, MI: Zondervan Publishing House, 1966.

——. *All the Men of the Bible*. Grand Rapids, MI: Zondervan Publishing House, 1958.

——. *All the Miracles of the Bible*. Grand Rapids, MI: Zondervan Publishing House, 1961.

——. *All the Parables of the Bible*. Grand Rapids, MI: Zondervan Publishing House, 1963.

——. *The Women of the Bible*. Grand Rapids, MI: Zondervan Publishing House, 1967.

Martin, Alfred. *Survey of the Scriptures*, Part I, II, III. Chicago, IL: Moody Bible Institute of Chicago, 1961.

McDowell, Josh. *Evidence That Demands A Verdict*, Vol.1. San Bernardino, CA: Here's Life Publishers, Inc., 1979.

Miller, Madeleine S. & J. Lane. *Harper's Bible Dictionary*. New York, NY: Harper & Row Publishers, 1961.

Nave, Orville J. *Nave's Topical Bible*. Nashville, TN: The Southwestern Company. Copyright © by J.B. Henderson, 1921.

Nelson's Complete Book of Bible Maps & Charts. Nashville, TN: Thomas Nelson Publishers, Inc., 1996.

New American Standard Bible, Reference Edition. La Habra, CA: The Lockman Foundation, 1975.

New American Standard Bible, Updated Edition. La Habra, CA: The Lockman Foundation, 1995.

New Bible Dictionary, 3rd Edition. Leicester, England: Universities & Colleges Christian Fellowship, 1996.

New International Version Study Bible. Grand Rapids, MI: Zondervan Bible Publishers, 1985.

New Living Translation, Holy Bible. Wheaton, IL: Tyndale House Publishers, Inc., 1996.

Orr, William. *How We May Know That God Is*. Wheaton, IL: Van Kampen Press, n.d.

Owens, John Joseph. *Analytical Key to the Old Testament*, Vols.1, 2, 3. Grand Rapids, MI: Baker Book House, 1989.

Payne, J. Barton. *Encyclopedia of Biblical Prophecy*. New York, NY: Harper & Row, Publishers, 1973.

Pilgrim Edition, Holy Bible. New York, NY: Oxford University Press, 1952.

Ridout, Samuel. *Lectures on the Tabernacle*. New York, NY: Loizeaux Brothers, Inc., 1914.

Smith, William. *Smith's Bible Dictionary*. Peabody, MA: Hendrickson Publishers, n.d.

Stone, Nathan J. *Names of God*. Chicago, IL: Moody Press, 1944.

Strong, James. *Strong's Exhaustive Concordance of the Bible*. Nashville, TN: Thomas Nelson, Inc., 1990.

——. *The Tabernacle Of Israel*. Grand Rapids, MI: Kregel Publications, 1987.

Strong's Greek and Hebrew Dictionary as compiled by iExalt Software. Database NavPress Software, 1990-1993.

The Amplified Bible. Scripture taken from THE AMPLIFIED BIBLE, Old Testament copyright © 1965, 1987 by the Zondervan Publishing House. The Amplified New Testament copyright © 1958, 1987 by The Lockman Foundation. Used by permission.

The Evangelical Dictionary of Theology. Elwell, Walter A., Editor. Grand Rapids, MI: Baker Book House, 1984.

The Hebrew-Greek Key Study Bible, New International Version. Spiros Zodhiates, Th.D., Executive Editor. Chattanooga, TN: AMG Publishers, 1996.

The Holy Bible in Four Translations. Minneapolis, MN: Worldwide Publications. Copyright © The Iversen-Norman Associates: New York, NY, 1972.

The Interlinear Bible, Vols.1, 2, 3. Translated by Jay P. Green, Sr. Grand Rapids, MI: Baker Book House, 1976.

The International Standard Bible Encyclopaedia, Edited by James Orr. Grand Rapids, MI: Eerdmans Publishing Co., 1939.

The NASB Greek/Hebrew Dictionary and Concordance. La Habra, CA: The Lockman Foundation, 1988.

The Nelson Study Bible, New King James Version. Nashville, TN: Thomas Nelson Publishers, Inc., 1997.

The New Compact Bible Dictionary. Edited by T. Alton Bryant. Grand Rapids, MI: Zondervan Publishing House, 1967. Used by permission of Zondervan Publishing House.

The New Scofield Reference Bible. Edited by C.I. Scofield. New York, NY: Oxford University Press, 1967.

The New Thompson Chain Reference Bible. Indianapolis, IN: B.B. Kirkbride Bible Co., Inc., 1964.

The New Unger's Bible Dictionary. Chicago, IL: Moody Press, 1998. Database NavPress Software, 1997.

The NIV Study Bible, New International Version. Grand Rapids, MI: Zondervan Publishing House, 1985.

The Open Bible. Nashville, TN: Thomas Nelson Publishers, 1975.

The Quest Study Bible. New International Version. Grand Rapids, MI: Zondervan Publishing House, 1994.

The Zondervan Pictorial Encyclopedia of the Bible, Vol.1. Merrill C. Tenney, Editor. Grand Rapids, MI: Zondervan Publishing House, 1982.

Theological Wordbook of the Old Testament. Edited by R. Laird Harris. Chicago, IL: Moody Bible Institute of Chicago, 1980.

Unger, Merrill F. & William White, Jr. *Nelson's Expository Dictionary of the Old Testament*. Nashville, TN: Thomas Nelson Publishers, 1980.

W.E. Vine, Merrill F. Unger, William White, Jr. *Vine's Complete Expository Dictionary of Old and New Testament Words*. Nashville, TN: Thomas Nelson Publishers, 1985.

Webster's Seventh New Collegiate Dictionary. Springfield, MA: G. & C. Merriam Company, Publishers, 1971.

Wilmington. Harold L. *The Outline Bible*. Wheaton, IL: Tyndale House Publishers, Inc., 1999.

Wilson, William. *Wilson's Old Testament Word Studies*. McLean, VA: MacDonald Publishing Company, n.d.

Wood, Leon. *A Survey of Israel's History*. Grand Rapids, MI: Zondervan Publishing House, 1982.

Young, Edward J. *An Introduction to the Old Testament*. Grand Rapids, MI: Eerdmans Publishing Co., 1964.

Young, Robert. *Young's Analytical Concordance to the Bible*. Grand Rapids, MI: Eerdmans Publishing Co., n.d.

Zondervan NIV Bible Library. Version 2.5. Grand Rapids, MI: Zondervan Publishing House.

THE COMMENTARIES

Archer, Gleason L. *Encyclopedia of Bible Difficulties*. Grand Rapids, MI: Zondervan, 1982.

Baldwin, Joyce G. *1 & 2 Samuel*. "The Tyndale Old Testament Commentaries." Downers Grove, IL: Inter-Varsity Press, 1988.

Barnes' Notes, Exodus to Esther. F.C. Cook, Editor. Grand Rapids, MI: Baker Book House, n.d.

Bergen, Robert D. *1, 2 Samuel*. "The New American Commentary," Vol.7. Nashville, TN: Broadman & Holman Publishers, 1996.

Burroughs, P.E., D.D. *Old Testament Studies*. Nashville, TN: Sunday School Board, Southern Baptist Convention, 1915.

Chafin, Kenneth. *The Preacher's Commentary on 1, 2 Samuel*. Nashville, TN: Word Publishing, 1989, 2003.

Crockett, William Day. *A Harmony of Samuel, Kings, and Chronicles*. Grand Rapids, MI: Baker Book House, 1985.

Evans, Mary J. *1 and 2 Samuel*. "New International Biblical Commentary." Peabody, MA: Hendrickson Publishers, Inc., 2000.

Gill, John. *Gill's Commentary*, Vol.1. Grand Rapids, MI: Baker Book House, 1980.

Henry, Matthew. *Matthew Henry's Commentary*, 6 Vols. Old Tappan, NJ: Fleming H. Revell Co., n.d.

Humphreys, W. Lee. *The Tragedy of King Saul: A Study of the Structure of 1 Samuel 9 – 31*. Sheffield: JSOT Press 6, 1978.

Keil-Delitzsch. *Commentary on the Old Testament*, Vol.2. Grand Rapids, MI: Eerdmans Publishing Co., n.d.

Longman, T., III and D.G. Reid. *God Is a Warrior*. Grand Rapids, MI: Zondervan Publishing House, 1966.

Maclaren, Alexander. *Expositions of Holy Scripture*, 11 Vols. Grand Rapids, MI: Eerdmans Publishing Co., 1952-59.

McCarter, P. Kyle, Jr. *1 Samuel*. "The Anchor Bible." Garden City, NY: Doubleday & Company, Inc., 1980.

McGee, J. Vernon. *Thru The Bible*, Vol.2. Nashville, TN: Thomas Nelson Publishers, 1981.

Morgan, G. Campbell. *Living Messages of the Books of the Bible*, Vol.1. Old Tappan, NJ: Fleming H. Revell, 1912.

Newsome, James D., Jr. *1 Samuel, 2 Samuel*. Atlanta, GA: John Knox Press, 1982.

Payne, D.F. *I and II Samuel*, DSB. Philadelphia, PA: Westminster Press, 1982.

Philip, James. *The Preacher's Commentary on Numbers*. Nashville, TN: Word Publishing, 1987, 2003.

Poole, Matthew. *Matthew Poole's Commentary on the Holy Bible*. Peabody, MA: Hendrickson Publishers, n.d.

ACKNOWLEDGMENTS AND BIBLIOGRAPHY
THE COMMENTARIES (continued)

Spurgeon, C.H. *Spurgeon's Sermon Notes. Genesis to Malachi*. Westwood, NJ: Fleming H. Revell Co., n.d.

Swindoll, Charles R. *A Man of Passion & Destiny, David*. Dallas, TX: Word Publishing, Inc., 1997.

The Interpreter's Bible, 12 Vols. New York, NY: Abingdon Press, 1956.

The Pulpit Commentary. 23 Vols. Edited by H.D.M. Spence & Joseph S. Exell. Grand Rapids, MI: Eerdmans Publishing Co., 1950.

Walvoord, John F. and Roy B. Zuck, Editors. *The Bible Knowledge Commentary*. Colorado Springs, CO: Chariot Victor Publishing, 1985.

Wiersbe, Warren W. *Be Available*. Colorado Springs, CO: Victor Books, 1994.

——. *Be Successful*. Colorado Springs, CO: Victor Books, 2001.

Wolf, Herbert, ed. *Judges*. "The Expositor's Bible Commentary," Vol.3. Grand Rapids, MI: Zondervan Publishing House, 1992.

Wood, Leon. *Distressing Days of the Judges*. Eugene, OR: Wips & Stock Publishers, 1998.

Youngblood, Ronald F. *1 Samuel*. "The Expositor's Bible Commentary," Vol.3. Grand Rapids, MI: Zondervan Publishing House, 1990.

ABBREVIATIONS

&	= and		O.T.	= Old Testament
Bc.	= because		p./pp.	= page/pages
Concl.	= conclusion		Pt.	= point
Cp.	= compare		Quest.	= question
Ct.	= contrast		Rel.	= religion
e.g.	= for example		Rgt.	= righteousness
f.	= following		Thru	= through
Illust.	= illustration		v./vv.	= verse/verses
N.T.	= New Testament		vs.	= versus

THE BOOKS OF THE OLD TESTAMENT

Book	Abbreviation	Chapters	Book	Abbreviation	Chapters
GENESIS	Gen. or Ge.	50	Ecclesiastes	Eccl. or Ec.	12
Exodus	Ex.	40	The Song of Solomon	S. of Sol. or Song	8
Leviticus	Lev. or Le.	27	Isaiah	Is.	66
Numbers	Num. or Nu.	36	Jeremiah	Jer. or Je.	52
Deuteronomy	Dt. or De.	34	Lamentations	Lam.	5
Joshua	Josh. or Jos.	24	Ezekiel	Ezk. or Eze.	48
Judges	Judg. or Jud.	21	Daniel	Dan. or Da.	12
Ruth	Ruth or Ru.	4	Hosea	Hos. or Ho.	14
1 Samuel	1 Sam. or 1 S.	31	Joel	Joel	3
2 Samuel	2 Sam. or 2 S.	24	Amos	Amos or Am.	9
1 Kings	1 Ki. or 1 K.	22	Obadiah	Obad. or Ob.	1
2 Kings	2 Ki. or 2 K.	25	Jonah	Jon. or Jona.	4
1 Chronicles	1 Chron. or 1 Chr.	29	Micah	Mic. or Mi.	7
2 Chronicles	2 Chron. or 2 Chr.	36	Nahum	Nah. or Na.	3
Ezra	Ezra or Ezr.	10	Habakkuk	Hab.	3
Nehemiah	Neh. or Ne.	13	Zephaniah	Zeph. or Zep.	3
Esther	Est.	10	Haggai	Hag.	2
Job	Job or Jb.	42	Zechariah	Zech. or Zec.	14
Psalms	Ps.	150	Malachi	Mal.	4
Proverbs	Pr.	31			

THE BOOKS OF THE NEW TESTAMENT

Book	Abbreviation	Chapters	Book	Abbreviation	Chapters
MATTHEW	Mt.	28	1 Timothy	1 Tim. or 1 Ti.	6
Mark	Mk.	16	2 Timothy	2 Tim. or 2 Ti.	4
Luke	Lk. or Lu.	24	Titus	Tit.	3
John	Jn.	21	Philemon	Phile. or Phm.	1
The Acts	Acts or Ac.	28	Hebrews	Heb. or He.	13
Romans	Ro.	16	James	Jas. or Js.	5
1 Corinthians	1 Cor. or 1 Co.	16	1 Peter	1 Pt. or 1 Pe.	5
2 Corinthians	2 Cor. or 2 Co.	13	2 Peter	2 Pt. or 2 Pe.	3
Galatians	Gal. or Ga.	6	1 John	1 Jn.	5
Ephesians	Eph. or Ep.	6	2 John	2 Jn.	1
Philippians	Ph.	4	3 John	3 Jn.	1
Colossians	Col.	4	Jude	Jude	1
1 Thessalonians	1 Th.	5	Revelation	Rev. or Re.	22
2 Thessalonians	2 Th.	3			

HOW TO USE
The Preacher's Outline & Sermon Bible®
Follow these easy steps to gain maximum benefit from The POSB.

① SUBJECT HEADING

② MAJOR POINTS

③ SUBPOINTS
&
SCRIPTURE

④ COMMENTARY

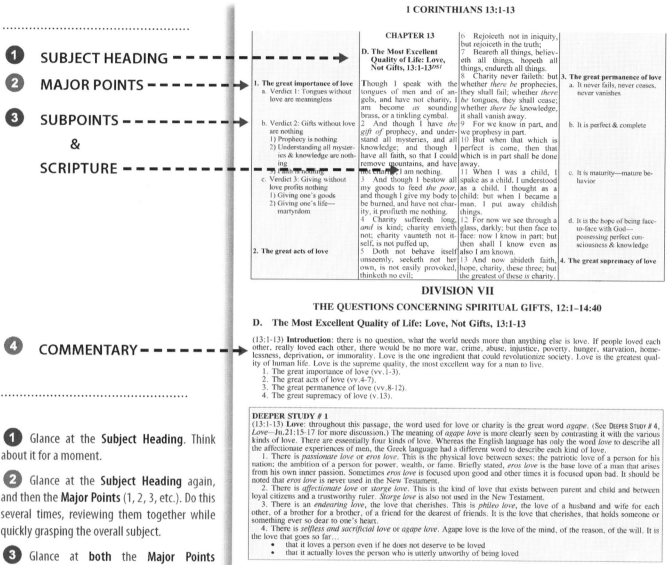

1 CORINTHIANS 13:1-13

CHAPTER 13

D. The Most Excellent Quality of Life: Love, Not Gifts, 13:1-13[DS1]

1. The great importance of love
   a. Verdict 1: Tongues without love are meaningless

   b. Verdict 2: Gifts without love are nothing
      1) Prophecy is nothing
      2) Understanding all mysteries & knowledge are nothing
      3) Faith is nothing
   c. Verdict 3: Giving without love profits nothing
      1) Giving one's goods
      2) Giving one's life—martyrdom

2. The great acts of love

Though I speak with the tongues of men and of angels, and have not charity, I am become as sounding brass, or a tinkling cymbal.
2 And though I have the gift of prophecy, and understand all mysteries, and all knowledge; and though I have all faith, so that I could remove mountains, and have not charity, I am nothing.
3 And though I bestow all my goods to feed the poor, and though I give my body to be burned, and have not charity, it profiteth me nothing.
4 Charity suffereth long, and is kind; charity envieth not; charity vaunteth not itself, is not puffed up,
5 Doth not behave itself unseemly, seeketh not her own, is not easily provoked, thinketh no evil;

6 Rejoiceth not in iniquity, but rejoiceth in the truth;
7 Beareth all things, believeth all things, hopeth all things, endureth all things.
8 Charity never faileth: but whether there be prophecies, they shall fail; whether there be tongues, they shall cease; whether there be knowledge, it shall vanish away.
9 For we know in part, and we prophesy in part.
10 But when that which is perfect is come, then that which is in part shall be done away.
11 When I was a child, I spake as a child, I understood as a child, I thought as a child: but when I became a man, I put away childish things.
12 For now we see through a glass, darkly; but then face to face: now I know in part; but then shall I know even as also I am known.
13 And now abideth faith, hope, charity, these three; but the greatest of these is charity.

3. The great permanence of love
   a. It never fails, never ceases, never vanishes

   b. It is perfect & complete

   c. It is maturity—mature behavior

   d. It is the hope of being face-to-face with God—possessing perfect consciousness & knowledge

4. The great supremacy of love

DIVISION VII
THE QUESTIONS CONCERNING SPIRITUAL GIFTS, 12:1–14:40

D. The Most Excellent Quality of Life: Love, Not Gifts, 13:1-13

(13:1-13) **Introduction:** there is no question, what the world needs more than anything else is love. If people loved each other, really loved each other, there would be no more war, crime, abuse, injustice, poverty, hunger, starvation, homelessness, deprivation, or immorality. Love is the one ingredient that could revolutionize society. Love is the greatest quality of human life. Love is the supreme quality, the most excellent way for a man to live.
1. The great importance of love (vv.1-3).
2. The great acts of love (vv.4-7).
3. The great permanence of love (vv.8-12).
4. The great supremacy of love (v.13).

DEEPER STUDY # 1
(13:1-13) **Love:** throughout this passage, the word used for love or charity is the great word *agape*. (See DEEPER STUDY # 4, *Love*—Jn.21:15-17 for more discussion.) The meaning of *agape* love is more clearly seen by contrasting it with the various kinds of love. There are essentially four kinds of love. Whereas the English language has only the word *love* to describe all the affectionate experiences of men, the Greek language had a different word to describe each kind of love.
   1. There is *passionate love* or *eros love*. This is the physical love between sexes; the patriotic love of a person for his nation; the ambition of a person for power, wealth, or fame. Briefly stated, *eros love* is the base love of a man that arises from his own inner passion. Sometimes *eros love* is focused upon good and other times it is focused upon bad. It should be noted that *eros love* is never used in the New Testament.
   2. There is *affectionate love* or *storge love*. This is the kind of love that exists between parent and child and between loyal citizens and a trustworthy ruler. *Storge love* is also not used in the New Testament.
   3. There is an *endearing love*, the love that cherishes. This is *phileo love*, the love of a husband and wife for each other, of a brother for a brother, of a friend for the dearest of friends. It is the love that cherishes, that holds someone or something ever so dear to one's heart.
   4. There is *selfless and sacrificial love* or *agape love*. Agape love is the love of the mind, of the reason, of the will. It is the love that goes so far...
   • that it loves a person even if he does not deserve to be loved
   • that it actually loves the person who is utterly unworthy of being loved

① Glance at the **Subject Heading**. Think about it for a moment.

② Glance at the **Subject Heading** again, and then the **Major Points** (1, 2, 3, etc.). Do this several times, reviewing them together while quickly grasping the overall subject.

③ Glance at **both** the **Major Points** and **Subpoints** together while reading the **Scripture**. Do this slower than Step 2. Note how these points sit directly beside the related verse and simply restate what the Scripture is saying—in Outline form.

④ Next read the **Commentary**. Note that the *Major Point Numbers* in the Outline match those in the Commentary. A small raised number (**DS1**, **DS2**, etc.) at the end of a Subject Heading or Outline Point, directs you to a related **Deeper Study** in the Commentary.

Finally, read the **Thoughts** and **Support Scripture** (not shown).

As you read and re-read, pray that the Holy Spirit will bring to your attention exactly what you should preach and teach. May God bless you richly as you study and teach His Word.

The POSB contains everything you need for sermon preparation:

1. **The Subject Heading** describes the overall theme of the passage, and is located directly above the Scripture (keyed *alphabetically*).

2. **Major Points** are keyed with an outline *number* guiding you to related commentary. Note that the Commentary includes "*Thoughts*" (life application) and abundant Supporting Scriptures.

3. **Subpoints** explain and clarify the Scripture as needed.

4. **Commentary** is fully researched and developed for every point.
   • **Thoughts** (in bold) help apply the Scripture to real life.
   • **Deeper Studies** provide in-depth discussions of key words.

***"Woe is unto me, if I
preach not the gospel"***
(1 Co.9:16)

TABLE OF CONTENTS
1 SAMUEL

THE
FIRST BOOK OF SAMUEL

OTHERWISE CALLED
THE FIRST BOOK OF THE KINGS

AUTHOR: uncertain. There is no direct claim to authorship and most of the events took place after Samuel's death. However, Jewish tradition says that Samuel wrote most of *1 Samuel,* recording the events that took place prior to his death (chapters 1-24). After Samuel's death, a history of important events was kept by the prophets Nathan and Gad.

> **"Now the acts of David the king, first and last, behold, they *are* written in the book of Samuel the seer, and in the book of Nathan the prophet, and in the book of Gad the seer" (1 Chr.29:29).**

It is also possible that Abiathar the priest, who was with David during both his exile and his reign, wrote much of *1 and 2 Samuel.* But other commentators suggest that the books were compiled by a prophet in one of the prophetic schools founded by Samuel.

In summary, the author is simply not known. There is no internal evidence or claim for authorship. However, the Divine Author is known: the Holy Spirit of God *breathed* or *inspired* the great books of *1 and 2 Samuel.* Through His inspiration, the Holy Spirit has given to the world a history of the very events God wanted recorded, events that give us hope and that serve both as an example and as a warning to us.

> **"For whatsoever things were written aforetime were written for our learning, that we through patience and comfort of the scriptures might have hope" (Ro.15:4).**
> **"Now all these things happened unto them for examples: and they are written for our admonition, upon whom the ends of the world are come" (1 Co.10:11).**

DATE: uncertain. There is a reference to the division of the monarchy, the time when Judah and Israel were ruled by different kings (1 S.27:6). This would mean that the material of *1 and 2 Samuel* was being compiled after Solomon's death, for the kingdom split right after his death (931 B.C.). Also, there is no mention of the Assyrian captivity, a very significant event that took place in 722 B.C. Based upon these two facts, the writing of *1 and 2 Samuel* most likely took place after the division of the kingdom and before the Assyrian captivity, between 931–722 B.C.

TO WHOM WRITTEN: the Israelites in particular and the human race in general. *First and Second Samuel* were written to the Israelites...

- to give them a historical record of their transition from the era of the judges to the era of the kings, a record of the birth and establishment of the monarchy.
- to teach them the importance of establishing the monarchy under the authority of God, teaching the utter necessity of obedience—of basing their lives and the rule of the king upon the commandments of God.

PURPOSE: three purposes are seen in the great books of *1 and 2 Samuel:*
1. The *Historical Purpose*:
   a. To record the transition from the corrupt era of the judges to the era of the kings or monarchy.
   b. To record the beginning of the monarchy, showing how the LORD Himself established and guided the monarchy from its inception.
   c. To give a permanent record of the lives of Samuel, Saul, and David.
   d. To show how the king was to rule and serve under the authority of God. His authority over the people was to be exercised under the authority of God, executing justice, righteousness, and compassion according to the laws and commandments of God.
   e. To show the significant role the prophets had played in the lives and reigns of the kings, thereby arousing both the king and the people to heed the Word of the LORD spoken through the prophets.
   f. To show how the Lord Himself raised up David to be king and promised to establish his dynasty forever.
2. The *Doctrinal or Spiritual Purpose*: to teach several important lessons to both Israel and all succeeding generations.
   a. To teach that both ruler and citizen must base their lives and government upon the Word of God, that they must execute justice, righteousness, and compassion according to the laws and commandments of God (13:13; 15:1-35; 24:1-22; 26:1-21).
   b. To teach how the sovereignty (power) of God moves events to bring about His purposes and to work all things out for good—the good of all who truly follow Him (1:1–31:13; see 29:1-11).
   c. To show how time and again God answers prayer (1:1-28; 7:1-14).
   d. To show that a society reaps what it sows: a people who execute justice and live righteously reap lives of peace and prosperity, but a people who commit injustice and live wicked lives will reap catastrophic judgment and terrible sufferings (3:11-18; 4:1b–6:21; 25:1-44; 26:21-25; 31:1-13).
3. The *Christological or Christ-Centered Purpose*: the great books of *1 and 2 Samuel* point to Jesus Christ.
   a. *First Samuel* actually uses the word *anointed* (mashiyach) to refer to an individual being the *Anointed One* or the *Messiah* (1 S.2:10). The *Anointed One* pointed to Jesus Christ who was to come as the Messiah and Savior of the world, the One who was to be *anointed* as King of the universe.
   b. The anointing and rule of David pointed to Jesus Christ as the coming Messiah who was predicted to be the Son of David (2 S.7:12f; Mt.21:9; 22:45).

INTRODUCTION TO 1 SAMUEL

SPECIAL FEATURES:

1. *First* and *Second Samuel* are "The Great Books That Were Originally One Book in the Hebrew Scriptures, Known as *The Book of Samuel*. However, when the Old Testament was translated into Greek (about 150 B.C.), the four books of Samuel and Kings were combined to give a complete history of Israel's kings and monarchy (titled First, Second, Third, and Fourth Kingdom). Later, *1 and 2 Samuel* were again separated from the two books of Kings, which is the way the books are divided in many Bibles today. However, in the Vulgate and Latin Bibles they are called First, Second, Third, and Fourth Kings.

2. *First* and *Second Samuel* are "The Great Books That Made Use of Other Written Sources in Recording the History of the Kings and Monarchy." The author used a source named *The Book of Jashar* (2 S.1:18). But note: four sources were used in compiling *First Chronicles*:

⇒ the court records of King David (1 Chr.27:24)
⇒ the records of Samuel the seer (1 Chr.29:29)
⇒ the records of Nathan the prophet (1 Chr.29:29)
⇒ the records of Gad the seer (1 Chr.29:29)

Most likely the author of *1 and 2 Samuel* had access to these sources. The detail given on David's government and his political and military personnel would strongly suggest that the author used the records of the Royal Court and of the court prophets, Nathan and Gad.

3. *First* and *Second Samuel* are "The Great Books That Give the Official Account of the Monarchy's History, Its Rise and Establishment under Samuel, Saul, and David" (1:1–31:13).

4. *First* and *Second Samuel* are "The Great Books That Cover the Lives of the Founders of the Monarchy." They cover the lives of Samuel, the last judge and the first prophet of Israel; Saul, the first king of Israel; and David, the young boy who was secretly anointed and became the greatest king of Israel.

5. *First Samuel* is "The Great Book That Closes the Era of the Judges and Begins the Rule of the Kings." It spans the history of Israel from the birth of Samuel, the last judge and the first prophet of the monarchy, to the death of Saul, who was the first king of Israel (1:1–31:13).

6. *First Samuel* is "The Great Book That Covers the Life of Samuel, the Man Chosen by God for a Very Special *Transitional Ministry* in the History of Israel." Samuel stood as the transitional figure who closed the era of the judges and prepared the Israelites for the rule of the kings. He himself was the last judge of Israel—the greatest of all the judges—and he was the first prophet of Israel, given the awesome task of anointing and nurturing the first two kings of Israel, as well as preparing the people to live under the rule of a monarchy. Under Samuel, the monarchy was born and nurtured by the Word of God. Both king and citizens were taught that the *authority of the king* was to be exercised under the *authority of God*. The king was just as responsible as the people to keep the commandments of God, living a righteous and holy life and executing justice with a heart full of compassion and service (1:1–16:23; 19:18-24; 25:1; 28:7-25).

7. *First Samuel* is "The Great Book That Covers the Disastrous Life of Israel's First King, King Saul" (8:1–31:13). Appointed by God Himself to rule Israel, Saul apparently had all the traits necessary to become a very successful king. But he failed to obey God's Word. As a result his life and reign were an utter failure, ending in terrible tragedy.

8. *First Samuel* is "The Great Book That Covers the Early Life of David, Who Was to Become the Greatest King in the History of Israel" (16:1–31:13). The record begins with the dramatic moment of David's secret anointing as a young boy to be the future king of the nation. Soon thereafter David is seen serving in the royal court of King Saul, being prepared for future rule, although Saul is unaware that the young boy has been anointed to succeed him. A few years later, David is shown killing the giant Goliath and being made a commander in the armed forces of Israel. Being very successful in every task assigned him and being victorious in every battle fought, David became more honored and more famous than the king himself. As a result, Saul became insanely jealous and paranoid, suspecting that David and others were plotting to seize the throne. Because of Saul's jealous rage, David—still a young man in his early twenties—was forced to flee for his life, leaving family, friends, and home. First Samuel covers the ten long years of David's life as a fugitive and then closes with Saul's tragic, tormented death.

9. *First Samuel* is "The Great Book That Covers the Years of David As a Fugitive from the Relentless Pursuit of King Saul" (21:1–31:13). For about seven years David lived under some of the most distressing circumstances imaginable, being a fugitive hunted down by a king who was determined to kill him. Living under these pressuring and agonizing circumstances, David was forced to flee every day of his life for these seven long years. Suspense and high drama filled the days of these years, and finally the strain took its toll upon David. A graphic description of his struggle to survive during these years is portrayed in *1 Samuel*.

10. *First Samuel* is "A Great Book That Shows the Importance of Training a Child in the Ways of the Lord." The book shows how righteous training led Samuel to live a godly and productive life as well as how the failure to train children in righteousness led the sons of Eli the priest to live wicked, ungodly lives (1:1-28; 2:1-11; 2:12-36; 4:1b-22).

11. *First Samuel* is "The Great Book That Exposes the Sins That Are Common to the Priesthood or Ministry." A sharp contrast is drawn between the wickedness of the priests (Eli's sons) with the righteousness of Samuel (2:12-36; 4:1b-22).

12. *First Samuel* is "The Great Book That Records the Capture and Return of the Ark by a Foreign Power, the Philistines (4:1b–6:21).

1 SAMUEL

THE PREACHER'S OUTLINE AND SERMON BIBLE® is *unique*. It differs from all other Study Bibles and Sermon Resource Materials in that every Passage and Subject is outlined right beside the Scripture. When you choose any *Subject* below and turn to the reference, you have not only the Scripture but also an outline of the Scripture and Subject *already prepared for you—verse by verse*.

For a quick example, choose one of the subjects below and turn over to the Scripture; you will find this to be a marvelous help for more organized and streamlined study.

In addition, every point of the Scripture and Subject is *fully developed in a Commentary with supporting Scripture* at the end of each point. Again, this arrangement makes sermon preparation much simpler and more efficient.

Note something else: the Subjects of *1 Samuel* have titles that are both Biblical and *practical*. The practical titles are often more appealing to people. This *benefit* is clearly seen for use on billboards, bulletins, church newsletters, etc.

A suggestion: for the *quickest* overview of *1 Samuel*, first read *all the Division titles* (I, II, III, etc.), then come back and read the individual outline titles.

OUTLINE OF 1 SAMUEL

I. **THE STORY OF ELI AND SAMUEL: THE LORD CLOSES THE ERA OF THE JUDGES AND PREPARES FOR THE RULE OF THE KINGS, 1:1–7:17**

    A. The Prayer of Hannah and the Birth of Samuel: A Lesson on Total Dedication, 1:1-28
    B. The Song of Hannah: A Lesson on Prayer, on Praising and Thanking God, 2:1-11
    C. The Wickedness of Eli's Sons Contrasted with the Righteousness of Samuel: A Lesson on a Corrupt Ministry, 2:12-36
    D. The Call of God to Samuel and His First Prophetic Message: A Lesson on God's Call to Service, 3:1-4:1a
    E. The Ark Captured and Eli's Family Destroyed—All in Fulfillment of Samuel's Prophecy: A Lesson on the Surety of God's Judgment, 4:1b-22
    F. The Ark Returned to Israel by the Philistines: A Lesson on God's Judgment upon All Unbelievers and False Worshippers, 5:1–6:21
    G. The Ministry of Samuel and the Events That Closed the Era of the Judges: A Lesson on How to Live Victoriously, 7:1-17

II. **THE STORY OF SAMUEL AND SAUL: THE LORD GIVES ISRAEL A KING JUST "LIKE ALL THE NATIONS," 8:1–15:35**

    A. The Demand of Israel for a King: Choosing the Ways of the World and Rejecting God, 8:1-22
    B. The Choice of Saul to Be King: A Look at a Promising Young Man, 9:1-27
    C. The Private Anointing and Public Installation of Saul as King: Receiving a New, Changed Heart, 10:1-27
    D. The First Military Victory of Saul and His Affirmation As King: Gaining the Victory over One's Enemies, 11:1-15
    E. The Message Preached by Samuel at the Coronation of King Saul: The Utter Necessity for Repentance and Faithful Service, 12:1-25
    F. The Unlawful Act That Made Saul Unfit to Be King: Being Disqualified to Serve the LORD, 13:1-23
    G. The Continued Decline of Saul: Weak Faith, Spiritual Insensitivity, and Misguided, Carnal Zeal, 14:1-52
    H. The LORD's Rejection of Saul As King: The Seriousness of Disobeying God, 15:1-55

III. **THE STORY OF SAUL AND DAVID (PART 1): THE LORD GIVES ISRAEL A KING "AFTER HIS OWN HEART," 16:1–20:42**

    A. The Story of David's Secret Anointing As King and His Service in Saul's Court: God Judges the Heart, Not the Appearance, of a Person, 16:1-23
    B. The Story of David and Goliath: Defeating the Oppressor of God's People, 17:1-58
    C. The Story of Saul's Jealous Rage and Attempts to Kill David (Part 1): A Look at the Evil of Jealousy, 18:1-30
    D. The Story of Saul's Jealous Rage and Attempts to Kill David (Part 2): A Look at the Evil of Jealousy, 19:1-24
    E. The Story of David and Jonathan's Friendship: A Lesson on Loyalty, 20:1-42

IV. **THE STORY OF SAUL AND DAVID (PART 2): DAVID THE FUGITIVE, 21:1–31:13**

    A. The Immediate, Desperate Flight of David from Saul: A Picture of Desperation and of God's Deliverance, 21:1–22:5
    B. The Insane Murder of the Priests by Saul: The Terrible Evil of Certain Sins, 22:6-23
    C. The Rescue of Keilah by David and the Insane Pursuit of David by Saul: A Picture of the Believer's Deliverance from All Enemies, 23:1-29

DIVISION I

THE STORY OF ELI AND SAMUEL: THE LORD CLOSES THE ERA OF THE JUDGES AND PREPARES FOR THE RULE OF THE KINGS, 1:1–7:17

(1:1–7:17) **DIVISION OVERVIEW**: the opening chapters of *1 Samuel* close the era of the judges and prepare for the rule of the kings. During the period of the judges, all forms of wickedness ran rampant: homosexuality, gang rape, wife abuse, savage brutality, murder, kidnapping, mob violence, terrorist attacks, rebellion, and civil war. The era of the judges was the darkest period in Israel's history, days that witnessed the utter spiritual and moral collapse of the people. As a result, the basic institutions of the nation collapsed:

⇒ the home
⇒ society
⇒ religion
⇒ government

Such a dark period of history called for great leaders, but there were no great leaders. Everyone did what was right in his own eyes, as he saw fit. No one obeyed God. The behavior of the Israelites, including the priests, was a disgraceful, detestable moral outrage.

But in the opening scene of *1 Samuel*, a glimpse of hope is seen. For a barren woman named Hannah began to pray and seek the LORD for a son whom she promised to dedicate to the LORD—if He would just hear her prayer. And God did: He granted Hannah a son named Samuel.

In obedience to her promise, Hannah dedicated Samuel to the LORD, and the LORD set apart the young boy to a very special ministry. He was chosen to close the dark, tragic era of the judges and to prepare the Israelites for the rule of the kings, especially for the rule of King David, the man "after God's own heart" (13:14).

In these seven brief chapters is seen the rise of Samuel as God's faithful priest and prophet; the decline and collapse of Eli and his priesthood; the twenty-plus years of Samuel's faithful preaching that led to Israel's repentance; and the close of the dark, wicked era of the judges.

THE STORY OF ELI AND SAMUEL: THE LORD CLOSES THE ERA OF THE JUDGES AND PREPARES FOR THE RULE OF THE KINGS, 1:1–7:17

A. **The Prayer of Hannah and the Birth of Samuel: A Lesson on Total Dedication, 1:1-28**

B. **The Song of Hannah: A Lesson on Prayer, on Praising and Thanking God, 2:1-11**

C. **The Wickedness of Eli's Sons Contrasted with the Righteousness of Samuel: A Lesson on a Corrupt Ministry, 2:12-36**

D. **The Call of God to Samuel and His First Prophetic Message: A Lesson on God's Call to Service, 3:1-4:1a**

E. **The Ark Captured and Eli's Family Destroyed—All in Fulfillment of Samuel's Prophecy: A Lesson on the Surety of God's Judgment, 4:1b-22**

F. **The Ark Returned to Israel by the Philistines: A Lesson on God's Judgment upon All Unbelievers and False Worshippers, 5:1–6:21**

G. **The Ministry of Samuel and the Events That Closed the Era of the Judges: A Lesson on How to Live Victoriously, 7:1-17**

THE
FIRST BOOK OF SAMUEL

OTHERWISE CALLED
THE FIRST BOOK OF THE KINGS

CHAPTER 1

I. THE STORY OF ELI & SAMUEL: THE LORD CLOSES THE ERA OF THE JUDGES & PREPARES FOR THE RULE OF THE KINGS, 1:1–7:17

A. The Prayer of Hannah & the Birth of Samuel: A Lesson on Total Dedication, 1:1-28

1. **The family into which Samuel was born: His parents were carnal bigamists who conformed to the culture of their day** [DS1]
   a. The father: Elkanah, a priest with no apparent religious function, 1 Chr.6:34
   b. The two wives of Elkanah
      1) Hannah: Had no child
      2) Peninnah: Had children

2. **The deep sorrow & broken heart of Samuel's mother, Hannah: She was helpless, hopeless, in anguish and agony**
   a. The family was devout: Made its annual trip to Shiloh to worship the LORD of hosts [DS2], Ex.34:23; De.12:5-7; Lu.2:41
   b. The family was deeply divided: Seen in the family's meal at the end of the feast
      1) Elkanah always gave a double portion of meat to Hannah because he especially loved her
      2) Peninnah—the rival wife—mocked & provoked Hannah because she was favored & childless
         • Taunted Hannah continually, especially at the annual festival
         • Irritated Hannah until she broke out in tears & could not eat
      3) Elkanah attempted to console & comfort Hannah

3. **The answer to the distressful circumstances of Samuel's mother: She prayed & trusted in God**
   a. Hannah's bitter misery: Peaked

Now there was a certain man of Ramathaim-zophim, of mount Ephraim, and his name was Elkanah, the son of Jeroham, the son of Elihu, the son of Tohu, the son of Zuph, an Ephrathite:

2 And he had two wives; the name of the one *was* Hannah, and the name of the other Peninnah: and Peninnah had children, but Hannah had no children.

3 And this man went up out of his city yearly to worship and to sacrifice unto the LORD of hosts in Shiloh. And the two sons of Eli, Hophni and Phinehas, the priests of the LORD, *were* there.

4 And when the time was that Elkanah offered, he gave to Peninnah his wife, and to all her sons and her daughters, portions:

5 But unto Hannah he gave a worthy portion; for he loved Hannah: but the LORD had shut up her womb.

6 And her adversary also provoked her sore, for to make her fret, because the LORD had shut up her womb.

7 And *as* he did so year by year, when she went up to the house of the LORD, so she provoked her; therefore she wept, and did not eat.

8 Then said Elkanah her husband to her, Hannah, why weepest thou? and why eatest thou not? and why is thy heart grieved? *am* not I better to thee than ten sons?

9 So Hannah rose up after they had eaten in Shiloh, and after they had drunk. Now Eli the priest sat upon a seat by a post of the temple of the LORD.

10 And she *was* in bitterness of soul, and prayed unto the LORD, and wept sore.

11 And she vowed a vow, and said, O LORD of hosts, if thou wilt indeed look on the affliction of thine handmaid, and remember me, and not forget thine handmaid, but wilt give unto thine handmaid a man child, then I will give him unto the LORD all the days of his life, and there shall no razor come upon his head.

12 And it came to pass, as she continued praying before the LORD, that Eli marked her mouth.

13 Now Hannah, she spake in her heart; only her lips moved, but her voice was not heard: therefore Eli thought she had been drunken.

14 And Eli said unto her, How long wilt thou be drunken? put away thy wine from thee.

15 And Hannah answered and said, No, my lord, I *am* a woman of a sorrowful spirit: I have drunken neither wine nor strong drink, but have poured out my soul before the LORD.

16 Count not thine handmaid for a daughter of Belial: for out of the abundance of my complaint and grief have I spoken hitherto.

17 Then Eli answered and said, Go in peace: and the God of Israel grant *thee* thy petition that thou hast asked of him.

18 And she said, Let thine handmaid find grace in thy sight. So the woman went her way, and did eat, and her countenance was no more *sad.*

19 And they rose up in the morning early, and worshipped before the LORD, and returned, and came to their house to Ramah: and Elkanah knew Hannah his wife; and the LORD remembered her.

20 Wherefore it came to pass, when the time was come about after Hannah had conceived, that she bare a son, and called his name

at one of the festivals, causing her to rush to the Tabernacle
   b. Hannah's intense weeping & silent prayer, 13
   c. Hannah's vow to the "LORD of hosts"
      1) Requested that the LORD give her a son

      2) Promised to give the son back to the LORD, to serve the LORD as a Nazarite

   d. Hannah's being misunderstood & condemned

      1) Eli, the High Priest, saw her distressful behavior & wrongly concluded that she was drunk

      2) Eli protested against her behavior at the Tabernacle

   e. Hannah's clarification
      1) Denied that she was drunk
      2) Declared that she was pouring her soul out to the LORD

      3) Insisted that she was not a wicked woman, that she was praying out of great anguish & sorrow

   f. Hannah's assurance & peace of heart
      1) Eli asked God to grant Hannah's prayer

      2) Hannah experienced a deep-seated assurance & confidence—peace of heart

4. **The result of the prayer & faith of Samuel's mother: God heard & healed her affliction—gave her a son, Samuel**
   a. The LORD remembered Hannah's prayer
   b. The son was born & was named Samuel

5. The faithfulness of Samuel's mother: She nursed the child & kept her promise to dedicate Samuel to the LORD	Samuel, *saying,* Because I have asked him of the LORD. 21 And the man Elkanah, and all his house, went up to offer unto the LORD the yearly sacrifice, and his vow.	weaned him, she took him up with her, with three bullocks, and one ephah of flour, and a bottle of wine, and brought him unto the house of the LORD in Shiloh: and the child *was* young.	LORD's service 1) She took the baby Samuel to the Tabernacle after he was weaned 2) She also took a bull, a half bushel of flour, and some wine for the dedication service
a. She was committed to diligently weaning the child—above all else, even above attending the annual festival	22 But Hannah went not up; for she said unto her husband, *I will not go up* until the child be weaned, and *then* I will bring him, that he may appear before the LORD, and there abide for ever.	25 And they slew a bullock, and brought the child to Eli. 26 And she said, Oh my lord, *as* thy soul liveth, my lord, I *am* the woman that stood by thee here, praying unto the LORD.	3) She had the bull presented to the LORD 4) She & her husband then took Samuel to Eli, the High Priest • She reminded Eli of her agonizing prayer for a child some years earlier
b. She was committed to fulfilling her promise: She informed her husband that the child would be dedicated to the LORD right after he was weaned	23 And Elkanah her husband said unto her, Do what seemeth thee good; tarry until thou have weaned him; only the LORD establish his word. So the woman abode, and		
c. She was supported by her husband in her decision to dedicate the child, give him up to the LORD	gave her son suck until she weaned him.	27 For this child I prayed; and the LORD hath given me my petition which I asked of him: 28 Therefore also I have lent him to the LORD; as long as	• She demonstrated a selfless devotion to God: She gave Samuel to the LORD, to serve the LORD
d. She dedicated Samuel to the	24 And when she had	he liveth he shall be lent to the LORD. And he worshipped the LORD there.	during his whole life

DIVISION I

THE STORY OF ELI AND SAMUEL: THE LORD CLOSES THE ERA OF THE JUDGES AND PREPARES FOR THE RULE OF THE KINGS, 1:1–7:17

A.   The Prayer of Hannah and the Birth of Samuel: A Lesson on Total Dedication, 1:1-28

(1:1-28) **Introduction—Society, Corruption—Israel, Corruption of—Lawlessness, of Society**: society had become a cesspool, a pit of depravity and corruption, when Samuel was born. His day was a time when people had slipped into an immoral, lawless, abusive, violent, compromising, and permissive lifestyle. The depth of their moral decay was seen in cases such as gang rape, homosexuality, wife abuse, child abuse, murder, kidnapping, widespread polygamy, greed, injustice, idolatry, and civil war (see outline and notes—Jud.17-21 for more discussion).

But in the midst of such an immoral and lawless society, there were a few persons who lived for God. Their lives demonstrated the light of God's Holy Word. They loved the LORD and obeyed Him, keeping His commandments. Such a person was Hannah, Samuel's mother. This chapter begins the story of Hannah and her son Samuel. This is: *The Prayer of Hannah and the Birth of Samuel: A Lesson on Total Dedication*, 1:1-28.

1. The family into which Samuel was born: carnal, bigamist parents who conformed to the culture of their day (vv.1-2).
2. The deep sorrow and broken heart of Samuel's mother, Hannah: a picture of anguish, agony, helplessness, and hopelessness (vv.3-8).
3. The answer to the distressful circumstances of Samuel's mother: prayer and trust in God (vv.9-18).
4. The result of the prayer and faith of Samuel's mother: God heard and healed her affection—gave her a son, Samuel (vv.19-20).
5. The faithfulness of Samuel's mother: she nursed the child and kept her promise to dedicate Samuel to the LORD (vv.21-28).

1 (1:1-2) **Society, Carnal Practices of—Samuel, Family of, Carnal—Carnal, Example of—Bigamy, Example of, a Priest—Elkanah, Samuel's Father—Hannah, Samuel's Mother—Peninnah, Second Wife of Samuel's Father**: there was the family into which Samuel was born. His parents were bigamists, parents who conformed to the carnal, social order and culture of their day. Note this fact in the two verses of this point:

OUTLINE	SCRIPTURE	SCRIPTURE	OUTLINE
1. The family into which Samuel was born: His parents were carnal bigamists who conformed to the culture of their day ᴰˢ¹ a. The father: Elkanah, a priest with no apparent religious function, 1 Chr.6:34	Now there was a certain man of Ramathaim-zophim, of mount Ephraim, and his name was Elkanah, the son of Jeroham, the son of Elihu, the son of Tohu, the son of Zuph, an Ephrathite:	2 And he had two wives; the name of the one *was* Hannah, and the name of the other Peninnah: and Peninnah had children, but Hannah had no children.	b. The two wives of Elkanah 1) Hannah: Had no child 2) Peninnah: Had children

a. The father of Samuel was Elkanah, a priest with no apparent religious function (v.1). We know that Elkanah was a priest from the genealogy of Samuel (1 Chr.6:25-27; 31-36). The family was of the Kohathite branch of the tribe of Levi or priests, and the family was to become ancestors of skilled musicians, musicians who served in the Tabernacle and temple (1 Chr.6:16, 23, 31-33).[1]

The family lived in Ramathaim Zophim, which is another name for Ramah, a town about five miles north of Jerusalem (v.19). Ramah was not one of the priestly cities that had originally been assigned to the tribe of Levi, but for some reason a branch of the tribe moved to the hill country of Ephraim (see outline and note—Jos.21:3-42 for more discussion). Just when is not known, but in the book of *Judges* there is the story of a priest coming from Bethlehem to Ephraim to serve a large property owner named Micah (Jud.17:1-13). We know from this passage that at least five generations of priests had lived in Ephraim (v.1).

b. Elkanah was a bigamist, marrying two wives: Hannah and Peninnah (v.2). By taking two wives, he conformed to the culture, the carnal, fleshly society of his day. The fact that a priest committed bigamy shows just how carnal, fleshly, and lawless God's people had become during Samuel's day. It was common practice for a man to take a second wife when his first wife could not bear children. Hannah had obviously been the first wife of Elkanah, but she could not bear a child; consequently, he married Peninnah who was able to bear him children. Apparently Elkanah lacked faith in the LORD, failing to trust Him to give Hannah a child.

DEEPER STUDY #1

(1:1-2) **Bigamy—Polygamy—Monogamy—One Wife—One Husband—One Spouse—One Flesh—Family, Union of**: bigamy or polygamy is a transgression of God's explicit will. Marrying two or more people violates God's Holy Word, His original institution for marriage. God's will is clearly stated: man and woman are to leave their parents and be *united* in marriage, becoming *one flesh*. God's clearly stated purpose is monogamy: one husband, one wife. Together they form a union, a union so tightly knit together that they become as *one flesh*. As *one flesh*, husband and wife become the foundation of the family and the very basic unit of society. Becoming *one flesh* or *one body,* the husband and wife are God's chosen way for the human race to continue and for the great values of human life to be learned. All the great values of life are to be found in the union of husband and wife and the family they establish: love, joy, peace, longsuffering, gentleness, goodness, faithfulness, meekness, control, fulfillment, satisfaction, purpose, meaning, significance. Again, bigamy and polygamy are not God's way for man and woman to be united; it is the practice of man's carnal, fleshly lust. This is the clear teaching of Scripture:

> "And Lamech took unto him two wives: the name of the one was Adah, and the name of the other Zillah" (Ge.4:19).
> "Therefore shall a man leave his father and his mother, and shall cleave unto his wife: and they shall be one flesh" (Ge.2:24).
> "Neither shall he multiply wives to himself, that his heart turn not away: neither shall he greatly multiply to himself silver and gold" (De.17:17).
> "And did not he make one? Yet had he the residue of the spirit. And wherefore one? That he might seek a godly seed. Therefore take heed to your spirit, and let none deal treacherously against the wife of his youth" (Mal.2:15).
> "And said, For this cause shall a man leave father and mother, and shall cleave to his wife: and they twain shall be one flesh....He saith unto them, Moses because of the hardness of your hearts suffered you to put away your wives: but from the beginning it was not so" (Mt.19:5, 8).
> "A bishop then must be blameless, the husband of one wife, vigilant, sober, of good behaviour, given to hospitality, apt to teach....Let the deacons be the husbands of one wife, ruling their children and their own houses well" (1 Ti.3:2, 12).
> "Love not the world, neither the things that are in the world. If any man love the world, the love of the Father is not in him. For all that is in the world, the lust of the flesh, and the lust of the eyes, and the pride of life, is not of the Father, but is of the world" (I Jn.2:15-16).

---

2 (1:3-8) **Sorrow, Example of—Heart, Broken, Example of—Distress, Example of—Agony and Anguish, Example of—Trouble, Example of—Family, Divided—Hannah, Distress and Sorrow of**: there was the deep sorrow and broken heart of Samuel's mother, Hannah. Her sorrow and broken heart were caused by strife within the family. The family was deeply divided, in particular the two wives. This is clearly seen in the Scripture and outline:

OUTLINE	SCRIPTURE	SCRIPTURE	OUTLINE
2. The deep sorrow & broken heart of Samuel's mother, Hannah: She was helpless, hopeless, in anguish and agony a. The family was devout: Made its annual trip to Shiloh to worship the LORD of hosts[DS2] (Ex.34:23; De.12:5-7; Lu.2:41) b. The family was deeply	3 And this man went up out of his city yearly to worship and to sacrifice unto the LORD of hosts in Shiloh. And the two sons of Eli, Hophni and Phinehas, the priests of the LORD, *were* there. 4 And when the time was	that Elkanah offered, he gave to Peninnah his wife, and to all her sons and her daughters, portions: 5 But unto Hannah he gave a worthy portion; for he loved Hannah: but the LORD had shut up her womb. 6 And her adversary also	divided: Seen in the family's meal at the end of the feast 1) Elkanah always gave a double portion of meat to Hannah because he especially loved her 2) Peninnah—the rival wife—

---

[1] Ronald F. Youngblood. *1 Samuel*. "The Expositor's Bible Commentary," Vol.3. (Grand Rapids, MI: Zondervan Publishing House, 1990), p.570.

OUTLINE	SCRIPTURE	SCRIPTURE	OUTLINE
mocked & provoked Hannah because she was favored & childless • Taunted Hannah continually, especially at the annual festival • Irritated Hannah until	provoked her sore, for to make her fret, because the LORD had shut up her womb. 7 And *as* he did so year by year, when she went up to the house of the LORD, so she provoked her; there-	fore she wept, and did not eat. 8 Then said Elkanah her husband to her, Hannah, why weepest thou? and why eatest thou not? and why is thy heart grieved? *am* not I better to thee than ten sons?	she broke out in tears & could not eat 3) Elkanah attempted to console & comfort Hannah

a. The family was devout, deeply religious. Year after year the family made an annual trip to Shiloh to worship the LORD (v.3). Remember, the Tabernacle and Ark had been at Shiloh for some time now (4:3-4; Jos.18:1; Jud.18:31). All Israelite men were required by law to attend the three major religious festivals each year, three festivals that were always held at the central worship center (Ex.34:23; De.12:5-7; Lu.2:41). Keep in mind the immoral and lawless society during the days of the judges. Few were obeying the law of God; consequently, there were probably few attending the religious feast in obedience to God's commandment. Thus, Elkanah's faithfulness and devotion to the LORD stood out as a strong testimony to his neighbors, setting a dynamic example for them. Note this fact as well: Elkanah was faithful in worshipping the LORD at the Tabernacle despite the hypocrisy of Eli's two sons who were serving as priests. Elkanah did not use their immoral, reprobate behavior as an excuse for not worshipping the LORD (see outline and notes 1 S.2:12-36 for more discussion).

b. The family was deeply divided despite its religious devotion (vv.4-8). The basic cause of the division was the bigamist relationship created by Elkanah. In ancient days, it was important for a man to have a son to perpetuate his name and to inherit his property. Thus, it was a devastating blow to Hannah when she could not bear a son for her husband. The great tragedy was that Elkanah and Hannah failed to trust God, for it was the LORD who closed her womb. And if He had closed the womb, the LORD could just as easily have opened the womb and caused Hannah to conceive a son. But their lack of trust led Elkanah to marry Peninnah. Consequently, when Peninnah bore children, she began to taunt, provoke, antagonize, and belittle Hannah. No doubt, Peninnah was filled with jealousy because her husband loved and favored Hannah more.

Apparently, the taunting and provoking of Hannah usually reached its peak at the annual festival attended by the family. Elkanah always gave a double portion of meat to Hannah because of his special love for her (vv.4-5). Of course, this only provoked the jealousy of Peninnah even more and caused her to badger and poke fun at Hannah until Hannah broke down in tears and could not eat (v.7). Year after year, Hannah experienced a deep, grieving sorrow, anguish, and agony. Her heart was plainly broken. No matter how much Elkanah attempted to console and comfort her, Hannah could not be consoled. She was gripped by a sense of helplessness and hopelessness, suffering deep pain, feeling that she was cursed by God and that she had failed her husband.

Thought 1. So many hearts are broken today, filled with sorrow, grief, agony, and anguish. So many people are suffering hurt and pain, gripped by a sense of helplessness and hopelessness. A broken heart may be caused by the inability to bear a child or by the loss of a child. But sorrow and pain can also be caused by the loss of a job, financial difficulties, disease, injury, death, or a host of other disturbances and problems that arise in our lives. Just as Hannah suffered deep sorrow and a broken heart, so we too can suffer the pain and agony of trials and the helplessness and hopelessness of circumstances. Listen to what Scripture says:

"That at that time ye were without Christ, being aliens from the commonwealth of Israel, and strangers from the covenants of promise, having no hope, and without God in the world" (Ep.2:12).

"But I would not have you to be ignorant, brethren, concerning them which are asleep, that ye sorrow not, even as others which have no hope" (1 Th.4:13).

"Wherefore is light given to him that is in misery, and life unto the bitter *in* soul; Which long for death, but it *cometh* not; and dig for it more than for hid treasures; Which rejoice exceedingly, *and* are glad, when they can find the grave" (Jb.3:20-22).

"My days are swifter than a weaver's shuttle, and are spent without hope" (Jb.7:6).

"So that my soul chooseth strangling, *and* death rather than my life" (Jb.7:15).

"My soul is weary of my life; I will leave my complaint upon myself; I will speak in the bitterness of my soul" (Jb.10:1).

"And where *is* now my hope? as for my hope, who shall see it" (Jb.17:15).

"O my God, my soul is cast down within me" (Ps.42:6).

"But as for me, my feet were almost gone; my steps had well nigh slipped. For I was envious at the foolish, *when* I saw the prosperity of the wicked" (Ps.73:2-3).

"Before I was afflicted I went astray: but now have I kept thy word" (Ps.119:67).

"Hope deferred maketh the heart sick: but *when* the desire cometh, *it is* a tree of life" (Pr.13:12).

"Therefore I hated life; because the work that is wrought under the sun is grievous unto me: for all *is* vanity and vexation of spirit" (Ec.2:17).

"So I returned, and considered all the oppressions that are done under the sun: and behold the tears of *such as were* oppressed, and they had no comforter; and on the side of their oppressors *there was* power; but they had no comforter. Wherefore I praised the dead which are already dead more than the living which are yet alive" (Ec.4:1-2).

"The LORD hath forsaken me, and my LORD hath forgotten me" (Is.49:14).

"They have heard that I sigh: *there is* none to comfort me: all mine enemies have heard of my trouble; they are glad that thou hast done *it*: thou wilt bring the day *that* thou hast called, and they shall be like unto me"(Lam.1:21).

"My strength and my hope is perished from the LORD" (Lam.3:18).

"Therefore now, O LORD, take, I beseech thee, my life from me; for *it is* better for me to die than to live"(Jona. 4:3).

DEEPER STUDY #2

(1:3) LORD of Hosts—LORD Almighty (YHWH Sebaot) God, Names of—Names, of God: this is the first time God is referred to as the LORD of hosts or armies. The term stresses God's sovereignty, rule, and supremacy—His ultimate leadership of Israel's armies and His supreme control over all the armies and hosts of the universe, both in heaven and earth. God is...

- the LORD of heavenly hosts such as angels (Jos. 5:14; 1 K.22:19; Ps.148:2)
- the LORD of human hosts such as human armies (Ex.7:4; Ps.44:9)
- the LORD of celestial hosts such as the sun, moon, and stars (Ge.2:1; De.4:19; Is.40:26)
- the LORD who will ultimately subject all who oppose Him and His dear people (Is.24:21-23; 34:1-10; Ph.2:9-11)

"The LORD of hosts" is a name of royalty, the name that refers to God as the Supreme Ruler over all the beings and powers of the universe. He is the Sovereign LORD over the entire universe. Samuel was probably the first person to use this term or to call upon the *LORD of hosts*. The LORD's supremacy over the people and powers of this earth was a message desperately needed. The Israelites were weak and their enemies strong. And the enemies were constantly attacking, brutalizing, oppressing, and enslaving them during the days of the judges. Their only hope was the intervention of God in their behalf, a mighty act of deliverance by the *LORD of hosts*.

LORD of hosts is a military term used over 260 times in the Old Testament, primarily by the prophets. Just picture the prophets ministering to God's people during the days of their terrible suffering, enslavement, and captivity. When they prayed and cried out to God, they did not often address Him simply as LORD nor use the term that we often use, "Father." But they cried to Him, "O LORD of hosts"—you who are LORD Almighty, the Supreme Ruler of the universe, the LORD in control of all the armies of earth and heaven...." For example, it is used by Isaiah (62 times), Jeremiah (79 times), Zechariah (53 times), and Malachi (24 times).

---

3 (1:9-18) **Prayer, Example of—Trust, Example of—Distress, Solution to—Sorrow, Solution to—Discouragement, Solution to—Agony and Anguish, Solution to—Hopelessness, Solution to—Helplessness, Solution to**: there was the answer to the distressful circumstances of Samuel's mother, that of prayer and trust in God.

OUTLINE	SCRIPTURE	SCRIPTURE	OUTLINE
3. The answer to the distressful circumstances of Samuel's mother: She prayed & trusted in God a. Hannah's bitter misery: Peaked at one of the festivals, causing her to rush to the Tabernacle b. Hannah's intense weeping & silent prayer, 13 c. Hannah's vow to the "LORD of hosts" 1) Requested that the LORD give her a son 2) Promised to give the son back to the LORD, to serve the LORD as a Nazarite d. Hannah's being misunderstood & condemned 1) Eli, the High Priest, saw her distressful behavior & wrongly concluded that she was drunk	9 So Hannah rose up after they had eaten in Shiloh, and after they had drunk. Now Eli the priest sat upon a seat by a post of the temple of the LORD. 10 And she *was* in bitterness of soul, and prayed unto the LORD, and wept sore. 11 And she vowed a vow, and said, O LORD of hosts, if thou wilt indeed look on the affliction of thine handmaid, and remember me, and not forget thine handmaid, but wilt give unto thine handmaid a man child, then I will give him unto the LORD all the days of his life, and there shall no razor come upon his head. 12 And it came to pass, as she continued praying before the LORD, that Eli marked her mouth. 13 Now Hannah, she spake in her heart; only her lips moved, but her voice was not heard: therefore Eli thought	she had been drunken. 14 And Eli said unto her, How long wilt thou be drunken? put away thy wine from thee. 15 And Hannah answered and said, No, my lord, I *am* a woman of a sorrowful spirit: I have drunken neither wine nor strong drink, but have poured out my soul before the LORD. 16 Count not thine handmaid for a daughter of Belial: for out of the abundance of my complaint and grief have I spoken hitherto. 17 Then Eli answered and said, Go in peace: and the God of Israel grant *thee* thy petition that thou hast asked of him. 18 And she said, Let thine handmaid find grace in thy sight. So the woman went her way, and did eat, and her countenance was no more *sad*.	2) Eli protested against her behavior at the Tabernacle e. Hannah's clarification 1) Denied that she was drunk 2) Declared that she was pouring her soul out to the LORD 3) Insisted that she was not a wicked woman, that she was praying out of great anguish & sorrow f. Hannah's assurance & peace of heart 1) Eli asked God to grant Hannah's prayer 2) Hannah experienced a deep-seated assurance & confidence—peace of heart

a., b. Hannah's bitter misery peaked at one of the festivals, and she rushed to the Tabernacle to pray and seek the LORD (vv.9-11). In deep anguish and bitterness of soul, Hannah wept and cried out to the LORD. In her prayer she made a special vow to the LORD, addressing him as the "LORD of hosts," the Almighty LORD who controlled all the events of human life (v.11). She first requested that the LORD give her a son, and then she made an astounding promise: to give the son back to the LORD. She promised to dedicate the son to God so the son could serve the LORD all the days of his life.

c. This vow was known as the Nazarite vow, a very special vow of *separation to the LORD*. By promising never to cut his hair, Hannah was fulfilling one of the requirements of the Nazarite vow (see outline and note—Nu.6:3-12 for more discussion).

Note the renewed commitment of Hannah: she calls herself God's servant (v.11). She asked God to look upon her affliction and to remember, not forget, His servant. Hannah was suffering deep, intense pain and anguish. Her heart was broken. She desperately needed the LORD to meet her need. She was doing all she could, praying and seeking the face of the LORD for help.

d. But note what happened: Hannah's lips were moving in silent prayer, and Eli, the High Priest, misunderstood and condemned her (vv.12-14). Eli had been sitting on a chair by the doorpost of the temple when Hannah rushed by him into the Tabernacle. Seeing her lips move silently, Eli wrongly concluded that she was drunk. He protested against her behavior in the Tabernacle and strongly rebuked her. In the corrupt, degenerate days of the judges, it was perhaps a common thing for the religious festival to become a drunken party. Thus, Eli simply assumed that Hannah was drunk.

e. Hannah clarified the situation, denying that she was intoxicated. She had not been drinking wine nor any other strong drink. She was merely pouring out her soul to the LORD, seeking for Him to meet her desperate need. In deep anguish, she continued to insist that she was not a wicked woman, that she had been praying out of painful agony and sorrow.

f. Hearing this, Eli gave great assurance and peace of heart to Hannah. He told her to go in peace and then asked God to grant Hannah's prayer (vv.17-18). From this point on, Hannah experienced a deep-seated assurance and confidence. Real peace gripped her heart. She went her way and ate. And note: her countenance was no longer sad or downcast (v.18).

Thought 1. Prayer is the answer to distressful circumstances. When we are in deep sorrow and our hearts are broken, prayer is the answer. When we are gripped by anguish, agony, grief, helplessness, or hopelessness—prayer is the answer. When we are sad, downcast, discouraged, or disheartened—prayer is the answer. Very simply stated, no matter the trouble or problem, situation or circumstance, trial or tribulation—prayer is the answer.

"**Ask, and it shall be given you; seek, and ye shall find; knock, and it shall be opened unto you**" (**Mt.7:7**).

"**Watch and pray, that ye enter not into temptation: the spirit indeed is willing, but the flesh is weak**" (**Mt.26:41**).

"**And he spake a parable unto them to this end, that men ought always to pray, and not to faint**" (**Lu.18:1**).

"**Hitherto have ye asked nothing in my name: ask, and ye shall receive, that your joy may be full**" (**Jn.16:24**).

"**Likewise the Spirit also helpeth our infirmities: for we know not what we should pray for as we ought: but the Spirit itself maketh intercession for us with groanings which cannot be uttered. And he that searcheth the hearts knoweth what is the mind of the Spirit, because he maketh intercession for the saints according to the will of God**" (**Ro.8:26-27**).

"**Is any among you afflicted? let him pray. Is any merry? let him sing psalms**" (**Js.5:13**).

"**Seek the LORD, and his strength: seek his face evermore**" (**Ps.105:4**).

"**Seek ye the LORD while he may be found, call ye upon him while he is near**" (**Is.55:6**).

4 (1:19-20) **Prayer, Results of—Hannah, Deliverance of—Deliverance, Example of—Hannah, Prayer Answered**: there were the results of Hannah's prayer. God heard and healed her affliction (vv.19-20). He remembered Hannah's prayer and quickened, empowered her body to conceive. Hannah bore a son and named him Samuel, which means *God heard*. Why this name? Because Hannah asked and God heard her prayer. And through the experience, Hannah learned a wonderful truth: God answers prayer. Samuel was a gift from the LORD: the LORD had given Samuel because she had prayed (v.20).

OUTLINE	SCRIPTURE	SCRIPTURE	OUTLINE
4. The result of the prayer & faith of Samuel's mother: God heard & healed her affliction—gave her a son, Samuel a. The LORD remembered Hannah's prayer	19 And they rose up in the morning early, and worshipped before the LORD, and returned, and came to their house to Ramah: and Elkanah knew Hannah his wife; and the LORD remembered her.	20 Wherefore it came to pass, when the time was come about after Hannah had conceived, that she bare a son, and called his name Samuel, *saying,* Because I have asked him of the LORD.	b. The son was born & was named Samuel

Thought 1. God answers prayer! From the beginning of human history, no matter what the distressful circumstance—sorrow, agony, anguish, discouragement, grief, sorrow, hurt, pain—no matter what the problem or trouble, God has always answered the prayers and met the needs of His dear people. And he will meet our needs when we are gripped by sorrow or a broken heart. No matter what trials or temptations we may face, God will answer our prayers and meet our needs.

"Therefore I say unto you, What things soever ye desire, when ye pray, believe that ye receive them, and ye shall have them" (Mk.11:24).

"Confess your faults one to another, and pray one for another, that ye may be healed. The effectual fervent prayer of a righteous man availeth much" (Js.5:16).

"If my people, which are called by my name, shall humble themselves, and pray, and seek my face, and turn from their wicked ways; then will I hear from heaven, and will forgive their sin, and will heal their land" (2 Chr.7:14).

"The LORD is my strength and my shield; my heart trusted in him, and I am helped: therefore my heart greatly rejoiceth; and with my song will I praise him" (Ps.28:7).

"But I am poor and needy; yet the LORD thinketh upon me: thou art my help and my deliverer; make no tarrying, O my God" (Ps.40:17).

"He shall call upon me, and I will answer him: I will be with him in trouble; I will deliver him, and honour him" (Ps.91:15).

"Fear thou not; for I am with thee: be not dismayed; for I am thy God: I will strengthen thee; yea, I will help thee; yea, I will uphold thee with the right hand of my righteousness" (Is.41:10).

"And it shall come to pass, that before they call, I will answer; and while they are yet speaking, I will hear" (Is.65:24).

"And I will bring the third part through the fire, and will refine them as silver is refined, and will try them as gold is tried: they shall call on my name, and I will hear them: I will say, It is my people: and they shall say, The LORD is my God" (Zec.13:9).

5 (1:21-28) **Faithfulness, Example of—Hannah, Faithfulness of—Dedication, of Children—Samuel, Dedicated to God—Promise, Duty**: there was the faithfulness of Samuel's mother. She nursed her child and kept her promise to dedicate him to the LORD.

OUTLINE	SCRIPTURE	SCRIPTURE	OUTLINE
5. The faithfulness of Samuel's mother: She nursed the child & kept her promise to dedicate Samuel to the LORD a. She was committed to diligently weaning the child—above all else, even above attending the annual festival b. She was committed to fulfilling her promise: She informed her husband that the child would be dedicated to the LORD right after he was weaned c. She was supported by her husband in her decision to dedicate the child, give him up to the LORD d. She dedicated Samuel to the LORD's service	21 And the man Elkanah, and all his house, went up to offer unto the LORD the yearly sacrifice, and his vow. 22 But Hannah went not up; for she said unto her husband, *I will not go up* until the child be weaned, and *then* I will bring him, that he may appear before the LORD, and there abide for ever. 23 And Elkanah her husband said unto her, Do what seemeth thee good; tarry until thou have weaned him; only the LORD establish his word. So the woman abode, and gave her son suck until she weaned him. 24 And when she had weaned him, she took him up	with her, with three bullocks, and one ephah of flour, and a bottle of wine, and brought him unto the house of the LORD in Shiloh: and the child *was* young. 25 And they slew a bullock, and brought the child to Eli. 26 And she said, Oh my lord, *as* thy soul liveth, my lord, I *am* the woman that stood by thee here, praying unto the LORD. 27 For this child I prayed; and the LORD hath given me my petition which I asked of him: 28 Therefore also I have lent him to the LORD; as long as he liveth he shall be lent to the LORD. And he worshipped the LORD there.	1) She took the baby Samuel to the Tabernacle after he was weaned 2) She also took a bull, a half bushel of flour, and some wine for the dedication service 3) She had the bull presented to the LORD 4) She & her husband then took Samuel to Eli, the High Priest • She reminded Eli of her agonizing prayer for a child some years earlier • She demonstrated a selfless devotion to God: She gave Samuel to the LORD, to serve the LORD during his whole life

a. Hannah was committed to weaning the child above all else, even above attending the annual festival (vv.21-22). When it came time to make the annual sacrifice to the LORD, Elkanah set out for the Tabernacle, but Hannah remained behind because she had not yet weaned the child.

b. But Hannah was committed to fulfilling her promise to the LORD. This is seen in her promise to dedicate the child right after he had been weaned.

c. Note that Hannah was totally supported by her husband in the decision to dedicate Samuel to the LORD. This is significant, for by law a husband's support was not required when a wife made a voluntary vow. The husband had the right to nullify the wife's vow (see outline and note—Nu.30:10-15 for more discussion). But not Elkanah: he was committed to the LORD and loved his wife too much to refuse her desire. Thus, he supported his wife even though it meant giving up the firstborn son of his beloved wife.[2] After Samuel had been weaned, they took the baby to the Tabernacle along with a bull, a half-bushel of flour, and some wine for the dedication service (v.24). Upon arriving, they had the bull presented in sacrifice to the LORD (v.25).

d. Then the momentous event took place: she and her husband dedicated Samuel to the LORD's service. Taking Samuel to Eli, Hannah reminded the High Priest of her agonizing prayer for a child some years earlier. And she proclaimed the glorious answer to her prayer: the LORD had given her what she had asked for, a son.

---

2 Robert D. Bergen. *1, 2 Samuel.* "The New American Commentary," Vol.7. (Nashville, TN: Broadman & Holman Publishers, 1996), p.72.

Hannah then demonstrated a strong, selfless devotion: she gave Samuel to the LORD, to serve the LORD during his whole life. She had promised to present Samuel "before the LORD" so that he could live in the sanctuary and in the presence of the LORD forever (see v.22). This phrase, "before the LORD," is one of the most prominent statements made about the life of Samuel. Samuel was to live "before the LORD" forever (2:11, 18, 21; 7:6; 10:19; 11:15; 12:3, 7; 15:33).[3]

Thought 1. Hannah, Samuel's mother, is a dynamic example of faithfulness to God. She was faithful to her commitments. When she made a promise to God, she kept her promise. She did exactly what she said. Her word was her bond. She was faithful to the LORD, and her faithfulness speaks volumes to us.

When we make a promise to God, we must fulfill our promise. We must keep our word, do exactly what we say. Often during a crisis, we will make some vow to God, a promise...

- to give up something
- to change our lives
- to make some gift to the church
- to repent and return to the LORD
- to receive Christ as our Savior
- to serve the LORD in the ministry

The example of Hannah is a strong example for us: we must be faithful to the LORD. We must keep our vows, our promises to the LORD. We must be faithful in following through for the LORD.

> **"And he said unto him, Well, thou good servant: because thou hast been faithful in a very little, have thou authority over ten cities" (Lu.19:17).**
>
> **"Moreover it is required in stewards, that a man be found faithful" (1 Co.4:2).**
>
> **"But Christ as a son over his own house; whose house are we, if we hold fast the confidence and the rejoicing of the hope firm unto the end" (He.3:6).**
>
> **"Fear none of those things which thou shalt suffer: behold, the devil shall cast some of you into prison, that ye may be tried; and ye shall have tribulation ten days: be thou faithful unto death, and I will give thee a crown of life" (Re.2:10).**
>
> **"When thou shalt vow a vow unto the LORD thy God, thou shalt not slack to pay it: for the LORD thy God will surely require it of thee; and it would be sin in thee. But if thou shalt forbear to vow, it shall be no sin in thee. That which is gone out of thy lips thou shalt keep and perform; even a freewill offering, according as thou hast vowed unto the LORD thy God, which thou hast promised with thy mouth" (De.23:21-23).**
>
> **"But the mercy of the LORD is from everlasting to everlasting upon them that fear him, and his righteousness unto children's children; To such as keep his covenant, and to those that remember his commandments to do them" (Ps.103:17-18).**
>
> **"When thou vowest a vow unto God, defer not to pay it; for he hath no pleasure in fools: pay that which thou hast vowed. Better is it that thou shouldest not vow, than that thou shouldest vow and not pay. Suffer not thy mouth to cause thy flesh to sin; neither say thou before the angel, that it was an error: wherefore should God be angry at thy voice, and destroy the work of thine hands" (Ec.5:4-6).**

---

[3] Robert D. Bergen. *1, 2 Samuel*, p.72.

CHAPTER 2

B. The Song of Hannah: A Lesson on Prayer, on Praising & Thanking God, 2:1-11

1. **Hannah thanked God for His personal deliverance**
   a. Her heart rejoiced
   b. Her strength conquered—through the LORD
   c. Her mouth boasted over her enemies (Peninnah's abuse)
2. **Hannah praised God for Himself**
   a. He is Holy
   b. He is the only living God
   c. He is the Rock of life
3. **Hannah issued a warning to the proud: God knows all things & judges or reverses the deeds of people**

   a. God reverses the strong & the weak, even military Jews who are strong

   b. God reverses the full & the hungry

   c. God reverses the barren woman & the fruitful

And Hannah prayed, and said, My heart rejoiceth in the LORD, mine horn is exalted in the LORD: my mouth is enlarged over mine enemies; because I rejoice in thy salvation.
2 *There is* none holy as the LORD: for *there is* none beside thee: neither *is there* any rock like our God.
3 Talk no more so exceeding proudly; let *not* arrogancy come out of your mouth: for the LORD is a God of knowledge, and by him actions are weighed.
4 The bows of the mighty men *are* broken, and they that stumbled are girded with strength.
5 *They that were* full have hired out themselves for bread; and *they that were* hungry ceased: so that the barren hath born seven; and she that hath many children is waxed feeble.
6 The LORD killeth, and maketh alive: he bringeth down to the grave, and bringeth up.
7 The LORD maketh poor, and maketh rich: he bringeth low, and lifteth up.
8 He raiseth up the poor out of the dust, *and* lifteth up the beggar from the dunghill, to set *them* among princes, and to make them inherit the throne of glory: for the pillars of the earth *are* the LORD'S, and he hath set the world upon them.
9 He will keep the feet of his saints, and the wicked shall be silent in darkness; for by strength shall no man prevail.
10 The adversaries of the LORD shall be broken to pieces; out of heaven shall he thunder upon them: the LORD shall judge the ends of the earth; and he shall give strength unto his king, and exalt the horn of his anointed.
11 And Elkanah went to Ramah to his house. And the child did minister unto the LORD before Eli the priest.

d. God reverses death & life, sickness & health

e. God reverses the poor & rich

f. God reverses the humble & the exalted

4. **Hannah predicted the future: The future lay in the hands of the LORD, the Creator of the world**
   a. The LORD will preserve the saints
   b. The LORD will judge the wicked

      1) Silence them in darkness
      2) Shatter them

   c. The LORD will strengthen His king & exalt His anointed (a prediction of David & of Christ)

DIVISION I

THE STORY OF ELI AND SAMUEL: THE LORD CLOSES THE ERA OF THE JUDGES AND PREPARES FOR THE RULE OF THE KINGS, 1:1–7:17

B.   The Song of Hannah: A Lesson on Prayer, on Praising and Thanking God, 2:1-11

(2:1-11) **Introduction—Prayer, Lack of—Praise, Lack of—Thanksgiving, Lack of**: there is a lack of prayer and praise today. Few people take time to seek the LORD and to praise Him for answered prayer. Yet all of our needs can be met through prayer. Just think! Not a single need ever has to go unmet. No matter what the problem is—fear, terror, insecurity, depression, sickness, hunger, destitution—God promises to meet our needs through prayer.

But there is a problem: most people simply do not believe God's promise. They do not believe God will actually answer their prayers. Consequently, there is little prayer offered up to God. As a result, there is little genuine praise and thanksgiving presented to God for answered prayer.

But this was not true with Hannah. Hannah prayed, and God answered her prayer. Once she had received the answer, she thanked God and praised His name. Her heart rejoiced in the LORD, for He had clearly met her desperate need.

This is a triumphant passage, an eloquent declaration of Hannah's faith in the LORD and in His promise to answer prayer. This is one of the great prayers and songs of the Old Testament, often referred to as "the Song of Hannah." It ranks right along with the other great songs of the Old Testament (the songs of Moses and Miriam, Ex.15:1-18, 21; De.32:1-43; the song of Deborah, Jud.5; and the song of David, 2 S.22).[1]

This prayer is the last recorded words of Hannah in Holy Scripture. It is a triumphant climax to the life of a person who believed in prayer, and who praised and thanked God for answering prayer. This is: *The Song of Hannah: A Lesson on Prayer, on Praising and Thanking God*, 2:1-11.

1. Hannah thanked God for His personal deliverance (v.1).
2. Hannah praised God for Himself (v.2).
3. Hannah issued a warning to the proud: God knows all things and judges or reverses the deeds of people (vv.3-7).
4. Hannah predicted the future: the future lay in the hands of the LORD, the Creator of the world (vv.8-11).

---

1 Ronald F. Youngblood. *1 Samuel*, p.578.

1 (2:1) **Prayer, Example of—Songs, Example of—Deliverance, from Enemies, Example of—Horn, Meaning—Hannah, Prayer of**: Hannah thanked God for His personal deliverance. God had done a wonderful thing for Hannah, delivered her from the ridicule, abuse, and taunting of Peninnah. God had given Hannah a son, Samuel. As a result, her heart had broken out in prayer, rejoicing in the LORD for His great deliverance. Note that the focus of her prayer was the LORD. She referred to the LORD over twenty-one times in these ten verses, praying, praising, and giving thanks to Him.

OUTLINE	SCRIPTURE
1. Hannah thanked God for His personal deliverance a. Her heart rejoiced b. Her strength conquered—through the LORD c. Her mouth boasted over her enemies (Peninnah's abuse)	And Hannah prayed, and said, My heart rejoiceth in the LORD, mine horn is exalted in the LORD: my mouth is enlarged over mine enemies; because I rejoice in thy salvation.

Note the reference to her "horn" being exalted, lifted high. The horn is a metaphor taken from the animal world, from creatures such as oxen, goats, deer, or rhinoceros. Horns are used by animals for both attack and defense; consequently, horns symbolize strength, power. God had given Hannah's body the strength, the power to conceive and bare a son. Hannah's horn—her strength and ability to bear a child—was exalted, lifted high in the LORD. She was now able to boast over her enemies because of the LORD's deliverance. Peninnah could no longer mock her over her barrenness. God had given her a son, the child Samuel. She had conquered the disgrace and shame of having no child.

Thought 1. God is our Deliverer. Through the LORD, we can be triumphant and victorious, conquering all the trials and temptations of life. Hannah conquered mockery and derision through the power of the LORD. Just as the LORD delivered her, He will deliver us. The LORD will help us conquer the trials and troubling circumstances that confront us. He will make us *more than conquerors* through Him.

"Behold, I give unto you power to tread on serpents and scorpions, and over all the power of the enemy: and nothing shall by any means hurt you" (Lu.10:19).

"Who shall separate us from the love of Christ? shall tribulation, or distress, or persecution, or famine, or nakedness, or peril, or sword....Nay, in all these things we are more than conquerors through him that loved us. For I am persuaded, that neither death, nor life, nor angels, nor principalities, nor powers, nor things present, nor things to come, Nor height, nor depth, nor any other creature, shall be able to separate us from the love of God, which is in Christ Jesus our LORD" (Ro.8:35, 37-39).

"There hath no temptation taken you but such as is common to man: but God is faithful, who will not suffer you to be tempted above that ye are able; but will with the temptation also make a way to escape, that ye may be able to bear it" (1 Co.10:13).

"And the LORD shall deliver me from every evil work, and will preserve me unto his heavenly kingdom: to whom be glory for ever and ever. Amen" (2 Ti.4:18).

"So that we may boldly say, The LORD is my helper, and I will not fear what man shall do unto me" (He.13:6).

"The LORD knoweth how to deliver the godly out of temptations, and to reserve the unjust unto the day of judgment to be punished" (2 Pe. 2:9).

"For whatsoever is born of God overcometh the world: and this is the victory that overcometh the world, even our faith. Who is he that overcometh the world, but he that believeth that Jesus is the Son of God" (1 Jn.5:4-5).

"The LORD is my strength and my shield; my heart trusted in him, and I am helped: therefore my heart greatly rejoiceth; and with my song will I praise him" (Ps.28:7).

"But I am poor and needy; yet the LORD thinketh upon me: thou art my help and my deliverer; make no tarrying, O my God" (Ps.40:17).

"Through thee will we push down our enemies: through thy name will we tread them under that rise up against us" (Ps.44:5).

"Surely he shall deliver thee from the snare of the fowler, and from the noisome pestilence" (Ps.91:3).

"Fear thou not; for I am with thee: be not dismayed; for I am thy God: I will strengthen thee; yea, I will help thee; yea, I will uphold thee with the right hand of my righteousness" (Is.41:10).

"Behold, the LORD GOD will help me; who is he that shall condemn me? lo, they all shall wax old as a garment; the moth shall eat them up" (Is.50:9).

2 (2:2) **Praise, Example of—Holiness, of God—Rock, Meaning—God, Title of, Rock—God, Nature of, Holy—God, None Like—God, Only Living**: Hannah praised God for Himself. Three features about the LORD in particular are spelled out by Hannah:

OUTLINE	SCRIPTURE
2. Hannah praised God for Himself a. He is Holy b. He is the only living God c. He is the Rock of life	2 *There is* none holy as the LORD: for *there is* none beside thee: neither *is there* any rock like our God.

a. Hannah praised God for His holiness. To be *holy* means to be set apart and marked as totally different, distinct from all other things. God's holiness is a holiness of perfection—perfect being, perfect essence, perfect character, and perfect behavior. God dwells in perfect righteousness, perfect morality, and perfect justice. God dwells in eternal holiness, perfect holiness. The LORD is holy in every detail of His being. All that He is and everything He does is perfect, totally set apart, different, distinct from all other things. Hannah declared that there was no one holy like the LORD.

> "Who shall not fear thee, O LORD, and glorify thy name? for *thou* only *art* holy: for all nations shall come and worship before thee; for thy judgments are made manifest" (Re.15:4).
>
> "But as he which hath called you is holy, so be ye holy in all manner of conversation; Because it is written, Be ye holy; for I am holy" (1 Pe.1:15-16).
>
> "Who *is* like unto thee, O LORD, among the gods? who *is* like thee, glorious in holiness, fearful *in* praises, doing wonders" (Ex.15:11).
>
> "For I am the LORD that bringeth you up out of the land of Egypt, to be your God: ye shall therefore be holy, for I *am* holy" (Le.11:45).
>
> "Exalt the LORD our God, and worship at his holy hill; for the LORD our God *is* holy" (Ps.99:9).
>
> "And one cried unto another, and said, Holy, holy, holy, *is* the LORD of hosts: the whole earth *is* full of his glory" (Is.6:3).

b. Hannah also declared that there is *no one besides the LORD*. He is the only living and true God, the only God who could have answered her prayer and taken away her barrenness. There is none other—no other God who lives and possesses such unlimited power. Only the LORD Himself could have heard her prayer and given her a child, delivering her from the scorn and insults of Peninnah. And this the LORD did because He is the living and true God. No one else could have helped her but Him and Him alone.

> "And the scribe said unto him, Well, Master, thou hast said the truth: for there is one God; and there is none other but he" (Mk.12:32).
>
> "As concerning therefore the eating of those things that are offered in sacrifice unto idols, we know that an idol is nothing in the world, and that there is none other God but one" (1 Co.8:4).
>
> "One God and Father of all, who is above all, and through all, and in you all" (Ep.4:6).
>
> "For there is one God, and one mediator between God and men, the man Christ Jesus" (1 Ti.2:5).
>
> "In the beginning God created the heaven and the earth" (Ge.1:1).
>
> "Who is like unto thee, O LORD, among the gods? who is like thee, glorious in holiness, fearful in praises, doing wonders" (Ex.15:11).
>
> "Unto thee it was showed, that thou mightest know that the LORD he is God; there is none else beside him" (De.4:35).
>
> "See now that I, even I, am he, and there is no god with me: I kill, and I make alive; I wound, and I heal: neither is there any that can deliver out of my hand" (De.32:39).
>
> "Wherefore thou art great, O LORD God: for there is none like thee, neither is there any God beside thee, according to all that we have heard with our ears" (2 S.7:22).
>
> "And he said, LORD God of Israel, there is no God like thee, in heaven above, or on earth beneath, who keepest covenant and mercy with thy servants that walk before thee with all their heart" (1 K.8:23).
>
> "O LORD, there is none like thee, neither is there any God beside thee, according to all that we have heard with our ears" (1 Chr.17:20).
>
> "That men may know that thou, whose name alone is Jehovah, art the most high over all the earth" (Ps.83:18).
>
> "For thou art great, and doest wondrous things: thou art God alone" (Ps.86:10).
>
> "For who in the heaven can be compared unto the LORD? *who* among the sons of the mighty can be likened unto the LORD?" (Ps.89:6).
>
> "To whom then will ye liken God? or what likeness will ye compare unto him" (Is.40:18).
>
> "Ye are my witnesses, saith the LORD, and my servant whom I have chosen: that ye may know and believe me, and understand that I am he: before me there was no God formed, neither shall there be after me. I, even I, am the LORD; and beside me there is no saviour" (Is.43:10-11).
>
> "For thus saith the LORD that created the heavens; God himself that formed the earth and made it; he hath established it, he created it not in vain, he formed it to be inhabited: I am the LORD; and there is none else" (Is.45:18).

c. Hannah praised the LORD for being the *Rock of Life*. She declared that there was no Rock like our God. The image of God as a rock means at least three things:

1) God is the support, the foundation and cornerstone of life. Just as a building must be constructed upon a solid, rocklike foundation, so our lives must be built upon the foundation of God. God and God alone can support us and provide the cornerstone necessary to uphold life. Hannah was declaring that God was her rock, and there is no rock like our God.

2) God is our protection, our security and safety. A rock gives protection; it is a picture of safety and security. Hannah is declaring that the LORD is her rock of protection, her rock of security and safety.

3) God is our strength. A rock is a symbol of strength and stability. Hannah declares there is no rock, no strength, and no stability like our God.

"Now to him that is of power to stablish you according to my gospel, and the preaching of Jesus Christ, according to the revelation of the mystery, which was kept secret since the world began" (Ro.16:25).

"He is the Rock, his work is perfect: for all his ways are judgment: a God of truth and without iniquity, just and right is he" (De.32:4).

"The LORD liveth; and blessed be my rock; and exalted be the God of the rock of my salvation" (2 S.22:47).

"And Elisha prayed, and said, LORD, I pray thee, open his eyes, that he may see. And the LORD opened the eyes of the young man; and he saw: and, behold, the mountain was full of horses and chariots of fire round about Elisha" (2 K.6:17).

"For the eyes of the LORD run to and fro throughout the whole earth, to show himself strong in the behalf of them whose heart is perfect toward him. Herein thou hast done foolishly: therefore from henceforth thou shalt have wars" (2 Chr.16:9).

"And thou shalt be secure, because there is hope; yea, thou shalt dig about thee, and thou shalt take thy rest in safety" (Jb.11:18).

"For who is God save the LORD? or who is a rock save our God" (Ps.18:31).

"Unto thee will I cry, O LORD my rock; be not silent to me: lest, if thou be silent to me, I become like them that go down into the pit" (Ps.28:1).

"He only is my rock and my salvation; he is my defence; I shall not be greatly moved" (Ps.62:2).

"Thou shalt not be afraid for the terror by night; nor for the arrow that flieth by day" (Ps.91:5).

"But the LORD is my defence; and my God is the rock of my refuge" (Ps.94:22).

"He shall not be afraid of evil tidings: his heart is fixed, trusting in the LORD" (Ps.112:7).

"His heart is established, he shall not be afraid, until he see his desire upon his enemies" (Ps.112:8).

"As the mountains are round about Jerusalem, so the LORD is round about his people from henceforth even for ever" (Ps.125:2).

---

3 (2:3-7) **Pride, Warning against—Warning, against the Proud—Judgment, How God Judges**: Hannah issued a warning to the proud, to all who go about talking proudly and speaking arrogantly. She warned that God knows all things and reverses and judges the deeds of people. No matter what a person may achieve on this earth—no matter how much power or wealth a person may possess—God knows the heart of a person. And God weighs the heart of the person by the deeds the person does. Just as a tree is known by its fruit, so a person's heart is known by the deeds (fruit) the person produces.

The point is striking and speaks to us all. God weighs the deeds of us all, and He will judge us by our deeds. Throughout life, God is constantly weighing and evaluating what we do. And if warranted or needed, God can reverse our lives here upon this earth. God can look upon us whenever we have a need and reverse our condition by giving us whatever we lack. On the other hand, when we have everything, God may take it away. God warns us through Hannah: He will reverse our condition, state, welfare, status, position, and wealth here on earth—if needed and if warranted or justified. This is God's clear warning given through Hannah:

OUTLINE	SCRIPTURE	SCRIPTURE	OUTLINE
3. Hannah issued a warning to the proud: God knows all things & judges or reverses the deeds of people	3 Talk no more so exceeding proudly; let *not* arrogancy come out of your mouth: for the LORD is a God of knowledge, and by him actions are weighed.	bread; and *they that were* hungry ceased: so that the barren hath born seven; and she that hath many children is waxed feeble.	c. God reverses the barren woman & the fruitful
a. God reverses the strong & the weak, even military Jews who are strong	4 The bows of the mighty men *are* broken, and they that stumbled are girded with strength.	6 The LORD killeth, and maketh alive: he bringeth down to the grave, and bringeth up.	d. God reverses death & life, sickness & health
b. God reverses the full & the hungry	5 *They that were* full have hired out themselves for	7 The LORD maketh poor, and maketh rich: he bringeth low, and lifteth up.	e. God reverses the poor & rich
			f. God reverses the humble & the exalted

a. God's judgment reverses the strong and the weak (v.4). Even military forces who are strong can be judged by God and victory given to the weak. If needed or warranted, God can weaken, disarm, or disable any of the proud who arrogantly boast of their strength. Through judgment, God can weaken any human body through sickness, disease, accident, or age. God can even weaken the human body to the point of death and the grave. Moreover, God can cause the mightiest army to collapse through intrigue and traitors, a surprise attack, some miscalculation, overconfidence, disarmament, or a host of other ways.

Likewise, God can take the weak and make them strong. He can raise them up from sickness or miraculously heal them; and He can protect, guide, and strengthen them. Furthermore, God can take the weak and give them insight and knowledge, making sure they receive the necessary weapons to defeat the proud and arrogant of this world. God can equip the weak to be victorious and triumphant throughout life. Through God, the weak can become *more than conquerors*.

b. God's judgment reverses the full and the hungry (v.5). If a person has plenty of food, so much that he never has to fear being hungry—his circumstances can change under the judgment of God. If needed or warranted, God can reverse his circumstances. A person's food supply or money can be wiped out by the hand of God's judgment.

So it is with the hungry: they will hunger no more. The day is coming when the hungry who have trusted God will be fed and filled. And they will always have plenty to eat. God's blessings will pour out upon them and give them an abundance. Their pain and despair will be wiped away by God; they will receive a constant provision of food and always be filled by God.

c. God's judgment reverses the barren woman and the fruitful one. Obviously, Hannah is thinking of herself in describing this situation of judgment. Hannah had been barren, but God had acted in her behalf and given her a son. Hannah eventually had six children (v.21). The point is striking: if needed and warranted, God can give children to the barren woman. And He can weaken the prideful woman who has born a child, weakened her to where she can bear no more children. If needed or warranted, God can make a woman frail and feeble long before her time.

d. God's judgment reverses death and life, sickness and health (v.6). God is sovereign, ruling and reigning over all beings and events throughout the universe. He is the LORD of life and death. If needed or warranted, God can act in judgment and bring death to a person, or He can raise a person from the bed of sickness, disease, or accident. God can protect human life, or He can remove His protective hand and leave a life to face the perils of this world. God can bring a person face-to-face with death and cause him to sink into the pit of the grave.

e. God's judgment reverses the poor and rich, poverty and wealth (v.7). If the wealthy talk proudly about their investments, property, or bank accounts, the judgment of God will fall upon them. It will fall either during this life or when they stand face-to-face with Christ. If needed or warranted, God may act during this life. He may act now by taking away the wealth and bringing the rich person into poverty.

For the poor, God gives a great promise: either in this life or the next, the poor who trust Christ will be made rich. The poor believer will receive wealth beyond human imagination. It is the LORD who gives wealth as well as poverty. He is the Sovereign Ruler who controls the wealth of the universe, either to give or to take away.

f. God's judgment reverses the humble and the exalted (vv.7-8). If needed or warranted, God takes the proud and brings them low, removing them from their position of esteem and honor. In judgment, God reverses their pride and turns it into shame, embarrassment, humiliation. He places the proud into a situation of being despised. The prideful will be humbled either upon this earth or when coming face-to-face with the Lord Jesus Christ in judgment.

But this is not to be the experience of the person who humbles himself before God. The person who is truly humble before God will be exalted. No matter who the humble are—no matter how poor or needy—God will take them and exalt them. He will raise the poor from the dust and lift up the needy from the ash heap. God will make them princes and cause them to inherit the throne of glory (v.8). The exaltation of the lowly will take place either upon this earth or in the new heavens and earth yet to come. This is definitely a prediction of the glory of the humble believer when he meets Christ face-to-face. But if needed or warranted, God will exalt the humble person during his life upon the earth.

Thought 1. This passage is definitely a warning to us and to all future generations. God will judge the *deeds* of us all. And the judgment may come right now, while we are living on this earth. If we keep talking so proudly and speaking so arrogantly, God's judgment will fall upon us. This judgment will definitely be executed against us when we come face-to-face with Christ. But if needed or warranted, His judgment may fall upon us even now, today, while we are living upon this earth. If we walk in pride, committing sin and evil, God can reverse our lives, turn them *upside down*.

But if we follow God, trusting Him to deliver, protect, and guide us—God will reverse our lives and turn them *right side up*. This is the promise to all genuine believers, either in this world or in the world to come when we stand before Him in the glory and majesty of heaven itself.

Hannah issued a warning to the proud of all generations: God knows all things and judges the deeds of us all. God is able to reverse the very deeds that we do. This is the strong declaration of Holy Scripture.

> **"For the Son of man shall come in the glory of his Father with his angels; and then he shall reward every man according to his works" (Mt.16:27).**
> **"For we must all appear before the judgment seat of Christ; that every one may receive the things done in his body, according to that he hath done, whether it be good or bad" (2 Co.5:10).**
> **"And if ye call on the Father, who without respect of persons judgeth according to every man's work, pass the time of your sojourning here in fear" (1 Pe.1:17).**
> **"And I saw a great white throne, and him that sat on it, from whose face the earth and the heaven fled away; and there was found no place for them. And I saw the dead, small and great, stand before God; and the books were opened: and another book was opened, which is the book of life: and the dead were judged out of those things which were written in the books, according to their works. And the sea gave up the dead which were in it; and death and hell delivered up the dead which were in them: and they were judged every man according to their works. And death and hell were cast into the lake of fire. This is the second death. And whosoever was not found written in the book of life was cast into the lake of fire" (Re.20:11-15).**
> **"And, behold, I come quickly; and my reward is with me, to give every man according as his work shall be" (Re.22:12).**
> **"Also unto thee, O LORD, belongeth mercy: for thou renderest to every man according to his work" (Ps.62:12).**
> **"I the LORD search the heart, I try the reins, even to give every man according to his ways, and according to the fruit of his doings" (Je.17:10).**

4 (2:8-11) **Prophecy, by Whom—Prophecy, about Christ—Prophecy, about David—Prophecy, of Judgment—Future, Prophecy about—Hannah, Prophecy of**: Hannah predicted the future of several wonderful truths. The future lay in the hands of the LORD, the Creator of the world. It is the LORD who has laid the foundations of the earth; consequently, it is He who controls the events of the world and gives order to the world. Because of God's sovereign control, three future events are guaranteed, three events that absolutely will take place:

OUTLINE	SCRIPTURE	SCRIPTURE	OUTLINE
4. Hannah predicted the future: The future lay in the hands of the LORD, the Creator of the world a. The LORD will preserve the saints b. The LORD will judge the wicked 1) Silence them in darkness 2) Shatter them	8 He raiseth up the poor out of the dust, *and* lifteth up the beggar from the dunghill, to set *them* among princes, and to make them inherit the throne of glory: for the pillars of the earth *are* the LORD'S, and he hath set the world upon them. 9 He will keep the feet of his saints, and the wicked shall be silent in darkness; for by strength shall no man pre-	vail. 10 The adversaries of the LORD shall be broken to pieces; out of heaven shall he thunder upon them: the LORD shall judge the ends of the earth; and he shall give strength unto his king, and exalt the horn of his anointed. 11 And Elkanah went to Ramah to his house. And the child did minister unto the LORD before Eli the priest.	c. The LORD will strengthen His king & exalt His anointed (a prediction of David & of Christ)

a. The LORD is in control: He will preserve the saints (v.9). Hannah declares that the LORD will keep—guard and protect—His saints. The word "saint" (*chaciyd* or *hasiyd*) means the consecrated ones, the godly, the faithful, the loving, the devoted, the favored, the holy, the merciful, and the good. A saint is a person who has made a covenant, a promise to love and obey God, to love and obey Him supremely, wholeheartedly. (Ps.12:1,8; 31:23; 34:9; 50:5; 16; 97:10; 145:10,20; 148:14).

Note that the *saints* belong to the LORD. They are His people, "His saints" (v.9). Because they are His, the LORD will guide, protect, and deliver them through all the trials and temptations of this life. And He will give them victory over all their enemies. They will be *more than conquerors* throughout life, triumphing over all the enemies and trials of this world. The LORD will preserve His saints, keeping them wherever their feet may walk.

> "For the which cause I also suffer these things: nevertheless I am not ashamed: for I know whom I have believed, and am persuaded that he is able to keep that which I have committed unto him against that day" (2 Ti.1:12).
>
> "And the LORD shall deliver me from every evil work, and will preserve me unto his heavenly kingdom: to whom be glory for ever and ever. Amen" (2 Ti.4:18).
>
> "And, behold, I am with thee, and will keep thee in all places whither thou goest, and will bring thee again into this land; for I will not leave thee, until I have done that which I have spoken to thee of" (Ge.28:15).
>
> "And the LORD commanded us to do all these statutes, to fear the LORD our God, for our good always, that he might preserve us alive, as it is at this day" (De.6:24).
>
> "O love the LORD, all ye his saints: for the LORD preserveth the faithful, and plentifully rewardeth the proud doer" (Ps.31:23).
>
> "For the LORD loveth judgment, and forsaketh not his saints; they are preserved for ever: but the seed of the wicked shall be cut off" (Ps.37:28).
>
> "Behold, he that keepeth Israel shall neither slumber nor sleep" (Ps.121:4).
>
> "He keepeth the paths of judgment, and preserveth the way of his saints" (Pr.2:8).

b. The LORD is in control: He will judge the wicked (vv.9-10a). The wicked will be silenced in darkness. The picture is descriptive: they will be blinded, unable to see, groping and grasping about trying to find their way through life. They may be strong, able to achieve here and there in life, but they are blind, walking and stumbling about in the dark. Consequently, they eventually fail to overcome or prevail and are unsuccessful. In their blindness and stumbling about, they fall and are broken. Their lives are to be shattered and their eternal fate is to face judgment and condemnation forever. The LORD's wrath will thunder against them from heaven in the day of judgment (v.10).

> "But if thine eye be evil, thy whole body shall be full of darkness. If therefore the light that is in thee be darkness, how great is that darkness" (Mt.6:23).
>
> "Let them alone: they be blind leaders of the blind. And if the blind lead the blind, both shall fall into the ditch" (Mt.15:14).
>
> "And this is the condemnation, that light is come into the world, and men loved darkness rather than light, because their deeds were evil" (Jn.3:19).
>
> "Marvel not at this: for the hour is coming, in the which all that are in the graves shall hear his voice. And shall come forth; they that have done good, unto the resurrection of life; and they that have done evil, unto the resurrection of damnation" (Jn.5:28-29).
>
> "The night is far spent, the day is at hand: let us therefore cast off the works of darkness, and let us put on the armour of light" (Ro.13:12).
>
> "But ye, brethren, are not in darkness, that that day should overtake you as a thief" (1 Th.5:4).

"The Lord knoweth how to deliver the godly out of temptations, and to reserve the unjust unto the day of judgment to be punished" (2 Pe.2:9).

"But the heavens and the earth, which are now, by the same word are kept in store, reserved unto fire against the day of judgment and perdition of ungodly men" (2 Pe.3:7).

"If we say that we have fellowship with him, and walk in darkness, we lie, and do not the truth" (1 Jn.1:6).

"And Enoch also, the seventh from Adam, prophesied of these, saying, Behold, the Lord cometh with ten thousands of his saints, To execute judgment upon all, and to convince all that are ungodly among them of all their ungodly deeds which they have ungodly committed, and of all their hard speeches which ungodly sinners have spoken against him" (Jude 14-15).

"And I saw a great white throne, and him that sat on it, from whose face the earth and the heaven fled away; and there was found no place for them. And I saw the dead, small and great, stand before God; and the books were opened: and another book was opened, which is the book of life: and the dead were judged out of those things which were written in the books, according to their works. And the sea gave up the dead which were in it; and death and hell delivered up the dead which were in them: and they were judged every man according to their works. And death and hell were cast into the lake of fire. This is the second death. And whosoever was not found written in the book of life was cast into the lake of fire" (Re.20:11-15).

"And thou shalt grope at noonday, as the blind gropeth in darkness, and thou shalt not prosper in thy ways: and thou shalt be only oppressed and spoiled evermore, and no man shall save thee" (De.28:29).

"They know not, neither will they understand; they walk on in darkness: all the foundations of the earth are out of course" (Ps.82:5).

"The way of the wicked is as darkness: they know not at what they stumble" (Pr.4:19).

"Therefore is judgment far from us, neither doth justice overtake us: we wait for light, but behold obscurity; for brightness, but we walk in darkness" (Is.59:9).

"Wherefore their way shall be unto them as slippery ways in the darkness: they shall be driven on, and fall therein: for I will bring evil upon them, even the year of their visitation, saith the Lord" (Je.23:12).

c. The Lord is in control: He will strengthen His king and exalt His anointed (v.10). The phrases "his king" and "his anointed" have a double meaning, referring to both David and Christ. This is a clear prediction of both David and the coming Messiah, the Lord Jesus Christ. This the first time the word "anointed" (*mashiyach* or *masiyah*) refers to an individual's being the *Anointed One* or the *Messiah*. The use of Hannah's prayer by Mary, the mother of Jesus, suggests that the very first believers considered this to be a prophecy of the coming Messiah (Lu.1:46-55). From this point on throughout the Old Testament, the Messiah or "Anointed One of God" is often referred to (Ps.2:6; Ps.89:20-24; Is.32:1; Je.23:5; Eze.22, 24; Ho.3:5; Zec.9:9).

When the child Samuel was born, Hannah saw how God was continuing to fulfill His promise to Abraham. God was continuing to send sons—the seed promised to Abraham—to bless the whole world. By seeing her son Samuel as part of the promised seed, she pointed to the Messiah. She foresaw the sending of the *promised seed*—the Messiah Himself—who would bless the whole world. Hannah declared that God would give strength to His king and exalt the strength of His anointed (v.10). She was predicting that the Lord would strengthen the king and the coming Messianic King...

- to accomplish their great tasks
- to march through the trials and temptations of life
- to conquer and gain victory over their enemies
- to reconcile their people and bring peace among them
- to give assurance and hope to their subjects

"For unto us a child is born, unto us a son is given: and the government shall be upon his shoulder: and his name shall be called Wonderful, Counsellor, The mighty God, The everlasting Father, The Prince of Peace. Of the increase of *his* government and peace *there shall be* no end, upon the throne of David, and upon his kingdom, to order it, and to establish it with judgment and with justice from henceforth even for ever. The zeal of the Lord of hosts will perform this" (Is.9:6-7).

"So then after the Lord had spoken unto them, he was received up into heaven, and sat on the right hand of God" (Mk.16:19).

"Therefore let all the house of Israel know assuredly, that God hath made that same Jesus, whom ye have crucified, both Lord and Christ" (Ac.2:36).

"For to this end Christ both died, and rose, and revived, that he might be Lord both of the dead and living" (Ro.14:9).

"Let this mind be in you, which was also in Christ Jesus: Who, being in the form of God, thought it not robbery to be equal with God: But made himself of no reputation, and took upon him the form of a servant, and was made in the likeness of men: And being found in fashion as a man, he humbled himself, and became obedient unto death, even the death of the cross. Wherefore God also hath highly exalted him, and given him a name which is above every name: That at the name of Jesus every knee should bow, of things in heaven, and things in earth, and things under the earth; And that every tongue should confess that Jesus Christ is Lord, to the glory of God the Father" (Ph.2:5-11).

"Saying with a loud voice, Worthy is the Lamb that was slain to receive power, and riches, and wisdom, and strength, and honour, and glory, and blessing" (Re.5:12).

C. The Wickedness of Eli's Sons Contrasted with the Righteousness of Samuel: A Lesson on a Corrupt Ministry, 2:12-36

1. The wickedness of Eli's sons

a. They were sons of Belial

b. They did not know the LORD

c. They desecrated the offerings

1) Insisted on getting some choice meat that belonged to the person presenting the offering

2) Insisted on getting raw meat before the LORD received His portion: Meat that was to be burned as a sweet aroma to the LORD (the act that symbolized the sacrifice was acceptable to God)

3) Insisted on getting some fat: Was clearly prohibited by the LORD, Le.7:22-25

d. They showed contempt for the LORD & His Word, sinning greatly

e. They committed immorality at the Tabernacle, 22

2. The sharp contrast of Samuel's commitment to the LORD: He served even as a child

a. He wore the priestly garment

b. He was visited by his parents & received a new coat from his mother each year: When she & Elkanah went up to offer the annual sacrifice

1) The priest would bless them, praying for the LORD to give them children to take the place of Samuel

2) The LORD was gracious to Hannah, giving her five more children

c. He continued to grow in the presence of the LORD: A sharp contrast of Samuel's growth in righteousness with the wicked behavior of Eli's sons

3. The failure & indulgence of Eli: He only mildly rebuked

12 Now the sons of Eli *were* sons of Belial; they knew not the LORD.

13 And the priest's custom with the people *was, that,* when any man offered sacrifice, the priest's servant came, while the flesh was in seething, with a fleshhook of three teeth in his hand;

14 And he struck *it* into the pan, or kettle, or caldron, or pot; all that the fleshhook brought up the priest took for himself. So they did in Shiloh unto all the Israelites that came thither.

15 Also before they burnt the fat, the priest's servant came, and said to the man that sacrificed, Give flesh to roast for the priest; for he will not have sodden flesh of thee, but raw.

16 And *if* any man said unto him, Let them not fail to burn the fat presently, and *then* take *as much* as thy soul desireth; then he would answer him, *Nay;* but thou shalt give *it me* now: and if not, I will take *it* by force.

17 Wherefore the sin of the young men was very great before the LORD: for men abhorred the offering of the LORD.

18 But Samuel ministered before the LORD, *being* a child, girded with a linen ephod.

19 Moreover his mother made him a little coat, and brought *it* to him from year to year, when she came up with her husband to offer the yearly sacrifice.

20 And Eli blessed Elkanah and his wife, and said, The LORD give thee seed of this woman for the loan which is lent to the LORD. And they went unto their own home.

21 And the LORD visited Hannah, so that she conceived, and bare three sons and two daughters. And the child Samuel grew before the LORD.

22 Now Eli was very old, and heard all that his sons did unto all Israel; and how they lay with the women that assembled *at* the door of the tabernacle of the congregation.

23 And he said unto them, Why do ye such things? for I hear of your evil dealings by all this people.

24 Nay, my sons; for *it is* no good report that I hear: ye make the LORD'S people to transgress.

25 If one man sin against another, the judge shall judge him: but if a man sin against the LORD, who shall intreat for him? Notwithstanding they hearkened not unto the voice of their father, because the LORD would slay them.

26 And the child Samuel grew on, and was in favour both with the LORD, and also with men.

27 And there came a man of God unto Eli, and said unto him, Thus saith the LORD, Did I plainly appear unto the house of thy father, when they were in Egypt in Pharaoh's house?

28 And did I choose him out of all the tribes of Israel *to be* my priest, to offer upon mine altar, to burn incense, to wear an ephod before me? and did I give unto the house of thy father all the offerings made by fire of the children of Israel?

29 Wherefore kick ye at my sacrifice and at mine offering, which I have commanded *in my* habitation; and honourest thy sons above me, to make yourselves fat with the chiefest of all the offerings of Israel my people?

30 Wherefore the LORD God of Israel saith, I said indeed *that* thy house, and the house of thy father, should walk before me for ever: but now the LORD saith, Be it far from me; for them that honour me I will honour, and they that despise me shall be lightly esteemed.

31 Behold, the days come, that I will cut off thine arm, and the arm of thy father's house, that there shall not be an old man in thine house.

32 And thou shalt see an enemy *in my* habitation, in all *the wealth* which *God* shall give Israel: and there shall

his sons, failing to stop the evil

a. Eli's sons continued their wicked decline: Committed immorality at the Tabernacle

b. Eli had heard about their evil through rumor: Their evil had been rumored far & wide

c. Eli confronted, rebuked, & warned his sons of God's judgment: Their deliberate, deceitful sin would be severely judged

d. Eli's rebuke was rejected by his sons

e. The result: The LORD marked them for judgment

4. The sharp contrast of young Samuel's growth: He grew physically & in favor with God & with people

5. The message of God's judgment against Eli & his sons: Sent by an unnamed prophet

a. The reminder of God's clear revelation of Himself & of His call to the priesthood

1) He chose the family of Levi (Aaron, Levi's son) to be His priest

2) He chose them to be His priests to carry on the ministry

b. The charge of God against Eli & his sons

1) They scorned the holy things of God: The Tabernacle, the offerings & sacrifices

2) Eli condoned his son's evil: Honored them more than God

c. The judgment of God against Eli & his sons

1) His house or descendants would be cut off as priests

2) His descendants would be dishonored, held in low esteem

3) His descendants would thereafter have only a short life span

4) His descendants would witness the blessings of God upon others, but only distress in their own families

5) His descendants would live in sadness & grief & die in the prime of life	not be an old man in thine house for ever. 33 And the man of thine, *whom* I shall not cut off from mine altar, *shall be* to consume thine eyes, and to grieve thine heart: and all the increase of thine house shall die in the flower of their age.	faithful priest, *that* shall do according to *that* which *is* in mine heart and in my mind: and I will build him a sure house; and he shall walk before mine anointed for ever.	**priest: Fulfilled first in Samuel (3:1, 20; 7:9; 9:12-13), then Zadok (2 S.8:17; 15:24-29; 1 K. 2:35), & finally Christ (He.5:10)**
6) His two sons would die on the same day: To serve as a sign that God's prophetic judgments would definitely take place	34 And this *shall be* a sign unto thee, that shall come upon thy two sons, on Hophni and Phinehas; in one day they shall die both of them.	36 And it shall come to pass, *that* every one that is left in thine house shall come *and* crouch to him for a piece of silver and a morsel of bread, and shall say, Put me, I pray thee, into one of the priests' offices, that I may eat a piece of bread.	a. Who would be faithful b. Who would minister to the anointed one (the king) c. Who would be sought by Eli's house: Seeking help from the appointed priest
6. The promise of a very special	35 And I will raise me up a	of bread.	

DIVISION I

THE STORY OF ELI AND SAMUEL: THE LORD CLOSES THE ERA OF THE JUDGES AND PREPARES FOR THE RULE OF THE KINGS, 1:1–7:17

C.   **The Wickedness of Eli's Sons Contrasted with the Righteousness of Samuel: A Lesson on a Corrupt Ministry, 2:12-36**

(2:12-36) **Introduction—Ministers, Fall of—Priests, Fall of**: when a minister falls into sin and commits wickedness, it is a terribly tragedy. Ministers are to point people to God, not lead them astray. Ministers are to proclaim the righteousness of God, not live unrighteous, immoral lives. Ministers are to meet the needs of people, not be focused upon lives of selfishness.

The present passage is a horrible picture of the sins of priests, the wickedness of ministers. A sharp contrast is drawn between wickedness and righteousness throughout the passage. This is: *The Wickedness of Eli's Sons Contrasted with the Righteousness of Samuel: A Lesson on a Corrupt Ministry*, 2:12-36.

1. The wickedness of Eli's sons (vv.12-17).
2. The sharp contrast of Samuel's commitment to the Lord: he served even as a child (vv.18-21).
3. The failure and indulgence of Eli: he only mildly rebuked his sons, failing to stop the evil (vv.22-25).
4. The sharp contrast of young Samuel's growth: he grew physically and in favor with God and with people (v.26).
5. The message of God's judgment against Eli and his sons: sent by an unnamed prophet (vv.27-34).
6. The promise of a very special priest: fulfilled first in Samuel (3:1, 20; 7:9; 9:12-13), then in Zadok (2 S.8:17; 15:24-29; 1 K.2:35), and finally in Christ (He.5:10) (vv.35-36).

☐1 (2:12-17) **Wickedness, of Priests and Ministers—Ministers, Sins of—Priesthood, Sins of—Eli, Sins of His Sons—Offerings, Abuse, Stealing**: there was the terrible wickedness of Eli's sons. A dark, menacing cloud now appeared over the horizon of Samuel's history and of the priesthood. The reader is being prepared for the terrible disasters that are to take place in chapter four. The wickedness of the priests was shameful, reaching the depth of corruption and immorality. The Scripture paints the picture of a rotten, defiled priesthood, a totally depraved priesthood:

OUTLINE	SCRIPTURE	SCRIPTURE	OUTLINE

1. The wickedness of Eli's sons
  a. They were sons of Belial
  b. They did not know the LORD
  c. They desecrated the offerings
    1) Insisted on getting some choice meat that belonged to the person presenting the offering
 	
  2) Insisted on getting raw
	12 Now the sons of Eli *were* sons of Belial; they knew not the LORD.
	13 And the priest's custom with the people *was, that,* when any man offered sacrifice, the priest's servant came, while the flesh was in seething, with a flesh-hook of three teeth in his hand;
	14 And he struck *it* into the pan, or kettle, or caldron, or pot; all that the fleshhook brought up the priest took for himself. So they did in Shiloh unto all the Israelites that came thither.
	15 Also before they burnt the
		fat, the priest's servant came, and said to the man that sacrificed, Give flesh to roast for the priest; for he will not have sodden flesh of thee, but raw.
		16 And *if* any man said unto him, Let them not fail to burn the fat presently, and *then* take *as much* as thy soul desireth; then he would answer him, *Nay;* but thou shalt give *it me* now: and if not, I will take *it* by force.
		17 Wherefore the sin of the young men was very great before the LORD: for men abhorred the offering of the LORD.
			meat before the LORD received His portion: Meat that was to be burned as a sweet aroma to the LORD (the act that symbolized the sacrifice was acceptable to God)
			  3) Insisted on getting some fat: Was clearly prohibited by the LORD, Le.7:22-25
			
			  d. They showed contempt for the LORD & His Word, sinning greatly
			  e. They committed immorality at the Tabernacle, 22

a. The priests, Eli's sons, had become sons of *Belial*. The Hebrew word means corrupt and wicked or scoundrels and troublemakers. The word is also used as a name for Satan himself, who is the very embodiment of wickedness, who stands for the very depths of lawlessness.[1] Eli's sons, the priests of that day, had become utterly corrupt. They were living as though they were sons of Belial, Satan himself.

b. The priests simply did not know the LORD (v.12). They did not respect nor show any regard for the LORD. To "know" in the Bible means to accept and believe the LORD; to commit one's life in following the LORD; to fellowship, commune, and worship the LORD. It does not mean merely having a mental knowledge of the LORD, just acknowledging that He exists in some abstract, spiritual, or theoretical sense. The sons of Eli plainly did not know the LORD—not personally, not intimately. They had no fellowship with the LORD, nor did they live for Him. As this Scripture describes, following and obeying the LORD was the furthest thing from their minds.

c. The priests desecrated the offerings that were being given to the LORD (vv.13-15). This wickedness was committed in three ways:

1) They insisted upon being given some of the choice meat that belonged to the person presenting the offering (vv.13-14). They were not satisfied with the portion of meat that was to be given to the priests; consequently, they would take a three-pronged fork and plunge it into the pot where the meat was boiling and take whatever portion they desired. Of course, their self-serving behavior was totally contrary to God's Word, the law that controlled the offerings.

2) They sometimes insisted upon some raw meat before the LORD received His portion, the meat that was to be burned as the sweet aroma to the LORD (v.15). Burning the LORD's portion as a sweet aroma was an act symbolizing that the sacrifice was acceptable to God.

3) They even insisted upon some of the fat that was clearly prohibited by the LORD. The fat also belonged to the LORD and was to be burned as a sweet aroma to Him (see outline and note—Le.7:22-25 for more discussion). The priests also abused and threatened the people if they objected to the meat being taken. They were willing to commit violence in order to provide the very best meat and food for their own families. Selfishness, greed, and lust had gripped their hearts to the point that they had become lawless and violent priests.

d. In showing such contempt for the LORD and His Word, the priests sinned greatly. The LORD had given clear instructions as to how the offerings were to be presented and how the meat was to be divided between the LORD, the offerer, and the priests (see outline and notes—Le.6:8-7:38 for more discussion). Yet Eli's sons disobeyed God's Holy Word. They showed utter disrespect and contempt for the LORD and His commandments.

e. The priests committed the terrible sin of immorality at the Tabernacle itself (v.22). This will be discussed in detail below (see note 5—1 S.2:27-34).

Thought 1. This is a picture of terrible corruption within the priesthood and ministry. The priests' wickedness had sunk to appalling depths of defilement and depravity. Just imagine the following sins:
⇒ a minister who has become so wicked that he is a very son of Belial, the devil himself.
⇒ a minister who does not know the LORD, who has never been genuinely converted, and does not follow the LORD nor live for Him.
⇒ a minister who desecrates and steals from the offerings.
⇒ a minister who abuses and threatens people in order to secure more and more—all because of a heart of greed and lust.
⇒ a minister who shows contempt for the LORD and His Word, who does not obey nor attempt to follow the commandments of the LORD.
⇒ a minister who commits immorality, adultery (v.22).

This was the depth of wickedness into which Eli's sons had fallen. And tragically, some ministers today sink to these very same depths. But God warns all ministers: they will be held accountable, and they will face the judgment of God for their wickedness.
(1) Listen to how Scripture describes unfaithful and false ministers.

> **"But the chief priests and elders persuaded the multitude that they should ask Barabbas, and destroy Jesus" (Mt.27:20).**
> **"But he that is an hireling, and not the shepherd, whose own the sheep are not, seeth the wolf coming, and leaveth the sheep, and fleeth: and the wolf catcheth them, and scattereth the sheep" (Jn.10:12).**
> **"When the chief priests therefore and officers saw him, they cried out, saying, Crucify him, crucify him. Pilate saith unto them, Take ye him, and crucify him: for I find no fault in him" (Jn.19:6).**
> **"Some indeed preach Christ even of envy and strife; and some also of good will" (Ph.1:15).**
> **"His watchmen are blind: they are all ignorant, they are all dumb dogs, they cannot bark; sleeping, lying down, loving to slumber. Yea, they are greedy dogs which can never have enough, and they are shepherds that cannot understand: they all look to their own way, every one for his gain, from his quarter. Come ye, say they, I will fetch wine, and we will fill ourselves with strong drink; and to morrow shall be as this day, and much more abundant" (Is.56:10-12).**
> **"My people hath been lost sheep: their shepherds have caused them to go astray, they have turned them away on the mountains: they have gone from mountain to hill, they have forgotten their restingplace" (Je.50:6).**

---

[1] *The NIV Study Bible, New International Version.* (Grand Rapids, MI: Zondervan Bible Publishers, 1985), De.13:13.

"For from the least of them even unto the greatest of them every one is given to covetousness; and from the prophet even unto the priest every one dealeth falsely" (Je.6:13).

"Her priests have violated my law, and have profaned mine holy things: they have put no difference between the holy and profane, neither have they showed difference between the unclean and the clean, and have hid their eyes from my sabbaths, and I am profaned among them" (Eze.22:26).

"But if the watchman see the sword come, and blow not the trumpet, and the people be not warned; if the sword come, and take any person from among them, he is taken away in his iniquity; but his blood will I require at the watchman's hand" (Eze.33:6).

"Son of man, prophesy against the shepherds of Israel, prophesy, and say unto them, Thus saith the Lord God unto the shepherds; Woe be to the shepherds of Israel that do feed themselves! should not the shepherds feed the flocks? Ye eat the fat, and ye clothe you with the wool, ye kill them that are fed: but ye feed not the flock " (Eze.34:2-3).

"The heads thereof judge for reward, and the priests thereof teach for hire, and the prophets thereof divine for money: yet will they lean upon the Lord, and say, Is not the Lord among us? none evil can come upon us" (Mi.3:11).

"Her prophets are light and treacherous persons: her priests have polluted the sanctuary, they have done violence to the law" (Zep.3:4).

(2) Listen to the judgment that will fall upon ministers who do not really know the LORD and who are corrupt and wicked.

"For the Son of man shall come in the glory of his Father with his angels; and then he shall reward every man according to his works" (Mt.16:27).

"So then every one of us shall give account of himself to God" (Ro.14:12).

"Moreover it is required in stewards, that a man be found faithful" (1 Co.4:2).

"For we must all appear before the judgment seat of Christ; that every one may receive the things done in his body, according to that he hath done, whether it be good or bad" (2 Co.5:10).

"And to you who are troubled rest with us, when the Lord Jesus shall be revealed from heaven with his mighty angels, In flaming fire taking vengeance on them that know not God, and that obey not the gospel of our Lord Jesus Christ" (2 Th.1:7-8).

"My brethren, be not many masters, knowing that we shall receive the greater condemnation" (Js.3:1).

"And I saw a great white throne, and him that sat on it, from whose face the earth and the heaven fled away; and there was found no place for them. And I saw the dead, small and great, stand before God; and the books were opened: and another book was opened, which is the book of life: and the dead were judged out of those things which were written in the books, according to their works. And the sea gave up the dead which were in it; and death and hell delivered up the dead which were in them: and they were judged every man according to their works. And death and hell were cast into the lake of fire. This is the second death. And whosoever was not found written in the book of life was cast into the lake of fire" (Re.20:11-15).

"And, behold, I come quickly; and my reward is with me, to give every man according as his work shall be" (Re.22:12).

"I the Lord search the heart, I try the reins, even to give every man according to his ways, and according to the fruit of his doings" (Je.17:10).

"Therefore thus saith the Lord God of Israel against the pastors that feed my people; Ye have scattered my flock, and driven them away, and have not visited them: behold, I will visit upon you the evil of your doings, saith the Lord" (Je.23:2).

"But if the watchman see the sword come, and blow not the trumpet, and the people be not warned; if the sword come, and take any person from among them, he is taken away in his iniquity; but his blood will I require at the watchman's hand" (Eze.33:6).

2 (2:18-21) **Commitment, Example of—Samuel, Example of—Children, Godly, Example of—Samuel, as a Boy—Righteousness, Contrasted with Wickedness, Example of**: Samuel served the LORD even as a child. The Scripture shows a sharp contrast between the boy Samuel's righteousness and the wickedness of Eli's sons.

OUTLINE	SCRIPTURE	SCRIPTURE	OUTLINE
2. The sharp contrast of Samuel's commitment to the LORD: He served even as a child	18 But Samuel ministered before the LORD, *being* a child, girded with a linen ephod.	and his wife, and said, The LORD give thee seed of this woman for the loan which is lent to the LORD. And they went unto their own home.	them, praying for the LORD to give them children to take the place of Samuel
a. He wore the priestly garment	19 Moreover his mother made him a little coat, and		2) The LORD was gracious to Hannah, giving her five more children
b. He was visited by his parents & received a new coat from his mother each year: When she & Elkanah went up to offer the annual sacrifice	brought *it* to him from year to year, when she came up with her husband to offer the yearly sacrifice.	21 And the LORD visited Hannah, so that she conceived, and bare three sons and two daughters. And the child Samuel	c. He continued to grow in the presence of the LORD: A sharp contrast of Samuel's growth in righteousness with the
1) The priest would bless	20 And Eli blessed Elkanah	grew before the LORD.	wicked behavior of Eli's sons

a. Samuel wore the priestly garment, the ephod (v.18). This was a sleeveless garment worn by the priest when he officiated at the altar. Note that Samuel ministered before the LORD, suggesting a *continued, ongoing activity* that was being ingrained into the very lifestyle of Samuel.[2]

b. Each year Samuel was visited by his parents and received a new coat from his mother (v.19). This visit took place when Elkanah and Hannah went up to offer the annual sacrifice to the LORD. During each visit, Eli would bless them, praying for the LORD to give them children to take the place of Samuel (v.20). In answer to Eli's prayer and, no doubt, Hannah's own seeking of the LORD, the LORD gave Hannah five more children, three sons and two daughters.

c. Throughout the years, Samuel continued to grow in the presence of the LORD (v.21). This is the striking emphasis of this passage, painting a sharp contrast between Samuel's growth and righteousness and the wicked behavior of Eli's sons, the priests of that day.

> **Thought 1**. The lesson for us is clear: we must grow in righteousness. We must follow the LORD and live righteous lives before Him. God demands righteousness, and anything short of righteousness exposes a defiled, corrupt, sinful heart.
>
> > **"For I say unto you, That except your righteousness shall exceed the righteousness of the scribes and Pharisees, ye shall in no case enter into the kingdom of heaven" (Mt.5:20).**
> > **"Awake to righteousness, and sin not; for some have not the knowledge of God: I speak this to your shame" (1 Co.15:34).**
> > **"Stand therefore, having your loins girt about with truth, and having on the breastplate of righteousness" (Ep.6:14).**
> > **"But thou, O man of God, flee these things; and follow after righteousness, godliness, faith, love, patience, meekness" (1 Ti.6:11).**
> > **"Teaching us that, denying ungodliness and worldly lusts, we should live soberly, righteously, and godly, in this present world; Looking for that blessed hope, and the glorious appearing of the great God and our Saviour Jesus Christ" (Tit.2:12-13).**
> > **"But the day of the Lord will come as a thief in the night; in the which the heavens shall pass away with a great noise, and the elements shall melt with fervent heat, the earth also and the works that are therein shall be burned up. Seeing then that all these things shall be dissolved, what manner of persons ought ye to be in all holy conversation [behavior, conduct] and godliness, Looking for and hasting unto the coming of the day of God, wherein the heavens being on fire shall be dissolved, and the elements shall melt with fervent heat? Nevertheless we, according to his promise, look for new heavens and a new earth, wherein dwelleth righteousness. Wherefore, beloved, seeing that ye look for such things, be diligent that ye may be found of him in peace, without spot, and blameless" (2 Pe.3:10-14).**
> > **"Wherefore, O king, let my counsel be acceptable unto thee, and break off thy sins by righteousness, and thine iniquities by showing mercy to the poor; if it may be a lengthening of thy tranquility" (Da.4:27).**
> > **"Sow to yourselves in righteousness, reap in mercy; break up your fallow ground: for it is time to seek the LORD, till he come and rain righteousness upon you" (Ho.10:12).**

3 (2:22-25) **Wickedness, of the Priesthood—Wickedness, Example of—Immorality, of Ministers—Ministers, Wickedness of—Eli, Sons of, Immorality of—Tabernacle, Sin within—Church, Sin within—Parents, Indulgence of Children**: there was the failure and indulgence of Eli. He was very aware of his sons' wickedness, but he only mildly rebuked them and failed to stop their sinful behavior. A terrible picture of Eli's parental neglect is painted by the Scripture:

OUTLINE	SCRIPTURE	SCRIPTURE	OUTLINE
3. The failure & indulgence of Eli: He only mildly rebuked his sons, failing to stop the evil a. Eli's sons continued their wicked decline: Committed immorality at the Tabernacle b. Eli had heard about their evil through rumor: Their evil had been rumored far & wide	22 Now Eli was very old, and heard all that his sons did unto all Israel; and how they lay with the women that assembled *at* the door of the tabernacle of the congregation. 23 And he said unto them, Why do ye such things? for I hear of your evil dealings by all this people. 24 Nay, my sons; for *it is* no	good report that I hear: ye make the LORD'S people to transgress. 25 If one man sin against another, the judge shall judge him: but if a man sin against the LORD, who shall intreat for him? Notwithstanding they hearkened not unto the voice of their father, because the LORD would slay them.	c. Eli confronted, rebuked, & warned his sons of God's judgment: Their deliberate, deceitful sin would be severely judged d. Eli's rebuke was rejected by his sons e. The result: The LORD marked them for judgment

a. Eli's sons continued their wicked decline into the depths of corruption (v.22). Unbelievable! Incomprehensible! They committed immorality with the women who came to worship the LORD at the Tabernacle. The implication is, they actually committed immorality at the Tabernacle. A horrendous, unimaginable evil and defilement.

b. Eventually Eli heard about their evil through the rumors that were obviously spreading far and wide throughout all Israel. Just imagine—the immoral, wicked behavior of the priests was so well-known, so pervasive that the scandal reached Eli himself!

---

2 Robert D. Bergen. *1, 2 Samuel*, p.79.

c. Far too late Eli rebuked and warned his sons of God's judgment (vv.24-25). He warned them that their deliberate, deceitful sin would be severely judged. Note that Eli used a legal dispute to illustrate God's judgment to his sons. When a legal case goes to court, God can use either the law or the circumstances to prove the innocence of the person. However, if a person is guilty of sinning against the LORD Himself, there is no one left to intercede for the person. The person *stands guilty* before the LORD and will be severely judged. The verdict against Eli's sons was clear: their deliberate, deceitful sin was against the LORD and against Him only. Consequently, they would be severely judged.

d. Eli's rebuke was to no avail: his sons hardened their hearts and defiantly rejected the warning of Eli (v.25). They stubbornly refused to repent of their wicked behavior.

e. The result was most tragic: the LORD marked them for judgment (v.25). Scripture clearly says that it was the LORD's will to put them to death, and chapter four will show how they died. It was the LORD's will for the priesthood to be pure, clean, and holy. The LORD does not take pleasure in killing people, for He is long-suffering and not willing that any should perish (2 Pe.3:9). But the LORD does execute justice upon the earth. In dealing with the priesthood and the ministry to God's people, it was both moral and just for God to begin removing these wicked priests who had corrupted the ministry.

This is the first recorded rebuke of Eli's sons. So far as Scripture records, Eli never rebuked his sons prior to this occasion. Eli's silence strongly suggests that he had always indulged the misbehavior of his sons—all throughout life. And their misbehavior continued to decline until they became totally wicked and corrupted the priesthood. Now all of a sudden, when he was an old man, he confronted and rebuked them. But it was too late. Wickedness and immorality had become ingrained into their very nature. Their hearts were hardened against the LORD and His commandments. Eli had indulged, given license to their bad behavior for too many years. His parental weakness was now public knowledge: he had pampered his sons, refusing to discipline them with a controlling hand.

> **Thought 1**. The lesson for us is a much needed lesson for parents. We must not pamper, indulge, or give license to the bad behavior of our children. Pampering, indulging, and giving license to misbehavior—whether mild or severe—is a clear sign of parental weakness. And, in most cases, failing to discipline our children will lead them to follow the immoral, wicked ways of the world.

> > "And the younger of them said to his father, Father, give me the portion of goods that falleth to me. And he divided unto them his living. And not many days after the younger son gathered all together, and took his journey into a far country, and there wasted his substance with riotous living" (Lu.15:12-13).
> >
> > "And these words, which I command thee this day, shall be in thine heart: And thou shalt teach them diligently unto thy children, and shalt talk of them when thou sittest in thine house, and when thou walkest by the way, and when thou liest down, and when thou risest up" (De.6:6-7).
> >
> > "For I have told him that I will judge his house for ever for the iniquity which he knoweth; because his sons made themselves vile, and he restrained them not" (1 S.3:13).
> >
> > "And his sons walked not in his ways, but turned aside after lucre, and took bribes, and perverted judgment" (1 S.8:3).
> >
> > "And his father had not displeased him at any time in saying, Why hast thou done so? and he also was a very goodly man; and his mother bare him after Absalom" (1 K.1:6).
> >
> > "He that spareth his rod hateth his son: but he that loveth him chasteneth him betimes" (Pr.13:24).
> >
> > "Chasten thy son while there is hope, and let not thy soul spare for his crying" (Pr.19:18).
> >
> > "Train up a child in the way he should go: and when he is old, he will not depart from it" (Pr.22:6).
> >
> > "Foolishness is bound in the heart of a child; but the rod of correction shall drive it far from him" (Pr.22:15).
> >
> > "Withhold not correction from the child: for if thou beatest him with the rod, he shall not die" (Pr.23:13).
> >
> > "The rod and reproof give wisdom: but a child left to himself bringeth his mother to shame" (Pr.29:15).
> >
> > "Whom shall he teach knowledge? and whom shall he make to understand doctrine? them that are weaned from the milk, and drawn from the breasts" (Is.28:9).

4 (2:26) **Growth, Spiritual, Example—Parents, Duty—Children, Growth—Samuel, Growth**: there was the contrast of young Samuel's growth in the LORD. A sharp contrast is again being emphasized between Samuel's spiritual growth and the depraved behavior of Eli's sons, the leading priests of that day. Note the strong emphasis that Samuel grew physically and in favor with God and with the *people*.

⇒ While the priests were declining in wickedness, Samuel was growing spiritually.

⇒ While the priests were being denounced by the people, Samuel was finding favor with the people and being commended by them.

⇒ While the priests were being condemned by God, Samuel was finding favor with the LORD.

Note how the childhood of Samuel stands as a picture of the childhood of Christ. God poured His grace into the life of Samuel, and Samuel's life as a child pictures the life of our LORD (Lu.2:52).

OUTLINE	SCRIPTURE
4. **The sharp contrast of young Samuel's growth: He grew physically & in favor with God & with people**	26 And the child Samuel grew on, and was in favour both with the LORD, and also with men.

Thought 1. The childhood of Samuel is a dynamic example for us and our children. We must rear our children to be healthy, both physically and spiritually. We must take care of their bodies, making sure that they eat balanced meals, get the proper exercise, and receive an adequate education. In addition, we must make sure that they grow spiritually and socially, in favor with God and with man. We must root our children in the Word of God and His commandments. And we must teach our children how to behave toward other people, teach them that they are to love their neighbors as themselves and treat others as they would like to be treated.

> **"And the second is like unto it, Thou shalt love thy neighbour as thyself" (Mt.22:39).**
>
> **"And as ye would that men should do to you, do ye also to them likewise" (Lu.6:31).**
>
> **"Let love be without dissimulation. Abhor that which is evil; cleave to that which is good" (Ro.12:9).**
>
> **"And, ye fathers, provoke not your children to wrath: but bring them up in the nurture and admonition of the Lord" (Ep.6:4).**
>
> **"And these words, which I command thee this day, shall be in thine heart: And thou shalt teach them diligently unto thy children, and shalt talk of them when thou sittest in thine house, and when thou walkest by the way, and when thou liest down, and when thou risest up" (De.6:6-7).**
>
> **"Train up a child in the way he should go: and when he is old, he will not depart from it" (Pr.22:6).**

5 (2:27-34) **Priesthood, Wickedness of, Seriousness of—Judgment, of Priesthood—Ministers, Judgment of—Eli, Judgment of—Hophni, Judgment of—Phinehas, Judgment of**: there was the message of God's judgment against Eli and his sons. An unnamed prophet was sent by God to pronounce the terrifying judgment. All three priests would soon die, and the priesthood of Eli's family was to be transferred to the family of a faithful priest who was to live during the time of Solomon, the priest Zadok (1 K.2:26, 27, 35). Note that this pronouncement was a prophecy, an event that was to take place in the future. Actually, the transfer of the priesthood had been predicted even prior to this during the days of Moses (see outline and note—Nu.25:6-13 for more discussion).

OUTLINE	SCRIPTURE	SCRIPTURE	OUTLINE
5. **The message of God's judgment against Eli & his sons: Sent by an unnamed prophet**	27 And there came a man of God unto Eli, and said unto him, Thus saith the LORD,	fore me for ever: but now the LORD saith, Be it far from me; for them that honour me I	would be cut off as priests
a. The reminder of God's clear revelation of Himself & of His call to the priesthood	Did I plainly appear unto the house of thy father, when they were in Egypt in Pharaoh's house?	will honour, and they that despise me shall be lightly esteemed.	2) His descendants would be dishonored, held in low esteem
1) He chose the family of Levi (Aaron, Levi's son) to be His priest	28 And did I choose him out of all the tribes of Israel *to be* my priest, to offer upon mine	31 Behold, the days come, that I will cut off thine arm, and the arm of thy father's	3) His descendants would thereafter have only a short life span
2) He chose them to be His priests to carry on the ministry	altar, to burn incense, to wear an ephod before me? and did I give unto the house of thy father all the offerings made by fire of the children of Israel?	house, that there shall not be an old man in thine house. 32 And thou shalt see an enemy *in my* habitation, in all *the wealth* which *God* shall give Israel: and there shall not be an old man in thine house for ever.	4) His descendants would witness the blessings of God upon others, but only distress in their own families
b. The charge of God against Eli & his sons	29 Wherefore kick ye at my sacrifice and at mine		
1) They scorned the holy things of God: The Tabernacle, the offerings & sacrifices	offering, which I have commanded *in my* habitation; and honourest thy sons above me, to make yourselves	33 And the man of thine, *whom* I shall not cut off from mine altar, *shall be* to consume thine eyes, and to grieve thine heart: and all the	5) His descendants would live in sadness & grief & die in the prime of life
2) Eli condoned his son's evil: Honored them more than God	fat with the chiefest of all the offerings of Israel my people?	increase of thine house shall die in the flower of their age.	
c. The judgment of God against Eli & his sons	30 Wherefore the LORD God of Israel saith, I said indeed	34 And this *shall be* a sign unto thee, that shall come upon thy two sons, on Hophni	6) His two sons would die on the same day: To serve as a sign that God's prophetic judgments would definitely take place
1) His house or descendants	*that* thy house, and the house of thy father, should walk be-	and Phinehas; in one day they shall die both of them.	

a. First, the unnamed prophet challenged Eli and his sons to remember the history of the priesthood. God had revealed Himself and chosen Aaron, Levi's son, to serve as the first priest of Israel (vv.27-28). Out of all the tribes of Israel, He had chosen the family of Levi to be His priests, to carry on the ministry among God's people. Aaron was the forefather of Eli and his sons, and they were to follow in the righteous steps of Aaron. For out of all the tribes and men of Israel, Eli and his sons had been chosen to carry on the ministry of God among the people: the ministry of the altar and of burning incense as a sweet aroma of acceptance before God, and of wearing the ephod, the very priestly garment that gave them access into the presence of God. Moreover, God had chosen them to approach the LORD with the sacrificial offerings that symbolized the redemption of God's people through the blood of the sacrifice.

b. Second, the unnamed prophet pronounced the charge of God against Eli and his sons (v.29). They scorned the holy things of God: the Tabernacle, the offerings, and sacrifices. They made themselves fat by stealing the choice parts of meat from the offerings being brought by the people. Note that Eli is included in this charge. He obviously had accepted and had been eating the sacrificial meat stolen by his sons. Condoning his sons' evil, Eli was honoring them instead of obeying God.

c. Third, the unnamed prophet pronounced the judgment of God against Eli and his sons (vv.30-34). The judgment was sixfold.

1) Eli's house or descendants would be cut off as priests (v.30). God had originally promised that his house or descendants would minister before Him forever. But the promise to Eli was *conditional*, just as all of God's promises to people are. Eli had to believe and obey the LORD in order to receive the promise. Consequently, when Eli and his sons scorned the holy things of God and committed immorality, God was left with no choice. He had to cut them off as priests. They were no longer fit to be ministers who served God's people.

2) Eli's descendants would be dishonored, held in low esteem (v.30). God's Word is clear: those who honor Him will be honored, and those who despise Him will be held in low esteem and condemned.

3) Eli's descendants would thereafter have only a short life span (v.31). This is a clear prediction of untimely deaths for Eli's descendants. Few of his male descendants, who would be serving as priests, would ever reach old age.

4) Eli's descendants would witness the blessings of God upon others, but only distress in their own families (v.32). In the future when God would be pouring out His blessings upon the Israelites, the house of Eli would be experiencing distress.

5) Eli's descendants would live in sadness and grief and die in the prime of life (v.33). Graphic, descriptive language is used to paint the picture of this point:
⇒ Many of Eli's descendants would be cut off from serving at God's altar. They would be denied the right to serve as priests and ministers.
⇒ Many of Eli's descendants would be spared, only to bear so much suffering that the eyes of the family would be blinded with tears and their hearts stricken with grief.
⇒ All Eli's descendants would die in the prime of life, none living to old age.

6) Eli's two sons would die on the same day (v.34). Their deaths were to serve as a sign that God's prophetic judgment would definitely take place.

Thought 1. Judgment upon the wicked and ungodly of this world will definitely take place. This is the strong prophetic message of God's Word. We will see in chapter four where the prophetic judgment against Eli and his sons took place. The judgment that had been foretold was never believed by Eli's sons. But it took place. In fact, judgment fell upon them very soon after the prediction.

Just when the judgment of God is going to fall upon this world is unknown. Just when each of us is going to stand before God is unknown. But the day is definitely coming. The only sure thing that we know about our lives is this: we will die. It is appointed unto us to die, but after this the judgment. Judgment is sure, definite, an absolute certainty. Judgment is coming.

> "And as it is appointed unto men once to die, but after this the judgment" (He.9:27).
> "When the Son of man shall come in his glory, and all the holy angels with him, then shall he sit upon the throne of his glory: And before him shall be gathered all nations: and he shall separate them one from another, as a shepherd divideth his sheep from the goats: And he shall set the sheep on his right hand, but the goats on the left" (Mt.25:31-33).
> "Marvel not at this: for the hour is coming, in the which all that are in the graves shall hear his voice, And shall come forth; they that have done good, unto the resurrection of life; and they that have done evil, unto the resurrection of damnation" (Jn.5:28-29).
> "And to you who are troubled rest with us, when the Lord Jesus shall be revealed from heaven with his mighty angels, In flaming fire taking vengeance on them that know not God, and that obey not the gospel of our Lord Jesus Christ" (2 Th.1:7-8).
> "The Lord knoweth how to deliver the godly out of temptations, and to reserve the unjust unto the day of judgment to be punished" (2 Pe.2:9).
> "But the heavens and the earth, which are now, by the same word are kept in store, reserved unto fire against the day of judgment and perdition of ungodly men" (2 Pe.3:7).
> "Behold, the Lord cometh with ten thousands of his saints, To execute judgment upon all, and to convince all that are ungodly among them of all their ungodly deeds which they have ungodly committed, and of all their hard speeches which ungodly sinners have spoken against him" (Jude 14-15).

6 (2:35-36) **Priesthood, of Christ—Priesthood, New, Promise of—Promise, of a New Priesthood—History, of Israel, Predicted—Prophecies, Concerning Christ**: there was the promise of a very special priest predicted by the unnamed prophet. This was a prophecy that was to be fulfilled first in Samuel, then in Zadok, and ultimately in Christ. Note exactly what the Scripture says:

OUTLINE	SCRIPTURE	SCRIPTURE	OUTLINE
6. The promise of a very special priest: Fulfilled first in Samuel (3:1, 20; 7:9; 9:12-13), then Zadok (2 S.8:17; 15:24-29; 1 K. 2:35), & finally Christ (He.5:10) a. Who would be faithful b. Who would minister to the anointed one (the king) c. Who would be sought by	35 And I will raise me up a faithful priest, *that* shall do according to *that* which *is* in mine heart and in my mind: and I will build him a sure house; and he shall walk before mine anointed for ever. 36 And it shall come to	pass, *that* every one that is left in thine house shall come *and* crouch to him for a piece of silver and a morsel of bread, and shall say, Put me, I pray thee, into one of the priests' offices, that I may eat a piece of bread.	Eli's house: Seeking help from the appointed priest

a. God was going to give a very special priest who would be faithful (v.35). The priest was to be raised up by God Himself, a priest who belonged to God and to Him alone. This priest would be obedient, do exactly what the heart and mind of God dictated. He would keep the commandments of God and follow God wholeheartedly.

b. This priest would always minister to the anointed one, the person chosen to be the king of God's people (v.35). God said that He would firmly establish the house or family of this priest. He would be given a permanent priesthood, a priesthood that would last forever. Note that God explained His purpose: it was His will for the priest to always minister before God's anointed king and people.

c. This priest would be sought by Eli's house (v.36). Everyone left in Eli's family line would seek help from the appointed priest. Everyone would come and bow down before him, asking for employment and food, pleading for work so that he could eat.

Thought 1. This prophetic promise of a very special priest was fulfilled first in Samuel, then in Zadok, and ultimately in Christ. Scripture clearly states this:

(1) Samuel served the LORD as both priest and prophet, and the people acknowledged him as God's priest and prophet.

> "And the child Samuel ministered unto the LORD before Eli. And the word of the LORD was precious in those days; there was no open vision" (1 S.3:1).
> "And all Israel from Dan even to Beer-sheba knew that Samuel was established to be a prophet of the LORD" (1 S.3:20).
> "And Samuel took a sucking lamb, and offered it for a burnt offering wholly unto the LORD: and Samuel cried unto the LORD for Israel; and the LORD heard him" (1 S.7:9).
> "And they answered them, and said, He is; behold, he is before you: make haste now, for he came to day to the city; for there is a sacrifice of the people to day in the high place: As soon as ye be come into the city, ye shall straightway find him, before he go up to the high place to eat: for the people will not eat until he come, because he doth bless the sacrifice; and afterwards they eat that be bidden. Now therefore get you up; for about this time ye shall find him" (1 S.9:12-13).

(2) Zadok was eventually appointed to serve God's people as priest. He was a faithful priest, faithful to God and to the line of David and Solomon.

> "And Zadok the son of Ahitub, and Ahimelech the son of Abiathar, were the priests; and Seraiah was the scribe" (2 S.8:17).
> "And lo Zadok also, and all the Levites were with him, bearing the ark of the covenant of God: and they set down the ark of God; and Abiathar went up, until all the people had done passing out of the city. And the king said unto Zadok, Carry back the ark of God into the city: if I shall find favour in the eyes of the LORD, he will bring me again, and show me both it, and his habitation: But if he thus say, I have no delight in thee; behold, here am I, let him do to me as seemeth good unto him. The king said also unto Zadok the priest, Art not thou a seer? return into the city in peace, and your two sons with you, Ahimaaz thy son, and Jonathan the son of Abiathar. See, I will tarry in the plain of the wilderness, until there come word from you to certify me. Zadok therefore and Abiathar carried the ark of God again to Jerusalem: and they tarried there" (2 S.15:24-29).
> "And he conferred with Joab the son of Zeruiah, and with Abiathar the priest: and they following Adonijah helped him. But Zadok the priest, and Benaiah the son of Jehoiada, and Nathan the prophet, and Shimei, and Rei, and the mighty men which belonged to David, were not with Adonijah" (1 K.1:7-8).
> "And unto Abiathar the priest said the king, Get thee to Anathoth, unto thine own fields; for thou art worthy of death: but I will not at this time put thee to death, because thou barest the ark of the Lord GOD before David my father, and because thou hast been afflicted in all wherein my father was afflicted. So Solomon thrust out Abiathar from being priest unto the LORD; that he might fulfil the word of the LORD, which he spake concerning the house of Eli in Shiloh....And the king put Benaiah the son of Jehoiada in his room over the host: and Zadok the priest did the king put in the room of Abiathar [a descendant of Eli]" (1 K.2:26-27, 35).

(3) The *appointed priest* ultimately referred to Christ. Jesus Christ is the supreme High Priest. He alone can stand before God declaring that He has been perfectly faithful and perfectly obedient, never failing to obey God. In perfection, Christ did exactly what was in God's heart and mind. He was *without sin*. It was the house of Christ

that God was to perfectly establish, and Christ was to perfectly minister before the anointed rulers and people of the world.

Everyone must come and bow down before Him to have a part in the work of God or to receive bread from heaven. Christ and Christ alone is the appointed supreme High Priest.

"Let this mind be in you, which was also in Christ Jesus: Who, being in the form of God, thought it not robbery to be equal with God: But made himself of no reputation, and took upon him the form of a servant, and was made in the likeness of men: And being found in fashion as a man, he humbled himself, and became obedient unto death, even the death of the cross. Wherefore God also hath highly exalted him, and given him a name which is above every name: That at the name of Jesus every knee should bow, of things in heaven, and things in earth, and things under the earth; And that every tongue should confess that Jesus Christ is Lord, to the glory of God the Father" (Ph.2:5-11).

"Wherefore in all things it behoved him to be made like unto his brethren, that he might be a merciful and faithful high priest in things pertaining to God, to make reconciliation for the sins of the people. For in that he himself hath suffered being tempted, he is able to succour them that are tempted" (He.2:17-18).

"Seeing then that we have a great high priest, that is passed into the heavens, Jesus the Son of God, let us hold fast our profession. For we have not an high priest which cannot be touched with the feeling of our infirmities; but was in all points tempted like as we are, yet without sin" (He.4:14-15).

"Though he were a Son, yet learned he obedience by the things which he suffered; And being made perfect, he became the author of eternal salvation unto all them that obey him; Called of God an high priest after the order of Melchisedec" (He.5:8-10).

"Whither the forerunner is for us entered, even Jesus, made an high priest for ever after the order of Melchisedec" (He.6:20).

"For such an high priest became us, who is holy, harmless, undefiled, separate from sinners, and made higher than the heavens" (He.7:26).

"Now of the things which we have spoken this is the sum: We have such an high priest, who is set on the right hand of the throne of the Majesty in the heavens" (He.8:1).

"And having an high priest over the house of God; Let us draw near with a true heart in full assurance of faith, having our hearts sprinkled from an evil conscience, and our bodies washed with pure water" (He.10:21-22).

"Forasmuch as ye know that ye were not redeemed with corruptible things, as silver and gold, from your vain conversation received by tradition from your fathers; But with the precious blood of Christ [our High Priest], as of a lamb without blemish and without spot" (1 Pe.1:18-19).

1. The need for God's call

a. Samuel was still young & tenderhearted: He had faithfully been serving the LORD, assisting Eli

b. A prophet was needed: God's Word & visions were rare

c. A replacement was needed for Eli: He was weak & almost blind (physically & spiritually), 2:22-36; 4:14-18

2. The call of God & the need to respond to God's call

a. God's call came at night after Samuel & Eli had gone to bed

b. God's call was given repeatedly, time & again

1) The first call was misunderstood: Thought to be from Eli, a human source
   • Samuel ran to Eli
   • Eli sent him back to bed

2) The second call was also misunderstood: Thought to be from Eli, a human source
   • Samuel ran to Eli again, but he was again sent back to bed
   • Samuel did not yet know how to recognize & discern the call of God, His Word

3) The third call was again misunderstood: Thought to be from Eli, a human source
   • Samuel ran to Eli
   • Eli finally realized the truth: God was calling the boy

c. God's call demanded a response

1) Eli told Samuel how to respond to God's call: "Speak, LORD, for your servant hears"

2) Samuel responded by making himself available to the LORD
   • The LORD called a fourth time
   • Samuel responded: "Speak,

CHAPTER 3

D. The Call of God to Samuel & His First Prophetic Message: A Lesson on God's Call to Service, 3:1–4:1ᵃ

And the child Samuel ministered unto the LORD before Eli. And the word of the LORD was precious in those days; *there was* no open vision.

2 And it came to pass at that time, when Eli *was* laid down in his place, and his eyes began to wax dim, *that* he could not see;

3 And ere the lamp of God went out in the temple of the LORD, where the ark of God *was,* and Samuel was laid down *to sleep;*

4 That the LORD called Samuel: and he answered, Here *am* I.

5 And he ran unto Eli, and said, Here *am* I; for thou calledst me. And he said, I called not; lie down again. And he went and lay down.

6 And the LORD called yet again, Samuel. And Samuel arose and went to Eli, and said, Here *am* I; for thou didst call me. And he answered, I called not, my son; lie down again.

7 Now Samuel did not yet know the LORD, neither was the word of the LORD yet revealed unto him.

8 And the LORD called Samuel again the third time. And he arose and went to Eli, and said, Here *am* I; for thou didst call me. And Eli perceived that the LORD had called the child.

9 Therefore Eli said unto Samuel, Go, lie down: and it shall be, if he call thee, that thou shalt say, Speak, LORD; for thy servant heareth. So Samuel went and lay down in his place.

10 And the LORD came, and stood, and called as at other times, Samuel, Samuel. Then Samuel answered, Speak; for thy servant

heareth.

11 And the LORD said to Samuel, Behold, I will do a thing in Israel, at which both the ears of every one that heareth it shall tingle.

12 In that day I will perform against Eli all *things* which I have spoken concerning his house: when I begin, I will also make an end.

13 For I have told him that I will judge his house for ever for the iniquity which he knoweth; because his sons made themselves vile, and he restrained them not.

14 And therefore I have sworn unto the house of Eli, that the iniquity of Eli's house shall not be purged with sacrifice nor offering for ever.

15 And Samuel lay until the morning, and opened the doors of the house of the LORD. And Samuel feared to show Eli the vision.

16 Then Eli called Samuel, and said, Samuel, my son. And he answered, Here *am* I.

17 And he said, What *is* the thing that *the LORD* hath said unto thee? I pray thee hide *it* not from me: God do so to thee, and more also, if thou hide *any* thing from me of all the things that he said unto thee.

18 And Samuel told him every whit, and hid nothing from him. And he said, It *is* the LORD: let him do what seemeth him good.

19 And Samuel grew, and the LORD was with him, and did let none of his words fall to the ground.

20 And all Israel from Dan even to Beersheba knew that Samuel *was* established *to be* a prophet of the LORD.

21 And the LORD appeared again in Shiloh: for the LORD revealed himself to Samuel in Shiloh by the word of the LORD.

CHAPTER 4:1ᵃ

And Samuel's word came to all Israel.

for your servant hears"

3. The message of God's call: Judgment

a. God was about ready to execute a terrifying, shocking judgment in Israel: Judgment was to be executed against Eli & his family, executed just as predicted, 2:27-36

1) Reason 1: Because Eli condoned the terrible, gross sin of his sons

2) Reason 2: Because the sin hardened them: They went too far—beyond repentance—beyond ever returning to God

b. Samuel feared sharing the message with Eli
   1) He lay down till morning
   2) He arose & did his chores

c. Eli heard Samuel stirring & called for him
   1) Insisted that Samuel share the message
   2) Charged Samuel with a threatening oath: He must share the entire message

d. Samuel shared faithfully the message of judgment

e. Eli demonstrated a submissive, understanding spirit: He knew he had failed

4. The proof of God's call

a. The LORD's presence & power: Speaking through Samuel, helping people

b. The people's recognition that God's hand was upon Samuel: He was God's prophet

c. The LORD's continued fellowship & revelation: Faithfully revealed Himself & His Word to Samuel

d. The obedience of Samuel

DIVISION I

THE STORY OF ELI AND SAMUEL: THE LORD CLOSES THE ERA OF THE JUDGES AND PREPARES FOR THE RULE OF THE KINGS, 1:1–7:17

D.   The Call of God to Samuel and His First Prophetic Message: A Lesson on God's Call to Service, 3:1–4:1a

(3:1–4:1a) **Introduction—Needs, List of—Needs, of People—Call, to Meet Needs**: people hurt and suffer all over the world today. Needs abound at every turn. Some people are hungry and thirsty, with little or no food or water. Other people are sick, diseased, or injured due to some accident. Still others are uneducated or untrained and unable to earn an adequate living. Some people are emotionally or mentally disturbed, depressed, discouraged, consumed with guilt or grief, brokenhearted or gripped by anxiety and stress. There are others who are bankrupt or in financial trouble. And still others who are lonely and empty, lacking satisfaction, fulfillment, purpose, meaning, or significance in life. Many are lost, having little or no contact with God. They are without God in this world, sensing that God is far off in space, unable to be reached and unwilling to truly help when they are suffering and in pain.

This is the condition of so many persons throughout society, some within every community of the world, your community and my community.

But note this wonderful truth: God issues a call to believers, a call for us to arise and go forth to meet the needs of the world. When that call comes—when God speaks to our hearts and says, "You are to arise and go forth"—we must respond; we must arise and go forth to help meet the desperate needs of this world.

The call of God is the wonderful subject of this passage of Scripture. God calls men and women, boys and girls to step forth and serve in ministering to the needs of people. In the present passage, a young boy is called to serve God, the young boy Samuel. This is: *The Call of God to Samuel and His First Prophetic Message: A Lesson on God's Call to Service, 3:1–4:1a.*

1. The need for God's call (vv.1-2).
2. The call of God and the need to respond to God's call (vv.3-10).
3. The message of God's call: Judgment (vv.11-18).
4. The proof of God's call (vv.3:19–4:1).

1 (3:1-2) **Call, of God, Need for—Society, Corrupt—Prophet, Need for—Samuel, Faithfulness of—Word of God, Rarity of—Eli, Blindness of, Physically and Spiritually—Samuel, Call of**: there was a desperate need for God to call someone to step forth and lead His dear people. Just why is clearly stated in the three reasons spelled out by the Scripture and outline:

OUTLINE	SCRIPTURE	SCRIPTURE	OUTLINE

1. The need for God's call
  a. Samuel was still young & tenderhearted: He had faithfully been serving the LORD, assisting Eli
  b. A prophet was needed: God's
	And the child Samuel ministered unto the LORD before Eli. And the word of the LORD was precious in those days; *there was* no open vision.	2 And it came to pass at that time, when Eli *was* laid down in his place, and his eyes began to wax dim, *that* he could not see;	Word & visions were rare
			  c. A replacement was needed for Eli: He was weak & almost blind (physically & spiritually), 2:22-36; 4:14-18

a. Samuel was still young and tenderhearted (v.1). Ever since childhood Samuel had been faithfully serving the LORD, assisting and learning from Eli, the High Priest. Now Samuel was no longer a small child (2:21, 26). He was a young man, a vigorous youth ready to enter manhood. Thus, it was time for God to issue a call to Samuel for service, time for a very special relationship to be established between God and Samuel. Samuel was hereafter to know the LORD personally and intimately. The young man was now to be set apart by God, set apart to begin his own ministry among God's people.

b. A prophet was desperately needed, for God's Word and visions were rare during the period of the judges (v.1). As the last verse of the great *Book of Judges* says:

> **"In those days there was no king in Israel: every man did that which was right in his own eyes" (Jud.21:25).**

Samuel was born during the days of the judges, and during those days there was no ruler. There was a terrible vacuum of leadership. No person seemed to have the moral character or the willingness to step forth and lead God's people in the ways of righteousness and justice. Every person did whatever seemed right in his own eyes, doing what he wanted when he wanted. There was no moral leader in Israel, not even among the priests—no leader who was obeying God's commandments and whose heart was full of mercy and justice. And the Israelites were not willing to acknowledge any king or ruler, either human or divine. Wickedness ran rampant, with every person forsaking God and doing his own thing. The most horrible evils imaginable were being committed by the people of that day:

⇒ adultery   ⇒ brutality   ⇒ child and spousal abuse
⇒ gang rape   ⇒ savagery   ⇒ terrorist attacks
⇒ homosexuality   ⇒ kidnapping   ⇒ rebellion
⇒ sexual perversion   ⇒ mob violence   ⇒ war
⇒ murder   ⇒ drunkenness

Vile, shameful, and wicked behavior was a constant threat to the people of Samuel's day. A cesspool of evil permeated society, infecting most families and influencing practically every person.

This was the reason there was no prophet in Israel, the reason God's Word was so rare in those days. There were very few committed and faithful persons. Few believed and obeyed God. Few loved and followed after God. For this reason, there was no person available for God to call and set apart to be a prophet among His people. Not until now, not until Hannah's renewed commitment and prayer, not until the birth of her son Samuel. But now, there was a young man who loved the LORD and who was following after the LORD, serving Him wholeheartedly. A young man whose mother had set him apart and given him to the service of the LORD, the young man Samuel. The word of the LORD had been rare because of the wickedness and lawlessness of the people. But now because of Samuel's faith and total commitment to the LORD, the Word of God could be proclaimed anew to the people.

c. A replacement was desperately needed for Eli. Eli was weak and almost blind (v.2). Physically, he could barely see and move about to carry on his ministry. And tragically, for years he had been spiritually blind. He had condoned the wicked behavior of his sons who were the two major priests serving with him in the Tabernacle of the LORD; and he apparently had participated to some degree in their wickedness (see outline and notes—1 S.2:12-36 for more discussion). Because of Eli's spiritual carnality and weak physical condition (he was aged and soon to die), it was time for God to issue the call for a replacement. That call was to be issued to Samuel.

Thought 1. Prophets are needed today, men and women who will take the Word of God to the world. Wickedness, immorality, and lawlessness are running rampant throughout society, contaminating and influencing almost every human being. If the truth of God's Holy Word, His commandments, have ever needed to be proclaimed, it is today. His Word must be proclaimed to a lost and dying world.

Who will step forth and become a prophet for God? What man? What woman? What boy? What girl? Who will step forth, believing and totally committing his or her life to Christ? Who will hear the call of God and become a prophet, a dynamic witness to a needy, lost, and dying world?

> **"Go ye therefore, and teach all nations, baptizing them in the name of the Father, and of the Son, and of the Holy Ghost: Teaching them to observe all things whatsoever I have commanded you: and, lo, I am with you alway, *even* unto the end of the world. Amen" (Mt.28:19-20).**

> **"And he said unto them, Go ye into all the world, and preach the gospel to every creature" (Mk.16:15).**

> **"Say not ye, There are yet four months, and *then* cometh harvest? behold, I say unto you, Lift up your eyes, and look on the fields; for they are white already to harvest" (Jn.4:35).**

> **"Go, stand and speak in the temple to the people all the words of this life. And when they heard *that,* they entered into the temple early in the morning, and taught. But the High Priest came, and they that were with him, and called the council together, and all the senate of the children of Israel and sent to the prison to have them brought" (Ac.5:20-21).**

> **"Then spake the Lord to Paul in the night by a vision, Be not afraid, but speak, and hold not thy peace: For I am with thee, and no man shall set on thee to hurt thee: for I have much people in this city" (Ac.18:9-10).**

> **"And he said, The God of our fathers hath chosen thee, that thou shouldest know his will, and see that Just One, and shouldest hear the voice of his mouth. For thou shalt be his witness unto all men of what thou hast seen and heard" (Ac.22:14-15).**

> **"And the things that thou hast heard of me among many witnesses, the same commit thou to faithful men, who shall be able to teach others also" (2 Ti.2:2).**

> **"These things speak, and exhort, and rebuke with all authority. Let no man despise thee" (Tit.2:15).**

> **"Ye *are* my witnesses, saith the LORD, and my servant whom I have chosen: that ye may know and believe me, and understand that I *am* he: before me there was no God formed, neither shall there be after me" (Is.43:10).**

[2] (3:3-10) **Call of God, Response to—Decision, Duty—Call of God, to Samuel—Samuel, Call of**: there was the call of God and the need to hear and respond to God's call. A graphic description of Samuel's encounter with the LORD is given in these verses:

OUTLINE	SCRIPTURE	SCRIPTURE	OUTLINE

2. The call of God & the need to respond to God's call
a. God's call came at night after Samuel & Eli had gone to bed
b. God's call was given repeatedly, time & again
  1) The first call was misunderstood: Thought to be from Eli, a human source
  • Samuel ran to Eli
  • Eli sent him back to bed
	3 And ere the lamp of God went out in the temple of the LORD, where the ark of God *was,* and Samuel was laid down *to sleep;*
	4 That the LORD called Samuel: and he answered, Here *am* I.
	5 And he ran unto Eli, and said, Here *am* I; for thou calledst me. And he said, I called not; lie down again.
		And he went and lay down.
		6 And the LORD called yet again, Samuel. And Samuel arose and went to Eli, and said, Here *am* I; for thou didst call me. And he answered, I called not, my son; lie down again.
		7 Now Samuel did not yet know the LORD, neither was the word of the LORD yet revealed unto him.
			2) The second call was also misunderstood: Thought to be from Eli, a human source
			  • Samuel ran to Eli again, but he was again sent back to bed
			  • Samuel did not yet know how to recognize & discern the call of God, His Word

OUTLINE	SCRIPTURE	SCRIPTURE	OUTLINE
3) The third call was again mis-understood: Thought to be from Eli, a human source • Samuel ran to Eli • Eli finally realized the truth: God was calling the boy c. God's call demanded a re-sponse 1) Eli told Samuel how to	8 And the LORD called Samuel again the third time. And he arose and went to Eli, and said, Here *am* I; for thou didst call me. And Eli per-ceived that the LORD had called the child. 9 Therefore Eli said unto Samuel, Go, lie down: and it shall be, if he call thee, that	thou shalt say, Speak, LORD; for thy servant heareth. So Samuel went and lay down in his place. 10 And the LORD came, and stood, and called as at other times, Samuel, Samuel. Then Samuel answered, Speak; for thy servant heareth.	respond to God's call: "Speak, LORD, for your servant hears" 2) Samuel responded by making himself available to the LORD • The LORD called a fourth time • Samuel responded: "Speak, for your servant hears"

a. God's call came to Samuel at night, came after he and Eli had gone to bed (v.3). Samuel was lying down in the temple, close to the Ark of God that symbolized God's holy presence. The lamp of God, the golden lampstand that was located in the Holy Place, had not yet gone out. Apparently, Samuel slept close by the lampstand, close to the entrance that led into the Most Holy Place where the Ark of God was kept. It was sometime during the night that the call of God came to the young man Samuel.

b. The call of God was given to Samuel repeatedly, time and again (vv.4-8). God issued His call to Samuel four differ-ent times, but Samuel misunderstood the call the first three times. He thought the voice he was hearing was that of Eli, merely a human voice. Each time Samuel ran to Eli saying, "Here am I." But each time Eli responded that he had not called Samuel and instructed him to go back to bed.

Note why Samuel did not respond to God's call: because he did not yet know the LORD and could not discern the call of God (v.7). He knew the written Word of the LORD, but he did not yet know the LORD personally. He did not have a personal, intimate relationship with the LORD. He did not yet know how the LORD reveals and speaks to the human heart.

c. There was a certain response demanded by God's call, a response that Samuel needed to learn (vv.9-10). No doubt, this was the purpose for God's repeated call to the young man. After God issued His third call, it dawned upon Eli that God was perhaps issuing a call to Samuel. Consequently, Eli instructed Samuel on how to respond to God's call. He was simply to respond, "Speak, LORD, for your servant hears and is listening." Thus when God issued His fourth call, Samuel responded exactly as he had been instructed: "Speak LORD, for your servant hears and is listening" (v.10).

Thought 1. The call of God demands a positive response; therefore, we must never reject it. At first, we may not understand God's call, just as Samuel did not understand. But when the call is repeated time and again, we must hear and listen to the call. We must submit ourselves, surrender our lives to serve God. Too many persons have re-jected God's call, turning away and refusing to serve God. As the Scripture says, many have been called, but few chosen. Many have been called...
• to accept Christ as their Savior and Lord
• to turn away from some fleshly, carnal sin
• to rededicate their lives and live wholeheartedly for Christ
• to serve in the ministry
• to serve in missions
• to minister to the poor
• to enter a certain profession
• to prepare and secure education for a certain task
• to earn money and give sacrificially
• to witness to a certain person or group
• to write in their wills some gift of money, property, or an entire estate to the cause of Christ

But when God called, they shut their ears and hardened their hearts, turning away. Almost every time a body of people gathers together, there are people present who have been called by God to make a specific decision. Yet they have refused, rejecting the call of God.

When God calls, there is a specific response demanded. The required response is straightforward and clear-cut: "Speak, LORD, for your servant hears and is listening." Or, very simply, "Here am I LORD. Send me."

> **"As they ministered to the Lord, and fasted, the Holy Ghost said, Separate me Barnabas and Saul for the work whereunto I have called them. And when they had fasted and prayed, and laid *their* hands on them, they sent *them* away" (Ac.13:2-3).**
>
> **"And a vision appeared to Paul in the night; There stood a man of Macedonia, and prayed him, saying, Come over into Macedonia, and help us. And after he had seen the vision, immediately we en-deavoured to go into Macedonia, assuredly gathering that the Lord had called us for to preach the gospel unto them" (Ac.16:9:10).**
>
> **"And when we were all fallen to the earth, I heard a voice speaking unto me, and saying in the Hebrew tongue, Saul, Saul, why persecutest thou me? *it is* hard for thee to kick against the pricks. And I said, Who art thou, Lord? And he said, I am Jesus whom thou persecutest. But rise, and stand upon thy feet: for I have appeared unto thee for this purpose, to make thee a minister and a witness both of these things which thou hast seen, and of those things in the which I will appear unto thee; De-livering thee from the people, and *from* the Gentiles, unto whom now I send thee, To open their eyes, *and* to turn *them* from dArkness to light, and *from* the power of Satan unto God, that they may receive**

forgiveness of sins, and inheritance among them which are sanctified by faith that is in me. Whereupon, O king Agrippa, I was not disobedient unto the heavenly vision" (Ac.26:14-19; see also Ac.9:1-16).

"Now the LORD had said unto Abram, Get thee out of thy country, and from thy kindred, and from thy father's house, unto a land that I will show thee: And I will make of thee a great nation, and I will bless thee, and make thy name great; and thou shalt be a blessing: And I will bless them that bless thee, and curse him that curseth thee: and in thee shall all families of the earth be blessed. So Abram departed, as the LORD had spoken unto him; and Lot went with him: and Abram *was* seventy and five years old when he departed out of Haran" (Ge.12:1-4).

"Come now therefore, and I will send thee unto Pharaoh, that thou mayest bring forth my people the children of Israel out of Egypt. And Moses said unto God, Who *am* I, that I should go unto Pharaoh, and that I should bring forth the children of Israel out of Egypt" (Ex.3:10-11).

"And the LORD looked upon him, and said, Go in this thy might, and thou shalt save Israel from the hand of the Midianites: have not I sent thee? And he said unto him, Oh my Lord, wherewith shall I save Israel? behold, my family is poor in Manasseh, and I *am* the least in my father's house" (Jud.6:14-15).

"Also I heard the voice of the Lord, saying, Whom shall I send, and who will go for us? Then said I, Here *am* I; send me" (Is.6:8).

"Then the word of the LORD came unto me, saying, Before I formed thee in the belly I knew thee; and before thou camest forth out of the womb I sanctified thee, *and* I ordained thee a prophet unto the nations. Then said I, Ah, Lord GOD! behold, I cannot speak: for I *am* a child. But the LORD said unto me, Say not, I *am* a child: for thou shalt go to all that I shall send thee, and whatsoever I command thee thou shalt speak. Be not afraid of their faces: for I *am* with thee to deliver thee, saith the LORD" (Je.1:4-8).

"Now the word of the LORD came unto Jonah the son of Amittai, saying, Arise, go to Nineveh, that great city, and cry against it; for their wickedness is come up before me. But Jonah rose up to flee unto Tarshish from the presence of the LORD, and went down to Joppa; and he found a ship going to Tarshish: so he paid the fare thereof, and went down into it, to go with them unto Tarshish from the presence of the LORD" (Jona.1:1-3).

---

3 (3:11-18) **Call of God, Message of—Message, of God's Call—Judgment, Cause of—Eli, Judgment of—Samuel, First Message of**: there was the message of God's call that Samuel was to deliver. It was a disturbing message for a young man to receive, a message of condemnation and judgment against the family of Eli.

OUTLINE	SCRIPTURE	SCRIPTURE	OUTLINE

3. The message of God's call: Judgment
a. God was about ready to execute a terrifying, shocking judgment in Israel: Judgment was to be executed against Eli & his family, executed just as predicted, 2:27-36
 	
1) Reason 1: Because Eli condoned the terrible, gross sin of his sons
 	
2) Reason 2: Because the sin hardened them: They went too far—beyond repentance—beyond ever returning to God
	11 And the LORD said to Samuel, Behold, I will do a thing in Israel, at which both the ears of every one that heareth it shall tingle.
	12 In that day I will perform against Eli all *things* which I have spoken concerning his house: when I begin, I will also make an end.
	13 For I have told him that I will judge his house for ever for the iniquity which he knoweth; because his sons made themselves vile, and he restrained them not.
	14 And therefore I have sworn unto the house of Eli, that the iniquity of Eli's house shall not be purged with sacrifice nor offering for ever.
		15 And Samuel lay until the morning, and opened the doors of the house of the LORD. And Samuel feared to shew Eli the vision.
		16 Then Eli called Samuel, and said, Samuel, my son. And he answered, Here *am* I.
		17 And he said, What *is* the thing that *the* LORD hath said unto thee? I pray thee hide *it* not from me: God do so to thee, and more also, if thou hide *any* thing from me of all the things that he said unto thee.
		18 And Samuel told him every whit, and hid nothing from him. And he said, It *is* the LORD: let him do what seemeth him good.
			b. Samuel feared sharing the message with Eli
			  1) He lay down till morning
			  2) He arose & did his chores
			
			c. Eli heard Samuel stirring & called for him
			
			  1) Insisted that Samuel share the message
			  2) Charged Samuel with a threatening oath: He must share the entire message
			
			d. Samuel shared faithfully the message of judgment
			e. Eli demonstrated a submissive, understanding spirit: He knew he had failed

a. God declared that He was ready to execute a severe, shocking judgment in Israel (v.11). Every ear that heard of the judgment would tingle, arousing terrifying fear and distress. Chapter four will describe exactly what happened:

⇒ Israel would be defeated in war by the Philistines, losing 30,000 foot soldiers.

⇒ Eli's two sons would be killed and Eli himself would die when receiving a report from the battlefield. The death of all three priests would mean a complete change in the priesthood, a cultural shock and transfer of power for the Israelites.

⇒ The Ark itself would be captured by the Philistines. Above all else, this would shock and strike terror in the hearts of the Israelites, for the Ark of God was the very symbol of God's presence among them. To many of the people, the loss of the Ark meant the loss of God's presence. God would no longer be present with them to guide, protect, and provide for them.

God knew exactly what was going to happen in the coming judgment upon Israel. Samuel and the people had no idea, but God did; therefore, He was able to pronounce that the judgment would be terrifying and shocking, a judgment so severe that it would shake the very culture of Israel. Not only would there be a massive loss of life, but the very religion and priesthood of the nation would be shaken to the core.

God pronounced that the judgment would be executed against the priesthood, against Eli and his family. And the judgment would be executed just as predicted (v.12; see outline and note—1 Sam.2:27-36 for more discussion). Two reasons were given for the coming judgment upon Eli's family:

1) Eli's family was to be judged because Eli had condoned the terrible, gross sins of his sons. Being the father and the chief priest, Eli should have restrained his sons and enforced a strict discipline upon them. Instead, he allowed them to become vile, contemptible, and blasphemous toward God—all because he refused to discipline and restrain them (v.13).

2) Eli's family was to be judged because their wickedness hardened their hearts (v.14). They became stiff-necked, stubborn against God. They went too far—beyond repentance, beyond ever returning to God. Consequently, God pronounced a tragic, terrifying judgment: their guilt could never be atoned for by sacrifice or offering. Only God can tell when a person's heart reaches this point, the point of never repenting and never returning to Him. These two sons of Eli—these wicked priests—had reached this point. Time and again, they had rejected the appeal of God's grace and mercy. And now they were being doomed to the judgment of God.

The message of God's judgment was now completed. God had finished speaking to Samuel. What kind of thoughts were bouncing around in the mind of this young man? What emotions was he experiencing? What were his thoughts, his emotions? Scripture does not elaborate; only our imaginations can tell us.

b. Fear struck the heart of Samuel (v.15). This is the only emotion experienced by Samuel that is mentioned in Scripture. Samuel feared sharing the message with Eli. After receiving the message from the LORD, he lay down until morning, and then he arose and went about his usual chores. He obviously did everything he could to avoid facing Eli, for he knew that Eli would ask about the message from the LORD.

c. But Eli heard Samuel stirring and called for him to come (vv.16-17). Insisting that Samuel share the message, Eli charged Samuel with a threatening oath. He threatened the young boy by pronouncing some severe judgment upon him if he refused to share the message. Eli's approach to Samuel in a threatening manner exposes his carnal, worldly heart.

d. Obediently, Samuel shared the message of judgment with Eli (v.18). He hid nothing, kept nothing from Eli.

e. On hearing the pronouncement upon him and his family, Eli demonstrated a submissive, understanding spirit (v.18). He knew that he had failed to rear his sons in the discipline of the LORD, and that he himself had lived a carnal, fleshly life. He was helpless to correct his failure, for he was now aged and physically disabled, about ready to leave this earth and face the LORD eternally.

Thought 1. Judgment is the one subject missing from most pulpits today. The message of the gospel is that of judgment: either the judgment of Christ upon the cross that brings salvation to us, or the judgment that we will confront when we come face-to-face with God. The message of judgment is intertwined with the very message of salvation. We are saved because of the judgment Christ bore, a judgment that we deserve, that was due us. Christ bore our judgment; therefore, we are saved from the wrath of God. But if we continue in our sin and wickedness, we must die and bear the judgment of God.

Judgment must be proclaimed by the faithful prophets of today: the judgment that Christ bore to save us and the judgment that we will bear if we continue in sin and wickedness. The faithful prophet of God cannot escape the message of judgment. He must proclaim the wrath of God, for we are appointed to die and then to face judgment.

"And as it is appointed unto men once to die, but after this the judgment" (He.9:27).

"And then shall appear the sign of the Son of man in heaven: and then shall all the tribes of the earth mourn, and they shall see the Son of man coming in the clouds of heaven with power and great glory" (Mt.24:30).

"When the Son of man shall come in his glory, and all the holy angels with him, then shall he sit upon the throne of his glory: And before him shall be gathered all nations: and he shall separate them one from another, as a shepherd divideth *his* sheep from the goats: And he shall set the sheep on his right hand, but the goats on the left" (Mt.25:31-33).

"And whosoever shall not receive you, nor hear you, when ye depart thence, shake off the dust under your feet for a testimony against them. Verily I say unto you, It shall be more tolerable for Sodom and Gomorrha in the day of judgment, than for that city" (Mk.6:11).

"Marvel not at this: for the hour is coming, in the which all that are in the graves shall hear his voice, And shall come forth; they that have done good, unto the resurrection of life; and they that have done evil, unto the resurrection of damnation" (Jn.5:28-29).

"And to you who are troubled rest with us, when the Lord Jesus shall be revealed from heaven with his mighty angels, In flaming fire taking vengeance on them that know not God, and that obey not the gospel of our Lord Jesus Christ" (2 Th.1:7-8).

"The Lord knoweth how to deliver the godly out of temptations, and to reserve the unjust unto the day of judgment to be punished" (2 Pt.2:9).

"But the heavens and the earth, which are now, by the same word are kept in store, reserved unto fire against the day of judgment and perdition of ungodly men" (2 Pt.3:7).

"Herein is our love made perfect, that we may have boldness in the day of judgment: because as he is, so are we in this world" (1 Jn.4:17).

"Behold, the Lord cometh with ten thousands of his saints, To execute judgment upon all, and to convince all that are ungodly among them of all their ungodly deeds which they have ungodly committed, and of all their hard *speeches* which ungodly sinners have spoken against him" (Jude 14-15).

"And I saw a great white throne, and him that sat on it, from whose face the earth and the heaven fled away; and there was found no place for them. And I saw the dead, small and great, stand before God; and the books were opened: and another book was opened, which is the book of life: and the dead were judged out of those things which were written in the books, according to their works. And the sea gave up the dead which were in it; and death and hell delivered up the dead which were in them: and they were judged every man according to their works. And death and hell were cast into the lake of fire. This is the second death. And whosoever was not found written in the book of life was cast into the lake of fire" (Re.20:11-15).

4 (3:19–4:1) **Call of God, Proof of—Samuel, Life of—Samuel, Title, Prophet—Prophets, Identified, Samuel**: there was the proof of God's call to Samuel. There are four evidences of God's call upon a life, and all four proofs were true of Samuel.

OUTLINE	SCRIPTURE	SCRIPTURE	OUTLINE
4. The proof of God's call a. The LORD's presence & power: Speaking through Samuel, helping people b. The people's recognition that God's hand was upon Samuel: He was God's prophet c. The LORD's continued fel-	19 And Samuel grew, and the LORD was with him, and did let none of his words fall to the ground. 20 And all Israel from Dan even to Beer-sheba knew that Samuel *was* established *to be* a prophet of the LORD. 21 And the LORD appeared	again in Shiloh: for the LORD revealed himself to Samuel in Shiloh by the word of the LORD. **CHAPTER 4a** And the word of Samuel came to all Israel.	lowship & revelation: Faithfully revealed Himself & His Word to Samuel d. The obedience of Samuel

a. First, the LORD's presence and power is proof of God's call upon a person (v.19). As Samuel grew up and matured, the LORD was with him, granting His presence and power to Samuel. God spoke through Samuel, helping and encouraging people. Note exactly how Scripture words this: God let "none of His words fall to the ground." "Everything Samuel said was wise and helpful" (NLT).

"Go ye therefore, and teach all nations, baptizing them in the name of the Father, and of the Son, and of the Holy Ghost: Teaching them to observe all things whatsoever I have commanded you: and, lo, I am with you alway, even unto the end of the world. Amen" (Mt.28:19-20).

"But ye shall receive power, after that the Holy Ghost is come upon you: and ye shall be witnesses unto me both in Jerusalem, and in all Judaea, and in Samaria, and unto the uttermost part of the earth" (Ac.1:8).

"That ye might walk worthy of the Lord unto all pleasing, being fruitful in every good work, and increasing in the knowledge of God; Strengthened with all might, according to his glorious power, unto all patience and longsuffering with joyfulness" (Col.1:10-11).

"Fear thou not; for I am with thee: be not dismayed; for I am thy God: I will strengthen thee; yea, I will help thee; yea, I will uphold thee with the right hand of my righteousness" (Is.41:10).

b. Second, the people's recognition of God's hand upon a person is proof of God's call (v.20). Samuel was definitely acknowledged to be a prophet of the LORD. As people came to the Tabernacle (central sanctuary) to worship, Samuel shared the Word of God with them. And when they returned home, they spread his reputation as a prophet throughout all Israel, from Dan to Beersheba. Dan was the northern boundary of the country and Beersheba the southern boundary.

"Wherefore, brethren, look ye out among you seven men of honest report, full of the Holy Ghost and wisdom, whom we may appoint over this business" (Ac.6:3).

"And they said, Cornelius the centurion, a just man, and one that feareth God, and of good report among all the nation of the Jews, was warned from God by an holy angel to send for thee into his house, and to hear words of thee" (Ac.10:22).

"And one Ananias, a devout man according to the law, having a good report of all the Jews which dwelt *there*" (Ac.22:12).

"And we have sent with him the brother, whose praise is in the gospel throughout all the churches" (2 Co.8:18).

"Demetrius hath good report of all *men*, and of the truth itself: yea, and we *also* bear record; and ye know that our record is true" (3 Jn.12).

c. Third, the LORD's continuous fellowship and revelation is proof of God's call upon a person. Faithfully, the LORD continued to manifest His presence at the Tabernacle—the worship center—and He continued to reveal Himself to Samuel through His Word.

"*Even* the Spirit of truth; whom the world cannot receive, because it seeth him not, neither knoweth him: but ye know him; for he dwelleth with you, and shall be in you" (Jn.14:17).

"He that hath my commandments, and keepeth them, he it is that loveth me: and he that loveth me shall be loved of my Father, and I will love him, and will manifest myself to him" (Jn.14:21).

"What? know ye not that your body is the temple of the Holy Ghost *which is* in you, which ye have of God, and ye are not your own? For ye are bought with a price: therefore glorify God in your body, and in your spirit, which are God's" (1 Co.6:19-20).

"I am crucified with Christ: nevertheless I live; yet not I, but Christ liveth in me: and the life which I now live in the flesh I live by the faith of the Son of God, who loved me, and gave himself for me" (Ga.2:20).

"That Christ may dwell in your hearts by faith; that ye, being rooted and grounded in love, May be able to comprehend with all saints what *is* the breadth, and length, and depth, and height; And to know the love of Christ, which passeth knowledge, that ye might be filled with all the fulness of God" (Ep.3:17-19).

"To whom God would make known what *is* the riches of the glory of this mystery among the Gentiles; which is Christ in you, the hope of glory" (Col.1:27).

"But the anointing which ye have received of him abideth in you, and ye need not that any man teach you: but as the same anointing teacheth you of all things, and is truth, and is no lie, and even as it hath taught you, ye shall abide in him" (1 Jn.2:27).

"And he that keepeth his commandments dwelleth in him, and he in him. And hereby we know that he abideth in us, by the Spirit which he hath given us" (1 Jn.3:24).

d. Fourth, obedience is proof of God's call upon a person. When God spoke to Samuel, Samuel gave God's Word to the people. Samuel faithfully and continually proclaimed the Word of the Living LORD (4:1).

"Not every one that saith unto me, Lord, Lord, shall enter into the kingdom of heaven; but he that doeth the will of my Father which is in heaven" (Mt.7:21).

"If ye keep my commandments, ye shall abide in my love; even as I have kept my Father's commandments, and abide in his love" (Jn.15:10).

"Blessed *are* they that do his commandments, that they may have right to the tree of life, and may enter in through the gates into the city" (Re.22:14).

"This day the LORD thy God hath commanded thee to do these statutes and judgments: thou shalt therefore keep and do them with all thine heart, and with all thy soul" (De.26:16).

"This book of the law shall not depart out of thy mouth; but thou shalt meditate therein day and night, that thou mayest observe to do according to all that is written therein: for then thou shalt make thy way prosperous, and then thou shalt have good success" (Jos.1:8).

E. The Ark Captured & Eli's Family Destroyed— All in Fulfillment of Samuel's Prophecy: A Lesson on the Surety of God's Judgment, 4:1ᵇ-22

1. The defeat of Israel by the Philistines: Judgment due to the departure of God's presence, His absence

a. The Israelites fought against the Philistines
1) Were attacked & defeated
2) Lost about 4,000 soldiers

b. The reason: The departure of God's presence

2. The capture of the Ark & the death of Eli's sons: Judgment due to superstitious idolatry & a corrupt priesthood

a. The Ark was viewed superstitiously, as an idol by the Israelites: Thought it could save them

1) The leaders sent for the Ark

2) The sons of Eli accompanied the Ark to the battlefield

3) The troops were encouraged when they saw the Ark: Began to shout with excitement

b. The Ark was viewed superstitiously, as an idol by the Philistines
1) They heard the uproar & learned that the Israelites had the Ark

2) They were stricken with fear
• Thought the Israelites had a god among them

• Had heard about the plagues inflicted upon the Egyptians by the Israelite God

3) They were aroused to fight more fiercely: To escape enslavement & death

Now Israel went out against the Philistines to battle, and pitched beside Ebenezer: and the Philistines pitched in Aphek.
2 And the Philistines put themselves in array against Israel: and when they joined battle, Israel was smitten before the Philistines: and they slew of the army in the field about four thousand men.
3 And when the people were come into the camp, the elders of Israel said, Wherefore hath the LORD smitten us to day before the Philistines? Let us fetch the ark of the covenant of the LORD out of Shiloh unto us, that, when it cometh among us, it may save us out of the hand of our enemies.
4 So the people sent to Shiloh, that they might bring from thence the ark of the covenant of the LORD of hosts, which dwelleth between the cherubims: and the two sons of Eli, Hophni and Phinehas, were there with the ark of the covenant of God.
5 And when the ark of the covenant of the LORD came into the camp, all Israel shouted with a great shout, so that the earth rang again.
6 And when the Philistines heard the noise of the shout, they said, What meaneth the noise of this great shout in the camp of the Hebrews? And they understood that the ark of the LORD was come into the camp.
7 And the Philistines were afraid, for they said, God is come into the camp. And they said, Woe unto us! for there hath not been such a thing heretofore.
8 Woe unto us! who shall deliver us out of the hand of these mighty Gods? these are the Gods that smote the Egyptians with all the plagues in the wilderness.
9 Be strong, and quit yourselves like men, O ye Philistines, that ye be not servants

unto the Hebrews, as they have been to you: quit yourselves like men, and fight.
10 And the Philistines fought, and Israel was smitten, and they fled every man into his tent: and there was a very great slaughter; for there fell of Israel thirty thousand footmen.
11 And the ark of God was taken; and the two sons of Eli, Hophni and Phinehas, were slain.
12 And there ran a man of Benjamin out of the army, and came to Shiloh the same day with his clothes rent, and with earth upon his head.
13 And when he came, lo, Eli sat upon a seat by the wayside watching: for his heart trembled for the ark of God. And when the man came into the city, and told it, all the city cried out.
14 And when Eli heard the noise of the crying, he said, What meaneth the noise of this tumult? And the man came in hastily, and told Eli.
15 Now Eli was ninety and eight years old; and his eyes were dim, that he could not see.
16 And the man said unto Eli, I am he that came out of the army, and I fled to day out of the army. And he said, What is there done, my son?
17 And the messenger answered and said, Israel is fled before the Philistines, and there hath been also a great slaughter among the people, and thy two sons also, Hophni and Phinehas, are dead, and the ark of God is taken.
18 And it came to pass, when he made mention of the ark of God, that he fell from off the seat backward by the side of the gate, and his neck brake, and he died: for he was an old man, and heavy. And he had judged Israel forty years.
19 And his daughter in law, Phinehas' wife, was with child, near to be delivered: and when she heard the tidings that the ark of God was taken, and that her father in law and her husband were dead, she bowed herself and travailed; for her pains came upon her.
20 And about the time of her

4) They fought & defeated the Israelites: Killed 30,000 soldiers

c. The Ark was captured & Eli's sons killed: Due to idolatry & a corrupt priesthood, 2:12-17, 22

3. The death of Eli: Judgment due to indulgence & the condoning of evil, 2:29
a. A messenger ran to Shiloh with news of the defeat
1) He ran right by Eli who was sitting by the road waiting for news: He feared for the Ark of God
2) He shouted out the disastrous news to the city: The people cried out in horror
b. Eli heard & asked about the outcry: Was not physically able to go to the messenger

1) He was aged: 98 years old
2) He was blind
3) He was obese, v.18

c. The messenger rushed over to Eli & shared the disastrous news

1) That Israel had been routed & suffered heavy losses
2) That Eli's two sons had been killed
3) That the Ark had been captured

d. Eli fell backward off his chair at the news of the Ark's capture: Broke his neck & died—had led Israel 40 years
e. The reason for Eli's death— the judgment: He was fat (indulgent) & condoned evil

4. The death of Eli's daughter-in-law & the birth of Ichabod: Judgment symbolized forever in the name of Ichabod, the departure of God's glory due to sin
a. The tragic news caused the pregnant wife of Eli's son Phinehas to go into labor

b. The tragic result

1) She died	death the women that stood by her said unto her, Fear not; for thou hast born a son. But she answered not, neither did she regard *it*.	is departed from Israel: because the ark of God was taken, and because of her father in law and her husband.	• Because the Ark had been captured
			• Because her loved ones had been killed
2) She named the boy "Ichabod": Means *no glory*	21 And she named the child Ichabod, saying, The glory	22 And she said, The glory is departed from Israel: for the ark of God is taken.	c. The reason: The glory of God had forsaken the wicked, departed because of sin

DIVISION I

THE STORY OF ELI AND SAMUEL: THE LORD CLOSES THE ERA OF THE JUDGES AND PREPARES FOR THE RULE OF THE KINGS, 1:1–7:17

E. The Ark Captured and Eli's Family Destroyed—All in Fulfillment of Samuel's Prophecy: A Lesson on the Surety of God's Judgment, 4:1ᵇ-22

(4:1ᵇ-22) **Introduction—Judgment, Surety of**: God's judgment is a surety. It will happen. And nothing will stop God's judgment from falling upon this earth. God is going to judge every human being who has ever lived. He will judge the secrets of men by Jesus Christ, just as the Word of God declares (Ro.2:16).

Judgment is the subject of this chapter of Scripture. God had forewarned Eli: because of his sin, he and his priesthood were to face the judgment of God and be destroyed (2:27-36). Now, God's pronouncement of judgment is executed. Using the Philistines to execute His judgment, God's warning is fulfilled upon the sinful, wicked Israelites and their priests. This is: *The Ark Captured and Eli's Family Destroyed—All in Fulfillment of Samuel's Prophecy: A Lesson on the Surety of God's Judgment,* 4:1ᵇ-22.

1. The defeat of Israel by the Philistines: Judgment due to the departure of God's presence, His absence (vv.1ᵇ-3a).
2. The capture of the Ark and the death of Eli's sons: Judgment due to superstitious idolatry and a corrupt priesthood (vv.3-11).
3. The death of Eli: Judgment due to indulgence and condoning of evil, 2:29 (vv.12-18).
4. The death of Eli's daughter-in-law and the birth of Ichabod: Judgment symbolized forever in the name of Ichabod, the departure of God's glory due to sin (vv.19-22).

1 (4:1ᵇ-3a) **Judgment, Cause of—God, Face Hidden—God, Distant, Absence of—Presence, of God, Departure of—Israel, Defeat of—Philistines, Defeat of Israel**: Israel went to war against the Philistines and was soundly defeated. This is a clear picture of judgment due to the departure of God's presence. This defeat took place soon after Samuel's prediction of judgment upon Israel and the family of the High Priest, Eli.

OUTLINE	SCRIPTURE	SCRIPTURE	OUTLINE
1. The defeat of Israel by the Philistines: Judgment due to the departure of God's presence, His absence	Now Israel went out against the Philistines to battle, and pitched beside Ebenezer: and the Philistines pitched in Aphek.	fore the Philistines: and they slew of the army in the field about four thousand men.	
a. The Israelites fought against the Philistines	2 And the Philistines put themselves in array against Israel: and when they joined battle, Israel was smitten be-	3 And when the people were come into the camp, the elders of Israel said, Wherefore hath the LORD smitten us to day before the Philistines?	b. The reason: The departure of God's presence
1) Were attacked & defeated			
2) Lost about 4,000 soldiers			

The Philistines were the bitter enemies of Israel, one of the fiercest oppressors of Israel during the days of Samson and of Saul and David. They began their fierce oppression of Israel during the period of the judges and continued their domination during the early years of Saul's reign. For example, they were so dominant that they are mentioned nearly 150 times in First and Second Samuel alone.[1] Scripture says that they came from the Island of Caphtor, which is Crete (Ge.10:14; 1 Chr.1:12; Je.47:4; Am.9:7). What happened was probably this: sometime earlier in history some of the Cretians or Caphtorians sailed down to northern Egypt and established settlements along the coast. Sometime later a branch of the Philistines migrated up along the east coast of the Mediterranean Sea. They became entrenched in the coastal areas and foothills of Canaan, so dominant that the area was eventually named after them (Palestine). Their aggressive migration into Israel took place shortly after 1200 B.C.[2]

In the present invasion the Philistines marched their soldiers into the territory of Israel and camped at Aphek, probably along the banks of the Yarkon River.[3] Marching out to meet the challenge, the Israelites camped at Ebenezer, which was two miles away. The Philistine army launched an attack and defeated the Israelites, killing about 4000 soldiers (vv.1-2). When the weary, defeated troops of Israel retreated to their camp, their leaders began to question the defeat. Why had the LORD allowed them to be defeated? Why had the LORD deserted them, hid His face from them?

---

[1] Ronald F. Youngblood. *1 Samuel*, p.594.

[2] *Ibid.,* p.594.

[3] Robert D. Bergen. *1, 2 Samuel*, p.90.

Thought 1. In answer to their question, the Israelites had been defeated for one reason and one reason only: they were guilty of the most horrible sins and wickedness:

⇒ adultery
⇒ homosexuality
⇒ sexual perversion
⇒ wife abuse
⇒ child abuse

⇒ brutality
⇒ savagery
⇒ gang rape
⇒ murder
⇒ kidnapping

⇒ drunkenness
⇒ mob violence
⇒ terrorist attacks
⇒ war

All these atrocities and criminal acts took place during the days of Samuel, the days of the judges. (See outline and notes—Jud.19:1-30; 20:1-48; 21:1-25 for more discussion.) Because of this vile, shameful behavior, God had no choice. His holiness demanded that He turn away from such vile wickedness, that He hide His face. His holiness and love cannot look upon sin and evil. Sin is an outrage to God, and wickedness is a cesspool of vileness and shame; consequently, God cannot bear to look upon such depravity. He is forced to turn away, to hide His face and remove His presence.

This is what happened to Israel, the reason for their defeat by the Philistines. God's face was hidden, His presence taken away because of their sin and wickedness.

So it is with us: our sins and wickedness cause God to turn away from us, to remove His presence. This is the strong declaration of Scripture.

"But your iniquities have separated between you and your God, and your sins have hid his face from you, that he will not hear" (Is.59:2).

"But he shall say, I tell you, I know you not whence ye are; depart from me, all ye workers of iniquity" (Lu.13:27).

"Follow peace with all men, and holiness, without which no man shall see the LORD: Looking diligently lest any man fail of the grace of God; lest any root of bitterness springing up trouble you, and thereby many be defiled; Lest there be any fornicator, or profane person, as Esau, who for one morsel of meat sold his birthright. For ye know how that afterward, when he would have inherited the blessing, he was rejected: for he found no place of repentance, though he sought it carefully with tears" (He.12:14-17).

"And I will surely hide my face in that day for all the evils which they shall have wrought, in that they are turned unto other gods" (De.31:18).

"If I regard iniquity in my heart, the LORD will not hear me" (Ps.66:18).

"And when ye spread forth your hands, I will hide mine eyes from you: yea, when ye make many prayers, I will not hear: your hands are full of blood" (Is.1:15).

"And there is none that calleth upon thy name, that stirreth up himself to take hold of thee: for thou hast hid thy face from us, and hast consumed us, because of our iniquities" (Is.64:7).

"And the heathen shall know that the house of Israel went into captivity for their iniquity: because they trespassed against me, therefore hid I my face from them, and gave them into the hand of their enemies: so fell they all by the sword" (Eze.39:23).

"They shall go with their flocks and with their herds to seek the LORD [to make sacrifice]; but they shall not find him; he hath withdrawn himself from them" (Ho.5:6).

"Then shall they cry unto the LORD, but he will not hear them: he will even hide his face from them at that time, as they have behaved themselves ill in their doings" (Mi.3:4).

2 (4:3-11) **Judgment, Caused by—Priesthood, Judgment of—Ministry, Judgment of—Hophni, Death of—Phinehas, Death of—Ark of God, Capture of—Idolatry, Example of—Superstition, Example of**: there was the capture of the Ark and the death of Eli's sons. These two events are a clear picture of God's judgment, judgment due to superstitious idolatry and a corrupt priesthood. Remember, the leaders were puzzled and bewildered, questioning why God had allowed them to be defeated by the Philistines. Why had He departed, not been present with them? Why had He hid His face from them? They came to one conclusion: they needed the Ark of God in battle with them, for the Ark was the very symbol of God's presence. No doubt, they recalled that Joshua had once carried the Ark into battle as a symbol of God's conquering, victorious power (Jos.3:3-7; 4:1-18; 6:6-21; see Nu.10:33-36). But when the Ark was brought to the battlefield, the result was catastrophic.

OUTLINE	SCRIPTURE	SCRIPTURE	OUTLINE
2. The capture of the Ark & the death of Eli's sons: Judgment due to superstitious idolatry & a corrupt priesthood	3 And when the people were come into the camp, the elders of Israel said, Wherefore hath the LORD smitten us	enemies.	
a. The Ark was viewed superstitiously, as an idol by the Israelites: Thought it could save them	to day before the Philistines? Let us fetch the ark of the covenant of the LORD out of Shiloh unto us, that, when it cometh among us, it may save us out of the hand of our	4 So the people sent to Shiloh, that they might bring from thence the ark of the covenant of the LORD of hosts, which dwelleth *between* the cherubims: and the two sons of Eli, Hophni and Phinehas, *were* there with the ark of the covenant of God.	1) The leaders sent for the Ark 2) The sons of Eli accompanied the Ark to the battlefield

OUTLINE	SCRIPTURE	SCRIPTURE	OUTLINE
3) The troops were encouraged when they saw the Ark: Began to shout with excitement b. The Ark was viewed superstitiously, as an idol by the Philistines 1) They heard the uproar & learned that the Israelites had the Ark 2) They were stricken with fear • Thought the Israelites had a god among them • Had heard about the plagues inflicted upon	5 And when the ark of the covenant of the LORD came into the camp, all Israel shouted with a great shout, so that the earth rang again. 6 And when the Philistines heard the noise of the shout, they said, What *meaneth* the noise of this great shout in the camp of the Hebrews? And they understood that the ark of the LORD was come into the camp. 7 And the Philistines were afraid, for they said, God is come into the camp. And they said, Woe unto us! for there hath not been such a thing heretofore. 8 Woe unto us! who shall deliver us out of the hand of	these mighty Gods? these *are* the Gods that smote the Egyptians with all the plagues in the wilderness. 9 Be strong, and quit yourselves like men, O ye Philistines, that ye be not servants unto the Hebrews, as they have been to you: quit yourselves like men, and fight. 10 And the Philistines fought, and Israel was smitten, and they fled every man into his tent: and there was a very great slaughter; for there fell of Israel thirty thousand footmen. 11 And the ark of God was taken; and the two sons of Eli, Hophni and Phinehas, were slain.	the Egyptians by the Israelite God 3) They were aroused to fight more fiercely: To escape enslavement & death 4) They fought & defeated the Israelites: Killed 30,000 soldiers c. The Ark was captured & Eli's sons killed: Due to idolatry & a corrupt priesthood, 2:12-17, 22

a. The Israelites viewed the Ark of God superstitiously, as an idol. To them it was like a good luck charm that could save them by turning the tide of the war with the Philistines (vv.3-5). Thus some leaders sent men to Shiloh for the Ark and the sons of Eli accompanied the Ark to the battlefield. Note the impressive description of the Ark:

⇒ "the Ark of the covenant of the LORD of Hosts, who dwells between the cherubim" (KJV; NKJV)
⇒ "the Ark of the covenant of the LORD Almighty, who is enthroned between the cherubim" (NIV; NLT)

As soon as Israel's troops saw the Ark entering the camp, a loud, exciting commotion broke loose. The soldiers shouted so loudly that the very ground itself shook.

b. The Philistines also viewed the Ark superstitiously, considering it to be an idol (vv.6-10). Hearing the uproar coming from the Hebrew camp, the enemy soldiers began to question what all the commotion was about. When they learned that the Ark of the LORD had been brought into the Hebrew camp, fear and panic struck them. They knew that the Ark was the throne of the Israelite gods. They also had some muddled knowledge of the supernatural deliverance of Israel from the Egyptians. To the Philistines, there had been many gods who had inflicted the plagues upon the Egyptians. Now, these "mighty gods" were again present with the Israelites and going to enter battle with them.

At first, terror struck the Philistines. But their leaders stood before them, challenging them to fight more fiercely to keep from being enslaved by the Israelites (v.9).

Emotionally aroused to fight for their lives, the Philistines launched a fierce attack and killed over 30,000 foot soldiers (v.10). The Israelites had expected the Ark to be a good luck charm, to assure God's presence with them. But judgment was to begin at home, first among God's people. Time and again throughout the period of the judges, the Israelites were guilty of the most gross wickedness, and God was forced to execute judgment against them. In the present case, God removed His presence and Israel suffered a catastrophic, devastating defeat: the loss of 30,000 foot soldiers.

c. It was also in this battle that the Ark was captured and Eli's sons killed (v.11). These two tragedies were a devastating blow to Israel, a catastrophic disaster to society. By losing the Ark, the very presence of God was removed from the nation. To the common Israelite, there would no longer be a need to worship at the Tabernacle, the central sanctuary of the nation, for the Ark or presence of God was no longer there.

But the loss of the Ark was not the only shocking change that took place within Israelite society. The family of Eli, the High Priest, had to be replaced. His two sons had been killed in battle, so a new family of priests needed to be installed at the Tabernacle.

Note why these two catastrophic disasters were allowed to devastate Israelite society: because of national wickedness and a corrupt priesthood (see outline and notes—1 S.2:12-36 for more discussion). The Israelites had become so wicked that the Ark itself was viewed superstitiously, as an idol. It was no longer seen as a symbol of God's presence, but rather as an idol, as possessing divine power within itself. In the people's mind, the Ark was thought to be supernatural, to possess the power to give them victory and conquest. This superstitious view of the Ark has been graphically portrayed in the twentieth century movie entitled *Raiders of the Lost Ark,* starring one of the leading movie actors of the day, Harrison Ford.

But it was not only the idolatry of the people that brought catastrophic disaster to the nation, it was also a corrupt priesthood. The two sons of Eli had been guilty of adultery and of stealing from the offerings of God and of a host of other sins. And most tragic of all, they had refused to repent and turn back to God. Instead, they had hardened their hearts and become embedded in wickedness, so embedded that they went too far, beyond repentance. For this reason, the hand of God's judgment fell upon them, and they were struck down by the Philistines.

Thought 1. Sinful, wicked behavior will result in judgment. The wicked behavior may be superstitious idolatry or a corrupt priesthood, a priesthood that is guilty of committing adultery and stealing from the LORD's offerings. But no matter what the sinful, wicked behavior is, if a priest or any other person continues to disobey God and break His holy commandments, that priest or person will be judged and condemned to eternal death, separation from God forever.

"Beware of false prophets, which come to you in sheep's clothing, but inwardly they are ravening wolves. Ye shall know them by their fruits. Do men gather grapes of thorns, or figs of thistles? Even so every good tree bringeth forth good fruit; but a corrupt tree bringeth forth evil fruit. A good tree cannot bring forth evil fruit, neither can a corrupt tree bring forth good fruit. Every tree that bringeth not forth good fruit is hewn down, and cast into the fire. Wherefore by their fruits ye shall know them. Not every one that saith unto me, LORD, LORD, shall enter into the kingdom of heaven; but he that doeth the will of my Father which is in heaven. Many will say to me in that day, LORD, LORD, have we not prophesied in thy name? and in thy name have cast out devils? and in thy name done many wonderful works? And then will I profess unto them, I never knew you: depart from me, ye that work iniquity" (Mt.7:15-23).

"For the wrath of God is revealed from heaven against all ungodliness and unrighteousness of men, who hold the truth in unrighteousness" (Ro.1:18).

"Being filled with all unrighteousness, fornication, wickedness, covetousness, maliciousness; full of envy, murder, debate, deceit, malignity; whisperers, Backbiters, haters of God, despiteful, proud, boasters, inventors of evil things, disobedient to parents, Without understanding, covenantbreakers, without natural affection, implacable, unmerciful: Who knowing the judgment of God, that they which commit such things are worthy of death, not only do the same, but have pleasure in them that do them" (Ro.1:29-32).

"Know ye not that the unrighteous shall not inherit the kingdom of God? Be not deceived: neither fornicators, nor idolaters, nor adulterers, nor effeminate, nor abusers of themselves with mankind, Nor thieves, nor covetous, nor drunkards, nor revilers, nor extortioners, shall inherit the kingdom of God" (1 Co.6:9-10).

"Now the works of the flesh are manifest, which are these; Adultery, fornication, uncleanness, lasciviousness, idolatry, witchcraft, hatred, variance, emulations, wrath, strife, seditions, heresies, envyings, murders, drunkenness, revellings, and such like: of the which I tell you before, as I have also told you in time past, that they which do such things shall not inherit the kingdom of God" (Ga.5:19-21).

"But the fearful, and unbelieving, and the abominable, and murderers, and whoremongers, and sorcerers, and idolaters, and all liars, shall have their part in the lake which burneth with fire and brimstone: which is the second death" (Re.21:8).

3 (4:12-18) **Judgment, Surety of—Indulgence, Example of—Obesity, Example of—Eli, Death of—Condoning, Evil**: there was the death of Eli when he received the report of the battle. This is a clear picture of judgment due to indulgence and the condoning of evil (2:29). The Scripture tells exactly what happened to Eli:

OUTLINE	SCRIPTURE	SCRIPTURE	OUTLINE

3. **The death of Eli: Judgment due to indulgence & the condoning of evil, 2:29**
a. A messenger ran to Shiloh with news of the defeat
  1) He ran right by Eli who was sitting by the road waiting for news: He feared for the Ark of God
  2) He shouted out the disastrous news to the city: The people cried out in horror
b. Eli heard & asked about the outcry: Was not physically able to go to the messenger
 	
  1) He was aged: 98 years old
  2) He was blind
  3) He was obese, v.18
c. The messenger rushed over
	12 And there ran a man of Benjamin out of the army, and came to Shiloh the same day with his clothes rent, and with earth upon his head. 13 And when he came, lo, Eli sat upon a seat by the wayside watching: for his heart trembled for the ark of God. And when the man came into the city, and told *it,* all the city cried out. 14 And when Eli heard the noise of the crying, he said, What *meaneth* the noise of this tumult? And the man came in hastily, and told Eli. 15 Now Eli was ninety and eight years old; and his eyes were dim, that he could not see. 16 And the man said unto	Eli, *I am* he that came out of the army, and I fled to day out of the army. And he said, What is there done, my son? 17 And the messenger answered and said, Israel is fled before the Philistines, and there hath been also a great slaughter among the people, and thy two sons also, Hophni and Phinehas, are dead, and the ark of God is taken. 18 And it came to pass, when he made mention of the ark of God, that he fell from off the seat backward by the side of the gate, and his neck brake, and he died: for he was an old man, and heavy. And he had judged Israel forty years.	to Eli & shared the disastrous news
			
			  1) That Israel had been routed & suffered heavy losses
			  2) That Eli's two sons had been killed
			  3) That the Ark had been captured
			
			d. Eli fell backward off his chair at the news of the Ark's capture: Broke his neck & died—had led Israel 40 years
			e. The reason for Eli's death—the judgment: He was fat (indulgent) & condoned evil

a. A messenger ran the twenty miles to Shiloh with news of the defeat (vv.12-13). He had torn his clothes and heaped dust upon his head as a symbolic expression of mourning over the defeat. As the messenger ran into the city, he ran right by Eli who was sitting at the city gate, watching and waiting for news from the battlefield. Note Eli's deepest concern: his heart feared for the Ark of God (v.13). Entering the city gates, the messenger ran to some central location and shouted out the disastrous news to the citizens. Upon hearing the devastating news, the people cried out in horror.

b. Eli heard and asked about the outcry of horror (vv.14-15). He was not physically able to go to the messenger himself, for he was 98 years old and blind and obese (vv.15, 18).

c. Rushing over to Eli the High Priest, the messenger shared the disastrous news with him (vv.16-17). He related the terrible report...

- that Israel had been routed and suffered heavy losses
- that Eli's two sons had been killed
- that the Ark had been captured

d. Upon hearing the news of the Ark's capture, Eli fell backward off his chair and broke his neck, dying (v.18). Note the brief statement that he had led Israel 40 years.

e. The reason for Eli's death was the judgment of God upon him (v.18). Scripture says he was obese, suggesting that he had lived an indulgent life. Because of this sin and the sin of condoning the wicked behavior of his sons, God had pronounced his judgment upon Eli (see outline and notes—1 S.2:22-36; 3:11-18 for more discussion).

Thought 1. Eli had indulged and condoned the wicked behavior of his sons. And he had even participated in their evil. He had accepted and eaten meat they had stolen from the sacrificial offerings of the people. Instead of rebuking them, he had taken part in their evil. It is interesting that he had become obese, that is, very heavy. His obesity suggests that he had readily accepted and reveled in the choice pieces of meat that had been stolen. God was left with no choice: judgment had to be executed upon Eli because of his indulgence and the condoning of his sons' wickedness. And now the judgment had fallen. Eli was dead.

The lesson for us is striking: it is the surety of judgment. God's judgment is fixed. It is definitely going to happen. All unbelievers, all who are sinful and wicked, will face the judgment of God.

"When the Son of man shall come in his glory, and all the holy angels with him, then shall he sit upon the throne of his glory: And before him shall be gathered all nations: and he shall separate them one from another, as a shepherd divideth his sheep from the goats: And he shall set the sheep on his right hand, but the goats on the left" (Mt.25:31-33).

"Whosoever therefore shall be ashamed of me and of my words in this adulterous and sinful generation; of him also shall the Son of man be ashamed, when he cometh in the glory of his Father with the holy angels" (Mk.8:38).

"Marvel not at this: for the hour is coming, in the which all that are in the graves shall hear his voice, And shall come forth; they that have done good, unto the resurrection of life; and they that have done evil, unto the resurrection of damnation" (Jn.5:28-29).

"And to you who are troubled rest with us, when the LORD Jesus shall be revealed from heaven with his mighty angels, In flaming fire taking vengeance on them that know not God, and that obey not the gospel of our LORD Jesus Christ" (2 Th.1:7-8).

"The LORD knoweth how to deliver the godly out of temptations, and to reserve the unjust unto the day of judgment to be punished" (2 Pe.2:9).

"But the heavens and the earth, which are now, by the same word are kept in store, reserved unto fire against the day of judgment and perdition of ungodly men" (2 Pe.3:7).

"And Enoch also, the seventh from Adam, prophesied of these, saying, Behold, the LORD cometh with ten thousands of his saints, To execute judgment upon all, and to convince all that are ungodly among them of all their ungodly deeds which they have ungodly committed, and of all their hard speeches which ungodly sinners have spoken against him" (Jude 14-15).

"Behold, he cometh with clouds; and every eye shall see him, and they also which pierced him: and all kindreds of the earth shall wail because of him. Even so, Amen" (Re.1:7).

4 (4:19-22) **Judgment, Surety of—Judgment, Caused by—Forsaken, the Wicked—Glory, of God, Departed—Ichabod, Meaning—Eli, Daughter-in-law:** there was the death of Eli's daughter-in-law and the birth of Ichabod. The judgment of God is symbolized forever in the name of Ichabod, for the name means *where is the glory*? God's glory had departed from Israel due to sinful, wicked behavior. Down through the centuries, the very word *Ichabod* has been used to symbolize the departure of God's presence or the loss of God's glory. This is the significance of Ichabod's birth, the event now graphically described by Scripture:

OUTLINE	SCRIPTURE	SCRIPTURE	OUTLINE
4. The death of Eli's daughter-in-law & the birth of Ichabod: Judgment symbolized forever in the name of Ichabod, the departure of God's glory due to sin a. The tragic news caused the pregnant wife of Eli's son Phinehas to go into labor b. The tragic result 　1) She died	19 And his daughter in law, Phinehas' wife, was with child, *near* to be delivered: and when she heard the tidings that the ark of God was taken, and that her father in law and her husband were dead, she bowed herself and travailed; for her pains came upon her. 20 And about the time of her death the women that stood by her said unto her, Fear not;	for thou hast born a son. But she answered not, neither did she regard *it.* 21 And she named the child Ichabod, saying, The glory is departed from Israel: because the ark of God was taken, and because of her father in law and her husband. 22 And she said, The glory is departed from Israel: for the ark of God is taken.	2) She named the boy "Ichabod": Means *no glory* 　• Because the Ark had been captured 　• Because her loved ones had been killed c. The reason: The glory of God had forsaken the wicked, departed because of sin

What happened was this: Eli's daughter-in-law, the wife of Phinehas, was pregnant and near her time of delivery. The tragic news of Israel's disastrous defeat caused the pregnant wife to go into labor (v.19). Hearing the news that her husband and father-in-law were dead and that the Ark of God had been captured was just too much for her to bear. Her labor pains began and she tragically died in childbirth. But as she was dying, the midwives told her that she had given birth to a son. In her few remaining breaths she named her child Ichabod: because the Ark had been captured and her loved ones had been killed (v.21). Weakly, she had murmured, "the glory has departed from Israel, for the Ark of God has been captured" (v.22).

Thought 1. God cannot live with wickedness. God's glory cannot shine upon the sinful. If we live in wickedness, God turns away from us. He cannot dwell in the midst of a cesspool, that of...
- filthy language and cursing
- immorality and adultery
- lying and stealing
- lawlessness and violence
- assault and murder
- mistreatment and abuse
- guilt and shame

God's holy nature cannot tolerate sinful, wicked behavior. If we choose to do evil and break God's commandments, we cannot expect God to be with us. We cannot expect Him to walk in sinful behavior, to approve our wickedness. God will not participate in sin. If we sin, He turns away, abandons, departs from us. He gives us up to our uncleanness if we choose to follow the lusts of this world.

"**Even so ye also outwardly appear righteous unto men, but within ye are full of hypocrisy and iniquity**" (Mt.23:38).
"**Then God turned, and gave them up to worship the host of heaven; as it is written in the book of the prophets, O ye house of Israel, have ye offered to me slain beasts and sacrifices** *by the space of* **forty years in the wilderness**" (Ac.7:42).
"**Wherefore God also gave them up to uncleanness through the lusts of their own hearts, to dishonour their own bodies between themselves: Who changed the truth of God into a lie, and worshipped and served the creature more than the Creator, who is blessed for ever. Amen. For this cause God gave them up unto vile affections: for even their women did change the natural use into that which is against nature: And likewise also the men, leaving the natural use of the woman, burned in their lust one toward another; men with men working that which is unseemly, and receiving in themselves that recompence of their error which was meet. And even as they did not like to retain God in** *their* **knowledge, God gave them over to a reprobate mind, to do those things which are not convenient; Being filled with all unrighteousness, fornication, wickedness, covetousness, maliciousness; full of envy, murder, debate, deceit, malignity; whisperers, Backbiters, haters of God, despiteful, proud, boasters, inventors of evil things, disobedient to parents, Without understanding, covenantbreakers, without natural affection, implacable, unmerciful: Who knowing the judgment of God, that they which commit such things are worthy of death, not only do the same, but have pleasure in them that do them**" (Ro.1:24-32).
"**But the Spirit of the LORD departed from Saul, and an evil spirit from the LORD troubled him**" (1 S.16:14).
"**And be not ye like your fathers, and like your brethren, which trespassed against the LORD God of their fathers,** *who* **therefore gave them up to desolation, as ye see**" (2 Chr.30:7).
"**So I gave them up unto their own hearts' lust:** *and* **they walked in their own counsels**" (Ps.81:12).
"**Then shall they call upon me, but I will not answer; they shall seek me early, but they shall not find me**" (Pr.1:28).

CHAPTER 5

F. The Ark Returned to Israel by the Philistines: A Lesson on God's Judgment upon All Unbelievers & False Worshippers, 5:1–6:21

1. God proved that idols are nothing: He alone is the only living & true God

a. The Ark of God was taken to Ashdod: Placed in the temple of Dagon, the chief Philistine god (a false god or idol)

b. The next morning, the idol was found lying facedown:
1) It was lying before the Ark of the LORD: A sign of reverence & submission
2) It was powerless to set itself back up

c. The following morning, the idol was again facedown on the ground
1) It was again prostrate before the Ark of the LORD
2) Its head & hands were broken off, lying on the threshold

d. The Philistines were spiritually blind: Used the event to begin a special ritual rather than repenting

2. God demonstrated that He would judge all unbelievers & false worshippers: He would put the fear of God in them

a. The LORD judged, afflicted the people of Ashdod with tumors
1) The people were stricken with panic, the fear of God

2) The city leaders requested a conference with the Philistine rulers, asking for advice

3) The rulers suggested moving the Ark to Gath

b. The LORD judged, afflicted the people of Gath
1) Afflicted both young & old
2) Struck the people with panic, the fear of God

And the Philistines took the ark of God, and brought it from Ebenezer unto Ashdod.
2 When the Philistines took the ark of God, they brought it into the house of Dagon, and set it by Dagon.
3 And when they of Ashdod arose early on the morrow, behold, Dagon *was* fallen upon his face to the earth before the ark of the LORD. And they took Dagon, and set him in his place again.
4 And when they arose early on the morrow morning, behold, Dagon *was* fallen upon his face to the ground before the ark of the LORD; and the head of Dagon and both the palms of his hands *were* cut off upon the threshold; only *the stump of* Dagon was left to him.
5 Therefore neither the priests of Dagon, nor any that come into Dagon's house, tread on the threshold of Dagon in Ashdod unto this day.
6 But the hand of the LORD was heavy upon them of Ashdod, and he destroyed them, and smote them with emerods, *even* Ashdod and the coasts thereof.
7 And when the men of Ashdod saw that *it was* so, they said, The ark of the God of Israel shall not abide with us: for his hand is sore upon us, and upon Dagon our god.
8 They sent therefore and gathered all the lords of the Philistines unto them, and said, What shall we do with the ark of the God of Israel? And they answered, Let the ark of the God of Israel be carried about unto Gath. And they carried the ark of the God of Israel about *thither*.
9 And it was *so*, that, after they had carried it about, the hand of the LORD was against the city with a very great destruction: and he smote the men of the city, both small and great, and they had

emerods in their secret parts.
10 Therefore they sent the ark of God to Ekron. And it came to pass, as the ark of God came to Ekron, that the Ekronites cried out, saying, They have brought about the ark of the God of Israel to us, to slay us and our people.
11 So they sent and gathered together all the lords of the Philistines, and said, Send away the ark of the God of Israel, and let it go again to his own place, that it slay us not, and our people: for there was a deadly destruction throughout all the city; the hand of God was very heavy there.
12 And the men that died not were smitten with the emerods: and the cry of the city went up to heaven.

CHAPTER 6

And the ark of the LORD was in the country of the Philistines seven months.
2 And the Philistines called for the priests and the diviners, saying, What shall we do to the ark of the LORD? tell us wherewith we shall send it to his place.
3 And they said, If ye send away the ark of the God of Israel, send it not empty; but in any wise return him a trespass offering: then ye shall be healed, and it shall be known to you why his hand is not removed from you.
4 Then said they, What *shall be* the trespass offering which we shall return to him? They answered, Five golden emerods, and five golden mice, *according to* the number of the lords of the Philistines: for one plague was on you all, and on your lords.
5 Wherefore ye shall make images of your emerods, and images of your mice that mar the land; and ye shall give glory unto the God of Israel: peradventure he will lighten his hand from off you, and from off your gods, and from off your land.
6 Wherefore then do ye harden your hearts, as the Egyptians and Pharaoh hardened their hearts? when he had wrought wonderfully among them, did they not let the people go, and they

3) Moved the Ark to Ekron

c. The LORD judged, afflicted the people of Ekron
1) The people—seeing the Ark enter the city—cried out in terror: Were stricken with the fear of God

2) The city leaders requested a conference with the Philistine rulers: Demanded that the Ark be sent away, back to Israel

3) The hand of God's judgment was heavy

- Many died
- Everyone else was afflicted with tumors

3. God proved His awesome power (sovereignty): Power to control human events

a. The decision of the Philistine rulers to return the Ark (after 7 months)
1) Called for the religious leaders
2) Sought their advice

b. The advice of the religious leaders
1) Should send a guilt offering to appease, pacify the god of Israel
2) The purpose: To stop the plague

c. The guilt offering suggested: A false approach to God—a detestable way to seek peace with God (His appeasement, His favor)
1) To make five gold images

2) To honor the god of Israel by sending the gold images back with the Ark

3) To remember the plagues inflicted upon the Egyptians when they hardened their hearts, Ex. 9; 10:1-2

d. The test suggested: To see if the afflictions wer caused by the Ark of God or by chance
   1) To secure a new cart & two cows that had calves never before yoked
   2) To pen up their calves
   3) To place the Ark & the chest with the gold of the guilt offering on the cart
   4) To send the cows on their way, letting them go where they would
   5) To watch the cart from a distance
   6) The purpose of the test: If the cows left their newborn calves & returned the Ark, the Philistines would know this fact: The affliction was the judgment of God upon them, not just coincidence

e. The test executed by the rulers: Convincingly proved God's power to control events & nature
   1) The instructions were followed exactly as suggested
   2) The result: God's power controlled the event
   • The cows went straight up the road to Beth Shemesh: Contrary to nature, with their calves pitifully crying or lowing after them
   • The rulers followed them to the border

4. God showed how people are to enter His presence: To approach Him through the substitute sacrifice & to honor Him as holy
a. The Israelites rejoiced over the returned Ark
   1) The cart stopped by a large rock in a field owned by Joshua of Beth Shemesh
   2) The joyful harvesters stopped work &

departed?

7 Now therefore make a new cart, and take two milch kine, on which there hath come no yoke, and tie the kine to the cart, and bring their calves home from them:

8 And take the ark of the LORD, and lay it upon the cart; and put the jewels of gold, which ye return him *for* a trespass offering, in a coffer by the side thereof; and send it away, that it may go.

9 And see, if it goeth up by the way of his own coast to Beth-shemesh, *then* he hath done us this great evil: but if not, then we shall know that *it is* not his hand *that* smote us; it *was* a chance *that* happened to us.

10 And the men did so; and took two milch kine, and tied them to the cart, and shut up their calves at home:

11 And they laid the ark of the LORD upon the cart, and the coffer with the mice of gold and the images of their emerods.

12 And the kine took the straight way to the way of Beth-shemesh, *and* went along the highway, lowing as they went, and turned not aside *to* the right hand or *to* the left; and the lords of the Philistines went after them unto the border of Beth-shemesh.

13 And *they of* Beth-shemesh *were* reaping their wheat harvest in the valley: and they lifted up their eyes, and saw the ark, and rejoiced to see *it.*

14 And the cart came into the field of Joshua, a Beth-shemite, and stood there, where *there was* a great stone: and they clave the wood of the cart, and offered the kine a burnt offering unto

the LORD.

15 And the Levites took down the ark of the LORD, and the coffer that *was* with it, wherein the jewels of gold *were,* and put *them* on the great stone: and the men of Beth-shemesh offered burnt offerings and sacrificed sacrifices the same day unto the LORD.

16 And when the five lords of the Philistines had seen *it,* they returned to Ekron the same day.

17 And these *are* the golden emerods which the Philistines returned *for* a trespass offering unto the LORD; for Ashdod one, for Gaza one, for Askelon one, for Gath one, for Ekron one;

18 And the golden mice, *according to* the number of all the cities of the Philistines *belonging* to the five lords, *both* of fenced cities, and of country villages, even unto the great *stone* of Abel, whereon they set down the ark of the LORD: *which stone remaineth* unto this day in the field of Joshua, the Beth-shemite.

19 And he smote the men of Beth-shemesh, because they had looked into the ark of the LORD, even he smote of the people fifty thousand and threescore and ten men: and the people lamented, because the LORD had smitten *many* of the people with a great slaughter.

20 And the men of Beth-shemesh said, Who is able to stand before this holy LORD God? and to whom shall he go up from us?

21 And they sent messengers to the inhabitants of Kirjath-jearim, saying, The Philistines have brought again the ark of the LORD; come ye down, *and* fetch it up to you.

worshipped the LORD
b. The Levites led the people in a day of worship
   1) Placed the Ark & chest on the large rock
   2) Offered many burnt offerings: Approached God through the substitute sacrifice
c. The Philistine rulers—watching from a distance—saw that their gold gifts were received & returned to Ekron
   1) The five gold tumors: Given as a guilt offering in behalf of the five rulers
   2) The five gold rats: Given as a guilt offering in behalf of the five cities or peoples controlled by the rulers
d. The large rock became a monument in honor of the event: The return of the Ark
e. The Israelites—many of them—violated the holiness of God: Failed to honor Him as holy
   1) Some looked into the Ark of the LORD & were stricken dead
   2) The other citizens were stricken with the fear of God, of His holiness
   3) The leaders sent messengers to Kiriath Jearim, asking them to take the Ark

DIVISION I

THE STORY OF ELI AND SAMUEL: THE LORD CLOSES THE ERA OF THE JUDGES AND PREPARES FOR THE RULE OF THE KINGS, 1:1–7:17

F. **The Ark Returned to Israel by the Philistines: A Lesson on God's Judgment upon All Unbelievers and False Worshippers, 5:1–6:21**

(5:1–6:21) **Introduction—Judgment, Truth of—Judgment, Surety of**: the judgment of God is coming upon all unbelievers and false worshippers. And the judgment of God cannot be escaped. We may not like the thought of God's judgment, but if we fail to believe and trust Christ, God forewarns us: we will face the condemnation and wrath of God. His hand of judgment will fall upon us. Time and again the truth of judgment is demonstrated in Scripture. The present passage is an example from which we are to draw lesson after lesson. This is: *The Ark Returned to Israel by the Philistines: A Lesson on God's Judgment upon All Unbelievers and False Worshippers*, 5:1–6:21.

1. God proved that idols are nothing: He alone is the only living and true God (vv.1-5).
2. God demonstrated that He would judge all unbelievers and false worshippers: He would put the fear of God in them (vv.6-12).
3. God proved His awesome power (sovereignty): power to control human events (ch.6:1-12).
4. God showed how people are to enter His presence: to approach Him through the substitute sacrifice and to honor Him as holy (vv.13-21).

1 (5:1-5) **Idolatry, Powerlessness of—Religion, Powerlessness of—Ark of God, Under the Philistines—Powerlessness, of Idolatry—Powerlessness, of False Religion—Dagon, a False God or Idol—Philistines, Idolatry of—Worship, False, Powerlessness of—God, Existence of—God, Proof of**: God proved that idols and false gods are nothing, that He and He alone is the only living and true God. This fact is clearly seen in the event that took place:

OUTLINE	SCRIPTURE	SCRIPTURE	OUTLINE
1. God proved that idols are nothing: He alone is the only living & true God	And the Philistines took the ark of God, and brought it from Ebenezer unto Ashdod.	ly on the morrow morning, behold, Dagon *was* fallen upon his face to the ground be-	idol was again facedown on the ground
a. The Ark of God was taken to Ashdod: Placed in the temple of Dagon, the chief Philistine god (a false god or idol)	2 When the Philistines took the ark of God, they brought it into the house of Dagon, and set it by Dagon.	fore the ark of the LORD; and the head of Dagon and both the palms of his hands *were* cut off upon the threshold;	1) It was again prostrate before the Ark of the LORD
b. The next morning, the idol was found lying facedown:	3 And when they of Ashdod arose early on the mor-	only *the stump of* Dagon was left to him.	2) Its head & hands were broken off, lying on the threshold
1) It was lying before the Ark of the LORD: A sign of reverence & submission	row, behold, Dagon *was* fallen upon his face to the earth before the ark of the LORD.	5 Therefore neither the priests of Dagon, nor any	
2) It was powerless to set itself back up	And they took Dagon, and set him in his place again.	that come into Dagon's house, tread on the threshold	d. The Philistines were spiritually blind: Used the event to begin a special ritual rather than repenting
c. The following morning, the	4 And when they arose ear-	of Dagon in Ashdod unto this day.	

a. Right after capturing the Ark of God, the Philistines took it to Ashdod, their capital city (vv.1-2). They placed it in the major temple of Dagon, who was the chief Philistine god. In their muddled understanding, they thought this: their god Dagon had led them to victory over the Israelites; therefore, their god was stronger than the LORD (Jehovah, Yahweh). The Ark, which they thought was an idol of the Israelite god(s), should therefore be placed in the temple of Dagon, showing reverence and submission before Dagon.

b. But note what happened: the very next morning, the idol was found lying facedown on the ground before the Ark, a clear sign that Dagon was *nothing* before the face of the LORD. When the people entered the temple, they were bound to be wondering what had happened. How could the idol have fallen facedown? And note: the idol was lifeless, powerless to set itself back up. The people had to pick up the idol and set it back in its place.

c. But the following morning when the people arose and entered the temple, the idol was again facedown on the ground, prostrate before the Ark of the LORD (v.4). This time, however, there was a shocking difference: the idol's head and hands were broken off, lying on the threshold. Only the trunk of the idol's body was left intact.

d. The spiritual blindness of the Philistines was astounding (v.5). Their false religion, belief in the power of the idol Dagon, should have been shaken. By their idol's being overthrown and broken in pieces, humiliated in reverence and submission before the Ark of God's presence, the Philistines should have acknowledged the LORD and repented before Him. The prostration of the idol Dagon before the LORD on two consecutive days was not an accident. One day might have been interpreted as an accident, but not two days. This was a clear sign that the LORD was the *only living and true God*. Consequently, the Philistines were without excuse when they failed to acknowledge the LORD and repent before Him. In fact, instead of repenting, they used the event to begin a special superstitious ritual. They began to look upon the threshold as possessing supernatural power because it had come in contact with the head and hands of Dagon. Consequently, the people adopted the policy of stepping over the threshold out of respect for Dagon.[1]

Thought 1. There is only one living and true God, the LORD Himself (Jehovah, Yahweh). There is none other. All other so-called gods are false, nothing but idols or ideas that people create within their minds. False gods are lifeless and powerless to help us when problems and trials confront us. Just think of the hardships and misfortunes that strike us throughout life:

- sickness
- disease
- accidents
- financial difficulties

- disturbed relationships
- broken promises
- pain
- depression

- loneliness
- guilt
- temptation
- death

No mental god—no god created by the imagination or thought—can deliver us through the hardships and misfortunes of life. False gods are lifeless, powerless. They are only ideas, pictures of the imagination. Only the LORD

---

1 *The NIV Study Bible*, 5:5.

Himself—the only living and true God—can help and deliver us through the trials and temptations of life. For this reason, the LORD demands two things of us:

(1) The LORD demands that we have absolutely nothing to do with false gods and idols.

> **"Forasmuch then as we are the offspring of God, we ought not to think that the Godhead is like unto gold, or silver, or stone, graven by art and man's device. And the times of this ignorance God winked at; but now commandeth all men every where to repent" (Ac.17:29-30).**

> **"For the invisible things of him from the creation of the world are clearly seen, being understood by the things that are made, *even* his eternal power and Godhead; so that they are without excuse: Because that, when they knew God, they glorified *him* not as God, neither were thankful; but became vain in their imaginations, and their foolish heart was darkened. Professing themselves to be wise, they became fools, And changed the glory of the uncorruptible God into an image made like to corruptible man, and to birds, and fourfooted beasts, and creeping things" (Ro.1:20-23).**

> **"Little children, keep yourselves from idols. Amen" (1 Jn.5:21).**

> **"Thou shalt not make unto thee any graven image, or any likeness *of any thing* that *is* in heaven above, or that *is* in the earth beneath, or that *is* in the water under the earth" (Ex.20:4).**

> **"Ye shall make you no idols nor graven image, neither rear you up a standing image, neither shall ye set up *any* image of stone in your land, to bow down unto it: for I *am* the LORD your God" (Le.26:1).**

> **"The graven images of their gods shall ye burn with fire: thou shalt not desire the silver or gold *that is* on them, nor take *it* unto thee, lest thou be snared therein: for it *is* an abomination to the LORD thy God" (De.7:25).**

> **"Therefore thou shalt love the LORD thy God, and keep his charge, and his statutes, and his judgments, and his commandments, alway" (De.11:1).**

> **"There shall no strange god be in thee; neither shalt thou worship any strange god" (Ps.81:9).**

> **"I *am* the LORD: that *is* my name: and my glory will I not give to another, neither my praise to graven images" (Is.42:8).**

> **"Assemble yourselves and come; draw near together, ye *that are* escaped of the nations: they have no knowledge that set up the wood of their graven image, and pray unto a god *that* cannot save" (Is.45:20).**

> **"For the customs of the people *are* vain: for *one* cutteth a tree out of the forest, the work of the hands of the workman, with the axe. They deck it with silver and with gold; they fasten it with nails and with hammers, that it move not. They *are* upright as the palm tree, but speak not: they must needs be borne, because they cannot go. Be not afraid of them; for they cannot do evil, neither also *is it* in them to do good" (Je.10:3-5).**

(2) The LORD demands that we acknowledge and worship Him, the only living and true God.

> **"My soul thirsteth for God, for the living God: when shall I come and appear before God?" (Ps.42:2).**

> **"For they themselves show of us what manner of entering in we had unto you, and how ye turned to God from idols to serve the living and true God" (1 Th.1:9).**

> **"And Jesus answered him, The first of all the commandments *is*, Hear, O Israel; The Lord our God is one Lord" (Mk.12:29).**

> **"And the scribe said unto him, Well, Master, thou hast said the truth: for there is one God; and there is none other but he" (Mk.12:32).**

> **"And saying, Sirs, why do ye these things? We also are men of like passions with you, and preach unto you that ye should turn from these vanities unto the living God, which made heaven, and earth, and the sea, and all things that are therein" (Ac.14:15).**

> **"One God and Father of all, who *is* above all, and through all, and in you all" (Ep.4:6).**

> **"For *there is* one God, and one mediator between God and men, the man Christ Jesus" (1 Ti.2:5).**

> **"*It is* a fearful thing to fall into the hands of the living God" (He.10:31).**

> **"Unto thee it was showed, that thou mightest know that the LORD he *is* God; *there is* none else beside him" (De.4:35).**

> **"Hear, O Israel: The LORD our God *is* one LORD" (De.6:4).**

> **"See now that I, *even* I, *am* he, and *there is* no god with me: I kill, and I make alive; I wound, and I heal: neither *is there any* that can deliver out of my hand" (De.32:39).**

> **"Thou, *even* thou, *art* LORD alone; thou hast made heaven, the heaven of heavens, with all their host, the earth, and all *things* that *are* therein, the seas, and all that *is* therein, and thou preservest them all; and the host of heaven worshippeth thee" (Ne.9:6).**

> **"That *men* may know that thou, whose name alone *is* JEHOVAH, *art* the most high over all the earth" (Ps.83:18).**

> **"My soul longeth, yea, even fainteth for the courts of the LORD: my heart and my flesh crieth out for the living God" (Ps.84:2).**

> **"For thou *art* great, and doest wondrous things: thou *art* God alone" (Ps.86:10).**

> **"Ye *are* my witnesses, saith the LORD, and my servant whom I have chosen: that ye may know and believe me, and understand that I *am* he: before me there was no God formed, neither shall there be after me. I, *even* I, *am* the LORD; and beside me *there is* no saviour" (Is.43:10-11).**

"For thus saith the LORD that created the heavens; God himself that formed the earth and made it; he hath established it, he created it not in vain, he formed it to be inhabited: I *am* the LORD; and *there is* none else" (Is.45:18).

"I make a decree, That in every dominion of my kingdom men tremble and fear before the God of Daniel: for he is the living God, and stedfast for ever, and his kingdom *that* which shall not be destroyed, and his dominion *shall be even* unto the end" (Da.6:26).

2 (5:6-12) **Judgment, Surety of—Worshippers, False, Judgment of—Judgment, of False Worshippers—Fear, of God, Example of—Unbelievers, Judgment of**: God used the capture of the Ark to teach a much needed lesson to the world: all unbelievers and false worshippers were to face the judgment of God. The "LORD's hand" was heavy against the Philistines and would be heavy against all who opposed Him. This term, "the LORD's hand," is the major theme throughout this Scripture. It is used seven times in describing God's dealings with the Philistines: His hand was heavy against them (5:6, 7, 9, 11; 6:3, 5, 9). Note how heavily God's hand or judgment moved against the Philistines:

OUTLINE	SCRIPTURE	SCRIPTURE	OUTLINE
2. God demonstrated that He would judge all unbelievers & false worshippers: He would put the fear of God in them a. The LORD judged, afflicted the people of Ashdod with tumors 　1) The people were stricken with panic, the fear of God 　2) The city leaders requested a conference with the Philistine rulers, asking for advice 　3) The rulers suggested moving the Ark to Gath b. The LORD judged, afflicted the people of Gath 　1) Afflicted both young &	6　But the hand of the LORD was heavy upon them of Ashdod, and he destroyed them, and smote them with emerods, *even* Ashdod and the coasts thereof. 7　And when the men of Ashdod saw that *it was* so, they said, The ark of the God of Israel shall not abide with us: for his hand is sore upon us, and upon Dagon our god. 8　They sent therefore and gathered all the lords of the Philistines unto them, and said, What shall we do with the ark of the God of Israel? And they answered, Let the ark of the God of Israel be carried about unto Gath. And they carried the ark of the God of Israel about *thither.* 9　And it was *so,* that, after they had carried it about, the hand of the LORD was against the city with a very great de-	struction: and he smote the men of the city, both small and great, and they had emerods in their secret parts. 10　Therefore they sent the ark of God to Ekron. And it came to pass, as the ark of God came to Ekron, that the Ekronites cried out, saying, They have brought about the ark of the God of Israel to us, to slay us and our people. 11　So they sent and gathered together all the lords of the Philistines, and said, Send away the ark of the God of Israel, and let it go again to his own place, that it slay us not, and our people: for there was a deadly destruction throughout all the city; the hand of God was very heavy there. 12　And the men that died not were smitten with the emerods: and the cry of the city went up to heaven.	old 　2) Struck the people with panic, the fear of God 　3) Moved the Ark to Ekron c. The LORD judged, afflicted the people of Ekron 　1) The people—seeing the Ark enter the city—cried out in terror: Were stricken with the fear of God 　2) The city leaders requested a conference with the Philistine rulers: Demanded that the Ark be sent away, back to Israel 　3) The hand of God's judgment was heavy 　• Many died 　• Everyone else was afflicted with tumors

a. The LORD judged, afflicted the people of Ashdod with tumors (vv.7-8). Apparently, these tumors were caused by disease-carrying rats (6:4). Because of their affliction, the people were stricken with panic and began to fear the God of the Israelites. They began to question whether the Ark of God should be taken to another city. Eventually, the city leaders requested a conference with all the Philistine rulers, asking for advice (v.8). Their conclusion was a suggestion that the Ark be moved to Gath.

b. But this was an ill-fated decision, for the LORD immediately struck again, judging and afflicting the people of Gath (v.8). Young and old alike felt the wrath of God's hand in judgment, suffering an outbreak of tumors. Panic and fear of the LORD again struck the people. So they too decided to move the Ark to another city, Ekron.

c. But the result was the same: the LORD judged and afflicted the people of Ekron (vv.10-12). It seems that God's hand of judgment fell suddenly as the Ark was being carried into the city of Ekron, for the people began to cry out in terror when they saw the Ark. An awful sense of distress gripped their hearts. Immediately, the city leaders requested a conference with all the other Philistine rulers and demanded that the Ark be sent away (v.11). In fact, note where they suggested it be sent: back to Israel.

Scripture graphically describes the scene of judgment upon Ekron: death filled the city, and panic struck the hearts of the citizens. God's hand was very heavy upon the city, moving in judgment among all the citizens. Many died, and everyone else was afflicted with tumors. The outcry of the city rose up to heaven itself. As a result, the Philistine rulers were considering sending the Ark back to Israel.

Thought 1. The hand of God's judgment will fall upon all unbelievers and false worshippers of this world. Often His judgment falls during this life. But if a person escapes the discipline and judgment of God upon this earth, he will face the judgment of God when he dies and comes face-to-face with God. There is no escape from the judgment of God. Every person will stand before God and give an account of his life. God warns all unbelievers and false worshippers: they will face the judgment of God.

"He that believeth on the Son hath everlasting life: and he that believeth not the Son shall not see life; but the wrath of God abideth on him" (Jn.3:36).

"I said therefore unto you, that ye shall die in your sins: for if ye believe not that I am *he,* ye shall die in your sins" (Jn.8:24).

"For the wrath of God is revealed from heaven against all ungodliness and unrighteousness of men, who hold the truth in unrighteousness; Because that which may be known of God is manifest in them; for God hath showed *it* unto them. For the invisible things of him from the creation of the world are clearly seen, being understood by the things that are made, *even* his eternal power and Godhead; so that they are without excuse: Because that, when they knew God, they glorified *him* not as God, neither were thankful; but became vain in their imaginations, and their foolish heart was darkened. Professing themselves to be wise, they became fools, And changed the glory of the uncorruptible God into an image made like to corruptible man, and to birds, and fourfooted beasts, and creeping things.... Being filled with all unrighteousness, fornication, wickedness, covetousness, maliciousness; full of envy, murder, debate, deceit, malignity; whisperers, Backbiters, haters of God, despiteful, proud, boasters, inventors of evil things, disobedient to parents, Without understanding, covenantbreakers, without natural affection, implacable, unmerciful: Who knowing the judgment of God, that they which commit such things are worthy of death, not only do the same, but have pleasure in them that do them" (Ro.1:18-23, 29-32).

"And to you who are troubled rest with us, when the Lord Jesus shall be revealed from heaven with his mighty angels, In flaming fire taking vengeance on them that know not God, and that obey not the gospel of our Lord Jesus Christ" (2 Th.1:7-8).

"The Lord knoweth how to deliver the godly out of temptations, and to reserve the unjust unto the day of judgment to be punished" (2 Pe.2:9).

"And Enoch also, the seventh from Adam, prophesied of these, saying, Behold, the Lord cometh with ten thousands of his saints, To execute judgment upon all, and to convince all that are ungodly among them of all their ungodly deeds which they have ungodly committed, and of all their hard *speeches* which ungodly sinners have spoken against him" (Jude 14-15).

"And I saw a great white throne, and him that sat on it, from whose face the earth and the heaven fled away; and there was found no place for them. And I saw the dead, small and great, stand before God; and the books were opened: and another book was opened, which is *the book* of life: and the dead were judged out of those things which were written in the books, according to their works. And the sea gave up the dead which were in it; and death and hell delivered up the dead which were in them: and they were judged every man according to their works. And death and hell were cast into the lake of fire. This is the second death. And whosoever was not found written in the book of life was cast into the lake of fire" (Re.20:11-15).

---

3 **(6:1-12) Sovereignty, of God—Power, of God, to Control Human Events—Ark of God, Returned by the Philistines—Philistines, Experience with the Ark of God**: God proved His sovereignty, His awesome power to control human events. The Philistines were eager, very eager, to get rid of the Ark, so they began to seek the best way to return the Ark to Israel.

OUTLINE	SCRIPTURE	SCRIPTURE	OUTLINE
3. God proved His awesome power (sovereignty): Power to control human events a. The decision of the Philistine rulers to return the Ark (after 7 months) 1) Called for the religious leaders 2) Sought their advice b. The advice of the religious leaders 1) Should send a guilt offering to appease, pacify the god of Israel 2) The purpose: To stop the plague c. The guilt offering suggested: A false approach to God—a detestable way to seek peace with God (His appeasement, His favor) 1) To make five gold images	And the ark of the LORD was in the country of the Philistines seven months. 2 And the Philistines called for the priests and the diviners, saying, What shall we do to the ark of the LORD? tell us wherewith we shall send it to his place. 3 And they said, If ye send away the ark of the God of Israel, send it not empty; but in any wise return him a trespass offering: then ye shall be healed, and it shall be known to you why his hand is not removed from you. 4 Then said they, What *shall be* the trespass offering which we shall return to him? They answered, Five golden emerods, and five golden mice, *according to* the number of the lords of the Philistines: for one plague was on you all, and on your lords.	5 Wherefore ye shall make images of your emerods, and images of your mice that mar the land; and ye shall give glory unto the God of Israel: peradventure he will lighten his hand from off you, and from off your gods, and from off your land. 6 Wherefore then do ye harden your hearts, as the Egyptians and Pharaoh hardened their hearts? when he had wrought wonderfully among them, did they not let the people go, and they departed? 7 Now therefore make a new cart, and take two milch kine, on which there hath come no yoke, and tie the kine to the cart, and bring their calves home from them: 8 And take the ark of the LORD, and lay it upon the	2) To honor the god of Israel by sending the gold images back with the Ark 3) To remember the plagues inflicted upon the Egyptians when they hardened their hearts, Ex. 9; 10:1-2 d. The test suggested: To see if the afflictions were caused by the Ark of God or by chance 1) To secure a new cart & two cows that had calves never before yoked 2) To pen up their calves 3) To place the Ark & the chest with the gold of the

OUTLINE	SCRIPTURE	SCRIPTURE	OUTLINE
guilt offering on the cart	cart; and put the jewels of gold, which ye return him *for* a trespass offering, in a coffer by the side thereof; and send it away, that it may go.	them to the cart, and shut up their calves at home:	God's power to control events & nature
4) To send the cows on their way, letting them go where they would		11 And they laid the ark of the LORD upon the cart, and the coffer with the mice of gold and the images of their emerods.	1) The instructions were followed exactly as suggested
5) To watch the cart from a distance	9 And see, if it goeth up by the way of his own coast to Beth-shemesh, *then* he hath done us this great evil: but if not, then we shall know that *it is* not his hand *that* smote us; it *was* a chance *that* happened to us.		2) The result: God's power controlled the event
6) The purpose of the test: If the cows left their newborn calves & returned the Ark, the Philistines would know this fact: The affliction was the judgment of God upon them, not just coincidence		12 And the kine took the straight way to the way of Beth-shemesh, *and* went along the highway, lowing as they went, and turned not aside *to* the right hand or *to* the left; and the lords of the Philistines went after them unto the border of Beth-shemesh.	• The cows went straight up the road to Beth Shemesh: Contrary to nature, with their calves pitifully crying or lowing after them
e. The test executed by the rulers: Convincingly proved	10 And the men did so; and took two milch kine, and tied		• The rulers followed them to the border

a. The Philistine rulers made the decision to return the Ark after seven months of suffering under the hand of God's judgment (vv.1-2). But in returning the Ark, they had to make sure that they did it properly. If they mishandled the Ark, they could arouse God's wrath against them even more heavily than before. Having suffered enough, the Philistine rulers summoned the religious leaders to seek their advice.

b. In advising the rulers, the religious leaders suggested sending a *guilt offering* back with the Ark. The purpose was to appease or pacify the God of Israel, arousing Him to stop the plague. If the plague did not stop, the rulers would know that the LORD had not sent the plague after all.

c. Note that the suggested *guilt offering* was a false approach to God, a detestable way to seek peace with God (His appeasement, His favor), (vv.4-6). The religious leaders instructed the rulers to make five gold images of tumors and five more of rats, a total of ten images to equal the number of the Philistine rulers (v.4). These gold images were to be sent back with the Ark in honor of the God of Israel (v.5). This brings up an interesting point. The name Dagon means *grain*. The Philistines were afraid that if they did not worship Dagon, they would not have a good harvest. It may be that the stores of grain were overrun by rats. But in any case, the God of Israel had been proven mightier than the Philistines' "grain god." This seems a likely reason for the offering of the five golden mice.

Questioning the rulers, the religious leaders asked why they had hardened their hearts against the Israelites. The rulers needed to remember the plagues that had been inflicted upon the Egyptians when they hardened their hearts against the God of Israel (v.6; Ex.9:1f; 10:1-2). The LORD's judgment and affliction upon the Egyptians had been so heavy that they were forced to free the Israelites from slavery. Remembering this fact, no doubt, aroused even more fear and a stronger determination to send the Ark back.

d. A test was suggested to determine if the afflictions were actually caused by the Ark of God or just by chance (vv.7-9). The rulers were to secure a new cart and two cows that had just had calves and never before been yoked to a cart. They were to hitch the cows to the cart and pen up the calves. Then they were to place the Ark and the chest with the gold (of the guilt offering) on the cart. After being loaded, they were to send the cows on their way, letting them go wherever they wanted (v.8). As the cows walked, the rulers were to keep watch over the cart from a distance (v.9). If the cows left their newborn calves and returned the Ark, the Philistines would know this fact: the affliction was the judgment of God upon them, not just a coincidence that happened by chance.

e. The test was executed by the Philistine rulers exactly as suggested by the religious leaders. And what happened next is convincing proof of God's power to control events and nature (vv.10-12). The cows went straight up the road to Beth Shemesh. This behavior of the cows was contrary to nature, for their calves were pitifully *crying*, *lowing* after them. It is most unusual for a cow not to go to the rescue of its calf when it is crying out in desperation for its mother.

The rulers followed the cows to the border of Beth Shemesh to observe this behavior of the cows and calves. By this event, they rightly concluded that the judgment and plagues were controlled by the LORD.

Thought 1. The LORD is sovereign, ruling and reigning over the earth and the entire universe. He is the great Creator of both heaven and earth, possessing the sovereign power to control all events, both seen and unseen. All kingdoms, power, and glory belong to Him. He and He alone made the world and all things therein, and He is the LORD of heaven and earth. There is no other sovereign power, controlling all that exists and that happens. All riches and all honor and all power and might—it all comes from Him. He gives and He takes away so that all people may know that He and He alone is the LORD (Jehovah, Yahweh). He is the Most High, the Sovereign LORD over all that exists throughout the universe. Whatever pleases the LORD, He does. And no person in heaven or earth can stop Him. The LORD God Almighty is sovereign, possessing awesome, unlimited power to control all events and happenings that take place throughout the whole universe.

> **"And lead us not into temptation, but deliver us from evil: For thine is the kingdom, and the power, and the glory, for ever. Amen" (Mt.6:13).**
>
> **"But Jesus beheld *them*, and said unto them, With men this is impossible; but with God all things are possible" (Mt.19:26).**
>
> **"God that made the world and all things therein, seeing that he is Lord of heaven and earth, dwelleth not in temples made with hands" (Ac.17:24).**

"Know therefore this day, and consider *it* in thine heart, that the LORD he *is* God in heaven above, and upon the earth beneath: *there is* none else" (De.4:39).

"Both riches and honour *come* of thee, and thou reignest over all; and in thine hand *is* power and might; and in thine hand *it is* to make great, and to give strength unto all" (1 Chr.29:12).

"He leadeth princes away spoiled, and overthroweth the mighty" (Jb.12:19).

"I know that thou canst do every *thing,* and *that* no thought can be withholden from thee" (Jb.42:2).

"Yea, all kings shall fall down before him: all nations shall serve him" (Ps.72:11).

"That *men* may know that thou, whose name alone *is* JEHOVAH, *art* the most high over all the earth" (Ps.83:18).

"The LORD reigneth, he is clothed with majesty; the LORD is clothed with strength, *wherewith* he hath girded himself: the world also is stablished, that it cannot be moved" (Ps.93:1).

"The LORD hath prepared his throne in the heavens; and his kingdom ruleth over all" (Ps.103:19).

"But our God *is* in the heavens: he hath done whatsoever he hath pleased" (Ps.115:3).

"Whatsoever the LORD pleased, *that* did he in heaven, and in earth, in the seas, and all deep places" (Ps.135:6).

"The king's heart *is* in the hand of the LORD, *as* the rivers of water: he turneth it whithersoever he will" (Pr.21:1).

"Yea, before the day *was* I *am* he; and *there is* none that can deliver out of my hand: I will work, and who shall let [hinder] it?" (Is.43:13).

"Daniel answered and said, Blessed be the name of God for ever and ever: for wisdom and might are his" (Da.2:20).

"And all the inhabitants of the earth *are* reputed as nothing: and he doeth according to his will in the army of heaven, and *among* the inhabitants of the earth: and none can stay his hand, or say unto him, What doest thou?" (Da.4:35).

4 (6:13-21) **Approach, to God, Duty—Access, to God, Duty—Holiness, of God—Sacrifice, Substitute, Duty—Presence, of God, How to Approach**: God showed how people are to enter His presence through the event that happened to the Israelites at Beth Shemesh. People must always approach God through the substitute sacrifice and honor Him as holy. But some of the citizens of Beth Shemesh violated the holiness of God, failing to show reverence and to fear His holy presence. The Scripture and outline clearly describe the scene:

OUTLINE	SCRIPTURE	SCRIPTURE	OUTLINE

4. God showed how people are to enter His presence: To approach Him through the substitute sacrifice & to honor Him as holy
a. The Israelites rejoiced over the returned Ark
  1) The cart stopped by a large rock in a field owned by Joshua of Beth Shemesh
 	
  2) The joyful harvesters stopped work & worshipped the LORD
b. The Levites led the people in a day of worship
  1) Placed the Ark & chest on the large rock
 	
  2) Offered many burnt offerings: Approached God through the substitute sacrifice
c. The Philistine rulers—watching from a distance—saw that their gold gifts were received & returned to Ekron
  1) The five gold tumors: Given as a guilt offering in behalf of the five rulers
	13 And *they of* Beth-shemesh *were* reaping their wheat harvest in the valley: and they lifted up their eyes, and saw the ark, and rejoiced to see *it.*
	14 And the cart came into the field of Joshua, a Beth-shemite, and stood there, where *there was* a great stone: and they clave the wood of the cart, and offered the kine a burnt offering unto the LORD.
	15 And the Levites took down the ark of the LORD, and the coffer that *was* with it, wherein the jewels of gold *were,* and put *them* on the great stone: and the men of Beth-shemesh offered burnt offerings and sacrificed sacrifices the same day unto the LORD.
	16 And when the five lords of the Philistines had seen *it,* they returned to Ekron the same day.
	17 And these *are* the golden emerods which the Philistines returned *for* a trespass offering unto the LORD; for Ashdod one, for Gaza one, for Askelon one, for Gath one,
		for Ekron one;
		18 And the golden mice, *according to* the number of all the cities of the Philistines *belonging* to the five lords, *both* of fenced cities, and of country villages, even unto the great *stone* of Abel, whereon they set down the ark of the LORD: *which stone remaineth* unto this day in the field of Joshua, the Beth-shemite.
		19 And he smote the men of Beth-shemesh, because they had looked into the ark of the LORD, even he smote of the people fifty thousand and threescore and ten men: and the people lamented, because the LORD had smitten *many* of the people with a great slaughter.
		20 And the men of Beth-shemesh said, Who is able to stand before this holy LORD God? and to whom shall he go up from us?
		21 And they sent messengers to the inhabitants of Kirjath-jearim, saying, The Philistines have brought again the ark of the LORD; come ye down, *and* fetch it up to you.
			2) The five gold rats: Given as a guilt offering in behalf of the five cities or peoples controlled by the rulers
			d. The large rock became a monument in honor of the event: The return of the Ark
			
			e. The Israelites—many of them—violated the holiness of God: Failed to honor Him as holy
			  1) Some looked into the Ark of the LORD & were stricken dead
			
			  2) The other citizens were stricken with the fear of God, of His holiness
			
			  3) The leaders sent messengers to Kiriath Jearim, asking them to take the Ark

a. When the Israelites saw the Ark approaching the city, they rejoiced over its return (vv.13-14). They were out harvesting their wheat in the valley when they looked up and saw the Ark approaching. The sight was bound to arouse great joy and rejoicing within their hearts. Beth Shemesh was a Levitical city, a city populated by a large number of priests from the clan of Kohath. The primary responsibility of the Kohath priests was to take care of the Ark of God (Num.4:4, 15). Thus, they in particular would be stirred over the Ark's being returned to Israel. The joyful harvesters stopped their work and worshipped the LORD right there on the spot. The cart had stopped beside a large rock. When the people reached it, they chopped up the wood of the cart and offered the two cows as a burnt offering to the LORD.

b. The priests actually led the people to take the whole day for worship (v.15). They placed the Ark and chest containing the gold gifts on the large rock. Then they began to present burnt offerings to the LORD, approaching God through the substitute sacrifice. But note this fact: they sacrificed the two cows as a burnt offering to the LORD. This was in direct disobedience to the LORD, to the law that governed the offerings (Le.1:3). The law of God prohibited the offering up of a heifer as a burnt sacrifice. Consequently, their reckless behavior was soon to face the judgment of God, for they had disobeyed His command and law. However, they were correct in approaching God through the substitute sacrifice, which is a clear symbol of the substitutionary sacrifice of the Lord Jesus Christ.

c. During all this activity, the Philistine rulers were watching from a distance. Once they saw that the cart had returned and that their gold gifts were received, they returned to Ekron (vv.16-18). Their five gold tumors and five gold rats that had been given as a *guilt offering* were received. Therefore, they concluded that the judgment and affliction of the LORD against them would be stopped. And they were correct. The hand of God's judgment against the Philistines was removed, at least for the present. However, God ceased His judgment, not because of the foolish strategy of the Philistines, but because of His sovereign mercy—and because He was using this event to teach all future generations that God will judge all unbelievers and false worshippers. He will even judge His own people when they approach Him falsely, disobediently.

d. The return of the Ark to Israel was a significant event in their history, so significant that the large rock upon which they had set the Ark became a monument (v.18). Note that the rock was still a monument when the great book of Samuel was written.

e. Tragically, during the festivities of the worship service, many of the Israelites violated the holiness of God, failing to honor Him as holy (vv.19-21). Some of the men did the most shocking, irreverent thing imaginable: they actually looked into the Ark of the LORD. And immediately they were stricken dead. Seventy of them were stricken dead by the hand of God's judgment. This, of course, put the fear of God in the Israelites' hearts and taught them a much needed lesson on the holiness of God. The leaders then sent messengers to Kiriath Jearim, asking them to take the Ark (v.21). As will be seen in the next chapter, that request was granted and the Ark was moved to Kiriath Jearim.

Thought 1. The lesson is dramatic: people must approach God just as He dictates. He and He alone is the LORD; therefore, He alone has the right to dictate how He is to be approached. God's holiness sets Him apart as distinct and different from all other creatures throughout the universe. God dwells in perfection, lives in perfect holiness, righteous, and purity. He is the very embodiment of perfection and holiness. Therefore, when God says that He must be approached through the substitute sacrifice and be honored as holy, a person must approach God exactly as dictated. This is precisely what Scripture declares:

(1) We must approach God acknowledging that He is holy, that He dwells in perfect holiness, righteousness, and purity. And because He is holy, we must live holy, righteous, and pure lives.

> "Follow peace with all *men,* and holiness, without which no man shall see the Lord" (He.12:14).
> "Because it is written, Be ye holy; for I am holy" (1 Pe.1:16).
> "*Seeing* then *that* all these things shall be dissolved, what manner *of persons* ought ye to be in *all* holy conversation and godliness, Looking for and hasting unto the coming of the day of God, wherein the heavens being on fire shall be dissolved, and the elements shall melt with fervent heat? Nevertheless we, according to his promise, look for new heavens and a new earth, wherein dwelleth righteousness. Wherefore, beloved, seeing that ye look for such things, be diligent that ye may be found of him in peace, without spot, and blameless" (2 Pe.11-14).
> "Who shall not fear thee, O Lord, and glorify thy name? for *thou* only *art* holy: for all nations shall come and worship before thee; for thy judgments are made manifest" (Re.15:4).
> "For I *am* the LORD that bringeth you up out of the land of Egypt, to be your God: ye shall therefore be holy, for I *am* holy" (Le.11:45).
> "Exalt the LORD our God, and worship at his holy hill; for the LORD our God *is* holy" (Ps.99:9).

(2) We must approach God through the substitute sacrifice, the Lord Jesus Christ Himself. He is the substitutionary sacrifice who died for our sins.

> "That it might be fulfilled which was spoken by Esaias the prophet, saying, Himself took our infirmities, and bare *our* sicknesses" (Mt.8:17).
> "The next day John seeth Jesus coming unto him, and saith, Behold the Lamb of God, which taketh away the sin of the world" (Jn.1:29).
> "Purge out therefore the old leaven, that ye may be a new lump, as ye are unleavened. For even Christ our passover is sacrificed for us" (1 Co.5:7).
> "So Christ was once offered to bear the sins of many; and unto them that look for him shall he appear the second time without sin unto salvation" (He.9:28).

"Forasmuch as ye know that ye were not redeemed with corruptible things, *as* silver and gold, from your vain conversation *received* by tradition from your fathers; But with the precious blood of Christ, as of a lamb without blemish and without spot" (1 Pe.1:18-19).

"Who his own self bare our sins in his own body on the tree, that we, being dead to sins, should live unto righteousness: by whose stripes ye were healed" (1 Pe.2:24).

"For Christ also hath once suffered for sins, the just for the unjust, that he might bring us to God, being put to death in the flesh, but quickened by the Spirit" (1 Pe.3:18).

"And ye know that he was manifested to take away our sins; and in him is no sin" (1 Jn.3:5).

"Surely he hath borne our griefs, and carried our sorrows: yet we did esteem him stricken, smitten of God, and afflicted" (Is.53:4).

1. Samuel led Israel to repentance: A call for confession & total commitment to LORD

a. The Ark was taken to Kiriath Jearim
1) Put in Abinadab's house
2) Guarded by Eleazar
3) Remained there for 20 years

b. The shock of having lost the Ark & worship center stirred the people to mourn & seek the LORD

c. The event aroused Samuel to preach one message for 20 years: Personal repentance & total commitment
1) The audience: All Israel
2) The message
• Repentance: Put away false gods & worship
• Total commitment: Serve the LORD only
• The result: Deliverance
3) The obedience of the Israelites: They repented & committed themselves

d. The repentance stirred Samuel to call for a nationwide assembly at Mizpah: To publicly confirm their renewal
1) They observed a ritual: Symbolized pouring out their hearts in repentance, Ps. 62:8
2) They fasted & confessed their sins
3) They began to look to Samuel as their nationwide leader or judge

2. Samuel stirred the Israelites to defeat the Philistines: Victory & deliverance from bondage through prayer

a. The mobilization of the Philistines & the gripping fear of the Israelites

CHAPTER 7

G. The Ministry of Samuel & the Events That Closed the Era of the Judges: A Lesson on How to Live Victoriously, 7:1-17

And the men of Kirjath-jearim came, and brought up the ark of the LORD, and brought it into the house of Abinadab in the hill, and sanctified Eleazar his son to keep the ark of the LORD.
2 And it came to pass, while the ark abode in Kirjath-jearim, that the time was long; for it was twenty years: and all the house of Israel lamented after the LORD.
3 And Samuel spake unto all the house of Israel, saying, If ye do return unto the LORD with all your hearts, then put away the strange gods and Ashtaroth from among you, and prepare your hearts unto the LORD, and serve him only: and he will deliver you out of the hand of the Philistines.
4 Then the children of Israel did put away Baalim and Ashtaroth, and served the LORD only.
5 And Samuel said, Gather all Israel to Mizpeh, and I will pray for you unto the LORD.
6 And they gathered together to Mizpeh, and drew water, and poured it out before the LORD, and fasted on that day, and said there, We have sinned against the LORD. And Samuel judged the children of Israel in Mizpeh.
7 And when the Philistines heard that the children of Israel were gathered together to Mizpeh, the lords of the Philistines went up against Israel. And when the children of Israel heard it, they were afraid of the Philistines.

8 And the children of Israel said to Samuel, Cease not to cry unto the LORD our God for us, that he will save us out of the hand of the Philistines.
9 And Samuel took a sucking lamb, and offered it for a burnt offering wholly unto the LORD: and Samuel cried unto the LORD for Israel; and the LORD heard him.
10 And as Samuel was offering up the burnt offering, the Philistines drew near to battle against Israel: but the LORD thundered with a great thunder on that day upon the Philistines, and discomfited them; and they were smitten before Israel.
11 And the men of Israel went out of Mizpeh, and pursued the Philistines, and smote them, until they came under Beth-car.
12 Then Samuel took a stone, and set it between Mizpeh and Shen, and called the name of it Ebenezer, saying, Hitherto hath the LORD helped us.
13 So the Philistines were subdued, and they came no more into the coast of Israel: and the hand of the LORD was against the Philistines all the days of Samuel.
14 And the cities which the Philistines had taken from Israel were restored to Israel, from Ekron even unto Gath; and the coasts thereof did Israel deliver out of the hands of the Philistines. And there was peace between Israel and the Amorites.
15 And Samuel judged Israel all the days of his life.
16 And he went from year to year in circuit to Bethel, and Gilgal, and Mizpeh, and judged Israel in all those places.
17 And his return was to Ramah; for there was his house; and there he judged Israel; and there he built an altar unto the LORD.

b. The appeal to Samuel for continued, unbroken prayer

c. The appeal & prayer to God by Samuel: Approached God through the Burnt Offering—seeking reconciliation through the blood of the substitute sacrifice

d. The miraculous answer to prayer by God: Achieved victory
1) The Philistines launched their attack just as Samuel was offering the sacrifice
2) The LORD struck the Philistines with a terrifying thunderstorm
3) The Philistine army was routed, pursued, & slaughtered by the Israelites

4) The victory was memorialized by Samuel: Set up a stone monument named Ebenezer, meaning "the stone of help"

e. The results of the victory
1) The Philistine enemy was subdued during Samuel's lifetime

2) The territory formerly conquered by the Philistine enemy was regained

3) The power of Israel struck fear in other enemies & secured peace

3. Samuel closed the era of the judges & launched the era of the kings: A lesson on faithfulness
a. He was faithful as a judge
1) Traveling as a circuit judge
2) Serving as the last judge: Closing the era of the judges & opening up the era of the kings
b. He was faithful as a prophet & priest or worship leader, 3:20; 4:1

DIVISION I

THE STORY OF ELI AND SAMUEL: THE LORD CLOSES THE ERA OF THE JUDGES AND PREPARES FOR THE RULE OF THE KINGS, 1:1–7:17

G.   The Ministry of Samuel and the Events That Closed the Era of the Judges: A Lesson on How to Live Victoriously, 7:1-17

(7:1-17) **Introduction—Victory, over Enemies—Conquest, over Enemies—Victorious Life, Seeking**: everyone desires to live a victorious, conquering life. Going through life depressed and discouraged—constantly feeling oppressed and defeated with no purpose or meaning to life—is not a pleasant picture. All of us yearn to be conquerors, to walk through life victoriously, triumphing over all the problems, temptations, and trials of life.

Living a life of conquest and victory is the subject of this great passage of Scripture. The Israelites had been defeated in war and subjected under the oppression of the Philistines. They were a downtrodden, defeated, and discouraged people. Even their worship center at Shiloh had been destroyed. The worst emotion that can grip the human heart had captured the spirit of the Israelites: that of being alienated, cut off, separated, and abandoned by God. The present passage covers a span of twenty-some years, years of mourning and crying out to God for deliverance. This is: *The Ministry of Samuel and the Events That Closed the Era of the Judges: A Lesson on How to Live Victoriously,* 7:1-17.

1. Samuel led Israel to repentance: a call for confession and total commitment to God (vv.1-6).
2. Samuel stirred the Israelites to defeat the Philistines: victory and deliverance from bondage through prayer (vv.7-14).
3. Samuel closed the era of the judges and launched the era of the kings: a lesson on faithfulness (vv.15-17).

1 (7:1-6) **Repentance, Duty—Confession, Duty—Commitment, Duty—Ministry, Duty—Message, Subject of—Renewal, Example of—Israel, Renewal and Revival—Ark of God, Recovered—Ark, Location of**: Samuel led Israel to repentance, calling upon the people to confess their sins and make a total commitment to God. What happened covered a twenty-year period of time.

OUTLINE	SCRIPTURE	SCRIPTURE	OUTLINE
1. Samuel led Israel to repentance: A call for confession & total commitment to LORD	And the men of Kirjath-jearim came, and brought up the ark of the LORD, and brought it into the house of Abinadab in the hill, and sanctified Eleazar his son to keep the ark of the LORD.	the LORD, and serve him only: and he will deliver you out of the hand of the Philistines.	false gods & worship
a. The Ark was taken to Kiriath Jearim			• Total commitment: Serve the LORD only
1) Put in Abinadab's house			• The result: Deliverance
2) Guarded by Eleazar		4 Then the children of Israel did put away Baalim and Ashtaroth, and served the LORD only.	3) The obedience of the Israelites: They repented & committed themselves
3) Remained there for 20 years	2 And it came to pass, while the ark abode in Kirjath-jearim, that the time was long; for it was twenty years: and all the house of Israel lamented after the LORD.	5 And Samuel said, Gather all Israel to Mizpeh, and I will pray for you unto the LORD.	d. The repentance stirred Samuel to call for a nationwide assembly at Mizpah: To publicly confirm their renewal
b. The shock of having lost the Ark & worship center stirred the people to mourn & seek the LORD	3 And Samuel spake unto all the house of Israel, saying, If ye do return unto the LORD with all your hearts, *then* put away the strange gods and Ashtaroth from among you, and prepare your hearts unto	6 And they gathered together to Mizpeh, and drew water, and poured *it* out before the LORD, and fasted on that day, and said there, We have sinned against the LORD. And Samuel judged the children of Israel in Mizpeh.	1) They observed a ritual: Symbolized pouring out their hearts in repentance, Ps. 62:8
c. The event aroused Samuel to preach one message for 20 years: Personal repentance & total commitment			2) They fasted & confessed their sins
1) The audience: All Israel			3) They began to look to Samuel as their nationwide leader or judge
2) The message			
• Repentance: Put away			

a. The Ark was carried to Kiriath Jearim and placed in the house of Abinadab and his son Eleazar (v.1). The son was actually consecrated, *officially set apart,* to look after and protect the Ark. This he did for over twenty years.

Why was the Ark not returned to Shiloh? Because Shiloh had evidently been destroyed earlier by the Philistines (1 S.4:10-11). Four facts seemed to point to Shiloh's destruction:[1]

⇒ First, Shiloh is never again mentioned as a worship center in 1 or 2 Samuel after the Philistine defeat.
⇒ Second, the center of Samuel's ministry became his hometown of Ramah after the Philistine defeat (7:17).
⇒ Third, the Ark was not returned to Shiloh after its recovery from the Philistines (7:1-2).
⇒ Fourth, the book of Psalms and Jeremiah mention the destruction of the sanctuary at Shiloh (Ps.78:60; Je.7:12-14; 26:6, 9).

However, there is a possibility that the Tabernacle escaped destruction even though the city of Shiloh was destroyed. The *NIV Study Bible* holds this position, pointing out that it was first moved to Nob (1 S.21:1-9). And then in the days of David and Solomon, it was located at Gibeon (1 Chr.16:39; 21:29; 2 Chr.1:3, 13). Later Solomon brought the Tabernacle to the temple after its construction had been completed (1 K.3:4; 8:4). There is, of course, the possibility that the furnishings of the Tabernacle had been quickly removed before the Philistine invasion and had been taken elsewhere for safekeeping. But the tent of the Tabernacle itself had been destroyed. And then sometime in the future, the tent of the Tabernacle was reconstructed and placed in the city of Nob; later in David's and Solomon's days, it was moved to Gibeon. Whatever the case, the important fact to note is that the Ark itself remained under the care of Eleazar for twenty years. During these twenty years, the Israelites experienced revival, a renewed commitment to the LORD.

b. It was the shock of having lost the Ark and worship center that stirred the people to seek after the LORD with a renewed commitment (v.2). With the loss of their central worship center and Ark, the people felt as though the presence of God had been lost. Remember that the Ark represented the presence of God among the people. Without the Ark, it was as

---

[1] Robert D. Bergen. *1, 2 Samuel*, p.92.

though God were not present with them, as though God were absent and unavailable to help, guide, and protect them. Consequently, the people began to mourn the loss of the Ark and their worship center and to seek after the LORD.

c. The renewed spiritual interest of the people aroused Samuel to preach one message for twenty years: the message of personal repentance and total commitment to the LORD (vv.3-4). Samuel challenged all Israel to repent by putting away their false gods and their false worship. The reference to "foreign gods" is synonymous with the false god "Baal" (v.4; 12:10; Jud.2:13; 10:6).[2] Baal dominated the false worship of the Canaanite nations. This false god's name means *master* or *lord,* and he was symbolized in the molten image of a bull. Baal was considered the god of fertility and of weather, being the Canaanite god who controlled the rain. He was thus responsible for the livestock of the farm.

Ashtaroth was the fertility goddess who was worshipped as the goddess of love (sex) and of war. Prostitute priestesses were a legalized part of the cult of this fertility goddess. She was closely associated with fornication and drunkenness.

Israel had forsaken the LORD, turned away from Him to serve Baal and Ashtaroth. This was an act of spiritual treason, an act that was reprehensible. It was gross idolatry, and such treachery had found its way into every part of Hebrew life. Thus, the message of repentance had to be preached by Samuel. He was forced to focus upon the utter necessity of turning away from false gods and false worship and of being totally committed to the LORD.

Note the promise that Samuel preached: if the people would repent and make a total commitment to the LORD, the LORD would deliver them from their enemies. He would even deliver them from that great enemy who stood so mightily opposed to them—the Philistines (v.3).

Gradually, over the twenty-year period of focusing upon this one single message, the Israelites obeyed the challenge of Samuel (v.4). They repented, put away their false gods and false worship. And they turned wholeheartedly to the LORD, serving Him and Him alone.

d. Once the mass movement of spiritual repentance had begun, Samuel immediately called for a nationwide assembly to be held at Mizpah. His purpose was to publicly confirm the people's decision to renew their commitment to the LORD (vv.5-6). In summoning the people to assemble, note exactly what Samuel said: he would pray, intercede for them. He would cry out for the LORD to accept the people's repentance, forgiving their sins and beginning once again to fulfill His promises to them, the promises of guiding and protecting them.

When the people assembled, three events of significance happened:

1) The people drew water and poured it out before the LORD (v.6). This was a ritual symbolizing the pouring out of a person's heart in repentance and commitment to the LORD (Ps.62:8). For twenty years, the people's hearts had been bearing the burden of sin, mourning and seeking for the LORD's presence. Now, the people had come together in a great period of public confession and repentance, seeking for a revival of their relationship with the LORD. To symbolize their seeking, they observed this ritual before the LORD.

2) The people fasted and confessed their sins, asking God to forgive and renew their relationship with Him. They stood in desperate need of His presence, provision, and protection against their archenemy, the Philistines. They cried out, "We have sinned against the LORD" (v.6).

3) The people began to look to Samuel as their nationwide leader, as the judge of all Israel (v.6). Beginning with this revival, Samuel took up the *mantle of leadership* and became the chief magistrate of all Israel. His nationwide ministry was now launched. Remember, the judge of that day and time not only rendered decisions and settled disputes among the people, but he was also the chief executive, the leader of the people. In Samuel's case, he became the judge of all Israel.

Thought 1. God demands repentance and wholehearted commitment to Him. If we sin, He demands repentance. If we worship false gods or become involved in false religion or false worship, God demands repentance. All idolatry and false worship must be renounced and abandoned. And we must return to God, seeking His forgiveness and cleansing and the revival of our relationship with Him. Our hearts must be poured out before God, completely given over to Him, to serve Him only.

Once we have repented and turned wholeheartedly to God, God will forgive our sins and cleanse us. And He will renew His relationship with us. God will grant a sense, a consciousness of His presence and begin anew to guide, protect, and provide for us. Repentance and true commitment are the only way to salvation and the fruitful, overflowing life promised by God.

(1) God demands repentance.

> "And saying, Repent ye: for the kingdom of heaven is at hand" (Mt.3:2).
>
> "Blessed *are* they that mourn: for they shall be comforted" (Mt.5:4).
>
> "And Jesus answering said unto them, Suppose ye that these Galilaeans were sinners above all the Galilaeans, because they suffered such things? I tell you, Nay: but, except ye repent, ye shall all likewise perish" (Lu.13:2-3).
>
> "Then Peter said unto them, Repent, and be baptized every one of you in the name of Jesus Christ for the remission of sins, and ye shall receive the gift of the Holy Ghost" (Ac.2:38).
>
> "Repent ye therefore, and be converted, that your sins may be blotted out, when the times of refreshing shall come from the presence of the Lord" (Ac.3:19).
>
> "Repent therefore of this thy wickedness, and pray God, if perhaps the thought of thine heart may be forgiven thee" (Ac.8:22).
>
> "If my people, which are called by my name, shall humble themselves, and pray, and seek my face, and turn from their wicked ways; then will I hear from heaven, and will forgive their sin, and will heal their land" (2 Chr.7:14).
>
> "Let the wicked forsake his way, and the unrighteous man his thoughts: and let him return unto the LORD, and he will have mercy upon him; and to our God, for he will abundantly pardon" (Is.55:7).

---

2 Ronald F. Youngblood. *1 Samuel*, p.607.

"But if the wicked will turn from all his sins that he hath committed, and keep all my statutes, and do that which is lawful and right, he shall surely live, he shall not die" (Eze.18:21).

"Cast away from you all your transgressions, whereby ye have transgressed; and make you a new heart and a new spirit: for why will ye die, O house of Israel?" (Eze.18:31).

"Therefore also now, saith the LORD, turn ye *even* to me with all your heart, and with fasting, and with weeping, and with mourning" (Joel 2:12).

(2) God demands that we wholeheartedly commit our lives to Him.

"And he said to *them* all, If any *man* will come after me, let him deny himself, and take up his cross daily, and follow me" (Lu.9:23).

"For if ye live after the flesh, ye shall die: but if ye through the Spirit do mortify the deeds of the body, ye shall live" (Ro.8:13).

"I beseech you therefore, brethren, by the mercies of God, that ye present your bodies a living sacrifice, holy, acceptable unto God, *which is* your reasonable service. And be not conformed to this world: but be ye transformed by the renewing of your mind, that ye may prove what is that good, and acceptable, and perfect, will of God" (Ro.12:1-2).

"And thou shalt love the LORD thy God with all thine heart, and with all thy soul, and with all thy might" (De.6:5).

"Create in me a clean heart, O God; and renew a right spirit within me" (Ps.51:10).

"Blessed *are* they that keep his testimonies, *and that* seek him with the whole heart" (Ps.119:2).

"Trust in the LORD with all thine heart; and lean not unto thine own understanding" (Pr.3:5).

"My son, give me thine heart, and let thine eyes observe my ways" (Pr.23:26).

"And ye shall seek me, and find *me,* when ye shall search for me with all your heart" (Je.29:13).

---

2 (7:7-14) **Victory, over Enemies—Deliverance, from Enemies—Bondage, Deliverance from, Through Prayer—Prayer, Results of—Philistines, Enemy of Israel—Israel, Victory over, Philistines**: Samuel stirred the Israelites to defeat the Philistines. This is a dramatic picture of the believer's victory from bondage, a victory that comes through prayer. This was to be a decisive victory over the Philistines, so decisive that it would break the back of Philistine power as a major military force.

OUTLINE	SCRIPTURE	SCRIPTURE	OUTLINE
2. Samuel stirred the Israelites to defeat the Philistines: Victory & deliverance from bondage through prayer	7 And when the Philistines heard that the children of Israel were gathered together to Mizpeh, the lords of the Philistines went up against Israel. And when the children of Israel heard *it,* they were afraid of the Philistines.	Israel. 11 And the men of Israel went out of Mizpeh, and pursued the Philistines, and smote them, until *they came* under Beth-car.	thunderstorm 3) The Philistine army was routed, pursued, & slaughtered by the Israelites
a. The mobilization of the Philistines & the gripping fear of the Israelites			
b. The appeal to Samuel for continued, unbroken prayer	8 And the children of Israel said to Samuel, Cease not to cry unto the LORD our God for us, that he will save us out of the hand of the Philistines.	12 Then Samuel took a stone, and set *it* between Mizpeh and Shen, and called the name of it Ebenezer, saying, Hitherto hath the LORD helped us.	4) The victory was memorialized by Samuel: Set up a stone monument named Ebenezer, meaning "the stone of help"
c. The appeal & prayer to God by Samuel: Approached God through the Burnt Offering—seeking reconciliation through the blood of the substitute sacrifice	9 And Samuel took a sucking lamb, and offered *it for a* burnt offering wholly unto the LORD: and Samuel cried unto the LORD for Israel; and the LORD heard him.	13 So the Philistines were subdued, and they came no more into the coast of Israel: and the hand of the LORD was against the Philistines all the days of Samuel.	e. The results of the victory 1) The Philistine enemy was subdued during Samuel's lifetime
d. The miraculous answer to prayer by God: Achieved victory 1) The Philistines launched their attack just as Samuel was offering the sacrifice 2) The LORD struck the Philistines with a terrifying	10 And as Samuel was offering up the burnt offering, the Philistines drew near to battle against Israel: but the LORD thundered with a great thunder on that day upon the Philistines, and discomfited them; and they were smitten before	14 And the cities which the Philistines had taken from Israel were restored to Israel, from Ekron even unto Gath; and the coasts thereof did Israel deliver out of the hands of the Philistines. And there was peace between Israel and the Amorites.	2) The territory formerly conquered by the Philistine enemy was regained 3) The power of Israel struck fear in other enemies & secured peace

a. When the Philistines heard that the Israelites had assembled at Mizpah, they immediately mobilized their armed forces and marched to attack Israel (v.7). Although the Israelites had assembled only for worship, the Philistines interpreted their assembly as a potential threat to them. Terror struck the Israelites, for they were not prepared for war. Many of them had traveled from the outer reaches of the nation and had neither weapon nor provision to engage in battle. Their assembly had been called for worship, not to mobilize for war.

b. Nevertheless, the Israelites did the only thing they could: they appealed to Samuel for continued, unbroken prayer (v.8). They begged him to cry to the LORD for rescue and not to stop his praying. They were desperate, standing on the brink of being totally wiped out by the attacking Philistines.

c. Note Samuel's response, his appeal and prayer to God (v.9). He approached God through the burnt offering, seeking reconciliation for the people, reconciliation through the blood of the substitute sacrifice. The burnt offering was the only way to approach God, the only acceptable way. Samuel knew that the people had to become acceptable if God was going to deliver them; consequently, he offered up the burnt offering just as God had instructed His people to do (see outline and notes—Le.1:1-17 for more discussion). Once the substitute sacrifice had been offered, Samuel cried out to the LORD on Israel's behalf, and the LORD wonderfully answered him.

d. The prayer was miraculously answered by God and victory was significantly achieved (vv.10-12). Just as Samuel was offering up the sacrifice, the Philistines launched their aggressive attack (v.10). But just as the Philistines struck, a terrifying thunderstorm broke loose upon the Philistines, a thunderstorm so fierce that it struck panic within them. Encouraged by the enemy's panic and flight, the Israelites grabbed what weapons they could and pursued the Philistines, slaughtering them all the way to Beth Car. The victory was significant, so much so that Samuel memorialized it by putting up a stone monument between Mizpah and Shen (v.12). The memorial was named Ebenezer, which means "the stone of help."

e. The results of the victory were extremely important for Israel (vv.13-14). Three momentous events took place as a result of the victory:

⇒ The backbone of the Philistine army as a major power was broken during Samuel's leadership and judgeship (v.13).

⇒ The territory formally conquered by the Philistine enemy was regained (v.14). It included the cities stretching from Ekron to Gath, cities that the Philistines had originally conquered and taken from Israel.

⇒ The power of Israel struck fear in the surrounding Amorite nations (Canaanites), so much fear that they sought and made peace with Israel (v.14).

Thought 1. Just as Samuel prayed and victory was given over the Philistines, so a triumphant life—victory, conquest, deliverance, and salvation—comes through prayer. It is God who delivers us and gives us victory, conquest over the enemies that confront and attempt to defeat us. Throughout life, enemy after enemy will attack, enemies such as...

• people who ridicule, slander, abuse, assault, or persecute us
• people or things that trap, enslave, or put us in bondage
• people who hurt us, causing pain and suffering, or who attempt to destroy us or to wreak utter havoc upon our lives
• people who act irresponsibly, involving us in accidents or bringing some disease upon us or death to a loved one

There are all kinds of enemies who attack us during life. In addition to people, there are other enemies in this corruptible world. There are enemies such as germs, diseases, drugs, alcohol, and tobacco. There are cravings of the flesh that enslave us such as immorality, adultery, and the resulting breakup of families that cause so much pain and suffering. Put simply, there are innumerable enemies that seek to destroy us as we walk throughout life.

The way of conquest—victory over the enemies of life—comes through prayer. God and God alone can deliver and save us from defeat, a life of enslavement to the flesh and the ways of this world. If we crave deliverance, prayer will arouse God to hear and save us.

(1) God will hear prayer.

> "**Ask, and it shall be given you; seek, and ye shall find; knock, and it shall be opened unto you**" (Mt.7:7).

> "**Watch and pray, that ye enter not into temptation: the spirit indeed** *is* **willing, but the flesh** *is* **weak**" (Mt.26:41).

> "**If ye abide in me, and my words abide in you, ye shall ask what ye will, and it shall be done unto you**" (Jn.15:7).

> "**Hitherto have ye asked nothing in my name: ask, and ye shall receive, that your joy may be full**" (Jn.16:24).

> "**Is any among you afflicted? let him pray. Is any merry? let him sing psalms**" (Js.5:13).

> "**He shall call upon me, and I will answer him: I** *will be* **with him in trouble; I will deliver him, and honour him**" (Ps.91:15).

> "**Then shalt thou call, and the LORD shall answer; thou shalt cry, and he shall say, Here I** *am*. **If thou take away from the midst of thee the yoke, the putting forth of the finger, and speaking vanity**" (Is.58:9).

> "**And it shall come to pass, that before they call, I will answer; and while they are yet speaking, I will hear**" (Is.65:24).

(2) God has answered the prayers of His people down through the ages.[3]

(a) God answered the prayer of Moses when the people were murmuring against Him.

> "**And the people murmured against Moses, saying, What shall we drink? And he cried unto the LORD; and the LORD showed him a tree,** *which* **when he had cast into the waters, the waters**

---

3 *The New Thompson Chain Reference Bible*. (Indianapolis, IN: B.B. Kirkbride Bible Co., Inc., 1964), #2818.

were made sweet: there he made for them a statute and an ordinance, and there he proved them" (Ex.15:24-25).

(b) God answered the prayer of Gideon when he feared the enemy and needed to know if it was God's will for him to attack the enemy.

"And Gideon said unto God, Let not thine anger be hot against me, and I will speak but this once: let me prove, I pray thee, but this once with the fleece; let it now be dry only upon the fleece, and upon all the ground let there be dew. And God did so that night: for it was dry upon the fleece only, and there was dew on all the ground" (Jud.6:39-40).

(c) God answered the prayer of Hannah for a child.

"For this child I prayed; and the LORD hath given me my petition which I asked of him" (1 S.1:27).

(d) God answered the prayer of Samuel in the present passage, a prayer beseeching God to deliver His people from their fierce enemy, the Philistines.

"And Samuel took a sucking lamb, and offered *it for* a burnt offering wholly unto the LORD: and Samuel cried unto the LORD for Israel; and the LORD heard him. And as Samuel was offering up the burnt offering, the Philistines drew near to battle against Israel: but the LORD thundered with a great thunder on that day upon the Philistines, and discomfited them; and they were smitten before Israel" (1 S.7:9-10).

(e) God heard the prayer of Solomon when Solomon asked God to pour out His presence upon the temple.

"And the LORD said unto him, I have heard thy prayer and thy supplication, that thou hast made before me: I have hallowed this house, which thou hast built, to put my name there for ever; and mine eyes and mine heart shall be there perpetually" (1 K.9:3).

(f) God heard the prayer of Elijah to prove that He and He alone was the LORD God.

"Hear me, O LORD, hear me, that this people may know that thou *art* the LORD God, and *that* thou hast turned their heart back again. Then the fire of the LORD fell, and consumed the burnt sacrifice, and the wood, and the stones, and the dust, and licked up the water that *was* in the trench" (1 K.18:37-38).

(g) God heard the prayer of Hezekiah when he prayed for deliverance from the king of Assyria.

"Now therefore, O LORD our God, I beseech thee, save thou us out of his hand, that all the kingdoms of the earth may know that thou *art* the LORD God, *even* thou only. Then Isaiah the son of Amoz sent to Hezekiah, saying, Thus saith the LORD God of Israel, *That* which thou hast prayed to me against Sennacherib king of Assyria I have heard" (2 K.19:19-20).

(h) God heard the prayer of Jehosophat when he prayed for deliverance from the enemy.

"And it came to pass, when the captains of the chariots saw Jehoshaphat, that they said, It *is* the king of Israel. Therefore they compassed about him to fight: but Jehoshaphat cried out, and the LORD helped him; and God moved them *to depart* from him" (2 Chr.18:31).

(i) God heard the prayer of Ezra.

"So we fasted and besought our God for this: and he was intreated of us" (Ezr.8:23).

(j) God heard the prayer of Zacharias when he prayed for a son.

"But the angel said unto him, Fear not, Zacharias: for thy prayer is heard; and thy wife Elisabeth shall bear thee a son, and thou shalt call his name John" (Lu.1:13).

(k) God heard the prayer of the early church when it prayed for the LORD to pour out His Spirit upon them.

"And when they had prayed, the place was shaken where they were assembled together; and they were all filled with the Holy Ghost, and they spake the word of God with boldness" (Ac.4:31).

3 (7:15-17) **Faithfulness, of Samuel—Ministry, of Samuel**: Samuel closed the era of the judges and launched the era of the kings. He stands as the pivotal figure between these two significant periods of Israel's history. This is exactly what Scripture declares:

OUTLINE	SCRIPTURE	SCRIPTURE	OUTLINE

3. Samuel closed the era of the judges & launched the era of the kings: A lesson on faithfulness
a. He was faithful as a judge
  1) Traveling as a circuit judge
  2) Serving as the last judge:
	15 And Samuel judged Israel all the days of his life.
	16 And he went from year to year in circuit to Bethel, and Gilgal, and Mizpeh, and judged Israel in all those
		places.
		17 And his return *was* to Ramah; for there *was* his house; and there he judged Israel; and there he built an altar unto the LORD.
			Closing the era of the judges & opening up the era of the kings
			b. He was faithful as a prophet & priest or worship leader, 3:20; 4:1

a. Samuel was faithful as a judge (vv.15-16; 8:1-4). From year to year—through all the days of his life—he traveled as a circuit judge to four major cities in the tribes of Benjamin, Ephraim, and Manasseh. These cities were...

- Bethel: where Jacob had his famous dream (Ge.28:10-22).
- Gilgal: a city close by Jericho, a city where the Israelites first camped after crossing the Jordan River to conquer the promised land (Jos.4:19-20).
- Mizpah: the city where Israel's national repentance or revival had taken place (1 S.7:5-6).
- Ramah: the home city of Samuel, the place where he had based his ministry since the destruction of Shiloh by the Philistines (1 S.7:17).

Note that these verses are a summary of Samuel's life, covering his ministry throughout the remainder of his life. The point here is striking: Samuel is serving as the last judge. He is closing the era of the judges and opening up the era of the kings. In the very next chapter, the Israelites will begin their cry for a king "just like other nations" (8:5, 19-20). Samuel is being presented as the last judge; after him, the Israelites will be ruled by kings.

b. Samuel was also faithful as a prophet and priest or worship leader (v.17). As we have just seen, Samuel called the people to repentance and wholehearted commitment to the LORD (vv.1-6). He was recognized by all the Israelites as a prophet and had a national influence (3:20; 4:1). From this point on, Samuel served as the priest or worship leader of Israel (v.17). He built an altar in his hometown which obviously became the worship center of the nation during his life and ministry.

Thought 1. God demands faithfulness. Whatever our profession or employment, God demands that we be faithful and do a good job. We are to work and labor as though we serve the LORD God Himself. In fact, when it comes to labor, God actually says that we do serve Him. In God's eyes, we are not working for an earthly employer but rather for the Creator of the universe, the Creator who placed the care and welfare of the world in our hands (Ge.2:15; 3:23). We are therefore to labor ever so diligently, doing our very best and giving our best effort and energy. We are to be faithful no matter what our call or labor.

"Not slothful in business; fervent in spirit; serving the Lord" (Ro.12:11).

"Moreover it is required in stewards, that a man be found faithful" (1 Co.4:2).

"Therefore, my beloved brethren, be ye stedfast, unmovable, always abounding in the work of the Lord, forasmuch as ye know that your labour is not in vain in the Lord" (1 Co.15:58).

"And whatsoever ye do in word or deed, do all in the name of the Lord Jesus, giving thanks to God and the Father by him" (Col.3:17).

"And whatsoever ye do, do it heartily, as to the Lord, and not unto men" (Col.3:23).

"Ye therefore, beloved, seeing ye know these things before, beware lest ye also, being led away with the error of the wicked, fall from your own stedfastness" (2 Pe.3:17).

"And the Lord God took the man, and put him into the garden of Eden to dress it and to keep it" (Ge.2:15).

"Therefore the Lord God sent him forth from the garden of Eden, to till the ground from whence he was taken" (Ge.3:23).

"The soul of the sluggard desireth, and hath nothing: but the soul of the diligent shall be made fat" (Pr.13:4).

THE STORY OF SAMUEL AND SAUL: THE LORD GIVES ISRAEL A KING JUST "LIKE ALL THE NATIONS," 8:1–15:35

(8:1–15:35) **DIVISION OVERVIEW**: after the great revival and the miraculous defeat of the Philistine army, Samuel led Israel for the next thirty-plus years. He served as the last judge the nation would ever have, for as Samuel aged and his sons proved to be unjust and corrupt judges, the people demanded that Samuel change the very form of government that ruled over Israel. In looking around, the people decided they wanted a government just like the surrounding states; they wanted to be ruled by a king "like all the nations" (8:5). There were at least three major reasons why the people pressured Samuel to place a king over them before his death.

1. Politically, there were not and never had been enough qualified judges to lead the nation. Samuel's two sons were just the latest examples of this tragic fact (8:3-5).

2. Militarily and economically, the nation was suffering under continued oppression from the Philistines and from other surrounding nations. Bands of marauders often swooped down upon Israelite villages and cities to steal their crops, livestock, and valuables, especially during harvest season (Jud.6:1-5). The stress of living under constant oppression and seeing their wives and children suffer (as so many war victims do) by being raped, abused, and enslaved, took its toll upon the people. The only answer seemed to be a king who would build a standing army to protect the citizens of Israel.

3. Spiritually, the people had failed to live righteous lives, failed to obey God's commandments. They were living sinful, wicked lives. By their sin, the people had alienated and separated themselves from God. As a result, they were living without God's...

- presence
- peace
- guidance
- provision
- protection

Since the days of Moses, the LORD had always given these wonderful promises to the Israelites. And when the people walked obediently, living righteous lives, they experienced God's wonderful promises. He Himself became the people's Savior, Guide, Provider, and Protector.

But now the Israelites had decided they no longer wanted to live under the *sole authority* of the LORD. They wanted to live first under the *authority* of an earthly king, a king who would be visibly present and who they thought could bring peace and security to their hearts and lives, guiding, protecting, and providing whatever they needed.

Surprisingly, the LORD granted the people's request. He told Samuel to give them a king. Why? Because their request for a king was not wrong. God had even made provision in His law for the appointment of a king to rule over His people (De.17:14-20; see also Ge.49:10; Nu.24:7, 17).

What then was wrong with the people's request for a king? Their motive, their purpose: they wanted a king "like all the nations" had (8:5), not a king "after God's own heart" (13:14). It was God's purpose to give His people a king "after His own heart," a king who would hold authority under the *supreme authority* of God, who would rule the people under the *supreme rule* of the LORD. The king was to be just as responsible as the people to love and obey the LORD. Therefore, he was to serve the people under the authority and commandments of God.

In granting the people's request, the LORD appointed a promising young man to become the first king of Israel. His name was Saul and he was a most impressive young man with enormous potential for leadership and service as the national leader of Israel. In appearance he was the ideal man. He was tall, standing head and shoulders above others, with a striking, handsome face and a charismatic appeal.

But King Saul was to fail, becoming unfit and disqualified to serve the LORD. He proved to be just what the people had requested: a king just "like all the nations" (8:5). He was a king who ignored God's Word and gave in to the craving lusts of his flesh. Consequently, his life and reign ended up being a disastrous tragedy.

THE STORY OF SAMUEL AND SAUL: THE LORD GIVES ISRAEL A KING JUST "LIKE ALL THE NATIONS," 8:1–15:35

A. The Demand of Israel for a King: Choosing the Ways of the World and Rejecting God, 8:1-22

DIVISION II
8:1–15:35

B. **The Choice of Saul to Be King: A Look at a Promising Young Man, 9:1-27**

C. **The Private Anointing and Public Installation of Saul As King: Receiving a New, Changed Heart, 10:1-27**

D. **The First Military Victory of Saul and His Affirmation As King: Gaining the Victory over One's Enemies, 11:1-15**

E. **The Message Preached by Samuel at the Coronation of King Saul: The Utter Necessity for Repentance and Faithful Service, 12:1-25**

F. **The Unlawful Act That Made Saul Unfit to Be King: Being Disqualified to Serve the LORD, 13:1-23**

G. **The Continued Decline of Saul: Weak Faith, Spiritual Insensitivity, and Misguided, Carnal Zeal, 14:1-52**

H. **The LORD's Rejection of Saul As King: The Seriousness of Disobeying God, 15:1-55**

1. The reasons for demanding a king: Corruption & worldliness
a. An aged leadership
b. A corrupt leadership & judicial system
   1) Samuel's sons were appointed to succeed him
   2) His sons were corrupt
   • Were dishonest, greedy for money
   • Accepted bribes
   • Perverted justice
c. A desire to be like the surrounding nations: A picture of carnality, seeking after the ways of the world
   1) The elders approached Samuel
   2) They demanded a king just "like all the nations"

2. The tragedy of demanding a king: A picture of forsaking God
a. The displeasure & prayer of Samuel
b. The response of God to Samuel
   1) Instructed him to grant their request
   2) Assured him that the people were not rejecting him, but God: They were forsaking God just as they had done since their deliverance from Egypt

   3) Told him to warn the people: Warn them of the consequences of being ruled by a king

3. The warning—the consequences of being ruled by a

CHAPTER 8

II. THE STORY OF SAMUEL & SAUL: THE LORD GIVES ISRAEL A KING JUST "LIKE ALL THE NATIONS," 8:1–15:35

A. The Demand of Israel for a King: Choosing the Ways of the World & Rejecting God, 8:1-22

And it came to pass, when Samuel was old, that he made his sons judges over Israel.
2 Now the name of his firstborn was Joel; and the name of his second, Abiah: *they were* judges in Beersheba.
3 And his sons walked not in his ways, but turned aside after lucre, and took bribes, and perverted judgment.
4 Then all the elders of Israel gathered themselves together, and came to Samuel unto Ramah,
5 And said unto him, Behold, thou art old, and thy sons walk not in thy ways: now make us a king to judge us like all the nations.
6 But the thing displeased Samuel, when they said, Give us a king to judge us. And Samuel prayed unto the LORD.
7 And the LORD said unto Samuel, Hearken unto the voice of the people in all that they say unto thee: for they have not rejected thee, but they have rejected me, that I should not reign over them.
8 According to all the works which they have done since the day that I brought them up out of Egypt even unto this day, wherewith they have forsaken me, and served other gods, so do they also unto thee.
9 Now therefore hearken unto their voice: howbeit yet protest solemnly unto them, and show them the manner of the king that shall reign over them.
10 And Samuel told all the words of the LORD unto the

people that asked of him a king.
11 And he said, This will be the manner of the king that shall reign over you: He will take your sons, and appoint *them* for himself, for his chariots, and to be his horsemen; and *some* shall run before his chariots.
12 And he will appoint him captains over thousands, and captains over fifties; and *will set them* to ear his ground, and to reap his harvest, and to make his instruments of war, and instruments of his chariots.
13 And he will take your daughters *to be* confectionaries, and *to be* cooks, and *to be* bakers.
14 And he will take your fields, and your vineyards, and your oliveyards, *even* the best *of them,* and give *them* to his servants.
15 And he will take the tenth of your seed, and of your vineyards, and give to his officers, and to his servants.
16 And he will take your menservants, and your maidservants, and your goodliest young men, and your asses, and put *them* to his work.
17 He will take the tenth of your sheep: and ye shall be his servants.
18 And ye shall cry out in that day because of your king which ye shall have chosen you; and the LORD will not hear you in that day.
19 Nevertheless the people refused to obey the voice of Samuel; and they said, Nay; but we will have a king over us;
20 That we also may be like all the nations; and that our king may judge us, and go out before us, and fight our battles.
21 And Samuel heard all the words of the people, and he rehearsed them in the ears of the LORD.
22 And the LORD said to Samuel, Hearken unto their voice, and make them a king. And Samuel said unto the men of Israel, Go ye every man unto his city.

king (a monarchy): A picture of reaping what one sows
a. There will be the severe restriction of liberty
   1) The oppressive, compulsory military service for sons
   • To serve as stable laborers
   • To serve as the king's honor guard
   • To build a large standing army
   2) The oppressive, compulsory service of laborers: To serve as support divisions in the fields & the factories

   3) The oppressive, compulsory service of daughters: To serve the royal palace

   4) The confiscation of property: To give to the king's loyal officials or nobles

   5) The taxation of crops: To give to the king's loyal officials or nobles

   6) The confiscation of the nation's labor force & of the best animals

   7) The taxation of animals
   8) The enslavement of the entire population: The loss, restriction of the people's freedom
b. There will be severe suffering, a cry for deliverance: But the LORD will not hear (His judicial judgment)

4. The insistent demands for a king: A picture of being stubborn, hard-hearted

a. The people's craving desire: To have a king just "like all the nations"
   1) To unite & lead them
   2) To build an army
b. The reseeking of the LORD by Samuel

c. The granting of the request by the LORD: Give them a king

DIVISION II

THE STORY OF SAMUEL AND SAUL: THE LORD GIVES ISRAEL A KING JUST "LIKE ALL THE NATIONS," 8:1–15:35

A. The Demand of Israel for a King: Choosing the Ways of the World and Rejecting God, 8:1-22

(8:1-22) **Introduction—World, Appeal of—Motive, Seeking the World—Focus, Seeking the World—Israel, Motive, Focus of, Seeking the World**: the world has much to offer any person who diligently pursues and seeks after the things of the world. The world can offer possessions, riches, recognition, honor, position, authority, power, pleasure, recreation, and a host of other benefits and enjoyments. There is nothing wrong with what the world offers unless the things of the world become the focus of our lives. Or unless we twist the benefits of this world and make them evil. However, our primary focus—our motivating drive in life—must be God, to know Him and to fellowship with Him.

Focusing upon the ways of this world was the tragic mistake of the Israelites. The driving motivation of their hearts became the ways of the world, not God and His righteousness. For thirty-plus years, the Israelites had followed the leadership of Samuel. But now Samuel had aged and would soon be passing from this world. As a result, the Israelites craved to establish a monarchy, the rule of a king just "like all the nations." Ever since the days of Moses, they had lived under a theocracy, the rule and reign of God Himself. In fact, under Moses' leadership, the Israelites had made a covenant, an agreement with the LORD. The terms of the agreement stipulated that the LORD was to be the Savior and Deliverer, the Protector and Provider of Israel. And all the Israelites had to do was obey the LORD, keep His commandments. Ever since the days of Moses, this covenant had been agreed upon by both the LORD and the Israelites. But now, after centuries of looking around at other nations and observing them, the Israelites began to covet the form of government adopted by them. They desired a king just "like all the nations." They wanted to break their covenant with the LORD and make an agreement with some charismatic man. They wanted this man to be just like the kings of most other nations: an attractive man, a charismatic leader, a man who would agree to rule over them and become their savior and deliverer, protector and provider.

The people's desire for a king became a craving lust, a lust that made them stubborn, stiff-necked, and hard-hearted. They insisted upon, even demanded, a king just "like all the nations." This is the subject of this pivotal Scripture: *The Demand of Israel for a King: Choosing the Ways of the World and Rejecting God*, 8:1-22.

1. The reasons for demanding a king: corruption and worldliness (vv.1-5).
2. The tragedy of demanding a king: a picture of forsaking God (vv.6-9).
3. The warning—the consequences of being ruled by a king (a monarchy): a picture of reaping what one sows (vv.10-18).
4. The insistent demands for a king: a picture of being stubborn, hard-hearted (vv.19-22).

1 (8:1-5) **King, Reasons for—Leadership, Need for—Leadership, Corrupt—Judicial System, Corrupt—Judges, Corrupt—Justice, Perverted—Bribes, Accepting—Greed, Example of—Israel, Demand for a King—King, of Israel, Demanded**: the reasons for Israel's demanding a king were threefold. The three reasons are clearly stated in the Scripture and outline:

OUTLINE	SCRIPTURE	SCRIPTURE	OUTLINE
1. The reasons for demanding a king: Corruption & worldliness a. An aged leadership b. A corrupt leadership & judicial system 　1) Samuel's sons were appointed to succeed him 　2) His sons were corrupt 　• Were dishonest, greedy for money	And it came to pass, when Samuel was old, that he made his sons judges over Israel. 2 Now the name of his firstborn was Joel; and the name of his second, Abiah: *they were* judges in Beersheba. 3 And his sons walked not in his ways, but turned aside after lucre, and took	bribes, and perverted judgment. 4 Then all the elders of Israel gathered themselves together, and came to Samuel unto Ramah, 5 And said unto him, Behold, thou art old, and thy sons walk not in thy ways: now make us a king to judge us like all the nations.	• Accepted bribes • Perverted justice c. A desire to be like the surrounding nations: A picture of carnality, seeking after the ways of the world 　1) The elders approached Samuel 　2) They demanded a king just "like all the nations"

a. An aged leader was clearly a reason for demanding new leadership (v.1). Samuel had grown old, and apparently his age was beginning to affect his ability to lead the nation. It appeared he would not live much longer and the people feared that the nation might slip back into the lawless days of the judges. To prevent this from happening, new leadership was demanded.

b. A corrupt leadership and judicial system was a reason for demanding a new system of government (vv.2-3). Because of his age, Samuel had appointed his two sons to succeed him: Joel, which means "the LORD is God," and Abijah, which means "my father is the LORD." With Samuel as their father, they had received a godly upbringing. But they lived hypocritical lives: they did not follow in the steps of their father. They turned away from God and became greedy for money. They accepted bribes and perverted justice. In determining controversial cases, they accepted bribes and ruled in favor of the oppressor or guilty party. This wickedness reminded the people of Eli's two sons, and they feared returning to the lawless, corrupt days of the judges (see outline and notes—1 Sam.2:12-36 for more discussion). Thus, a desire arose within the people for new leadership, the leadership of a king.

c. A desire to be like the surrounding nations was a reason the Israelites requested a king (vv.4-5). Note that the tribal leaders of Israel gathered together and traveled to Ramah. In conference with Samuel, they laid out their three reasons for desiring a king: Samuel was old, and his sons did not walk in his godly ways; therefore, they desired to have a king just "like all the nations." Note what they emphasized and what they did not emphasize:

⇒ they demanded a king just "like all the nations."
⇒ they did not demand a king "after God's own heart."

The people should have desired a king who had the *heart of God*, a man who was totally, wholeheartedly committed to God. This should have been their emphasis, their focus; but instead, they emphasized a king just "like all the nations." Their eyes and hearts were set upon the world and its ways instead of upon God and His way of righteousness. They were interested in the world's way of securing peace, security, prosperity, position, authority, power, honor, ceremony, and pleasure. They would never deny that they had an interest in the man's being a godly ruler, but their emphasis was not upon the spiritual or righteous commitment of the man. Having a king with a heart "just like God's" was not their focus. They wanted a king just "like all the nations."

Thought 1. There are two strong lessons for us in this point:

(1) We must not be controlled by greed: coveting money, position, fame, or power. And we must not pervert justice: accepting bribes, kickbacks, or payoffs, a practice common in politics, construction projects, and far too often in legal cases. God forbids these sins time and again:

"And when they heard *it,* they were glad, and promised to give him money. And he sought how he might conveniently betray him" (Mk.14:11).

"And when Simon saw that through laying on of the apostles' hands the Holy Ghost was given, he offered them money" (Ac.8:18).

"For the love of money is the root of all evil: which while some coveted after, they have erred from the faith, and pierced themselves through with many sorrows" (1 Ti.6:10).

"Thou shalt not wrest the judgment of thy poor in his cause....And thou shalt take no gift: for the gift blindeth the wise, and perverteth the words of the righteous" (Ex.23:6, 8).

"Judges and officers shalt thou make thee in all thy gates, which the LORD thy God giveth thee, throughout thy tribes: and they shall judge the people with just judgment. Thou shalt not wrest judgment; thou shalt not respect persons, neither take a gift: for a gift doth blind the eyes of the wise, and pervert the words of the righteous" (De.16:18-19).

"Thou shalt not pervert the judgment of the stranger, *nor* of the fatherless; nor take a widow's raiment to pledge" (De.24:17).

"Cursed *be* he that perverteth the judgment of the stranger, fatherless, and widow. And all the people shall say, Amen" (De.27:19).

"And his sons walked not in his ways, but turned aside after lucre, and took bribes, and perverted judgment" (1 S.8:3).

"*There is* a league between me and thee, *and* between my father and thy father: behold, I have sent unto thee a present of silver and gold; come and break thy league with Baasha king of Israel, that he may depart from me" (1 K.15:19).

"*He that* putteth not out his money to usury, nor taketh reward against the innocent. He that doeth these *things* shall never be moved" (Ps.15:5).

"He that is greedy of gain troubleth his own house; but he that hateth gifts shall live" (Pr.15:27).

"He coveteth greedily all the day long: but the righteous giveth and spareth not" (Pr.21:26).

"The heads thereof judge for reward, and the priests thereof teach for hire, and the prophets thereof divine for money: yet will they lean upon the LORD, and say, *Is* not the LORD among us? none evil can come upon us" (Mi.3:11).

(2) We must not focus upon this world, seeking after the ways of this world. We must not develop carnal, fleshly minds, desiring the things of this world more than we desire the things of God. The Christian believer lives *in* this world, but he must not become a part *of* this world. This is the strong declaration of Scripture.

"And take heed to yourselves, lest at any time your hearts be overcharged with surfeiting, and drunkenness, and cares of this life, and so that day come upon you unawares" (Lu.21:34).

"And be not conformed to this world: but be ye transformed by the renewing of your mind, that ye may prove what is that good, and acceptable, and perfect, will of God" (Ro.12:2).

"And they that use this world, as not abusing *it:* for the fashion of this world passeth away" (1 Co.7:31).

"This I say therefore, and testify in the Lord, that ye henceforth walk not as other Gentiles walk, in the vanity of their mind" (Ep.4:17).

"Put on therefore, as the elect of God, holy and beloved, bowels of mercies, kindness, humbleness of mind, meekness, longsuffering" (Col.3:12).

"No man that warreth entangleth himself with the affairs of *this* life; that he may please him who hath chosen him to be a soldier" (2 Ti.2:4).

"Teaching us that, denying ungodliness and worldly lusts, we should live soberly, righteously, and godly, in this present world; Looking for that blessed hope, and the glorious appearing of the great God and our Saviour Jesus Christ" (Tit.2:12-13).

"By faith Moses, when he was come to years, refused to be called the son of Pharaoh's daughter; Choosing rather to suffer affliction with the people of God, than to enjoy the pleasures of sin for a season" (He.11:24-25).

"Love not the world, neither the things *that are* in the world. If any man love the world, the love of the Father is not in him. For all that *is* in the world, the lust of the flesh, and the lust of the eyes, and the pride of life, is not of the Father, but is of the world" (1 Jn.2:15-16).

"The LORD knoweth the thoughts of man, that they *are* vanity" (Ps.94:11).

2 (8:6-9) **Rejection, of God—Forsaking, of God—Israel, Demand for a King—Israel, Rejecting God—King, of Israel, Demand for**: the demand of Israel for a king was most tragic. By demanding a king, they were forsaking God and rejecting His kingship, His authority and rule over their lives. Note that this is exactly what Scripture says:

OUTLINE	SCRIPTURE	SCRIPTURE	OUTLINE

2. The tragedy of demanding a king: A picture of forsaking God
a. The displeasure & prayer of Samuel
b. The response of God to Samuel
  1) Instructed him to grant their request
  2) Assured him that the people were not rejecting him, but God: They were forsaking God just as
	6 But the thing displeased Samuel, when they said, Give us a king to judge us. And Samuel prayed unto the LORD.
	7 And the LORD said unto Samuel, Hearken unto the voice of the people in all that they say unto thee: for they have not rejected thee, but they have rejected me, that I should not reign over them.
	8 According to all the
		works which they have done since the day that I brought them up out of Egypt even unto this day, wherewith they have forsaken me, and served other gods, so do they also unto thee.
		9 Now therefore hearken unto their voice: howbeit yet protest solemnly unto them, and show them the manner of the king that shall reign over them.
			they had done since their deliverance from Egypt
			
			3) Told him to warn the people: Warn them of the consequences of being ruled by a king

a. The request of the elders for a king displeased Samuel and clearly caught him off guard—a complete surprise (v.8). Apparently, he had had no idea what the elders were going to be requesting. Requesting a king meant that there were grumblings against his leadership among the citizens of the nation and that some had already rejected his leadership. The elders would never have come on their own unless there were serious grumblings and complaints from the people. Utterly shocked, Samuel requested time to seek the LORD in prayer. But the shocking request of the elders was not to be the only surprise Samuel received. God's response also amazed him.

b. God instructed Samuel to grant the elders' request for a king (vv.7-9). To relieve Samuel's uneasiness, God assured him that the people were not rejecting Samuel, but God Himself. Just as the Israelites had done since their deliverance from Egypt, so they were now doing once again: they were rejecting their Savior and Deliverer, their Protector and Provider. Remember, the Israelites had a covenant relationship with the LORD, an agreement that the LORD would be their Savior, their Provider and Protector—if they would just obey Him, accepting His rule of righteousness. But here they were, ready to break their covenant with the LORD in order to make an agreement with a king just "like all the nations." Forgetting how often the LORD had saved and delivered them in the past and forgetting how He had constantly provided for them throughout their lives, the Israelites requested the right to establish a monarchy, to live under the authority of a king.

Note this fact: their desire for a king was not wrong, not in and of itself. God Himself had even made provisions in His law for the appointment and rule of a king over His people (De.17:14-20; see also Ge.49:10; Nu.24:7, 17). What, therefore, was wrong with Israel's request for a king? It was their motive, their purpose. They wanted a king just "like all the nations," not a king "after God's own heart" (13:14). Consequently, in requesting a king just "like all the nations," they were rejecting God. They were breaking their covenant, their agreement with Him.

> **Thought 1.** There is a strong lesson for us in this point: we must never forsake God, rejecting and turning away from Him. Our desires may not be the desire expressed by Israel, the craving for a king to rule over us, a king just "like all the nations." But if we have other desires that focus upon the worldly or carnal ways of this earth, then we too reject God. If we turn to any sinful or wicked way of this world, we reject God. For God cannot look upon evil. God will have nothing to do with the sinful, wicked ways of this world. Scripture warns us against rejecting the LORD.
>
> "For God hath not called us unto uncleanness, but unto holiness. He therefore that despiseth, despiseth not man, but God, who hath also given unto us his holy Spirit" (1 Th.4:7-8).
>
> "Having eyes full of adultery, and that cannot cease from sin; beguiling unstable souls: an heart they have exercised with covetous practices; cursed children: Which have forsaken the right way, and are gone astray, following the way of Balaam *the son* of Bosor, who loved the wages of unrighteousness; But was rebuked for his iniquity: the dumb ass speaking with man's voice forbad the madness of the prophet. These are wells without water, clouds that are carried with a tempest; to whom the mist of darkness is reserved for ever" (2 Pe.2:14-17).
>
> "The LORD shall send upon thee cursing, vexation, and rebuke, in all that thou settest thine hand unto for to do, until thou be destroyed, and until thou perish quickly; because of the wickedness of thy doings, whereby thou hast forsaken me" (De.28:20).

"Yet ye have forsaken me, and served other gods: wherefore I will deliver you no more" (Jud.10:13).

"But my people would not hearken to my voice; and Israel would none of me. So I gave them up unto their own hearts' lust: *and* they walked in their own counsels. Oh that my people had hearkened unto me, *and* Israel had walked in my ways!" (Ps.81:11-13).

"Because I have called, and ye refused; I have stretched out my hand, and no man regarded; But ye have set at nought all my counsel, and would none of my reproof: I also will laugh at your calamity; I will mock when your fear cometh; When your fear cometh as desolation, and your destruction cometh as a whirlwind; when distress and anguish cometh upon you. Then shall they call upon me, but I will not answer; they shall seek me early, but they shall not find me: For that they hated knowledge, and did not choose the fear of the LORD: They would none of my counsel: they despised all my reproof. Therefore shall they eat of the fruit of their own way, and be filled with their own devices" (Pr.1:24-31).

"And I will utter my judgments against them touching all their wickedness, who have forsaken me, and have burned incense unto other gods, and worshipped the works of their own hands" (Je.1:16).

"For my people have committed two evils; they have forsaken me the fountain of living waters, *and* hewed them out cisterns, broken cisterns, that can hold no water" (Je.2:13).

"O LORD, the hope of Israel, all that forsake thee shall be ashamed, *and* they that depart from me shall be written in the earth, because they have forsaken the LORD, the fountain of living waters" (Je.17:13).

---

3 (8:10-18) **Reaping, What One Sows—Judgment, Judicial—Judgment, Cause of—King, Rights of—King, Prerogatives of—Monarchy, Rights of—Warning, against Living under Kings—Monarchy, Consequences of**: there was the warning of Samuel: there would be consequences if Israel was to be ruled by a king. This is a sober, thought-provoking picture of just what Israel could expect from a king.

OUTLINE	SCRIPTURE	SCRIPTURE	OUTLINE
3. The warning—the consequences of being ruled by a king (a monarchy): A picture of reaping what one sows a. There will be the severe restriction of liberty 1) The oppressive, compulsory military service for sons • To serve as stable laborers • To serve as the king's honor guard • To build a large standing army 2) The oppressive, compulsory service of laborers: To serve as support divisions in the fields & the factories 3) The oppressive, compulsory service of daughters: To serve the royal palace	10 And Samuel told all the words of the LORD unto the people that asked of him a king. 11 And he said, This will be the manner of the king that shall reign over you: He will take your sons, and appoint *them* for himself, for his chariots, and to be his horsemen; and *some* shall run before his chariots. 12 And he will appoint him captains over thousands, and captains over fifties; and *will* set *them* to ear his ground, and to reap his harvest, and to make his instruments of war, and instruments of his chariots. 13 And he will take your daughters *to be* confectionaries, and *to be* cooks, and *to*	*be* bakers. 14 And he will take your fields, and your vineyards, and your oliveyards, *even* the best *of them,* and give *them* to his servants. 15 And he will take the tenth of your seed, and of your vineyards, and give to his officers, and to his servants. 16 And he will take your menservants, and your maidservants, and your goodliest young men, and your asses, and put *them* to his work. 17 He will take the tenth of your sheep: and ye shall be his servants. 18 And ye shall cry out in that day because of your king which ye shall have chosen you; and the LORD will not hear you in that day.	4) The confiscation of property: To give to the king's loyal officials or nobles 5) The taxation of crops: To give to the king's loyal officials or nobles 6) The confiscation of the nation's labor force & of the best animals 7) The taxation of animals 8) The enslavement of the entire population: The loss, restriction of the people's freedom b. There will be severe suffering, a cry for deliverance: But the LORD will not hear (His judicial judgment)

a. There would be the severe restriction of liberty if the people chose to live under a monarchy, the rule of a king. Eight oppressive restrictions of liberty are spelled out by Samuel.

1) Under a king, there would be oppressive, compulsory military service for sons (vv.11-12). Men would be needed to care for the military horses and chariots and other equipment, as well as to serve in the king's honor guard. A large standing army would be required to protect the nation. Manpower for the military would be an absolute essential; consequently, the sons of the nation would be taken from their homes and be compelled to serve the king.

2) Under a king, there would be oppressive, compulsory service for a core of laborers (v.12). A large force of laborers would be necessary to work in the fields and factories of the nation. Both food and weapons of war and equipment for the king's chariots would have to be mass-produced.

3) Under a king, there would be oppressive, compulsory service for the daughters of the nation. They would be required to serve the royal palace as perfumers, cooks, and bakers (v.13).

4) Under a king, there would be confiscation of property (v.14). The very best fields, vineyards, and groves would be needed to provide food and supplies for the king's attendants. Daily supplies and provisions would be needed by the people serving in the royal court, the loyal officials or nobles, the military, and the core of laborers serving the king and his administration.

5) Under a king, there would be a system of taxation instituted. Taxes would be an absolute essential to maintain the government of the king and to ensure the continued loyalty of the king's officials and nobles.

6) Under a king, there would be confiscation of the nation's labor force and of the best animals (v.16). This is a reference to the menial, common labor force of the nation. Even they would be enlisted by the king when needed. Moreover, the farmers and ranchers of the nation would be forced to give their very best animals to the king.

7) Under a king, there would be additional taxation instituted when needed (v.17). Animals, as well as crops, could be taxed as needed. Indeed, as much as one-tenth of the flocks could be confiscated by the king.

8) Under a king, the entire population would, in a sense, be enslaved. People would be forced to surrender some rights, some freedoms. There would be the loss and restriction of people's freedom. The demands of the king and his decrees would receive first priority, stripping and eating away at the freedom and liberty of the people. Just how much freedom the people would have would depend upon the righteousness and morality of the king.

b. The restriction of liberty would not be the only consequence of living within a monarchy, under the rule of a king. There would also be severe suffering, a cry for deliverance (v.18). Note, this was a prediction that would definitely happen to the Israelites (v.18). Under a king, the day would come when they would cry out for deliverance from his oppression and enslavement. They would cry out for relief from their own king who had become their oppressive enemy.

But note what God's response would be: the LORD would not answer the cry of His people. When that day came, it would be too late. The oppressive, lawless, and violent ways of this world would have become too embedded in both the king and his subjects. Thus, the LORD would allow them to continue in the way they had chosen, to have a king just "like all the nations." They would suffer under the judicial judgment of God, reaping exactly what they had sowed.

Thought 1. The lesson for us is strong: we reap what we sow. Just as Israel requested a king just "like all the nations," so God would give them a worldly king, a king just "like all the nations." The result would be catastrophic: they would reap the results of a worldly king. They would reap exactly what they had sown.

So it is with us: we reap what we sow. If we live a life of wickedness, we will reap a wicked end, the judgment of God—an eternity of doom, separated from the presence of God forever and ever. Listen to what God's Holy Word says about the sowing and reaping:

"For with what judgment ye judge, ye shall be judged: and with what measure ye mete, it shall be measured to you again" (Mt.7:2).

"But after thy hardness and impenitent heart treasurest up unto thyself wrath against the day of wrath and revelation of the righteous judgment of God; Who will render to every man according to his deeds" (Ro.2:5-6).

"Be not deceived; God is not mocked: for whatsoever a man soweth, that shall he also reap. For he that soweth to his flesh shall of the flesh reap corruption; but he that soweth to the Spirit shall of the Spirit reap life everlasting" (Ga.6:7-8).

"But my people would not hearken to my voice; and Israel would none of me. So I gave them up unto their own hearts' lust: *and* they walked in their own counsels" (Ps.81:11-12).

"He, that being often reproved hardeneth *his* neck, shall suddenly be destroyed, and that without remedy" (Pr.29:1).

"For I will not contend for ever, neither will I be always wroth: for the spirit should fail before me, and the souls *which* I have made" (Is.57:16).

4 (8:19-22) **Stubbornness, Example of—King, Israel's Demand for—Israel, History of, Demand for a King**: tragically, Israel insisted on—stubbornly demanded—a king. They refused to listen to Samuel and his warnings, even shouting out "No!" They refused to continue under the authority of God alone. They wanted a king to rule over them. They were deaf to reason and blind to the evil of their craving desire. They wanted a king who could unite the nation, build an army, and lead them to victory over their enemies. Simply stated, they wanted a king who could be...

- their savior and deliverer
- their protector and provider

OUTLINE	SCRIPTURE	SCRIPTURE	OUTLINE
4. The insistent demands for a king: A picture of being stubborn, hard-hearted	19 Nevertheless the people refused to obey the voice of Samuel; and they said, Nay; but we will have a king over us;	21 And Samuel heard all the words of the people, and he rehearsed them in the ears of the LORD.	b. The reseeking of the LORD by Samuel
a. The people's craving desire: To have a king just "like all the nations" 1) To unite & lead them 2) To build an army	20 That we also may be like all the nations; and that our king may judge us, and go out before us, and fight our battles.	22 And the LORD said to Samuel, Hearken unto their voice, and make them a king. And Samuel said unto the men of Israel, Go ye every man unto his city.	c. The granting of the request by the LORD: Give them a king

Rejecting God as their Savior and Deliverer, their Protector and Provider, the Israelites were now ready to put their destiny into the hands of a human being rather than into the hands of God. They were ready to make a covenant, an agreement with a man and to forget their covenant with God.

Again, Samuel did all he could: he went before the LORD, seeking His will (v.21). Once more, the LORD commanded the prophet to give them a king. Granting their request, Samuel sent the leaders or elders home (v.22).

Thought 1. The Israelites persisted in their stubborn desire for a king. They stiffened their necks against God, hardened their hearts against Him and insisted on living as they wanted. History has shown that their stubborn resistance to God was tragic. Down through the centuries, Israel had suffered terribly for their continued stubbornness against God.

There is a strong lesson for us in this experience of the Israelites. We must not be stubborn, stiff-necked, and hard-hearted against God.

"Ye stiffnecked and uncircumcised in heart and ears, ye do always resist the Holy Ghost: as your fathers *did,* so *do* ye" (Ac.7:51).

"But exhort one another daily, while it is called To day; lest any of you be hardened through the deceitfulness of sin" (He.3:13).

"Yet he sent prophets to them, to bring them again unto the Lord; and they testified against them: but they would not give ear" (2 Chr.24:19).

"Be ye not as the horse, *or* as the mule, *which* have no understanding: whose mouth must be held in with bit and bridle, lest they come near unto thee. Many sorrows *shall be* to the wicked: but he that trusteth in the Lord, mercy shall compass him about" (Ps.32:9-10).

"For he established a testimony in Jacob, and appointed a law in Israel, which he commanded our fathers, that they should make them known to their children:...And might not be as their fathers, a stubborn and rebellious generation; a generation *that* set not their heart aright, and whose spirit was not stedfast with God" (Ps.78:5, 8).

"Harden not your heart, as in the provocation, *and as in* the day of temptation in the wilderness: When your fathers tempted me, proved me, and saw my work. Forty years long was I grieved with *this* generation, and said, It *is* a people that do err in their heart, and they have not known my ways: Unto whom I sware in my wrath that they should not enter into my rest" (Ps.95:8-11).

"Happy *is* the man that feareth alway: but he that hardeneth his heart shall fall into mischief" (Pr.28:14).

"He, that being often reproved hardeneth *his* neck, shall suddenly be destroyed, and that without remedy" (Pr.29:1).

"Hearken unto me, ye stouthearted, that *are* far from righteousness" (Is.46:12).

"Because I knew that thou *art* obstinate, and thy neck *is* an iron sinew, and thy brow brass;...*There is* no peace, saith the Lord, unto the wicked" (Is.48:4, 22).

"And they have turned unto me the back, and not the face: though I taught them, rising up early and teaching *them,* yet they have not hearkened to receive instruction" (Je.32:33).

"*As for* the word that thou hast spoken unto us in the name of the Lord, we will not hearken unto thee" (Je.44:16).

"But they refused to hearken, and pulled away the shoulder, and stopped their ears, that they should not hear" (Zec.7:11).

"If ye will not hear, and if ye will not lay *it* to heart, to give glory unto my name, saith the Lord of hosts, I will even send a curse upon you, and I will curse your blessings: yea, I have cursed them already, because ye do not lay *it* to heart" (Mal.2:2).

CHAPTER 9

B. The Choice of Saul to Be King: A Look at a Promising Young Man, 9:1-27

1. Saul was an impressive young man
a. His heritage was four generations strong
b. His father was powerful & wealthy, 9:2; 11:5
c. His personal appearance was striking: Handsome, tall, with no equal among the Israelites

2. Saul was a trustworthy young man whose steps were guided by God
a. He was given an important task: That of finding a herd of lost donkeys
b. He was diligent, steadfast, very industrious in carrying out his task
   1) Crisscrossed throughout the land between the borders of Benjamin & Ephraim
   2) Was unsuccessful: Could not find the donkeys
c. He demonstrated a tender heart: Became concerned for his father, that he would worry something had happened to him & the servant
d. He was being led by God, guided step by step
   1) God's guidance is seen in the servant's suggestion: That they seek the counsel of a local "man of God" in finding the donkeys

   • Saul points out that they have nothing to give the man of God for his advice

   • The servant responded that he had a small silver piece that they could use to pay the man of God

   • An historical footnote: When special insight or discernment was needed,

Now there was a man of Benjamin, whose name *was* Kish, the son of Abiel, the son of Zeror, the son of Bechorath, the son of Aphiah, a Benjamite, a mighty man of power.
2 And he had a son, whose name *was* Saul, a choice young man, and a goodly: and *there was* not among the children of Israel a goodlier person than he: from his shoulders and upward *he was* higher than any of the people.
3 And the asses of Kish Saul's father were lost. And Kish said to Saul his son, Take now one of the servants with thee, and arise, go seek the asses.
4 And he passed through mount Ephraim, and passed through the land of Shalisha, but they found *them* not: then they passed through the land of Shalim, and *there they were* not: and he passed through the land of the Benjamites, but they found *them* not.
5 *And* when they were come to the land of Zuph, Saul said to his servant that *was* with him, Come, and let us return; lest my father leave *caring* for the asses, and take thought for us.
6 And he said unto him, Behold now, *there is* in this city a man of God, and *he is* an honourable man; all that he saith cometh surely to pass: now let us go thither; peradventure he can show us our way that we should go.
7 Then said Saul to his servant, But, behold, *if* we go, what shall we bring the man? for the bread is spent in our vessels, and *there is* not a present to bring to the man of God: what have we?
8 And the servant answered Saul again, and said, Behold, I have here at hand the fourth part of a shekel of silver: *that* will I give to the man of God, to tell us our way.
9 (Beforetime in Israel, when a man went to enquire of God, thus he spake, Come,

and let us go to the seer: for *he that is* now *called* a Prophet was beforetime called a Seer.)
10 Then said Saul to his servant, Well said; come, let us go. So they went unto the city where the man of God *was*.
11 *And* as they went up the hill to the city, they found young maidens going out to draw water, and said unto them, Is the seer here?
12 And they answered them, and said, He is; behold, *he is* before you: make haste now, for he came to day to the city; for *there is* a sacrifice of the people to day in the high place:
13 As soon as ye be come into the city, ye shall straightway find him, before he go up to the high place to eat: for the people will not eat until he come, because he doth bless the sacrifice; *and* afterwards they eat that be bidden. Now therefore get you up; for about this time ye shall find him.
14 And they went up into the city: *and* when they were come into the city, behold, Samuel came out against them, for to go up to the high place.
15 Now the LORD had told Samuel in his ear a day before Saul came, saying,
16 To morrow about this time I will send thee a man out of the land of Benjamin, and thou shalt anoint him *to be* captain over my people Israel, that he may save my people out of the hand of the Philistines: for I have looked upon my people, because their cry is come unto me.
17 And when Samuel saw Saul, the LORD said unto him, Behold the man whom I spake to thee of! this same shall reign over my people.
18 Then Saul drew near to Samuel in the gate, and said, Tell me, I pray thee, where the seer's house *is*.
19 And Samuel answered Saul, and said, I *am* the seer: go up before me unto the high place; for ye shall eat with me to day, and to morrow I will let thee go, and will tell thee all that *is* in thine heart.
20 And as for thine asses

a person sought a *man of God* or prophet, formerly called a *seer*

   • Saul agreed to seek counsel from the man of God

   2) God's guidance is seen in the directions given by some girls
   • Saul & the servant asked if the seer was there
   • The girls informed them that the seer was there, that he had just come to their town to lead the people in worship at the high place[DS1]: "He is ahead of you, Hurry… you will catch him before he leaves for worship."

   3) God's guidance is seen in the LORD'S using stray donkeys to lead Saul to Samuel: Saul, entering the city, met Samuel

3. Saul was chosen to be king by the LORD Himself, chosen to help & to deliver God's people
a. The LORD had revealed His choice to Samuel: "I will send you a man"
b. The LORD had instructed Samuel to anoint the man as leader over Israel
   1) The purpose: To deliver God's people
   2) The reason: God had heard their cry
c. The LORD now revealed that Saul was the man: Immediately, as Samuel caught sight of Saul approaching him

4. Saul was a humble, respectful young man
a. Saul met Samuel & was immediately informed of three significant facts
   1) He was to eat & spend the night with Samuel & be told all that was in his heart

   2) The donkeys had already

OUTLINE	SCRIPTURE	SCRIPTURE	OUTLINE

been found
 	
3) The desire of Israel was now turned, focused upon Saul
 	
b. Saul demonstrated a lowly, humble spirit
  1) He was from the smallest tribe of Israel
  2) He was from a clan that was the least of all the clans
c. Saul demonstrated a respectful attitude
  1) Respect in humbly, willingly letting Samuel seat him at the head of the feast table
 	
  2) Respect in willingly receiving the main portion of meat—the leg—the portion usually given to the priest
	that were lost three days ago, set not thy mind on them; for they are found. And on whom is all the desire of Israel? Is it not on thee, and on all thy father's house?
	21 And Saul answered and said, Am not I a Benjamite, of the smallest of the tribes of Israel? and my family the least of all the families of the tribe of Benjamin? wherefore then speakest thou so to me?
	22 And Samuel took Saul and his servant, and brought them into the parlour, and made them sit in the chiefest place among them that were bidden, which were about thirty persons.
	23 And Samuel said unto the cook, Bring the portion which I gave thee, of which I said unto thee, Set it by thee.
	24 And the cook took up the shoulder, and that which was upon it, and set it before
		Saul. And Samuel said, Behold that which is left! set it before thee, and eat: for unto this time hath it been kept for thee since I said, I have invited the people. So Saul did eat with Samuel that day.
		25 And when they were come down from the high place into the city, Samuel communed with Saul upon the top of the house.
		26 And they arose early: and it came to pass about the spring of the day, that Samuel called Saul to the top of the house, saying, Up, that I may send thee away. And Saul arose, and they went out both of them, he and Samuel, abroad.
		27 And as they were going down to the end of the city, Samuel said to Saul, Bid the servant pass on before us, (and he passed on,) but stand thou still a while, that I may show thee the word of God.
			3) Respect in accepting Samuel's invitation to spend the night & to converse together
			
			4) Respect in following the routine instructions of Samuel
			  • In getting ready to leave to return home
			
			  • In sending the servant on ahead & remaining behind to talk more with Samuel
			5) Respect in listening to God's message: Sent to him from God through Samuel

DIVISION II

THE STORY OF SAMUEL AND SAUL: THE LORD GIVES ISRAEL A KING JUST "LIKE ALL THE NATIONS," 8:1–15:35

B. The Choice of Saul to Be King: A Look at a Promising Young Man, 9:1-27

(9:1-27) **Introduction—Young People, Potential, Excites People**: to see a young person with great promise is an exciting thing. A child with unusual potential excites a parent. A student with an unusual hunger for knowledge excites a teacher. A young athlete with special skills excites a coach. A young politician with charisma and wisdom excites the public. A young artist with special talents stirs the audience. Whatever the area or profession, a *promising young person* stirs excitement within people.

In response to Israel's stubborn, stiff-necked demand for a king, God raised up a promising young man to become the first king of Israel. Saul is introduced for the very first time on the pages of Scripture, and the portrait painted is that of a very promising young man, a man with great potential for leadership and service as the national leader of the Israelites. Saul was impressive in appearance and carriage, very tall, handsome, and charismatic. In addition, he was trustworthy, diligent, steadfast, and industrious in carrying out his employment or whatever task was assigned to him. He was also a humble, respectful young man, indicating that his parents had trained him well. Just how Saul would turn out, the kind of leader he would prove to be, will be seen later. For now, in the present passage of Scripture, the portrait of Saul to be seen is that of a young man with enormous potential for leadership and service to the nation. This is: *The Choice of Saul to Be King: A Look at a Promising Young Man*, 9:1-27.

1. Saul was an impressive young man, very tall and handsome (vv.1-2).
2. Saul was a trustworthy young man whose steps were guided by God (vv.3-14).
3. Saul was chosen to be king by the LORD Himself, chosen to help and deliver God's people (vv.15-17).
4. Saul was a humble, respectful young man (vv.18-27)

1 (9:1-2) **Appearance, Deceitful—Judging, by Appearance—Appearance, Judging by—Appearance, Outward, Judging—Appearance, Glorying in—Appearance, Pride in—Charisma, Dependence upon—Saul, Appearance**: Saul was a very impressive young man—very tall and handsome—and he came from a powerful, wealthy family. Note what Scripture says about him:

OUTLINE	SCRIPTURE	SCRIPTURE	OUTLINE
1. Saul was an impressive young man a. His heritage was four generations strong b. His father was powerful & wealthy, 9:2; 11:5 c. His personal appearance	Now there was a man of Benjamin, whose name was Kish, the son of Abiel, the son of Zeror, the son of Bechorath, the son of Aphiah, a Benjamite, a mighty man of power. 2 And he had a son, whose	name was Saul, a choice young man, and a goodly: and there was not among the children of Israel a goodlier person than he: from his shoulders and upward he was higher than any of the people.	was striking: Handsome, tall, with no equal among the Israelites

Saul was from the tribe of Benjamin, the smallest of the twelve tribes of Israel. His father was obviously one of the leaders of the tribe of Benjamin, a very wealthy land owner, a powerful man who was something like a feudal lord who took a leadership role during times of war.[1]

In describing Saul, note what is stressed: not his character, integrity, righteousness, or wisdom, but his appearance. His outward appearance was striking, very impressive. Saul was handsome and tall, without equal among the Israelites (v.2). His personal appearance and charisma struck the onlooker. Judging from outward appearance, Saul seemed to have great potential for leadership and service.[2]

The name Saul means "asked for." This is interesting, for the people had actually asked for *a king* and God gave them Saul, a man whose very name means "asked for." What a striking point. This recalls the naming of Samuel (1:20). Remember, Samuel means "God heard." Yet, The Scripture clearly states that Hannah had asked God for a son out of a broken heart that was focused totally upon God and His wonderful blessing. Therefore, Hannah was given a son because she was seeking God with *all of her heart*. Saul on the other hand was the king who had been requested by the people, a people whose heart was focused upon the world and its distrustful ways. God gave the people a king, but not in answer to their worldly, fleshly prayer. He chose to use their carnal prayer to teach them a much-needed lesson: faith must be placed in the LORD, not in man and the ways of the world. When the people looked at Saul, they would be able to take great pride in him, for his stature, good looks, and charisma were striking—just the appearance people wanted in their leader. But note this fact: this is fleshly pride, judging a person by outward appearance. The inner qualities of the heart and mind were simply not mentioned, as though they did not exist with Saul.

> **Thought 1**. Appearances can be deceitful, so deceitful that they lead to utter failure and destruction. Later we will see that this is exactly what happened to Saul. Despite his impressive appearance, he failed God terribly and utterly destroyed his life and service for God and the Israelites. Saul's miserable failure teaches us that we must never judge by appearance, for appearances are deceitful and can lead to utter destruction.
>
> Leaders are often chosen because of their charisma or appearance, more so than for their character, integrity, wisdom, and moral values. But this should never be, for it leads to weakness, failure, and sometimes destruction. This is true within families as well as government, businesses, and organizations. For example, if a man or woman marries because of the spouse's outward appearance instead of the inner qualities, the marriage will be weak and perhaps doomed to divorce. If a person is chosen to head up a business or organization because of his or her charisma, the business or organization can suffer loss.
>
> God's Word is clear: we must not judge by appearance, by a person's charm or attractiveness. Decisions and judgments are to be based upon the heart and mind, upon the inner character, integrity, skill, initiative, and trustworthiness of a person. This is the true measure of any person, including leaders. It is the heart, not outward appearance, that truly matters.
>
> > "Woe unto you, scribes and Pharisees, hypocrites! for ye are like unto whited sepulchres, which indeed appear beautiful outward, but are within full of dead men's bones, and of all uncleanness." (Mt.23:27).
> > "Even so ye also outwardly appear righteous unto men, but within ye are full of hypocrisy and iniquity" (Mt.23:28).
> > "Judge not according to the appearance, but judge righteous judgment" (Jn.7:24).
> > "For we commend not ourselves again unto you, but give you occasion to glory on our behalf, that ye may have somewhat to answer them which glory in appearance, and not in heart" (2 Co.5:12)
> > "Do ye look on things after the outward appearance? If any man trust to himself that he is Christ's, let him of himself think this again, that, as he is Christ's, even so are we Christ's" (2 Co.10:7).
> > "But the LORD said unto Samuel, Look not on his countenance, or on the height of his stature; because I have refused him: for the LORD seeth not as man seeth; for man looketh on the outward appearance, but the LORD looketh on the heart" (1 S.16:7).

2 (9:3-14) **Trustworthy, Example of—Guidance, by God, Example of—God, Guidance of—Saul, Character, Trustworthy—Saul, Life of, Guided by God**: Saul was a trustworthy young man whose steps were guided by God. This is seen clearly in the incident that happened next:

OUTLINE	SCRIPTURE	SCRIPTURE	OUTLINE
2. Saul was a trustworthy young man whose steps were guided by God a. He was given an important task: That of finding a herd of lost donkeys b. He was diligent, steadfast, very industrious in carrying out his task	3 And the asses of Kish Saul's father were lost. And Kish said to Saul his son, Take now one of the servants with thee, and arise, go seek the asses. 4 And he passed through mount Ephraim, and passed through the land of Shalisha,	but they found *them* not: then they passed through the land of Shalim, and *there they* were not: and he passed through the land of the Benjamites, but they found *them* not. 5 *And* when they were come to the land of Zuph,	• Crisscrossed throughout the land between the borders of Benjamin & Ephraim • Was unsuccessful: Could not find the donkeys c. He demonstrated a tender heart: Became concerned for

---

1 *The Nelson Study Bible, New King James Version.* (Nashville, TN: Thomas Nelson Publishers, Inc., 1997), 9:1.
2 *The Nelson Study Bible, NKJV*, 9:2.

OUTLINE	SCRIPTURE	SCRIPTURE	OUTLINE
his father, that he would worry something had happened to him and the servant	Saul said to his servant that *was* with him, Come, and let us return; lest my father leave *caring* for the asses, and take thought for us.	10 Then said Saul to his servant, Well said; come, let us go. So they went unto the city where the man of God *was*.	• Saul agreed to seek counsel from the man of God
d. He was being led by God, guided step by step	6 And he said unto him, Behold now, *there is* in this city a man of God, and *he is*	11 *And* as they went up the hill to the city, they found young maidens going out to	2) God's guidance is seen in the directions given by some girls
1) God's guidance is seen in the servant's suggestion: That they seek the counsel of a local "man of God" in finding the donkeys	an honourable man; all that he saith cometh surely to pass: now let us go thither; peradventure he can shew us our way that we should go.	draw water, and said unto them, Is the seer here? 12 And they answered them, and said, He is; behold, *he is* before you: make haste now,	• Saul & the servant asked if the seer was there • The girls informed them that the seer was there, that he had just come to their town to lead the
• Saul points out that they have nothing to give the man of God for his advice	7 Then said Saul to his servant, But, behold, *if* we go, what shall we bring the man? for the bread is spent in our vessels, and *there is* not a present to bring to the man of God: what have we?	for he came to day to the city; for *there is* a sacrifice of the people to day in the high place: 13 As soon as ye be come into the city, ye shall straightway find him, before he go	people in worship at the high place[DSI]: "He is ahead of you, Hurry... you will catch him before he leaves for worship."
• The servant responded that he had a small silver piece that they could use to pay the man of God	8 And the servant answered Saul again, and said, Behold, I have here at hand the fourth part of a shekel of silver: *that* will I give to the man of God, to tell us our way.	up to the high place to eat: for the people will not eat until he come, because he doth bless the sacrifice; *and* afterwards they eat that be bidden. Now therefore get you up; for about this time ye shall find him.	
• An historical footnote: When special insight or discernment was needed, a person sought a *man of God* or prophet, formerly called a *seer*	9 (Beforetime in Israel, when a man went to enquire of God, thus he spake, Come, and let us go to the seer: for *he that is* now *called* a Prophet was beforetime called a Seer.)	14 And they went up into the city: *and* when they were come into the city, behold, Samuel came out against them, for to go up to the high place.	3) God's guidance is seen in the LORD's using stray donkeys to lead Saul to Samuel: Saul, entering the city, met Samuel

a. Saul was given an important task, that of finding a herd of lost donkeys (v.3). These lost donkeys were to be used by God to bring Saul in contact with Samuel. Note that Saul's father Kish owned this herd of donkeys, a sign of extreme wealth.

b. Saul was diligent and very industrious in carrying out his tasks (v.4). He crisscrossed throughout the land between the borders of Benjamin and Ephraim searching for the donkeys. But he was unsuccessful; he could not find the animals.

c. Saul demonstrated a tender heart (v.5). He and the servant with him had been searching for the donkeys for over three days, having traveled far and wide, all the way into the district of Zuph, the home district of Samuel. Saul became concerned for his father, that his father would worry something had happened to him and the servant. Therefore, Saul suggested that they return home.

d. But Saul was being led by God step-by-step (vv.6-14). Thus Saul's suggestion to return home was not acceptable. God was working, guiding this event to bring about the meeting between Saul and Samuel, the meeting that was to appoint Saul as king of Israel. The guidance of God is seen in three events:

1) God's guidance is seen in the servant's suggestion that they seek the counsel of a local man of God in finding the donkeys (vv.6-10). The term "man of God" refers to a prophet, a man who had a prophetic ministry and was recognized as a prophet.

   Saul pointed out that they had nothing to give the man of God for his advice (v.7). But the servant responded that he had a small silver piece that could be used to pay for his services (v.8).

   Note the historical footnote given by the author of Samuel: the man of God or prophet was formerly called a seer. A seer referred to a person who could give some special insight, some special discernment to those in need (v.9). Both terms, *prophet* and *seer*, were used during the days of Samuel and Saul, but the term *seer* was the more popular term used among the people when they needed some special insight or discernment.

   Fully knowing the value of the herd of lost donkeys, Saul immediately agreed with the servant to seek counsel from the man of God (v.10).

2) God's guidance is also seen in the directions given by some girls as they were coming out of the city of Ramah to draw water (vv.11-13). It was early evening when Saul and the servant entered the city, for that was when the women of ancient days came out of the cities to draw water. Seeing the girls, Saul asked if the seer was there (v.11). The girls informed him that the seer was indeed there, that he had just come to their town to lead the people in worship at the high place (v.12). In fact, the seer was just ahead of them. If Saul hurried, he would catch him before he left for worship (v.13).

3) God's guidance is seen in the LORD's using stray donkeys to lead Saul to Samuel (v.14). Rushing, following the information just given by the girls, Saul saw Samuel coming toward them on his way up to the high place.

Thought 1. The steps of a good man are ordered by the LORD (Ps.37:23). At this point in Saul's life, he was apparently a good, trustworthy young man. He was certainly diligent and very industrious in carrying out his tasks. He also demonstrated a tender heart, unusual feelings and concern for his father. And there is no question, God was guiding the steps of Saul to meet Samuel. God was in the process of appointing Saul to become king of Israel.

There is a strong lesson for us in God's guidance of Saul. If we are faithful in following God, seeking to be responsible and to live righteous lives, God will guide us as well. God will be with us day by day and guide us step-by-step. No matter how rocky the terrain, no matter how many obstacles in the path, no matter how many dangers, threats, trials, or temptations facing us—God will guide us over, around, under, or through the problem or circumstance. God will show the way. This is the wonderful promise of the Holy Bible.

> **"Through the tender mercy of our God; whereby the dayspring from on high hath visited us, To give light to them that sit in darkness and *in* the shadow of death, to guide our feet into the way of peace" (Lu.1:78-79).**

> **"Howbeit when he, the Spirit of truth, is come, he will guide you into all truth: for he shall not speak of himself; but whatsoever he shall hear, *that* shall he speak: and he will show you things to come" (Jn.16:13).**

> **"The LORD *is* my shepherd; I shall not want. He maketh me to lie down in green pastures: he leadeth me beside the still waters. He restoreth my soul: he leadeth me in the paths of righteousness for his name's sake. Yea, though I walk through the valley of the shadow of death, I will fear no evil: for thou *art* with me; thy rod and thy staff they comfort me. Thou preparest a table before me in the presence of mine enemies: thou anointest my head with oil; my cup runneth over. Surely goodness and mercy shall follow me all the days of my life: and I will dwell in the house of the LORD for ever" (Ps.23:1-6).**

> **"The meek will he guide in judgment: and the meek will he teach his way" (Ps.25:9).**

> **"The steps of a *good* man are ordered by the LORD: and he delighteth in his way" (Ps.37:23).**

> **"For this God *is* our God for ever and ever: he will be our guide *even* unto death" (Ps.48:14).**

> **"Thou shalt guide me with thy counsel, and afterward receive me *to* glory" (Ps.73:24).**

> **"*If* I take the wings of the morning, *and* dwell in the uttermost parts of the sea; Even there shall thy hand lead me, and thy right hand shall hold me" (Ps.139:9-10).**

> **"And thine ears shall hear a word behind thee, saying, This *is* the way, walk ye in it, when ye turn to the right hand, and when ye turn to the left" (Is.30:21).**

> **"And I will bring the blind by a way *that* they knew not; I will lead them in paths *that* they have not known: I will make darkness light before them, and crooked things straight. These things will I do unto them, and not forsake them" (Is.42:16).**

DEEPER STUDY #1

(9:12) High Place—Worship: from earliest history, people have tended to use elevated sights for worship, whether on hills or platforms constructed in temples. This was particularly true of the Canaanites (Nu.33:52; De.12:2-5). But Israel also made use of the "high place." Samuel had apparently constructed a sacred sight in his hometown at Ramah to replace the worship center at Shiloh that had been destroyed by the Philistines. Since the destruction of Shiloh, a number of worship centers or high places had been constructed throughout Israel. However, later in the history of the nation, the high places became easy targets for the infiltration of false gods and false worship. The high places became centers of idolatry and were fiercely condemned by God (1 K.11:7; 12:26-33; 2 K.17:7-18; 21:2-9; 23:4-25).

---

3 **(9:15-17) Deliverance, Duty—Chosen, by God, Saul—Appointment, to Leadership—Call, Purpose of—Saul, Appointment of—King, Of Israel, Saul**: Saul was chosen to be king by the LORD Himself, chosen to help and to deliver God's people. Note that God calls Israel "my people" four times in these three verses.

OUTLINE	SCRIPTURE	SCRIPTURE	OUTLINE
3. Saul was chosen to be king by the LORD Himself, chosen to help & to deliver God's people a. The LORD had revealed His choice to Samuel: "I will send you a man" b. The LORD had instructed Samuel to anoint the man as leader over Israel	15 Now the LORD had told Samuel in his ear a day before Saul came, saying, 16 To morrow about this time I will send thee a man out of the land of Benjamin, and thou shalt anoint him *to be* captain over my people Israel, that he may save my	people out of the hand of the Philistines: for I have looked upon my people, because their cry is come unto me. 17 And when Samuel saw Saul, the LORD said unto him, Behold the man whom I spake to thee of! this same shall reign over my people.	1) The purpose: To deliver God's people 2) The reason: God had heard their cry c. The LORD now revealed that Saul was the man: Immediately, as Samuel caught sight of Saul approaching him

Although He was choosing Saul to be king of Israel, the LORD was not relinquishing His authority over the people, nor was He giving up His claim to be the true ruler over the people. He was the LORD God of the universe; consequently, the true believers among the Israelites would remain the LORD's own "treasured possession" (Ex.19:5; De.7:6; 14:2; 26:18). Saul was to be just what all leaders are, mere caretakers of God's flock (1 Pe.5:2).[3] Saul was just as responsible as the people were for living a righteous and holy life and for serving the LORD. His authority as king was to be exercised under the authority of the King of kings and LORD of lords.

---

3 Robert D. Bergen. *1, 2 Samuel*, p.123.

Sometime the day before, the LORD had revealed His choice of Saul to Samuel, telling him that He would send Samuel the young man who was to be anointed leader over Israel (vv.15-16). The purpose for the appointment of Saul was clearly stated: he was to deliver God's people from their oppressive enemy, the Philistines. Since the very beginning of the judges, the Israelites had been suffering terrible oppression from the surrounding nations. With broken hearts, the Israelites had finally repented and turned to the LORD under the leadership of Samuel (see outline and notes—1 S.7:1-6 for more discussion). In compassion and mercy, the LORD had heard their cry and was now determined to begin preparation for their deliverance. Part of that preparation was the appointment of Saul to be their leader, the first king of Israel. Thus, as Samuel first caught sight of Saul in the distance, God spoke to his heart saying, "This is the man...he will reign over, rule, and govern my people" (v.17).

Thought 1. It is God who chooses the rulers and leaders of this world. It is God who appoints men and women to serve and govern the people of this earth. Certain gifts and abilities are given to specific persons so that they can serve and carry on the functions of government, organizations, businesses, and other institutions of society. Serving others is a privilege, a privilege that is given to certain people by God. But far too often leaders violate the privilege given them, abusing their power and rights. To such abusive leaders, God warns: they will face the severest wrath of God's judgment.

But the lesson for us in this point is God's appointment. It is God who appoints men and women to leadership positions. Whether the ruler of a nation or the floor manager of a department store, the person placed in leadership is placed there by the sovereignty of God. God gifted the person with leadership ability and worked to open up the opportunity to serve. This is the clear teaching of God's Holy Word:

"**Ye have not chosen me, but I have chosen you, and ordained you, that ye should go and bring forth fruit, and *that* your fruit should remain: that whatsoever ye shall ask of the Father in my name, he may give it you**" (Jn.15:16).

"**But the LORD said unto him, Go thy way: for he is a chosen vessel unto me, to bear my name before the Gentiles, and kings, and the children of Israel**" (Ac.9:15).

"**Let every soul be subject unto the higher powers. For there is no power but of God: the powers that be are ordained of God**" (Ro.13:1).

"**So now *it was* not you *that* sent me [Joseph] hither, but God: and he hath made me a father to Pharaoh, and lord of all his house, and a ruler throughout all the land of Egypt**" (Ge.45:8).

"**Come now therefore, and I will send thee unto Pharaoh, that thou mayest bring forth my people the children of Israel out of Egypt**" (Ex.3:10).

"**The LORD maketh poor, and maketh rich: he bringeth low, and lifteth up**" (1 S.2:7).

"**Now therefore so shalt thou say unto my servant David, Thus saith the LORD of hosts, I took thee from the sheepcote, from following the sheep, to be ruler over my people, over Israel**"(2 S.7:8).

"**Go, tell Jeroboam, Thus saith the LORD God of Israel, Forasmuch as I exalted thee from among the people, and made thee prince over my people Israel**" (1 K.14:7).

"**But God *is* the judge: he putteth down one, and setteth up another**" (Ps.75:7).

"**And he changeth the times and the seasons: he removeth kings, and setteth up kings: he giveth wisdom unto the wise, and knowledge to them that know understanding**" (Da.2:21).

4 (9:18-27) **Humility, Example of—Respect, Example of**: Saul was a very humble, respectful young man. This is seen throughout the meeting between Saul and Samuel.

OUTLINE	SCRIPTURE	SCRIPTURE	OUTLINE

4. Saul was a humble, respectful young man
a. Saul met Samuel & was immediately informed of three significant facts
  1) He was to eat & spend the night with Samuel & be told all that was in his heart
 	
  2) The donkeys had already been found
 	
  3) The desire of Israel was now turned, focused upon Saul
 	
b. Saul demonstrated a lowly,
	18 Then Saul drew near to Samuel in the gate, and said, Tell me, I pray thee, where the seer's house *is*.
	19 And Samuel answered Saul, and said, I *am* the seer: go up before me unto the high place; for ye shall eat with me to day, and to morrow I will let thee go, and will tell thee all that *is* in thine heart.
	20 And as for thine asses that were lost three days ago, set not thy mind on them; for they are found. And on whom *is* all the desire of Israel? *Is it* not on thee, and on all thy father's house?
	21 And Saul answered and
		said, *Am* not I a Benjamite, of the smallest of the tribes of Israel? and my family the least of all the families of the tribe of Benjamin? wherefore then speakest thou so to me?
		22 And Samuel took Saul and his servant, and brought them into the parlour, and made them sit in the chiefest place among them that were bidden, which *were* about thirty persons.
		23 And Samuel said unto the cook, Bring the portion which I gave thee, of which I said unto thee, Set it by thee.
		24 And the cook took up the shoulder, and *that* which *was*
			humble spirit
			  1) He was from the smallest tribe of Israel
			  2) He was from a clan that was the least of all the clans
			
			c. Saul demonstrated a respectful attitude
			  1) Respect in humbly, willingly letting Samuel seat him at the head of the feast table
			
			  2) Respect in willingly receiving the main portion of meat—the leg—the portion usually given to the priest

OUTLINE	SCRIPTURE	SCRIPTURE	OUTLINE
	upon it, and set *it* before Saul. And *Samuel* said, Behold that which is left! set *it* before thee, *and* eat: for unto this time hath it been kept for thee since I said, I have invited the people. So Saul did eat with Samuel that day. 25 And when they were come down from the high place into the city, *Samuel* communed with Saul upon the top of the house. 26 And they arose early: and it came to pass about the	spring of the day, that Samuel called Saul to the top of the house, saying, Up, that I may send thee away. And Saul arose, and they went out both of them, he and Samuel, abroad. 27 *And* as they were going down to the end of the city, Samuel said to Saul, Bid the servant pass on before us, (and he passed on,) but stand thou still a while, that I may show thee the word of God.	Samuel • In getting ready to leave to return home • In sending the servant on ahead & remaining behind to talk more with Samuel 5) Respect in listening to God's message: Sent to him from God through Samuel
3) Respect in accepting Samuel's invitation to spend the night & to converse together 4) Respect in following the routine instructions of			

a. Saul, not knowing who Samuel was, approached Samuel at the gateway of the city, asking where the seer's house was. After identifying himself as the seer or prophet, Samuel immediately informed Saul of three significant facts (vv.18-20):

⇒ Saul was to eat and spend the night with Samuel and to be told all that was within his heart (v.19). Imagine having the questions of one's heart, one's innermost thoughts, explained. No doubt, this was a reference to the lengthy conversations Samuel was to have with Saul through the long overnight stay. But Saul did not know this yet. Imagine his shock when he heard Samuel say that he would tell him all that was in his heart.

⇒ Samuel told Saul not to worry about the donkeys, for they had already been found (v.20).

⇒ Then Samuel revealed a fact to Saul that must have shaken him to the core of his being: all the desire of Israel was now turned, focused upon Saul (v.20).

b. Hearing these words, Saul demonstrated a most lowly, humble spirit (v.21). He exclaimed that he was from Benjamin, the smallest tribe of Israel and from a family that was the least of all families of Benjamin. Why, then, would Samuel say such a thing to him?

This response by Saul demonstrates a lowly, humble spirit. Despite his impressive, charismatic appearance, Saul was a humble young man.

c. Saul demonstrated not only humility, but also a respectful attitude (vv.22-27). Samuel took Saul and his servant along with him, bringing them into the hall where he was to conduct the worship service. Note the humble respect shown by Saul during the worship feast and during his overnight stay with Samuel.

1) Saul's respect was seen in his humility and willingness to let Samuel seat him at the head of the table during the feast (v.22). The young man was a stranger in the community, and there were over thirty persons present. Uneasy feelings must have surged through his body when Samuel began to seat him at the head of the table. But he respectfully submitted to Samuel's wishes instead of protesting.

2) Saul's respect is also seen in his willingness to receive the main portion of meat, the leg, the portion usually given to the priest (vv.23-24). Once the LORD had revealed to Samuel that the future king was to be his guest, Samuel had a meal prepared for the occasion (v.24).

3) Saul showed respect in accepting Samuel's invitation to spend the night and converse with him (v.25). Just what they talked about is not covered by Scripture. However, the subject must have focused upon God's appointment of Saul to be king and upon the desperate needs of Israel, in particular their need to be delivered from the oppression of the Philistines.

4) Saul showed respect in following the routine instructions of Samuel after they arose the next morning (v.26). Samuel instructed the young man to get ready to return home. He even instructed Saul to send the servant on ahead but to remain behind to talk more with him (v.27). Respectfully, obediently, Saul did just as Samuel instructed.

5) Saul showed respect by listening to God's message that had been sent to him through Samuel (v.27). Just what the message was will be seen in the next chapter. For now, the point to note is Saul's humble spirit and respectful attitude.

Thought 1. Saul's example of humility and respect is a strong lesson for us. Humility is essential throughout society. Lawlessness would run rampant without humility and respect. A peaceful and just society demands respect of human life and property. If there is no respect for life, there is violence, abuse, assaults, and the taking of human life. If there is no respect for property, there is stealing or destruction of property. If there is no respect for mannerly or decent behavior, there is rudeness and vulgarity.

So it is with humility. If we do not walk humbly and consider others, we exalt ourselves above others and put them down. We squash, embarrass, humiliate, mistreat, and abuse others. Humility and respect are two absolute essentials for a peaceful and just society.

(1) We must walk in humility.

> **"And he said unto them, The kings of the Gentiles exercise lordship over them; and they that exercise authority upon them are called benefactors. But ye *shall* not *be* so: but he that is greatest among you, let him be as the younger; and he that is chief, as he that doth serve" (Lu.22:25-26).**

"For I say, through the grace given unto me, to every man that is among you, not to think *of himself* more highly than he ought to think; but to think soberly, according as God hath dealt to every man the measure of faith" (Ro.12:3).

"*Let* nothing *be done* through strife or vainglory; but in lowliness of mind let each esteem other better than themselves. Look not every man on his own things, but every man also on the things of others. Let this mind be in you, which was also in Christ Jesus" (Ph.2:3-5).

"Humble yourselves in the sight of the LORD, and he shall lift you up" (Js.4:10).

"Likewise, ye younger, submit yourselves unto the elder. Yea, all *of you* be subject one to another, and be clothed with humility: for God resisteth the proud, and giveth grace to the humble. Humble yourselves therefore under the mighty hand of God, that he may exalt you in due time" (1 Pe.5:5-6).

"He hath showed thee, O man, what *is* good; and what doth the LORD require of thee, but to do justly, and to love mercy, and to walk humbly with thy God" (Mi.6:8).

(2) We must walk in respect for others. We must show respect to others.

"Thou shalt love thy neighbour as thyself" (Mt.22:39).

"Let all bitterness, and wrath, and anger, and clamour, and evil speaking, be put away from you, with all malice: And be ye kind one to another, tenderhearted, forgiving one another, even as God for Christ's sake hath forgiven you" (Ep.4:31-32).

"Children, obey your parents in the LORD: for this is right" (Ep.6:1).

"Receive him therefore in the LORD with all gladness; and hold such in reputation" (Ph.2:29).

"And to esteem them very highly in love for their work's sake. And be at peace among yourselves" (1 Th.5:13).

"Rebuke not an elder, but intreat him as a father; and the younger men as brethren; The elder women as mothers; the younger as sisters, with all purity" (1 Ti.5:1-2).

"Remember them which have the rule over you, who have spoken unto you the word of God: whose faith follow, considering the end of their conversation [behavior, conduct]" (He.13:7).

"Thou shalt rise up before the hoary [gray] head, and honour the face of the old man, and fear thy God: I am the LORD" (Le.19:32).

"Hearken unto thy father that begat thee, and despise not thy mother when she is old" (Pr.23:22).

CHAPTER 10

C. The Private Anointing & Public Installation of Saul as King: Receiving a New, Changed Heart, 10:1-27

1. Saul was privately anointed as king by Samuel: A symbol of being set apart & empowered by God's Spirit
a. Saul was anointed to be the leader of God's inheritance
b. Saul was given four signs to confirm that he was God's choice to be king
 1) Sign 1: He would meet two men who would assure him that the herd of lost donkeys had been found

 2) Sign 2: He would then meet three travelers going up to worship God at Bethel

 • They would offer him the *holy bread* to be used in their worship

 • He was to accept it, for he was the LORD's anointed, 21:6

 3) Sign 3: He would later meet a procession of prophets returning from worship who would be playing music & prophesying[DS1]

 4) Sign 4: God's Spirit would come upon him
 • He would prophesy
 • He would be changed, transformed, converted
c. Saul was to carry out his duty as king to the very best of his ability

d. Saul was to wait seven days at Gilgal for Samuel
 1) To wait for Samuel to lead in worship & to offer sacrifices
 2) To wait for Samuel to give further instructions

Then Samuel took a vial of oil, and poured *it* upon his head, and kissed him, and said, *Is it* not because the LORD hath anointed thee *to be* captain over his inheritance?
2 When thou art departed from me to day, then thou shalt find two men by Rachel's sepulchre in the border of Benjamin at Zelzah; and they will say unto thee, The asses which thou wentest to seek are found: and, lo, thy father hath left the care of the asses, and sorroweth for you, saying, What shall I do for my son?
3 Then shalt thou go on forward from thence, and thou shalt come to the plain of Tabor, and there shall meet thee three men going up to God to Bethel, one carrying three kids, and another carrying three loaves of bread, and another carrying a bottle of wine:
4 And they will salute thee, and give thee two *loaves* of bread; which thou shalt receive of their hands.
5 After that thou shalt come to the hill of God, where *is* the garrison of the Philistines: and it shall come to pass, when thou art come thither to the city, that thou shalt meet a company of prophets coming down from the high place with a psaltery, and a tabret, and a pipe, and a harp, before them; and they shall prophesy:
6 And the Spirit of the LORD will come upon thee, and thou shalt prophesy with them, and shalt be turned into another man.
7 And let it be, when these signs are come unto thee, *that* thou do as occasion serve thee; for God *is* with thee.
8 And thou shalt go down before me to Gilgal; and, behold, I will come down unto thee, to offer burnt offerings, *and* to sacrifice sacrifices of peace offerings: seven days shalt thou tarry, till I come to

thee, and show thee what thou shalt do.
9 And it was *so,* that when he had turned his back to go from Samuel, God gave him another heart: and all those signs came to pass that day.
10 And when they came thither to the hill, behold, a company of prophets met him; and the Spirit of God came upon him, and he prophesied among them.
11 And it came to pass, when all that knew him beforetime saw that, behold, he prophesied among the prophets, then the people said one to another, What *is* this *that* is come unto the son of Kish? *Is* Saul also among the prophets?
12 And one of the same place answered and said, But who *is* their father? Therefore it became a proverb, *Is* Saul also among the prophets?
13 And when he had made an end of prophesying, he came to the high place.
14 And Saul's uncle said unto him and to his servant, Whither went ye? And he said, To seek the asses: and when we saw that *they were* no where, we came to Samuel.
15 And Saul's uncle said, Tell me, I pray thee, what Samuel said unto you.
16 And Saul said unto his uncle, He told us plainly that the asses were found. But of the matter of the kingdom, whereof Samuel spake, he told him not.
17 And Samuel called the people together unto the LORD to Mizpeh;
18 And said unto the children of Israel, Thus saith the LORD God of Israel, I brought up Israel out of Egypt, and delivered you out of the hand of the Egyptians, and out of the hand of all kingdoms, *and* of them that oppressed you:
19 And ye have this day rejected your God, who himself saved you out of all your adversities and your tribulations; and ye have said unto him, *Nay,* but set a king over us. Now therefore present yourselves before the LORD by your tribes, and by your thousands.
20 And when Samuel had

2. Saul was transformed, given a new, changed heart by God: A picture of conversion
a. The signs were fulfilled

b. The Spirit of God came upon Saul in power & he prophesied

 1) His prophesying in public bore strong testimony to his transformation, his change

 2) His prophesying aroused one man to ask who the father or man was who could cause such a transformation
c. The spirit of humility & wisdom gripped Saul
 1) He went to worship
 2) He humbly & wisely concealed from his relatives his private anointing as king

 • Guarded against pride

 • Trusted God to carry out His plan & timing through Samuel

3. Saul was publicly installed as king: A picture of feeling unfit & fleeing from God's call
a. The charge of Samuel against the Israelites
 1) The LORD had saved them from Egypt & all other enemies: A symbol of deliverance from the world & its bondages

 2) They were now rejecting God—His rule (as their Savior, Guide, Protector, & Provider)—& choosing to be ruled by an earthly king, 8:10-18

b. The choosing of a king by lot

1) The tribe of Benjamin was chosen	caused all the tribes of Israel to come near, the tribe of Benjamin was taken.	the people, See ye him whom the LORD hath chosen, that *there is* none like him among all the people? And all the people shouted, and said, God save the king.	public acclamation of Saul as king
2) The LORD directed the lots to fall upon Saul	21 When he had caused the tribe of Benjamin to come near by their families, the family of Matri was taken, and Saul the son of Kish was taken: and when they sought him, he could not be found.		
c. The fleeing from God's call by Saul: He could not be found		25 Then Samuel told the people the manner of the kingdom, and wrote *it* in a book, and laid *it* up before the LORD. And Samuel sent all the people away, every man to his house.	e. The regulations to govern the king
1) The LORD led the leaders to Saul's hiding place	22 Therefore they enquired of the LORD further, if the man should yet come thither. And the LORD answered, Behold, he hath hid himself among the stuff.		1) Were written down by Samuel
			2) Were placed in the Tabernacle: A symbol that the regulations & God's Word were to govern the king
		26 And Saul also went home to Gibeah; and there went with him a band of men, whose hearts God had touched.	f. The meeting adjourned & the response to Saul's appointment as king
2) The leaders presented him to the people: He stood a head taller than anyone else, an impressive height & appearance, 9:2	23 And they ran and fetched him thence: and when he stood among the people, he was higher than any of the people from his shoulders and upward.	27 But the children of Belial said, How shall this man save us? And they despised him, and brought him no presents. But he held his peace.	1) Some valiant men escorted Saul: Stirred by God to be his personal (honor) guard
d. The presentation & the	24 And Samuel said to all		2) Some troublemakers despised Saul: Rejected his kingship: Saul did not react or have them executed

DIVISION II

SAMUEL AND SAUL: THE LORD GIVES ISRAEL A KING JUST "LIKE ALL THE NATIONS," 8:1–15:35

C. The Private Anointing and Public Installation of Saul as King: Receiving a New, Changed Heart, 10:1-27

(10:1-27) **Introduction—Second Chance, Fact—Conversion, Fact—Life, Fact, Can Be Changed—Deliverance, Fact—Transformation, Fact**: a second chance, a new opportunity, a changed life—many a person would give anything to have such a possibility in life. They would do anything for a new opportunity to live life, to be able to alter their lives. Many have made a mess out of their lives through bad decisions that led to financial difficulties, terrible loss, painful divorce, severe accident or injury, inadequate training and education, or some addiction to alcohol, drugs, or food. Many persons would give anything to change the suffering they have to endure due to disease, sin and wickedness, guilt, discouragement, depression, stress, anxiety, and a host of other emotional and psychotic problems.

But there is wonderful, marvelous news: we can have a second chance, a new opportunity, a changed life. With whatever time remains in our lives, God will give us that chance, that new opportunity, that changed life. How? How is this possible? By conversion! Being transformed by the power of the Lord Jesus Christ. God will take our lives and *convert* them, *transform* them into new lives. God will make us into *new creations—new persons, new men, new women, new boys, new girls*—all by His power to quicken and regenerate our lives.

The wonderful truth of conversion—the transformation of a human life—is seen in this present Scripture. God took Saul and converted or transformed him into a changed man. He raised him up to become the very first king of Israel. This is the subject of this passage in the Holy Bible: *The Private Anointing and Public Installation of Saul as King: Receiving a New, Changed Heart,* 10:1-27.

1. Saul was privately anointed as king by Samuel: a symbol of being set apart and empowered by God's Spirit (vv.1-8).
2. Saul was transformed, given a new, changed heart by God: a picture of conversion (vv.9-16).
3. Saul was publicly installed as king: a picture of feeling unfit and fleeing from God's call (vv.17-27).

1 (10:1-8) **Power, Source of—Set Apart, Source of—Anointing, Source of—Anointing, Persons Anointed—Anointing, Symbol of—Conversion, Example of—Saul, Conversion—Samuel, Ministry of**: Saul was privately anointed by Samuel. Being anointed was a symbol of being set apart and empowered by God's Spirit. This is the first time a person was anointed other than the Aaronic priest and sacred objects (Le.8:10-11, 30; Nu.7:1).[1] Remember, Saul and Samuel had just met the day before when Samuel had first revealed to Saul that he was God's choice to be king of Israel. At the invitation of Samuel, Saul had spent the night with him so they could discuss the appointment. Now, the next morning, they were walking together, probably along the path of some garden or vineyard. All kinds of emotions were bound to be running through Saul's heart and mind: utter shock and bewilderment, fear and apprehension, and all kinds of

---

[1] Robert D. Bergen. *1, 2 Samuel,* p.126.

questions. But God is faithful: He always meets the needs of those He sets apart for service. Note how He dealt with Saul's doubts and met his need:

OUTLINE	SCRIPTURE	SCRIPTURE	OUTLINE

1. **Saul was privately anointed as king by Samuel: A symbol of being set apart & empowered by God's Spirit**
  a. Saul was anointed to be the leader of God's inheritance
  b. Saul was given four signs to confirm that he was God's choice to be king
    1) Sign 1: He would meet two men who would assure him that the herd of lost donkeys had been found
	Then Samuel took a vial of oil, and poured *it* upon his head, and kissed him, and said, *Is it* not because the LORD hath anointed thee *to be* captain over his inheritance?
	2 When thou art departed from me to day, then thou shalt find two men by Rachel's sepulchre in the border of Benjamin at Zelzah; and they will say unto thee, The asses which thou wentest to seek are found: and, lo, thy father hath left the care of the asses, and sorroweth for you, saying, What shall I do for my son?
		bread; which thou shalt receive of their hands.
		5 After that thou shalt come to the hill of God, where *is* the garrison of the Philistines: and it shall come to pass, when thou art come thither to the city, that thou shalt meet a company of prophets coming down from the high place with a psaltery, and a tabret, and a pipe, and a harp, before them; and they shall prophesy:
			anointed, 21:6
			
			3) Sign 3: He would later meet a procession of prophets returning from worship who would be playing music & prophesying[DS1]

2) Sign 2: He would then meet three travelers going up to worship God at Bethel
 	
      • They would offer him the *holy bread* to be used in their worship
 	
      • He was to accept it, for he was the LORD's
	3 Then shalt thou go on forward from thence, and thou shalt come to the plain of Tabor, and there shall meet thee three men going up to God to Bethel, one carrying three kids, and another carrying three loaves of bread, and another carrying a bottle of wine:
	4 And they will salute thee, and give thee two *loaves* of
		6 And the Spirit of the LORD will come upon thee, and thou shalt prophesy with them, and shalt be turned into another man.
		7 And let it be, when these signs are come unto thee, *that* thou do as occasion serve thee; for God *is* with thee.
		8 And thou shalt go down before me to Gilgal; and, behold, I will come down unto thee, to offer burnt offerings, *and* to sacrifice sacrifices of peace offerings: seven days shalt thou tarry, till I come to thee, and show thee what thou shalt do.
			4) Sign 4: God's Spirit would come upon him
			  • He would prophesy
			  • He would be changed, transformed, converted
			c. Saul was to carry out his duty as king to the very best of his ability
			
			d. Saul was to wait seven days at Gilgal for Samuel
			  1) To wait for Samuel to lead in worship & to offer sacrifices
			  2) To wait for Samuel to give further instructions

a. Saul was anointed to be the leader of God's inheritance (v.1). "God's inheritance" refers to both the people of God and the promised land (Ex.15:17; 34:9). By anointing Saul, Samuel was assuring him that God had chosen him to be the king of His people and of His land, the promised land.

Note that Samuel also kissed Saul. A kiss was simply a sign of respect, acknowledging the position of Saul, that he was hereafter the anointed leader of God's people.

b. Saul was then given four signs to confirm that he was God's choice to be king (vv.2-8). All four signs were to come to pass immediately, that very day. Once the signs had taken place, they would help to reinforce Saul's conviction that he was definitely God's choice to be king of Israel. All doubt hopefully would be erased.

    1) The first sign was this: as Saul traveled back home, he would meet two men who would assure him that the herd of lost donkeys had been found (v.2). This encounter would take place near Rachel's tomb, at Zelzah, on the border of Benjamin. Moreover, the men would inform Saul that his father was no longer thinking about the herd of lost donkeys, but rather, was worried about the welfare of Saul. Keep in mind, this event had not yet taken place. Samuel was predicting a future event that was to take place that day, an event that was to help prove Saul's appointment. After the encounter with the two men, Saul should be assured that he was God's anointed leader.

    2) The second sign was this: soon after the first sign, Saul would meet three travelers going up to worship at Bethel (v.3). Note that the very spot where the men would meet Saul was predicted by Samuel: at the great tree of Tabor. Moreover, what each of the three men would be carrying was predicted by Samuel: one would be carrying three young goats, another three loaves of bread, and the third a skin bottle of wine. But this was not all: Samuel predicted that they would greet Saul and offer him two loaves of holy bread that they had intended to use in their worship (v.4). Samuel instructed Saul that he was to accept the bread, for he was the Lord's anointed (21:6). By accepting the "holy bread," Saul would be symbolizing that he accepted the legitimacy of his appointment to be king.[2]

    3) The third sign was this: as Saul continued traveling home, he would meet a procession of prophets returning from worship who would be playing music and prophesying (v.5). This event was to take place at the hill of God or Gibeah of GOD, where there was a Philistine outpost. There was obviously a *school of prophets* in the city, a school that had been founded by Samuel to train young men for a prophetic ministry among God's people. In the corrupt days of the judges and prophets, it was necessary for *schools of prophets* to be founded in order to train young men for the prophetic ministry (1 K.20:35; 2 K.2:3-7, 15; 4:1, 38; 5:22; 6:1; 9:1). The prophesying referred to here is most likely an enthusiastic, ecstatic praising of God inspired by the Holy Spirit.[3]

---

[2] Robert D. Bergen. *1, 2 Samuel*, p.128.
[3] *The NIV Study Bible*, 10:5, p.385.

4) The fourth sign was this: God's Spirit would come upon Saul so that he himself would begin to prophesy (v.6). In fact, he would be a changed, transformed person. His whole being would be converted: he would be prepared by God to be king, to serve God's people. Saul would be wonderfully transformed by the Spirit of God.

c. Once these signs were fulfilled, Saul was to carry out his duty as king to the very best of his ability (v.7). Note the wonderful assurance Samuel gave Saul: "God is with you." God would show Saul how to lead the people and how to establish the kingdom of Israel. No greater assurance could be given Saul than the assurance of God's presence. Saul could not fail, not if he trusted and followed after God, for God was with him.

d. Samuel then instructed Saul to go to Gilgal and wait seven days for his coming (v.8). At the end of the seven days, Samuel promised to come and conduct a worship service, presenting offerings and sacrifices to the LORD. At that time, Samuel would give Saul further instructions, telling him exactly how he was to become established as the king of Israel.

Thought 1. It is God's Spirit who comes upon us, enabling us to live life to the fullest and to do our work or to carry out the task given to us. Without the Spirit of God, we are left to confront life all alone. There is no one to help us other than the little help our families and other people might be able to give us. And the help of others is limited, coming up ever so short when we are facing the severe crises of this life. Medicine and technology can help us only so much and only for so long. Eventually some terrible hardship, misfortune, accident, or disease happens or else the inevitable declining health of age grips us and we die. The Spirit of God is needed to give us the fullness of life and to help us carry out the tasks and duties of life. For this reason, we must cry out for the Spirit of God to come upon us and equip us for life.

"If ye then, being evil, know how to give good gifts unto your children: how much more shall your heavenly Father give the Holy Spirit to them that ask him" (Lu.11:13).

"It is the spirit that quickeneth; the flesh profiteth nothing: the words that I speak unto you, they are spirit, and they are life" (Jn.6:63).

"And I will pray the Father, and he shall give you another Comforter, that he may abide with you for ever; Even the Spirit of truth; whom the world cannot receive, because it seeth him not, neither knoweth him: but ye know him; for he dwelleth with you, and shall be in you" (Jn.14:16-17).

"But the Comforter, which is the Holy Ghost, whom the Father will send in my name, he shall teach you all things, and bring all things to your remembrance, whatsoever I have said unto you" (Jn.14:26).

"But when the Comforter is come, whom I will send unto you from the Father, even the Spirit of truth, which proceedeth from the Father, he shall testify of me"(Jn.15:26).

"Nevertheless I tell you the truth; It is expedient for you that I go away: for if I go not away, the Comforter will not come unto you; but if I depart, I will send him unto you. And when he is come, he will reprove the world of sin, and of righteousness, and of judgment" (Jn.16:7-8).

"Howbeit when he, the Spirit of truth, is come, he will guide you into all truth: for he shall not speak of himself; but whatsoever he shall hear, that shall he speak: and he will show you things to come" (Jn.16:13).

"But ye shall receive power, after that the Holy Ghost is come upon you: and ye shall be witnesses unto me both in Jerusalem, and in all Judaea, and in Samaria, and unto the uttermost part of the earth" (Ac.1:8).

"Then Peter said unto them, Repent, and be baptized every one of you in the name of Jesus Christ for the remission of sins, and ye shall receive the gift of the Holy Ghost" (Ac.2:38).

"But if the Spirit of him that raised up Jesus from the dead dwell in you, he that raised up Christ from the dead shall also quicken your mortal bodies by his Spirit that dwelleth in you" (Ro.8:11).

"The Spirit itself beareth witness with our spirit, that we are the children of God" (Ro.8:16).

"But the fruit of the Spirit is love, joy, peace, longsuffering, gentleness, goodness, faith, Meekness, temperance: against such there is no law" (Ga.5:22-23).

"But the anointing which ye have received of him abideth in you, and ye need not that any man teach you: but as the same anointing teacheth you of all things, and is truth, and is no lie, and even as it hath taught you, ye shall abide in him" (1 Jn.2:27).

DEEPER STUDY #1

(10:5, 10-11): **Prophecy—Prophesying—School, of the Prophets—Prophets, School of**: Samuel apparently founded a school to train young men to become prophets throughout the nation of Israel. Lawlessness and wickedness were running rampant throughout the society of Samuel's day, even among the priesthood. Consequently, there was a desperate need for prophets to be sent out across the nation, proclaiming the Word of God and challenging the people to repent and renew their relationship, their covenant with God.

Just when the first school for prophets was founded is unknown. But there is the possibility that Samuel remembered how meaningful his own training had been under his tutor Eli, the High Priest (see outline and notes—1 S.1:1-28; 2:12-36; 3:1-21 for more discussion). Thus, Samuel started the movement by gathering small bands of young men together for prophetic training in the Word of God and in the methods of ministering to God's people. Whatever the case, groups of prophets began to emerge during the rise of the kings and continued their prophetic training throughout the era of the monarchy. They were a refreshing alternative to the habitual rituals, cold ceremony, and formal worship of the priesthood. In the words of *The Expositor's Bible Commentary*:

> The bands of companies (vv.5, 10; 19:20; 2 Kings 2:15-17) were often large in number ("fifty," 2 Kings 2:7; "one hundred." 1 Kings 18:4, 13; 2 Kings 4:43). They were frequently associated with time-honored places, often at or near shrines, such as Ramah (19:18-20), Bethel (2 Kings 2:3), Jericho (2:5), and Gilgal (4:38).
>
> The characteristic activity of the prophetic bands was "prophesying" (v.5), usually interpreted in these contexts to mean "uttering ecstatic praises/oracles" or the like (BDB, Delitzsch, Klein). A strong case can be made in vv.5-13 and 19:20-24 however, for the meaning "being in" or "falling into a possession trance":
>
> > In the first passage the behavior is accompanied, perhaps fostered, by music. It is interpreted as a radical transformation of the personality, and may confer extraordinary powers on the person so affected. According to the second it may entail stripping off one's clothes, and may issue in a coma. In both its onset is described as an invasion, or at least as visitation, by a divine spirit. It is a group behavior and is contagious. It seems clear that we have to do with some kind of trance state, or altered state of consciousness. (Simon B. Parker, "Possession Trance and Prophecy in Pre-exilic Israel," VetTest 28, 3 [1978]: 272)....
>
> Individual or group prophesying, ecstatic or not, was often induced when the Spirit of the Lord came on a person in power (v.6; 19:20, 23; Num 11:25, 29). At such times the prophet would experience an altered state of consciousness and would be "changed into a different person" (cf. also v.9). Such ecstasy was often contagious.[4]

2 (10:9-16) **Conversion, Picture of—Transformation, Example of—Heart, Changed—Saul, Conversion of—Holy Spirit, Came upon—Prophecying, Example of—Humility, Example—Saul, Humility of**: Saul was transformed, given a new, changed heart by God. This is definitely a picture of Saul's spiritual conversion or either a significant moment of spiritual growth for Saul.[5] The Scripture graphically describes the experience of Saul:

OUTLINE	SCRIPTURE	SCRIPTURE	OUTLINE
2. Saul was transformed, given a new, changed heart by God: A picture of conversion a. The signs were fulfilled b. The Spirit of God came upon Saul in power & he prophesied 1) His prophesying in public bore strong testimony to his transformation, his change 2) His prophesying aroused one man to ask who the	9 And it was *so,* that when he had turned his back to go from Samuel, God gave him another heart: and all those signs came to pass that day. 10 And when they came thither to the hill, behold, a company of prophets met him; and the Spirit of God came upon him, and he prophesied among them. 11 And it came to pass, when all that knew him beforetime saw that, behold, he prophesied among the prophets, then the people said one to another, What *is* this *that is* come unto the son of Kish? *Is* Saul also among the prophets? 12 And one of the same place answered and said, But	who *is* their father? Therefore it became a proverb, *Is* Saul also among the prophets? 13 And when he had made an end of prophesying, he came to the high place. 14 And Saul's uncle said unto him and to his servant, Whither went ye? And he said, To seek the asses: and when we saw that *they were* no where, we came to Samuel. 15 And Saul's uncle said, Tell me, I pray thee, what Samuel said unto you. 16 And Saul said unto his uncle, He told us plainly that the asses were found. But of the matter of the kingdom, whereof Samuel spake, he told him not.	father or man was who could cause such a transformation c. The spirit of humility & wisdom gripped Saul 1) He went to worship 2) He humbly & wisely concealed from his relatives his private anointing as king • Guarded against pride • Trusted God to carry out His plan & timing through Samuel

a. All four signs predicted by Samuel were fulfilled that very day. But it was the fourth sign that was significant.

b. The Spirit of God came upon Saul in power, and he prophesied just as predicted (vv.10-12). As Saul was entering the city of Gibeah, the procession of prophets met him as predicted by Samuel. Immediately, the Spirit of God overpowered him, and he joined in their prophesying. Note how this bore a strong testimony to his transformation, his changed heart. People walking by or either standing around noted the change in Saul and began to question what exactly had happened to him. Had he now become a disciple of the prophets? One man who lived there in the city asked who the father or leader of the prophet was. He wondered who could bring about such a transformation, so powerful a change in the life of Saul. The change in this promising young man's life was so dramatic that the question became a proverb throughout the land: "Is Saul also among the prophets?"

c. After the experience, a spirit of humility and wisdom gripped Saul (vv.13-16). He immediately went up to worship, and then returned home. Note how he humbly and wisely concealed from his relatives the experience of being privately anointed as king (vv.14-16). Saul's uncle asked him and his servant where they had been. In reply, Saul simply said they had been looking for the donkeys, but when they could not find them, they went to Samuel for help. Hearing this, Saul's uncle asked him what Samuel had said. Saul simply replied that Samuel had assured them that the donkeys had been

---

4 Ronald F. Youngblood. *1 Samuel*, p.624-625.
5 *The Nelson Study Bible, NKJV*, 10:6.

found. He said nothing whatsoever about being anointed king of Israel. Note two simple facts: Saul guarded against pride and boasting, trusting God to carry out His plan and the timing to inform the public of his appointment as king.

Thought 1. A changed, transformed life—this is the will of God for every human being. If we are to conquer the trials and temptations, problems and difficulties of this life; if we are to be victorious over sin and wickedness, over enemies and those who attempt to defeat and destroy us; if we are to triumph over death and hell—we must be *converted*. We must be *born again* by the Spirit of God. This is the clear teaching of God's Holy Word.

"**And said, Verily I say unto you, Except ye be converted, and become as little children, ye shall not enter into the kingdom of heaven" (Mt.18:3).**

"**But as many as received him, to them gave he power to become the sons of God, even to them that believe on his name: Which were born, not of blood, nor of the will of the flesh, nor of the will of man, but of God" (Jn.1:12-13).**

"**Jesus answered and said unto him, Verily, verily, I say unto thee, Except a man be born again, he cannot see the kingdom of God" (Jn.3:3).**

"**Repent ye therefore, and be converted, that your sins may be blotted out, when the times of refreshing shall come from the presence of the Lord" (Ac.3:19).**

"**Therefore if any man be in Christ, he is a new creature: old things are passed away; behold, all things are become new" (2 Co.5:17).**

"**Not by works of righteousness which we have done, but according to his mercy he saved us, by the washing of regeneration, and renewing of the Holy Ghost" (Tit.3:5).**

"**Brethren, if any of you do err from the truth, and one convert him; Let him know, that he which converteth the sinner from the error of his way shall save a soul from death, and shall hide a multitude of sins" (Js.5:19-20).**

"**Being born again, not of corruptible seed, but of incorruptible, by the word of God, which liveth and abideth for ever" (1 Pe.1:23).**

"**For whatsoever is born of God overcometh the world: and this is the victory that overcometh the world, even our faith. Who is he that overcometh the world, but he that believeth that Jesus is the Son of God" (I Jn.5:4-5).**

"**A new heart also will I give you, and a new spirit will I put within you: and I will take away the stony heart out of your flesh, and I will give you an heart of flesh" (Eze.36:26).**

[3] (10:17-27) **Call, of God, Fleeing from—Ministry, Fleeing from—Service, Fleeing from—Minister, Inadequacy of—Service, Inadequacy of—King, Installation of—Saul, Installation as King**: Saul was publically installed as king. As quickly as he could, Samuel sent messengers all over Israel to summon the leaders and people to Mizpah. There they would meet for the installation service of their first king. Saul had already experienced a private anointing by Samuel that was for his own personal benefit and encouragement, assuring him that he was definitely God's appointed king. But now, it was time for Saul to be publically proclaimed and installed as the first king of Israel. What happened is most interesting:

OUTLINE	SCRIPTURE	SCRIPTURE	OUTLINE

3. Saul was publicly installed as king: A picture of feeling unfit & fleeing from God's call
a. The charge of Samuel against the Israelites
  1) The LORD had saved them from Egypt & all other enemies: A symbol of deliverance from the world & its bondages
 	
  2) They were now rejecting God—His rule (as their Savior, Guide, Protector, & Provider)—& choosing to be ruled by an earthly king, 8:10-18
 	
b. The choosing of a king by lot
  1) The tribe of Benjamin was chosen
	17 And Samuel called the people together unto the LORD to Mizpeh;
	18 And said unto the children of Israel, Thus saith the LORD God of Israel, I brought up Israel out of Egypt, and delivered you out of the hand of the Egyptians, and out of the hand of all kingdoms, *and* of them that oppressed you:
	19 And ye have this day rejected your God, who himself saved you out of all your adversities and your tribulations; and ye have said unto him, *Nay,* but set a king over us. Now therefore present yourselves before the LORD by your tribes, and by your thousands.
	20 And when Samuel had caused all the tribes of Israel to come near, the tribe of Benjamin was taken.
		21 When he had caused the tribe of Benjamin to come near by their families, the family of Matri was taken, and Saul the son of Kish was taken: and when they sought him, he could not be found.
		22 Therefore they enquired of the LORD further, if the man should yet come thither. And the LORD answered, Behold, he hath hid himself among the stuff.
		23 And they ran and fetched him thence: and when he stood among the people, he was higher than any of the people from his shoulders and upward.
		24 And Samuel said to all the people, See ye him whom the LORD hath chosen, that *there is* none like him among all the people? And all the people shouted, and said,
			2) The LORD directed the lots to fall upon Saul
			
			c. The fleeing from God's call by Saul: He could not be found
			  1) The LORD led the leaders to Saul's hiding place
			
			  2) The leaders presented him to the people: He stood a head taller than anyone else, an impressive height & appearance, 9:2
			
			d. The presentation & the public acclamation of Saul as king

OUTLINE	SCRIPTURE	SCRIPTURE	OUTLINE
e. The regulations to govern the king 1) Were written down by Samuel 2) Were placed in the Tabernacle: A symbol that the regulations & God's Word were to govern the king f. The meeting adjourned &	God save the king. 25 Then Samuel told the people the manner of the kingdom, and wrote *it* in a book, and laid *it* up before the LORD. And Samuel sent all the people away, every man to his house. 26 And Saul also went home	to Gibeah; and there went with him a band of men, whose hearts God had touched. 27 But the children of Belial said, How shall this man save us? And they despised him, and brought him no presents. But he held his peace.	the response to Saul's appointment as king 1) Some valiant men escorted Saul: Stirred by God to be his personal (honor) guard 2) Some troublemakers despised Saul: Rejected his kingship: Saul did not react or have them executed

a. Surprisingly, as soon as the leaders and people had assembled for the installation service, Samuel leveled a strong charge against the Israelites (vv.18-19). The LORD had given Samuel a very special message for the people, a message of severe condemnation, a strong indictment against them. Samuel declared that the LORD had saved them from Egypt and delivered them from all the surrounding kings who had oppressed them. But now, tragically, they had rejected God. Ever since their deliverance from Egypt, God had been their Ruler, their Savior and Guide, their Protector. But now here they were, demanding to be ruled by an earthly king, demanding that their deliverance and provision be dependent upon an earthly ruler.

Nevertheless, God would not reject their demand: they would be given their earthly ruler. They would be allowed to live under the dominating authority of an earthly king. Thus, Samuel called upon the people to present themselves before the LORD by their tribes and clans or families.

b. After the people had gathered together by their tribes and clans, Samuel began to choose the king by lot (v.21). Obviously, this act was carried out for the sake of the people—to publically substantiate that Saul was definitely God's anointed choice to be king. Samuel already knew the fact, but the public needed clear evidence. Thus, Samuel cast the sacred lots, depending upon God to publically indicate that Saul was His choice. At the first casting of the lots, the tribe of Benjamin was chosen. Then with each cast, clan by clan and family by family were eliminated until, finally, Saul was chosen. The LORD directed the lots to fall upon His appointed choice to be the first king of Israel, the young man Saul.

c. But note what had happened: Saul had fled from God's call. He could not be found (v.21). Even after an extensive search, he still could not be found. The leaders had no choice but to seek the LORD as to his whereabouts. Somehow, the LORD gave indication that he was hiding in the baggage or equipment storage area (v.22). Hearing this, some of the leaders ran and brought him out, presenting him to the people. As Saul stood there, he stood a head taller than anyone else, an impressive height and appearance (v.23).

d. Samuel then made the public presentation and acclamation of Saul as king. No doubt standing upon a platform or elevated spot, he cried out for the multitude to look and see the man the LORD had chosen. There was no one like him among the people, no one who stood head and shoulders above others, presenting such an impressive, charasmatic appearance. At this, the people shouted out: "God save the king" or "Long live the king."

e. Samuel then explained the regulations that were to govern the king of Israel (v.25). There was a dire need to clearly spell out the difference between the king of God's people and the kings of the surrounding nations. God's king was to rule under the authority of God and His holy commandments. Just what were the regulations that Samuel explained to the people? Scripture does not say, but most likely they included instructions of the LORD given earlier by Moses and Samuel himself (De.17:14-20; 1 Sam.8:11-18). Note that the regulations were written down by Samuel and then placed in the Tabernacle. This was a clear symbol that the regulations in God's Word were to govern the king.

f. Samuel then adjourned the meeting and dismissed the people to return home. Saul returned to his home in Gibeah, which became the temporary capital city of Israel. Note that some valiant men accompanied Saul, stirred by God to become his personal honor guard (v.26). However, scattered throughout the nation, there were some troublemakers who despised Saul and rejected his kingship (v.27). Scripture calls them "sons of Belial," which means wicked men, scoundrels or men under the control and influence of the devil. These men refused to bring gifts and pay honor to Saul. But Saul, showing patience, did not react. He did not have them executed. Instead, he kept silent and ignored them.

Thought 1. Saul ran from the call of God. No doubt he felt inadequate, insufficient, unqualified for the task. In his flight and feelings of inadequacy, he is a picture of so many who flee from God's call. Within every community and church, and practically every family, God has called some persons to reach out and minister to others. Often, He has called persons to serve full time in the church. Others have been called to the great cause of world evangelism and service. But in many cases, individuals have fled from God's call, hiding themselves and refusing to surrender their lives to the LORD. But the Holy Bible warns:

"And every one that heareth these sayings of mine, and doeth them not, shall be likened unto a foolish man, which built his house upon the sand: And the rain descended, and the floods came, and the winds blew, and beat upon that house; and it fell: and great was the fall of it" (Mt.7:26-27).

"Therefore say I unto you, The kingdom of God shall be taken from you, and given to a nation bringing forth the fruits thereof" (Mt.21:43).

"Then he which had received the one talent came and said, Lord, I knew thee that thou art an hard man, reaping where thou hast not sown, and gathering where thou hast not strawed: And I was afraid, and went and hid thy talent in the earth: lo, there thou hast that is thine. His lord answered and said unto him, Thou wicked and slothful servant, thou knewest that I reap where I sowed not, and gather where I have not strawed: Thou oughtest therefore to have put my money to the exchangers, and then at my coming I should have received mine own with usury. Take therefore the talent from him, and give it unto him which hath ten talents. For unto every one that hath shall be given, and he shall have abundance: but from him that hath not shall be taken away even that which he hath. And cast ye the unprofitable servant into outer darkness: there shall be weeping and gnashing of teeth" (Mt.25:24-30).

"And he said unto them, Why are ye so fearful? how is it that ye have no faith" (Mk.4:40).

"And that servant, which knew his lord's will, and prepared not himself, neither did according to his will, shall be beaten with many stripes" (Lu.12:47).

"Then said he unto him, A certain man made a great supper, and bade many: And sent his servant at supper time to say to them that were bidden, Come; for all things are now ready. And they all with one consent began to make excuse. The first said unto him, I have bought a piece of ground, and I must needs go and see it: I pray thee have me excused. And another said, I have bought five yoke of oxen, and I go to prove them: I pray thee have me excused. And another said, I have married a wife, and therefore I cannot come. So that servant came, and showed his lord these things. Then the master of the house being angry said to his servant, Go out quickly into the streets and lanes of the city, and bring in hither the poor, and the maimed, and the halt, and the blind. And the servant said, Lord, it is done as thou hast commanded, and yet there is room. And the lord said unto the servant, Go out into the highways and hedges, and compel them to come in, that my house may be filled. For I say unto you, That none of those men which were bidden shall taste of my supper" (Lu.14:16-24).

"What doth it profit, my brethren, though a man say he hath faith, and have not works? can faith save him" (Js.2:14).

"Therefore to him that knoweth to do good, and doeth it not, to him it is sin" (Js.4:17).

CHAPTER 11

D. The First Military Victory of Saul & His Affirmation As King: Gaining Victory over One's Enemies, 11:1-15

1. The Ammonite siege & cruel threat against Jabesh-Gilead: A picture of the cruel persecution of believers by unbelievers
a. The Israelites attempted to surrender

b. The cruel condition demanded by Nahash: That the right eye of everyone be gouged out
  1) To disgrace all Israel as weak & cowardly
  2) To hamper their sight, prevent a future revolt
c. The appeal of the leaders of Jabesh

2. The mobilization of Israel's army by Saul: A picture of righteous anger & victory over enemies who besiege us
a. A report of the siege was sent to Saul
  1) He was just returning from plowing the fields
  2) He saw the people weeping & asked why

b. A spirit of righteous anger burned within Saul at the news: The Spirit of God came upon him
c. A graphic message was sent by Saul to all Israel
  1) He cut up two oxen
  2) He sent a piece to each tribe with the demand that the army be mobilized
  3) The results:
    • The fear of the LORD gripped the people

Then Nahash the Ammonite came up, and encamped against Jabesh-gilead: and all the men of Jabesh said unto Nahash, Make a covenant with us, and we will serve thee.
2 And Nahash the Ammonite answered them, On this *condition* will I make *a covenant* with you, that I may thrust out all your right eyes, and lay it *for* a reproach upon all Israel.
3 And the elders of Jabesh said unto him, Give us seven days' respite, that we may send messengers unto all the coasts of Israel: and then, if *there be* no man to save us, we will come out to thee.
4 Then came the messengers to Gibeah of Saul, and told the tidings in the ears of the people: and all the people lifted up their voices, and wept.
5 And, behold, Saul came after the herd out of the field; and Saul said, What *aileth* the people that they weep? And they told him the tidings of the men of Jabesh.
6 And the Spirit of God came upon Saul when he heard those tidings, and his anger was kindled greatly.
7 And he took a yoke of oxen, and hewed them in pieces, and sent *them* throughout all the coasts of Israel by the hands of messengers, saying, Whosoever cometh not forth after Saul and after Samuel, so shall it be done unto his oxen. And the fear of the LORD fell on

the people, and they came out with one consent.
8 And when he numbered them in Bezek, the children of Israel were three hundred thousand, and the men of Judah thirty thousand.
9 And they said unto the messengers that came, Thus shall ye say unto the men of Jabesh-gilead, To morrow, by *that time* the sun be hot, ye shall have help. And the messengers came and showed *it* to the men of Jabesh; and they were glad.
10 Therefore the men of Jabesh said, To morrow we will come out unto you, and ye shall do with us all that seemeth good unto you.
11 And it was *so* on the morrow, that Saul put the people in three companies; and they came into the midst of the host in the morning watch, and slew the Ammonites until the heat of the day: and it came to pass, that they which remained were scattered, so that two of them were not left together.
12 And the people said unto Samuel, Who *is* he that said, Shall Saul reign over us? bring the men, that we may put them to death.
13 And Saul said, There shall not a man be put to death this day: for to day the LORD hath wrought salvation in Israel.
14 Then said Samuel to the people, Come, and let us go to Gilgal, and renew the kingdom there.
15 And all the people went to Gilgal; and there they made Saul king before the LORD in Gilgal; and there they sacrificed sacrifices of peace offerings before the LORD; and there Saul and all the men of Israel rejoiced greatly.

• A large army was mobilized: Numbered 330,000

d. A message of support & assurance was sent back to the leaders of Jabesh-Gilead: They would be rescued the next day

e. A brilliant military plan & trap were launched by Saul
  1) He had the leaders of Jabesh give false security to the Ammonites
  2) He separated his men into three divisions
  3) He secretly attacked at night: During the third watch (3-6 am)
f. A glorious victory was achieved: The Ammonites were routed & totally defeated

3. The forgiving spirit of Saul & his reaffirmation as king: The picture of a forgiving spirit & of supporting God's leader
a. The people made a threat against Saul's opposition
b. Saul demonstrated a dynamic example of forgiveness

c. Samuel suggested that Saul be reaffirmed as king at Gilgal
d. Saul was reconfirmed as king by all the people
e. Saul & the people worshipped & rejoiced greatly: Sacrificed peace or fellowship offerings, Le.3

DIVISION II

THE STORY OF SAMUEL AND SAUL: THE LORD GIVES ISRAEL A KING JUST "LIKE ALL THE NATIONS," 8:1–15:35

D. The First Military Victory of Saul and His Affirmation As King: Gaining Victory over One's Enemies, 11:1-15

(11:1-15) **Introduction—Tongue, Evils of—Enemies, Evil of—Victorious Life, Need for**: gossip, slander, ridicule, backbiting, belittling, grumbling, murmuring, complaining—all of these are evils of the tongue. And sometimes, unfortunately, people use their tongues to launch these evils against us, taking a stand as enemies against us. But enemies who oppose us will sometimes use not only their tongues but also physical attacks such as assault, rape, abuse, and even murder. But even this is not all that an enemy will do. An enemy will steal from us, lie about us, and do all he can to oppress us.

What are we to do when an enemy attacks? When a person seeks to harm us either verbally or physically, how can we conquer the attack and overcome the situation? How can we be victorious over our enemies? The answer will be found in this present passage of Holy Scripture.

Almost immediately after Saul was appointed king, a distant region of Israel was attacked by one of its archenemies, the Ammonites. Saul mobilized the army and defeated the Ammonites. Studying his conquest, we can learn how to gain victory over all enemies who oppress us and seek to defeat us. This is: *The First Military Victory of Saul and His Affirmation As King: Gaining Victory over One's Enemies,* 11:1-15.

1. The Ammonite siege and cruel threat against Jabesh-Gilead: a picture of the cruel persecution of believers by unbelievers (vv.1-3).
2. The mobilization of Israel's army by Saul: a picture of righteous anger and victory over enemies who besiege us (vv.4-11).
3. The forgiving spirit of Saul and his reaffirmation as king: the picture of a forgiving spirit and of supporting God's leader (vv.12-15).

---

1 (11:1-3) **Persecution, Example of—Siege, of Jabesh-Gilead—Jabesh-Gilead, Siege of—Ammonites, Wars Against Israel—Nahash, King of the Ammonites**: there was the Ammonite siege and threat against Jabesh-Gilead. Jabesh-Gilead was an important city within the tribe of Manasseh that was located on the east side of the Jordan River. The Ammonites were desert marauders or raiders who controlled the territory east of Gad and Manasseh. They were descendants of Lot who became fierce, cruel enemies of the Israelites. An example of their cruelty is seen in the present passage:

OUTLINE	SCRIPTURE	SCRIPTURE	OUTLINE
1. The Ammonite siege & cruel threat against Jabesh-Gilead: A picture of the cruel persecution of believers by unbelievers a. The Israelites attempted to surrender b. The cruel condition demanded by Nahash: That the right eye of everyone be gouged out	Then Nahash the Ammonite came up, and encamped against Jabesh-gilead: and all the men of Jabesh said unto Nahash, Make a covenant with us, and we will serve thee. 2 And Nahash the Ammonite answered them, On this *condition* will I make *a covenant* with you, that I may	thrust out all your right eyes, and lay it *for* a reproach upon all Israel. 3 And the elders of Jabesh said unto him, Give us seven days' respite, that we may send messengers unto all the coasts of Israel: and then, if *there be* no man to save us, we will come out to thee.	1) To disgrace all Israel as weak & cowardly 2) To hamper their sight, prevent a future revolt c. The appeal of the leaders of Jabesh

a. When the Ammonites set up a siege around Jabesh-Gilead, the city was helpless and unable to defend itself against the massive army of the enemy. Consequently, the city attempted to surrender, offering to sign a treaty whereby they would become subjects of the Ammonites.

b. But note the cruel condition by Nahash, the Ammonite king. He would agree to a treaty only on the condition that he gouge out the right eye of all the citizens (v.2). His stated purpose for this condition was to disgrace all Israel as weak and cowardly. However, the king also knew that blindness in one eye would handicap the men and help prevent any future revolt. Partial blindness would almost ensure the continued subjection of Jabesh-Gilead to the Ammonites.

c. Hearing this cruel condition, the leaders of Jabesh-Gilead made two appeals to the Ammonite king:
⇒ that they have seven days to consider the condition
⇒ that they be allowed to send messengers appealing to the rest of Israel for help to defend themselves

No doubt, King Nahash was confident of his military superiority and confident that the Israelites would not rally to the support of Jabesh-Gilead, for he agreed to this appeal. For these two reasons and to prevent from having to fight and deplete his own military resources, he allowed the leaders of Jabesh to send messages throughout Israel. Most likely, he was also convinced that any army the Israelites could mobilize against him would meet with defeat and that defeating a larger army would only mean more spoils and wealth for his own people. Whatever his reason, King Nahash agreed to the proposal and made a deadly miscalculation. [1]

Thought 1. The Ammonite siege against the city of Jabesh is a clear picture of unbelievers persecuting believers. A true follower of Jesus Christ will be persecuted, for the true follower will live a righteous life and bear strong testimony for Christ. And many unbelievers want nothing to do with righteousness nor with Christ. They stand opposed to righteousness, choosing to live as they wish, pleasing their flesh and living lives given over to sexual immorality, impurity, partying, drunkenness, debauchery, false worship, dissension, hatred, jealousy, selfish ambition, orgies, and deceptions that depend upon the world of the occult and of the zodiac.

When the believer lives and proclaims the righteousness of God, many unbelievers will oppose him. Unbelievers will ridicule, mock, curse, and downplay the message of righteousness and the witness for Christ. And sometimes, the reaction of unbelievers against believers is that of physical persecution, involving imprisonment or assault or even death.

---

[1] Robert D. Bergen. *1, 2 Samuel*, p.136.

"Blessed are ye, when *men* shall revile you, and persecute *you,* and shall say all manner of evil against you falsely, for my sake" (Mt.5:11).

"But beware of men: for they will deliver you up to the councils, and they will scourge you in their synagogues; And ye shall be brought before governors and kings for my sake, for a testimony against them and the Gentiles. But when they deliver you up, take no thought how or what ye shall speak: for it shall be given you in that same hour what ye shall speak. For it is not ye that speak, but the Spirit of your Father which speaketh in you. And the brother shall deliver up the brother to death, and the father the child: and the children shall rise up against *their* parents, and cause them to be put to death. And ye shall be hated of all *men* for my name's sake: but he that endureth to the end shall be saved" (Mt.10:17-22).

"And ye shall be hated of all *men* for my name's sake: but he that endureth to the end shall be saved" (Mt.10:22).

"And every one that hath forsaken houses, or brethren, or sisters, or father, or mother, or wife, or children, or lands, for my name's sake, shall receive an hundredfold, and shall inherit everlasting life" (Mt.19:29).

"Then shall they deliver you up to be afflicted, and shall kill you: and ye shall be hated of all nations for my name's sake" (Mt.24:9).

"Blessed are ye, when men shall hate you, and when they shall separate you *from their company,* and shall reproach *you,* and cast out your name as evil, for the Son of man's sake" (Lu.6:22).

"Remember the word that I said unto you, The servant is not greater than his lord. If they have persecuted me, they will also persecute you; if they have kept my saying, they will keep yours also" (Jn.15:20).

"They shall put you out of the synagogues: yea, the time cometh, that whosoever killeth you will think that he doeth God service" (Jn.16:2).

"And they departed from the presence of the council, rejoicing that they were counted worthy to suffer shame for his name" (Ac.5:41).

"The Spirit itself beareth witness with our spirit, that we are the children of God: And if children, then heirs; heirs of God, and joint-heirs with Christ; if so be that we suffer with *him,* that we may be also glorified together" (Ro.8:16-17).

"For unto you it is given in the behalf of Christ, not only to believe on him, but also to suffer for his sake" (Ph.1:29).

"Always bearing about in the body the dying of the LORD Jesus, that the life also of Jesus might be made manifest in our body" (2 Co.4:10).

"Yea, and all that will live godly in Christ Jesus shall suffer persecution" (2 Ti.3:12).

"For therefore we both labour and suffer reproach, because we trust in the living God, who is the Saviour of all men, specially of those that believe" (1 Ti.4:10).

"By faith Moses, when he was come to years, refused to be called the son of Pharaoh's daughter; Choosing rather to suffer affliction with the people of God, than to enjoy the pleasures of sin for a season; Esteeming the reproach of Christ greater riches than the treasures in Egypt: for he had respect unto the recompence of the reward" (He.11:24-26).

"Take, my brethren, the prophets, who have spoken in the name of the LORD, for an example of suffering affliction, and of patience" (Js.5:10).

"For what glory *is it,* if, when ye be buffeted for your faults, ye shall take it patiently? but if, when ye do well, and suffer *for it,* ye take it patiently, this *is* acceptable with God" (1 Pe.2:20).

"If ye be reproached for the name of Christ, happy *are ye;* for the spirit of glory and of God resteth upon you: on their part he is evil spoken of, but on your part he is glorified" (1 Pe.4:14).

"But the God of all grace, who hath called us unto his eternal glory by Christ Jesus, after that ye have suffered a while, make you perfect, stablish, strengthen, settle *you*" (1 Pe.5:10).

"Fear none of those things which thou shalt suffer: behold, the devil shall cast *some* of you into prison, that ye may be tried; and ye shall have tribulation ten days: be thou faithful unto death, and I will give thee a crown of life" (Re.2:10).

"My times *are* in thy hand: deliver me from the hand of mine enemies, and from them that persecute me" (Ps.31:15).

O LORD my God, in thee do I put my trust: save me from all them that persecute me, and deliver me" (Ps.7:1).

"Many are my persecutors and mine enemies; yet do I not decline from thy testimonies" (Ps.119:157).

2 (11:4-11) **Anger, Righteous—Victory, over Enemies—Conquest, over Enemies—Israel, Victory over Enemies—Saul, Conquest of—Ammonites, Defeat of**: there was Saul's mobilization of Israel's army to march against the Ammonites. This is a dramatic description of the first military victory of Saul:

OUTLINE	SCRIPTURE	SCRIPTURE	OUTLINE
2. The mobilization of Israel's army by Saul: A picture of righteous anger & victory over enemies who besiege us a. A report of the siege was sent to Saul	4 Then came the messengers to Gibeah of Saul, and told the tidings in the ears of the people: and all the people lifted up their voices, and wept.	5 And, behold, Saul came after the herd out of the field; and Saul said, What *aileth* the people that they weep? And they told him the tidings of the men of Jabesh.	1) He was just returning from plowing the fields 2) He saw the people weeping & asked why

OUTLINE	SCRIPTURE	SCRIPTURE	OUTLINE

b. A spirit of righteous anger burned within Saul at the news: The Spirit of God came upon him
c. A graphic message was sent by Saul to all Israel
   1) He cut up two oxen
   2) He sent a piece to each tribe with the demand that the army be mobilized
   3) The results:
   • The fear of the LORD gripped the people
 	
   • A large army was mobilized: Numbered 330,000
 	
d. A message of support & assurance was sent back to the
	6 And the Spirit of God came upon Saul when he heard those tidings, and his anger was kindled greatly. 7 And he took a yoke of oxen, and hewed them in pieces, and sent *them* throughout all the coasts of Israel by the hands of messengers, saying, Whosoever cometh not forth after Saul and after Samuel, so shall it be done unto his oxen. And the fear of the LORD fell on the people, and they came out with one consent. 8 And when he numbered them in Bezek, the children of Israel were three hundred thousand, and the men of Judah thirty thousand. 9 And they said unto the messengers that came, Thus	shall ye say unto the men of Jabesh-gilead, To morrow, by *that time* the sun be hot, ye shall have help. And the messengers came and showed *it* to the men of Jabesh; and they were glad. 10 Therefore the men of Jabesh said, To morrow we will come out unto you, and ye shall do with us all that seemeth good unto you. 11 And it was *so* on the morrow, that Saul put the people in three companies; and they came into the midst of the host in the morning watch, and slew the Ammonites until the heat of the day: and it came to pass, that they which remained were scattered, so that two of them were not left together.	leaders of Jabesh-Gilead: They would be rescued the next day
			
			e. A brilliant military plan & trap were launched by Saul
			   1) He had the leaders of Jabesh give false security to the Ammonites
			   2) He separated his men into three divisions
			   3) He secretly attacked at night: During the third watch (3-6 am)
			f. A glorious victory was achieved: The Ammonites were routed & totally defeated

a. As soon as the leaders of Jabesh-Gilead were able, they sent messengers to Saul, informing him of the siege by the Ammonites (vv.4-5). Note that Saul had been out in the fields working despite the fact that he had been appointed king. Right after his appointment, he had returned home to wait for the LORD's leadership as to what he should do next (10:7, 26). As he was returning from plowing the fields, he saw the people in the city weeping and asked what was wrong with them and why they were weeping.

b. After being told about the siege of the Ammonites, a spirit of righteous anger burned within Saul at the news. Then the Spirit of God came upon him in power, and he made the immediate decision to mobilize the army and march (v.6).

c. Saul issued a call all across the nation for the troops to report for duty, and he used a graphic picture to coerce the troops to mobilize (v.7). He cut up two oxen and sent a piece to each tribe with the demand that they mobilize their troops. If anyone failed to follow Saul and Samuel in battle, then that person's oxen would be slaughtered just as Saul had slaughtered his two oxen as a warning (see Jud.19:29; 20:6 for a similar act carried out by a Levite). The result of Saul's dramatic picture was just what he had hoped to achieve: the fear of the LORD gripped the people and the troops—a large army numbering 330,000 soldiers—mobilized at Bezek.

d. After the army had gathered, a message of support and assurance was immediately sent back to the leaders of Jabesh, stating that they would be rescued the very next day at high noon (v.9).

e. Saul had planned a brilliant military strategy, a strategy that included deception and a surprise attack at night (vv.10-11). He had the leaders of Jabesh give false security to King Nahash by informing him that they would surrender and become subjects of the Ammonites the next day. While the leaders of Jabesh were carrying out the deceptive strategy against the Ammonites, Saul was separating his men into three divisions for a surprise attack (v.11). At the start of the next day, Saul launched his surprise attack during the early morning hours of the third watch, which was somewhere between 3:00 and 6:00 a.m.

f. A glorious victory was achieved as the soldiers fiercely fought until the heat of the day, approximately noon. The Ammonites were eventually routed, so totally defeated that no two of them were left standing or fleeing together.

Thought 1. There are two striking lessons for us in this point:

(1) Saul was gripped by righteous anger, an anger that was aroused by the Spirit of God Himself. His anger burned against the Ammonites because of their cruel, savage threats against the city of Jabesh.

A righteous anger should always be aroused against evil. We should be angered every time we see people mistreating others. A righteous indignation should swell up within our hearts against...

- abuse
- assault
- murder
- adultery
- extortion

- stealing, shoplifting
- lying
- deception
- slothful work
- ridicule

- mockery
- gossip
- false accusations
- drunkenness, drunk driving
- drug addiction

The list of evil behaviors could go on and on. But the point is well made: a righteous anger or indignation should arise within our hearts against all evil, against all mistreatment of other people. This is the clear declaration of Holy Scripture.

"Be ye angry, and sin not: let not the sun go down upon your wrath" (Ep.4:26).

"And it came to pass, as soon as he came nigh unto the camp, that he saw the calf, and the dancing: and Moses' anger waxed hot, and he cast the tables out of his hands, and brake them beneath the mount" (Ex.32:19).

"And Moses diligently sought the goat of the sin offering, and, behold, it was burnt: and he was angry with Eleazar and Ithamar, the sons of Aaron *which were* left *alive,* saying, Wherefore have ye not eaten the sin offering in the holy place, seeing it *is* most holy, and *God* hath given it you to bear the iniquity of the congregation, to make atonement for them before the LORD? Behold, the blood of it was not brought in within the holy *place:* ye should indeed have eaten it in the holy *place,* as I commanded" (Le.10:16-18).

"And I was very angry when I heard their cry and these words. Then I consulted with myself, and I rebuked the nobles, and the rulers, and said unto them, Ye exact usury, every one of his brother. And I set a great assembly against them" (Ne.5:6-7).

(2) The power of God's Spirit came upon Saul, and he achieved a glorious victory over the enemies who had besieged the city of Jabesh. So it is with genuine believers. The Spirit of God gives power to conquer the enemies that oppress us. Just think of the enemies that attack us, seeking either to enslave or to destroy us...

- illicit sexual pleasure
- pornographic films
- pornographic literature
- violent and immoral television programs
- greed
- selfishness
- uncontrolled thoughts

- hatred
- disease
- depression
- discouragement
- purposelessness
- hopelessness
- helplessness

- financial difficulty
- bigotry
- prejudice
- discrimination
- slander
- gossip
- false accusations

There are numerous enemies that confront us throughout life, enemies ranging from people to personal emotions to events that cause all kinds of problems for us. Any of these can overwhelm and defeat us. And in some cases, they can even kill us or cause premature death.

But there is hope, wonderful hope through the power of God's Spirit. By His power, we can conquer the enemies that besiege and oppress us. We can be victorious and triumphant over all the enemies of this life.

"These things I have spoken unto you, that in me ye might have peace. In the world ye shall have tribulation: but be of good cheer; I have overcome the world" (Jn.16:33).

"Who shall separate us from the love of Christ? *shall* tribulation, or distress, or persecution, or famine, or nakedness, or peril, or sword....Nay, in all these things we are more than conquerors through him that loved us. For I am persuaded, that neither death, nor life, nor angels, nor principalities, nor powers, nor things present, nor things to come, Nor height, nor depth, nor any other creature, shall be able to separate us from the love of God, which is in Christ Jesus our LORD" (Ro.8:35, 37-39).

"There hath no temptation taken you but such as is common to man: but God *is* faithful, who will not suffer you to be tempted above that ye are able; but will with the temptation also make a way to escape, that ye may be able to bear *it*" (1 Co.10:13).

"Now thanks *be* unto God, which always causeth us to triumph in Christ, and maketh manifest the savour of his knowledge by us in every place" (2 Co.2:14).

"Wherefore take unto you the whole armour of God, that ye may be able to withstand in the evil day, and having done all, to stand" (Ep.6:13).

"For whatsoever is born of God overcometh the world: and this is the victory that overcometh the world, *even* our faith. Who is he that overcometh the world, but he that believeth that Jesus is the Son of God" (1 Jn.5:4-5).

"Through thee will we push down our enemies: through thy name will we tread them under that rise up against us" (Ps.44:5).

"The LORD shall fight for you, and ye shall hold your peace" (Ex.14:14).

"With him *is* an arm of flesh; but with us *is* the LORD our God to help us, and to fight our battles. And the people rested themselves upon the words of Hezekiah king of Judah" (2 Chr.32:8).

3 (11:12-15) **Forgiveness, of Others—Leaders, Duty Toward—Support, of Leaders—Saul, Kingship of, Reaffirmed**: there was the forgiving spirit of Saul and his reaffirmation as king. After the decisive victory over the Ammonites, excitement and joy filled the air of the Israelite camp. A strong conviction gripped the heart of the army, the conviction that Saul was definitely God's choice to be king. Thus, the military wanted all the citizens to commit their loyalty to Saul as king and to the new form of government. Note what happened:

OUTLINE	SCRIPTURE	SCRIPTURE	OUTLINE
3. The forgiving spirit of Saul & his reaffirmation as king: The picture of a forgiving spirit & of supporting God's leader a. The people made a threat against Saul's opposition	12 And the people said unto Samuel, Who *is* he that said, Shall Saul reign over us? bring the men, that we may put them to death.	13 And Saul said, There shall not a man be put to death this day: for to day the LORD hath wrought salvation in Israel. 14 Then said Samuel to the	b. Saul demonstrated a dynamic example of forgiveness c. Samuel suggested that Saul

OUTLINE	SCRIPTURE	SCRIPTURE	OUTLINE
be reaffirmed as king at Gil-gal	people, Come, and let us go to Gilgal, and renew the kingdom there.	Saul king before the LORD in Gilgal; and there they sacri-ficed sacrifices of peace of-	e. Saul & the people wor-shipped & rejoiced greatly: Sacrificed peace or fellow-
d. Saul was reconfirmed as king by all the people	15 And all the people went to Gilgal; and there they made	ferings before the LORD; and there Saul and all the men of	ship offerings, Le.3

a. Some soldiers—apparently some military officers—made a threat against the men who had originally opposed Saul as king (vv.12; 10:27).

b. But Saul set a dynamic example of forgiveness and of bearing strong testimony to God's deliverance (v.13). He re-sponded to the officers, declaring that no one would be put to death that day, for it was the day the LORD had rescued Is-rael. In making this decision, Saul demonstrated godly character and statesmanlike conduct and ability.

c. Being present, Samuel saw a unique opportunity to unify the nation. He could use the victory and the excitement of the troops to rally the entire nation to support both the new king and the new order of government now instituted in Israel. So, Samuel suggested that Saul be reaffirmed as king at Gilgal (v.14). With one stroke, the monarchy—the kingship it-self—could be firmly established and solidified in the minds of the Israelites.

d. All Israel responded to the summons to assemble at Gilgal and confirm Saul as king (v.15). Note that he was con-firmed "before the LORD" or "in the presence of the LORD," and that the people worshipped by sacrificing fellowship of-ferings before the LORD. Most likely, this points toward a renewing of the covenant between the people and the LORD, a renewing of their commitment to obey the commandments of the LORD and to follow His newly appointed king.

Thought 1. Two lessons can be gleaned from this point.
(1) Saul demonstrated a dynamic example of forgiveness, of forgiving some troublemakers who despised him (10:27). In the Holy Bible, God commands that we forgive others. If we harden our hearts and refuse to forgive others, God declares that He will not forgive us.

> **"But I say unto you, Love your enemies, bless them that curse you, do good to them that hate you, and pray for them which despitefully use you, and persecute you" (Mt.5:44).**
> **"For if ye forgive men their trespasses, your heavenly Father will also forgive you: But if ye forgive not men their trespasses, neither will your Father forgive your trespasses" (Mt.6:14-15).**
> **"But I say unto you which hear, Love your enemies, do good to them which hate you....But love ye your enemies, and do good, and lend, hoping for nothing again; and your reward shall be great, and ye shall be the children of the Highest: for he is kind unto the unthankful and *to the* evil" (Lu.6:27, 35).**
> **"And if he trespass against thee seven times in a day, and seven times in a day turn again to thee, saying, I repent; thou shalt forgive him" (Lu.17:4).**
> **"And when ye stand praying, forgive, if ye have ought against any: that your Father also which is in heaven may forgive you your trespasses" (Mk.11:25).**
> **"Therefore if thine enemy hunger, feed him; if he thirst, give him drink: for in so doing thou shalt heap coals of fire on his head" (Ro.12:20).**
> **"And be ye kind one to another, tenderhearted, forgiving one another, even as God for Christ's sake hath forgiven you" (Ep.4:32).**
> **"Forbearing one another, and forgiving one another, if any man have a quarrel against any: even as Christ forgave you, so also *do* ye" (Col.3:13).**
> **"See that none render evil for evil unto any *man;* but ever follow that which is good, both among yourselves, and to all *men*" (1 Th.5:15).**
> **"If thine enemy be hungry, give him bread to eat; and if he be thirsty, give him water to drink" (Pr.25:21).**

(2) The Israelites were called upon to support God's leader, King Saul. So it is with us: we are expected to support and honor our leaders throughout society, both secular and religious leaders. This is the clear declaration of the Holy Bible:

> **"Let every soul be subject unto the higher powers. For there is no power but of God: the pow-ers that be are ordained of God" (Ro.13:1).**
> **"Receive him therefore in the LORD with all gladness; and hold such in reputation" (Ph.2:29).**
> **"That ye submit yourselves unto such, and to every one that helpeth with *us,* and laboureth" (1 Co.16:16).**
> **"And we beseech you, brethren, to know them which labour among you, and are over you in the LORD, and admonish you; And to esteem them [all leaders] very highly in love for their work's sake. *And* be at peace among yourselves" (1 Th.5:12-13).**
> **"Let the elders that rule well be counted worthy of double honour, especially they who labour in the word and doctrine" (1 Ti.5:17).**
> **"Put them in mind to be subject to principalities and powers, to obey magistrates, to be ready to every good work" (Tit.3:1).**

"Remember them which have the rule over you, who have spoken unto you the word of God: whose faith follow, considering the end of *their* conversation [conduct, behavior]" (He.13:7).

"Honour all *men*. Love the brotherhood. Fear God. Honour the king" (1 Pe.2:17).

"Likewise, ye younger, submit yourselves unto the elder. Yea, all *of you* be subject one to another, and be clothed with humility: for God resisteth the proud, and giveth grace to the humble" (1 Pe.5:5).

"Thou shalt not...curse the ruler of thy people" (Ex.22:28).

CHAPTER 12

E. The Message Preached by Samuel at the Coronation of King Saul: The Utter Necessity for Repentance & Faithful Service, 12:1-25

1. Samuel closed & vindicated his ministry: A faithful minister
 a. He had listened to the people: Given them a king, selecting the king even over Samuel's own sons
 b. He was now elderly, & he had served faithfully since his youth

 c. He pictured himself in a courtroom with the people as his witnesses: He called upon them to vindicate his ministry
  1) Had he ever stolen, cheated, or oppressed anyone?
  2) Had he ever taken or condoned a bribe, favoring the rich & powerful?
  3) If he was guilty of any wrong, he would immediately make it right.
 d. He heard the desired verdict: The people declared that Samuel was innocent of all evil; he had served faithfully
 e. He declared that the LORD & Saul were witnesses to the truth of his righteous, faithful life & service

2. Samuel vindicated the LORD: His work of salvation
 a. The LORD delivered Israel from Egypt, working through Moses & Aaron
 b. The LORD & all His righteous acts were vindicated by the evidence, the bar of justice: "Stand still that I may reason with you" (the scene of a courtroom)
 c. The LORD heard the cry of the Israelites for help and established them as a nation: He delivered them from Egypt & settled them in the promised land of Canaan, Ex.2:23-24
 d. The LORD delivered the Israelites through the repeated cycle of a compromising, inconsistent life, Jud.2:11-19
  1) They forsook the LORD
  2) The LORD judged,

And Samuel said unto all Israel, Behold, I have hearkened unto your voice in all that ye said unto me, and have made a king over you.
2 And now, behold, the king walketh before you: and I am old and grayheaded; and, behold, my sons *are* with you: and I have walked before you from my childhood unto this day.
3 Behold, here I *am:* witness against me before the LORD, and before his anointed: whose ox have I taken? or whose ass have I taken? or whom have I defrauded? whom have I oppressed? or of whose hand have I received *any* bribe to blind mine eyes therewith? and I will restore it you.
4 And they said, Thou hast not defrauded us, nor oppressed us, neither hast thou taken ought of any man's hand.
5 And he said unto them, The LORD *is* witness against you, and his anointed *is* witness this day, that ye have not found ought in my hand. And they answered, *He is* witness.
6 And Samuel said unto the people, *It is* the LORD that advanced Moses and Aaron, and that brought your fathers up out of the land of Egypt.
7 Now therefore stand still, that I may reason with you before the LORD of all the righteous acts of the LORD, which he did to you and to your fathers.
8 When Jacob was come into Egypt, and your fathers cried unto the LORD, then the LORD sent Moses and Aaron, which brought forth your fathers out of Egypt, and made them dwell in this place.
9 And when they forgat the LORD their God, he sold them into the hand of Sisera, captain of the host of Hazor, and into the hand of the Philistines, and into the hand of

the king of Moab, and they fought against them.
10 And they cried unto the LORD, and said, We have sinned, because we have forsaken the LORD, and have served Baalim and Ashtaroth: but now deliver us out of the hand of our enemies, and we will serve thee.
11 And the LORD sent Jerubbaal, and Bedan, and Jephthah, and Samuel, and delivered you out of the hand of your enemies on every side, and ye dwelled safe.
12 And when ye saw that Nahash the king of the children of Ammon came against you, ye said unto me, Nay; but a king shall reign over us: when the LORD your God *was* your king.
13 Now therefore behold the king whom ye have chosen, *and* whom ye have desired! and, behold, the LORD hath set a king over you.
14 If ye will fear the LORD, and serve him, and obey his voice, and not rebel against the commandment of the LORD, then shall both ye and also the king that reigneth over you continue following the LORD your God:
15 But if ye will not obey the voice of the LORD, but rebel against the commandment of the LORD, then shall the hand of the LORD be against you, as *it was* against your fathers.
16 Now therefore stand and see this great thing, which the LORD will do before your eyes.
17 *Is it* not wheat harvest to day? I will call unto the LORD, and he shall send thunder and rain; that ye may perceive and see that your wickedness *is* great, which ye have done in the sight of the LORD, in asking you a king.
18 So Samuel called unto the LORD; and the LORD sent thunder and rain that day: and all the people greatly feared the LORD and Samuel.
19 And all the people said unto Samuel, Pray for thy servants unto the LORD thy God, that we die not: for we have added unto all our sins *this* evil, to ask us a king.
20 And Samuel said unto the people, Fear not: ye have done all this wickedness:

chastised them through the suffering of war & oppression
  3) They cried out to the LORD for deliverance, confessing their sin

  4) The LORD delivered them by raising up the judges (Gideon, Jud. 6:1f; Barak, Jud. 4:6-7; Jephthah, Jud.11:1)

3. Samuel pointed out the terrible sin of Israel & issued a strong warning: Rejecting the LORD leads to terrifying judgments
 a. The sin: Rejected the LORD
  1) Demanded an earthly king to protect them
  2) Received their wish: God gave them their desires, a king

 b. The warning: God blesses & God curses
  1) God blesses the obedient: Must fear, serve, & obey the LORD

  2) God curses—chastises, judges—the disobedient: His hand of judgment is aroused against a person

 c. The call to stand still & witness a dramatic sign of God's power to execute judgment:
  1) The sign was a thunderstorm in the midst of the dry, harvest season
  2) The purpose was to arouse the people to acknowledge & confess their terrible evil

  3) The LORD sent the thunderstorm: It most likely destroyed some of the crop, symbolizing God's power to execute judgment
  4) The response of the people was fear & awe
   • Asked Samuel to pray
   • Confessed their sin: Rejected God & demanded a king to be their savior, guide, & provider

4. Samuel called for Israel to repent: A need for repentance
 a. The condition

OUTLINE	SCRIPTURE	SCRIPTURE	OUTLINE

1) Must not forsake the LORD again
2) Must serve the LORD
3) Must not turn to idols & false worship
  • That cannot save you
  • That are useless
b. The assurance of God's acceptance given to the people
1) He honors His great name
2) He chose His people
 	
c. The assurance of Samuel's
	yet turn not aside from following the LORD, but serve the LORD with all your heart;
	21 And turn ye not aside: for *then should ye go* after vain *things,* which cannot profit nor deliver; for they *are* vain.
	22 For the LORD will not forsake his people for his great name's sake: because it hath pleased the LORD to make you his people.
	23 Moreover as for me, God
		forbid that I should sin against the LORD in ceasing to pray for you: but I will teach you the good and the right way:
		24 Only fear the LORD, and serve him in truth with all your heart: for consider how great *things* he hath done for you.
		25 But if ye shall still do wickedly, ye shall be consumed, both ye and your king.
			prayer & continued ministry of teaching
			
			d. The final challenge & warning to the people
			1) The challenge: Fear & serve the LORD faithfully
			
			2) The warning: If you continue in sin, God will judge— destroy

DIVISION II

THE STORY OF SAMUEL AND SAUL: THE LORD GIVES ISRAEL A KING JUST "LIKE ALL THE NATIONS," 8:1–15:35

E. The Message Preached by Samuel at the Coronation of King Saul: The Utter Necessity for Repentance and Faithful Service, 12:1-25

(12:1-25) **Introduction—Repentance, Essential—Service, Faithful, Essential—Faithfulness, Essential—Theocracy, Meaning—Israel, Demand for a King—Monarchy, Desire for**: two things are absolute essentials, utter necessities as we walk throughout this life: repentance before God and faithful service in whatever we do. Before God will ever accept us, He demands repentance and faithful service. No person can expect to be accepted by God if he rejects God and lives selfishly, rejecting and refusing to help other people.

Repentance and faithful service are the messages of this passage of Scripture. These two subjects were the theme of the message preached by Samuel at the coronation of King Saul. Repentance and faithful service were the very messages that both King Saul and the Israelites needed to hear. The people had demanded a king just "like all the nations," demanded a new order of government. Prior to their demand, the Israelites had been ruled by God. God was the Supreme Authority of the nation Israel, a form of government known as a *theocracy*. This simply meant that the Israelites looked to God as their Savior, Guide, Provider, and Protector. They trusted and depended upon God to meet their every need. And when they followed God wholeheartedly, God never failed them. He always met their need. But the Israelites had recently rejected the LORD and demanded a king just "like all the nations." In and of itself, there is nothing wrong with being ruled by a monarchy, a king. The Israelites' request for a king would have been acceptable if they had been living for God and had requested a king "after God's own heart." Instead they had been living wicked, disobedient lives and demanded a king just "like all the nations." They had turned away from the LORD, forsaken Him, forgetting that He had always been their Savior, Guide, Provider, and Protector. Forgetting all the blessings of the LORD, the Israelites began to look at all other nations and desire a leader like their kings. And God granted their desires.

Now, it was the task of Samuel to prepare the people to live under the monarchy, the new form of government. And the first step in this preparation was that of repentance. Once they had repented, they could begin to live lives of faithful service. For the new form of government to succeed, it would be necessary for both the king and the people to faithfully fulfill their tasks. Success could be guaranteed only if they faithfully served and fulfilled their calling upon this earth. To do all he could to assure the success of the monarchy, Samuel preached the following message at the coronation of King Saul: *The Message Preached by Samuel at the Coronation of King Saul: The Utter Necessity for Repentance and Faithful Service,* 12:1-25.

1. Samuel closed and vindicated his ministry: a faithful minister (vv.1-5).
2. Samuel vindicated the LORD: his work of salvation (vv.6-11).
3. Samuel pointed out the terrible sin of Israel and issued a strong warning: rejecting the LORD leads to terrifying judgments (vv.12-19).
4. Samuel called for Israel to repent: a need for repentance (vv.20-25).

1 (12:1-5) **Faithfulness, of Minister—Vindication, of Minister—Minister, Faithfulness of—Samuel, Faithfulness of**: Samuel closed and vindicated his ministry before the people. A new leader—King Saul, the very first king of Israel—had been appointed to rule over the people. It was now time for Samuel to step aside and turn the reigns of leadership over to King Saul. But in stepping aside, he wanted to stress the utter necessity for Saul to be faithful. This he did by vindicating his own ministry, showing how he had lived a righteous life and executed justice among the people. Just imagine the impact upon Saul as he stood there and heard these words from Samuel:

OUTLINE	SCRIPTURE	SCRIPTURE	OUTLINE
1. Samuel closed & vindicated his ministry: A faithful minister a. He had listened to the people: Given them a king,	And Samuel said unto all Israel, Behold, I have hearkened unto your voice in all that ye said unto me,	and have made a king over you. 2 And now, behold, the king walketh before you:	selecting the king even over Samuel's own sons b. He was now elderly, & he had served faithfully since

OUTLINE	SCRIPTURE	SCRIPTURE	OUTLINE
his youth	and I am old and grayheaded; and, behold, my sons *are* with you: and I have walked before you from my childhood unto this day.	bribe to blind mine eyes therewith? and I will restore it you.	3) If he was guilty of any wrong, he would immediately make it right.
c. He pictured himself in a courtroom with the people as his witnesses: He called upon them to vindicate his ministry	3 Behold, here I *am:* witness against me before the LORD, and before his anointed: whose ox have I taken? or whose ass have I taken? or whom have I defrauded? whom have I oppressed? or of whose hand have I received *any*	4 And they said, Thou hast not defrauded us, nor oppressed us, neither hast thou taken ought of any man's hand.	d. He heard the desired verdict: The people declared that Samuel was innocent of all evil; he had served faithfully
1) Had he ever stolen, cheated, or oppressed anyone?		5 And he said unto them, The LORD *is* witness against you, and his anointed *is* witness this day, that ye have not found ought in my hand. And they answered, *He is* witness.	e. He declared that the LORD & Saul were witnesses to the truth of his righteous, faithful life & service
2) Had he ever taken or condoned a bribe, favoring the rich & powerful?			

a. Samuel declared that he had listened to the people and done exactly as they had asked: he had given them King Saul, selecting him even over his own sons (v.1). Samuel was stressing that a leader had to have an open heart and mind and had to be available to his people. A leader had to listen to the requests and demands of the people.

b. Samuel declared that he was now elderly and that he had been their leader from the days of his youth, serving faithfully (v.2). But now it was time for him to step aside and for King Saul to take up the mantle of leadership, assuming responsibility for the people. But Saul needed to remember one fact: he must serve faithfully throughout all the years just as Samuel had served faithfully since the days of his youth.

c. Samuel then painted the picture of a courtroom scene, a courtroom in which he stood before the people who were witnesses to the life he had lived (v.3). Samuel called upon the people to vindicate his ministry:

⇒ Had he ever stolen, cheated, or oppressed anyone?
⇒ Had he ever taken or condoned a bribe, favoring the rich and powerful?
⇒ If he was guilty of any wrong, he would immediately make it right.

d. Samuel heard the desired verdict: the people declared that Samuel was innocent of all wrongdoing. He had lived a righteous life and served faithfully throughout all the years (v.4).

e. Samuel then declared that the LORD and Saul were witnesses to the truth of his righteous, faithful life and service (v.5). His life and ministry were vindicated.

Thought 1. Just imagine the impact upon Saul as he heard Samuel's life and ministry vindicated by the people. This servant of God had lived righteously and been faithful throughout all the days of his life. What a testimony! What a dynamic, living example for us. We must live righteous lives, keep all the commandments of God, obeying Him in all that He says. We must be faithful, diligent in all that we do. This is the strong declaration of God's Holy Word:

"And so he that had received five talents came and brought other five talents, saying, LORD, thou deliveredst unto me five talents: behold, I have gained beside them five talents more. His lord said unto him, Well done, *thou* good and faithful servant: thou hast been faithful over a few things, I will make thee ruler over many things: enter thou into the joy of thy lord" (Mt.25:20-21; see vv.14-30).

"And he said unto him, Well, thou good servant: because thou hast been faithful in a very little, have thou authority over ten cities" (Lu.19:17).

"Moreover it is required in stewards, that a man be found faithful" (1 Co.4:2).

"For this cause have I sent unto you Timotheus, who is my beloved son, and faithful in the LORD, who shall bring you into remembrance of my ways which be in Christ, as I teach every where in every church" (1 Co.4:17).

"What? know ye not that your body is the temple of the Holy Ghost *which is* in you, which ye have of God, and ye are not your own? For ye are bought with a price: therefore glorify God in your body, and in your spirit, which are God's" (1 Co.6:19-20).

"Therefore, my beloved brethren, be ye stedfast, unmovable, always abounding in the work of the LORD, forasmuch as ye know that your labour is not in vain in the LORD" (1 Co.15:58).

"As ye also learned of Epaphras our dear fellowservant, who is for you a faithful minister of Christ" (Col.1:7).

"O Timothy, keep that which is committed to thy trust, avoiding profane *and* vain babblings, and oppositions of science falsely so called"(1 Ti.6:20).

"As every man hath received the gift, *even so* minister the same one to another, as good stewards [managers] of the manifold grace of God" (1 Pe.4:10).

"Fear none of those things which thou shalt suffer: behold, the devil shall cast *some* of you into prison, that ye may be tried; and ye shall have tribulation ten days: be thou faithful unto death, and I will give thee a crown of life" (Re.2:10).

"These shall make war with the Lamb, and the Lamb shall overcome them: for he is LORD of lords, and King of kings: and they that are with him *are* called, and chosen, and faithful" (Re.17:14).

"Now therefore, if ye will obey my voice indeed, and keep my covenant, then ye shall be a peculiar treasure unto me above all people: for all the earth *is* mine" (Ex.19:5).

"But the mercy of the LORD _is_ from everlasting to everlasting upon them that fear him, and his righteousness unto children's children; To such as keep his covenant, and to those that remember his commandments to do them" (Ps.103:17-18).

2 (12:6-11) **Salvation, Work of—Vindication, of God's Salvation—Vindication, of the LORD—History, of Israel—Deliverance, Source of**: having closed and vindicated his own ministry, Samuel now vindicated the LORD, His work of salvation. Samuel proclaimed all the righteous acts the LORD had done for the Israelites down through history. This was a very critical time in the history of Israel. The people had demanded a king just "like all the nations." This meant a totally new form of government. Now the people had their new king and the new form of government; the monarchy had been established. The only question was, would the people totally forget God and look to the new king as their savior, guide, and provider? Or would they acknowledge that the new king ruled under the _authority_ of God, that he himself was dependent upon God just as much as the people, that he himself must look to God as the Savior, Guide, and Protector of both the king and the people? Would the new king live a righteous life and use his power to serve the people and minister to the needs of society, or would he use his power for selfish purposes, to amass wealth and to enjoy the sinful, wicked pleasures of the world? Samuel knew that these were key questions, questions that would determine the destiny of Israel. For this reason, it was essential that the people remember the LORD, remember all His righteous acts, His glorious work of salvation throughout the history of the nation:

OUTLINE	SCRIPTURE	SCRIPTURE	OUTLINE
2. Samuel vindicated the LORD: His work of salvation a. The LORD delivered Israel from Egypt, working through Moses & Aaron b. The LORD & all His righteous acts were vindicated by the evidence, the bar of justice: "Stand still that I may reason with you" (the scene of a courtroom) c. The LORD heard the cry of the Israelites for help and established them as a nation: He delivered them from Egypt & settled them in the promised land of Canaan, Ex.2:23-24 d. The LORD delivered the Israelites through the repeated	6 And Samuel said unto the people, _It is_ the LORD that advanced Moses and Aaron, and that brought your fathers up out of the land of Egypt. 7 Now therefore stand still, that I may reason with you before the LORD of all the righteous acts of the LORD, which he did to you and to your fathers. 8 When Jacob was come into Egypt, and your fathers cried unto the LORD, then the LORD sent Moses and Aaron, which brought forth your fathers out of Egypt, and made them dwell in this place. 9 And when they forgat the LORD their God, he sold them	into the hand of Sisera, captain of the host of Hazor, and into the hand of the Philistines, and into the hand of the king of Moab, and they fought against them. 10 And they cried unto the LORD, and said, We have sinned, because we have forsaken the LORD, and have served Baalim and Ashtaroth: but now deliver us out of the hand of our enemies, and we will serve thee. 11 And the LORD sent Jerubbaal, and Bedan, and Jephthah, and Samuel, and delivered you out of the hand of your enemies on every side, and ye dwelled safe.	cycle of a compromising, inconsistent life, Jud.2:11-19 1) They forsook the LORD 2) The LORD judged, chastised them through the suffering of war & oppression 3) They cried out to the LORD for deliverance, confessing their sin 4) The LORD delivered them by raising up the judges (Gideon, Jud. 6:1f; Barak, Jud. 4:6-7; Jephthah, Jud.11:1)

a. Samuel reminded the people of the LORD's great deliverance from Egypt (v.6). The LORD had worked through Moses and Aaron to deliver their forefathers out of bondage, saving them from a life of slavery.

b. Samuel then declared that the LORD and all His righteous acts were vindicated by the evidence at the bar of justice (v.7). He cried out for the people to stand still so that he could reason with them.

c. It was the LORD who had heard the cry of the Israelites for help and established them as a nation (v.8). It was the LORD who had delivered them from Egypt and settled them in this place, the promised land of Canaan (Ex.2:23-24).

d. Samuel reminded the people of another _very significant_ fact: the LORD had delivered the Israelites through the repeated cycle of a compromising, inconsistent life (see outline and notes—Judg.2:11-19 for more discussion). Samuel spelled out the steps involved in the repeated cycle of their compromising, inconsistent life.

1) Their forefathers had consistently forsaken the LORD (v.9). They had turned away from the LORD, living life as they wished and doing their own thing. They had lived sinful, wicked lives, continually disobeying the LORD and breaking His holy commandments.

2) As a consequence, the LORD had judged and chastised them through the suffering and oppression (v.9). The LORD had "sold" them, given them over to be conquered by Sisera, the commander of a Canaanite army. Moreover, God had given them up to be conquered by the Philistines and the king of Moab.

3) But eventually, the forefathers had cried out to the LORD for deliverance, confessing their sins (v.10). They had forsaken the LORD and turned to false worship, serving the Baals and the Ashtoreths. But the chastisement of God's judgment had snapped them out of their insanity of sin and brought them to their senses. And the forefathers had eventually cried out to the LORD for deliverance from their enemies, promising that they would serve God with a renewed heart.

4) Samuel reminded the people that the LORD then delivered their forefathers by raising up the judges (v.11). He mentioned three judges in particular: Gideon (Jud.6:11f), Barak, (Jud.4:6-7), and Jephthah (Jud.11:1f).

Thought 1. Throughout history the LORD has been vindicated by His righteous acts. God has worked and moved upon the scene of world history, saving and delivering all who turned to Him by faith in Jesus Christ. Millions of people have been saved by the work of God's salvation. Millions have been removed from the bondage of sin and wickedness, bondages such as...

- alcohol
- drugs
- pornography
- immorality
- gluttony
- greed

- covetousness
- foul language
- shoplifting
- homosexuality
- smoking
- false worship

- slothfulness
- ignorance
- gossiping
- hatred
- hostility
- depression

The things in life that can enslave us are innumerable. But there is glorious hope: we can be delivered, saved from all the bondages and enslavements of this life. Deliverance is found in God. God will save us, deliver us from any bondage, from anything that enslaves us in this life. This is the wonderful promise of God's Holy Word:

"**For unto you is born this day in the city of David a Saviour, which is Christ the LORD**" (Lu.2:11).

"**For God so loved the world, that he gave his only begotten Son, that whosoever believeth in him should not perish, but have everlasting life. For God sent not his Son into the world to condemn the world; but that the world through him might be saved**" (Jn.3:16-17).

"**Know ye not that the unrighteous shall not inherit the kingdom of God? Be not deceived: neither fornicators, nor idolaters, nor adulterers, nor effeminate, nor abusers of themselves with mankind, Nor thieves, nor covetous, nor drunkards, nor revilers, nor extortioners, shall inherit the kingdom of God. And such were some of you: but ye are washed, but ye are sanctified, but ye are justified in the name of the LORD Jesus, and by the Spirit of our God. All things are lawful unto me, but all things are not expedient: all things are lawful for me, but I will not be brought under the power of any. Meats for the belly, and the belly for meats: but God shall destroy both it and them. Now the body *is* not for fornication, but for the LORD; and the LORD for the body. And God hath both raised up the LORD, and will also raise up us by his own power**" (1 Co.6:9-14).

"**There hath no temptation taken you but such as is common to man: but God *is* faithful, who will not suffer you to be tempted above that ye are able; but will with the temptation also make a way to escape, that ye may be able to bear *it*"** (1 Co.10:13).

"**Now the works of the flesh are manifest, which are *these;* Adultery, fornication, uncleanness, lasciviousness, Idolatry, witchcraft, hatred, variance, emulations, wrath, strife, seditions, heresies, Envyings, murders, drunkenness, revellings, and such like: of the which I tell you before, as I have also told *you* in time past, that they which do such things shall not inherit the kingdom of God. But the fruit of the Spirit is love, joy, peace, longsuffering, gentleness, goodness, faith, Meekness, temperance: against such there is no law. And they that are Christ's have crucified the flesh with the affections and lusts. If we live in the Spirit, let us also walk in the Spirit**" (Ga.5:19-25).

"**And the LORD shall deliver me from every evil work, and will preserve *me* unto his heavenly kingdom: to whom *be* glory for ever and ever. Amen**" (2 Ti.4:18).

"**Forasmuch then as the children are partakers of flesh and blood, he also himself likewise took part of the same; that through death he might destroy him that had the power of death, that is, the devil; And deliver them who through fear of death were all their lifetime subject to bondage**" (He.2:14-15).

"**Wherefore he is able also to save them to the uttermost that come unto God by him, seeing he ever liveth to make intercession for them**" (He.7:25).

"**Surely he shall deliver thee from the snare of the fowler, *and* from the noisome pestilence**" (Ps.91:3).

"**And *even* to *your* old age I *am* he; and *even* to hoar [gray] hairs will I carry *you*: I have made, and I will bear; even I will carry, and will deliver *you***" (Is.46:4).

"**Be not afraid of their faces: for I *am* with thee to deliver thee, saith the LORD**" (Je.1:8).

3 (12:12-19) **Judgment, Warning against—Rejection, of the LORD, Result of—Israel, Sin of—Warning, Against Rejection of God**: Samuel pointed out the terrible sin of Israel and issued a forceful warning: if the people *continued* to reject God, they would face His terrifying judgment. By demanding a king, the people standing before Samuel had rejected God. They had failed to remember the work of God's salvation in the lives of their forefathers, and they had turned away from the LORD. Because of their rejection, they faced the threat of God's terrifying judgment falling upon them. This is the thrust of what Samuel now preached at the coronation of King Saul:

OUTLINE	SCRIPTURE	SCRIPTURE	OUTLINE

3. Samuel pointed out the terrible sin of Israel & issued a strong warning: Rejecting the LORD leads to terrifying judgments
a. The sin: Rejected the LORD
  1) Demanded an earthly king to protect them
  2) Received their wish: God gave them their desires, a king
	12 And when ye saw that Nahash the king of the children of Ammon came against you, ye said unto me, Nay; but a king shall reign over us: when the LORD your God *was* your king.
	13 Now therefore behold the king whom ye have chosen, *and* whom ye have desired! and, behold, the LORD hath set a king over you.
		14 If ye will fear the LORD, and serve him, and obey his voice, and not rebel against the commandment of the LORD, then shall both ye and also the king that reigneth over you continue following the LORD your God:
		15 But if ye will not obey the voice of the LORD, but rebel against the commandment of the LORD, then shall the hand
			b. The warning: God blesses & God curses
			  1) God blesses the obedient: Must fear, serve, & obey the LORD
			
			  2) God curses—chastises, judges—the disobedient: His hand of judgment is aroused against a person

OUTLINE	SCRIPTURE	SCRIPTURE	OUTLINE
c. The call to stand still & witness a dramatic sign of God's power to execute judgment: 1) The sign was a thunderstorm in the midst of the dry, harvest season 2) The purpose was to arouse the people to acknowledge & confess their terrible evil	of the LORD be against you, as *it was* against your fathers. 16 Now therefore stand and see this great thing, which the LORD will do before your eyes. 17 *Is it* not wheat harvest today? I will call unto the LORD, and he shall send thunder and rain; that ye may perceive and see that your wickedness *is* great, which ye have done in the sight of the LORD, in asking you a	king. 18 So Samuel called unto the LORD; and the LORD sent thunder and rain that day: and all the people greatly feared the LORD and Samuel. 19 And all the people said unto Samuel, Pray for thy servants unto the LORD thy God, that we die not: for we have added unto all our sins *this* evil, to ask us a king.	3) The LORD sent the thunderstorm: It most likely destroyed some of the crop, symbolizing God's power to execute judgment 4) The response of the people was fear & awe • Asked Samuel to pray • Confessed their sin: Rejected God & demanded a king to be their savior, guide, & provider

a. Samuel charged the people with sin, the sin of rejecting the LORD (v.12). When they demanded an earthly king, they rejected the LORD. Prior to their demand, the Israelites had always been ruled by God, a form of government known as a *theocracy*. This simply means that the people looked to God as their Savior, Guide, Provider, and Protector. But in choosing a king, they were choosing to be ruled by another form of government, a monarchy. Demanding a king was not wrong in and of itself. The *wrong* or *evil* of the Israelites' demand was the kind of king they had requested: a king just "like all the nations." They should have asked for a king "after God's own heart." Instead they were looking for an earthly king who would be their savior, guide, provider, and protector. They had taken their eyes off the LORD and looked to an earthly king who could bring them peace, security, and a robust economy. Their trust in an earthly king had betrayed, exposed their hearts. They had lost confidence in God, forgotten His work of salvation throughout their history. They were guilty of terrible sin, that of rejecting the LORD and putting their trust in an earthly king. Note that Samuel says it was the threat of the Ammonites in the east that had aroused the people to demand an earthly king. No doubt, they were also thinking of the threat of the Philistines in the west (9:16).

At this point, Samuel apparently turned and pointed toward Saul, shouting out: "Behold! Here is the king you have chosen, the one you have desired and demanded. The LORD has granted your request and set a king over you" (v.13).

b. Turning back to the people, Samuel issued his strong warning: God blesses and God curses (vv.14-15). Under the new system of government the people could be blessed, for God always blesses the obedient. If the people feared the LORD, served and obeyed Him, the LORD would bless them. But note: the people must not rebel against the LORD's commandments. And both they and the king must continue to follow the LORD, looking to Him as the Supreme Authority of the nation. They must continue to look to the LORD Himself as their Savior, Guide, Provider, and Protector. Note that even the king must look to the LORD as the Supreme Authority, the Sovereign Majesty under which the king himself must serve. The king must be the servant of God who ministers and executes justice among the people of God.

Furthermore, God not only blesses the obedient, He also curses—chastises and judges—the disobedient (v.15). If the king and people did not obey the LORD—if they rebelled against His commandments—God's hand of judgment would be aroused against them. Judgment would fall upon them even as it had fallen upon their forefathers.

c. At this point, Samuel cried out for the people to stand still and witness the power of God to execute judgment (vv.16-19). A dramatic sign of God's power was to be given to the people. The sign was a thunderstorm in the midst of the dry, hot harvest season (v.17). The purpose for the miraculous thunderstorm was to arouse the people to acknowledge and confess their terrible evil of rejecting God. Picture the scene: Samuel stood upon an elevated platform before the massive crowd standing all around him. All of a sudden, he called out to the LORD for a thunderstorm to break forth. And soon the dark, threatening clouds began to form off in the distance. And the LORD sent thunder and rain. As in most large thunderstorms, this storm most likely destroyed some of the crop, a symbol of God's power to execute His judgment upon the people.

The impact upon the people was striking: they feared both the LORD and Samuel, feared the power demonstrated in the thunderstorm. They knew that the LORD definitely had the power to execute judgment when Samuel sought His face.

What Samuel had hoped for happened. The people requested that Samuel pray for God to restrain, hold back His judgment. And they confessed that they had added to all their other sins the evil of asking for a king. They confessed their rejection of God and their turning to an earthly king as their savior, guide, provider, and protector.

Note that Samuel had led the people to the point of confession, the exact place they needed to be. Their hearts had been moved to confess their sin, their rejection of God. They had been dramatically reminded of the judgment of God as they witnessed a dramatic demonstration of God's power to judge. Now they were crying out for deliverance from God's hand of judgment, crying out and confessing their sins to the LORD. This was exactly what the people needed to do.

Thought 1. Rejecting God will arouse the hand of God's judgment against us. If we forsake the LORD—forget, ignore, and neglect the LORD—we will face the judgment of God. And the judgment will be severe. For this reason, we must guard our lives. We must make absolutely sure that we walk righteously and godly in this present life. If we disobey the commandments of God, living sinful, selfish, wicked lives, we will be condemned by God. Judgment will fall upon all who...

- curse and use vulgarity
- commit adultery and immorality
- lie, steal, and cheat
- abuse, assault, and murder
- despise, hate, and seek vengeance
- commit acts of lawlessness

All immoral, lawless, and violent behavior and all acts of injustice will be condemned. God will execute justice and judgment upon all the sinful, wicked, and evil of this earth.

"He that believeth on him is not condemned: but he that believeth not is condemned already, because he hath not believed in the name of the only begotten Son of God. And this is the condemnation, that light is come into the world, and men loved darkness rather than light, because their deeds were evil" (Jn.3:18-19).

"He that rejecteth me, and receiveth not my words, hath one that judgeth him: the word that I have spoken, the same shall judge him in the last day" (Jn.12:48).

"And to you who are troubled rest with us, when the LORD Jesus shall be revealed from heaven with his mighty angels, In flaming fire taking vengeance on them that know not God, and that obey not the gospel of our Lord Jesus Christ" (2 Th.1:7-8).

"For *it is* impossible for those who were once enlightened, and have tasted of the heavenly gift, and were made partakers of the Holy Ghost, And have tasted the good word of God, and the powers of the world to come, If they shall fall away, to renew them again unto repentance; seeing they crucify to themselves the Son of God afresh, and put *him* to an open shame" (He.6:4-6).

"The LORD knoweth how to deliver the godly out of temptations, and to reserve the unjust unto the day of judgment to be punished" (2 Pe.2:9).

"But the heavens and the earth, which are now, by the same word are kept in store, reserved unto fire against the day of judgment and perdition of ungodly men" (2 Pe.3:7).

"And Enoch also, the seventh from Adam, prophesied of these, saying, Behold, the LORD cometh with ten thousands of his saints, To execute judgment upon all, and to convince all that are ungodly among them of all their ungodly deeds which they have ungodly committed, and of all their hard *speeches* which ungodly sinners have spoken against him" (Jude 14-15).

"And I saw a great white throne, and him that sat on it, from whose face the earth and the heaven fled away; and there was found no place for them. And I saw the dead, small and great, stand before God; and the books were opened: and another book was opened, which is *the book* of life: and the dead were judged out of those things which were written in the books, according to their works. And the sea gave up the dead which were in it; and death and hell delivered up the dead which were in them: and they were judged every man according to their works. And death and hell were cast into the lake of fire. This is the second death. And whosoever was not found written in the book of life was cast into the lake of fire" (Re.20:11-15).

"...The LORD *is* with you, while ye be with him; and if ye seek him, he will be found of you; but if ye forsake him, he will forsake you" (2 Chr.15:2).

"...The hand of our God *is* upon all them for good that seek him; but his power and his wrath *is* against all them that forsake him" (Ezr.8:22).

"And I will utter my judgments against them touching all their wickedness, who have forsaken me, and have burned incense unto other gods, and worshipped the works of their own hands" (Je.1:16).

"Thou hast forsaken me, saith the LORD, thou art gone backward: therefore will I stretch out my hand against thee, and destroy thee; I am weary with repenting" (Je.15:6).

4 (12:20-25) **Repentance, Call to—Repentance, Condition for—Assurance, Source—Idols, Weakness of—Challenge, Message of—Acceptance, Conditions or Requirements for—False Worship, Inadequacy of**: Samuel called for the Israelites to repent. Keep in mind the people had just confessed their sins, including their sin of rejecting God when they requested an earthly king. It was now time for Samuel to point the people to the LORD. His message was simple and very straightforward:

OUTLINE	SCRIPTURE	SCRIPTURE	OUTLINE

4. Samuel called for Israel to repent: A need for repentance
a. The condition
  1) Must not forsake the LORD again
  2) Must serve the LORD
  3) Must not turn to idols & false worship
   • That cannot save you
   • That are useless
 	
b. The assurance of God's acceptance given to the people
  1) He honors His great name
  2) He chose His people
	20 And Samuel said unto the people, Fear not: ye have done all this wickedness: yet turn not aside from following the LORD, but serve the LORD with all your heart;
	21 And turn ye not aside: for *then should ye go* after vain *things,* which cannot profit nor deliver; for they *are* vain.
	22 For the LORD will not forsake his people for his great name's sake: because it hath pleased the LORD to
		make you his people.
		23 Moreover as for me, God forbid that I should sin against the LORD in ceasing to pray for you: but I will teach you the good and the right way:
		24 Only fear the LORD, and serve him in truth with all your heart: for consider how great *things* he hath done for you.
		25 But if ye shall still do wickedly, ye shall be consumed, both ye and your king.
			c. The assurance of Samuel's prayer & continued ministry of teaching
			
			d. The final challenge & warning to the people
			  1) The challenge: Fear & serve the LORD faithfully
			  2) The warning: If you continue in sin, God will judge—destroy

a. Samuel laid down the conditions for repentance (vv.20-21). Spelling out three conditions, he shouted out:

⇒ You must not turn away from the LORD, never forsake Him ever again.
⇒ You must serve the LORD wholeheartedly.
⇒ You must not turn away to idols and false worship. They are empty, useless things that cannot help or rescue you (v.21).

b. Samuel proclaimed the assurance of God's acceptance to the people (v.22). God accepts any person who repents and turns to Him. For the sake of His name, He will not reject His people, not ever—not if they turn to Him in true repentance. Samuel gave two reasons why God would never reject His people:
⇒ because He always honors His great name, the name of the LORD (Jehovah, Yahweh)
⇒ because the LORD had chosen the Israelites (true believers) to be His people

Standing before Samuel and hearing these two great assurances being preached, the people knew exactly what Samuel was saying. The Israelites who truly followed God and served Him would be accepted and blessed by God (vv.14, 20-21). But the Israelites who turned away from the LORD, following after false believers and false worship, would face the hand of God's curse and judgment (v.15).

c. After giving the people the assurance of God's acceptance, Samuel assured the people of his own prayers and continued ministry of teaching. As long as he lived, he would continue to teach and pray for the people (v.23).

d. In closing his coronation message, Samuel gave the people a final challenge and warning (vv.24-25). He challenged them to fear the LORD and to serve Him faithfully, wholeheartedly. One thing in particular they were to keep in mind: the great things the LORD had done for them down through the years of history.

Finally, in one brief sentence, Samuel closed his coronation message, a message preached both to King Saul and to the Israelite nation. He closed with a warning that summarized all the judgments of the law and that foresaw the future of the new order of government being instituted in Israel, the monarchy. In fact, the warning proclaimed by Samuel has proven true not only with every form of government instituted by Israel but also with every nation upon the face of the earth. The warning was brief and straightforward: if you continue in sin, both you and your king (leader) will be swept away (judged, destroyed). Ultimately the judgment of God's hand would fall upon Israel, and they would be led into captivity and exile from the promised land (see outline and notes—De.28:15-68 for more discussion). Robert D. Bergen gives an excellent summary of the coronation of Samuel:

> The message is a pointed one, and strikes at the heart of Israel's problem. The nation's real threat was not external, that is, one that could be faced and defeated by a king who would go out and lead Israel in battle (cf. 8:20). Rather it was internal and spiritual. The malignant faith condition that caused Israel to demand a king in preference to restoring a relationship with God was what would ultimately cause the nation to "be swept away" (v. 25; a form of sapâ). No king, however mighty, could stop the tide of divine judgment that would roll against Israel in the day of the LORD's wrath.[1]

Thought 1. When approaching God, repentance is essential, an absolute essential. Every person must turn away from sin when turning to God. Samuel did an excellent job in spelling out the conditions for repentance: we must repent if we have turned away from the LORD—forsaking, ignoring, or neglecting Him; denying or questioning His existence. If we have turned to false religion, false worship, or idolatry, we must repent. If we are trusting anything or any person to save us other than the LORD Himself, we must repent. Emphatically, the Word of God declares that we must repent:

"And saying, Repent ye: for the kingdom of heaven is at hand" (Mt.3:2).
"Then Peter said unto them, Repent, and be baptized every one of you in the name of Jesus Christ for the remission of sins, and ye shall receive the gift of the Holy Ghost" (Ac.2:38).
"Repent ye therefore, and be converted, that your sins may be blotted out, when the times of refreshing shall come from the presence of the LORD" (Ac.3:19).
"Repent therefore of this thy wickedness, and pray God, if perhaps the thought of thine heart may be forgiven thee" (Ac.8:22).
"And the times of this ignorance God winked at; but now commandeth all men every where to repent" (Ac.17:30).
"If my people, which are called by my name, shall humble themselves, and pray, and seek my face, and turn from their wicked ways; then will I hear from heaven, and will forgive their sin, and will heal their land" (2 Chr.7:14).
"Therefore also now, saith the LORD, turn ye *even* to me with all your heart, and with fasting, and with weeping, and with mourning" (Joel 2:12).
"Let the wicked forsake his way, and the unrighteous man his thoughts: and let him return unto the LORD, and he will have mercy upon him; and to our God, for he will abundantly pardon" (Is.55:7).
"But if the wicked will turn from all his sins that he hath committed, and keep all my statutes, and do that which is lawful and right, he shall surely live, he shall not die" (Eze.18:21).
"Cast away from you all your transgressions, whereby ye have transgressed; and make you a new heart and a new spirit: for why will ye die, O house of Israel" (Eze.18:31).

---

[1] Robert D. Bergen. *1, 2 Samuel*, p.145.

1. The full-scale war with the Philistines: The believer's fear & panic in facing trials

a. The mobilizing of a standing army in the second year of Saul's reign as king[DS1]
  1) He stationed 2000 soldiers with him
  2) He stationed 1000 soldiers with his son Jonathan
  3) He sent the rest of the army home

b. The attack of a Philistine outpost at Geba by Jonathan

c. The mobilizing of the entire army by Saul: To prepare for a counterattack

  1) The attack inflamed the Philistines

  2) The army was summoned to Gilgal

d. The mobilizing of the Philistine army
  1) Mobilized 30,000 chariots, 6000 horsemen, a multitude of soldiers
  2) Camped at Micmash, east of Beth Aven

e. The fear & panic of the Israelites: A mass defection & desertion
  1) They fled & hid in caves, thickets, pits, cisterns, & among the rocks

  2) Some even fled across the Jordan River into East Jordan
  3) All the troops were gripped with a paralyzing fear

2. The unlawful act that made Saul unfit to be king: Being disqualified from serving the LORD

a. The delay of Samuel & Saul's impatient fear
b. The unlawful act of Saul: Did not wait for Samuel & assumed the role of priest, offering up the burnt offering

CHAPTER 13

F. The Unlawful Act That Made Saul Unfit to Be King: Being Disqualified from Serving the LORD, 13:1-23

Saul reigned one year; and when he had reigned two years over Israel,

2 Saul chose him three thousand *men* of Israel; *whereof* two thousand were with Saul in Michmash and in mount Bethel, and a thousand were with Jonathan in Gibeah of Benjamin: and the rest of the people he sent every man to his tent.

3 And Jonathan smote the garrison of the Philistines that *was* in Geba, and the Philistines heard *of it*. And Saul blew the trumpet throughout all the land, saying, Let the Hebrews hear.

4 And all Israel heard say *that* Saul had smitten a garrison of the Philistines, and *that* Israel also was had in abomination with the Philistines. And the people were called together after Saul to Gilgal.

5 And the Philistines gathered themselves together to fight with Israel, thirty thousand chariots, and six thousand horsemen, and people as the sand which *is* on the sea shore in multitude: and they came up, and pitched in Michmash, eastward from Beth-aven.

6 When the men of Israel saw that they were in a strait, (for the people were distressed,) then the people did hide themselves in caves, and in thickets, and in rocks, and in high places, and in pits.

7 And *some of* the Hebrews went over Jordan to the land of Gad and Gilead. As for Saul, he *was* yet in Gilgal, and all the people followed him trembling.

8 And he tarried seven days, according to the set time that Samuel *had appointed*: but Samuel came not to Gilgal; and the people were scattered from him.

9 And Saul said, Bring hither a burnt offering to me, and peace offerings. And he offered the burnt offering.

10 And it came to pass, that as soon as he had made an end of offering the burnt offering, behold, Samuel came; and Saul went out to meet him, that he might salute him.

11 And Samuel said, What hast thou done? And Saul said, Because I saw that the people were scattered from me, and *that* thou camest not within the days appointed, and *that* the Philistines gathered themselves together at Michmash;

12 Therefore said I, The Philistines will come down now upon me to Gilgal, and I have not made supplication unto the LORD: I forced myself therefore, and offered a burnt offering.

13 And Samuel said to Saul, Thou hast done foolishly: thou hast not kept the commandment of the LORD thy God, which he commanded thee: for now would the LORD have established thy kingdom upon Israel for ever.

14 But now thy kingdom shall not continue: the LORD hath sought him a man after his own heart, and the LORD hath commanded him *to be* captain over his people, because thou hast not kept *that* which the LORD commanded thee.

15 And Samuel arose, and gat him up from Gilgal unto Gibeah of Benjamin. And Saul numbered the people *that were* present with him, about six hundred men.

16 And Saul, and Jonathan his son, and the people *that were* present with them, abode in Gibeah of Benjamin: but the Philistines encamped in Michmash.

17 And the spoilers came out of the camp of the Philistines in three companies: one company turned unto the way *that leadeth to* Ophrah, unto the land of Shual:

18 And another company turned the way *to* Bethhoron: and another company turned *to* the way of the border that looketh to the valley of Zeboim toward the wilderness.

19 Now there was no smith found throughout all the land of Israel: for the Philistines said, Lest the Hebrews

c. The confrontation with Samuel: Samuel arrived just as Saul was completing the offering

  1) Samuel questioned Saul
  2) Saul gave four excuses
  • The fleeing of the troops
  • The delay of Samuel
  • The massive mobilization of the Philistines

  • The desperate need to seek the LORD's favor before the attack of the Philistines was launched against him

d. The rebuke & pronouncement of God's judgment upon Saul
  1) He acted foolishly: He had disobeyed the LORD
  2) He had lost the permanent establishment of his kingdom: It would not last

e. The bypassing of Saul: The LORD had chosen another man—"a man after His own heart"—to be the leader of God's people

3. The critical situation confronted by Saul: A desperate need for God's help

a. He was alienated from God & God's prophet due to sin
b. He had only 600 troops left to fight the overwhelming Philistine army

c. He faced three major raiding parties: Sent to harass & plunder & to demoralize the population

d. He had no weapons developed from metal nor from the latest technology
  1) The Israelites had been

forbidden to have black-smiths 2) The Israelites were totally dependent upon the Philistines for all metal tools e. He had no money to manufacture or purchase weapons: Because of the high price charged for services by the Philistines	make *them* swords or spears: 20 But all the Israelites went down to the Philistines, to sharpen every man his share, and his coulter, and his axe, and his mattock. 21 Yet they had a file for the mattocks, and for the coulters, and for the forks, and for the axes, and to sharpen the goads.	22 So it came to pass in the day of battle, that there was neither sword nor spear found in the hand of any of the people that *were* with Saul and Jonathan: but with Saul and with Jonathan his son was there found. 23 And the garrison of the Philistines went out to the passage of Michmash.	f. He & his son Jonathan had the only two swords among the entire army g. He faced the major road being blocked by a detachment of enemy soldiers

DIVISION II

THE STORY OF SAMUEL AND SAUL: THE LORD GIVES ISRAEL A KING JUST "LIKE ALL THE NATIONS," 8:1–15:35

F. The Unlawful Act That Made Saul Unfit to Be King: Being Disqualified from Serving the LORD, 13:1-23

(13:1-23) **Introduction—Disqualified, Tragedy of—Rejection, Tragedy of—Unfit, Tragedy of—Ineligible, Tragedy of**: "Disqualified!" Merely hearing or seeing the word can cut the heart of a person. Pain, even severe pain, can shoot through the heart of a person when he hears that he has been *disqualified* or *barred* or *put out*. Likewise, all kinds of emotions grip us when we find out we have been disqualified:

⇒ disqualified from a promotion
⇒ disqualified from a job
⇒ disqualified from a sports' team
⇒ disqualified from an organization
⇒ disqualified from gaining credit
⇒ disqualified from an athletic event
⇒ disqualified from a competition
⇒ disqualified, counted unacceptable, by some person

Saul heard the heartrending word *disqualified*, a word that must have cut him to the core. This chapter begins the decline of Saul. Saul was disqualified from being king of Israel, disqualified from serving the LORD and His people. His decline and disqualification are highlighted in chapters 13 through 15, but his decline continues throughout the story of David's rise to power (16:1–31:13).[1] This present chapter is: *The Unlawful Act That Made Saul Unfit to Be King: Being Disqualified from Serving the LORD,* 13:1-23.

1. The full-scale war with the Philistines: the believer's fear and panic in facing trials (vv.1-7).
2. The unlawful act that made Saul unfit to be king: being disqualified from serving the LORD (vv.8-14).
3. The critical situation confronted by Saul: a desperate need for God's help (vv.15-23).

[1] (13:1-7) **Fear, Caused by—Panic, Caused by—Saul, Wars of—Wars, of Israel—Philistines, Wars Against Israel**: there was the full-scale war with the Philistines. This is a clear picture of the believer's fear and sometimes panic in facing the trials and problems of life.

OUTLINE	SCRIPTURE	SCRIPTURE	OUTLINE

1. The full-scale war with the Philistines: The believer's fear & panic in facing trials
a. The mobilizing of a standing army in the second year of Saul's reign as king[DS1]
  1) He stationed 2000 soldiers with him
  2) He stationed 1000 soldiers with his son Jonathan
  3) He sent the rest of the army home
b. The attack of a Philistine outpost at Geba by Jonathan
	Saul reigned one year; and when he had reigned two years over Israel,
	2 Saul chose him three thousand *men* of Israel; *whereof* two thousand were with Saul in Michmash and in mount Bethel, and a thousand were with Jonathan in Gibeah of Benjamin: and the rest of the people he sent every man to his tent.
	3 And Jonathan smote the garrison of the Philistines that
		was in Geba, and the Philistines heard *of it*. And Saul blew the trumpet throughout all the land, saying, Let the Hebrews hear.
		4 And all Israel heard say *that* Saul had smitten a garrison of the Philistines, and *that* Israel also was had in abomination with the Philistines. And the people were called together after Saul to Gilgal.
		5 And the Philistines gathered
			c. The mobilizing of the entire army by Saul: To prepare for a counterattack
			
			1) The attack inflamed the Philistines
			
			2) The army was summoned to Gilgal
			
			d. The mobilizing of the

---

1 Ronald F. Youngblood. *1 Samuel*, p.652.

OUTLINE	SCRIPTURE	SCRIPTURE	OUTLINE
Philistine army 1) Mobilized 30,000 chariots, 6000 horsemen, a multitude of soldiers 2) Camped at Micmash, east of Beth Aven e. The fear & panic of the Israelites: A mass defection &	themselves together to fight with Israel, thirty thousand chariots, and six thousand horsemen, and people as the sand which *is* on the sea shore in multitude: and they came up, and pitched in Michmash, eastward from Beth-aven. 6 When the men of Israel saw that they were in a strait,	(for the people were distressed,) then the people did hide themselves in caves, and in thickets, and in rocks, and in high places, and in pits. 7 And *some of* the Hebrews went over Jordan to the land of Gad and Gilead. As for Saul, he *was* yet in Gilgal, and all the people followed him trembling.	desertion 1) They fled & hid in caves, thickets, pits, cisterns, & among the rocks 2) Some even fled across the Jordan River into East Jordan 3) All the troops were gripped with a paralyzing fear

a. Saul mobilized a standing army of 3,000 soldiers in the second year of his reign as king (vv.1-2). He stationed 2,000 soldiers with him at Micmash and in the hill country of Bethel. The remaining 1,000 soldiers were placed under the command of his son Jonathan at Gibeah in the territory of Benjamin. The rest of the troops were sent home.

The city of Micmash was about seven miles north of Jerusalem and about five miles northeast of Gibeah, which was the city chosen by Saul to be his capital. This was a strategic positioning of Saul's troops, most likely to eliminate the Philistine outpost at Geba, which was less than three miles from Saul's capital. Jonathan's troops were guarding a strategic pass that led to Geba, apparently to block any attempt to escape by the Philistines.[2]

b. At some point the decision was made for Jonathan to attack and take over the Philistine outpost at Geba (v.3). Soon after his attack, the news spread quickly among the Philistines that Israel had revolted.

c. Sensing that the Philistines were going to launch a counterattack, Saul sent messengers throughout all Israel warning the people that the Philistines had become inflamed and now hated the Israelites more than ever. Israel had become an abomination to, a stench in the very nostrils of the Philistines. Strong hostility flooded the hearts of the Philistines against the Israelites.

d. For that reason, the Philistines mobilized a massive army to march against Israel (v.5). Note the forces mobilized: 30,000 chariots (some manuscripts of the Septuagint say 3,000); 6,000 horsemen; and an innumerable legion of soldiers. The army marched up and took over the military site that Saul had originally occupied at Micmash.

e. Fear and panic struck the Israelite troops when they saw the overwhelming army that opposed them. It was clearly evident that their situation was critical, that the bloody, savage maiming and slaughter that take place in war were about to happen. The heaviest casualties would undoubtedly be suffered by the Israelites, for they were far outnumbered. And because of the deep-seated hostility of the Philistines, they likely would leave no survivors. Terror swept through the Israelite camp, and a mass defection and desertion set in. Thousands of troops fled and hid in caves, thickets, pits, cisterns, and among the rocks (v.6). Some even fled across the Jordan River into East Jordan, to the land of Gad and Gilead (v.7). All the troops were gripped with a paralyzing fear.

Thought 1. In facing the Philistines, the Israelites confronted an overwhelming enemy. And so it is with us. As we walk throughout life, we often face enormous trials and problems, trials and problems that seem overwhelming, such as...

- disease
- accidents
- financial troubles
- difficulties at school, work, home, or in society
- divorce
- the death of a loved one
- emotional disturbance
- purposelessness
- depression
- dissatisfaction

Some hardship or temptation confronts each of us every day of our lives. And far too often, we begin to question our ability to handle the difficulty. Fear—and sometimes panic—strikes our hearts, and we begin to wonder what we will do next.

It is at this point that we must learn to turn to the LORD. For He promises to uphold us, to strengthen us, to help us through any trial or any problem. This is the strong declaration of God's Holy Word:

"But the very hairs of your head are all numbered. Fear ye not therefore, ye are of more value than many sparrows" (Mt.10:30-31).

"Only let your conversation [behavior, conduct] be as it becometh the gospel of Christ: that whether I come and see you, or else be absent, I may hear of your affairs, that ye stand fast in one spirit, with one mind striving together for the faith of the gospel; And in nothing terrified by your adversaries: which is to them an evident token of perdition, but to you of salvation, and that of God" (Ph.1:27-28).

"For God hath not given us the spirit of fear; but of power, and of love, and of a sound mind" (2 Ti.1:7).

"The LORD *is* my light and my salvation; whom shall I fear? the LORD *is* the strength of my life; of whom shall I be afraid? When the wicked, *even* mine enemies and my foes, came upon me to eat up my

---

2 Robert D. Bergen. *1, 2 Samuel*, p.148.

flesh, they stumbled and fell. Though an host should encamp against me, my heart shall not fear: though war should rise against me, in this *will* I *be* confident" (Ps.27:1-3).

"I will say of the LORD, *He is* my refuge and my fortress: my God; in him will I trust. Surely he shall deliver thee from the snare of the fowler, *and* from the noisome pestilence. He shall cover thee with his feathers, and under his wings shalt thou trust: his truth *shall be thy* shield and buckler. Thou shalt not be afraid for the terror by night; *nor* for the arrow *that* flieth by day; *Nor* for the pestilence *that* walketh in darkness; *nor* for the destruction *that* wasteth at noonday" (Ps.91:2-6).

"The LORD *is* on my side; I will not fear: what can man do unto me" (Ps.118:6).

"When thou liest down, thou shalt not be afraid: yea, thou shalt lie down, and thy sleep shall be sweet" (Pr.3:24).

"Fear thou not; for I *am* with thee: be not dismayed; for I *am* thy God: I will strengthen thee; yea, I will help thee; yea, I will uphold thee with the right hand of my righteousness" (Is.41:10).

"For I the LORD thy God will hold thy right hand, saying unto thee, Fear not; I will help thee" (Is.41:13).

"Fear not: for I have redeemed thee, I have called *thee* by thy name; thou *art* mine. When thou passest through the waters, I *will be* with thee; and through the rivers, they shall not overflow thee: when thou walkest through the fire, thou shalt not be burned; neither shall the flame kindle upon thee" (Is.43:1-2).

DEEPER STUDY #1

(13:1) **Saul, Reign of—Hebrew Text, Explanation**: the Hebrew in this verse is unclear, literally saying: "Saul was the son of one year." Most commentators agree that the exact meaning is unknown, and that perhaps something has been lost in the manuscript throughout the years of copying the original manuscript. Because of this, most modern-day translations differ from one another. Just when Saul began to reign over Israel is unknown; however, it is known that he reigned for a period of forty-two years. As Matthew Henry and Robert D. Bergen say, perhaps the author was simply saying that Saul reigned one year and the second year the events of this chapter took place, a tragically significant year when Saul disqualified himself from serving as king.

---

2 (13:8-14) **Disqualification, Caused by—Disobedience, Results of—Saul, Disqualification of—Kings, Saul, Disqualification of—Ruler, Disqualification of**: there was the unlawful act that made Saul unfit to be king. This is the clear picture of being disqualified from serving the LORD. Saul committed a serious offense in what he now did, an offense that was to change his life forever, an offense that was to doom his kingdom. Note his unlawful act that disqualified him from being king:

OUTLINE	SCRIPTURE	SCRIPTURE	OUTLINE

2. The unlawful act that made Saul unfit to be king: Being disqualified from serving the LORD
a. The delay of Samuel & Saul's impatient fear
b. The unlawful act of Saul: Did not wait for Samuel & assumed the role of priest, offering up the burnt offering
c. The confrontation with Samuel: Samuel arrived just as Saul was completing the offering
 	
1) Samuel questioned Saul
2) Saul gave four excuses
  • The fleeing of the troops
  • The delay of Samuel
  • The massive mobilization of the Philistines
	8 And he tarried seven days, according to the set time that Samuel *had appointed:* but Samuel came not to Gilgal; and the people were scattered from him. 9 And Saul said, Bring hither a burnt offering to me, and peace offerings. And he offered the burnt offering. 10 And it came to pass, that as soon as he had made an end of offering the burnt offering, behold, Samuel came; and Saul went out to meet him, that he might salute him. 11 And Samuel said, What hast thou done? And Saul said, Because I saw that the people were scattered from me, and *that* thou camest not within the days appointed, and *that* the Philistines gathered themselves together at	Michmash; 12 Therefore said I, The Philistines will come down now upon me to Gilgal, and I have not made supplication unto the LORD: I forced myself therefore, and offered a burnt offering. 13 And Samuel said to Saul, Thou hast done foolishly: thou hast not kept the commandment of the LORD thy God, which he commanded thee: for now would the LORD have established thy kingdom upon Israel for ever. 14 But now thy kingdom shall not continue: the LORD hath sought him a man after his own heart, and the LORD hath commanded him *to be* captain over his people, because thou hast not kept *that* which the LORD commanded thee.	• The desperate need to seek the LORD's favor before the attack of the Philistines was launched against him
			
			d. The rebuke & pronouncement of God's judgment upon Saul
			1) He acted foolishly: He had disobeyed the LORD
			2) He had lost the permanent establishment of his kingdom: It would not last
			e. The bypassing of Saul: The LORD had chosen another man—"a man after His own heart"—to be the leader of God's people

a. For some reason, Samuel had delayed his arrival to the battlefield, and Saul became impatient—very impatient (v.8). Apparently, Samuel had instructed Saul to always wait at least seven days, if possible, before engaging in any military battle. Seven days would give Samuel time to reach the battlefield to lead the troops in worship and sacrifice, and to give spiritual, military guidance to Saul (10:8). Whatever the case, in this particular instance Samuel had definitely instructed Saul to wait seven days for his arrival. However, some of Saul's few remaining troops began to scatter.

b. In desperation, Saul committed a terrible, unlawful act (v.9). Not waiting for Samuel, he assumed the role of a priest and led the men in worship, offering up the burnt offering. But note that he never had time to offer up the fellowship sacrifices (v.9).

c. Just as Saul had finished offering up the burnt sacrifice, Samuel arrived (v.10). Seeing him off in the distance, Saul went out to greet Samuel. Immediately Samuel questioned Saul, asking what he had done. In response, Saul gave four excuses for his unlawful act of disobedience and blamed the troops, Samuel, and the Philistines. His excuses were:

⇒ the fleeing of the troops
⇒ the delay of Samuel
⇒ the massive mobilization of the Philistines
⇒ the desperate need to seek the LORD's favor before the attack of the Philistines was launched against him (v.12)

Saul confessed his fear of facing the Philistines without having sought the LORD's favor. Therefore he felt compelled to offer the burnt offering since Samuel had not yet arrived.

d. Hearing this, Samuel immediately pronounced God's judgment upon Saul (v.13). He declared that Saul had acted foolishly, that he had tragically disobeyed the LORD's command. He had disobeyed by not waiting the seven days (10:8) and by assuming the place of a priest in worship and offering the burnt sacrifices.

No crisis could ever justify such an offense against God, such terrible disobedience. Saul had disobeyed God; consequently, he had to face the judgment of God. He had to pay the penalty for his disobedience. Samuel pronounced the judgment: Saul was to lose the permanent establishment of his kingdom, the rule of his dynasty in the future. His dynasty or kingdom would not last (v.13).

e. Saul was to be bypassed and another kingdom or dynasty established. The LORD would thereafter choose another man—"a man after His own heart"—to be the leader of His people (v.14; see v.5). The future ruler of God's people would be a person totally committed to the LORD.

Thought 1. The lesson for us is simple, yet very straightforward: disobedience disqualifies us from serving the LORD. If we disobey the LORD, we make ourselves unclean instruments for the LORD. The LORD cannot use...

• a disobedient person to proclaim obedience
• a sinful person to proclaim holiness
• a wicked person to proclaim righteousness
• an immoral person to proclaim morality
• an unjust person to proclaim justice
• a foul-mouthed person to proclaim spiritual truths
• an irresponsible person to proclaim responsibility
• a thief to proclaim honesty
• a liar to proclaim truth

"Not every one that saith unto me, LORD, LORD, shall enter into the kingdom of heaven; but he that doeth the will of my Father which is in heaven" (Mt.7:21).

"Jesus said unto him, If thou wilt be perfect, go *and* sell that thou hast, and give to the poor, and thou shalt have treasure in heaven: and come *and* follow me. But when the young man heard that saying, he went away sorrowful: for he had great possessions. Then said Jesus unto his disciples, Verily I say unto you, That a rich man shall hardly enter into the kingdom of heaven" (Mt.19:21-23).

"And he said to *them* all, If any *man* will come after me, let him deny himself, and take up his cross daily, and follow me" (Lu.9:23).

"And it came to pass, that, as they went in the way, a certain *man* said unto him, LORD, I will follow thee whithersoever thou goest. And Jesus said unto him, Foxes have holes, and birds of the air *have* nests; but the Son of man hath not where to lay *his* head. And he said unto another, Follow me. But he said, LORD, suffer me first to go and bury my father. Jesus said unto him, Let the dead bury their dead: but go thou and preach the kingdom of God. And another also said, LORD, I will follow thee; but let me first go bid them farewell, which are at home at my house. And Jesus said unto him, No man, having put his hand to the plough, and looking back, is fit for the kingdom of God" (Lu.9:57-62).

"And that servant, which knew his lord's will, and prepared not *himself,* neither did according to his will, shall be beaten with many *stripes*" (Lu.12:47).

"If any *man* come to me, and hate not his father, and mother, and wife, and children, and brethren, and sisters, yea, and his own life also, he cannot be my disciple. And whosoever doth not bear his cross, and come after me, cannot be my disciple" (Lu.14:26-27).

"For if ye live after the flesh, ye shall die: but if ye through the Spirit do mortify the deeds of the body, ye shall live" (Ro.8:13).

"But I keep under my body, and bring *it* into subjection: lest that by any means, when I have preached to others, I myself should be a castaway" (1 Co.9:27).

"And they that are Christ's have crucified the flesh with the affections and lusts" (Ga.5:24).

"But in a great house there are not only vessels of gold and of silver, but also of wood and of earth; and some to honour, and some to dishonour. If a man therefore purge himself from these, he shall be a vessel unto honour, sanctified, and meet for the master's use, *and* prepared unto every good work" (2 Ti.2:20-21).

"Now the just shall live by faith: but if *any man* draw back, my soul shall have no pleasure in him" (He.10:38).

"Nevertheless I have *somewhat* against thee, because thou hast left thy first love. Remember therefore from whence thou art fallen, and repent, and do the first works; or else I will come unto thee quickly, and will remove thy candlestick out of his place, except thou repent" (Re.2:4-5).

"Cursed be he that doeth the work of the LORD deceitfully, and cursed be he that keepeth back his sword from blood" (Je.48:10).

3 (13:15-23) **Defeat, Danger of—Enemy, Danger of—Believer, Danger Facing—Israel, Weapons of**: there was the critical situation confronted by Saul. Since he had just become disqualified from serving the LORD, he faced the possibility of being utterly defeated by the Philistines.

OUTLINE	SCRIPTURE	SCRIPTURE	OUTLINE
3. The critical situation confronted by Saul: A desperate need for God's help a. He was alienated from God & God's prophet due to sin b. He had only 600 troops left to fight the overwhelming Philistine army c. He faced three major raiding parties: Sent to harass & plunder & to demoralize the population d. He had no weapons	15 And Samuel arose, and gat him up from Gilgal unto Gibeah of Benjamin. And Saul numbered the people *that were* present with him, about six hundred men. 16 And Saul, and Jonathan his son, and the people *that were* present with them, abode in Gibeah of Benjamin: but the Philistines encamped in Michmash. 17 And the spoilers came out of the camp of the Philistines in three companies: one company turned unto the way *that leadeth to* Ophrah, unto the land of Shual: 18 And another company turned the way *to* Beth-horon: and another company turned *to* the way of the border that looketh to the valley of Zeboim toward the wilderness. 19 Now there was no smith	found throughout all the land of Israel: for the Philistines said, Lest the Hebrews make *them* swords or spears: 20 But all the Israelites went down to the Philistines, to sharpen every man his share, and his coulter, and his axe, and his mattock. 21 Yet they had a file for the mattocks, and for the coulters, and for the forks, and for the axes, and to sharpen the goads. 22 So it came to pass in the day of battle, that there was neither sword nor spear found in the hand of any of the people that *were* with Saul and Jonathan: but with Saul and with Jonathan his son was there found. 23 And the garrison of the Philistines went out to the passage of Michmash.	developed from metal nor from the latest technology 1) The Israelites had been forbidden to have blacksmiths 2) The Israelites were totally dependent upon the Philistines for all metal tools e. He had no money to manufacture or purchase weapons: Because of the high price charged for services by the Philistines f. He & his son Jonathan had the only two swords among the entire army g. He faced the major road being blocked by a detachment of enemy soldiers

a. Because of his terrible disobedience, Saul had been alienated from God, and he was now to be alienated from God's prophet (v.15). Samuel turned and walked away from Saul, leaving Saul to face the enemy by himself. Apparently Samuel neither prayed with nor gave any direction to Saul. Saul had made the tragic decision of doing his own thing, disobeying God, and taking matters into his own hands. As a result, God's prophet was to leave the scene, allowing Saul to exercise his free will and do just what he had wanted. Neither the LORD nor His prophet Samuel could have anything to do with such self-centered behavior and disobedience.

b. Being left all alone, Saul counted his men and discovered that there were only 600 troops left to fight the overwhelming Philistine army (vv.15-16). At this time, Saul and Jonathan were camped in Gibeah, while the Philistines were camped at Micmash.

c. Three major raiding parties were sent out by the Philistines to harass and plunder and to demoralize the population of Israel (v.17). By using this strategy, the Philistines were obviously seeking to achieve an easy victory, perhaps even a surrender by the Israelites. If they could demoralize the population, Saul might be forced to surrender, and the Philistines would gain a victory without the loss of any troops.

d. Note that the Israelites had no weapons developed from metal nor any other of the latest technologies (vv.19-20). They had only weapons made of wood and stone such as knives, slings, javelins, clubs, bows, and arrows.[3]

In their oppression and occupation of Israel, the Philistines had forbidden the Israelites to have blacksmiths. This made the Israelites totally dependent upon the Philistines for all their metal tools (vv.19-20). If an Israelite needed to purchase or repair some agricultural tool, he was forced to go to the Philistines.

e. Moreover, the Israelites had no money to manufacture or to purchase weapons, for the Philistines charged outrageous prices for servicing agricultural tools (v.21). Economically, the Israelites were a poor people with little money to spend on anything, much less weapons.

f. In fact, on the day of the battle there were only two swords among the entire army, the swords carried by Saul and Jonathan themselves (v.22). The Philistine oppression had forced a harsh, poverty-stricken life upon the Israelites.

g. At some point, the Philistines sent a detachment of soldiers to block the pass at Micmash (v.23). The pass was the major road between the two armies. By blocking the pass, the Philistines prevented a surprise attack and assured a

---

3 Robert D. Bergen. *1, 2 Samuel*, p.154.

delaying action in the event of an attack, a delay that would allow them time to mobilize their forces to withstand any attack by the Israelites.

Thought 1. Saul had disobeyed and separated himself from the LORD. Tragically, he sinned when he most desperately needed the LORD. If he ever needed divine guidance, it was now. He and his troops faced a terrifying, critical situation.

There is a strong lesson for us in Saul's experience. When we are facing terrible, terrifying situations, God will help us. If we will confess and repent of our sins, turn away from sin and turn to God—God will help us. No matter what the hardship or misfortune is, if our hearts are cleansed from sin, God will deliver us. He will deliver us through...

- sickness
- disease
- accident
- injury
- financial difficulties
- bankruptcy
- broken relationships
- divorce
- loneliness
- depression
- distress
- emptiness
- purposelessness
- guilt
- temptation

God will deliver us through any hardship or misfortune if we genuinely follow after Him, seeking Him with a repentant, clean heart. This is the wonderful declaration of God's Holy Word:

"And the LORD shall deliver me from every evil work, and will preserve *me* unto his heavenly kingdom: to whom *be* glory for ever and ever. Amen" (2 Ti.4:18).

"*Let your* conversation [behavior, conduct] *be* without covetousness; *and be* content with such things as ye have: for he hath said, I will never leave thee, nor forsake thee. So that we may boldly say, The LORD *is* my helper, and I will not fear what man shall do unto me" (He.13:5-6).

"Casting all your care upon him; for he careth for you" (1 Pe.5:7).

"And, behold, I *am* with thee, and will keep thee in all *places* whither thou goest, and will bring thee again into this land; for I will not leave thee, until I have done *that* which I have spoken to thee of" (Ge.28:15).

"The eternal God *is thy* refuge, and underneath *are* the everlasting arms: and he shall thrust out the enemy from before thee; and shall say, Destroy *them*" (De.33:27).

"The LORD *is* my strength and my shield; my heart trusted in him, and I am helped: therefore my heart greatly rejoiceth; and with my song will I praise him" (Ps.28:7).

"But I *am* poor and needy; *yet* the LORD thinketh upon me: thou *art* my help and my deliverer; make no tarrying, O my God" (Ps.40:17).

"Be merciful unto me, O God, be merciful unto me: for my soul trusteth in thee: yea, in the shadow of thy wings will I make my refuge, until *these* calamities be overpast" (Ps.57:1).

"For thou hast been a strength to the poor, a strength to the needy in his distress, a refuge from the storm, a shadow from the heat, when the blast of the terrible ones *is* as a storm *against* the wall" (Is.25:4).

"Fear thou not; for I *am* with thee: be not dismayed; for I *am* thy God: I will strengthen thee; yea, I will help thee; yea, I will uphold thee with the right hand of my righteousness" (Is.41:10).

"And *even* to *your* old age I *am* he; and *even* to hoar [gray] hairs will I carry *you:* I have made, and I will bear; even I will carry, and will deliver *you*" (Is.46:4).

CHAPTER 14

G. The Continued Decline of Saul: Weak Faith, Spiritual Insensitivity, & Misguided, Carnal Zeal, 14:1-52

1. Saul's weak, wavering faith contrasted with Jonathan's strong, fearless faith

a. Jonathan's suggestion to his armor-bearer: That they spy out the Philistine outpost

b. Saul's weak, wavering faith: His indecisiveness seen in his withdrawal to the outskirts of Gibeah
  1) With his 600 soldiers

  2) With Ahijah
  • Was wearing an ephod, the dress of a priest
  • Was the great-grandson of Eli: To bear the judgment pronounced on Eli's family, 2:27-36; 3:11-14

c. Jonathan's strong, fearless faith
  1) The dangerous, jagged cliffs that confronted Jonathan in his attempt to spy out the Philistine outpost
  • One was Bozez: Faced north toward Micmash
  • The other was Seneh: Faced south toward Geba

  2) The suggestion of Jonathan restated: To spy out the outpost of the "uncircumcised" (unbelievers)
  3) The strong faith & confidence of Jonathan in the LORD's power to give victory against all odds
  4) The unified spirit & encouragement of the armorbearer

  5) The trust of Jonathan in the LORD, that He would give a clear sign of victory

  • A Philistine challenge to Jonathan & his aide to stay where they were would be a sign from the LORD not to attack
  • A Philistine challenge to climb up the cliffs would

Now it came to pass upon a day, that Jonathan the son of Saul said unto the young man that bare his armour, Come, and let us go over to the Philistines' garrison, that *is* on the other side. But he told not his father.
2 And Saul tarried in the uttermost part of Gibeah under a pomegranate tree which is in Migron: and the people that *were* with him *were* about six hundred men;
3 And Ahiah, the son of Ahitub, Ichabod's brother, the son of Phinehas, the son of Eli, the LORD'S priest in Shiloh, wearing an ephod. And the people knew not that Jonathan was gone.
4 And between the passages, by which Jonathan sought to go over unto the Philistines' garrison, *there was* a sharp rock on the one side, and a sharp rock on the other side: and the name of the one *was* Bozez, and the name of the other Seneh.
5 The forefront of the one *was* situate northward over against Michmash, and the other southward over against Gibeah.
6 And Jonathan said to the young man that bare his armour, Come, and let us go over unto the garrison of these uncircumcised: it may be that the LORD will work for us: for *there is* no restraint to the LORD to save by many or by few.
7 And his armourbearer said unto him, Do all that *is* in thine heart: turn thee; behold, I *am* with thee according to thy heart.
8 Then said Jonathan, Behold, we will pass over unto *these* men, and we will discover ourselves unto them.
9 If they say thus unto us, Tarry until we come to you; then we will stand still in our place, and will not go up unto them.
10 But if they say thus, Come up unto us; then we will go up:

for the LORD hath delivered them into our hand: and this *shall be* a sign unto us.
11 And both of them discovered themselves unto the garrison of the Philistines: and the Philistines said, Behold, the Hebrews come forth out of the holes where they had hid themselves.
12 And the men of the garrison answered Jonathan and his armourbearer, and said, Come up to us, and we will show you a thing. And Jonathan said unto his armourbearer, Come up after me: for the LORD hath delivered them into the hand of Israel.
13 And Jonathan climbed up upon his hands and upon his feet, and his armourbearer after him: and they fell before Jonathan; and his armourbearer slew after him.
14 And that first slaughter, which Jonathan and his armourbearer made, was about twenty men, within as it were an half acre of land, *which* a yoke *of oxen might plow.*
15 And there was trembling in the host, in the field, and among all the people: the garrison, and the spoilers, they also trembled, and the earth quaked: so it was a very great trembling.
16 And the watchmen of Saul in Gibeah of Benjamin looked; and, behold, the multitude melted away, and they went on beating down *one another.*
17 Then said Saul unto the people that were with him, Number now, and see who is gone from us. And when they had numbered, behold, Jonathan and his armourbearer *were* not *there.*
18 And Saul said unto Ahiah, Bring hither the ark of God. For the ark of God was at that time with the children of Israel.
19 And it came to pass, while Saul talked unto the priest, that the noise that *was* in the host of the Philistines went on and increased: and Saul said unto the priest, Withdraw thine hand.
20 And Saul and all the people that *were* with him assembled themselves, and they came to the battle: and, behold, every man's sword was against his fellow, *and*

be a sign from the LORD to attack & gain the victory

6) The sign was given to Jonathan by God
  • The Philistine outpost spotted Jonathan & his armor-bearer: Ridiculed them

  • The Philistine soldiers challenged them to climb up the cliffs & face death

7) The amazing victory of Jonathan & his armorbearer—against all odds: They scaled the cliffs & killed 20 soldiers within an area of about half an acre

8) The result of Jonathan's strong, fearless faith
  • God sent a terrifying earthquake
  • Panic struck the Philistine army

2. Saul's spiritual insensitivity: He refused to wait upon the LORD & follow His ways

a. The panic & flight of the Philistines: Was spotted by Saul's lookouts
b. The command of Saul for a roll call & an investigation to see who had routed the Philistines: Discovered that it was Jonathan & his armor-bearer

c. The command of Saul for the High Priest Ahijah to bring the Ark of God: To seek God— whether or not to join in the battle
d. The sinful, disobedient command of Saul: Ordered the High Priest to suspend his priestly duties, to stop seeking the LORD, De.20:1-4

e. The command of Saul for his troops to immediately assemble & join in the battle
  1) The Philistine troops were found in utter confusion, striking out at each other

2) The Hebrews—some bandits with divided loyalties—betrayed the Philistines & joined ranks with the Israelite troops

3) The Israelite troops who had earlier fled in fear heard about the Philistine defeat & returned to join the victorious battle

4) The victorious result: The LORD saved, rescued Israel

3. **Saul's misguided, carnal zeal in seeking the LORD's favor & blessing**
   a. Saul's misguided zeal in seeking personal revenge
   b. Saul's misguided zeal in imposing a rash, unwise fast & oath upon his troops—all to secure God's favor
      1) The loyalty of the troops to Saul's command to fast: Saw plenty of honey throughout the forest, but refused to eat

      2) The violation of the oath by Jonathan: Was committed in ignorance
         • He had not heard of the fast & oath
         • He ate some honey & his strength was renewed

         • He was immediately informed of the fast & oath by another soldier & informed that the troops were weakened because of the fast

      3) The criticism by Jonathan: Accused Saul of causing trouble by the fasting oath
         • Weakened the troops
         • Kept the troops from achieving a greater victory because of their weakened strength

   c. Saul's misguided zeal in correcting the conduct of his

---

there was a very great discomfiture.
21 Moreover the Hebrews *that* were with the Philistines before that time, which went up with them into the camp *from the country* round about, even they also *turned* to be with the Israelites that *were* with Saul and Jonathan.
22 Likewise all the men of Israel which had hid themselves in mount Ephraim, *when* they heard that the Philistines fled, even they also followed hard after them in the battle.
23 So the LORD saved Israel that day: and the battle passed over unto Beth-aven.
24 And the men of Israel were distressed that day: for Saul had adjured the people, saying, Cursed *be* the man that eateth *any* food until evening, that I may be avenged on mine enemies. So none of the people tasted *any* food.
25 And all *they of* the land came to a wood; and there was honey upon the ground.
26 And when the people were come into the wood, behold, the honey dropped; but no man put his hand to his mouth: for the people feared the oath.
27 But Jonathan heard not when his father charged the people with the oath: wherefore he put forth the end of the rod that *was* in his hand, and dipped it in an honeycomb, and put his hand to his mouth; and his eyes were enlightened.
28 Then answered one of the people, and said, Thy father straitly charged the people with an oath, saying, Cursed *be* the man that eateth *any* food this day. And the people were faint.
29 Then said Jonathan, My father hath troubled the land: see, I pray you, how mine eyes have been enlightened, because I tasted a little of this honey.
30 How much more, if haply the people had eaten freely to day of the spoil of their enemies which they found? for had there not been now a much greater slaughter among the Philistines?
31 And they smote the Philistines that day from Mich-

---

mash to Aijalon: and the people were very faint.
32 And the people flew upon the spoil, and took sheep, and oxen, and calves, and slew *them* on the ground: and the people did eat *them* with the blood.
33 Then they told Saul, saying, Behold, the people sin against the LORD, in that they eat with the blood. And he said, Ye have transgressed: roll a great stone unto me this day.
34 And Saul said, Disperse yourselves among the people, and say unto them, Bring me hither every man his ox, and every man his sheep, and slay *them* here, and eat; and sin not against the LORD in eating with the blood. And all the people brought every man his ox with him that night, and slew *them* there.
35 And Saul built an altar unto the LORD: the same was the first altar that he built unto the LORD.
36 And Saul said, Let us go down after the Philistines by night, and spoil them until the morning light, and let us not leave a man of them. And they said, Do whatsoever seemeth good unto thee. Then said the priest, Let us draw near hither unto God.
37 And Saul asked counsel of God, Shall I go down after the Philistines? wilt thou deliver them into the hand of Israel? But he answered him not that day.
38 And Saul said, Draw ye near hither, all the chief of the people: and know and see wherein this sin hath been this day.
39 For, *as* the LORD liveth, which saveth Israel, though it be in Jonathan my son, he shall surely die. But *there was* not a man among all the people *that* answered him.
40 Then said he unto all Israel, Be ye on one side, and I and Jonathan my son will be on the other side. And the people said unto Saul, Do what seemeth good unto thee.
41 Therefore Saul said unto the LORD God of Israel, Give a perfect *lot*. And Saul and Jonathan were taken: but the people escaped.
42 And Saul said, Cast *lots* between me and Jonathan my

---

troops while he himself was ignorant of God's laws & failing to live righteously
   1) The utter exhaustion & sinful behavior of the troops: Eating meat with blood, Ge.9:4; Le.3:17; 7:26
   2) The sinful violation pointed out to Saul
      • He was obviously ignorant of God's commandment

      • He corrected the troops
      • He had an elevated surface prepared—a large stone—upon which the animals could be slaughtered

   d. Saul's misguided zeal in seeking God's favor by building an altar when he was living a self-centered, distrustful life
   e. Saul's misguided zeal in seeking God's will when he was not wholly committed
      1) Saul planned to launch a nighttime raid to plunder & wipe out all the Philistines
      2) The High Priest Ahijah suggested they first seek God
      3) Saul sought an answer from God

      4) God did not answer him

   f. Saul's misguided zeal in seeking to discover the sinner when he himself was guilty of being a sinner

      1) The command of Saul for the officers to launch an investigation: Vowed to execute the person, even if it was his own son Jonathan
      2) The officers said nothing
      3) The guidance sought by Saul in exposing the sinner.
         • By lining up the officers in front of him & Jonathan

         • By praying & asking God to guide the casting of lots between them
      4) The lot fell upon Saul & Jonathan
      5) The lot then fell upon Jonathan

g. Saul's misguided zeal in seeking to justify himself before God while condemning his innocent son, a believer filled with strong, fearless faith
1) Jonathan gave an explanation
2) Saul attempted to justify himself: Even if it meant the execution of his son
3) The troops rescued Jonathan
• They argued the case before Saul: It was Jonathan who had brought about the great victory over the Philistines
• They insisted Jonathan not be executed
• They won the case: Saul was forced to rescind his order, to let Jonathan live
4) Saul & the army withdrew from pursuing the enemy, returned home

4. Saul's military victories over the enemies of Israel & his family line
a. Saul's military victories
1) East: Moab, Ammon, Edom
2) North: Kings of Zobah
3) West: The Philistines
4) South: The Amalekites

b. Saul's family
1) His sons: Three listed here; one son, Abinadab, listed elsewhere, 31:2
2) His two daughters
3) His wife
4) His cousin Abner: Made commander of the armed forces

c. Saul's most bitter enemies: The Philistines
d. Saul's answer to the continued threat of the Philistines: A permanent draft system

son. And Jonathan was taken. 43 Then Saul said to Jonathan, Tell me what thou hast done. And Jonathan told him, and said, I did but taste a little honey with the end of the rod that *was* in mine hand, *and,* lo, I must die. 44 And Saul answered, God do so and more also: for thou shalt surely die, Jonathan. 45 And the people said unto Saul, Shall Jonathan die, who hath wrought this great salvation in Israel? God forbid: *as* the LORD liveth, there shall not one hair of his head fall to the ground; for he hath wrought with God this day. So the people rescued Jonathan, that he died not. 46 Then Saul went up from following the Philistines: and the Philistines went to their own place. 47 So Saul took the kingdom over Israel, and fought against all his enemies on every side, against Moab, and against the children of Ammon, and against Edom, and against the kings of Zobah, and against the Philistines: and whithersoever he turned himself, he vexed *them.* 48 And he gathered an host, and smote the Amalekites, and delivered Israel out of the hands of them that spoiled them. 49 Now the sons of Saul were Jonathan, and Ishui, and Melchi-shua: and the names of his two daughters *were these;* the name of the firstborn Merab, and the name of the younger Michal: 50 And the name of Saul's wife *was* Ahinoam, the daughter of Ahimaaz: and the name of the captain of his host *was* Abner, the son of Ner, Saul's uncle. 51 And Kish *was* the father of Saul; and Ner the father of Abner *was* the son of Abiel. 52 And there was sore war against the Philistines all the days of Saul: and when Saul saw any strong man, or any valiant man, he took him unto him.

DIVISION II

THE STORY OF SAMUEL AND SAUL: THE LORD GIVES ISRAEL A KING JUST "LIKE ALL THE NATIONS," 8:1–15:35

G. The Continued Decline of Saul: Weak Faith, Spiritual Insensitivity, and Misguided, Carnal Zeal, 14:1-52

(14:1-52) **Introduction—Faith, Weak—Hope, Weak, Results—Hopelessness, Caused by—Helplessness, Caused by**: a weak, wavering faith will lead to defeat. A person with weak faith has little hope in the future, little to hang on to. If a person does not believe in the future, what hope does he have? His heart is empty, with little purpose and hope of achieving. To achieve, a person must believe that he can accomplish the task. For a person to sense purpose, he must believe in something. Weak faith leads to a life of helplessness and hopelessness.

This passage of Scripture also covers spiritual insensitivity. It shows what happens to a person who is insensitive and has a hard, indifferent heart toward the LORD. But this is not all, for the passage also covers a misguided, carnal zeal. It paints a picture of what happens to a person who allows his zeal to run wild, contrary to the Word of God. This is the subject of the present passage of Scripture: *The Continued Decline of Saul: Weak Faith, Spiritual Insensitivity, and Misguided, Carnal Zeal,* 14:1-52.

1. Saul's weak, wavering faith contrasted with Jonathan's strong, fearless faith (vv.1-15).
2. Saul's spiritual insensitivity: he refused to wait upon the LORD and follow His ways (vv.16-23).
3. Saul's misguided, carnal zeal in seeking the LORD's favor and blessing (vv.24-46).
4. Saul's military victories over the enemies of Israel and his family line (vv.47-52).

1 (14:1-15) **Faith, Wavering—Faith, Fearless—Saul, Weakness of—Jonathan, Faith of**: Saul's continued decline is seen in his weak, wavering faith contrasted with Jonathan's strong, fearless faith. Remember, the Philistines had mobilized a huge army with thousands of chariots and division after division of foot soldiers. Setting up their base camp at Micmash, the Philistines were poised to attack and prepared to subject the Israelites to Philistine oppression. Three raiding parties had been sent out by the Philistines to harass and plunder and to demoralize the population (13:17). Later, a fourth detachment of soldiers had been sent out to set up an outpost and guard the pass at Micmash, protecting the Philistines from a surprise attack by the Israelite army. What now happened is one of the most daring, fearless feats by an individual in the annals of military history. The scene also pictures a sharp contrast between weak, wavering faith and strong, fearless faith:

OUTLINE	SCRIPTURE	SCRIPTURE	OUTLINE
1. Saul's weak, wavering faith contrasted with Jonathan's strong, fearless faith a. Jonathan's suggestion to his armor-bearer: That they spy out the Philistine outpost b. Saul's weak, wavering faith: His indecisiveness seen in his withdrawal to the outskirts of Gibeah 1) With his 600 soldiers 2) With Ahijah • Was wearing an ephod, the dress of a priest • Was the great-grandson of Eli: To bear the judgment pronounced on Eli's family, 2:27-36; 3:11-14 c. Jonathan's strong, fearless faith 1) The dangerous, jagged cliffs that confronted Jonathan in his attempt to spy out the Philistine outpost • One was Bozez: Faced north toward Micmash • The other was Seneh: Faced south toward Geba 2) The suggestion of Jonathan restated: To spy out the outpost of the "uncircumcised" (unbelievers) 3) The strong faith & confidence of Jonathan in the LORD's power to give victory against all odds 4) The unified spirit & encouragement of the armor-bearer	Now it came to pass upon a day, that Jonathan the son of Saul said unto the young man that bare his armour, Come, and let us go over to the Philistines' garrison, that *is* on the other side. But he told not his father. 2 And Saul tarried in the uttermost part of Gibeah under a pomegranate tree which is in Migron: and the people that *were* with him *were* about six hundred men; 3 And Ahiah, the son of Ahitub, Ichabod's brother, the son of Phinehas, the son of Eli, the LORD'S priest in Shiloh, wearing an ephod. And the people knew not that Jonathan was gone. 4 And between the passages, by which Jonathan sought to go over unto the Philistines' garrison, *there was* a sharp rock on the one side and a sharp rock on the other side: and the name of the one *was* Bozez, and the name of the other Seneh. 5 The forefront of the one *was* situate northward over against Michmash, and the other southward over against Gibeah. 6 And Jonathan said to the young man that bare his armour, Come, and let us go over unto the garrison of these uncircumcised: it may be that the LORD will work for us: for *there is* no restraint to the LORD to save by many or by few. 7 And his armourbearer said unto him, Do all that *is* in thine heart: turn thee; behold, I *am* with thee according to thy heart.	8 Then said Jonathan, Behold, we will pass over unto *these* men, and we will discover ourselves unto them. 9 If they say thus unto us, Tarry until we come to you; then we will stand still in our place, and will not go up unto them. 10 But if they say thus, Come up unto us; then we will go up: for the LORD hath delivered them into our hand: and this *shall be* a sign unto us. 11 And both of them discovered themselves unto the garrison of the Philistines: and the Philistines said, Behold, the Hebrews come forth out of the holes where they had hid themselves. 12 And the men of the garrison answered Jonathan and his armourbearer, and said, Come up to us, and we will show you a thing. And Jonathan said unto his armourbearer, Come up after me: for the LORD hath delivered them into the hand of Israel. 13 And Jonathan climbed up upon his hands and upon his feet, and his armourbearer after him: and they fell before Jonathan; and his armourbearer slew after him. 14 And that first slaughter, which Jonathan and his armourbearer made, was about twenty men, within as it were an half acre of land, *which* a yoke *of oxen might plow.* 15 And there was trembling in the host, in the field, and among all the people: the garrison, and the spoilers, they also trembled, and the earth quaked: so it was a very great trembling.	5) The trust of Jonathan in the LORD, that He would give a clear sign of victory • A Philistine challenge to Jonathan & his aide to stay where they were would be a sign from the LORD not to attack • A Philistine challenge to climb up the cliffs would be a sign from the LORD to attack & gain the victory 6) The sign was given to Jonathan by God • The Philistine outpost spotted Jonathan & his armor-bearer: Ridiculed them • The Philistine soldiers challenged them to climb up the cliffs & face death 7) The amazing victory of Jonathan & his armor-bearer—against all odds: They scaled the cliffs & killed 20 soldiers within an area of about half an acre 8) The result of Jonathan's strong, fearless faith • God sent a terrifying earthquake • Panic struck the Philistine army

a. Jonathan made a suggestion to his armor-bearer that they spy out the Philistine outpost guarding the pass at Micmash (v.1). Only Jonathan and his armor-bearer were to know about the spy mission. It was to be kept totally secret, with Jonathan not telling even his father.

b. While Jonathan was showing bold, courageous initiative, note the picture that is painted of Saul: that of a man with weak, wavering faith (v.2). Saul had withdrawn to the outskirts of Gibeah, and Scripture actually says that he was sitting under a pomegranate tree. The picture painted here is that of a commander who has withdrawn and is gripped by a spirit of fear and indecisiveness, dejection and utter discouragement. Remember that Saul had been strongly rebuked by the prophet Samuel and that judgment had been pronounced upon Saul (13:13-14).

Picture the scene: there was Saul sitting under the pomegranate tree being consumed by a spirit of helplessness and hopelessness, expecting at any moment to be attacked, captured, and executed by the Philistines. With Saul were his 600 soldiers and the priest Ahijah who was wearing an ephod, the very dress of a priest. References made to Ahijah's being the great-grandson of Eli meant he was to bear the judgment pronounced on Eli's family; that is, he was to have a very short ministry and brief life (2:27-36; 3:11-14). Reference is also made to Ahijah's being a grandson within the family of Ichabod whose name means "no glory" (4:21). Obviously, the point being made by Scripture is that the rejected Saul is in the presence of the rejected High Priest, that the glory and appointment of God upon Saul had been taken away by God even as God had removed His glory and appointment from the house of Eli (13:14).

c. Now note Jonathan's strong, fearless faith (vv.4-15). While Saul was gripped by a weak, wavering faith of dejection and utter hopelessness, Jonathan demonstrated a strong, fearless faith.

1) In attempting to spy out the Philistine outpost, Jonathan and his armor-bearer had to climb the face of a dangerous, jagged cliff. The pass was actually flanked by two rock formations, one called Bozez and the other Seneh.

2) Jonathan restated his suggestion to his armor-bearer that they spy out the outpost of the Philistines. But this time he referred to the Philistines as the "uncircumcised," meaning that they were unbelievers. They were Gentiles who did not bear the mark of God's people, that of circumcision, and who had no covenant relationship, no agreement with the only living and true God. Calling someone *uncircumcised* was a term of contempt (17:26, 36; 31:4; 2 S.1:20; Jud.14:3; 15:18; 1 Chr.10:4).[1]

3) In speaking to his armor-bearer, Jonathan declared a strong faith and confidence in the LORD's power to give victory against all odds (v.6). Despite the impossible odds and the utter hopelessness of the situation, Jonathan actually believed that the LORD could and would save His people, that absolutely nothing could keep the LORD from saving them.

4) Jonathan's armor-bearer declared his loyalty, that he was with Jonathan in heart and soul. His unified spirit was bound to be an encouragement to Jonathan.

5) Note the total trust of Jonathan in the LORD, believing that the LORD would give a clear sign of victory (vv.8-10). Just as Gideon had done centuries earlier (Jud.6:36-40), Jonathan laid out a fleece before the LORD, trusting the LORD to give a clear indication of the upcoming conquest. Defying military logic, Jonathan suggested that they cross over toward the Philistine outpost and actually let the enemy soldiers see them (v.8).
   ⇒ The sign from the LORD not to attack the outpost would come in the form of a challenge from the Philistines that Jonathan and his armor-bearer would remain where they were.
   ⇒ The sign from the LORD to attack and gain the victory would be a challenge shouted out by the Philistines for Jonathan and his armor-bearer to climb up the cliffs and fight.

6) The sign was clearly given by God to Jonathan (vv.11-12). The Philistine outpost spotted him and his armor-bearer, ridiculing them, shouting out that the Hebrews were like animals who had crawled out of the holes in which they had been hiding. And then the enemy soldiers shouted their challenge, daring Jonathan and his armor-bearer to climb up the cliffs and face them in battle.

7) Against all odds, Jonathan and his armor-bearer gained an amazing victory over the outpost (vv.13-14). Scaling the dangerous and jagged cliffs, the two men reached the top. In hand-to-hand combat, they killed twenty soldiers within an area of about half an acre.

8) As a result of Jonathan's strong and fearless faith, God moved with miraculous power by sending a strong earthquake and tremors throughout the whole area (v.15). With the earth quaking under their feet, their tents collapsing, their supplies falling and being scattered upon the earth, and perhaps their chariots being damaged—panic struck the entire army of the Philistines. In utter confusion the enemy soldiers fled for their lives, including those in the camp and field and those in the raiding parties and outposts. God was miraculously moving to save His people from their helpless and hopeless situation—all because of the strong, fearless faith of one man, Jonathan.

Thought 1. A weak, wavering faith leads to a defeated life. If we have no faith, we have no hope. Without faith, without believing in the future, there is no purpose, meaning, or significance in life. There is no rest of soul, no inner peace, no sense of fulfillment or accomplishment or satisfaction.

But a strong, fearless faith brings to the human soul a *spiritual rest*. When Scripture speaks of God's *spiritual rest* it means a spirit of confidence, assurance, purpose, hope, fulfillment, satisfaction.

(1) God warns us against weak and wavering faith. If we are gripped by unbelief and doubt, we will miss the *spiritual rest* promised by God.

> **"And he said unto them, Why are ye so fearful? how is it that ye have no faith" (Mk.4:40).**
>
> **"He that believeth on the Son hath everlasting life: and he that believeth not the Son shall not see life; but the wrath of God abideth on him" (Jn.3:36).**
>
> **"Harden not your hearts, as in the provocation, in the day of temptation in the wilderness: When your fathers tempted me, proved me, and saw my works forty years. Wherefore I was grieved with that generation, and said, They do alway err in their heart; and they have not known my ways. So I sware in my wrath, They shall not enter into my rest" (He.3:8-11).**
>
> **"And to whom sware he that they should not enter into his rest, but to them that believed not? So we see that they could not enter in because of unbelief" (He.3:18-19).**
>
> **"Let us therefore fear, lest, a promise being left us of entering into his rest, any of you should seem to come short of it. For unto us was the gospel preached, as well as unto them: but the word preached did not profit them, not being mixed with faith in them that heard it. For we which have believed do enter into rest, as he said, As I have sworn in my wrath, if they shall enter into my rest: although the works were finished from the foundation of the world" (He.4:1-3).**
>
> **"Let us labour therefore to enter into that rest, lest any man fall after the same example of unbelief" (He.4:11).**
>
> **"But without faith it is impossible to please him: for he that cometh to God must believe that he is, and that he is a rewarder of them that diligently seek him" (He.11:6).**

---

[1] *The NIV Study Bible*, 14:6.

(2) God gives the most wonderful promises to those with strong, fearless faith.

> "That whosoever believeth in him should not perish, but have eternal life. For God so loved the world, that he gave his only begotten Son, that whosoever believeth in him should not perish, but have everlasting life" (Jn.3:15-16).

> "Verily, verily, I say unto you, He that heareth my word, and believeth on him that sent me, hath everlasting life, and shall not come into condemnation; but is passed from death unto life" (Jn.5:24).

> "Jesus said unto her, I am the resurrection, and the life: he that believeth in me, though he were dead, yet shall he live: And whosoever liveth and believeth in me shall never die. Believest thou this" (Jn.11:25-26).

> "Therefore being justified by faith, we have peace with God through our Lord Jesus Christ" (Ro.5:1).

> "That if thou shalt confess with thy mouth the LORD Jesus, and shalt believe in thine heart that God hath raised him from the dead, thou shalt be saved. For with the heart man believeth unto righteousness; and with the mouth confession is made unto salvation" (Ro.10:9-10).

> "Above all, taking the shield of faith, wherewith ye shall be able to quench all the fiery darts of the wicked" (Ep.6:16).

> "Even as Abraham believed God, and it was accounted to him for righteousness" (Ga.3:6).

> "Who through faith subdued kingdoms, wrought righteousness, obtained promises, stopped the mouths of lions" (He.11:33).

> "If any of you lack wisdom, let him ask of God, that giveth to all men liberally, and upbraideth not; and it shall be given him. But let him ask in faith, nothing wavering. For he that wavereth is like a wave of the sea driven with the wind and tossed" (Js.1:5-6).

> "And they rose early in the morning, and went forth into the wilderness of Tekoa: and as they went forth, Jehoshaphat stood and said, Hear me, O Judah, and ye inhabitants of Jerusalem; Believe in the LORD your God, so shall ye be established; believe his prophets, so shall ye prosper" (2 Chr.20:20).

> "I laid me down and slept; I awaked; for the LORD sustained me" (Ps.3:5).

> "Oh how great is thy goodness, which thou hast laid up for them that fear thee; which thou hast wrought for them that trust in thee before the sons of men" (Ps.31:19).

> "Trust in the LORD, and do good; so shalt thou dwell in the land, and verily thou shalt be fed" (Ps.37:3).

> "Commit thy way unto the LORD; trust also in him; and he shall bring it to pass" (Ps.37:5).

> "Thou wilt keep him in perfect peace, whose mind is stayed on thee: because he trusteth in thee" (Is.26:3).

---

2 (14:16-23) **Insensibility, Spiritual—Insensitivity, Spiritual—Indifference, Spiritual—Callousness, Spiritual—Hardness, Spiritual—Impatience—Disobedience**: Saul's decline is also seen in his spiritual insensitivity and hardness of heart. He demonstrated a spirit of indifference and impatience by refusing to wait upon the LORD and to obey His commands. As the Philistine army fled in panic, note what happened:

OUTLINE	SCRIPTURE	SCRIPTURE	OUTLINE
2. Saul's spiritual insensitivity: He refused to wait upon the LORD & follow His ways a. The panic & flight of the Philistines: Was spotted by Saul's lookouts b. The command of Saul for a roll call & an investigation to see who had routed the Philistines: Discovered that it was Jonathan & his armorbearer c. The command of Saul for the High Priest Ahijah to bring the Ark of God: To seek God— whether or not to join in the battle d. The sinful, disobedient command of Saul: Ordered the High Priest to suspend his priestly duties, to stop seeking the LORD, De.20:1-4 e. The command of Saul for	16 And the watchmen of Saul in Gibeah of Benjamin looked; and, behold, the multitude melted away, and they went on beating down *one another.* 17 Then said Saul unto the people that *were* with him, Number now, and see who is gone from us. And when they had numbered, behold, Jonathan and his armourbearer *were* not *there.* 18 And Saul said unto Ahiah, Bring hither the ark of God. For the ark of God was at that time with the children of Israel. 19 And it came to pass, while Saul talked unto the priest, that the noise that *was* in the host of the Philistines went on and increased: and Saul said unto the priest, Withdraw thine hand. 20 And Saul and all the peo-	ple that *were* with him assembled themselves, and they came to the battle: and, behold, every man's sword was against his fellow, *and there was* a very great discomfiture. 21 Moreover the Hebrews *that* were with the Philistines before that time, which went up with them into the camp *from the country* round about, even they also *turned* to be with the Israelites that *were* with Saul and Jonathan. 22 Likewise all the men of Israel which had hid themselves in mount Ephraim, *when* they heard that the Philistines fled, even they also followed hard after them in the battle. 23 So the LORD saved Israel that day: and the battle passed over unto Beth-aven.	his troops to immediately assemble & join in the battle 1) The Philistine troops were found in utter confusion, striking out at each other 2) The Hebrews—some bandits with divided loyalties—betrayed the Philistines & joined ranks with the Israelite troops 3) The Israelite troops who had earlier fled in fear heard about the Philistine defeat & returned to join the victorious battle 4) The victorious result: The LORD saved, rescued Israel

a. The panic and flight of the Philistines was immediately spotted by Saul's lookouts (v.16). Saul's watchmen could hear the noise and commotion of the soldiers as thousands and thousands of them scattered in all directions fleeing the quaking earth.

b. As soon as Saul received the report of the panic-stricken enemy, he issued the command for a roll call and investigation to see who had routed the Philistines (v.17). Only two men were found to be missing from his small force: Jonathan and his armor-bearer.

c. In obedience to the command of God, Saul summoned for the High Priest Ahijah to bring the Ark of God (v.18). God had earlier stipulated that the priest was always to lead the soldiers in a brief worship service before they engaged in battle (De.20:1-4). At this point Saul was obeying the commandment of God.

d. But note what happened: while Saul was still talking with Ahijah, the noise and commotion in the enemy's camp grew louder and louder. Consequently, Saul commanded the High Priest to suspend his priestly duties, to stop seeking the LORD (v.19). In the words of Robert D. Bergen:

> *Sensing that he was about to lose a golden opportunity to rout the enemy, Saul did the unthinkable—he ordered Ahijah to suspend his priestly activities before they were completed. This incredible interruption of the divine pattern—an action without precedent in the Bible—was intended to enable Israel to win an even greater victory over the Philistines. But for readers who were informed by the [law], it meant that Saul was unfit to fulfill the task of leading Israel against their enemies (cf. 8:20). It also added one more image in the narrative...that depicts Saul as spiritually benighted and insensitive to the Lord's ways. Furthermore, in light of Israel's diminished victory against the Philistines, it reinforced a fundamental teaching of the [law]; any breach of the Lord's instruction diminishes the good that could have resulted (cf. 14:30).*[2]

e. Immediately Saul commanded his troops to assemble and march against the fleeing, panic-stricken enemy (vv.20-23). When Saul and his troops reached the camp of the Philistines, they found the enemy in utter confusion, striking out at each other with their swords (v.20). Some Hebrew bandits who had divided loyalties had earlier joined the Philistines, but now they were betraying them and joining ranks with the Israelites (v.21). Moreover, when the Israelite troops who had earlier fled in fear heard about the Philistine defeat, they turned to join in the intense pursuit of the enemy (v.22). But note this significant fact: the victory over the Philistines was due to the LORD, not to the army of Israel. It was the LORD who had caused an earthquake and routed the enemy. It was the LORD who had saved and rescued Israel from their helpless and hopeless situation. The overpowering army of the Philistines was defeated by the LORD Himself. And note why: it was due to the strong and fearless faith of Jonathan, not Saul. Saul demonstrated a spiritual insensitivity, a hard and indifferent heart, as well as an impatience in waiting upon the LORD.

Thought 1. God warns us against spiritual insensitivity, against being indifferent, impatient, and hard-hearted. Troublesome things happen to us if we are insensitive to spiritual matters. If we are callous, hard, and cold toward God, we separate ourselves from God. The Lord is no longer present with us. We are left to ourselves. And walking throughout life without God means that we...

- have no lasting help through the terrible crises of life, such as a severe accident, permanent injury, serious illness, terminal disease
- have no permanent assurance beyond this life, no sure hope of eternity
- have no lasting purpose, meaning, or significance in life
- lack a lasting sense of peace, security, satisfaction, and fulfillment
- have no true spiritual help in moments of loneliness, distress, depression, discouragement, hopelessness, helplessness, financial difficulty, broken relationships, divorce

An insensitive, callous, indifferent heart toward God will cut us off from God. And being separated from God means that we walk through life without God's presence, guidance, and provision.

"For the heart of this people is waxed gross, and their ears are dull of hearing, and their eyes have they closed; lest they should see with their eyes, and hear with their ears, and understand with their heart, and should be converted, and I should heal them" (Ac.28:27).

"But after thy hardness and impenitent heart treasurest up unto thyself wrath against the day of wrath and revelation of the righteous judgment of God" (Ro.2:5).

"This I say therefore, and testify in the LORD, that ye henceforth walk not as other Gentiles walk, in the vanity of their mind, Having the understanding darkened, being alienated from the life of God through the ignorance that is in them, because of the blindness of their heart: Who being past feeling have given themselves over unto lasciviousness, to work all uncleanness with greediness" (Ep.4:17-19).

"Now the Spirit speaketh expressly, that in the latter times some shall depart from the faith, giving heed to seducing spirits, and doctrines of devils; Speaking lies in hypocrisy; having their conscience seared with a hot iron" (1 Ti.4:1-2).

"But exhort one another daily, while it is called To day; lest any of you be hardened through the deceitfulness of sin" (He.3:13).

"Harden not your heart, as in the provocation, and as in the day of temptation in the wilderness: When your fathers tempted me, proved me, and saw my work. Forty years long was I grieved with this

---

2 Robert D.Bergen. *1, 2 Samuel*, p.157-158.

generation, and said, It is a people that do err in their heart, and they have not known my ways: Unto whom I sware in my wrath that they should not enter into my rest" (Ps.95:8-11).

"Happy is the man that feareth alway: but he that hardeneth his heart shall fall into mischief" (Pr.28:14).

"He, that being often reproved hardeneth his neck, shall suddenly be destroyed, and that without remedy" (Pr.29:1).

3 (14:24-46) **Zeal, Carnal—Zeal, Misguided—Carnal, Zeal—Saul, Decline of:** Saul's decline is also seen in his misguided, carnal zeal. Right before his fierce pursuit of the panic-stricken enemy, Saul actually sought the LORD's favor and blessing, but he approached God with a carnal spirit. Note that he referred to the Philistines as *my enemies*. He sought to take vengeance on personal enemies, not to secure a victory for the glory of the LORD and for the sake of the LORD's people, the Israelites. Obviously, Saul's heart was gripped by a spirit of selfishness and carnality. He was zealous to gain the victory, but primarily for himself. His zeal was misguided, a fact that is clearly seen in seven specific steps he took.

OUTLINE	SCRIPTURE	SCRIPTURE	OUTLINE
3. Saul's misguided, carnal zeal in seeking the LORD's favor & blessing a. Saul's misguided zeal in seeking personal revenge b. Saul's misguided zeal in imposing a rash, unwise fast & oath upon his troops—all to secure God's favor 1) The loyalty of the troops to Saul's command to fast: Saw plenty of honey throughout the forest, but refused to eat	24 And the men of Israel were distressed that day: for Saul had adjured the people, saying, Cursed *be* the man that eateth *any* food until evening, that I may be avenged on mine enemies. So none of the people tasted *any* food. 25 And all *they of* the land came to a wood; and there was honey upon the ground. 26 And when the people were come into the wood, behold, the honey dropped; but no man put his hand to his mouth: for the people feared the oath.	32 And the people flew upon the spoil, and took sheep, and oxen, and calves, and slew *them* on the ground: and the people did eat *them* with the blood. 33 Then they told Saul, saying, Behold, the people sin against the LORD, in that they eat with the blood. And he said, Ye have transgressed: roll a great stone unto me this day. 34 And Saul said, Disperse yourselves among the people, and say unto them, Bring me hither every man his ox, and	1) The utter exhaustion & sinful behavior of the troops: Eating meat with blood, Ge.9:4; Le.3:17; 7:26 2) The sinful violation pointed out to Saul • He was obviously ignorant of God's commandment • He corrected the troops • He had an elevated surface prepared—a large
2) The violation of the oath by Jonathan: Was committed in ignorance • He had not heard of the fast & oath • He ate some honey & his strength was renewed • He was immediately informed of the fast & oath by another soldier & informed that the troops were weakened because of the fast 3) The criticism by Jonathan: Accused Saul of causing trouble by the fasting oath • Weakened the troops • Kept the troops from achieving a greater victory because of their weakened strength c. Saul's misguided zeal in correcting the conduct of his troops while he himself was ignorant of God's laws & failing to live righteously	27 But Jonathan heard not when his father charged the people with the oath: wherefore he put forth the end of the rod that *was* in his hand, and dipped it in an honeycomb, and put his hand to his mouth; and his eyes were enlightened. 28 Then answered one of the people, and said, Thy father straitly charged the people with an oath, saying, Cursed *be* the man that eateth *any* food this day. And the people were faint. 29 Then said Jonathan, My father hath troubled the land: see, I pray you, how mine eyes have been enlightened, because I tasted a little of this honey. 30 How much more, if haply the people had eaten freely to day of the spoil of their enemies which they found? for had there not been now a much greater slaughter among the Philistines? 31 And they smote the Philistines that day from Michmash to Aijalon: and the people were very faint.	every man his sheep, and slay *them* here, and eat; and sin not against the LORD in eating with the blood. And all the people brought every man his ox with him that night, and slew *them* there. 35 And Saul built an altar unto the LORD: the same was the first altar that he built unto the LORD. 36 And Saul said, Let us go down after the Philistines by night, and spoil them until the morning light, and let us not leave a man of them. And they said, Do whatsoever seemeth good unto thee. Then said the priest, Let us draw near hither unto God. 37 And Saul asked counsel of God, Shall I go down after the Philistines? wilt thou deliver them into the hand of Israel? But he answered him not that day. 38 And Saul said, Draw ye near hither, all the chief of the people: and know and see wherein this sin hath been this day. 39 For, *as* the LORD liveth, which saveth Israel, though it be in Jonathan my son, he shall surely die. But *there*	stone—upon which the animals could be slaughtered d. Saul's misguided zeal in seeking God's favor by building an altar when he was living a self-centered, distrustful life e. Saul's misguided zeal in seeking God's will when he was not wholly committed 1) Saul planned to launch a nighttime raid to plunder & wipe out all the Philistines 2) The High Priest Ahijah suggested they first seek God 3) Saul sought an answer from God 4) God did not answer him f. Saul's misguided zeal in seeking to discover the sinner when he himself was guilty of being a sinner 1) The command by Saul for the officers to launch an investigation: Vowed to execute the person, even if it

OUTLINE	SCRIPTURE	SCRIPTURE	OUTLINE
was his own son Jonathan 2) The officers said nothing 3) The guidance sought by Saul in exposing the sinner • By lining up the officers in front of him & Jonathan • By praying & asking God to guide the casting of lots between them 4) The lot fell upon Saul & Jonathan 5) The lot then fell upon Jonathan g. Saul's misguided zeal in seeking to justify himself before God while condemning his innocent son, a believer filled with strong, fearless	*was* not a man among all the people *that* answered him. 40 Then said he unto all Israel, Be ye on one side, and I and Jonathan my son will be on the other side. And the people said unto Saul, Do what seemeth good unto thee. 41 Therefore Saul said unto the LORD God of Israel, Give a perfect *lot.* And Saul and Jonathan were taken: but the people escaped. 42 And Saul said, Cast *lots* between me and Jonathan my son. And Jonathan was taken. 43 Then Saul said to Jonathan, Tell me what thou hast done. And Jonathan told him, and said, I did but taste a lit-	tle honey with the end of the rod that *was* in mine hand, *and,* lo, I must die. 44 And Saul answered, God do so and more also: for thou shalt surely die, Jonathan. 45 And the people said unto Saul, Shall Jonathan die, who hath wrought this great salvation in Israel? God forbid: *as* the LORD liveth, there shall not one hair of his head fall to the ground; for he hath wrought with God this day. So the people rescued Jonathan, that he died not. 46 Then Saul went up from following the Philistines: and the Philistines went to their own place.	faith 1) Jonathan gave an explanation 2) Saul attempted to justify himself: Even if it meant the execution of his son 3) The troops rescued Jonathan • They argued the case before Saul: It was Jonathan who had brought about the great victory over the Philistines • They insisted Jonathan not be executed • They won the case: Saul was forced to rescind his order, to let Jonathan live 4) Saul & the army withdrew from pursuing the enemy, returned home

a. Saul's misguided zeal is seen in his seeking *personal revenge* against the Philistines (v.24).

b. Saul's misguided zeal is seen in the rash, unwise fast and oath he forced upon the troops—all to secure God's favor (v.24). Fasting to seek God's favor is commendable, but there is a time and a place for fasting. And combat is not a time to be denying food to troops. Soldiers need food, especially when they are about to enter combat or when they are able to gain a break during combat missions.

Note the loyalty of the troops to Saul's command (vv.25-26). They saw plenty of honey throughout the forest, but they refused to eat, because they feared the oath Saul had placed them under. However, Jonathan was unaware of his father's oath so he reached out with the end of his staff and dipped it into a honeycomb. He raised the staff to his mouth and ate the honey, renewing his strength. Immediately one of the soldiers informed him of the fast and oath, explaining that the troops were weakened because of the fast. Hearing this, Jonathan criticized his father, accusing Saul of weakening the troops and of preventing them from achieving a greater victory because of their weakened strength (vv.29-30).

c. Saul's misguided zeal is seen in his correcting the conduct of his troops while he himself was ignorant of God's laws in failing to live righteously (vv.31-34). Despite their hunger, the Israelite soldiers pursued the Philistines all day from Micmash to Aijalon, killing the Philistines all along the way. By the end of the day they were utterly exhausted, and they pounced on the animals from the plunder, butchering them on the ground rather than hanging them up and letting the blood drain from their bodies. As a result, they ate the blood right along with the meat. This was in direct violation of God's law (Ge.9:4; Le.3:17; 7:26).

This sinful violation was immediately pointed out to Saul by someone standing close by him (vv.33-34). Apparently Saul had been ignorant of God's commandment, for after being informed that the troops were in violation of God's law, he immediately corrected them. He had an elevated surface prepared, a large stone rolled over, so the men could slaughter their animals upon it.

d. Saul's misguided zeal is also seen in his seeking God's favor by building an altar while he was living a self-centered, distrustful life before God (v.35). His self-centered, distrustful life has already been seen in his weak, wavering faith (vv.2-3), his spiritual insensitivity (vv.16-23), and in the rash oath he placed upon his troops (vv.24-30). Now Saul—despite his corrupt heart—sought God's favor by building an altar. He built a place for worship, most likely a place where sacrifices were offered in thanksgiving to God for the victory He had given. But this practice was forbidden. It had been a direct violation of God's law ever since the Israelites had entered the promised land (De.12:13-14).[3]

e. Saul's misguided zeal is seen in his seeking God's will when he was not wholly committed to the LORD (vv.36-37). Saul planned to launch a nighttime raid to plunder and wipe out all the Philistines. But the High Priest Ahijah suggested that they first seek God's approval. Agreeing with Ahijah, Saul sought an answer from God. But God did not answer him. This passage does not say why, but other Scriptures do. If a person regards or holds iniquity in his heart, the LORD will not hear him (Ps.66:18). Saul's carnal, selfish, distrustful heart had separated him from God. Consequently, God could not answer him.

f. Saul's misguided zeal is seen in his seeking to discover the sinner when he himself was guilty of being a sinner (vv.38-42). God's refusing to answer Saul's prayer led Saul to a misguided conclusion: that there was some sinner in the camp, some person with whom the LORD was displeased. Saul commanded the officers to launch an investigation, and then he exposed his misguided zeal once again. For the second time he issued an unwise oath, vowing to execute the guilty person, even if it was his own son Jonathan (v.39). But the officers said nothing, refusing to expose Jonathan's violation of the oath. Saul lined up the officers in front of him and Jonathan. Then he prayed, asking God to guide the casting of lots between them (vv.40-41). The lot fell first upon Saul and Jonathan, and next upon Jonathan alone, identifying him as the guilty party.

---

3 Robert D. Bergen. *1, 2 Samuel*, p.160.

g. Saul's misguided zeal is also seen in his seeking to justify himself before God while condemning his innocent son, a believer filled with strong and fearless faith (vv.43-46). When Saul asked Jonathan what he had done, Jonathan replied that he had merely tasted a little honey on the end of his staff. Then Jonathan asked if such a small act deserved death. Keep in mind that Jonathan had never broken the vow, for he was totally unaware of the rash oath imposed upon the troops by his father. Nevertheless, Saul attempted to justify his oath by calling upon God to strike him (Saul) dead if he did not execute Jonathan (v.44). Hearing this, some of the troops and leaders came to the defense and rescue of Jonathan (vv.45-46). They argued Jonathan's case, that it had been Jonathan who had brought victory over the Philistines. And they strongly insisted that Jonathan not be executed, going so far as to declare that not a hair of his head would be touched. Their opposition won the case, forcing Saul to rescind his order and to let Jonathan live. But the chance to pursue and wipe out the enemy was now lost. Saul's misguided zeal, his preoccupation with carrying out his unwise oath against his own son, kept him from delivering a fatal blow to the Philistines.

Thought 1. The lesson for us is striking: we must have zeal, be diligent in all that we do. But our zeal and diligence must not be misguided. Misguided zeal results in such behavior as…

- fanaticism
- rash and unwise behavior
- unrighteous acts
- selfishness
- self-justification
- spiritual blindness
- brutality
- abuse
- arrogance
- unwise choices
- ignorant behavior
- injustice

Zeal and diligence are to be traits deeply embedded within our lives. We are always to do the very best we can, demonstrating zeal and diligence. But knowledge is an absolute essential. We must know what should consume our lives, where to place our zeal and diligence. We must be zealous over that which is wise, diligent over that which is good. We must never give our hearts to that which is wicked, immoral, or unjust. We must be zealous for righteousness, morality, and justice.

(1) The zeal demonstrated by Christ is a dynamic example for us.

"And he said unto them, How is it that ye sought me? wist [knew] ye not that I must be about my Father's business" (Lu.2:49).

"And his disciples remembered that it was written, The zeal of thine house hath eaten me up" (Jn.2:17).

"Jesus saith unto them, My meat is to do the will of him that sent me, and to finish his work" (Jn.4:34).

"I must work the works of him that sent me, while it is day: the night cometh, when no man can work" (Jn.9:4).

"How God anointed Jesus of Nazareth with the Holy Ghost and with power: who went about doing good, and healing all that were oppressed of the devil; for God was with him" (Ac.10:38).

"For he put on righteousness as a breastplate, and an helmet of salvation upon his head; and he put on the garments of vengeance for clothing, and was clad with zeal as a cloke" (Is.59:17).

(2) God commands us to be zealous and diligent in all that we do.

"Not slothful in business; fervent in spirit; serving the LORD" (Ro.12:11).

"Even so ye, forasmuch as ye are zealous of spiritual gifts, seek that ye may excel to the edifying of the church" (1 Co.14:12).

"And whatsoever ye do in word or deed, do all in the name of the LORD Jesus, giving thanks to God and the Father by him" (Col.3:17).

"And whatsoever ye do, do it heartily, as to the LORD, and not unto men" (Col.3:23).

"Wherefore I put thee in remembrance that thou stir up the gift of God, which is in thee by the putting on of my hands" (2 Ti.1:6).

"Wherefore I will not be negligent to put you always in remembrance of these things, though ye know them, and be established in the present truth. Yea, I think it meet, as long as I am in this tabernacle, to stir you up by putting you in remembrance" (2 Pe.1:12-13).

"Wherefore, beloved, seeing that ye look for such things, be diligent that ye may be found of him in peace, without spot, and blameless" (2 Pe.3:14).

"As many as I love, I rebuke and chasten: be zealous therefore, and repent" (Re.3:19).

"He becometh poor that dealeth with a slack hand: but the hand of the diligent maketh rich" (Pr.10:4).

"Whatsoever thy hand findeth to do, do it with thy might; for there is no work, nor device, nor knowledge, nor wisdom, in the grave, whither thou goest" (Ec.9:10).

---

4 (14:47-52) **Victory, Military, of Saul—Saul, Victories of—Israel, Military Victories of—Saul, Family**: this is a summary of Saul's military victories over the enemies of Israel and a summary of his family line. (See *The Family Line of Saul* in the Resource Section on page 276. The summary given here covers all the military campaigns and conquests of Saul. The Scripture and outline are sufficient to cover this particular point.

OUTLINE	SCRIPTURE	SCRIPTURE	OUTLINE

4. Saul's military victories over the enemies of Israel & his family line
a. Saul's military victories
  1) East: Moab, Ammon, Edom
  2) North: Kings of Zobah
  3) West: The Philistines
 	
  4) South: The Amalekites
 	
b. Saul's family
  1) His sons: Three listed here; one son, Abinadab,
	47 So Saul took the kingdom over Israel, and fought against all his enemies on every side, against Moab, and against the children of Ammon, and against Edom, and against the kings of Zobah, and against the Philistines: and whithersoever he turned himself, he vexed *them*.
	48 And he gathered an host, and smote the Amalekites, and delivered Israel out of the hands of them that spoiled them.
	49 Now the sons of Saul were Jonathan, and Ishui, and Melchi-shua: and the names
		of his two daughters *were these;* the name of the firstborn Merab, and the name of the younger Michal:
		50 And the name of Saul's wife *was* Ahinoam, the daughter of Ahimaaz: and the name of the captain of his host *was* Abner, the son of Ner, Saul's uncle.
		51 And Kish *was* the father of Saul; and Ner the father of Abner *was* the son of Abiel.
		52 And there was sore war against the Philistines all the days of Saul: and when Saul saw any strong man, or any valiant man, he took him unto him.
			listed elsewhere, 31:2
			2) His two daughters
			
			3) His wife
			
			4) His cousin Abner: Made commander of the armed forces
			c. Saul's most bitter enemies: The Philistines
			d. Saul's answer to the continued threat of the Philistines: A permanent draft system

Thought 1. Note that Saul never gained complete victory over the Philistines. They were a constant thorn in his side, continually oppressing the people of God. But the constant oppression did not have to be. If Saul and the Israelites had trusted the LORD, God would have given them permanent victory over their enemies.

The lesson for us is clear: victory over all the enemies of life is possible. This is the promise of God. We can walk through all trials and problems of this life, no matter what they may be:

- being orphaned
- being widowed
- being imprisoned
- being brokenhearted
- being backslidden
- being diseased
- being injured
- being hungry
- being thirsty
- being poverty-stricken
- being lonely
- being without purpose
- being homeless
- being unemployed
- experiencing financial difficulties
- experiencing broken relationships
- suffering physical pain
- suffering mental anguish

A spirit of conquest and triumph can rule in our lives. All the trials and problems can be conquered, overcome by the power of Christ in our lives.

"Who shall separate us from the love of Christ? shall tribulation, or distress, or persecution, or famine, or nakedness, or peril, or sword....Nay, in all these things we are more than conquerors through him that loved us. For I am persuaded, that neither death, nor life, nor angels, nor principalities, nor powers, nor things present, nor things to come, Nor height, nor depth, nor any other creature, shall be able to separate us from the love of God, which is in Christ Jesus our LORD" (Ro.8:35, 37-39).

"There hath no temptation taken you but such as is common to man: but God is faithful, who will not suffer you to be tempted above that ye are able; but will with the temptation also make a way to escape, that ye may be able to bear it" (1 Co.10:13).

"Now unto him that is able to do exceeding abundantly above all that we ask or think, according to the power that worketh in us" (Ep.3:20).

"Finally, my brethren, be strong in the LORD, and in the power of his might. Put on the whole armour of God, that ye may be able to stand against the wiles of the devil. For we wrestle not against flesh and blood, but against principalities, against powers, against the rulers of the darkness of this world, against spiritual wickedness in high places. Wherefore take unto you the whole armour of God, that ye may be able to withstand in the evil day, and having done all, to stand" (Ep.6:10-13).

"But thou, O man of God, flee these things; and follow after righteousness, godliness, faith, love, patience, meekness. Fight the good fight of faith, lay hold on eternal life, whereunto thou art also called, and hast professed a good profession before many witnesses" (1 Ti.6:11-12).

"For whatsoever is born of God overcometh the world: and this is the victory that overcometh the world, even our faith. Who is he that overcometh the world, but he that believeth that Jesus is the Son of God" (1 Jn.5:4-5).

"He that overcometh, the same shall be clothed in white raiment; and I will not blot out his name out of the book of life, but I will confess his name before my Father, and before his angels" (Re.3:5).

"To him that overcometh will I grant to sit with me in my throne, even as I also overcame, and am set down with my Father in his throne" (Re.3:21).

"He that overcometh shall inherit all things; and I will be his God, and he shall be my son" (Re.21:7).

"Through thee will we push down our enemies: through thy name will we tread them under that rise up against us" (Ps.44:5).

1. The clear command of God to totally destroy the Amalekites: A picture of the need to obey God in conquering spiritual enemies

a. The source of the command: The LORD of hosts

b. The reason for God's judgment: The savage behavior of the Amalekites—were beyond repentance, change, Ex.17:8-16; Nu.24:20; De.25:17-19

c. The command: To totally destroy everything—not sparing anything^{DS1}

d. The mobilization of the army by Saul: 200,000 foot soldiers plus 10,000 more from Judah gathered at Telaim

e. The strategy of Saul: To set an ambush against the city of Amalek

f. The secret warning given to the Kenites: Because of their alliance & friendly relations with Israel; Ex. 2:16-22; 3:1; 4:18-20; 18:1-5; Num.10:29-32; Jdg.1:16; 4:11, 17-23; 5:24; 1 Ch.2:55

g. The victory over the Amalekites

h. The refusal of Saul & his army to destroy everything: An unwillingness to completely obey God
  1) Spared the king, Agag
  2) Spared the best animals & everything else that was of value

  3) Destroyed only the weak animals & the things of no value or of poor quality

2. The sins of Saul & his failure to obey God

a. The message of God
  1) Saul's disobedience grieved, broke the heart

CHAPTER 15

H. The LORD's Rejection of Saul As King: The Seriousness of Disobeying God, 15:1-35

Samuel also said unto Saul, The LORD sent me to anoint thee *to be* king over his people, over Israel: now therefore hearken thou unto the voice of the words of the LORD.

2 Thus saith the LORD of hosts, I remember *that* which Amalek did to Israel, how he laid *wait* for him in the way, when he came up from Egypt.

3 Now go and smite Amalek, and utterly destroy all that they have, and spare them not; but slay both man and woman, infant and suckling, ox and sheep, camel and ass.

4 And Saul gathered the people together, and numbered them in Telaim, two hundred thousand footmen, and ten thousand men of Judah.

5 And Saul came to a city of Amalek, and laid wait in the valley.

6 And Saul said unto the Kenites, Go, depart, get you down from among the Amalekites, lest I destroy you with them: for ye showed kindness to all the children of Israel, when they came up out of Egypt. So the Kenites departed from among the Amalekites.

7 And Saul smote the Amalekites from Havilah *until* thou comest to Shur, that *is* over against Egypt.

8 And he took Agag the king of the Amalekites alive, and utterly destroyed all the people with the edge of the sword.

9 But Saul and the people spared Agag, and the best of the sheep, and of the oxen, and of the fatlings, and the lambs, and all *that was* good, and would not utterly destroy them: but every thing *that was* vile and refuse, that they destroyed utterly.

10 Then came the word of the LORD unto Samuel, saying,

11 It repenteth me that I have set up Saul *to be* king:

for he is turned back from following me, and hath not performed my commandments. And it grieved Samuel; and he cried unto the LORD all night.

12 And when Samuel rose early to meet Saul in the morning, it was told Samuel, saying, Saul came to Carmel, and, behold, he set him up a place, and is gone about, and passed on, and gone down to Gilgal.

13 And Samuel came to Saul: and Saul said unto him, Blessed *be* thou of the LORD: I have performed the commandment of the LORD.

14 And Samuel said, What *meaneth* then this bleating of the sheep in mine ears, and the lowing of the oxen which I hear?

15 And Saul said, They have brought them from the Amalekites: for the people spared the best of the sheep and of the oxen, to sacrifice unto the LORD thy God; and the rest we have utterly destroyed.

16 Then Samuel said unto Saul, Stay, and I will tell thee what the LORD hath said to me this night. And he said unto him, Say on.

17 And Samuel said, When thou *wast* little in thine own sight, *wast* thou not *made* the head of the tribes of Israel, and the LORD anointed thee king over Israel?

18 And the LORD sent thee on a journey, and said, Go and utterly destroy the sinners the Amalekites, and fight against them until they be consumed.

19 Wherefore then didst thou not obey the voice of the LORD, but didst fly upon the spoil, and didst evil in the sight of the LORD?

20 And Saul said unto Samuel, Yea, I have obeyed the voice of the LORD, and have gone the way which the LORD sent me, and have brought Agag the king of Amalek, and have utterly destroyed the Amalekites.

21 But the people took of the spoil, sheep and oxen, the chief of the things which should have been utterly destroyed, to sacrifice unto the LORD thy God in Gilgal.

of God
  2) God regretted having made Saul king

b. The agonizing prayer of Samuel
  1) Cried out all night to God
  2) Arose early in the morning to go find Saul

c. The terrible sins of Saul
  1) The sin of pride
    • Built a monument in his own honor
    • Built at Carmel

  2) The sin of boasting
    • Samuel reached Saul
    • Saul greeted him with a boast of obedience

  3) The sin of blaming others: Seeking to justify oneself
    • Samuel asked about the animal noise he heard

    • Saul blamed the soldiers
  4) The sin of deception, lying
    • Saul claimed the best animals were spared so they could be sacrificed to the LORD
    • Samuel interrupted & commanded Saul to stop making excuses, to stop lying & trying to deceive: Saul must hear the Word of the LORD

  5) The sin of losing the spirit of humility
    • Saul was now arrogant
    • Saul had forgotten that it was the LORD who had appointed him king

  6) The sin of disobedience
    • The LORD had sent Saul on a very special mission: To totally destroy the Amalekites

    • Saul disobeyed
  7) The sin of covetousness: Lusted, grasped after the plunder

  8) The sin of an argumentative, stubborn, unrepentant heart
    • Saul insisted he had obeyed the LORD

    • Saul again insisted the best animals had been spared to offer as a sacrifice to God

3. The weak, inadequate confession of sin
a. The supreme demand of God's Word: Obedience
   1) To obey is better than sacrifice
   2) To obey is better than the most choice gift
b. The seriousness of disobedience
   1) Rebellion is as bad as witchcraft
   2) Arrogance is as bad as idolatry
   3) Disobedience results in judgment & rejection
c. The weak, inadequate confession of Saul: He fell to his knees
   1) He confessed his sinful disobedience: He had feared the people, their covetousness
   2) He called upon Samuel, not God, to forgive his sin; see also v.15, 21, 30, "the LORD your God"
4. The irrevocable, unchanging judgment of God
a. The verdict, judgment upon Saul restated: The LORD had rejected him as king
   1) The desperation of Saul: Caught & tore Samuel's robe
   2) The symbolism of the torn robe declared by Samuel: The kingdom had been torn from Saul & given to
	22 And Samuel said, Hath the LORD *as great* delight in burnt offerings and sacrifices, as in obeying the voice of the LORD? Behold, to obey *is* better than sacrifice, *and* to hearken than the fat of rams.
	23 For rebellion *is as* the sin of witchcraft, and stubbornness *is as* iniquity and idolatry. Because thou hast rejected the word of the LORD, he hath also rejected thee from *being* king.
	24 And Saul said unto Samuel, I have sinned: for I have transgressed the commandment of the LORD, and thy words: because I feared the people, and obeyed their voice.
	25 Now therefore, I pray thee, pardon my sin, and turn again with me, that I may worship the LORD.
	26 And Samuel said unto Saul, I will not return with thee: for thou hast rejected the word of the LORD, and the LORD hath rejected thee from being king over Israel.
	27 And as Samuel turned about to go away, he laid hold upon the skirt of his mantle, and it rent.
	28 And Samuel said unto him, The LORD hath rent the kingdom of Israel from thee this day, and hath given it to
		a neighbour of thine, *that is* better than thou.
		29 And also the Strength of Israel will not lie nor repent: for he *is* not a man, that he should repent.
		30 Then he said, I have sinned: *yet* honour me now, I pray thee, before the elders of my people, and before Israel, and turn again with me, that I may worship the LORD thy God.
		31 So Samuel turned again after Saul; and Saul worshipped the LORD.
		32 Then said Samuel, Bring ye hither to me Agag the king of the Amalekites. And Agag came unto him delicately. And Agag said, Surely the bitterness of death is past.
		33 And Samuel said, As thy sword hath made women childless, so shall thy mother be childless among women. And Samuel hewed Agag in pieces before the LORD in Gilgal.
		34 Then Samuel went to Ramah; and Saul went up to his house to Gibeah of Saul.
		35 And Samuel came no more to see Saul until the day of his death: nevertheless Samuel mourned for Saul: and the LORD repented that he had made Saul king over Israel.
			someone else—a better person than Saul
			b. The irrevocable nature & judgment of God, *the Strength or Glory of Israel*: He does not lie nor change His mind
			5. The sharp contrast of Samuel's faithfulness with Saul's unfaithfulness
			a. Samuel's faithfulness to Saul
			   1) Saul begged Samuel to return with him to lead in worship: To save face
			   2) Samuel agreed: To assure an effective rule until Saul was replaced
			b. Samuel's faithfulness to the LORD's command
			   1) Samuel completed Saul's task: Executed King Agag
			   • Agag thought he had escaped death
			   • Agag was executed because of the savage evil committed by him & his people
			   2) Samuel accepted God's judgment upon Saul
			   • Separated from Saul
			   • Would never again go to see Saul
			   3) Samuel mourned for Saul: Showed compassion
			c. The permanent judgment of God: Regretted having made Saul king

DIVISION II

THE STORY OF SAMUEL AND SAUL: THE LORD GIVES ISRAEL A KING JUST "LIKE ALL THE NATIONS," 8:1–15:35

H. The LORD's Rejection of Saul As King: The Seriousness of Disobeying God, 15:1-35

(15:1-35) **Introduction—Disobedience to God**: one of the most serious behaviors in all the world is an act of disobedience. When a person disobeys those in authority, trouble follows. The trouble may be minor or it may be major; nevertheless, trouble is aroused and problems take place. If a child disobeys a parent and touches a hot stove, a minor problem arises: the child's finger is burned. But if the child disobeys a parent and plays with matches around some flammable object, a major consequence occurs: the child is severely burned or causes some major destruction to property. So it is with employees when they disobey their supervisors. The result of their disobedience may be a minor infraction requiring only a reprimand, or it may be a major infraction demanding termination and loss of income or bankruptcy. Example after example of disobedience and its consequences could be listed, but the point is clearly seen. Again, an act of disobedience is one of the most serious behaviors committed by people.

Disobedience to God is the practical subject of this present passage of Scripture. The LORD gave Saul a very special privilege, a unique opportunity to fulfill a prophecy that God had given to Moses generations before. This prophecy was the prediction that the Amalekites would face the judgment of God and be erased from the face of the earth (Ex.17:14). It was now time for the prophecy to be executed, time for the hand of God's judgment to fall upon the Amalekites. And the instrument of God's judgment was to be King Saul. Thus the command of God was given to Saul: he was to carry out the execution of God's judgment. But Saul disobeyed and failed God miserably. And in his disobedience, his decline reached its climax: Saul was finally rejected by God. The final straw of God's patience was broken, and the hand of God's judgment fell upon Saul himself—all because of his disobedience. This is: *The LORD's Rejection of Saul As King: The Seriousness of Disobeying God,* 15:1-35.

1. The clear command of God to totally destroy the Amalekites: a picture of the need to obey God in conquering spiritual enemies (vv.1-9).
2. The sins of Saul and his failure to obey God (vv.10-21).

3. The weak, inadequate confession of sin (vv.22-25).
4. The irrevocable, unchanging judgment of God (vv.26-29).
5. The sharp contrast of Samuel's faithfulness with Saul's unfaithfulness (vv.30-35).

[1] (15:1-9) **Judgment, Caused by—Nations, Judgment of, Caused by—Disobedience, Example of—Spiritual Warfare, Picture of—Saul, Disobedience of—Amalekites, Defeated by Israel**: there was the clear command of God to Saul: he was to totally destroy the Amalekites. The Amalekites were descendants of Esau, a nomadic people who lived south of Judea in the Sinai Desert and the region of the Negev (Ge.36:12, 16). Amalekite marauders or bandits were constantly attacking and oppressing the Israelites (Ex.17:8-13; Nu.14:43-45; De.25:17-19; Jud.3:13; 6:1-16, 33; 7:12; 10:12). Just why God would give a command to *totally* destroy the Amalekites, or any other people for that matter, is covered below (see DEEPER STUDY #1—1 S.15:3). For now, the point to grasp is Saul's response to the command of God:

OUTLINE	SCRIPTURE	SCRIPTURE	OUTLINE
1. The clear command of God to totally destroy the Amalekites: A picture of the need to obey God in conquering spiritual enemies a. The source of the command: The LORD of hosts b. The reason for God's judgment: The savage behavior of the Amalekites—were beyond repentance, change, Ex.17:8-16; Nu.24:20; De.25:17-19 c. The command: To totally destroy everything—not sparing anything[DS1] d. The mobilization of the army by Saul: 200,000 foot soldiers plus 10,000 more from Judah gathered at Telaim e. The strategy of Saul: To set an ambush against the city of Amalek	Samuel also said unto Saul, The LORD sent me to anoint thee *to be* king over his people, over Israel: now therefore hearken thou unto the voice of the words of the LORD. 2 Thus saith the LORD of hosts, I remember *that* which Amalek did to Israel, how he laid *wait* for him in the way, when he came up from Egypt. 3 Now go and smite Amalek, and utterly destroy all that they have, and spare them not; but slay both man and woman, infant and suckling, ox and sheep, camel and ass. 4 And Saul gathered the people together, and numbered them in Telaim, two hundred thousand footmen, and ten thousand men of Judah. 5 And Saul came to a city of Amalek, and laid wait in the valley.	6 And Saul said unto the Kenites, Go, depart, get you down from among the Amalekites, lest I destroy you with them: for ye showed kindness to all the children of Israel, when they came up out of Egypt. So the Kenites departed from among the Amalekites. 7 And Saul smote the Amalekites from Havilah *until* thou comest to Shur, that *is* over against Egypt. 8 And he took Agag the king of the Amalekites alive, and utterly destroyed all the people with the edge of the sword. 9 But Saul and the people spared Agag, and the best of the sheep, and of the oxen, and of the fatlings, and the lambs, and all *that was* good, and would not utterly destroy them: but every thing *that was* vile and refuse, that they destroyed utterly.	f. The secret warning given to the Kenites: Because of their alliance & friendly relations with Israel; Ex. 2:16-22; 3:1; 4:18-20; 18:1-5; Nu.10:29-32; Jud.1:16; 4:11, 17-23; 5:24; 1 Chr.2:55 g. The victory over the Amalekites h. The refusal of Saul & his army to destroy everything: An unwillingness to completely obey God 1) Spared the king, Agag 2) Spared the best animals & everything else that was of value 3) Destroyed only the weak animals & the things of no value or of poor quality

a. It was the "LORD of hosts," the "LORD Almighty" who gave the command to Saul. He and He alone was the source of the command (v.1). Samuel was only the prophet sent to declare the message of the LORD of hosts, the message of the LORD Almighty, the Sovereign Creator and Ruler of the universe. (See DEEPER STUDY #2—1 S.1:3 for more discussion.) As the LORD Almighty, the ruler over all nations, He has the right to execute judgment against any nation when the people deserve to be judged.

b. Note the reason for God's judgment against the Amalekites (v.2). For generations they had been a cruel, savage, evil people, brutal oppressors of the Israelites and no doubt other people as well. Their brutality and evil had become so embedded within their nature that they were beyond repentance, beyond ever changing and turning to the LORD. If left upon the earth, this nation of people would only continue to oppress and slaughter other people, in particular the Israelites.

c. For this reason God issued the command to Saul to totally destroy the Amalekites and everything that belonged to them, not sparing a single thing. Centuries before the LORD had told Moses that the day was coming when the Amalekites would be utterly destroyed, when they would feel the hand of His judgment falling upon them (Ex.17:8-16; Nu.24:20; De.25:17-19). The LORD had said that He would completely blot out the memory of the Amalekites and personally be at war with them from generation to generation until the day they were to be erased from the face of the earth (Ex.17:15-16). Now, the final order for God's judgment to be executed against the Amalekites was being given to Saul. Nothing of the Amalekites—no human life, no animal, and no object—was to be left upon the face of the earth. All of the Amalekites and everything that belonged to them were to be destroyed. God's hand of judgment was to fall upon them, being executed by the hand of Saul. And the command given to Saul was perfectly clear (see DEEPER STUDY #1—1 S.15:3 for more discussion).

d. Saul immediately summoned and mobilized the army to march against the Amalekites (v.4). Over 200,000 foot soldiers plus 10,000 soldiers from the tribe of Judah gathered at Telaim, a city that was located someplace in the Negev.

e. The strategy of Saul was to set an ambush against the city of Amalek (v.5). He positioned his troops in the ravine which was probably the brook of Egypt.[1] The major road leading out of Amalek most likely ran through the ravine.

---

[1] Robert D. Bergen. *1, 2 Samuel*, p.169.

Therefore the Israelite army was poised to launch a secret attack against the city and to prevent any of the Amalekites from escaping.

f. Note the secret warning given by Saul to the Kenites (v.6). The Kenites were a nomadic people who lived in the Desert of Sinai. The Israelites had an alliance with the people and were on friendly relations with them. Moses had actually married a Kenite woman and some of the Kenites had accompanied the Israelites and settled with them in the promised land (Ex.2:16-22; 3:1; 4:18-20; 18:1-5; Nu.10:29-32; Jud.1:16; 4:11, 17-23; 5:24; 1 Chr.2:55).

g. Victory was achieved over the Amalekites. Saul attacked and pursued the fleeing Amalekites all the way from Havilah to Shur, the full length and breadth of the Amalekite nation.

h. But note the refusal of Saul and his army to destroy everything, a deliberate unwillingness to completely obey God (vv.8-9). Saul spared King Agag and the best animals and everything else that was of value. He and the army destroyed only the weak animals and the things of no value or of poor quality. They allowed greed and covetousness to grip their hearts, lusting after the wealth of the Amalekites. Consequently, instead of being the agents of God's judgment, they became the agents of their own selfish desires for wealth. Saul failed to obey God. He was clearly disobedient.

Thought 1. God promises to give us victory over all the enemies of this life. If people oppress us through ridicule, mockery, degradation, neglect, abuse, assaults, threats, persecution, attacks, even murder—God promises to give us victory, a victory so triumphant that even death itself is conquered through eternal life.

But this is not the only victory that God gives us. As we walk day by day, trial after trial and temptation after temptation combat us. Here again God promises to give us victory, to make us more than conquerors throughout life.

However, note this fact: victory is conditional. We must believe God and obey God completely, keeping *all* His commandments. Faith and obedience are essential to be victorious. This is the clear teaching of God's Holy Word:

"Not every one that saith unto me, LORD, LORD, shall enter into the kingdom of heaven; but he that doeth the will of my Father which is in heaven" (Mt.7:21).

"Jesus answered and said unto him, If a man love me, he will keep my words: and my Father will love him, and we will come unto him, and make our abode with him" (Jn.14:23).

"If ye keep my commandments, ye shall abide in my love; even as I have kept my Father's commandments, and abide in his love" (Jn.15:10).

"For whatsoever is born of God overcometh the world: and this is the victory that overcometh the world, *even* our faith. Who is he that overcometh the world, but he that believeth that Jesus is the Son of God" (1 Jn.5:4-5).

"Blessed *are* they that do his commandments, that they may have right to the tree of life, and may enter in through the gates into the city" (Re.22:14).

"Finally, my brethren, be strong in the LORD, and in the power of his might. Put on the whole armour of God, that ye may be able to stand against the wiles of the devil. For we wrestle not against flesh and blood, but against principalities, against powers, against the rulers of the darkness of this world, against spiritual wickedness in high *places*. Wherefore take unto you the whole armour of God, that ye may be able to withstand in the evil day, and having done all, to stand. Stand therefore, having your loins girt about with truth, and having on the breastplate of righteousness; And your feet shod with the preparation of the gospel of peace; Above all, taking the shield of faith, wherewith ye shall be able to quench all the fiery darts of the wicked. And take the helmet of salvation, and the sword of the Spirit, which is the word of God: Praying always with all prayer and supplication in the Spirit, and watching thereunto with all perseverance and supplication for all saints" (Ep.6:10-18).

"But whoso looketh into the perfect law of liberty, and continueth *therein,* he being not a forgetful hearer, but a doer of the work, this man shall be blessed in his deed" (Js.1:25).

"Now therefore, if ye will obey my voice indeed, and keep my covenant, then ye shall be a peculiar treasure unto me above all people: for all the earth *is* mine" (Ex.19:5).

"O that there were such an heart in them, that they would fear me, and keep all my commandments always, that it might be well with them, and with their children for ever" (De.5:29).

"This book of the law shall not depart out of thy mouth; but thou shalt meditate therein day and night, that thou mayest observe to do according to all that is written therein: for then thou shalt make thy way prosperous, and then thou shalt have good success" (Jos.1:8).

"And if thou wilt walk in my ways, to keep my statutes and my commandments, as thy father David did walk, then I will lengthen thy days" (1 K.3:14).

"Through thee will we push down our enemies: through thy name will we tread them under that rise up against us" (Ps.44:5).

DEEPER STUDY # 1
(15:3) **Iniquity, Cup of—Harem Principle—Nations, Destruction of—Nations, Evil of—Nations, Judgment of—Canaanites, Destruction of—Judgment, Why God Judges**: because of the length of this DEEPER STUDY, it is being placed at the end of this outline and commentary.

---

[2] (15:10-21) **Sins, List of—Disobedience, Example of—Saul, Sins of—Saul, Disobedience of**: there were the sins of Saul and his failure to obey God. Above all the other failures of Saul, this passage exposes the deceitfulness and depravity of Saul's heart. It paints a clear picture of just how corrupt and self-deceiving a human heart can become.

OUTLINE	SCRIPTURE	SCRIPTURE	OUTLINE

2. The sins of Saul & his failure to obey God
  a. The message of God
    1) Saul's disobedience grieved, broke the heart of God
    2) God regretted having made Saul king
  b. The agonizing prayer of Samuel
    1) Cried out all night to God
    2) Arose early in the morning to go find Saul
  c. The terrible sins of Saul
    1) The sin of pride
      • Built a monument in his own honor
      • Built at Carmel
 	
    2) The sin of boasting
      • Samuel reached Saul
      • Saul greeted him with a boast of obedience
 	
    3) The sin of blaming others: Seeking to justify oneself
      • Samuel asked about the animal noise he heard
      • Saul blamed the soldiers
    4) The sin of deception, lying
      • Saul claimed the best animals were spared so they could be sacrificed to the LORD
      • Samuel interrupted &
	10 Then came the word of the LORD unto Samuel, saying,
	11 It repenteth me that I have set up Saul *to be* king: for he is turned back from following me, and hath not performed my commandments. And it grieved Samuel; and he cried unto the LORD all night.
	12 And when Samuel rose early to meet Saul in the morning, it was told Samuel, saying, Saul came to Carmel, and, behold, he set him up a place, and is gone about, and passed on, and gone down to Gilgal.
	13 And Samuel came to Saul: and Saul said unto him, Blessed *be* thou of the LORD: I have performed the commandment of the LORD.
	14 And Samuel said, What *meaneth* then this bleating of the sheep in mine ears, and the lowing of the oxen which I hear?
	15 And Saul said, They have brought them from the Amalekites: for the people spared the best of the sheep and of the oxen, to sacrifice unto the LORD thy God; and the rest we have utterly destroyed.
	16 Then Samuel said unto
		Saul, Stay, and I will tell thee what the LORD hath said to me this night. And he said unto him, Say on.
		17 And Samuel said, When thou *wast* little in thine own sight, *wast* thou not *made* the head of the tribes of Israel, and the LORD anointed thee king over Israel?
		18 And the LORD sent thee on a journey, and said, Go and utterly destroy the sinners the Amalekites, and fight against them until they be consumed.
		19 Wherefore then didst thou not obey the voice of the LORD, but didst fly upon the spoil, and didst evil in the sight of the LORD?
		20 And Saul said unto Samuel, Yea, I have obeyed the voice of the LORD, and have gone the way which the LORD sent me, and have brought Agag the king of Amalek, and have utterly destroyed the Amalekites.
		21 But the people took of the spoil, sheep and oxen, the chief of the things which should have been utterly destroyed, to sacrifice unto the LORD thy God in Gilgal.
			commanded Saul to stop making excuses, to stop lying & trying to deceive: Saul must hear the Word of the LORD
			    5) The sin of losing the spirit of humility
			      • Saul was now arrogant
			      • Saul had forgotten that it was the LORD who had appointed him king
			    6) The sin of disobedience
			      • The LORD had sent Saul on a very special mission: To totally destroy the Amalekites
			
			      • Saul disobeyed
			    7) The sin of covetousness: Lusted, grasped after the plunder
			
			    8) The sin of an argumentative, stubborn, unrepentant heart
			      • Saul insisted he had obeyed the LORD
			
			      • Saul again insisted the best animals had been spared to offer as a sacrifice to God

a. Once again the LORD had a message to give to Saul. Saul was to be called to account for his disobedience. He had deliberately disobeyed God in failing to execute judgment upon the Amalekites; consequently, he himself must face the judgment of God. But note the first point of God's message: He was grieved; His heart was cut, broken over the disobedience of Saul. The word "repenteth" or "grieved" (*nacham* or *naham*) means to sigh; to breathe strongly; to be sorry in the sense of pitying, consoling, comforting, easing, expressing sympathy, or having compassion. It also means to regret in the sense of suffering remorse and being grieved, so much so that one repents, relents, reconsiders, and changes one's mind. The Hebrew word involves deep emotional feelings, intense concern. The LORD was grieved, for Saul's disobedience cut or broke His heart, causing the LORD to sigh deeply and to suffer intense pain. He regretted having made Saul king.

b. This message from the LORD struck Samuel to the core of his heart. Samuel was deeply troubled, and he cried out all night in agonizing prayer. Early the next morning, he arose with the message of God burning in his heart, and he set out to find Saul (v.12). When he arrived where he expected Saul to be, he was told that Saul had gone to Carmel, a city located someplace in the Negev.

c. From this point on, eight terrible sins of Saul are covered (vv.12-21).

1) There was the sin of pride (v.12). Samuel was told that Saul had gone to Carmel to set up a monument in his own honor. Apparently, the monument was to commemorate the recent victory he had achieved over the Amalekites. From there Saul had traveled on down to Gilgal, the very place where Samuel had earlier rebuked Saul, a place that had become a center for religious worship (7:16; 10:8; 13:7-14; 15:21).

Note that the monument was not built to honor the LORD, but to honor Saul. Saul was taking credit for the victory over the Amalekites; he was not giving credit to the LORD. His heart had been gripped by the sin of pride. And God warns us against pride.

"And whosoever shall exalt himself shall be abased; and he that shall humble himself shall be exalted" (Mt.23:12).

"Love not the world, neither the things *that are* in the world. If any man love the world, the love of the Father is not in him. For all that *is* in the world, the lust of the flesh, and the lust of the eyes, and the pride of life, is not of the Father, but is of the world" (1 Jn.2:15-16).

"*When* pride cometh, then cometh shame: but with the lowly *is* wisdom" (Pr.11:2).

"Pride *goeth* before destruction, and an haughty spirit before a fall" (Pr.16:18).

"Though thou exalt *thyself* as the eagle, and though thou set thy nest among the stars, thence will I bring thee down, saith the LORD" (Ob.4).

2) There was the sin of boasting (v.13). When Samuel reached Saul, Saul spoke up first, greeting Samuel. And he did not wait for Samuel to respond, but immediately boasted of his obedience. He proudly declared that he had carried out the LORD's instructions. Of course, this was not true. But to divert attention from his disobedience, Saul attempted to deceive Samuel by boasting, bragging about his obedience. He was committing a sin that God warns against, the sin of boasting.

"Wherefore let him that thinketh he standeth take heed lest he fall" (1 Co.10:12).
"For the wicked boasteth of his heart's desire, and blesseth the covetous, whom the Lord abhorreth" (Ps.10:3).
"He that trusteth in his own heart is a fool: but whoso walketh wisely, he shall be delivered" (Pr.28:26).
"Be not wise in thine own eyes: fear the Lord, and depart from evil" (Pr.3:7).
"Woe unto *them that are* wise in their own eyes, and prudent in their own sight" (Is.5:21).

3) There was the sin of blaming others, the sin of seeking to justify oneself (v.14). Standing there, Samuel had heard the noise of animals crying out in the background. In response to Saul's boasting, Samuel demanded to know where Saul had secured the animals. Note Saul's answer: he blamed the soldiers, saying that they had brought them as plunder from the Amalekite victory. Saul followed the course of human nature, that of blaming others. He declared it was not he who had been disobedient; it was the soldiers.

Thought 1. This is the way of sin, blaming others and trying to escape as much guilt as possible. Whatever happens to us—no matter the circumstances—we often lay the major blame at the feet of...

- husband
- wife
- parent
- child
- in-laws
- neighbors
- employer
- employees
- government
- economy
- environment
- special situations or circumstances

"Therefore thou art inexcusable, O man, whosoever thou art that judgest: for wherein thou judgest another, thou condemnest thyself; for thou that judgest doest the same things" (Ro.2:1).
"If I justify myself, mine own mouth shall condemn me: if I say, I am perfect, it shall also prove me perverse" (Jb.9:20).
"Most men will proclaim every one his own goodness: but a faithful man who can find" (Pr.20:6).
"There is a generation that are pure in their own eyes, and yet is not washed from their filthiness" (Pr.30:12).
"Yet thou sayest, Because I am innocent, surely his anger shall turn from me. Behold, I will plead with thee, because thou sayest, I have not sinned" (Je.2:35).

4) There was the sin of deception, of lying (vv.15-16). Shockingly, Saul told a bold-faced lie. He claimed that the best animals had been spared so they could be sacrificed to the LORD. He and his soldiers felt a greater good could be accomplished, that the LORD would be far better pleased if the animals were actually sacrificed in His honor.
    At this point—immediately before Saul could say anything else—Samuel interrupted his conversation. He demanded that Saul stop making excuses, stop his lying and attempts to deceive. It was time for Saul to hush and hear the Word of the LORD.

"Lie not one to another, seeing that ye have put off the old man with his deeds" (Col.3:9).
"Ye shall not steal, neither deal falsely, neither lie one to another" (Le.19:11).
"He that worketh deceit shall not dwell within my house: he that telleth lies shall not tarry in my sight" (Ps.101:7).
"Lying lips are abomination to the Lord: but they that deal truly are his delight" (Pr.12:22).
"The getting of treasures by a lying tongue *is* a vanity tossed to and fro of them that seek death" (Pr.21:6).

5) There was the sin of losing the spirit of humility (v.17). Samuel declared the Word of the LORD to Saul in a very forceful and straightforward manner: when Saul began his service as king, he possessed a spirit of humility. He had considered himself to be inadequate for the task. If he was appointed by the LORD to be king, the LORD would have to equip him. In the beginning he had been dependent upon the LORD. But now Saul had forgotten that it was the LORD who had anointed and equipped him. He had lost his spirit of humility, the very spirit that God demands of His followers.

"For I say, through the grace given unto me, to every man that is among you, not to think *of himself* more highly than he ought to think; but to think soberly" (Ro.12:3).
"Humble yourselves in the sight of the Lord, and he shall lift you up" (Js.4:10).

"Better it is to be of an humble spirit with the lowly, than to divide the spoil with the proud" (Pr.16:19).

"A man's pride shall bring him low: but honour shall uphold the humble in spirit" (Pr.29:23).

"For thus saith the high and lofty One that inhabiteth eternity, whose name is Holy; I dwell in the high and holy place, with him also that is of a contrite and humble spirit, to revive the spirit of the humble, and to revive the heart of the contrite ones" (Is.57:15).

"He hath showed thee, O man, what is good; and what doth the Lord require of thee, but to do justly, and to love mercy, and to walk humbly with thy God" (Mi.6:8).

6) There was the sin of disobedience (vv.18-19). Simply stated, the LORD had sent Saul on a very special mission, that of totally destroying the wicked Amalekites. But Saul had disobeyed. And God warns all generations against disobedience.

"For this ye know, that no whoremonger, nor unclean person, nor covetous man, who is an idolater, hath any inheritance in the kingdom of Christ and of God. Let no man deceive you with vain words: for because of these things cometh the wrath of God upon the children of disobedience" (Ep.5:5-6).

"And to you who are troubled rest with us, when the Lord Jesus shall be revealed from heaven with his mighty angels, In flaming fire taking vengeance on them that know not God, and that obey not the gospel of our Lord Jesus Christ: Who shall be punished with everlasting destruction from the presence of the Lord, and from the glory of his power" (2 Th.1:7-9).

"And a curse, if ye will not obey the commandments of the Lord your God, but turn aside out of the way which I command you this day, to go after other gods, which ye have not known" (De.11:28).

"But if ye will not obey the voice of the Lord, but rebel against the commandment of the Lord, then shall the hand of the LORD be against you, as it was against your fathers" (1 S.12:15).

7) There was the sin of covetousness (v.19). Saul and the army had lusted, grasped after the riches or wealth of the plunder. They coveted the animals of the Amalekites to increase their own herds. And when they saw the money and valuables of the Amalekites, a burning lust arose within their hearts to increase their own wealth and estates. Saul and his men became greedy, committing the sin of covetousness.

"And he said unto them, Take heed, and beware of covetousness: for a man's life consisteth not in the abundance of the things which he possesseth" (Lu.12:15).

"Mortify therefore your members which are upon the earth; fornication, uncleanness, inordinate affection, evil concupiscence, and covetousness, which is idolatry: For which things' sake the wrath of God cometh on the children of disobedience" (Col.3:5-6).

"Woe to him that coveteth an evil covetousness to his house, that he may set his nest on high, that he may be delivered from the power of evil" (Hab.2:9).

8) There was the sin of an argumentative, stubborn, unrepentant heart (vv.20-21). Picture the scene: there stood Samuel, the prophet of God, before King Saul, laying charge after charge of sin against him. Instead of falling to his knees and crying out for the LORD to forgive him, Saul stubbornly and repeatedly argued that he was innocent. He insisted that he had obeyed the LORD, that he had completely followed the instructions of the LORD. He had destroyed all the enemies except one, King Agag. Moreover, Saul continued to insist that only the best animals had been spared and, then, only to be offered as a sacrifice to God (v.21). Imagine the audacity of his standing before the prophet of God and continuing to lie and justify his sinful behavior. Saul had become hardhearted, stiff-necked against God. He was unrepentant.

"But after thy hardness and impenitent heart treasurest up unto thyself wrath against the day of wrath and revelation of the righteous judgment of God" (Ro.2:5).

"Harden not your heart, as in the provocation, and as in the day of temptation in the wilderness: When your fathers tempted me, proved me, and saw my work. Forty years long was I grieved with this generation, and said, It is a people that do err in their heart, and they have not known my ways: Unto whom I sware in my wrath that they should not enter into my rest" (Ps.95:8-11).

"Happy is the man that feareth alway: but he that hardeneth his heart shall fall into mischief" (Pr.28:14).

3 (15:22-25) **Confession, Example of—Confession, Weak and Inadequate—Saul, Confession, Weak and Inadequate**: there was the weak, inadequate confession of Saul. A confrontation with the prophet of God failed to drive Saul to his knees. But one thing would humble Saul: the pronouncement of God's judgment. Thus God's message of judgment was delivered to Saul. Hearing the judgment pronounced against him, Saul immediately fell to his knees in confession. The scene is dramatically pictured in the Scripture:

OUTLINE	SCRIPTURE	SCRIPTURE	OUTLINE
3. The weak, inadequate confession of sin a. The supreme demand of	22 And Samuel said, Hath the LORD as great delight in burnt offerings and sacrifices,	as in obeying the voice of the LORD? Behold, to obey is better than sacrifice, and to	God's Word: Obedience 1) To obey is better than sacrifice

OUTLINE	SCRIPTURE	SCRIPTURE	OUTLINE

2) To obey is better than the most choice gift
b. The seriousness of disobedience
  1) Rebellion is as bad as witchcraft
  2) Arrogance is as bad as idolatry
  3) Disobedience results in judgment & rejection
c. The weak, inadequate
	hearken than the fat of rams.
	23 For rebellion *is as* the sin of witchcraft, and stubbornness *is as* iniquity and idolatry. Because thou hast rejected the word of the LORD, he hath also rejected thee from *being* king.
	24 And Saul said unto Sam-
		uel, I have sinned: for I have transgressed the commandment of the LORD, and thy words: because I feared the people, and obeyed their voice.
		25 Now therefore, I pray thee, pardon my sin, and turn again with me, that I may worship the LORD.
			confession of Saul: He fell to his knees
			  1) He confessed his sinful disobedience: He had feared the people, their covetousness
			  2) He called upon Samuel, not God, to forgive his sin; see also v.15, 21, 30, "the LORD your God"

a. Samuel declared the supreme demand of God's Word: obedience (v.22). One thing above all others pleases God and makes a person acceptable to God: obedience, devotion to the LORD. God wants a heart of devotion, a heart that is set upon obedience. Note two facts:

⇒ To obey is better than sacrifice. Sacrifice is important, but it is acceptable only when it is brought to the LORD with a heart of devotion, a heart of obedience.

⇒ To obey is better than the most choice gift given to God. The fat of a sacrifice was the portion of meat that belonged to the LORD, that was to be burned so that the aroma could ascend up toward the sky, symbolizing that the sacrifice was acceptable to God. The fat, the portion that belonged to God, was considered the most choice gift. But even the most choice gift was no substitute for obedience.

The supreme gift that could be given to God was *obedience*. This was the message of God to Saul, and it is the message that God proclaims to all generations.

b. Samuel declared the seriousness of disobedience (v.23). Nothing provokes the LORD like rebelliousness or defiance of His commandments. After all, the LORD is the Creator who has given us life and all the wonderful benefits and experiences of life. All the fruitfulness and abundance of life comes from God. He is the wonderful Savior, Provider, Protector, and Guide throughout life, making the way to escape death and to inherit eternal life. Therefore, nothing hurts or angers the great Creator and Provider of life more than our disobedience. Note exactly what the LORD says about disobedience:

⇒ Rebellion is equivalent to witchcraft. To rebel against God is as bad as seeking to be saved, protected, and guided by an evil spirit or the world of the occult.

⇒ Being stubborn or arrogant is equivalent to idolatry. Stubbornly standing against God, refusing to obey the commandments of God, is as bad as committing idolatry. It is equivalent to turning to other gods, for stubbornness exalts a person as his own god. A stubborn person does his own thing, acts as he wishes to act, not as God commands.

Note that disobedience results in the judgment and rejection of God. Samuel pronounced God's judgment upon Saul: Saul was rejected as king. He had rejected the Word of the LORD; consequently the LORD had rejected him as king. Saul would continue to reign for a while, but the judgment was an accomplished fact. He was soon to be removed as king, and his descendants would never be allowed to serve as leaders of God's people.

c. Hearing these words of judgment, Saul fell to his knees and confessed his disobedience (vv.24-25). But note how weak and inadequate his confession was. Bowing before Samuel he confessed his sin, but note why: not because he feared the LORD, but because he was afraid of the people. Obviously, when the soldiers saw the enormous wealth of the Amalekites, their spirit of covetousness put enormous pressure upon Saul to keep the plunder instead of destroying it as commanded by God. The result was catastrophic: Saul confessed that he was more afraid of the soldiers than he was of disobeying God and facing the judgment of God.

But again note the weak, inadequate confession of Saul: he called upon Samuel, not God, to forgive his sin (v.25). He was looking to the prophet of God, not to the LORD Himself, for forgiveness. Three times throughout this passage he refers to "the LORD your God" (vv.15, 21, 30). He never addresses the LORD as "my LORD." A personal, vibrant relationship with the LORD seems to be missing. Note that he also felt he could not worship the LORD apart from Samuel. He begged Samuel to return home with him so he could worship the LORD. In every way the confession of Saul is weak and inadequate. He seeks forgiveness, but not from the LORD. He looks to the prophet of God, not to the LORD Himself.

Thought 1. Only the LORD can forgive sins, not man. No prophet, priest, minister, teacher, or self-professed messiah can forgive the sins of another person. Sins can be forgiven only by the LORD Himself. If we wish to be forgiven, we must confess our sins to the LORD and to Him alone.

> **"Then Peter said unto them, Repent, and be baptized every one of you in the name of Jesus Christ for the remission of sins, and ye shall receive the gift of the Holy Ghost" (Ac.2:38).**
>
> **"Repent ye therefore, and be converted, that your sins may be blotted out, when the times of refreshing shall come from the presence of the LORD" (Ac.3:19).**
>
> **"Repent therefore of this thy wickedness, and pray God, if perhaps the thought of thine heart may be forgiven thee" (Ac.8:22).**
>
> **"If we confess our sins, he is faithful and just to forgive us *our* sins, and to cleanse us from all unrighteousness" (1 Jn.1:9).**
>
> **"If my people, which are called by my name, shall humble themselves, and pray, and seek my face, and turn from their wicked ways; then will I hear from heaven, and will forgive their sin, and will heal their land" (2 Chr.7:14).**

"He that covereth his sins shall not prosper: but whoso confesseth and forsaketh *them* shall have mercy" (Pr.28:13).

"Let the wicked forsake his way, and the unrighteous man his thoughts: and let him return unto the LORD, and he will have mercy upon him; and to our God, for he will abundantly pardon" (Is.55:7).

"Only acknowledge thine iniquity, that thou hast transgressed against the LORD thy God, and hast scattered thy ways to the strangers under every green tree, and ye have not obeyed my voice, saith the LORD" (Je.3:13).

"Now therefore make confession unto the LORD God of your fathers, and do his pleasure: and separate yourselves from the people of the land, and from the strange wives" (Ezr.10:11).

4 (15:26-29) **Judgment, Surety of—Saul, Judgment of—God, Title, the Glory of Israel**: there was the irrevocable, unchanging judgment of God pronounced upon Saul. The scene is dramatic:

OUTLINE	SCRIPTURE	SCRIPTURE	OUTLINE
4. The irrevocable, unchanging judgment of God a. The verdict, judgment upon Saul restated: The LORD had rejected him as king 1) The desperation of Saul: Caught & tore Samuel's robe	26 And Samuel said unto Saul, I will not return with thee: for thou hast rejected the word of the LORD, and the LORD hath rejected thee from being king over Israel. 27 And as Samuel turned about to go away, he laid hold upon the skirt of his mantle, and it rent.	28 And Samuel said unto him, The LORD hath rent the kingdom of Israel from thee this day, and hath given it to a neighbour of thine, *that is* better than thou. 29 And also the Strength of Israel will not lie nor repent: for he *is* not a man, that he should repent.	2) The symbolism of the torn robe declared by Samuel: The kingdom had been torn from Saul & given to someone else—a better person than Saul b. The irrevocable nature & judgment of God, *the Strength or Glory of Israel*: He does not lie nor change His mind

a. The verdict or judgment upon Saul was restated: the LORD had rejected him as king (vv.26-27). Remember that Saul had just requested Samuel to return home with him to conduct a worship service. Refusing, Samuel repeated the sentence passed upon him by God. Saul had rejected the Word of the LORD; consequently, the LORD had rejected him as king over His people.

Having said this, Samuel turned to leave. However, Saul, trying to hold Samuel back, grabbed him and tore the hem of Samuel's robe. Immediately, Samuel drew a dramatic picture, a symbolic lesson from the torn robe: he declared that the LORD had torn the kingdom from Saul that very day and given it to someone else, a far better person than Saul. By "better" was meant that the person would obey God, keep His commandments. This is a reference to David (vv.16:11-13; 2 S.7:11-16).

b. Samuel then declared the irrevocable nature and judgment of God. And note that he called God the "Enduring, Lasting One of Israel" or "the Glory of Israel." This is the only time this title for God is used in Scripture. The Strength or Glory of Israel does not lie or change his mind. He is not like a man who often says one thing but later changes his mind. Once God has pronounced judgment, the judgment is irrevocable. The surety of judgment is unchangeable. Consequently, Saul would bear the judgment of God.

Thought 1. The lesson for us is as clearly stated as can be: the judgment of God is irrevocable. It is set, fixed, established, unchangeable. God's judgment is inevitable and irreversible. Coming judgment cannot be altered: it is predestined and predetermined. If we fail to repent of our sins—to turn away from wickedness and turn to the LORD—we will face the judgment of God. This is the irrevocable, unchangeable truth proclaimed by the living LORD:

"And as it is appointed unto men once to die, but after this the judgment" (He.9:27).

"When the Son of man shall come in his glory, and all the holy angels with him, then shall he sit upon the throne of his glory: And before him shall be gathered all nations: and he shall separate them one from another, as a shepherd divideth *his* sheep from the goats: And he shall set the sheep on his right hand, but the goats on the left....Then shall he say also unto them on the left hand, Depart from me, ye cursed, into everlasting fire, prepared for the devil and his angels: For I was an hungred, and ye gave me no meat: I was thirsty, and ye gave me no drink: I was a stranger, and ye took me not in: naked, and ye clothed me not: sick, and in prison, and ye visited me not. Then shall they also answer him, saying, LORD, when saw we thee an hungred, or athirst, or a stranger, or naked, or sick, or in prison, and did not minister unto thee? Then shall he answer them, saying, Verily I say unto you, Inasmuch as ye did *it* not to one of the least of these, ye did *it* not to me. And these shall go away into everlasting punishment: but the righteous into life eternal" (Mt.25:31-33, 41-46).

"The LORD knoweth how to deliver the godly out of temptations, and to reserve the unjust unto the day of judgment to be punished" (2 Pe.2:9).

"And Enoch also, the seventh from Adam, prophesied of these, saying, Behold, the LORD cometh with ten thousands of his saints, To execute judgment upon all, and to convince all that are ungodly among them of all their ungodly deeds which they have ungodly committed, and of all their hard *speeches* which ungodly sinners have spoken against him" (Jude 14-15).

"And I saw a great white throne, and him that sat on it, from whose face the earth and the heaven fled away; and there was found no place for them. And I saw the dead, small and great, stand before God; and the books were opened: and another book was opened, which is *the book* of life: and the dead were judged out of those things which were written in the books, according to their works. And the sea gave up the dead which were in it; and death and hell delivered up the dead which were in them: and they were judged every man according to their works. And death and hell were cast into the lake of fire. This is the second death. And whosoever was not found written in the book of life was cast into the lake of fire" (Re.20:11-15).

5 (15:30-35) **Faithfulness, Example of—Samuel, Faithfulness of**: there was the sharp contrast of Samuel's faithfulness with Saul's unfaithfulness. What now happened paints a dramatic picture of what it means to be faithful to God:

OUTLINE	SCRIPTURE	SCRIPTURE	OUTLINE

5. The sharp contrast of Samuel's faithfulness with Saul's unfaithfulness
a. Samuel's faithfulness to Saul
  1) Saul begged Samuel to return with him to lead in worship: To save face
  2) Samuel agreed: To assure an effective rule until Saul was replaced
b. Samuel's faithfulness to the LORD's command
  1) Samuel completed Saul's task: Executed King Agag
    • Agag thought he had escaped death
	30 Then he said, I have sinned: *yet* honour me now, I pray thee, before the elders of my people, and before Israel, and turn again with me, that I may worship the LORD thy God.
	31 So Samuel turned again after Saul; and Saul worshipped the LORD.
	32 Then said Samuel, Bring ye hither to me Agag the king of the Amalekites. And Agag came unto him delicately. And Agag said, Surely the bitterness of death is past.
		33 And Samuel said, As thy sword hath made women childless, so shall thy mother be childless among women. And Samuel hewed Agag in pieces before the LORD in Gilgal.
		34 Then Samuel went to Ramah; and Saul went up to his house to Gibeah of Saul.
		35 And Samuel came no more to see Saul until the day of his death: nevertheless Samuel mourned for Saul: and the LORD repented that he had made Saul king over Israel.
			• Agag was executed because of the savage evil committed by him & his people
			
			2) Samuel accepted God's judgment upon Saul
			  • Separated from Saul
			  • Would never again go to see Saul
			3) Samuel mourned for Saul: Showed compassion
			c. The permanent judgment of God: Regretted having made Saul king

a. Note that Samuel remained faithful to Saul to the very end (v.30). Desperate to save face before the people and to publicly show that Samuel still supported him, Saul begged Samuel to return with him and to lead in a public service of worship. Finally Samuel agreed, realizing that his support was needed to assure an effective rule in government until Saul was replaced. This was necessary, for Saul was to continue ruling for about fifteen more years although his fate was sealed right then and there (15:23, 26, 28; 16:14).[2]

b. Samuel demonstrated a strong faithfulness to the LORD's command (v.32). Remember that Samuel was the last person to serve in the position of Israel's judge, the judge who was supremely responsible to execute justice and to carry out the judgment of God among the people. In one final act of executing justice, Samuel issued an order that King Agag of the Amalekites be brought before him (vv.32-33). Up to this point, Agag thought he had escaped death. But standing before Samuel, he heard the charge against him and the verdict pronounced: he was guilty of the most cruel, savage evil imaginable—that of oppressing, brutalizing, and slaughtering people. Consequently, just as he had made many mothers childless by killing their sons, so would his mother be childless. He was to be executed, and his executioner was Samuel. Samuel was faithful to the LORD's command.

Note that Samuel accepted God's judgment upon Saul (v.34). He returned home to Ramah, and Saul went home to Gibeah. The two men were separated for the last time, for Samuel would never again go to see Saul. But Samuel mourned, showing the deepest compassion for him.

c. Nonetheless, the judgment against Saul was permanent (v.35). The LORD repented, regretted having made Saul king of Israel. The LORD grieved over Saul.

Thought 1. God demands faithfulness. If God commands us to do something, we must be faithful to do it. If God calls us to perform some service by meeting some need, we are to be faithful and perform that service. No matter where we are and no matter what we are doing, we are to be faithful to God. We are to keep His commandments and serve Him by helping our neighbor and meeting the needs of the world. Faithfulness—obeying and serving God—is an absolute essential. The task can be any task and the commandment can be any commandment: we are still to be faithful. Whatever our position or call in life, we are to be faithful. We are to perform the functions, the work, the labor of our position and our call in life. Once again, God demands faithfulness.

"Not slothful in business; fervent in spirit; serving the LORD" (Ro.12:11).

"Therefore, my beloved brethren, be ye stedfast, unmovable, always abounding in the work of the LORD, forasmuch as ye know that your labour is not in vain in the LORD" (1 Co.15:58).

"Stand fast therefore in the liberty wherewith Christ hath made us free, and be not entangled again with the yoke of bondage" (Ga.5:1).

"Only let your conversation be as it becometh the gospel of Christ: that whether I come and see you, or else be absent, I may hear of your affairs, that ye stand fast in one spirit, with one mind striving together for the faith of the gospel" (Ph.1:27).

"And whatsoever ye do in word or deed, *do* all in the name of the LORD Jesus, giving thanks to God and the Father by him" (Col.3:17).

"And whatsoever ye do, do *it* heartily, as to the LORD, and not unto men" (Col.3:23).

---

2 John F. Walvoord and Roy B. Zuck, Editors. *The Bible Knowledge Commentary*. (Colorado Springs, CO: Chariot Victor Publishing, 1985), p.47.

"Moreover it is required in stewards, that a man be found faithful" (1 Co.4:2).

"Be sober, be vigilant; because your adversary the devil, as a roaring lion, walketh about, seeking whom he may devour: Whom resist stedfast in the faith, knowing that the same afflictions are accomplished in your brethren that are in the world" (1 Pe.5:8-9).

"But the day of the LORD will come as a thief in the night; in the which the heavens shall pass away with a great noise, and the elements shall melt with fervent heat, the earth also and the works that are therein shall be burned up. *Seeing* then *that* all these things shall be dissolved, what manner *of persons* ought ye to be in *all* holy conversation and godliness, Looking for and hasting unto the coming of the day of God, wherein the heavens being on fire shall be dissolved, and the elements shall melt with fervent heat? Nevertheless we, according to his promise, look for new heavens and a new earth, wherein dwelleth righteousness. Wherefore, beloved, seeing that ye look for such things, be diligent that ye may be found of him in peace, without spot, and blameless....Ye therefore, beloved, seeing ye know *these things* before, beware lest ye also, being led away with the error of the wicked, fall from your own stedfastness" (2 Pe.3:10-14, 17).

"And Moses verily *was* faithful in all his house, as a servant, for a testimony of those things which were to be spoken after" (He.3:5).

DEEPER STUDY # 1

(15:3) Iniquity, Cup of—Harem Principle—Nations, Destruction of—Nations, Evil of—Nations, Judgment of—Canaanites, Destruction of—Judgment, Why God Judges: Why did God command Israel to drive out the Canaanites from the promised land? To actually exterminate them? The command was for them to be "utterly destroyed" or "totally and completely destroyed" (*harami* or *charam*). The word means to annihilate, exterminate, eliminate, abolish. The word is related to the Hebrew *herem* which means "to devote to the ban."[3] Once something had been promised or devoted to God, it was placed under the ban: it could not be removed. If it was a gift, it had to be given to God. If it was the promise to do something, then it had to be done. If it was a vow to devote something to destruction, then it had to be destroyed or exterminated. In ancient days, this was known as the *harem principal or law*. Once a person or thing had been *devoted* to the LORD, it could not be removed. It went to the LORD.

"And Israel vowed a vow unto the LORD, and said, If thou wilt indeed deliver this people into my hand, then I will utterly destroy their cities. And the LORD hearkened to the voice of Israel, and delivered up the Canaanites; and they utterly destroyed them and their cities: and he called the name of the place Hormah" (Nu.21:2-3).

"But of the cities of these people, which the LORD thy God doth give thee *for* an inheritance, thou shalt save alive nothing that breatheth: But thou shalt utterly destroy them; *namely*, the Hittites, and the Amorites, the Canaanites, and the Perizzites, the Hivites, and the Jebusites; as the LORD thy God hath commanded thee: That they teach you not to do after all their abominations, which they have done unto their gods; so should ye sin against the LORD your God" (De.20:16-18).

"For it was of the LORD to harden their hearts, that they should come against Israel in battle, that he might destroy them utterly, *and* that they might have no favour, but that he might destroy them, as the LORD commanded Moses" (Jos.11:20).

The very idea that God and moral people would be set on the total destruction of a people is offensive to some persons. How could God and moral people possibly endorse such an act? In looking at this, certain factors need to be kept in mind:

1. People can become so savage, evil, and corrupt that they are beyond repair or repentance, beyond hope or correction. This is what is known as the "cup of iniquity being full"—filled to the point that it overflows and continues to overflow with...

- savagery
- violence
- brutality
- slavery
- rape

- ruthlessness
- lawlessness
- abuse
- cruelty
- atrocities

- barbarism
- corruption
- evil
- immorality
- injustice

History has shown that such behavior can be true of both individuals and nations. A person's or a nation's "cup of iniquity" can become full—well beyond repair or repentance, well beyond hope or correction. God declares this fact time and again as the Scriptures below show (Ge.15:16).

God wants justice executed against people who are totally given over to evil. Scripture is clear about this fact: this is the very purpose for the judgment of God.

"But in the fourth generation they shall come hither again: for the iniquity of the Amorites is not yet full" (Ge.15:16).

"Defile not ye yourselves in any of these things: for in all these the nations are defiled which I cast out before you: And the land is defiled: therefore I do visit the iniquity thereof upon it, and the land itself vomiteth out her inhabitants" (Le.18:24-25).

"And ye shall not walk in the manners of the nation, which I cast out before you: for they committed all these things, and therefore I abhorred them" (Le.20:23).

---

3 *Judges.* "The Expositor's Bible Commentary," Vol.3. Herbert Wolf, Editor. (Grand Rapids, MI: Zondervan Publishing House, 1992), p.874.

> "Speak not thou in thine heart, after that the LORD thy God hath cast them out from before thee, saying, For my righteousness the LORD hath brought me in to possess this land: but for the wickedness of these nations the LORD doth drive them out from before thee. Not for thy righteousness, or for the uprightness of thine heart, dost thou go to possess their land: but for the wickedness of these nations the LORD thy God doth drive them out from before thee, and that he may perform the word which the LORD sware unto thy fathers, Abraham, Isaac, and Jacob" (De.9:4-5).

> "And he did that which was evil in the sight of the LORD, after the abominations of the heathen, whom the LORD cast out before the children of Israel" (2 K.21:2).

> "Moreover he burnt incense in the valley of the son of Hinnom, and burnt his children in the fire, after the abominations of the heathen whom the LORD had cast out before the children of Israel" (2 Chr.28:3).

> "But did that which was evil in the sight of the LORD, like unto the abominations of the heathen, whom the LORD had cast out before the children of Israel" (2 Chr.33:2).

> "For in the hand of the Lord there is a cup, and the wine is red; it is full of mixture; and he poureth out of the same: but the dregs thereof, all the wicked of the earth shall wring them out, and drink them" (Ps.75:8).

> "And shed innocent blood, even the blood of their sons and of their daughters, whom they sacrificed unto the idols of Canaan: and the land was polluted with blood" (Ps.106:38).

> "The earth also is defiled under the inhabitants thereof; because they have transgressed the laws, changed the ordinance, broken the everlasting covenant" (Is.24:5).

> "...thou hast polluted the land with thy whoredoms and with thy wickedness" (Je.3:2).

> "And first I will recompense their iniquity and their sin double; because they have defiled my land, they have filled mine inheritance with the carcases of their detestable and abominable things" (Je.16:18).

2. God is a just God as well as a God of love. God loves all people—every individual and all the people of every nation upon earth. His love continually flows out to everyone. But God is also a just God, the Sovereign LORD who executes justice upon the earth. God is not an *indulgent-grandfather* type of person who pampers the evil and savage of this world. To allow injustice to go unpunished, He would be a God of evil, a God who showed partiality and favoritism. He would be favoring the evil of the earth by allowing them to go unpunished and showing injustice to the moral of the earth by allowing them to continue to suffer under the injustices of evil people.

When the "cup of iniquity becomes full"—well beyond repair or repentance, well beyond hope or correction—that person or people are to be judged. Justice is to be executed upon them. God wants justice executed against such persons. This is the reason He has appointed a day in which He Himself will judge the world.

> "For the Son of man shall come in the glory of his Father with his angels; and then he shall reward every man according to his works" (Mt.16:27).

> "When the Son of man shall come in his glory, and all the holy angels with him, then shall he sit upon the throne of his glory: And before him shall be gathered all nations: and he shall separate them one from another, as a shepherd divideth his sheep from the goats: And he shall set the sheep on his right hand, but the goats on the left" (Mt.25:31-33).

> "Because he hath appointed a day, in the which he will judge the world in righteousness by that man whom he hath ordained; whereof he hath given assurance unto all men, in that he hath raised him from the dead" (Ac.17:31).

> "In the day when God shall judge the secrets of men by Jesus Christ according to my gospel" (Ro.2:16).

> "I charge thee therefore before God, and the Lord Jesus Christ, who shall judge the quick and the dead at his appearing and his kingdom" (2 Ti.4:1).

> "And as it is appointed unto men once to die, but after this the judgment" (He.9:27).

> "The LORD knoweth how to deliver the godly out of temptations, and to reserve the unjust unto the day of judgment to be punished" (2 Pe.2:9).

> "The LORD is not slack concerning his promise, as some men count slackness; but is longsuffering to us-ward, not willing that any should perish, but that all should come to repentance" (2 Pe.3:9).

> "Behold, the LORD cometh with ten thousands of his saints, To execute judgment upon all, and to convince all that are ungodly among them of all their ungodly deeds which they have ungodly committed, and of all their hard speeches which ungodly sinners have spoken against him" (Jude 14-15).

> "And I saw the dead, small and great, stand before God; and the books were opened: and another book was opened, which is the book of life: and the dead were judged out of those things which were written in the books, according to their works" (Re.20:12).

3. Israel was used by God as His instrument of justice and judgment against the nations of Canaan. The Israelites did not receive the promised land of Canaan because of some merit or value within themselves nor because of their own strength or power. In justice and judgment, God Himself destroyed the Canaanites, and it was because of their wickedness that He destroyed them.

Again, it is critical to note this fact: Israel as a people did not receive the promised land because of their merit or value nor because of some righteousness they possessed. The Canaanites were destroyed because they were evil and their "cup of iniquity" had been filled to the brim. They reached the point of no repentance; they were beyond correction. Moses himself declared to the Israelites:

a. "It is not because of any personal righteousness within you, not because you have pure hearts, that you inherit the promised land" (De.9:5). The enemies of the land are to be conquered and destroyed for two reasons:
  ⇒ "Because of their wickedness and because they are an evil people; their 'cup of iniquity' is full."
  ⇒ Because God is faithful; He fulfills His promise to the forefathers, to Abraham, Isaac, and Jacob. God has promised to give the promised land to their descendants, to all those down through the centuries who believe His Word, His promises.
b. "Understand this warning: it is not because of your righteousness that God gives you the promised land. On the contrary, you are a stiff-necked, stubborn people (De.9:6). You are a sinful people. You have no righteousness within yourselves that merits God's favor. Your hearts are not upright nor pure enough to make God accept you and give you victory over the enemies of the promised land. You are a stiff-necked, stubborn people."

> **"Not for thy righteousness, or for the uprightness of thine heart, dost thou go to possess their land: but for the wickedness of these nations the LORD thy God doth drive them out from before thee, and that he may perform the word which the LORD sware unto thy fathers, Abraham, Isaac, and Jacob. Understand therefore, that the LORD thy God giveth thee not this good land to possess it for thy righteousness; for thou *art* a stiffnecked people" (De.9:5-6).**

4. God shows no partiality, no favoritism—not to any person or to any nation. God warned the Israelites that they too would face the justice and judgment of God if they disobeyed Him, if they failed to keep His commandments.

The Canaanites were destroyed because they lived immoral and unrighteous lives. If the Israelites adopted the immoral and unrighteous lifestyle of the Canaanites, they too would be destroyed.

> **"Defile not ye yourselves in any of these things: for in all these the nations are defiled which I cast out before you: And the land is defiled: therefore I do visit the iniquity thereof upon it, and the land itself vomiteth out her inhabitants. Ye shall therefore keep my statutes and my judgments, and shall not commit *any* of these abominations; *neither* any of your own nation, nor any stranger that sojourneth among you: (For all these abominations have the men of the land done, which *were* before you, and the land is defiled;) That the land spue not you out also, when ye defile it, as it spued out the nations that *were* before you. For whosoever shall commit any of these abominations, even the souls that commit *them* shall be cut off from among their people. Therefore shall ye keep mine ordinance, that *ye* commit not *any one* of these abominable customs, which were committed before you, and that ye defile not yourselves therein: I *am* the LORD your God" (Le.18:24-30).**
> **"Ye shall therefore keep all my statutes, and all my judgments, and do them: that the land, whither I bring you to dwell therein, spue you not out. And ye shall not walk in the manners of the nation, which I cast out before you: for they committed all these things, and therefore I abhorred them. But I have said unto you, Ye shall inherit their land, and I will give it unto you to possess it, a land that floweth with milk and honey: I *am* the LORD your God, which have separated you from *other* people" (Le.20:22-24).**
> **"When the LORD thy God shall bring thee into the land whither thou goest to possess it, and hath cast out many nations before thee, the Hittites, and the Girgashites, and the Amorites, and the Canaanites, and the Perizzites, and the Hivites, and the Jebusites, seven nations greater and mightier than thou; And when the LORD thy God shall deliver them before thee; thou shalt smite them, *and* utterly destroy them; thou shalt make no covenant with them, nor show mercy unto them: Neither shalt thou make marriages with them; thy daughter thou shalt not give unto his son, nor his daughter shalt thou take unto thy son. For they will turn away thy son from following me, that they may serve other gods: so will the anger of the LORD be kindled against you, and destroy thee suddenly" (De.7:1-4).**
> **"Speak not thou in thine heart, after that the LORD thy God hath cast them out from before thee, saying, For my righteousness the LORD hath brought me in to possess this land: but for the wickedness of these nations the LORD doth drive them out from before thee. Not for thy righteousness, or for the uprightness of thine heart, dost thou go to possess their land: but for the wickedness of these nations the LORD thy God doth drive them out from before thee, and that he may perform the word which the LORD sware unto thy fathers, Abraham, Isaac, and Jacob. Understand therefore, that the LORD thy God giveth thee not this good land to possess it for thy righteousness; for thou *art* a stiffnecked people" (De.9:4-6).**

Thought 1. James Philip makes an excellent statement on the justice and judgment of God that is well worth quoting in full.

> *God was using His people as the rod of His anger against peoples whose cup of iniquity was full to overflowing. They were being judged for their sins and their depravities. This is, of course, stated explicitly more than once in the Old Testament itself (cf. Gen. 15:16 and Lev. 18:24-30). The time of their destruction was ripe. This is why they were thus dealt with, and it was no arbitrary act of injustice that drove them out of their land. They had forfeited the right to live as nations in Canaan by the extremes of their debauchery and depravity, just as Sodom and Gomorrah had done (Ge. 19), and just as the Cainite civilization as a whole had done, bringing upon itself the judgment of the Flood (Ge. 6). Furthermore, it should be remembered that God dealt with His own people in similar fashion when they proved themselves unworthy to life in the land of promise, and He brought them into the captivity of Babylon in 586 B.C. To understand God's burning passion for righteousness in His creatures*

is to understand the basic reason for these judgments upon men and nations that refused to be righteous, and who rendered themselves incapable of being so by their continued sin.[4]

Thought 2. *The Nelson Study Bible* says this:

> *Of Israel's attacks on the northern part of Canaanite cities, the Bible states, "but they struck every man with the edge of the sword until they had destroyed them, and they left none breathing. As the LORD had commanded Moses his servant, so Moses commanded Joshua, and so Joshua did" (Jos. 11:14, 15). God clearly commanded Israel to annihilate the Canaanites, and that is exactly what Joshua did.*
>
> *Headlines such as this have caused many people to question God's basic justice. How can a holy, just, and loving God command such extreme violence? Indeed, many have thought of this issue as the Old Testament's biggest challenge to modern readers. Some have gone so far as to allege that there is no connection between the "God of the Old Testament" and "God of the New Testament revealed in Jesus."*
>
> *However, this stereotype breaks down under examination. The Bible gives reasons for the Canaanites' destruction—and these reasons are in concert with the whole tenor of the Bible in both Testaments.*
>
> *The primary reason for the Canaanites' destruction was that they were guilty of gross sin. Abraham got a preview of this when God promised him the land. God said fulfillment of the promise would be delayed in part because "the iniquity of the Amorites is not yet complete" (Ge. 15:16; the Amorites were the Canaanites). For many years, the Canaanites' sins would not justify annihilation. But that time would arrive, and it did arrive by the time of Joshua.*
>
> *What were the sins of the Canaanites? The gruesome list in Lev. 18 gives some of the details, including incest, adultery, child sacrifice, homosexuality, and bestiality. Of course, every person has sinned in some fashion (Ps. 14:3). On this level, the Canaanites only received what all peoples deserved; others were spared only by God's grace. But Canaan was not a community of upstanding citizens. It was a thoroughly debased society, hostile to all God's ways (Deut. 9:4, 5).*
>
> *To a lesser degree, God was merely protecting His people. God promised Abraham that He would curse anyone who cursed Israel (Ge. 12:3). The Canaanites sought to destroy Israel on at least two occasions (Jos. 9:1, 2; 11:1-5), and God would not allow that.*
>
> *The stereotype also breaks down because it overlooks the highly localized nature of the judgment on Canaan. The Israelites did not have a license to kill. They had no right to do the same to whatever peoples they encountered, at any time or in any place. This destruction targeted the sinful Canaanites of that time only. As harsh as it may seem to us, the Canaanites brought God's judgment on themselves by their own sin.*
>
> *The New Testament states that one day Jesus Christ will judge the wicked nations of the earth (Matt. 25:31-46). God once judged all the wicked with an overwhelming flood (Ge. 6-9), and the same God will one day again judge everyone who has ever lived (2 Pet. 3:10-13). The judgment against the Canaanites is merely one instance of His judgment on the wicked even as He extends forgiveness to others.*[5]

Thought 3. Warren Wiersbe gives an excellent statement on God's command to exterminate the Canaanite nations.

> *But wasn't it cruel and unjust for God to command Israel to exterminate the nations in Canaan? Not in the least! To begin with, He had been patient with these nations for centuries and had mercifully withheld His judgment (Ge. 15:16; 2 Peter 3:9). Their society, and especially their religion, was unspeakably wicked (Rom. 1:18ff) and should have been wiped out years before Israel appeared on the scene.*
>
> *Something else is true: These nations had been warned by the judgments God had inflicted on others, especially on Egypt and the nations east of the Jordan (Jos. 2:8-13). Rahab and her family had sufficient information to be able to repent and believe, and God saved them (Jos. 2; 6:22-25). Therefore, we have every right to conclude that God would have saved anybody who had turned to Him. These nations were sinning against a flood of light in rejecting God's truth and going their own way.*
>
> *God didn't want the filth of the Canaanite society and religion to contaminate His people Israel. Israel was God's special people, chosen to fulfill divine purposes in this world. Israel would give the world the knowledge of the true God, the Holy Scriptures, and the Savior. In order to accomplish God's purposes, the nation had to be separated from all other nations....God is perpetually at war with sin, wrote G. Campbell Morgan.*[6]
>
> *The main deity in Canaan was Baal, god of rainfall and fertility, and Ashtoreth was his spouse. If you wanted to have fruitful orchards and vineyards, flourishing crops, and increasing flocks and herds, you worshiped Baal by visiting a temple prostitute. This combination of idolatry, immorality, and agricultural success was difficult for men to resist, which explains why God told Israel to wipe out the Canaanite religion completely (Num. 33:51-56; Deut. 7:1-5).*[7]

---

4   James Philip. *The Preacher's Commentary on Numbers*. (Nashville, TN: Word Publishing, 1987, 2000), p.311.

5   *The Nelson Study Bible*, NKJV, p.375.

6   G. Campbell Morgan. *Living Messages of the Books of the Bible*, Vol.1 (Old Tappan, NJ: Fleming H. Revell, 1912), p.104.

7   Warren Wiersbe. *Be Available*. (Colorado Springs, CO: Victor Books, 1994), pp.15-16.

DIVISION III

THE STORY OF SAUL AND DAVID (PART 1):
THE LORD GIVES ISRAEL A KING
"AFTER HIS OWN HEART," 16:1–20:42

(16:1–20:42) **DIVISION OVERVIEW**: the LORD had given the people just what they wanted, a king "like all the nations" had (8:5). But King Saul had failed miserably and been rejected by the LORD. Now it was time for the LORD to give Israel not the leader they wanted but the leader they needed, a man "after God's own heart" (13:14). Sometime earlier the LORD had predicted that He would raise up a man "after His own heart" (13:14; 16:1). Although Saul was to rule about 15 more years, it was time for the LORD to unfold His plan for raising up the righteous king who was to rule His people after Saul. At the time of Saul's rejection by the LORD, the future ruler was only a small boy whose name was David. Nevertheless, the LORD wanted the young boy *secretly anointed* as the future king so that his preparation could begin and be guided by Samuel himself. A suspenseful picture of high drama took place with the secret anointing of David. This event marked a shift in power within Israel, power secretly transferred from the ruling monarch to a young boy who was destined to become king.

From the very day of David's secret anointing, the LORD began to move events to prepare the young boy for future rule. Soon thereafter, although Saul knew nothing about David's secret anointing, the king brought David into his royal court to serve as the king's very own harpist. As a member of the royal court, David was able to observe and learn about the nation's economic, military, and justice systems, as well as about the morality and character needed by its officials.

A few years later, although still too young to serve in the military (age 20), David demonstrated an unusual courage and fearlessness by defeating the giant Goliath. Because of his stunning victory over Goliath, Saul promoted David and brought him permanently into the king's court and service. Such a brave, courageous man was just the kind of person the king wanted serving him in his royal court. After serving the king faithfully for some time, David was given a command in the army of Israel. As commander, he proved very successful, winning victories over one enemy after another, never losing a single battle. Almost immediately David became a hero in the minds of the people, becoming even more popular than Saul himself. Because of David's popularity, Saul became extremely jealous and convinced that David and others were plotting to overthrow his kingdom. From this moment on, Saul launched a fierce pursuit to kill David, a pursuit that was to consume the rest of Saul's life. The king made attempt after attempt to assassinate the young man whom God had appointed to be the future ruler of His people, the young man "after God's own heart."

THE STORY OF SAUL AND DAVID (PART 1):
THE LORD GIVES ISRAEL A KING
"AFTER HIS OWN HEART," 16:1–20:42

A. The Story of David's Secret Anointing As King and His Service in Saul's Court: God Judges the Heart, Not the Appearance, of a Person, 16:1-23

B. The Story of David and Goliath: Defeating the Oppressor of God's People, 17:1-58

C. The Story of Saul's Jealous Rage and Attempts to Kill David (Part 1): A Look at the Evil of Jealousy, 18:1-30

D. The Story of Saul's Jealous Rage and Attempts to Kill David (Part 2): A Look at the Evil of Jealousy, 19:1-24

E. The Story of David and Jonathan's Friendship: A Lesson on Loyalty, 20:1-42

CHAPTER 16

III. THE STORY OF SAUL & DAVID (PART 1): THE LORD GIVES ISRAEL A KING "AFTER HIS OWN HEART," 16:1–20:42

A. The Story of David's Secret Anointing As King & His Service in Saul's Court: God Judges the Heart, Not the Appearance, of a Person, 16:1-23

1. The mission of Samuel to arise & anoint a new king: Conquering grief & sorrow
a. The LORD's rebuke of Samuel: He had grieved over His rejection of Saul far too long

b. The protest by Samuel: He feared that if he went to Bethlehem Saul would kill him
c. The LORD's solution: He was to go for the purpose of offering a sacrifice to prevent Saul from being suspicious
1) To invite Jesse & his sons to the sacrifice
2) To anoint the son indicated by God
d. The obedience of Samuel
e. The fear felt by Bethlehem's officials
1) They feared Samuel had come to execute judgment

2) Samuel assured them he had come to offer sacrifice, & he charged them to consecrate themselves
3) Samuel consecrated Jesse & his sons

2. The secret anointing of David: Being empowered by God's Spirit
a. The choice of Samuel
1) He chose the firstborn
2) He was rebuked by God: God had not chosen Eliab to be king
b. The basic qualification of God for service: Not physical appearance, but the heart

c. The choice of the father Jesse: He brought each of his seven sons before Samuel
1) Abinadab: Was rejected

And the LORD said unto Samuel, How long wilt thou mourn for Saul, seeing I have rejected him from reigning over Israel? fill thine horn with oil, and go, I will send thee to Jesse the Bethlehemite: for I have provided me a king among his sons.
2 And Samuel said, How can I go? if Saul hear *it*, he will kill me. And the LORD said, Take an heifer with thee, and say, I am come to sacrifice to the LORD.
3 And call Jesse to the sacrifice, and I will shew thee what thou shalt do: and thou shalt anoint unto me *him* whom I name unto thee.
4 And Samuel did that which the LORD spake, and came to Bethlehem. And the elders of the town trembled at his coming, and said, Comest thou peaceably?
5 And he said, Peaceably: I am come to sacrifice unto the LORD: sanctify yourselves, and come with me to the sacrifice. And he sanctified Jesse and his sons, and called them to the sacrifice.
6 And it came to pass, when they were come, that he looked on Eliab, and said, Surely the LORD'S anointed *is* before him.
7 But the LORD said unto Samuel, Look not on his countenance, or on the height of his stature; because I have refused him: for *the LORD seeth* not as man seeth; for man looketh on the outward appearance, but the LORD looketh on the heart.
8 Then Jesse called Abinadab, and made him pass before Samuel. And he said, Neither hath the LORD chosen this.

9 Then Jesse made Shammah to pass by. And he said, Neither hath the LORD chosen this.
10 Again, Jesse made seven of his sons to pass before Samuel. And Samuel said unto Jesse, The LORD hath not chosen these.
11 And Samuel said unto Jesse, Are here all *thy* children? And he said, There remaineth yet the youngest, and, behold, he keepeth the sheep. And Samuel said unto Jesse, Send and fetch him: for we will not sit down till he come hither.
12 And he sent, and brought him in. Now he *was* ruddy, *and* withal of a beautiful countenance, and goodly to look to. And the LORD said, Arise, anoint him: for this *is* he.
13 Then Samuel took the horn of oil, and anointed him in the midst of his brethren: and the Spirit of the LORD came upon David from that day forward. So Samuel rose up, and went to Ramah.
14 But the Spirit of the LORD departed from Saul, and an evil spirit from the LORD troubled him.
15 And Saul's servants said unto him, Behold now, an evil spirit from God troubleth thee.
16 Let our lord now command thy servants, *which are* before thee, to seek out a man, *who is* a cunning player on an harp: and it shall come to pass, when the evil spirit from God is upon thee, that he shall play with his hand, and thou shalt be well.
17 And Saul said unto his servants, Provide me now a man that can play well, and bring *him* to me.
18 Then answered one of the servants, and said, Behold, I have seen a son of Jesse the Bethlehemite, *that is* cunning in playing, and a mighty valiant man, and a man of war, and prudent in matters, and a comely person, and the LORD *is* with him.
19 Wherefore Saul sent messengers unto Jesse, and said, Send me David thy son, which *is* with the sheep.
20 And Jesse took an ass *laden* with bread, and a bottle

2) Shammah was rejected

3) All seven sons brought by Jesse were rejected

d. The choice of the LORD: The youngest son
1) Samuel was perplexed: Asked Jesse if he had any other sons
2) David, the youngest, had been left tending the sheep

3) Samuel immediately sent for David: When he arrived, he was seen to have striking features
4) The LORD identified David as His choice to be king

e. The secret anointing of David
1) He was anointed in the presence of his brothers
2) He was equipped, empowered by the Spirit of the LORD

3. The beginning of David's preparation to be king: A picture of God's sovereignty
a. The removal of God's Spirit from Saul
1) The advice of Saul's attendants: To find a harpist who could soothe Saul when he was tormented by an evil spirit (spiritually, mentally, & emotionally)

2) Saul agreed & ordered that a musician be found
b. The introduction of David's name to Saul
1) One of Saul's attendants knew about David, his qualifications & abilities

2) Saul was impressed & sent for David

c. The beginning of David's service in Saul's court

1) Jesse sent a gift to Saul along with his son David	of wine, and a kid, and sent *them* by David his son unto Saul.	hath found favour in my sight.	his court
2) Saul was impressed with David • He made David one of his armor-bearers • He asked Jesse to allow his son to become a permanent member of	21 And David came to Saul, and stood before him: and he loved him greatly; and he became his armourbearer. 22 And Saul sent to Jesse, saying, Let David, I pray thee, stand before me; for he	23 And it came to pass, when the *evil* spirit from God was upon Saul, that David took an harp, and played with his hand: so Saul was refreshed, and was well, and the evil spirit departed from him.	3) David played the harp for Saul • He played when some mental disturbance—the evil spirit—came upon him • He was able to soothe, bring relief to King Saul

DIVISION III

THE STORY OF SAUL AND DAVID (PART 1): THE LORD GIVES ISRAEL A KING "AFTER HIS OWN HEART," 16:1–20:42

A. The Story of David's Secret Anointing As King and His Service in Saul's Court: God Judges the Heart, Not the Appearance, of a Person, 16:1-23

(16:1-23) **Introduction—Anointing, Secret, of a King—King, Secret Anointing of**: picture a king sitting upon his throne, ruling over a nation and people he had governed for years. But unknown to him, some distance away, a young boy is about to be secretly anointed to replace him, a young boy who was to become the future king of the nation. And not only is a secret anointing taking place, but this young boy would soon be serving in the royal court at the very feet of the king he would someday replace. And the king would be totally unaware that the young boy was the future anointed king.

What a picture of high drama! A suspenseful picture of the shift of power, the highest power of a nation being secretly transferred from a ruling king over to a young boy who was destined to become king.

This is the dramatic story unfolded in this present chapter of God's Holy Word. Because of disobedience, King Saul was destined to be removed as king of Israel by the hand of God's judgment. But the work of God among the Israelites and upon this earth was to go on. And to carry on the work of God, God had chosen a young boy who had a heart "after God's own heart" (13:14). This young boy was to become the future king of God's people. From the day of David's secret anointing to the end of Saul's life, David would be a threat to Saul's claim to the throne. And Saul would seek to kill David time and again. This drama is played out in the remaining chapters of this great book, *1 Samuel*. This is: *The Story of David's Secret Anointing As King and His Service in Saul's Court: God Judges the Heart, Not the Appearance, of a Person*, 16:1-23.

1. The mission of Samuel to arise and anoint a new king: conquering grief and sorrow (vv.1-5).
2. The secret anointing of David: being empowered by God's Spirit (vv.6-13).
3. The beginning of David's preparation to be king: a picture of God's sovereignty (vv.14-23).

1 (16:1-5) **Grief, Conquering, Example of—Sorrow, Conquering, Example of—Discouragement, Example—Rebuke, of God, Example—Samuel, Charges to**: there was the mission of Samuel to arise and anoint a new king. Remember that the LORD had rejected Saul and promised to raise up another king, "a man after [God's] own heart" (13:14), and a man who was "better than" Saul (15:28). This was a specific reference to David, and it was now time to anoint the young boy to become the future king of Israel. As mentioned in the introduction above, this is high drama at its best, for Saul was still king and would continue ruling for many more years. But here the LORD commissions Samuel to secretly anoint a young boy who was to be the future king of the nation. From this point on, the story focuses upon the jealousy of Saul toward David and his many attempts to kill the future king of Israel. The present scene launches the suspenseful adventure of this high drama:

OUTLINE	SCRIPTURE	SCRIPTURE	OUTLINE
1. The mission of Samuel to arise & anoint a new king: Conquering grief & sorrow a. The LORD's rebuke of Samuel: He had grieved over His rejection of Saul far too long	And the LORD said unto Samuel, How long wilt thou mourn for Saul, seeing I have rejected him from reigning over Israel? fill thine horn with oil, and go, I will send thee to Jesse the Bethlehemite: for I have provided me a king among his sons.	rifice, and I will show thee what thou shalt do: and thou shalt anoint unto me *him* whom I name unto thee. 4 And Samuel did that which the LORD spake, and came to Bethlehem. And the elders of the town trembled at his coming, and said, Comest thou peaceably?	1) To invite Jesse & his sons to the sacrifice 2) To anoint the son indicated by God d. The obedience of Samuel e. The fear felt by Bethlehem's officials 1) They feared Samuel had come to execute judgment
b. The protest by Samuel: He feared that if he went to Bethlehem Saul would kill him c. The LORD's solution: He was to go for the purpose of offering a sacrifice to prevent Saul from being suspicious	2 And Samuel said, How can I go? if Saul hear *it,* he will kill me. And the LORD said, Take an heifer with thee, and say, I am come to sacrifice to the LORD. 3 And call Jesse to the sac-	will kill me. And the LORD am come to sacrifice unto the LORD: sanctify yourselves, and come with me to the sacrifice. And he sanctified Jesse and his sons, and called them to the sacrifice.	2) Samuel assured them he had come to offer sacrifice, & he charged them to consecrate themselves 3) Samuel consecrated Jesse & his sons

a. The LORD rebuked Samuel, for he had grieved over His rejection of Saul far too long. Because of Saul's disobedience, the LORD had rejected him as king and the kingdom was to be torn from him. It had been the sad duty of Samuel to inform Saul of his rejection by the LORD (15:22-23, 26, 28). Delivering the message of Saul's rejection had been a difficult mission for Samuel. From the beginning Samuel had held great hope for Saul, for Saul appeared to have all the attributes needed to be a very successful ruler. He was tall, handsome, and had a charismatic personality. More importantly, when he first began to rule, he had both a humble, respectful spirit and a bold, courageous spirit (9:1-27; 10:1-27; 11:1-15). Moreover, Saul had been chosen to be king by the LORD Himself, and the LORD had transformed him, giving him a new and changed heart (9:15-17; 10:9-15). Saul had been just the kind of man people desired in a leader, and he had the additional qualification of having been chosen and equipped by the LORD Himself. Outwardly—from all appearances—no man had more to offer than Saul.

But Saul had failed and been condemned by God, rejected as king. Someday out in the future, Saul would be removed from the throne and another dynasty of kings would rule Israel. The dynasty of Saul's kingdom would never be established. This was a terrible tragedy for Saul and his household. And the tragedy of Saul's failure gripped the soul of Samuel: he became discouraged, depressed, downhearted, and began to grieve over the situation. As Scripture says, for some long period of time he mourned. A sorrowful, grief-stricken spirit gripped his emotions. He mourned for Saul personally, because Saul had been so disobedient and so disappointing both to the LORD and to him personally. In addition, Saul was to lose his kingdom and dynasty.

But the day came when God was ready to begin preparation for the new king. It was time for Samuel to snap out of his grief and mourning over Saul, time for Samuel to arise and secretly anoint a new king. Thus, God confronted Samuel and strongly rebuked him. He had been mourning far too long. He must now arise and fill his horn with oil and go to Bethlehem to the household of Jesse, for God had chosen one of his sons to be the new king.

b. Note the response of Samuel: he protested because he feared that Saul would hear about the secret anointing and kill him (v.2). This was a dangerous mission for Samuel, for Saul would interpret the anointing as a serious threat to his own claim to the throne.

c. The LORD's solution to this problem was for Samuel to go for the purpose of offering a sacrifice (v.2). Traveling to Bethlehem to offer sacrifice would prevent the arousal of suspicion. As a levitical judge, it was the common practice of Samuel to travel from place to place for the purpose of holding court to deal with legal matters and to offer sacrifice to atone for unsolved murder cases (De.21:1-9).[1]

In the present situation, the LORD instructed Samuel to invite Jesse and his sons to the sacrifice (v.3). At some point during the sacrifice, the LORD would indicate which son was to be anointed as the secret king.

d. Samuel obeyed, did exactly what the LORD commanded (v.4).

e. But note the fear of Bethlehem's officials (vv.4-5). When Samuel arrived in Bethlehem, the officials feared that he had come to hold court and to execute some judgment. And they were apparently unaware of any criminal action that required his presence (7:15-16; De.21:1-9). But Samuel assured them that he had come only to offer sacrifice to the LORD (v.5). He charged them to *sanctify* themselves and to come to the sacrifice with him. The word "sanctify" means to set one apart spiritually and ceremonially or ritually. A person sanctified or consecrated himself by taking a bath, putting on clean clothes, abstaining from sex, and avoiding contact with any dead body (Ex.19:10, 14; Le.7:19-21; 15:2-33; Nu.19:1-22; De.23:10-11). But more important than the outward rituals of cleansing oneself, a person was to seek the LORD for spiritual cleansing, confessing and repenting of his sins. The *outward* acts of sanctification or cleansing were merely symbols of *inner* cleansing. At some point Samuel visited Jesse in order to become acquainted with him and his family. And he invited Jesse and his sons to the sacrifice.

Thought 1. Samuel was wallowing around in grief, being gripped by a spirit of dejection, discouragement, and depression. Looking at him, a person saw a man with a very sorrowful, grief-stricken countenance. A victorious, conquering spirit was absent.

But this was not the way God intended His servant to live. And it is not the way God intends us to live. Sorrowful experiences do arise in the lives of us all. But they are not to grip us. We are to conquer and overcome such experiences. No matter what confronts us, we are to be triumphant over the circumstance. God will help us conquer and overcome any tragedy or sorrowful experience. He will help us conquer and overcome...

- poverty
- financial difficulty
- the death of a loved one
- alcohol or drug addiction
- rejection and divorce
- loss of employment
- failure
- a sense of purposelessness
- helplessness
- hopelessness
- emptiness
- sin and guilt

Conquering power—the power to overcome and triumph over the trials and temptations, problems and tragedies of this life—can be ours through the LORD. The LORD will empower us to live victorious lives, conquering all the sorrowful tragedies that strike us. We are not to wallow around in grief and despair, displaying a sad countenance. We are to live victoriously, for we are more than conquerors through Christ who has loved us and given Himself for us.

> **"Who shall separate us from the love of Christ? *shall* tribulation, or distress, or persecution, or famine, or nakedness, or peril, or sword....Nay, in all these things we are more than conquerors through him that loved us. For I am persuaded, that neither death, nor life, nor angels, nor principalities, nor powers, nor things present, nor things to come, Nor height, nor depth, nor any**

---

1 Robert D. Bergen. *1, 2 Samuel*, p.178.

other creature, shall be able to separate us from the love of God, which is in Christ Jesus our LORD" (Ro.8:35, 37-39).

"There hath no temptation taken you but such as is common to man: but God *is* faithful, who will not suffer you to be tempted above that ye are able; but will with the temptation also make a way to escape, that ye may be able to bear *it*" (1 Co.10:13).

"And the LORD shall deliver me from every evil work, and will preserve *me* unto his heavenly kingdom: to whom *be* glory for ever and ever. Amen" (2 Ti.4:18).

"*Let your* conversation [behavior, conduct] *be* without covetousness; *and be* content with such things as ye have: for he hath said, I will never leave thee, nor forsake thee. So that we may boldly say, The LORD *is* my helper, and I will not fear what man shall do unto me" (He.13:5-6).

"For whatsoever is born of God overcometh the world: and this is the victory that overcometh the world, *even* our faith. Who is he that overcometh the world, but he that believeth that Jesus is the Son of God" (1 Jn.5:4-5).

"The eternal God *is thy* refuge, and underneath *are* the everlasting arms: and he shall thrust out the enemy from before thee; and shall say, Destroy *them*" (De.33:27).

"Thou hast also given me the shield of thy salvation: and thy right hand hath holden me up, and thy gentleness hath made me great" (Ps.18:35).

"The LORD *is* my strength and my shield; my heart trusted in him, and I am helped: therefore my heart greatly rejoiceth; and with my song will I praise him" (Ps.28:7).

"But I *am* poor and needy; *yet* the LORD thinketh upon me: thou *art* my help and my deliverer; make no tarrying, O my God" (Ps.40:17).

"Fear thou not; for I *am* with thee: be not dismayed; for I *am* thy God: I will strengthen thee; yea, I will help thee; yea, I will uphold thee with the right hand of my righteousness" (Is.41:10).

"And *even* to *your* old age I *am* he; and *even* to hoar [gray] hairs will I carry *you:* I have made, and I will bear; even I will carry, and will deliver *you*" (Is.46:4).

---

2 (16:6-13) **Anointing, Example of—Empowering, Example of—Holy Spirit, Anointing of, Example—David, Anointing of—David, Empowering—David, Spirit-Filled**: there was the secret anointing of David and the coming of the Holy Spirit upon him. When the Spirit of God came upon David, it was a symbol that he was equipped and empowered by God to become the future leader of Israel. Keep in mind that this was a secret anointing:

OUTLINE	SCRIPTURE	SCRIPTURE	OUTLINE
2. The secret anointing of David: Being empowered by God's Spirit a. The choice of Samuel 　1) He chose the firstborn 　2) He was rebuked by God: God had not chosen Eliab to be king b. The basic qualification of God for service: Not physical appearance, but the heart c. The choice of the father Jesse: He brought each of his seven sons before Samuel 　1) Abinadab: Was rejected 　2) Shammah was rejected 　3) All seven sons brought by Jesse were rejected	6 And it came to pass, when they were come, that he looked on Eliab, and said, Surely the LORD'S anointed *is* before him. 7 But the LORD said unto Samuel, Look not on his countenance, or on the height of his stature; because I have refused him: for *the LORD seeth* not as man seeth; for man looketh on the outward appearance, but the LORD looketh on the heart. 8 Then Jesse called Abinadab, and made him pass before Samuel. And he said, Neither hath the LORD chosen this. 9 Then Jesse made Shammah to pass by. And he said, Neither hath the LORD chosen this. 10 Again, Jesse made seven of his sons to pass before	Samuel. And Samuel said unto Jesse, The LORD hath not chosen these. 11 And Samuel said unto Jesse, Are here all *thy* children? And he said, There remaineth yet the youngest, and, behold, he keepeth the sheep. And Samuel said unto Jesse, Send and fetch him: for we will not sit down till he come hither. 12 And he sent, and brought him in. Now he *was* ruddy, *and* withal of a beautiful countenance, and goodly to look to. And the LORD said, Arise, anoint him: for this *is* he. 13 Then Samuel took the horn of oil, and anointed him in the midst of his brethren: and the Spirit of the LORD came upon David from that day forward. So Samuel rose up, and went to Ramah.	d. The choice of the LORD: The youngest son 　1) Samuel was perplexed: Asked Jesse if he had any other sons 　2) David, the youngest, had been left tending the sheep 　3) Samuel immediately sent for David: When he arrived, he was seen to have striking features 　4) The LORD identified David as His choice to be king e. The secret anointing of David 　1) He was anointed in the presence of his brothers 　2) He was equipped, empowered by the Spirit of the LORD

a. Note that Samuel's choice was not God's choice (vv.6-7). When Jesse and his sons first arrived at the worship service, Samuel's attention was immediately drawn to the oldest son, Eliab. The young man was tall and attractive, with a charismatic personality (v.7). Samuel thought that surely this was God's choice. But immediately the LORD rebuked Samuel. He was not to consider the young man's appearance nor height, for the LORD had not chosen Eliab to be king.

b. Note the basic qualification of God for service: it is not physical appearance but the heart that the LORD looks at. Man usually looks at the outward things, but the LORD looks at the heart of a person. The LORD judges a person by his heart and his heart alone.

c. Note who the father would choose to be the future king: he had each of his seven sons in descending order by age pass in front of Samuel (vv.8-10). After the oldest son Eliab had been rejected, Jesse presented Abinadab to Samuel. But Abinadab was rejected. Then Jesse had Shammah pass before Samuel, but he too was rejected (v.9). One by one in descending order, Jesse had his sons pass before Samuel. But in each case, Samuel pronounced the fateful words, each was rejected (v.10). Had it been left to Samuel and Jesse, one of these seven would have been chosen to be the future king of Israel. But God knew the *hearts*, and the *heart* that He was after was not present.

d. Note the choice of the LORD: it was the youngest son, a son who was considered by his father not even to be eligible or qualified to be the future king (vv.11-12). Samuel had been perplexed, puzzled by the LORD's rejection of Jesse's seven sons. He was bound to be mentally, silently questioning what was going on. Did Jesse have other sons? If so, why would he not have brought them? Finally, he asked Jesse if these seven were all the sons he had. Jesse replied that he did have a younger son who had been left behind to tend the sheep. Hearing this, Samuel immediately sent for David.

When David arrived, note the favorable impression he made upon Samuel, and keep in mind that he was just a young boy. He was "ruddy" which means that he had a healthy bronze complexion. And he was good looking with piercing, bright eyes. As soon as young David walked into Samuel's presence, the LORD immediately identified David as His choice to be king. But keep in mind why he was God's choice: not because of his striking physical features, but because of his heart. He was a young boy with a heart "after God's own heart" (13:14), and his heart was to make him a better man than Saul (15:28).

"But God is the judge: he putteth down one, and setteth up another" (Ps.75:7).

e. Note the secret anointing of David (v.13). And remember that this *secret* anointing was totally unknown to King Saul. David was anointed in the presence of his brothers and apparently no one else. While he was being anointed, the Spirit of the LORD came upon him. Note what Scripture says: the Spirit of the LORD remained on him from that day forward. God's Spirit never left David. In the words of Robert D. Bergen:

> The shapeless, invasive fluid [anointing oil] used in the ceremony served fittingly as a symbol of the mystical presence of God. As the oil worked its way into the individual's hair and pores, it symbolized the divine presence entering into the one being anointed.[2]

Thought 1. The greatest gift in all the world is the gift of God's Spirit. When we approach God through Christ, God places His own Spirit in us, in the very core of our being. We become indwelt by God's Spirit. It is God's Spirit who convicts and saves and gives us assurance of salvation. He guides, teaches, protects, and provides the necessities of life for us, meeting all our needs.

What more could a person ask? It is the Spirit of God who empowers us to conquer all the trials and temptations of life, who enables us to live a victorious and triumphant life day by day.

"It is the spirit that quickeneth; the flesh profiteth nothing: the words that I speak unto you, *they* are spirit, and *they* are life" (Jn.6:63).

"*Even* the Spirit of truth; whom the world cannot receive, because it seeth him not, neither knoweth him: but ye know him; for he dwelleth with you, and shall be in you" (Jn.14:17).

"But the Comforter, *which is* the Holy Ghost, whom the Father will send in my name, he shall teach you all things, and bring all things to your remembrance, whatsoever I have said unto you" (Jn.14:26).

"But when the Comforter is come, whom I will send unto you from the Father, *even* the Spirit of truth, which proceedeth from the Father, he shall testify of me" (Jn.15:26).

"Howbeit when he, the Spirit of truth, is come, he will guide you into all truth: for he shall not speak of himself; but whatsoever he shall hear, *that* shall he speak: and he will show you things to come" (Jn.16:13).

"But ye shall receive power, after that the Holy Ghost is come upon you: and ye shall be witnesses unto me both in Jerusalem, and in all Judaea, and in Samaria, and unto the uttermost part of the earth" (Ac.1:8).

"As they ministered to the LORD, and fasted, the Holy Ghost said, Separate me Barnabas and Saul for the work whereunto I have called them" (Ac.13:2).

"But if the Spirit of him that raised up Jesus from the dead dwell in you, he that raised up Christ from the dead shall also quicken your mortal bodies by his Spirit that dwelleth in you" (Ro.8:11).

"The Spirit itself beareth witness with our spirit, that we are the children of God: And if children, then heirs; heirs of God, and joint-heirs with Christ; if so be that we suffer with *him*, that we may be also glorified together" (Ro.8:16-17).

"Now we have received, not the spirit of the world, but the spirit which is of God; that we might know the things that are freely given to us of God" (1 Co.2:12).

"Know ye not that ye are the temple of God, and *that* the Spirit of God dwelleth in you? If any man defile the temple of God, him shall God destroy; for the temple of God is holy, which *temple* ye are. Let no man deceive himself. If any man among you seemeth to be wise in this world, let him become a fool, that he may be wise. For the wisdom of this world is foolishness with God. For it is written, He taketh the wise in their own craftiness. And again, The LORD knoweth the thoughts of the wise, that they are vain" (1 Co.3:16-20).

---

2 Robert D. Bergen. *1, 2 Samuel*, p.180.

"And because ye are sons, God hath sent forth the Spirit of his Son into your hearts, crying, Abba, Father" (Ga.4:6).

"For Christ also hath once suffered for sins, the just for the unjust, that he might bring us to God, being put to death in the flesh, but quickened by the Spirit" (1 Pe.3:18).

"But the anointing which ye have received of him abideth in you, and ye need not that any man teach you: but as the same anointing teacheth you of all things, and is truth, and is no lie, and even as it hath taught you, ye shall abide in him" (1 Jn.2:27).

"And thine ears shall hear a word behind thee, saying, This is the way, walk ye in it, when ye turn to the right hand, and when ye turn to the left" (Is.30:21).

"And I will put my spirit within you, and cause you to walk in my statutes, and ye shall keep my judgments, and do them" (Eze.36:27).

---

3 (16:14-23) **Sovereignty, of God—Leadership, of God—Guidance, of God—David, in Saul's Court—Saul, and David, First Meeting**: there was the beginning of David's preparation to be king. What now happened is a clear picture of God's sovereignty and His guidance throughout David's life:

OUTLINE	SCRIPTURE	SCRIPTURE	OUTLINE

3. **The beginning of David's preparation to be king: A picture of God's sovereignty**
a. The removal of God's Spirit from Saul
  1) The advice of Saul's attendants: To find a harpist who could soothe Saul when he was tormented by an evil spirit (spiritually, mentally, & emotionally)
 	
  2) Saul agreed & ordered that a musician be found
 	
b. The introduction of David's name to Saul
  1) One of Saul's attendants knew about David, his qualifications & abilities
	14 But the Spirit of the LORD departed from Saul, and an evil spirit from the LORD troubled him. 15 And Saul's servants said unto him, Behold now, an evil spirit from God troubleth thee. 16 Let our lord now command thy servants, which are before thee, to seek out a man, who is a cunning player on an harp: and it shall come to pass, when the evil spirit from God is upon thee, that he shall play with his hand, and thou shalt be well. 17 And Saul said unto his servants, Provide me now a man that can play well, and bring him to me. 18 Then answered one of the servants, and said, Behold, I have seen a son of Jesse the Bethlehemite, that is cunning in playing, and a mighty valiant man, and a man of war, and prudent in matters, and a	comely person, and the LORD is with him. 19 Wherefore Saul sent messengers unto Jesse, and said, Send me David thy son, which is with the sheep. 20 And Jesse took an ass laden with bread, and a bottle of wine, and a kid, and sent them by David his son unto Saul. 21 And David came to Saul, and stood before him: and he loved him greatly; and he became his armourbearer. 22 And Saul sent to Jesse, saying, Let David, I pray thee, stand before me; for he hath found favour in my sight. 23 And it came to pass, when the evil spirit from God was upon Saul, that David took an harp, and played with his hand: so Saul was refreshed, and was well, and the evil spirit departed from him.	
			
			2) Saul was impressed & sent for David
			
			c. The beginning of David's service in Saul's court
			  1) Jesse sent a gift to Saul along with his son David
			
			  2) Saul was impressed with David
			    • He made David one of his armor-bearers
			    • He asked Jesse to allow his son to become a permanent member of his court
			
			  3) David played the harp for Saul
			    • He played when some mental disturbance—the evil spirit—came upon him
			    • He was able to soothe, bring relief to King Saul

a. Note the removal of God's Spirit from Saul. Simply stated, the Spirit of the LORD departed from Saul. But even more tragic than this, an evil spirit was sent by the LORD to torment Saul (v.14). What does this mean? It certainly means that the Spirit of God was no longer present to guide, protect, or provide for Saul as he walked daily throughout the remainder of his life. It certainly also means that the Spirit of God no longer empowered Saul to serve as king. But what does it mean when it says that the LORD sent a tormenting spirit upon him, a spirit that troubled and distressed him, that filled him with depression and fear? Various commentators have interpreted this to mean:[3]

⇒ demon-possession sent upon Saul as a judgment because of his disobedience.
⇒ some demonic attack or influence allowed by God because of Saul's disobedience.
⇒ some evil messenger allowed by God to oppress Saul, an evil messenger such as the one sent to deceive Ahab (1 K.22:20-23).
⇒ a deep sense of guilt, depression, and fear—all kinds of emotional and psychological problems—aroused by God within Saul because of his disobedience.

Whatever the case, Saul had disobeyed God and was now reaping what he had sown. The hand of God's judgment had fallen upon him, and an evil spirit was creating a sense of guilt, depression, and fear within him. God's Spirit had left Saul to live the sinful, wicked, and disobedient life Saul had chosen. Just as Scripture teaches, God had given Saul up to live just as Saul wanted, given him up to do his own thing (Ro.1:24). As a result, an evil spirit troubled and tormented Saul.

---

3 *The Nelson Study Bible, NKJV*, 16:14, 15.

Noticing this radical change in Saul's behavior, some of his attendants suggested that a harpist be found who could soothe Saul when he was stricken with an episode of depression and fear (vv.15-16). Saul agreed and ordered for a musician to be found, one who played well.

b. Note the introduction of David's name to Saul (vv.18-19). One of Saul's attendants immediately spoke up, sharing that he knew about a young boy who had the needed qualifications and abilities to serve in the court of the king. He was a son of Jesse from Bethlehem, a young boy who was brave, courageous, and a potential warrior. The young man also had good judgment and was a fine looking young boy. And even more significant, the LORD was with him. Hearing this, Saul was very impressed and sent for David to be brought to him.

c. Note the beginning of David's service in Saul's court (vv.20-23). Obviously, Jesse was excited about his youngest son's being called upon to serve in the court of the king. Remember, Jesse already knew that his son was eventually to become the king of Israel. Perhaps he thought that the LORD had moved upon Saul's heart to begin preparing David to assume the office of king upon Saul's death. Whatever the case, Jesse sent a gift to Saul along with his son David (v.20). When David began serving Saul, the king was very impressed with him, so impressed that he made David one of his armor-bearers. And he requested that David's father Jesse allow his son to become a permanent member of his court. By keeping David close to him, Saul would be assured of David's availability to play the harp when he (Saul) was attacked with a tormenting episode of guilt, depression, or fear. And note this is exactly what happened: when some spiritual or mental disturbance struck Saul, David played the harp for him. David was able to soothe, bring relief to King Saul. Saul would feel much better, and in the words of Scripture, the evil spirit would leave him.

Thought 1. In the sovereignty of God, God moved events in order to place David in the court of Saul. God worked all things out, moving the events so that the preparation of the future king could begin. By being in the court of Saul, David would learn how a king should rule a nation. He would learn exactly what a king should and should not do. He would be exposed to the nation's economic, military, and justice systems and to the morality and character of its officials. God moved events so that David could learn how to fulfill his task upon this earth.

The lesson for us is clear: God is sovereign. He rules and reigns over the earth. He and He alone is God Almighty, the LORD of hosts who stands over every creature of this universe, both in heaven and in earth. It is He and He alone who is the Creator and Sovereign LORD of the universe. And because of who He is, He has the power to move events in order to help us. When we need help, God has the power to help us. No matter what our need—no matter how small or how great—God will meet it. He is sovereign, looking after us every step of our lives, taking care of us if we will simply trust Him. God has the sovereign power to help us no matter what we may need.

"And lead us not into temptation, but deliver us from evil: For thine is the kingdom, and the power, and the glory, for ever. Amen" (Mt.6:13).

"But Jesus beheld *them,* and said unto them, With men this is impossible; but with God all things are possible" (Mt.19:26).

"For with God nothing shall be impossible" (Lu.1:37).

"Now to him that is of power to stablish you according to my gospel, and the preaching of Jesus Christ, according to the revelation of the mystery, which was kept secret since the world began, But now is made manifest, and by the Scriptures of the prophets, according to the commandment of the everlasting God, made known to all nations for the obedience of faith. To God only wise, *be* glory through Jesus Christ for ever. Amen" (Ro.16:25-27).

"Now unto him that is able to do exceeding abundantly above all that we ask or think, according to the power that worketh in us" (Ep.3:20).

"Now unto the King eternal, immortal, invisible, the only wise God, *be* honour and glory for ever and ever. Amen" (1 Ti.1:17).

"*Let your* conversation [behavior, conduct] *be* without covetousness; *and be* content with such things as ye have: for he hath said, I will never leave thee, nor forsake thee. So that we may boldly say, The LORD *is* my helper, and I will not fear what man shall do unto me" (He.13:5-6).

"Now unto him that is able to keep you from falling, and to present *you* faultless before the presence of his glory with exceeding joy, To the only wise God our Saviour, *be* glory and majesty, dominion and power, both now and ever. Amen" (Jude 24-25).

"Know therefore this day, and consider *it* in thine heart, that the LORD he *is* God in heaven above, and upon the earth beneath: *there is* none else" (De.4:39).

"Both riches and honour *come* of thee, and thou reignest over all; and in thine hand *is* power and might; and in thine hand *it is* to make great, and to give strength unto all" (1 Chr.29:12).

"And said, O LORD God of our fathers, *art* not thou God in heaven? and rulest *not* thou over all the kingdoms of the heathen? and in thine hand *is there not* power and might, so that none is able to withstand thee" (2 Chr.20:6).

"But if thou wilt go, do *it,* be strong for the battle: God shall make thee fall before the enemy: for God hath power to help, and to cast down" (2 Chr.25:8).

"He divideth the sea with his power, and by his understanding he smiteth through the proud" (Jb.26:12).

"I know that thou canst do every *thing,* and *that* no thought can be withholden from thee" (Jb.42:2).

"Fear thou not; for I *am* with thee: be not dismayed; for I *am* thy God: I will strengthen thee; yea, I will help thee; yea, I will uphold thee with the right hand of my righteousness" (Is.41:10).

CHAPTER 17

**B. The Story of David &
Goliath: Defeating the
Oppressor of God's Peo-
ple, 17:1-58**

**1. The war launched by the Phil-
istines & the defiance of Goliath: Confronting an aggressive, frightening enemy**
a. The Philistines invaded Israel
at Shochoh in Judah

1) The invasion: Saul & his
army countered in the valley of Elah

2) The battle lines: The armies faced each other on
opposite hills surrounding
the valley

b. The Philistines sent forth a
giant warrior named Goliath
who issued a hostile challenge to the Israelites
1) His size: Over 9 feet tall
2) His armor
• A bronze helmet
• A coat of scale armor
that weighed 125
pounds

• A pair of bronze leg-
gings

3) His weapon: A bronze
spear with a tip that
weighed 15 pounds
4) His shield: An armor-
bearer carried it before him

5) His defiant mockery: Why
did the Israelites line up to
fight when not a single
soldier would face Goliath?
6) His hostile challenge:
That the mightiest warrior
of Israel fight a personal
dual with him
7) His aggressive proposal:
That the dual be a *representative war*, the nation
of the loser would become
subject to the winner

c. The impact of Goliath's defiance was a paralyzed army:
The Israelites were shaken,
terrorized

Now the Philistines gathered
together their armies to battle, and were gathered together at Shochoh, which *belongeth* to Judah, and pitched
between Shochoh and Aze-
kah, in Ephes-dammim.
2 And Saul and the men of
Israel were gathered together,
and pitched by the valley of
Elah, and set the battle in array against the Philistines.
3 And the Philistines stood
on a mountain on the one
side, and Israel stood on a
mountain on the other side:
and *there was* a valley between them.
4 And there went out a
champion out of the camp of
the Philistines, named Goliath, of Gath, whose height
was six cubits and a span.
5 And *he had* an helmet of
brass upon his head, and he
was armed with a coat of
mail; and the weight of the
coat *was* five thousand shekels of brass.
6 And *he had* greaves of
brass upon his legs, and a
target of brass between his
shoulders.
7 And the staff of his spear
was like a weaver's beam;
and his spear's head *weighed*
six hundred shekels of iron:
and one bearing a shield went
before him.
8 And he stood and cried
unto the armies of Israel, and
said unto them, Why are ye
come out to set *your* battle in
array? *am* not I a Philistine,
and ye servants to Saul?
choose you a man for you, and
let him come down to me.
9 If he be able to fight with
me, and to kill me, then will
we be your servants: but if I
prevail against him, and kill
him, then shall ye be our
servants, and serve us.
10 And the Philistine said, I
defy the armies of Israel this
day; give me a man, that we
may fight together.
11 When Saul and all Israel
heard those words of the
Philistine, they were dismayed, and greatly afraid.

12 Now David *was* the son
of that Ephrathite of Bethle-
hemjudah, whose name *was*
Jesse; and he had eight sons:
and the man went among
men *for* an old man in the
days of Saul.
13 And the three eldest sons
of Jesse went *and* followed
Saul to the battle: and the
names of his three sons that
went to the battle *were* Eliab
the first born, and next unto
him Abinadab, and the third
Shammah.
14 And David *was* the
youngest: and the three eldest
followed Saul.
15 But David went and re-
turned from Saul to feed his
father's sheep at Bethlehem.
16 And the Philistine drew
near morning and evening,
and presented himself forty
days.
17 And Jesse said unto David his son, Take now for thy
brethren an ephah of this
parched *corn,* and these ten
loaves, and run to the camp
to thy brethren;
18 And carry these ten
cheeses unto the captain of
their thousand, and look how
thy brethren fare, and take
their pledge.
19 Now Saul, and they, and
all the men of Israel, *were* in
the valley of Elah, fighting
with the Philistines.
20 And David rose up early
in the morning, and left the
sheep with a keeper, and
took, and went, as Jesse had
commanded him; and he
came to the trench, as the
host was going forth to the
fight, and shouted for the battle.
21 For Israel and the Philistines had put the battle in array, army against army.
22 And David left his carriage in the hand of the keeper of the carriage, and ran into the army, and came and sa-
luted his brethren.
23 And as he talked with
them, behold, there came up
the champion, the Philistine
of Gath, Goliath by name,
out of the armies of the Philistines, and spake according
to the same words: and David
heard *them.*
24 And all the men of Israel,
when they saw the man, fled
from him, and were sore afraid.

**2. The family of David & his du-
ties as a youth: The picture of
a very responsible young boy**
a. The elderly father Jesse
1) Was from Bethlehem
2) Had eight sons

b. The three oldest brothers:
Were soldiers

c. The duties of David, the
youngest son

1) Served Saul
2) Tended his father's sheep
in between, 16:11
**3. The righteous anger of David
over Goliath's defiance & Israel's fear: A need for courage**
a. The 40-day defiance of Goliath
b. The very special duty assigned to David by his father
1) To take supplies to the front
lines
• For his three brothers

• For the commander of
their unit
2) To check on his brothers'
welfare

c. The obedience, faithfulness
of David to his father's instructions
1) He left early morning,
leaving the sheep with another shepherd
2) He arrived just as the
troops were going out to
their daily battle positions

3) He took the provisions to
the supply officer
4) He ran to the front lines to
his brothers

d. The first sighting of Goliath
by David
1) He saw Goliath step out
from the Philistine ranks
& shout out his terroriz-
ing, hostile challenge

2) He witnessed the fear &
the utter panic of the Israelite forces

e. The reward offered by Saul to any soldier who killed Goliath
  1) Great wealth

  2) His daughter in marriage

  3) Tax exemption for his entire family
f. The surge of courage aroused in David over Israel's fear & Goliath's defiance
  1) David demonstrated a courageous anger
    • At the insult, hostility hurled at Israel by Goliath
    • At the defiance, insult against "the living God"

  2) The soldiers shared with David the promises of Saul to the man who killed Goliath
g. The jealousy & anger of David's oldest brother Eliab
  1) He was jealous of the courage shown by David
  2) He made three accusations against David
    • Accused him of pride, a haughty spirit
    • Accused him of neglecting his duty
    • Accused him of a wicked curiosity, coming to watch the battle
  3) David's firm response
    • The cause, issue being discussed is important
    • David turned to others & continued to discuss the issue of Goliath's defiance & Saul's promises

4. The utter trust of David in God: His power to deliver
a. Saul heard of David's courage & outrage
b. David demonstrated strong confidence before Saul: Declared he would fight Goliath

c. Saul rejected David's offer: Thought he was only a boy caught up in youthful idealism & would be fighting a trained, experienced soldier

d. David humbly but strongly argued that he had the very experience that could defeat Goliath
  1) He was a shepherd who had faced bears & lions
  2) He had actually seized the creatures & clubbed them to death

25 And the men of Israel said, Have ye seen this man that is come up? surely to defy Israel is he come up: and it shall be, *that* the man who killeth him, the king will enrich him with great riches, and will give him his daughter, and make his father's house free in Israel.
26 And David spake to the men that stood by him, saying, What shall be done to the man that killeth this Philistine, and taketh away the reproach from Israel? for who *is* this uncircumcised Philistine, that he should defy the armies of the living God?
27 And the people answered him after this manner, saying, So shall it be done to the man that killeth him.
28 And Eliab his eldest brother heard when he spake unto the men; and Eliab's anger was kindled against David, and he said, Why camest thou down hither? and with whom hast thou left those few sheep in the wilderness? I know thy pride, and the naughtiness of thine heart; for thou art come down that thou mightest see the battle.
29 And David said, What have I now done? *Is there* not a cause?
30 And he turned from him toward another, and spake after the same manner: and the people answered him again after the former manner.
31 And when the words were heard which David spake, they rehearsed *them* before Saul: and he sent for him.
32 And David said to Saul, Let no man's heart fail because of him; thy servant will go and fight with this Philistine.
33 And Saul said to David, Thou art not able to go against this Philistine to fight with him: for thou *art but* a youth, and he a man of war from his youth.
34 And David said unto Saul, Thy servant kept his father's sheep, and there came a lion, and a bear, and took a lamb out of the flock:
35 And I went out after him, and smote him, and delivered *it* out of his mouth: and when

he arose against me, I caught *him* by his beard, and smote him, and slew him.
36 Thy servant slew both the lion and the bear: and this uncircumcised Philistine shall be as one of them, seeing he hath defied the armies of the living God.
37 David said moreover, The LORD that delivered me out of the paw of the lion, and out of the paw of the bear, he will deliver me out of the hand of this Philistine. And Saul said unto David, Go, and the LORD be with thee.
38 And Saul armed David with his armour, and he put an helmet of brass upon his head; also he armed him with a coat of mail.
39 And David girded his sword upon his armour, and he assayed to go; for he had not proved *it*. And David said unto Saul, I cannot go with these; for I have not proved *them*. And David put them off him.
40 And he took his staff in his hand, and chose him five smooth stones out of the brook, and put them in a shepherd's bag which he had, even in a scrip; and his sling *was* in his hand: and he drew near to the Philistine.
41 And the Philistine came on and drew near unto David; and the man that bare the shield *went* before him.
42 And when the Philistine looked about, and saw David, he disdained him: for he was *but* a youth, and ruddy, and of a fair countenance.
43 And the Philistine said unto David, *Am* I a dog, that thou comest to me with staves? And the Philistine cursed David by his gods.
44 And the Philistine said to David, Come to me, and I will give thy flesh unto the fowls of the air, and to the beasts of the field.
45 Then said David to the Philistine, Thou comest to me with a sword, and with a spear, and with a shield: but I come to thee in the name of the LORD of hosts, the God of the armies of Israel, whom thou hast defied.
46 This day will the LORD deliver thee into mine hand; and I will smite thee, and

e. David boldly declared his confidence & trust in God
  1) The unbelieving Goliath would be nothing more than the lion & the bear: Because of the "living God"
  2) The LORD would deliver him from the hand of Goliath—just as He had delivered him from the paws of the lion & the bear
f. Saul finally agreed to let David fight & blessed him

  1) Saul demonstrated a trust in the armor of men: He gave David his armor & sword

  2) David felt uncomfortable, burdened down with the armor: He took them off

5. The victory of David over Goliath: God's power to overcome the oppressor of His people
a. The weapons of David—the weapons of a shepherd: A staff, sling, & five stones

b. The strategy & advance of Goliath
  1) He advanced with his shield-bearer in front
  2) He mocked & ridiculed David
    • Because David was only a boy

    • Because David carried only a staff
  3) He cursed David by the name of his false gods

  4) He shouted a boastful threat: That he would kill David & feed his flesh to the birds & beasts

c. The strategy & advance of David
  1) He shouted out the difference between himself & Goliath
    • Goliath trusted in his man-made weapons
    • David trusted in the LORD Almighty
  2) He shouted out that the victory would be the LORD's
    • The LORD would enable

him to strike Goliath down
- The LORD would give a great victory over the Philistine army

3) He shouted out the impact upon the whole world, that they would know…
  - There is *a living God*
  - It is not by military might that the LORD saves
  - It is the LORD Himself who gives victory

4) He suddenly began to run toward Goliath, zigzagging & maneuvering all about

5) He rapidly swirled his sling shot with ferocious, deadly force toward Goliath: The stone sank into Goliath's forehead & he fell facedown

d. The stunning victory of David over Goliath
1) David triumphed with just a sling & a stone—without a sword

2) David ran over & stood over Goliath: Stripped him of his sword & cut off his head

3) The result: The Philistine army was stricken with panic & fled

take thine head from thee; and I will give the carcases of the host of the Philistines this day unto the fowls of the air, and to the wild beasts of the earth; that all the earth may know that there is a God in Israel. 47 And all this assembly shall know that the LORD saveth not with sword and spear: for the battle *is* the LORD's, and he will give you into our hands. 48 And it came to pass, when the Philistine arose, and came and drew nigh to meet David, that David hasted, and ran toward the army to meet the Philistine. 49 And David put his hand in his bag, and took thence a stone, and slang *it,* and smote the Philistine in his forehead, that the stone sunk into his forehead; and he fell upon his face to the earth. 50 So David prevailed over the Philistine with a sling and with a stone, and smote the Philistine, and slew him; but *there was* no sword in the hand of David. 51 Therefore David ran, and stood upon the Philistine, and took his sword, and drew it out of the sheath thereof, and slew him, and cut off his head therewith. And when the Philistines saw their champion was dead, they fled.

52 And the men of Israel and of Judah arose, and shouted, and pursued the Philistines, until thou come to the valley, and to the gates of Ekron. And the wounded of the Philistines fell down by the way to Shaaraim, even unto Gath, and unto Ekron. 53 And the children of Israel returned from chasing after the Philistines, and they spoiled their tents. 54 And David took the head of the Philistine, and brought it to Jerusalem; but he put his armour in his tent. 55 And when Saul saw David go forth against the Philistine, he said unto Abner, the captain of the host, Abner, whose son *is* this youth? And Abner said, *As* thy soul liveth, O king, I cannot tell. 56 And the king said, Enquire thou whose son the stripling *is.* 57 And as David returned from the slaughter of the Philistine, Abner took him, and brought him before Saul with the head of the Philistine in his hand. 58 And Saul said to him, Whose son *art* thou, *thou* young man? And David answered, *I am* the son of thy servant Jesse the Bethlehemite.

e. The crushing victory of Israel & Judah over the Philistine army
1) They chased the Philistines all the way to their coastal cities, Gath & Ekron
2) They executed every soldier they were able to catch
3) They returned & plundered the Philistine camp

f. The foreshadow of David's military spirit
1) He hung Goliath's head in Jerusalem to warn all
2) He kept Goliath's weapons

g. The investigation of David by Saul
1) Saul had asked Abner who David was as David marched out to fight Goliath: Abner did not know

2) Saul charged Abner to find out

3) Abner brought David to Saul right after the combat was over: David was still holding Goliath's head

4) Saul asked about David's family: David identified himself as the son of Jesse

DIVISION III

THE STORY OF SAUL AND DAVID (PART 1): THE LORD GIVES ISRAEL A KING "AFTER HIS OWN HEART," 16:1–20:42

B.   The Story of David and Goliath: Defeating the Oppressor of God's People, 17:1-58

(17:1-58) **Introduction—Victory, Source—Conquest, Assurance—Triumph, Source**: enemies can be defeated. And any oppressor, whether a person or some trial, can be conquered. Victory and triumph are promised to the person who will trust God and call upon Him for power and help.

One of the most famous stories in all the Bible, the story of David and Goliath, teaches us this great lesson. The story is a captivating drama that attracts both the storyteller and the hearer. Furthermore, it is one of the most well-known stories in all literature. Overcoming impossible odds, the young boy David defeated a mighty warrior who stood over nine feet tall. An impossible feat, yet through the power of God David did the impossible. And because of his victory, he stands as a dynamic example before the world—an example of what can be accomplished by the person who truly believes in God. David teaches us that we can defeat any oppressor and conquer any enemy through the power of God. This is: *The Story of David and Goliath: Defeating the Oppressor of God's People,* 17:1-58.

1. The war launched by the Philistines and the defiance of Goliath: confronting an aggressive, frightening enemy (vv.1-11).
2. The family of David and his duties as a youth: the picture of a very responsible young boy (vv.12-15).
3. The righteous anger of David over Goliath's defiance and Israel's fear: a need for courage (vv.16-30).
4. The utter trust of David in God: His power to deliver (vv.31-39).
5. The victory of David over Goliath: God's power to overcome the oppressor of His people (vv.40-58).

1 (17:1-11) **Fear, of Enemy—War, of Israel—Philistines, Conflict with Israel—Defiance, Example of—Hostility, Example of—Goliath, Defiance of—Spiritual Warfare, Symbolized by Philistines**: there was the war launched by the Philistines and the defiance of Goliath. This is a clear picture of the believer confronting an aggressive, defiant, frightening enemy. This is only one of many conflicts between the Philistines and Israel throughout Saul's reign, for the Philistines were bitter enemies of God's people (13:1-23; 14:1-52; 14:47; 14:52). In this present passage, the Philistines again launched an invasion against Israel:

OUTLINE	SCRIPTURE	SCRIPTURE	OUTLINE
1. The war launched by the Philistines & the defiance of Goliath: Confronting an aggressive, frightening enemy	Now the Philistines gathered together their armies to battle, and were gathered together at Shochoh, which *belongeth* to Judah, and pitched between Shochoh and Azekah, in Ephes-dammim.	target of brass between his shoulders.	
a. The Philistines invaded Israel at Shochoh in Judah		7 And the staff of his spear *was* like a weaver's beam; and his spear's head *weighed* six hundred shekels of iron: and one bearing a shield went before him.	3) His weapon: A bronze spear with a tip that weighed 15 pounds
1) The invasion: Saul & his army countered in the valley of Elah	2 And Saul and the men of Israel were gathered together, and pitched by the valley of Elah, and set the battle in array against the Philistines.	8 And he stood and cried unto the armies of Israel, and said unto them, Why are ye come out to set *your* battle in array? *am* not I a Philistine, and ye servants to Saul? choose you a man for you, and let him come down to me.	4) His shield: An armor-bearer carried it before him
2) The battle lines: The armies faced each other on opposite hills surrounding the valley	3 And the Philistines stood on a mountain on the one side, and Israel stood on a mountain on the other side: and *there was* a valley between them.		5) His defiant mockery: Why did the Israelites line up to fight when not a single soldier would face Goliath?
b. The Philistines sent forth a giant warrior named Goliath who issued a hostile challenge to the Israelites	4 And there went out a champion out of the camp of the Philistines, named Goliath, of Gath, whose height *was* six cubits and a span.	9 If he be able to fight with me, and to kill me, then will we be your servants: but if I prevail against him, and kill him, then shall ye be our servants, and serve us.	6) His hostile challenge: That the mightiest warrior of Israel fight a personal dual with him
1) His size: Over 9 feet tall	5 And *he had* an helmet of brass upon his head, and he *was* armed with a coat of mail; and the weight of the coat *was* five thousand shekels of brass.	10 And the Philistine said, I defy the armies of Israel this day; give me a man, that we may fight together.	7) His aggressive proposal: That the dual be a *representative war*, the nation of the loser would become subject to the winner
2) His armor			
• A bronze helmet			
• A coat of scale armor that weighed 125 pounds		11 When Saul and all Israel heard those words of the Philistine, they were dismayed, and greatly afraid.	c. The impact of Goliath's defiance was a paralyzed army: The Israelites were shaken, terrorized
• A pair of bronze leggings	6 And *he had* greaves of brass upon his legs, and a		

a. The Philistines invaded Israel at Shochoh, which was located about fifteen miles west of Bethlehem in the territory of Judea (2 Chr.28:18). They actually pitched their camp at Ephes-dammim, which was between Shochoh and Azekah.

The invasion was immediately countered by Saul and his army. They camped in the valley of Elah. Thus the battle lines were drawn: the armies faced each other on opposite hills surrounding the valley (vv.2-3). Picture the scene: there were the Israelite forces, thousands and thousands of soldiers, battalion after battalion, standing in their battle lines. Opposite them was an invading army of thousands who bitterly hated the Israelites and sought to enslave and subject them to serve the Philistine nation. The Israelite forces knew they were in a fight for their very survival. A spirit of apprehension and fear was bound to be gripping their hearts. But an even greater fear was about to surge through their veins, a paralyzing fear.

b. All of a sudden, a frightening, giant warrior named Goliath stepped forth from the Philistine ranks crying out a hostile challenge to the Israelites (vv.4-10). Note the terrifying description given of this giant warrior:

⇒ He was approximately nine feet nine inches tall (v.4).
⇒ His armor consisted of a bronze helmet, a coat of scale armor weighing about 125 pounds (v.5), and a pair of bronze leggings (v.6).
⇒ His weapons were a bronze spear with a fifteen-pound tip, a sword, and a javelin (vv.7, 45).
⇒ His shield was carried by an armor-bearer who walked before him (v.7).

Standing there in the valley, Goliath presented an awesome appearance. He was a mighty warrior who could overpower any enemy. Then he spoke, crying out in defiance, mocking and ridiculing the Israelites: Why did they line up to fight when not a single soldier would come out to face him (v.8)? He shouted out a hostile challenge, that of representative combat: that is, that the mightiest warrior of Israel fight a personal dual with him, Goliath. This dual would be a representative war with the nation of the loser becoming subject to the winner, serving the winning nation (vv.9-10).

c. The defiance and appearance of Goliath as a mighty warrior paralyzed the Israelite army. A chilling, unnerving fear gripped their hearts. The Israelites were shaken, terrorized by Goliath.

Thought 1. Enemy after enemy confronts us as we walk throughout life. Sometimes these enemies are defiant and frightening, and we feel overpowered and overwhelmed. These enemies may be...

• people who ridicule, mock, oppose, bypass, ignore, abuse, assault, curse, lie, or steal

- circumstances that create all kinds of trials, temptations, accidents, disease, financial difficulty, depression, discouragement, purposelessness, or the death of a loved one

Enemies that overwhelm us can be persons or trials or temptations. As we walk throughout life we will face enemies, defiant and frightening enemies, who will seek to oppress and defeat us. Listen to what the Word of God says about our conflict with these enemies:

"And the LORD said, Simon, Simon, behold, Satan hath desired *to have* you, that he may sift *you* as wheat" (Lu.22:31).

"And that, knowing the time, that now *it is* high time to awake out of sleep: for now *is* our salvation nearer than when we believed. The night is far spent, the day is at hand: let us therefore cast off the works of darkness, and let us put on the armour of light" (Ro.13:11-12).

"(For the weapons of our warfare *are* not carnal, but mighty through God to the pulling down of strong holds;) Casting down imaginations, and every high thing that exalteth itself against the knowledge of God, and bringing into captivity every thought to the obedience of Christ" (2 Co.10:4-5).

"Finally, my brethren, be strong in the LORD, and in the power of his might. Put on the whole armour of God, that ye may be able to stand against the wiles of the devil. For we wrestle not against flesh and blood, but against principalities, against powers, against the rulers of the darkness of this world, against spiritual wickedness in high *places*. Wherefore take unto you the whole armour of God, that ye may be able to withstand in the evil day, and having done all, to stand" (Ep.6:10-13).

"And take the helmet of salvation, and the sword of the Spirit, which is the word of God" (Ep.6:17).

"But let us, who are of the day, be sober, putting on the breastplate of faith and love; and for an helmet, the hope of salvation. For God hath not appointed us to wrath, but to obtain salvation by our Lord Jesus Christ" (1 Th.5:8-9).

"This charge I commit unto thee, son Timothy, according to the prophecies which went before on thee, that thou by them mightest war a good warfare; Holding faith, and a good conscience; which some having put away concerning faith have made shipwreck" (1 Ti.1:18-19).

"But thou, O man of God, flee these things; and follow after righteousness, godliness, faith, love, patience, meekness. Fight the good fight of faith, lay hold on eternal life, whereunto thou art also called, and hast professed a good profession before many witnesses" (1 Ti.6:11-12).

"Thou therefore endure hardness, as a good soldier of Jesus Christ. No man that warreth entangleth himself with the affairs of *this* life; that he may please him who hath chosen him to be a soldier" (2 Ti.2:3-4).

"For the word of God *is* quick, and powerful, and sharper than any twoedged sword, piercing even to the dividing asunder of soul and spirit, and of the joints and marrow, and *is* a discerner of the thoughts and intents of the heart" (He.4:12).

"Be sober, be vigilant; because your adversary the devil, as a roaring lion, walketh about, seeking whom he may devour: Whom resist stedfast in the faith, knowing that the same afflictions are accomplished in your brethren that are in the world. But the God of all grace, who hath called us unto his eternal glory by Christ Jesus, after that ye have suffered a while, make you perfect, stablish, strengthen, settle *you*" (1 Pe.5:8-10).

"And they overcame him by the blood of the Lamb, and by the word of their testimony; and they loved not their lives unto the death" (Re.12:11).

"O God, the proud are risen against me, and the assemblies of violent *men* have sought after my soul; and have not set thee before them" (Ps.86:14).

2 (17:12-15) **Responsible, Example of—Trustworthy, Example of—Faithful, Example of—Obedience, Example of—David, Family of—David, as a Child**: there was the family of David and his duties as a youth. He was a very responsible, obedient young boy. This is the first time the roots or genealogy of David has been given. The picture of David as a young shepherd boy is also gleaned from this passage:

OUTLINE	SCRIPTURE	SCRIPTURE	OUTLINE
2. The family of David & his duties as a youth: The picture of a very responsible young boy	12 Now David *was* the son of that Ephrathite of Bethlehemjudah, whose name *was* Jesse; and he had eight sons: and the man went among men *for* an old man in the days of Saul.	went to the battle *were* Eliab the first born, and next unto him Abinadab, and the third Shammah.	
a. The elderly father Jesse		14 And David *was* the youngest: and the three eldest followed Saul.	c. The duties of David, the youngest son
1) Was from Bethlehem			
2) Had eight sons	13 And the three eldest sons of Jesse went *and* followed Saul to the battle: and the names of his three sons that	15 But David went and returned from Saul to feed his father's sheep at Bethlehem.	1) Served Saul
b. The three oldest brothers: Were soldiers			2) Tended his father's sheep in between, 16:11

David's father was Jesse, an Ephrathite, one of the important families or clans in the tribe of Judah (v.12; 1 Chr.2:19; 4:4). The family lived in Bethlehem. Jesse had eight sons, and by the time of Saul's reign Jesse was already an elderly man. His three oldest sons had enlisted in the army and were serving under Saul's command in the war with the Philistines. The names of these sons are given: the firstborn, Eliab; the second, Abinadab; and the third, Shammah (v.13). David was the youngest son (v.14). Note what David's duties were during the days after his enlistment by Saul to serve in his court: he went back and forth between working for Saul and tending his father's sheep in Bethlehem (v.15; 16:11). Apparently, he was not yet twenty years of age, the minimum age for military service in Israel (Nu.1:3).

Thought 1. The lesson for us is that of responsible service, of doing a good job with the task assigned to us. No matter what the task is—carrying out the trash, making up the bed, working at our employment, fighting a war, or serving the LORD—we must be responsible. We must be diligent and faithful, wholeheartedly performing the task or work. This is the teaching of God's Holy Word:

"Not slothful in business; fervent in spirit; serving the LORD" (Ro.12:11).

"Moreover it is required in stewards, that a man be found faithful" (1 Co.4:2).

"Therefore, my beloved brethren, be ye stedfast, unmovable, always abounding in the work of the LORD, forasmuch as ye know that your labour is not in vain in the LORD" (1 Co.15:58).

"Stand fast therefore in the liberty wherewith Christ hath made us free, and be not entangled again with the yoke of bondage" (Ga.5:1).

"Only let your conversation [behavior, conduct] be as it becometh the gospel of Christ: that whether I come and see you, or else be absent, I may hear of your affairs, that ye stand fast in one spirit, with one mind striving together for the faith of the gospel" (Ph.1:27).

"And whatsoever ye do in word or deed, *do* all in the name of the LORD Jesus, giving thanks to God and the Father by him" (Col.3:17).

"And whatsoever ye do, do *it* heartily, as to the LORD, and not unto men" (Col.3:23).

"And Moses verily *was* faithful in all his house, as a servant, for a testimony of those things which were to be spoken after" (He.3:5).

"Be sober, be vigilant; because your adversary the devil, as a roaring lion, walketh about, seeking whom he may devour: Whom resist stedfast in the faith, knowing that the same afflictions are accomplished in your brethren that are in the world" (1 Pe.5:8-9).

---

3 (17:16-30) **Anger, Justified, Example of—Courage, Example of—David, Courage of—Goliath, Defiance of—David, Confrontation with Goliath—Jealousy, Example of, David's Brother**: there was the righteous anger of David over Goliath's defiance and Israel's fear. This is a descriptive picture showing the need for courage among God's people:

OUTLINE	SCRIPTURE	SCRIPTURE	OUTLINE
3. **The righteous anger of David over Goliath's defiance & Israel's fear: A need for courage**	16 And the Philistine drew near morning and evening, and presented himself forty days.	22 And David left his carriage in the hand of the keeper of the carriage, and ran into the army, and came and saluted his brethren.	3) He took the provisions to the supply officer
a. The 40-day defiance of Goliath	17 And Jesse said unto David his son, Take now for thy brethren an ephah of this parched *corn,* and these ten loaves, and run to the camp to thy brethren;	23 And as he talked with them, behold, there came up the champion, the Philistine of Gath, Goliath by name, out of the armies of the Philistines, and spake according to the same words: and David heard *them.*	4) He ran to the front lines to his brothers
b. The very special duty assigned to David by his father			d. The first sighting of Goliath by David
1) To take supplies to the front lines	18 And carry these ten cheeses unto the captain of *their* thousand, and look how thy brethren fare, and take their pledge.		1) He saw Goliath step out from the Philistine ranks & shout out his terrorizing, hostile challenge
• For his three brothers		24 And all the men of Israel, when they saw the man, fled from him, and were sore afraid.	
• For the commander of their unit	19 Now Saul, and they, and all the men of Israel, *were* in the valley of Elah, fighting with the Philistines.		2) He witnessed the fear & the utter panic of the Israelite forces
2) To check on his brothers' welfare		25 And the men of Israel said, Have ye seen this man that is come up? surely to defy Israel is he come up: and it shall be, *that* the man who killeth him, the king will enrich him with great riches, and will give him his daughter, and make his father's house free in Israel.	e. The reward offered by Saul to any soldier who killed Goliath
c. The obedience, faithfulness of David to his father's instructions	20 And David rose up early in the morning, and left the sheep with a keeper, and took, and went, as Jesse had commanded him; and he came to the trench, as the host was going forth to the fight, and shouted for the battle.		1) Great wealth
1) He left early morning, leaving the sheep with another shepherd			2) His daughter in marriage
			3) Tax exemption for his entire family
2) He arrived just as the troops were going out to their daily battle positions	21 For Israel and the Philistines had put the battle in array, army against army.	26 And David spake to the men that stood by him, saying, What shall be done to the man that killeth this	f. The surge of courage aroused in David over Israel's fear & Goliath's defiance
			1) David demonstrated a

OUTLINE	SCRIPTURE	SCRIPTURE	OUTLINE
courageous anger • At the insult, hostility hurled at Israel by Goliath • At the defiance, insult against "the living God" 2) The soldiers shared with David the promises of Saul to the man who killed Goliath g. The jealousy & anger of David's oldest brother Eliab 1) He was jealous of the courage shown by David 2) He made three accusa-	Philistine, and taketh away the reproach from Israel? for who *is* this uncircumcised Philistine, that he should defy the armies of the living God? 27 And the people answered him after this manner, saying, So shall it be done to the man that killeth him. 28 And Eliab his eldest brother heard when he spake unto the men; and Eliab's anger was kindled against David, and he said, Why camest	thou down hither? and with whom hast thou left those few sheep in the wilderness? I know thy pride, and the naughtiness of thine heart; for thou art come down that thou mightest see the battle. 29 And David said, What have I now done? *Is there* not a cause? 30 And he turned from him toward another, and spake after the same manner: and the people answered him again after the former manner.	tions against David • Accused him of pride, a haughty spirit • Accused him of neglecting his duty • Accused him of a wicked curiosity, coming to watch the battle 3) David's firm response • The cause, issue being discussed is important • David turned to others & continued to discuss the issue of Goliath's defiance & Saul's promises

a. For forty long, frightful days and nights Goliath defied the army of Israel. Every morning and evening during the forty days, Goliath stepped forth into the valley below mocking, ridiculing, and taunting the Israelites. Gripped by fear, Saul and his troops were shaken and terrorized. They became a paralyzed army. No man, not even Saul who stood a head taller than any other Israelite, dared to step forth to engage Goliath in hand-to-hand combat. A standoff between the two armies had developed. But note what was taking place behind the scenes.

b. A very special duty was being assigned to David by his father (vv.17-19). David's father charged him to take supplies to the front lines and to check on the welfare of his brothers. Note that the supplies were also for the commander of their unit. Soldiers of that day usually lived off the land that they occupied or else supplies and rations were sent to them by family members who remained at home.

c. David was obedient, faithful to his father's instructions (vv.20-22). When early morning arrived, he left for the battlefield, leaving the sheep with another shepherd. David arrived just as the troops were going out to their daily battle positions (v.21). He immediately took the provisions to the supply officer, then ran to the front lines to check on his brothers (v.22).

d. While talking with his brothers, David caught his very first sight of Goliath (vv.23-24). He saw the giant soldier step out from the Philistine ranks and shout out his terrorizing challenge. And David witnessed the paralyzing effect on the Israelite forces: they all shrunk back and ran away in fright.

e. Desperately needing a courageous volunteer to accept Goliath's challenge, Saul had offered an enormous reward to any soldier who killed Goliath (v.25). The reward included great wealth, his own daughter in marriage, and tax exemption for the soldier's entire family.

f. A deep concern and righteous anger were aroused in David when he saw Goliath defy Israel's troops and saw the soldiers flee from him (vv.26-27). He was angered at the insult hurled at Israel, the armies of the Living God. By insulting the army of Israel, Goliath was insulting and defying God Himself. This disturbed David deeply as he stood there listening to such insults and curses against the Living God. Suddenly a surge of courage was aroused within the heart of David. He asked the men standing near him what would be done for the man who stepped forth and killed this Philistine, stopping this reproach, this abuse upon Israel. In anger, he asked just who this uncircumcised, pagan Philistine thought he was, that he should defy the armies of the Living God. In response to David's question, the soldiers standing nearby spelled out the reward that Saul had promised to give to the soldier who killed Goliath (v.27).

g. Seeing the bold anger arising within David and hearing David ask the courageous questions irritated the older brother Eliab (vv.28-30). After all, David was the youngest brother, not even old enough to enter military service; yet here he was, demonstrating a bold and courageous anger that suggested he could face Goliath. Obviously, Eliab was jealous of the courage shown by David. Consequently, he made three accusations against David:

⇒ He accused David of pride, of having a haughty spirit.
⇒ He accused David of neglecting his duty, suggesting that he should be back home tending the sheep.
⇒ He accused David of a wicked curiosity, of coming just to watch the battle take place.

Keep in mind that Samuel had rejected Eliab as future king of Israel and had appointed David instead, and the older brother had witnessed the secret anointing (16:6-13). Moreover, David had already been taken into the court of Saul to serve the king. An irritating jealousy had obviously captured the heart of the older brother. As a result, witnessing the bold, courageous anger of David against Goliath only deepened the jealousy within Eliab.

But note the firm response of David to his older brother (vv.29-30). He asked what he had done to irritate Eliab. Was he not even allowed to speak, to ask questions? David was insisting that the cause, the issue being discussed was important. Turning away to someone else, David continued to discuss the issues of Goliath's defiance and the promises of reward made by Saul.

Thought 1. Courage—bold courage—is desperately needed as we face the enemies of this life. Shrinking back and running from enemies will only lead to humiliation, defeat, destruction, and sometimes even death. All kinds of enemies will confront and threaten us as we walk throughout life:

⇒ trials and temptations
⇒ unfavorable circumstances and difficult problems
⇒ persecution and hatred
⇒ hardship and misfortune

⇒ criminals and terrorists
⇒ mockers and slanderers
⇒ evil men and warmongers

We must therefore be noble and stir up a spirit of courage and boldness. We must arouse a strong determination to conquer and triumph over the enemy. A bold, courageous spirit that depends upon the LORD will conquer all enemies and live a victorious life. This is the promise of God's Holy Word:

"Watch ye, stand fast in the faith, quit you like men, be strong" (1 Co.16:13).

"Finally, my brethren, be strong in the LORD, and in the power of his might" (Ep.6:10).

"Only let your conversation [behavior, conduct] be as it becometh the gospel of Christ: that whether I come and see you, or else be absent, I may hear of your affairs, that ye stand fast in one spirit, with one mind striving together for the faith of the gospel; And in nothing terrified by your adversaries: which is to them an evident token of perdition, but to you of salvation, and that of God" (Ph.1:27-28).

"Thou therefore, my son, be strong in the grace that is in Christ Jesus" (2 Ti.2:1).

"Be strong and of a good courage, fear not, nor be afraid of them: for the LORD thy God, he *it is* that doth go with thee; he will not fail thee, nor forsake thee" (De.31:6).

"Be strong and of a good courage: for unto this people shalt thou divide for an inheritance the land, which I sware unto their fathers to give them" (Jos.1:6).

"And Joshua said unto them, Fear not, nor be dismayed, be strong and of good courage: for thus shall the LORD do to all your enemies against whom ye fight" (Jos.10:25).

"Be ye therefore very courageous to keep and to do all that is written in the book of the law of Moses, that ye turn not aside therefrom *to* the right hand or *to* the left; That ye come not among these nations, these that remain among you; neither make mention of the names of their gods, nor cause to swear *by them,* neither serve them, nor bow yourselves unto them: But cleave unto the LORD your God, as ye have done unto this day" (Jos.23:6-8).

"Be of good courage, and let us play the men for our people, and for the cities of our God: and the LORD do that which seemeth him good" (2 S.10:12).

"Be of good courage, and let us behave ourselves valiantly for our people, and for the cities of our God: and let the LORD do *that which is* good in his sight" (1 Chr.19:13).

"Then shalt thou prosper, if thou takest heed to fulfil the statutes and judgments which the LORD charged Moses with concerning Israel: be strong, and of good courage; dread not, nor be dismayed" (1 Chr.22:13).

"And David said to Solomon his son, Be strong and of good courage, and do *it:* fear not, nor be dismayed: for the LORD God, *even* my God, *will be* with thee; he will not fail thee, nor forsake thee, until thou hast finished all the work for the service of the house of the LORD" (1 Chr.28:20).

"The LORD *is* my light and my salvation; whom shall I fear? the LORD *is* the strength of my life; of whom shall I be afraid? When the wicked, *even* mine enemies and my foes, came upon me to eat up my flesh, they stumbled and fell. Though an host should encamp against me, my heart shall not fear: though war should rise against me, in this *will* I *be* confident" (Ps.27:1-3).

"I will say of the LORD, *He is* my refuge and my fortress: my God; in him will I trust. Surely he shall deliver thee from the snare of the fowler, *and* from the noisome pestilence. He shall cover thee with his feathers, and under his wings shalt thou trust: his truth *shall be thy* shield and buckler. Thou shalt not be afraid for the terror by night; *nor* for the arrow *that* flieth by day; *Nor* for the pestilence *that* walketh in darkness; *nor* for the destruction *that* wasteth at noonday" (Ps.91:2-6).

"The LORD *is* on my side; I will not fear: what can man do unto me" (Ps.118:6).

"Behold, God *is* my salvation; I will trust, and not be afraid: for the LORD JEHOVAH *is* my strength and *my* song; he also is become my salvation" (Is.12:2).

4 (17:31-39) **Faith, Example of—Trust, Example of—Confidence, Example of—David, Faith of—God, Power, Faith in—Power, God, Trust in**: there was David's utter trust in God, in His power to deliver him and God's people from their enemies, Goliath and the Philistines. Note the Scripture and outline:

OUTLINE	SCRIPTURE	SCRIPTURE	OUTLINE
4. The utter trust of David in God: His power to deliver	31 And when the words were heard which David spake, they rehearsed *them* before Saul: and he sent for him.	33 And Saul said to David, Thou art not able to go against this Philistine to fight with him: for thou *art but* a youth, and he a man of war from his youth.	c. Saul rejected David's offer: Thought he was only a boy caught up in youthful idealism & would be fighting a trained, experienced soldier
a. Saul heard of David's courage & outrage			
b. David demonstrated strong confidence before Saul: Declared he would fight Goliath	32 And David said to Saul, Let no man's heart fail because of him; thy servant will go and fight with this Philistine.	34 And David said unto Saul, Thy servant kept his father's sheep, and there came a lion, and a bear,	d. David humbly but strongly argued that he had the very experience that could defeat Goliath

OUTLINE	SCRIPTURE	SCRIPTURE	OUTLINE
1) He was a shepherd who had faced bears & lions 2) He had actually seized the creatures & clubbed them to death e. David boldly declared his confidence & trust in God 1) The unbelieving Goliath would be nothing more than the lion & the bear: Because of the "living God" 2) The LORD would deliver him from the hand of Goliath—just as He had delivered him from the	and took a lamb out of the flock: 35 And I went out after him, and smote him, and delivered *it* out of his mouth: and when he arose against me, I caught *him* by his beard, and smote him, and slew him. 36 Thy servant slew both the lion and the bear: and this uncircumcised Philistine shall be as one of them, seeing he hath defied the armies of the living God. 37 David said moreover, The LORD that delivered me out of the paw of the lion, and out of the paw of the bear,	he will deliver me out of the hand of this Philistine. And Saul said unto David, Go, and the LORD be with thee. 38 And Saul armed David with his armour, and he put an helmet of brass upon his head; also he armed him with a coat of mail. 39 And David girded his sword upon his armour, and he assayed to go; for he had not proved *it*. And David said unto Saul, I cannot go with these; for I have not proved *them*. And David put them off him.	paws of the lion & the bear f. Saul finally agreed to let David fight & blessed him 1) Saul demonstrated a trust in the armor of men: He gave David his armor & sword 2) David felt uncomfortable, burdened down with the armor: He took them off

a. David's courage and outrage against the blasphemies of Goliath were reported to King Saul (v.31). After forty days, and having no one else with the courage to step forward, Saul wanted to talk with this young man who was showing such bold anger against the defiance of Goliath. Thus, Saul summoned David to the royal command quarters.

b. Standing before Saul, David demonstrated a strong confidence, declaring that the army should not lose heart, not let their hearts fail them. He personally would go and fight Goliath.

c. Instantly, Saul rejected David's offer, exclaiming that he was only a boy caught up in the youthful idealism and excitement of warfare (v.33). His engaging in hand-to-hand combat was an impossibility, for Goliath was a trained, experienced soldier and he was only a shepherd boy.

d. But David was gripped by a determination, apparently from the LORD: he humbly but strongly argued that he had the very experience that could defeat Goliath (vv.34-35). True, he was only a shepherd, but he had already been engaged in mortal combat: he had faced bears and lions. When a lion or bear caught and carried off a sheep, he had pursued the creature. With only a club in his hand, he would snatch the lamb from the mouth of the creature. And if the animal turned on him, he would seize its hair and club it to death.

e. But even more important than his combat experience with bears and lions, David boldly declared his confidence and trust in God. With God's help, fighting the unbelieving Goliath would be no more dangerous than fighting the lion or the bear (vv.36-37). The *Living God* would make it so, for Goliath had defied both the Living God and His armies. Just as the LORD had delivered him from the paws of the lion and bear, He would deliver him from the hand of Goliath (v.37). The LORD had the power to deliver him, and he was convinced that the LORD would infuse His power into him. He would be empowered to defeat Goliath. This was the strong trust and faith David had in the *Living God*.

f. Seeing David's bold determination and hearing of his courageous experiences against the ferocious beasts of the wilderness, Saul finally agreed to let him go to fight Goliath. In sharing his decision with David, he uttered a brief blessing that no doubt was also intended to be a prayer, asking the LORD to be with the young shepherd boy.

Note that Saul demonstrated a trust in the armor of men: he gave David his armor and sword. But David felt uncomfortable, burdened down because he was not used to wearing such heavy protective armor. Explaining his awkwardness to Saul, he removed the armor.

Thought 1. David's faith, his trust in God, is a dynamic example for us. David's trust challenges us to trust God. God has the power to deliver us from all enemies. No matter who or what the enemy is, God can and will deliver us. But we must trust God, have faith in him. If we believe in God and trust God to empower us, He will infuse His power within us. God will strengthen us to withstand and conquer any trial or temptation. But we must always remember that belief—trusting God—is an absolute essential. Listen to the exhortations of God's Holy Word:

> **"That whosoever believeth in him should not perish, but have eternal life. For God so loved the world, that he gave his only begotten Son, that whosoever believeth in him should not perish, but have everlasting life" (Jn.3:15-16).**

> **"Verily, verily, I say unto you, He that heareth my word, and believeth on him that sent me, hath everlasting life, and shall not come into condemnation; but is passed from death unto life" (Jn.5:24).**

> **"Above all, taking the shield of faith, wherewith ye shall be able to quench all the fiery darts of the wicked" (Ep.6:16).**

> **"But without faith *it is* impossible to please *him:* for he that cometh to God must believe that he is, and *that* he is a rewarder of them that diligently seek him" (He.11:6).**

> **"If any of you lack wisdom, let him ask of God, that giveth to all *men* liberally, and upbraideth not; and it shall be given him. But let him ask in faith, nothing wavering. For he that wavereth is like a wave of the sea driven with the wind and tossed" (Js.1:5-6).**

> **"For whatsoever is born of God overcometh the world: and this is the victory that overcometh the world, *even* our faith. Who is he that overcometh the world, but he that believeth that Jesus is the Son of God" (1 Jn.5:4-5).**

"And they rose early in the morning, and went forth into the wilderness of Tekoa: and as they went forth, Jehoshaphat stood and said, Hear me, O Judah, and ye inhabitants of Jerusalem; Believe in the LORD your God, so shall ye be established; believe his prophets, so shall ye prosper" (2 Chr.20:20).

"*Oh* how great *is* thy goodness, which thou hast laid up for them that fear thee; *which* thou hast wrought for them that trust in thee before the sons of men" (Ps.31:19).

"Many sorrows *shall be* to the wicked: but he that trusteth in the LORD, mercy shall compass him about" (Ps.32:10).

"The LORD redeemeth the soul of his servants: and none of them that trust in him shall be desolate" (Ps.34:22).

"Trust in the LORD, and do good; *so* shalt thou dwell in the land, and verily thou shalt be fed" (Ps.37:3).

"Commit thy way unto the LORD; trust also in him; and he shall bring *it* to pass" (Ps.37:5).

"*It is* better to trust in the LORD than to put confidence in man" (Ps.118:8).

"Trust in the LORD with all thine heart; and lean not unto thine own understanding. In all thy ways acknowledge him, and he shall direct thy paths" (Pr.3:5-6).

"The fear of man bringeth a snare: but whoso putteth his trust in the LORD shall be safe" (Pr.29:25).

"Thou wilt keep *him* in perfect peace, *whose* mind *is* stayed *on thee:* because he trusteth in thee" (Is.26:3).

"Trust ye in the LORD for ever: for in the LORD JEHOVAH *is* everlasting strength" (Is.26:4).

---

5 (17:40-58) **Victory, over Enemies, Example of—Conquest, of Enemies, Example of—Spiritual Warfare, Deliverance from—David, Victories of—Goliath, Defeated by David**: there was the victory of David over Goliath. This is a clear picture of God's power to overcome the enemy, the oppressor of His people. A graphic description is pictured of this famous combat, this stunning victory of David over Goliath:

OUTLINE	SCRIPTURE	SCRIPTURE	OUTLINE
5. The victory of David over Goliath: God's power to overcome the oppressor of His people	40 And he took his staff in his hand, and chose him five smooth stones out of the brook, and put them in a shepherd's bag which he had, even in a scrip; and his sling *was* in his hand: and he drew near to the Philistine.	deliver thee into mine hand; and I will smite thee, and take thine head from thee; and I will give the carcases of the host of the Philistines this day unto the fowls of the air, and to the wild beasts of the earth; that all the earth may know that there is a God in Israel.	victory would be the LORD's
a. The weapons of David—the weapons of a shepherd: A staff, sling, & five stones			• The LORD would enable him to strike Goliath down
			• The LORD would give a great victory over the Philistine army
b. The strategy & advance of Goliath	41 And the Philistine came on and drew near unto David; and the man that bare the shield *went* before him.	47 And all this assembly shall know that the LORD saveth not with sword and spear: for the battle *is* the LORD'S, and he will give you into our hands.	3) He shouted out the impact upon the whole world, that they would know…
1) He advanced with his shield-bearer in front			• There is *a living God*
2) He mocked & ridiculed David	42 And when the Philistine looked about, and saw David, he disdained him: for he was *but* a youth, and ruddy, and of a fair countenance.		• It is not by military might that the LORD saves
• Because David was only a boy			• It is the LORD Himself who gives victory
• Because David carried only a staff	43 And the Philistine said unto David, *Am* I a dog, that thou comest to me with staves? And the Philistine cursed David by his gods.	48 And it came to pass, when the Philistine arose, and came and drew nigh to meet David, that David hasted, and ran toward the army to meet the Philistine.	4) He suddenly began to run toward Goliath, zigzagging & maneuvering all about
3) He cursed David by the name of his false gods			
4) He shouted a boastful threat: That he would kill David & feed his flesh to the birds & beasts	44 And the Philistine said to David, Come to me, and I will give thy flesh unto the fowls of the air, and to the beasts of the field.	49 And David put his hand in his bag, and took thence a stone, and slang *it,* and smote the Philistine in his forehead, that the stone sunk into his forehead; and he fell upon his face to the earth.	5) He rapidly swirled his sling shot with ferocious, deadly force toward Goliath: The stone sank into Goliath's forehead & he fell facedown
c. The strategy & advance of David	45 Then said David to the Philistine, Thou comest to me with a sword, and with a spear, and with a shield: but I come to thee in the name of the LORD of hosts, the God of the armies of Israel, whom thou hast defied.	50 So David prevailed over the Philistine with a sling and with a stone, and smote the Philistine, and slew him; but *there was* no sword in the hand of David.	d. The stunning victory of David over Goliath
1) He shouted out the difference between himself & Goliath			1) David triumphed with just a sling & a stone—without a sword
• Goliath trusted in his man-made weapons			
• David trusted in the LORD Almighty			
2) He shouted out that the	46 This day will the LORD	stood upon the Philistine, and	2) David ran over & stood over Goliath: Stripped

OUTLINE	SCRIPTURE	SCRIPTURE	OUTLINE
him of his sword & cut off his head 3) The result: The Philistine army was stricken with panic & fled e. The crushing victory of Israel & Judah over the Philistine army 1) They chased the Philistines all the way to their coastal cities, Gath & Ekron 2) They executed every soldier they were able to catch 3) They returned & plundered the Philistine camp f. The foreshadow of David's military spirit 1) He hung Goliath's head in Jerusalem to warn all	took his sword, and drew it out of the sheath thereof, and slew him, and cut off his head therewith. And when the Philistines saw their champion was dead, they fled. 52 And the men of Israel and of Judah arose, and shouted, and pursued the Philistines, until thou come to the valley, and to the gates of Ekron. And the wounded of the Philistines fell down by the way to Shaaraim, even unto Gath, and unto Ekron. 53 And the children of Israel returned from chasing after the Philistines, and they spoiled their tents. 54 And David took the head of the Philistine, and brought it to Jerusalem; but he put his armour in his	tent. 55 And when Saul saw David go forth against the Philistine, he said unto Abner, the captain of the host, Abner, whose son *is* this youth? And Abner said, *As* thy soul liveth, O king, I cannot tell. 56 And the king said, Enquire thou whose son the stripling *is*. 57 And as David returned from the slaughter of the Philistine, Abner took him, and brought him before Saul with the head of the Philistine in his hand. 58 And Saul said to him, Whose son *art* thou, *thou* young man? And David answered, *I am* the son of thy servant Jesse the Bethlehemite.	2) He kept Goliath's weapons g. The investigation of David by Saul 1) Saul had asked Abner who David was as David marched out to fight Goliath: Abner did not know 2) Saul charged Abner to find out 3) Abner brought David to Saul right after the combat was over: David was still holding Goliath's head 4) Saul asked about David's family: David identified himself as the son of Jesse

a. David's weapons were those of a shepherd: a staff, a sling, stones, and a pouch to hold the stones. David reached down and picked up five stones from a stream and put them in the pouch of his shepherd's bag. Then, armed only with his staff and sling, he began to approach Goliath.

b. Note the strategy and advance of Goliath (vv.41-44). He began to advance with his shield-bearer in front of him. As he moved forward, he mocked and ridiculed David, despising him because the Israelites had sent only a small boy to fight him, the famous warrior of the Philistines. And they had equipped the small boy with only a staff as a weapon (vv.42-43).

To some degree, Goliath felt insulted, for he was a famous warrior; and to defeat a young boy such as David armed only with a staff could become the target of jokes among the soldiers and citizens of the Philistines.

Consequently, Scripture says that Goliath disdained, despised David, holding him in contempt. He began to curse David by the name of his false gods, and he shouted a boastful threat: that he would kill David and feed his flesh to the birds and beasts of the field (vv.43-44).

c. Note the strategy and advance of David (vv.45-49). Unmoved by the defiance and threats of Goliath, David launched a verbal counterattack.[1] He shouted out the difference between him and Goliath: that Goliath trusted in his man-made weapons, the weapons of sword and spear and javelin. But he, David, trusted in *the LORD of hosts*, the "LORD Almighty"—the God of the armies of Israel whom Goliath had defied (v.45). Then David shouted out that the victory would be the LORD's. The LORD would enable David to strike Goliath down and even cut off his head. Moreover, the LORD would give a great victory over the Philistine army, and the carcasses of the army would be given to the birds of the air and the beasts of the fields.

Note what David then shouted out: he declared that this event would become historically famous, that it would have an impact upon the whole world (vv.46-47). By the victory God was going to give David, the world would know that the LORD is the only living and true God. And the world would know that it is not by military might that the LORD saves. The LORD saves by the might of His own power (v.47).

Suddenly, the verbal assaults were over, and all the defiance that could be uttered had been shouted out by each combatant. They were almost within range of each other's weapons. Unexpectedly—quickly and abruptly—David broke into a run toward Goliath, zigzagging and maneuvering all about, rapidly swirling his slingshot. Then with ferocious, deadly force, he slung a stone through the air, striking and sinking into Goliath's forehead, causing the giant to fall facedown on the ground (v.49).

d. Just as quickly as the conflict had begun, David had gained a quick, stunning victory over Goliath (vv.50-51). He had triumphed over the enemy without a sword, using only a sling and a stone.

Quickly David ran and stood over Goliath (v.51). He stripped Goliath of his sword and thrust it through the giant's body, making sure the brutal enemy was dead. Then using Goliath's own sword, David cut off the head of the giant. Witnessing the quick defeat and death of their hero, the Philistine army was utterly shocked and stricken with panic. Hurriedly, they fled the battlefield in utter confusion.

e. Now note the crushing victory of Israel and Judah over the Philistine army (vv.52-53). Excited over witnessing David's quick defeat of Goliath, the Israelites shouted out the joy of their triumph. And being encouraged by the strong faith and courage of David, they rushed forth and chased the Philistines all the way to the gates of their coastal cities, Gath and Ekron. They executed every soldier they were able to catch, and the dead and wounded lay all along the road right up to the city gates of the two cities. Once the enemy had fled behind their fortified walls, the Israelites returned from chasing the Philistines and plundered their camp (v.53).

---

[1] Robert D. Bergen. *1, 2 Samuel*, p.195.

f. A foreshadowing of David's military spirit then emerged: he hung Goliath's head in Jerusalem (v.54). Just why he did this is not stated. But most likely it was for the purpose of intimidation, to strike fear in the heart of any enemy who entertained thoughts of attacking Israel. As for Goliath's weapons, David kept them as a personal trophy of his victory.

g. Earlier Saul had watched David march out to meet Goliath, wondering who this courageous young man was. He asked Abner, who was the commander of the army, but Abner did not know. Thus Saul charged Abner to find out (v.56). Consequently, right after the combat was over, Abner brought David to Saul.

Note the scene: standing before King Saul, David was still holding Goliath's head (v.57). It would be interesting to know what the thoughts of Saul were. Here was this courageous young man standing before him with the head of the giant he had just slain. And the courageous young man had just achieved a victory that had delivered King Saul and his army from utter devastation at the hands of the Philistines. Saul wanted to know what any ruler—or for that matter what any person—would want to know. Just who was this young man who had more courage than an army of over 200,000 soldiers? Of course, Saul had met David earlier when he enlisted him to be his harpist (16:18-21), but Saul did not remember David, for that had been several years earlier when David was just a young boy, perhaps no more than twelve years old. Now he was probably somewhere around sixteen to eighteen years old.[2] Moreover, David's services as a harpist had been needed only occasionally by Saul and most likely had been for only a brief period of time. This seems to be indicated by the fact that David had been back home tending sheep for his father (v.15). Whatever the case, Saul obviously did not remember David as one of the young men serving in his court.

King Saul also needed to know who the father of David was. As soon as David was brought into his presence, King Saul asked him for the identity of his father. It was necessary for Saul to gain knowledge of the family, for David had earned the right to marry his daughter. Furthermore, the entire family was to be exempted from taxes. The *conquering hero* David had earned the rewards promised by King Saul.

> **Thought 1**. God will give us the power to conquer all enemies. All the trials and temptations of this life can be conquered, even the climatic trial of death itself. Through the power of God, we can walk through any trial or temptation, conquering and triumphing over all. Victory is ours through the power of God.
>
> **"For with God nothing shall be impossible" (Lu.1:37).**
>
> **"But ye shall receive power, after that the Holy Ghost is come upon you: and ye shall be witnesses unto me both in Jerusalem, and in all Judaea, and in Samaria, and unto the uttermost part of the earth" (Ac.1:8).**
>
> **"Now to him that is of power to stablish you according to my gospel, and the preaching of Jesus Christ, according to the revelation of the mystery, which was kept secret since the world began" (Ro.16:25).**
>
> **"But God hath chosen the foolish things of the world to confound the wise; and God hath chosen the weak things of the world to confound the things which are mighty" (1 Co.1:27).**
>
> **"And he said unto me, My grace is sufficient for thee: for my strength is made perfect in weakness. Most gladly therefore will I rather glory in my infirmities, that the power of Christ may rest upon me. Therefore I take pleasure in infirmities, in reproaches, in necessities, in persecutions, in distresses for Christ's sake: for when I am weak, then am I strong" (2 Co.12:9-10).**
>
> **"That he would grant you, according to the riches of his glory, to be strengthened with might by his Spirit in the inner man" (Ep.3:16).**
>
> **"Now unto him that is able to do exceeding abundantly above all that we ask or think, according to the power that worketh in us" (Ep.3:20).**
>
> **"Strengthened with all might, according to his glorious power, unto all patience and longsuffering with joyfulness" (Col.1:11).**
>
> **"For God hath not given us the spirit of fear; but of power, and of love, and of a sound mind" (2 Ti.1:7).**
>
> **"And what shall I more say? for the time would fail me to tell of Gedeon, and *of* Barak, and *of* Samson, and *of* Jephthae; *of* David also, and Samuel, and *of* the prophets: Who through faith subdued kingdoms, wrought righteousness, obtained promises, stopped the mouths of lions, Quenched the violence of fire, escaped the edge of the sword, out of weakness were made strong, waxed valiant in fight, turned to flight the armies of the aliens" (He.11:32-34).**
>
> **"For thou hast girded me with strength to battle: them that rose up against me hast thou subdued under me" (2 S.22:40).**
>
> **"I know that thou canst do every *thing,* and *that* no thought can be withholden from thee" (Jb.42:2).**
>
> **"Out of the mouth of babes and sucklings hast thou ordained strength because of thine enemies, that thou mightest still the enemy and the avenger" (Ps.8:2).**
>
> **"But they that wait upon the LORD shall renew *their* strength; they shall mount up with wings as eagles; they shall run, and not be weary; *and* they shall walk, and not faint" (Is.40:31).**
>
> **"Fear thou not; for I *am* with thee: be not dismayed; for I *am* thy God: I will strengthen thee; yea, I will help thee; yea, I will uphold thee with the right hand of my righteousness" (Is.41:10).**
>
> **"But truly I am full of power by the spirit of the LORD, and of judgment, and of might, to declare unto Jacob his transgression, and to Israel his sin" (Mi.3:8).**

---

[2] John F. Walvoord and Roy B. Zuck, Editors. *The Bible Knowledge Commentary*, p.448.

Thought **2**. Robert D. Bergen has an excellent statement on Goliath that is well worth quoting in full:

> *As David viewed it, Goliath was outnumbered and would soon be overpowered, for the Lord would fight with David against the giant. In the battle that would occur "this day" (v.46), the Lord would "hand [Goliath] over" to David; then for his part the young shepherd would "strike [Goliath] down and cut off [his] head." David's efforts would not be limited to slaying Goliath; he also would slaughter and humiliate the Philistine army. Yet the Philistines would not die in vain. In fact, their destruction would serve a high theological purpose; it would be a revelatory event by which "the whole world will know that there is a God in Israel" (cf. Josh 2:10-11). Achieving a depth of insight remarkable for a person of any age, young David perceived that the events of this day would give rise to narrative accounts that would reveal the Lord's power and reality to all who might hear them. Eyewitnesses to the ensuing battle would learn an additional truth from the Lord, "that it is not by sword or spear that the LORD saves, for the battle is the LORD's" (v.47; cf. 2:9-10; 13:22; Jer 9:23-24; Zech 4:6).*
>
> *David, the Lord's anointed one, discerned a theological purpose in warfare. This perspective is one that must be examined because it is of utmost importance for understanding the mind-set of orthodox Israelites in the Old Testament. For David—and, we judge, for all Old Testament Israelites of true faith in God—armed conflict was fundamentally a religious event.[3] Only when the Lord willed it were Israelites under David's command to engage in it (cf. 2 Sam 5:19). And when the Lord ordained battle for David's troops, it was to be performed in accordance with divine directives (cf. 2 Sam 5:23-25). Furthermore, because soldiers were performing God's work, only individuals who were in a state of ritual purity were to participate in military missions (cf. 1 Sam 21:5). The Lord was the one who gave victory to David and his troops in battle (cf. v. 47; 2 Sam 22:30, 36, 51), and thus the Lord alone was worthy of praise for David's and Israel's military successes (2 Sam 22:47-48).[4]*

---

[3] T. Longman III and D.G. Reid. *God Is a Warrior.* (Grand Rapids, MI: Zondervan Publishing House, 1966).

[4] Robert D. Bergen. *1, 2 Samuel*, p.196.

CHAPTER 18

C. The Story of Saul's Jealous Rage & Attempts to Kill David (Part 1): A Look at the Evil of Jealousy & Envy, 18:1-30

1. **The jealousy of Saul over the success of David: A picture of jealousy & envy**
   a. Jonathan, Saul's son, loved David like a brother

   b. Saul honored David by elevating him in the king's court & service—permanently

   c. Jonathan, the king's son & future prince, made a covenant with David
      1) Acknowledged David as the future king
      2) Gave David his own royal clothing & weapons

   d. David succeeded greatly in every task assigned to him
   e. Saul made David a commander in the army: An act that pleased the people & the officers

   f. The people acknowledged David as a hero & he become more popular than Saul
      1) The triumphant march: The people celebrated David's triumph over Goliath & the army's victory over the Philistines

      2) The women composed a song that honored David more than Saul: Placed Saul in second place

   g. The result: A spirit of jealous rage gripped Saul
      1) He was galled, very angry
      2) He became paranoid, suspicious of treason: Thought David was a threat to his throne & dynasty

      3) He began to keep a jealous eye, a close watch, on David

2. **The first attempt to kill David: Bitter hatred, a spirit of rage & fury aroused by jealousy**
   a. Saul was gripped by an evil spirit & began to prophesy— "rave[d] like a madman," NLT
   b. Saul attempted to kill David:

And it came to pass, when he had made an end of speaking unto Saul, that the soul of Jonathan was knit with the soul of David, and Jonathan loved him as his own soul.
2 And Saul took him that day, and would let him go no more home to his father's house.
3 Then Jonathan and David made a covenant, because he loved him as his own soul.
4 And Jonathan stripped himself of the robe that *was* upon him, and gave it to David, and his garments, even to his sword, and to his bow, and to his girdle.
5 And David went out whithersoever Saul sent him, *and* behaved himself wisely: and Saul set him over the men of war, and he was accepted in the sight of all the people, and also in the sight of Saul's servants.
6 And it came to pass as they came, when David was returned from the slaughter of the Philistine, that the women came out of all cities of Israel, singing and dancing, to meet king Saul, with tabrets, with joy, and with instruments of musick.
7 And the women answered *one another* as they played, and said, Saul hath slain his thousands, and David his ten thousands.
8 And Saul was very wroth, and the saying displeased him; and he said, They have ascribed unto David ten thousands, and to me they have ascribed *but* thousands: and *what* can he have more but the kingdom?
9 And Saul eyed David from that day and forward.
10 And it came to pass on the morrow, that the evil spirit from God came upon Saul, and he prophesied in the midst of the house: and David played with his hand, as at other times: and *there was* a javelin in Saul's hand.
11 And Saul cast the javelin;

for he said, I will smite David even to the wall *with it.* And David avoided out of his presence twice.
12 And Saul was afraid of David, because the LORD was with him, and was departed from Saul.
13 Therefore Saul removed him from him, and made him his captain over a thousand; and he went out and came in before the people.
14 And David behaved himself wisely in all his ways; and the LORD *was* with him.
15 Wherefore when Saul saw that he behaved himself very wisely, he was afraid of him.
16 But all Israel and Judah loved David, because he went out and came in before them.
17 And Saul said to David, Behold my elder daughter Merab, her will I give thee to wife: only be thou valiant for me, and fight the LORD'S battles. For Saul said, Let not mine hand be upon him, but let the hand of the Philistines be upon him.
18 And David said unto Saul, Who *am* I? and what *is* my life, *or* my father's family in Israel, that I should be son in law to the king?
19 But it came to pass at the time when Merab Saul's daughter should have been given to David, that she was given unto Adriel the Meholathite to wife.
20 And Michal Saul's daughter loved David: and they told Saul, and the thing pleased him.
21 And Saul said, I will give him her, that she may be a snare to him, and that the hand of the Philistines may be against him. Wherefore Saul said to David, Thou shalt this day be my son in law in the one of the twain.
22 And Saul commanded his servants, *saying,* Commune with David secretly, and say, Behold, the king hath delight in thee, and all his servants love thee: now therefore be the king's son in law.
23 And Saul's servants spake those words in the ears of David. And David said, Seemeth it to you *a* light *thing* to be a king's son in law, seeing that I *am* a poor

Threw his spear at David twice, but David escaped

3. **The second attempt to kill David: Fear, division, & a sinister plot aroused by jealousy**
   a. Saul was abandoned by God
   b. Saul used a sinister tactic to try to kill David: Sent David to fight risky battles, hoping he would lose & be discredited or killed
   c. The result: David succeeded in everything because the LORD was with him
      1) Saul feared David even more

      2) All Israel loved David even more

4. **The third attempt to kill David: Lies & deception aroused by jealousy**
   a. The deceptive promise of Saul: To give his daughter to David if he proved himself in battle
   b. The purpose of Saul: To expose David to armed conflict so he might be killed
   c. The response & humility of David: He was not worthy of such honor, the honor of marrying the princess & of being a part of the king's family
   d. The broken promise of Saul—for the second time (17:25): He gave his daughter Merab in marriage to Adriel

5. **The fourth attempt to kill David: Seduction & evil influence aroused by jealousy**
   a. Saul's seductive plot
      1) Plotted to use his younger daughter's love for David as a snare
         • By having her seduce & corrupt David spiritually (19:13)
         • The result: God's protection would be removed
      2) Offered Michal in marriage to David
      3) Sent attendants to speak confidentially with David—seducing, enticing him with misinformation, lies
   b. David's rejection of the marriage proposal
      1) He lacked the wealth to pay the dowry
      2) He lacked the social status

c. Saul's second seductive offer to David	man, and lightly esteemed? 24 And the servants of Saul told him, saying, On this manner spake David.	brought their foreskins, and they gave them in full tale to the king, that he might be the king's son in law. And Saul	fulfillment of the terms 1) Saul was forced to give his daughter in marriage to David
1) David could earn the dowry, the "bride price," for Saul's daughter by killing 100 Philistines	25 And Saul said, Thus shall ye say to David, The king desireth not any dowry, but an	gave him Michal his daughter to wife. 28 And Saul saw and knew	
2) Saul's hidden motive & secret hope: That David would be killed in battle	hundred foreskins of the Philistines, to be avenged of the king's enemies. But Saul thought to make David fall	that the LORD *was* with David, and *that* Michal Saul's daughter loved him.	2) Saul realized the LORD was with David & his daughter truly loved him
d. David's acceptance of the terms	by the hand of the Philistines. 26 And when his servants told David these words, it	29 And Saul was yet the more afraid of David; and Saul became David's enemy	3) Saul feared David even more & went beyond repentance, beyond ever
1) David agreed to become the king's son-in-law	pleased David well to be the king's son in law: and the days were not expired.	continually. 30 Then the princes of the Philistines went forth: and it	changing
2) David went out & exceeded the terms before the deadline, killing 200 Philistines	27 Wherefore David arose and went, he and his men, and slew of the Philistines	came to pass, after they went forth, *that* David behaved himself more wisely than all	f. David's continued success in battle & in becoming more famous
e. David's exploits resulted in	two hundred men; and David	the servants of Saul; so that his name was much set by.	

DIVISION III

THE STORY OF SAUL AND DAVID (PART 1): THE LORD GIVES ISRAEL A KING "AFTER HIS OWN HEART," 16:1–20:42

C. The Story of Saul's Jealous Rage and Attempts to Kill David (Part 1): A Look at the Evil of Jealousy and Envy, 18:1-30

(18:1-30) **Introduction—Jealousy, Evil of—Envy, Evil of**: jealousy and envy are terrible evils. Envy is the resentful feeling we have when we see someone with something we want or see a person achieve something we wish to achieve. If a person has something that we want and cannot get, what are we going to do? If the passion to have the thing is strong enough, we go after it. The driving force of the passion compels us to pursue whatever we want. It is the passion of envy or jealousy that causes people to steal, abuse, assault, and even commit murder. We may be jealous or envious of...

- a person's beauty or good looks
- a person's wealth or possessions
- a person's house or cars
- a person's position or authority
- a person's job or income
- a person's husband or wife, boyfriend or girlfriend

We can be jealous or envious of any person or of any thing in this world. And jealousy or envy that has become deep-seated is what causes so much lawlessness, immorality, violence, power seeking, and war within society and among the nations of the earth. Being jealous of people and the possessions, power, and wealth of this world is a cancerous sore that eats away at the human heart and destroys human lives. Jealousy will destroy the life of any person who gives in to its passion. And the jealous person far too often damages the lives of those he envies through rumor and covetousness, lust and abuse, and even attacks—either verbal or physical.

This present passage is a picture of the terrible evils of jealousy and envy. King Saul became so jealous, so envious of David that he progressively deteriorated mentally and spiritually. He became insanely jealous, gripped with extreme paranoia. He experienced episodes of insanity and made attempt after attempt upon David's life. This is: *The Story of Saul's Jealous Rage and Attempts to Kill David (Part 1): A Look at the Evil of Jealousy and Envy, 18:1-30.*

1. The jealousy of Saul over the success of David: a picture of jealousy and envy (vv.1-9).
2. The first attempt to kill David: bitter hatred, a spirit of rage and fury aroused by jealousy (vv.10-11).
3. The second attempt to kill David: fear, division, and a sinister plot aroused by jealousy (vv.12-16).
4. The third attempt to kill David: lies and deception aroused by jealousy (vv.17-19).
5. The fourth attempt to kill David: seduction and evil influence aroused by jealousy (vv.20-30).

1 (18:1-9) **Jealousy, Example of—Envy, Example of—Saul, Sin and Weakness of, Jealousy—Jonathan, Relationship with David—David, Relationship with Jonathan—Saul, Evil Spirit of**: there was the jealousy of Saul over the success of David. Remember that David was just a youth, most likely somewhere between 16 and 18 years old. He was not yet of military age (20 years old). He had just shown the most unusual valor, courageously facing and killing Goliath, the heroic warrior of the Philistines. His extraordinary bravery aroused the fearful Israelite army to attack and gain a significant victory over the Philistine forces. Because of David, Saul and his army were victorious. Immediately after the battle had settled down, Saul had summoned David to be brought before him, and they had apparently had a long conversation. As a result of the conversation, David's life was to be changed forever, both for good and for bad. The Scripture and outline paint the scene of just how David's life was redirected:

OUTLINE	SCRIPTURE	SCRIPTURE	OUTLINE

1. The jealousy of Saul over the success of David: A picture of jealousy & envy
a. Jonathan, Saul's son, loved David like a brother
 	
b. Saul honored David by elevating him in the king's court & service—permanently
c. Jonathan, the king's son & future prince, made a covenant with David
  1) Acknowledged David as the future king
  2) Gave David his own royal clothing & weapons
 	
d. David succeeded greatly in every task assigned to him
e. Saul made David a commander in the army: An act that pleased the people & the officers
	And it came to pass, when he had made an end of speaking unto Saul, that the soul of Jonathan was knit with the soul of David, and Jonathan loved him as his own soul.
	2 And Saul took him that day, and would let him go no more home to his father's house.
	3 Then Jonathan and David made a covenant, because he loved him as his own soul.
	4 And Jonathan stripped himself of the robe that *was* upon him, and gave it to David, and his garments, even to his sword, and to his bow, and to his girdle.
	5 And David went out whithersoever Saul sent him, *and* behaved himself wisely: and Saul set him over the men of war, and he was accepted in the sight of all the
		people, and also in the sight of Saul's servants.
		6 And it came to pass as they came, when David was returned from the slaughter of the Philistine, that the women came out of all cities of Israel, singing and dancing, to meet king Saul, with tabrets, with joy, and with instruments of musick.
		7 And the women answered *one another* as they played, and said, Saul hath slain his thousands, and David his ten thousands.
		8 And Saul was very wroth, and the saying displeased him; and he said, They have ascribed unto David ten thousands, and to me they have ascribed *but* thousands: and *what* can he have more but the kingdom?
		9 And Saul eyed David from that day and forward.
			f. The people acknowledged David as a hero & he became more popular than Saul
			  1) The triumphant march: The people celebrated David's triumph over Goliath & the army's victory over the Philistines
			  2) The women composed a song that honored David more than Saul: Placed Saul in second place
			
			g. The result: A spirit of jealous rage gripped Saul
			  1) He was galled, very angry
			  2) He became paranoid, suspicious of treason: Thought David was a threat to his throne & dynasty
			
			  3) He began to keep a jealous eye, a close watch, on David

a. Saul's son Jonathan developed a strong fellowship with David, even a brotherly love for him (v.1). Keep in mind that both of these young men had courageous spirits and possessed great faith in the LORD (14:1-48; 17:1-58). But Jonathan was obviously older, probably by quite a few years, for a man had to be at least 20 years old to serve in the army, and Jonathan was already a seasoned soldier. In fact, he was one of the major commanders in the army and had already won two significant victories (13:1-4; 14:1-48). It was probably David's courageous boldness that attracted Jonathan to David and that led him to take David under his care in order to train him in the affairs of the royal court and in military tactics. As a result, a close bond of friendship grew into a oneness of spirit and brotherly love.

b. Immediately after David's victory over Goliath, Saul honored David by bringing him permanently into the king's court and service (v.2). Such a brave, courageous young man was just the kind of person any king would want serving in his royal court.

c. At some point in time Jonathan made an unusual covenant with David (vv.3-4). And keep in mind that Jonathan was the king's son and was looked upon as the future prince of the nation. The initiative for the covenant came from Jonathan himself. Just what the terms of the covenant were is not stated; however, at the very least the two young men would have pledged their friendship and loyalty to one another. They would always look after the needs and welfare of one another. But note this fact as well: Jonathan seemed to be acknowledging that David was to be the future king, for he gave David his own royal clothing and weapons. The royal robe and weapons were to be used only by the future heir to the throne. In effect, Jonathan was transferring the right to the throne over to David.[1]

Why would Jonathan transfer his right to rule over to David? Obviously, Jonathan had somehow learned of David's secret anointing, that David was the appointed future ruler of Israel. Because of their close friendship and Jonathan's love for the LORD, Jonathan was able to accept the fact. This is clearly indicated in later passages (20:13-16, 31; 23:17).

d. David was very wise in the way he handled every task assigned him. And he was very successful in every assignment given him by Saul (v.5).

e. Because of David's military successes and faithful service to the royal court, Saul soon made David a commander in the army (v.5). Note that this was an act that pleased both the people and the military officers.

f. In the minds of the people, David was a hero and became even more popular than Saul (vv.6-7). After the defeat of the Philistines, the army marched triumphantly from city to city celebrating the glorious victory over the archenemy. Note what happened: in celebrating David's triumph over Goliath and the army's victory over the Philistines, the women composed a song that honored David more than Saul, placing Saul in second place. The women danced about, singing that Saul had slain his thousands, but David his tens of thousands (v.7).

g. The result was catastrophic: Saul was gripped with a spirit of jealous rage (v.8). He was very angry and displeased. The song galled him. He became paranoid, suspicious of treason, that there was a plot by David and others to overthrow his kingdom. And from that moment on, he began to keep a jealous, watchful eye on David.

Thought 1. Jealousy and envy can cause all kinds of problems for us. Envying a person's beauty or good looks can cause us to feel unattractive and lead us to degrade ourselves. Envying a person's position can arouse covetousness

---

[1] Ronald F. Youngblood. *1 Samuel*, p.707.

within us and cause us to attack the person either verbally or physically. Envying a person's success or achievement can create bitter hatred within us, a bitter hatred that causes us to react in all kinds of ways.

Being jealous or envious of a person because he has something we want can consume us, can absorb all our thoughts, time, and passion. It can eat away at our hearts and minds just like a cancer. A man can be so jealous of another's wealth that he claws or grasps after wealth, becoming consumed with gaining wealth. A woman can become so jealous of another's beauty that she is consumed with becoming more attractive, spending all kinds of money on clothing, jewelry, hairdos, or plastic surgery—all to gain more beauty or better looks. We can become jealous or envious over anything to such a degree that it consumes our lives. Listen to what the Word of God says about jealousy and envy:

> "Now his elder son was in the field: and as he came and drew nigh to the house, he heard music and dancing. And he called one of the servants, and asked what these things meant. And he said unto him, Thy brother is come; and thy father hath killed the fatted calf, because he hath received him safe and sound. And he was angry, and would not go in: therefore came his father out, and intreated him" (Lu.15:25-28).
>
> "Let us walk honestly, as in the day; not in rioting and drunkenness, not in chambering and wantonness, not in strife and envying" (Ro.13:13).
>
> "Charity suffereth long, *and* is kind; charity envieth not; charity vaunteth not itself, is not puffed up" (1 Co.13:4).
>
> "Let us not be desirous of vain glory, provoking one another, envying one another" (Ga.5:26).
>
> "And when his brethren saw that their father loved him more than all his brethren, they hated him, and could not speak peaceably unto him" (Ge.37:4).
>
> "And Saul was very wroth, and the saying displeased him; and he said, They have ascribed unto David ten thousands, and to me they have ascribed *but* thousands: and *what* can he have more but the kingdom" (1 S.18:8).
>
> "Fret not thyself because of evildoers, neither be thou envious against the workers of iniquity" (Ps.37:1).
>
> "Envy thou not the oppressor, and choose none of his ways" (Pr.3:31).
>
> "A sound heart *is* the life of the flesh: but envy the rottenness of the bones" (Pr.14:30).
>
> "Let not thine heart envy sinners: but *be thou* in the fear of the LORD all the day long" (Pr.23:17).
>
> "Be not thou envious against evil men, neither desire to be with them" (Pr.24:1).

2 (18:10-11) **Jealousy, Result of—Envy, Result of—Murder, Attempted—Saul, Attempts at David's Life—David, Attempts to Murder, Kill**: there was the first attempt of Saul to kill David. Saul was filled with bitter hatred, a spirit of rage and fury against David—all aroused by his jealousy and the possible threat to his throne. Note that this event took place the very day after the army's triumphal march through the cities. A tranquil scene is pictured with David playing the harp. Then it happened: a tormenting, evil spirit came upon Saul and he began to prophesy; that is, to experience some kind of ecstatic, uncontrollable behavior, acting and raving like a madman (NLT). All of a sudden Saul hurled a spear at David, attempting to kill him. And note, this was not the only attempt on this particular day. While David was playing the harp for Saul, attempting to calm his episode of insanity, Saul again attempted to kill him. But David eluded him both times. This is a strong testimony to the loyalty and commitment of David to whatever task was assigned him. He was loyal to Saul and committed to helping the king overcome his episodes of insanity.

OUTLINE	SCRIPTURE	SCRIPTURE	OUTLINE
2. The first attempt to kill David: Bitter hatred, a spirit of rage & fury aroused by jealousy a. Saul was gripped by an evil spirit & began to prophesy—"rave[d] like a mad-	10 And it came to pass on the morrow, that the evil spirit from God came upon Saul, and he prophesied in the midst of the house: and David played with his hand, as at other times: and *there was a*	javelin in Saul's hand. 11 And Saul cast the javelin; for he said, I will smite David even to the wall *with it.* And David avoided out of his presence twice.	man," NLT b. Saul attempted to kill David: Threw his spear at David twice, but David escaped

Thought 1. Saul's jealousy aroused a spirit of bitter hatred against David. Hatred can consume the soul as much as the most dangerous cancer can consume the body. Hatred will cause all kinds of strife and problems, destroying relationships within families, businesses, communities, and nations, as well as among co-workers, neighbors, and schoolmates. Hatred can cause various problems such as...

- abuse
- assault
- murder
- lies and rumors
- theft
- loss of property
- loss of employment
- broken friendships
- ulcers
- depression
- revenge
- insanity

The problems created by bitter hatred are innumerable. Listen to what the Word of God says about hatred:

> "For John had said unto Herod, It is not lawful for thee to have thy brother's wife. Therefore Herodias had a quarrel against him, and would have killed him; but she could not" (Mk.6:18-19).

"And they were filled with madness; and communed one with another what they might do to Jesus" (Lu.6:11).

"And when it was day, certain of the Jews banded together, and bound themselves under a curse, saying that they would neither eat nor drink till they had killed Paul" (Ac.23:12).

"He that saith he is in the light, and hateth his brother, is in darkness even until now" (1 Jn.2:9).

"Whosoever hateth his brother is a murderer: and ye know that no murderer hath eternal life abiding in him" (1 Jn.3:15).

"If a man say, I love God, and hateth his brother, he is a liar: for he that loveth not his brother whom he hath seen, how can he love God whom he hath not seen" (1 Jn.4:20).

"And Esau hated Jacob because of the blessing wherewith his father blessed him: and Esau said in his heart, The days of mourning for my father are at hand; then will I slay my brother Jacob" (Ge.27:41).

"And when his brethren saw that their father loved him more than all his brethren, they hated him, and could not speak peaceably unto him" (Ge.37:4).

"Thou shalt not hate thy brother in thine heart: thou shalt in any wise rebuke thy neighbour, and not suffer sin upon him" (Le.19:17).

"...then was Haman full of wrath. And he thought scorn to lay hands on Mordecai alone; for they had showed him the people of Mordecai: wherefore Haman sought to destroy all the Jews that *were* throughout the whole kingdom of Ahasuerus, *even* the people of Mordecai" (Esth.3:5-6).

"Hatred stirreth up strifes: but love covereth all sins" (Pr.10:12).

"Better *is* a dinner of herbs where love is, than a stalled ox and hatred therewith" (Pr.15:17).

3 (18:12-16) **Jealousy, Result of—Envy, Result of—Fear, Caused by, Jealousy—Division, Caused by, Jealousy—Plots – Schemes, Caused by, Jealousy—Saul, Attempts to Kill David**: there was the second attempt of Saul to kill David through a sinister plot. Saul's jealousy and suspicious nature aroused within his heart a deep-seated fear of David. Because of his fear he wanted David out of his presence, nowhere around. And if possible, he wanted David dead in order to remove him as a threat against his throne. Note why: because the LORD was with David but had abandoned Saul. In Saul's mind, David was a threat to Saul's claim to the throne and to the dynasty he hoped to establish through Jonathan. Thus Saul used a sinister tactic in an attempt to kill David: he made David the commander of 1000 troops, sending him out to fight risky battles, hoping that David would lose and be discredited by the people or else be killed in battle (vv.13, 17).

But note the result: David succeeded in every battle and in everything else he did because the LORD was with him (vv.14-16). And David's success only made Saul fear him even more. On the other hand, David's success in military campaigns stirred the people to love him more and more.

OUTLINE	SCRIPTURE	SCRIPTURE	OUTLINE
3. The second attempt to kill David: Fear, division, & a sinister plot aroused by jealousy a. Saul was abandoned by God b. Saul used a sinister tactic to try to kill David: Sent David to fight risky battles, hoping he would lose & be discredited or killed	12 And Saul was afraid of David, because the LORD was with him, and was departed from Saul. 13 Therefore Saul removed him from him, and made him his captain over a thousand; and he went out and came in before the people.	14 And David behaved himself wisely in all his ways; and the LORD *was* with him. 15 Wherefore when Saul saw that he behaved himself very wisely, he was afraid of him. 16 But all Israel and Judah loved David, because he went out and came in before them.	c. The result: David succeeded in everything because the LORD was with him 1) Saul feared David even more 2) All Israel loved David even more

Thought 1. Jealousy or envy will cause fear and division between people. Naturally, if a person is envious of someone else, there is division between the two and sometimes fear. Being afraid of what the envious person will do often becomes a problem. For an envious person may lie, steal, or cheat to get what he or she wants. Envy may lead a person to slander, ridicule, persecute, abuse, assault, and even murder to get what he or she wants. If a person is envious of us, he may be a threat to us and arouse fear within us. But this is not the way God intends us to live. We are not to be jealous or envious of one another. Neither are we to live in fear and division with one another. We have already dealt with jealousy and envy in point one. Now, we need to see what God has to say about fear and division:

"But he, knowing their thoughts, said unto them, Every kingdom divided against itself is brought to desolation; and a house *divided* against a house falleth" (Lu.11:17).

"Nevertheless among the chief rulers also many believed on him; but because of the Pharisees they did not confess *him,* lest they should be put out of the synagogue" (Jn.12:42).

"Now I beseech you, brethren, by the name of our Lord Jesus Christ, that ye all speak the same thing, and *that* there be no divisions among you; but *that* ye be perfectly joined together in the same mind and in the same judgment" (1 Co.1:10).

"For ye are yet carnal: for whereas *there is* among you envying, and strife, and divisions, are ye not carnal, and walk as men" (1 Co.3:3).

"Finally, brethren, farewell. Be perfect, be of good comfort, be of one mind, live in peace; and the God of love and peace shall be with you" (2 Co.13:11).

"For before that certain came from James, he did eat with the Gentiles: but when they were come, he withdrew and separated himself, fearing them which were of the circumcision" (Ga.2:12).

"For God hath not given us the spirit of fear; but of power, and of love, and of a sound mind" (2 Ti.1:7).

"Finally, be ye all of one mind, having compassion one of another, love as brethren, be pitiful, be courteous" (1 Pt.3:8).

"Ye shall not respect persons in judgment; *but* ye shall hear the small as well as the great; ye shall not be afraid of the face of man; for the judgment *is* God's: and the cause that is too hard for you, bring *it* unto me, and I will hear it" (De.1:17).

"The LORD *is* my light and my salvation; whom shall I fear? the LORD *is* the strength of my life; of whom shall I be afraid? When the wicked, *even* mine enemies and my foes, came upon me to eat up my flesh, they stumbled and fell. Though an host should encamp against me, my heart shall not fear: though war should rise against me, in this *will* I *be* confident" (Ps.27:1-3).

"I will say of the LORD, *He is* my refuge and my fortress: my God; in him will I trust. Surely he shall deliver thee from the snare of the fowler, *and* from the noisome pestilence. He shall cover thee with his feathers, and under his wings shalt thou trust: his truth *shall be thy* shield and buckler. Thou shalt not be afraid for the terror by night; *nor* for the arrow *that* flieth by day; *Nor* for the pestilence *that* walketh in darkness; *nor* for the destruction *that* wasteth at noonday" (Ps.91:2-6).

"The LORD *is* on my side; I will not fear: what can man do unto me" (Ps.118:6).

"The fear of man bringeth a snare: but whoso putteth his trust in the LORD shall be safe" (Pr.29:25).

"I, *even* I, *am* he that comforteth you: who *art* thou, that thou shouldest be afraid of a man *that* shall die, and of the son of man *which* shall be made as grass" (Is.51:12).

---

4 (18:17-19) **Lies, Caused by—Deception, Caused by—Jealousy, Results of—David, Attempts Against His Life— Saul, Attempts to Kill David**: there was the third attempt by Saul to kill David, a sinister attempt that was based upon lies and deception. Sometime after David had been promoted to commander in the armed forces, Saul promised to give his older daughter Merab to David if he proved himself in battle against the Philistines (v.17). Remember, however, that Saul had earlier promised his oldest daughter to the man who killed Goliath (17:25). By right David was already entitled to have Merab's hand in marriage, but now Saul was making their marriage dependent upon David's being engaged in several more armed conflicts. Note why: Saul wanted David exposed to armed conflict in order that he might be killed in battle (v.17). To Saul, David was his archrival, a very serious threat to his throne and dynasty; consequently, he wanted David eliminated.

Note David's humble response to the offer of Saul's daughter in marriage: he was not worthy of such honor, the honor of being a part of the king's family (v.18; see v.23).

The depth of Saul's antagonism toward David is clearly seen in what now happened: he broke this promise to David for a second time. He gave Merab in marriage to Adriel (vv.19; 17:25). From the very first day that the people honored David more than Saul, Saul had determined to kill David and eliminate what he perceived to be a threat against his throne. Thus he never intended to give his daughter's hand in marriage to David. He was only lying to and deceiving David, using his daughter as the bait to expose David to armed conflict in order that he might be killed.

OUTLINE	SCRIPTURE	SCRIPTURE	OUTLINE
4. The third attempt to kill David: Lies & deception aroused by jealousy a. The deceptive promise of Saul: To give his daughter to David if he proved himself in battle b. The purpose of Saul: To expose David to armed conflict so he might be killed c. The response & humility of	17 And Saul said to David, Behold my elder daughter Merab, her will I give thee to wife: only be thou valiant for me, and fight the LORD'S battles. For Saul said, Let not mine hand be upon him, but let the hand of the Philistines be upon him. 18 And David said unto	Saul, Who *am* I? and what *is* my life, *or* my father's family in Israel, that I should be son in law to the king? 19 But it came to pass at the time when Merab Saul's daughter should have been given to David, that she was given unto Adriel the Meholathite to wife.	David: He was not worthy of such honor, the honor of marrying the princess & of being a part of the king's family d. The broken promise of Saul—for the second time (17:25): He gave his daughter Merab in marriage to Adriel

Thought 1. Jealousy or envy will give rise to lies and deception. If we are jealous or envious of a person, we may be tempted to lie and spread rumors in order to hurt and damage the reputation of the person and thereby gain an advantage over him. Or we might attempt to deceive the person in order to hurt him or to secure his property, wealth, position, or honor. If a person has something we want and we allow jealousy or envy to consume our hearts, covetousness will grip our souls. And covetousness will drive us to lie and deceive in order to secure whatever we desire.

Lies and deception hurt people, destroying reputations, families, businesses, civic clubs, and governments. Lies and deception cause all kinds of problems such as financial difficulties, loss of position or employment, broken relationships, divorce, low grades in school, and loss of friends. There is no end to the damage that lies and deception can cause. For this reason, the LORD warns us against lying to and deceiving others:

"Lie not one to another, seeing that ye have put off the old man with his deeds" (Col.3:9).

"But the fearful, and unbelieving, and the abominable, and murderers, and whoremongers, and sorcerers, and idolaters, and all liars, shall have their part in the lake which burneth with fire and brimstone: which is the second death" (Re.21:8).

"Ye shall not steal, neither deal falsely, neither lie one to another" (Le.19:11).

"Thou shalt destroy them that speak leasing [lying]: the LORD will abhor the bloody and deceitful man" (Ps.5:6).

"But the king shall rejoice in God; every one that sweareth by him shall glory: but the mouth of them that speak lies shall be stopped" (Ps.63:11).

"He that worketh deceit shall not dwell within my house: he that telleth lies shall not tarry in my sight" (Ps.101:7).

"Lying lips *are* abomination to the LORD: but they that deal truly *are* his delight" (Pr.12:22).

"A false witness shall not be unpunished, and *he that* speaketh lies shall not escape" (Pr.19:5).

"The getting of treasures by a lying tongue *is* a vanity tossed to and fro of them that seek death" (Pr.21:6).

5 (18:20-30) **Seduction, Caused by—Evil Influence, Caused by—Enticement, Caused by—Jealousy, Results of—David, Attempts Against His Life—Saul, Attempts to Kill David**: there was the fourth attempt by Saul to kill David, an attempt that revolved around seduction and evil influence. When the Philistines failed to kill David, Saul was determined more than ever to eliminate this rival to his throne. One day Saul noticed an event that caught his eye, some interaction between his daughter Michal and David that indicated Michal was in love with David. Always looking for a way to get rid of David, Saul saw yet another opportunity to plot his death. The Scripture and outline paint a startling picture of Saul's sinister plot:

OUTLINE	SCRIPTURE	SCRIPTURE	OUTLINE
5. The fourth attempt to kill David: Seduction & evil influence aroused by jealousy a. Saul's seductive plot 1) Plotted to use his younger daughter's love for David as a snare • By having her seduce & corrupt David spiritually (19:13) • The result: God's protection would be removed 2) Offered Michal in marriage to David 3) Sent attendants to speak confidentially with David—seducing, enticing him with misinformation, lies b. David's rejection of the marriage proposal 1) He lacked the wealth to pay the dowry 2) He lacked the social status c. Saul's second seductive offer to David 1) David could earn the dowry, the "bride price," for Saul's daughter by killing 100 Philistines 2) Saul's hidden motive &	20 And Michal Saul's daughter loved David: and they told Saul, and the thing pleased him. 21 And Saul said, I will give him her, that she may be a snare to him, and that the hand of the Philistines may be against him. Wherefore Saul said to David, Thou shalt this day be my son in law in *the one of* the twain. 22 And Saul commanded his servants, *saying,* Commune with David secretly, and say, Behold, the king hath delight in thee, and all his servants love thee: now therefore be the king's son in law. 23 And Saul's servants spake those words in the ears of David. And David said, Seemeth it to you *a light thing* to be a king's son in law, seeing that I *am* a poor man, and lightly esteemed? 24 And the servants of Saul told him, saying, On this manner spake David. 25 And Saul said, Thus shall ye say to David, The king desireth not any dowry, but an hundred foreskins of the Philistines, to be avenged of the	king's enemies. But Saul thought to make David fall by the hand of the Philistines. 26 And when his servants told David these words, it pleased David well to be the king's son in law: and the days were not expired. 27 Wherefore David arose and went, he and his men, and slew of the Philistines two hundred men; and David brought their foreskins, and they gave them in full tale to the king, that he might be the king's son in law. And Saul gave him Michal his daughter to wife. 28 And Saul saw and knew that the LORD *was* with David, and *that* Michal Saul's daughter loved him. 29 And Saul was yet the more afraid of David; and Saul became David's enemy continually. 30 Then the princes of the Philistines went forth: and it came to pass, after they went forth, *that* David behaved himself more wisely than all the servants of Saul; so that his name was much set by.	secret hope: That David would be killed in battle d. David's acceptance of the terms 1) David agreed to become the king's son-in-law 2) David went out & exceeded the terms before the deadline, killing 200 Philistines e. David's exploits resulted in fulfillment of the terms 1) Saul was forced to give his daughter in marriage to David 2) Saul realized the LORD was with David & his daughter truly loved him 3) Saul feared David even more & went beyond repentance, beyond ever changing f. David's continued success in battle & in becoming more famous

a. The seductive scheme of Saul was to use his daughter's love for David as a snare against David (vv.20-22). Saul's sinister plot included his daughter's hand in marriage to David, hoping that she would seduce and corrupt David with her idolatrous worship and false gods. If David began to engage in idolatry and false worship, the judgment of God would fall upon him. David's success would begin to decline and he would begin to lose popularity with the people and perhaps even be killed in battle. God would not bless David if he was engaging in false worship; God's protection would be removed from his life.

Saul sent some attendants to speak confidentially with David, seducing and enticing him with lies and misinformation (v.22). They told David that Saul liked him and really wanted him to become his son-in-law.

b. Again David rejected the marriage proposed by Saul (v.23). His reason was the same as before: he did not have the wealth needed to marry the king's daughter, to pay the dowry that would be required. Neither did he have the social status to marry a princess. But Saul was not about to give up in his attempt to snare and eliminate David.

c. Saul made a second seductive offer to David: David could earn the dowry, the "bride price," for Saul's daughter by killing 100 Philistines (vv.24–25). But note, David would have to prove that he had killed that many soldiers by presenting the foreskins to King Saul. Of course, Saul's hidden motive and secret hope was that David would be killed in battle.

d. David accepted the terms laid down by Saul, agreeing to become his son-in-law by marrying his daughter. He went out against the Philistines and actually exceeded the terms of the agreements before the deadline, killing not 100 of the enemy, but 200 soldiers.

e. The results of David's surprising exploit were threefold:
⇒ Saul was forced to give his daughter in marriage to David (v.27).
⇒ Saul realized that the LORD was with David and that his daughter truly loved him (v.28).
⇒ Saul began to fear David even more and went beyond repentance, beyond ever changing (v.29). In Saul's mind, David was to remain his enemy for the rest of his days, which means that Saul was to stand permanently opposed to God. Saul would never repent, never change from seeking to kill David, the man he perceived to be a serious threat to his throne and dynasty.

f. Nevertheless David continued to win battle after battle against the Philistines, being far more successful than any other military officers. As a result, David's name became known more and more throughout the land. He became a heroic warrior, highly esteemed and acclaimed by the people (v.30).

Thought 1. Saul had plotted to use the evil influence of his daughter to seduce and corrupt David. He had wanted her to influence and encourage David to participate in her false worship. By her evil influence, he hoped to destroy David's spiritual life, his witness and testimony for God.

This is a strong warning for us: we must stand against all seduction and evil influence and associations that might corrupt us. God's Word is clear: we live *in the world*, but we must not be a part *of the world*. Spiritually, we are to be separated from the world and its evil influences and associations. We are not to participate in the evil, corrupt, wicked ways of the world. This is the clear teaching of God's Holy Word:

"**And take heed to yourselves, lest at any time your hearts be overcharged with surfeiting, and drunkenness, and cares of this life, and so that day come upon you unawares**" (Lu.21:34).

"**And be not conformed to this world: but be ye transformed by the renewing of your mind, that ye may prove what is that good, and acceptable, and perfect, will of God**" (Ro.12:2).

"**But now I have written unto you not to keep company, if any man that is called a brother be a fornicator, or covetous, or an idolater, or a railer, or a drunkard, or an extortioner; with such an one no not to eat**" (1 Co.5:11).

"**Be not deceived: evil communications [companionships] corrupt good manners**" (1 Co.15:33).

"**Be ye not unequally yoked together with unbelievers: for what fellowship hath righteousness with unrighteousness? and what communion hath light with darkness? And what concord hath Christ with Belial? or what part hath he that believeth with an infidel? And what agreement hath the temple of God with idols? for ye are the temple of the living God; as God hath said, I will dwell in them, and walk in** *them;* **and I will be their God, and they shall be my people**" (2 Co.6:14-16).

"**Wherefore come out from among them, and be ye separate, saith the LORD, and touch not the unclean** *thing;* **and I will receive you, And will be a Father unto you, and ye shall be my sons and daughters, saith the LORD Almighty**" (2 Co.6:17-18).

"**And have no fellowship with the unfruitful works of darkness, but rather reprove** *them*" (Ep.5:11).

"**Now we command you, brethren, in the name of our Lord Jesus Christ, that ye withdraw yourselves from every brother that walketh disorderly, and not after the tradition which he received of us**" (2 Th.3:6).

"**Thou therefore endure hardness, as a good soldier of Jesus Christ. No man that warreth entangleth himself with the affairs of** *this* **life; that he may please him who hath chosen him to be a soldier**" (2 Ti.2:3-4).

"**Love not the world, neither the things** *that are* **in the world. If any man love the world, the love of the Father is not in him. For all that** *is* **in the world, the lust of the flesh, and the lust of the eyes, and the pride of life, is not of the Father, but is of the world**" (1 Jn.2:15-16).

"**Thou shalt not follow a multitude to** *do* **evil; neither shalt thou speak in a cause to decline after many to wrest** *judgment*" (Ex.23:2).

"**Blessed** *is* **the man that walketh not in the counsel of the ungodly, nor standeth in the way of sinners, nor sitteth in the seat of the scornful**" (Ps.1:1).

"**Be not thou envious against evil men, neither desire to be with them**" (Pr.24:1).

"**Depart ye, depart ye, go ye out from thence, touch no unclean** *thing;* **go ye out of the midst of her; be ye clean, that bear the vessels of the LORD**" (Is.52:11).

1. The fifth attempt to kill David: Jealousy counteracted by friendship & brotherly love

a. Saul ordered Jonathan & his servants to kill David

b. Jonathan warned David of the assassination plot

   1) By revealing the time & suggesting that he escape

   2) By assuring David that he would intervene, plead David's case before his father

c. Jonathan urged Saul to reverse his conspiracy to kill David

   1) Because David was innocent

   2) Because David had helped Saul greatly by killing a feared enemy (Goliath & the Philistines, 17:55-58)

   3) Because the LORD was with David, & Saul would be committing a terrible evil: Shedding innocent blood

d. Saul listened to Jonathan & pledged not to kill David

e. Jonathan informed David of the reconciliation & brought him back to the royal court

2. The sixth attempt to kill David: An evil & murderous assault aroused by jealousy

a. David was again victorious in battle against the Philistines

b. Saul was again overcome by an evil spirit

   1) David was playing the harp for Saul

   2) Saul tried to kill David with his spear

CHAPTER 19

D. The Story of Saul's Jealous Rage & Attempts to Kill David (Part 2): A Look at the Evil of Jealousy & Envy, 19:1-24

And Saul spake to Jonathan his son, and to all his servants, that they should kill David.
2 But Jonathan Saul's son delighted much in David: and Jonathan told David, saying, Saul my father seeketh to kill thee: now therefore, I pray thee, take heed to thyself until the morning, and abide in a secret *place,* and hide thyself:
3 And I will go out and stand beside my father in the field where thou *art,* and I will commune with my father of thee; and what I see, that I will tell thee.
4 And Jonathan spake good of David unto Saul his father, and said unto him, Let not the king sin against his servant, against David; because he hath not sinned against thee, and because his works *have been* to thee-ward very good:
5 For he did put his life in his hand, and slew the Philistine, and the LORD wrought a great salvation for all Israel: thou sawest *it,* and didst rejoice: wherefore then wilt thou sin against innocent blood, to slay David without a cause?
6 And Saul hearkened unto the voice of Jonathan: and Saul sware, *As* the LORD liveth, he shall not be slain.
7 And Jonathan called David, and Jonathan showed him all those things. And Jonathan brought David to Saul, and he was in his presence, as in times past.
8 And there was war again: and David went out, and fought with the Philistines, and slew them with a great slaughter; and they fled from him.
9 And the evil spirit from the LORD was upon Saul, as he sat in his house with his javelin in his hand: and David played with *his* hand.
10 And Saul sought to smite David even to the wall with the javelin; but he slipped

away out of Saul's presence, and he smote the javelin into the wall: and David fled, and escaped that night.
11 Saul also sent messengers unto David's house, to watch him, and to slay him in the morning: and Michal David's wife told him, saying, If thou save not thy life to night, to morrow thou shalt be slain.
12 So Michal let David down through a window: and he went, and fled, and escaped.
13 And Michal took an image, and laid *it* in the bed, and put a pillow of goats' *hair* for his bolster, and covered *it* with a cloth.
14 And when Saul sent messengers to take David, she said, He *is* sick.
15 And Saul sent the messengers *again* to see David, saying, Bring him up to me in the bed, that I may slay him.
16 And when the messengers were come in, behold, *there was* an image in the bed, with a pillow of goats' *hair* for his bolster.
17 And Saul said unto Michal, Why hast thou deceived me so, and sent away mine enemy, that he is escaped? And Michal answered Saul, He said unto me, Let me go; why should I kill thee?
18 So David fled, and escaped, and came to Samuel to Ramah, and told him all that Saul had done to him. And he and Samuel went and dwelt in Naioth.
19 And it was told Saul, saying, Behold, David *is* at Naioth in Ramah.
20 And Saul sent messengers to take David: and when they saw the company of the prophets prophesying, and Samuel standing *as* appointed over them, the Spirit of God was upon the messengers of Saul, and they also prophesied.
21 And when it was told Saul, he sent other messengers, and they prophesied likewise. And Saul sent messengers again the third time, and they prophesied also.
22 Then went he also to Ramah, and came to a great well that *is* in Sechu: and he asked and said, Where *are*

c. David eluded Saul & escaped

3. The seventh attempt to kill David: Family strife & division aroused by jealousy

a. Saul sent some men to watch David's house & to kill him

b. Michal warned David & helped him escape

   1) Let him down through a window

   2) Put an idol under the bed coverings to deceive the assassins

   3) Claimed that David was ill, unable to get up

c. Saul sent the assassins back to arrest David, even if he was ill

d. Michal's deception was discovered by the men

e. Saul questioned Michal about her deception

   1) Saul's question: Why had she deceived him?

   2) Michal's response: David had threatened her, forced her to lie

4. The eighth attempt to kill David: Repeated rebellion against God's Spirit aroused by jealousy

a. David fled & went to seek counsel from Samuel

b. Saul heard that David was with Samuel in Naioth at Ramah

c. God's Spirit protected David

   1) Saul sent men to capture David

   • They saw a group of prophets prophesying under Samuel's leadership

   • They themselves were stricken by the Spirit of God & began to prophesy

   2) Saul sent a second & third group of men to arrest David: They too were stricken by God's Spirit & began to prophesy

   3) Saul himself left for Ramah & discovered that David & Samuel had gone to Naioth

• Saul was overcome by God's Spirit & gripped by a trance of prophesying as he walked along, traveling to Naioth	Samuel and David? And *one* said, Behold, *they be* at Naioth in Ramah. 23 And he went thither to Naioth in Ramah: and the Spirit of God was upon him also, and he went on, and prophesied, until he came to	Naioth in Ramah. 24 And he stript off his clothes also, and prophesied before Samuel in like manner, and lay down naked all that day and all that night. Wherefore they say, *Is* Saul also among the prophets?	• Saul stripped off his royal robes & prophesied before Samuel, lying that way all day & night: A symbol of God's Spirit stripping Saul of his throne

DIVISION III

THE STORY OF SAUL AND DAVID (PART 1): THE LORD GIVES ISRAEL A KING "AFTER HIS OWN HEART," 16:1–20:42

D. The Story of Saul's Jealous Rage and Attempts to Kill David (Part 2): A Look at the Evil of Jealousy and Envy, 19:1-24

(19:1-24) **Introduction—Jealousy, Example of—Paranoia, Example of—David, Threats Against, by Saul**: this passage is a continuation of the former Scripture, chapter 18. Because of David's popularity with both the army and the citizens of the nation, Saul perceived David to be a serious threat to his throne and dynasty. Consequently, Saul continued to scheme and plot, laying plan after plan to secretly assassinate David or to openly execute him. The king was driven by an insane, paranoid jealousy over David's success and his public acclaim by the people. This is: *The Story of Saul's Jealous Rage and Attempts to Kill David (Part 2): A Look at the Evil of Jealousy and Envy,* 19:1-24.

1. The fifth attempt to kill David: jealousy counteracted by friendship and brotherly love (vv.1-7).
2. The sixth attempt to kill David: an evil and murderous assault aroused by jealousy (vv.8-10).
3. The seventh attempt to kill David: family strife and division aroused by jealousy (vv.11-17).
4. The eighth attempt to kill David: repeated rebellion against God's Spirit aroused by jealousy (vv.18-24).

1 (19:1-7) **Jealousy, How to Conquer—Envy, How to Conquer—Friendship, Example of—Brotherly Love, Example of—David, Attempts Against His Life—Saul, Attempts to Kill David**: there was the fifth attempt by Saul to kill David. This particular attempt was counteracted by Jonathan's close friendship with David and the brotherly love that existed between the two.

OUTLINE	SCRIPTURE	SCRIPTURE	OUTLINE
1. The fifth attempt to kill David: Jealousy counteracted by friendship & brotherly love a. Saul ordered Jonathan & his servants to kill David b. Jonathan warned David of the assassination plot 1) By revealing the time & suggesting that he escape 2) By assuring David that he would intervene, plead David's case before his father c. Jonathan urged Saul to reverse his conspiracy to kill David 1) Because David was innocent	And Saul spake to Jonathan his son, and to all his servants, that they should kill David. 2 But Jonathan Saul's son delighted much in David: and Jonathan told David, saying, Saul my father seeketh to kill thee: now therefore, I pray thee, take heed to thyself until the morning, and abide in a secret *place,* and hide thyself: 3 And I will go out and stand beside my father in the field where thou *art,* and I will commune with my father of thee; and what I see, that I will tell thee. 4 And Jonathan spake good of David unto Saul his father, and said unto him, Let not the king sin against his servant,	against David; because he hath not sinned against thee, and because his works *have* been to thee-ward very good: 5 For he did put his life in his hand, and slew the Philistine, and the LORD wrought a great salvation for all Israel: thou sawest *it,* and didst rejoice: wherefore then wilt thou sin against innocent blood, to slay David without a cause? 6 And Saul hearkened unto the voice of Jonathan: and Saul sware, *As* the LORD liveth, he shall not be slain. 7 And Jonathan called David, and Jonathan showed him all those things. And Jonathan brought David to Saul, and he was in his presence, as in times past.	2) Because David had helped Saul greatly by killing a feared enemy (Goliath & the Philistines, 17:55-58) 3) Because the LORD was with David, & Saul would be committing a terrible evil: Shedding innocent blood d. Saul listened to Jonathan & pledged not to kill David e. Jonathan informed David of the reconciliation & brought him back to the royal court

a. Saul now publicly ordered the killing of David, charging his own son Jonathan and all his attendants to assassinate David (v.1). Up to this point, Saul's attempts had apparently not been publicly known. Saul's sinister plots to kill David had been borne in his own mind, and the first attempt against David's life had actually been carried out by the hand of Saul himself (18:10-11). After his own personal failure to murder David, Saul crafted a scheme to have David murdered in what would appear to be a natural, normal consequence, that of engaging in armed conflict (18:12-19). When the Philistines failed to kill David, he attempted to manipulate David's relationship with God Himself in order to corrupt David (v.20). Every attempt had failed, and Saul's fear of David's threat to the throne now totally consumed him. Saul had acted so wickedly for so long that he was now beyond repentance, beyond ever changing (18:29). He was consumed with jealousy toward David and hated him with bitter animosity. Consequently, he gave the explicit order to his son Jonathan and to all his attendants: kill David.

b. But note what happened: Jonathan warned David of the assassination plot (vv.1-3). Remember, Jonathan and David had earlier made a permanent covenant of friendship, a promise of loyalty and help in meeting each other's needs and looking after each other's welfare (18:3-4; 19:2-3; 20:8, 13-16, 41-42; 23:17-18). Jonathan revealed the actual time of the assassination attempt and suggested a way for David to escape. He assured David that he would intervene, pleading David's case before his father.

c. Jonathan urged his father Saul to reverse his conspiracy to kill David (vv.4-5). Declaring David's innocence, he reminded his father of the great service David had performed for the king and the nation. It was, after all, David who had killed Goliath and motivated the Israelites to defeat the oppressive Philistines (17:55-58). Also there was a clear, undeniable fact that King Saul knew: the LORD was with David, and Saul would be committing a terrible evil if he killed David, that of shedding innocent blood (v.5).

d. Saul listened to the logical reasoning of Jonathan, agreed, and pledged not to kill David (v.6).

e. Excitedly, Jonathan rushed to inform David of the reconciliation (v.7). And note, Jonathan brought David before Saul and the relationship was restored, at least temporarily.

Thought 1. One thing will counteract jealousy and envy: a close bond of friendship, brotherly love. Loving one's neighbor as oneself will help prevent and erase a spirit of jealousy and envy. If two people are close friends, they help and encourage one another. They are loyal to one another, standing ready to help and to meet the needs of the other when facing trial or temptation. They are always looking after the welfare of each other, sharing together and building each other up, encouraging and praising and strengthening one another. This is the kind of world God wants us to have: families, communities, societies, and nations that are closely bound together in friendship and brotherly love.

"And the second *is* like unto it, Thou shalt love thy neighbour as thyself" (Mt.22:39).

"A new commandment I give unto you, That ye love one another; as I have loved you, that ye also love one another. By this shall all *men* know that ye are my disciples, if ye have love one to another" (Jn.13:34-35).

"This is my commandment, That ye love one another, as I have loved you" (Jn.15:12).

"Greater love hath no man than this, that a man lay down his life for his friends. Ye are my friends, if ye do whatsoever I command you" (Jn.15:13-14).

"*Let* love be without dissimulation [hypocrisy]. Abhor that which is evil; cleave to that which is good" (Ro.12:9).

"And the LORD make you to increase and abound in love one toward another, and toward all *men*, even as we *do* toward you" (1 Th.3:12).

"But as touching brotherly love ye need not that I write unto you: for ye yourselves are taught of God to love one another" (1 Th.4:9).

"Seeing ye have purified your souls in obeying the truth through the Spirit unto unfeigned love of the brethren, *see that ye* love one another with a pure heart fervently" (1 Pe.1:22).

"And above all things have fervent charity among yourselves: for charity shall cover the multitude of sins" (1 Pe.4:8).

"He that loveth his brother abideth in the light, and there is none occasion of stumbling in him" (1 Jn.2:10).

"And this commandment have we from him, That he who loveth God love his brother also" (1 Jn.4:21).

"Love ye therefore the stranger: for ye were strangers in the land of Egypt" (De.10:19).

"A friend loveth at all times, and a brother is born for adversity" (Pr.17:17).

"Thine own friend, and thy father's friend, forsake not; neither go into thy brother's house in the day of thy calamity: *for* better *is* a neighbour *that is* near than a brother far off" (Pr.27:10).

"Two *are* better than one; because they have a good reward for their labour. For if they fall, the one will lift up his fellow: but woe to him *that is* alone when he falleth; for *he hath* not another to help him up" (Ec.4:9-10).

2 (19:8-10) **Murder, Caused by—Jealousy, Result of—Assault, Caused by—David, Attempts Against His Life—Saul, Attempts to Kill David**: there was the sixth attempt by Saul to kill David, an evil and murderous assault aroused by his jealousy. Note the strong contrast between the character of David and Saul in this passage:

OUTLINE	SCRIPTURE	SCRIPTURE	OUTLINE
2. The sixth attempt to kill David: An evil & murderous assault aroused by jealousy a. David was again victorious in battle against the Philistines b. Saul was again overcome by an evil spirit 1) David was playing the harp for Saul	8 And there was war again: and David went out, and fought with the Philistines, and slew them with a great slaughter; and they fled from him. 9 And the evil spirit from the LORD was upon Saul, as he sat in his house with his	javelin in his hand: and David played with *his* hand. 10 And Saul sought to smite David even to the wall with the javelin; but he slipped away out of Saul's presence, and he smote the javelin into the wall: and David fled, and escaped that night.	2) Saul tried to kill David with his spear c. David eluded Saul & escaped

a. David's character is seen in his spirit of responsibility and loyalty to both Saul and the nation. Once more war broke out, and David was again victorious in battle against the Philistines (v.8). Apparently, he gained a quick and significant victory against them, for Scripture says that he struck them with such force that they were routed and fled for their lives.

b. Saul's character was exposed by the tormenting, evil spirit that again came upon him (vv.9-10). Most likely it had been David's recent victory over the Philistines that agitated Saul, arousing the spirit of insane jealousy and extreme paranoia within his heart. Note that David was playing the harp for him during this episode of insanity just as he had earlier done (18:10-11; also see 16:14-23). Sitting there holding a spear in his hand, Saul suddenly hurled the spear at David, attempting to kill him.

c. But just as before, David dodged out of the way and the spear went flying by. That night, David eluded Saul and escaped out of the city, fleeing for his life.

Thought 1. The Word of God teaches two striking, forceful lessons about murder:
(1) God forbids murder.

"For this, Thou shalt not commit adultery, Thou shalt not kill, Thou shalt not steal, Thou shalt not bear false witness, Thou shalt not covet; and if *there be* any other commandment, it is briefly comprehended in this saying, namely, Thou shalt love thy neighbour as thyself" (Ro.13:9).
"But let none of you suffer as a murderer, or *as* a thief, or *as* an evildoer, or as a busybody in other men's matters" (1 Pe.4:15).
"Thou shalt not kill" (Ex.20:13).

(2) The murderer will not inherit eternal life. A person who deliberately murders another person will not inherit the kingdom of God. Only one hope remains for the murderer: a genuine repentance, a complete turning away from the life of sin to the life of righteousness found only in the Lord Jesus Christ.

"For the wrath of God is revealed from heaven against all ungodliness and unrighteousness of men, who hold the truth in unrighteousness....Being filled with all unrighteousness, fornication, wickedness, covetousness, maliciousness; full of envy, murder, debate, deceit, malignity; whisperers, Backbiters, haters of God, despiteful, proud, boasters, inventors of evil things, disobedient to parents, Without understanding, covenantbreakers, without natural affection, implacable, unmerciful: Who knowing the judgment of God, that they which commit such things are worthy of death, not only do the same, but have pleasure in them that do them" (Ro.1:18, 29-32).
"Now the works of the flesh are manifest, which are *these;* Adultery, fornication, uncleanness, lasciviousness, Idolatry, witchcraft, hatred, variance, emulations, wrath, strife, seditions, heresies, Envyings, murders, drunkenness, revellings, and such like: of the which I tell you before, as I have also told *you* in time past, that they which do such things shall not inherit the kingdom of God" (Ga.5:19-21).
"Whosoever hateth his brother is a murderer: and ye know that no murderer hath eternal life abiding in him" (1 Jn.3:15).
"But the fearful, and unbelieving, and the abominable, and murderers, and whoremongers, and sorcerers, and idolaters, and all liars, shall have their part in the lake which burneth with fire and brimstone: which is the second death" (Re.21:8).

3 (19:11-17) **Strife, Caused by—Division, Caused by—Jealousy, Results of—David, Attempts Against His Life— Saul, Attempts to Kill David**: there was the seventh attempt to kill David, and this attempt caused strife and division between Saul and his daughter. A high crescendo of suspense and drama is reached in this pursuit to assassinate David:

OUTLINE	SCRIPTURE	SCRIPTURE	OUTLINE
3. The seventh attempt to kill David: Family strife & division aroused by jealousy a. Saul sent some men to watch David's house & to kill him b. Michal warned David & helped him escape 1) Let him down through a window 2) Put an idol under the bed coverings to deceive the assassins 3) Claimed that David was ill, unable to get up	11 Saul also sent messengers unto David's house, to watch him, and to slay him in the morning: and Michal David's wife told him, saying, If thou save not thy life to night, to morrow thou shalt be slain. 12 So Michal let David down through a window: and he went, and fled, and escaped. 13 And Michal took an image, and laid *it* in the bed, and put a pillow of goats' *hair* for his bolster, and covered *it* with a cloth. 14 And when Saul sent messengers to take David, she	said, He *is* sick. 15 And Saul sent the messengers *again* to see David, saying, Bring him up to me in the bed, that I may slay him. 16 And when the messengers were come in, behold, *there was* an image in the bed, with a pillow of goats' *hair* for his bolster. 17 And Saul said unto Michal, Why hast thou deceived me so, and sent away mine enemy, that he is escaped? And Michal answered Saul, He said unto me, Let me go; why should I kill thee?	c. Saul sent the assassins back to arrest David, even if he was ill d. Michal's deception was discovered by the men e. Saul questioned Michal about her deception 1) Saul's question: Why had she deceived him? 2) Michal's response: David had threatened her, forced her to lie

a. Saul sent some men to watch David's house throughout the night so that he could not escape out of the city. The men were ordered to kill David first thing in the morning (v.11).

b. But Michal's love for her husband was to override her father's sinister, evil plot. Michal warned David and helped him escape (vv.12-14). She helped him climb through an unguarded window, and David was able to flee unnoticed and escape. Michal then put an idol under the bed coverings to deceive the assassins when they questioned her. When morning arrived and the men entered the home to capture David, Michal claimed that David was ill and unable to get up (vv.13-14).

c. When the assassins returned to Saul, he sent them right back to arrest David, even if they had to bring him in his bed (v.15). In Saul's mind, absolutely nothing was going to keep him from killing David (v.15).

d. Naturally, when the men returned to arrest David, Michal's deception was discovered and she, instead of David, was hauled in before King Saul (v.16).

e. Standing in court before her father, Michal was ordered to give an account for her behavior. Why had she helped David, her father's enemy, to escape (v.17)? Michal's response was probably the only response that could have saved her life: that David had threatened her, forcing her to deceive and lie to the assassins.

Thought 1. Strife and division are terrible evils, causing all kinds of problems. If we are striving and reacting against a person, there can be no peace. There can be only...

- evil imaginations
- plotting of mischief
- destruction of property
- abuse
- divorce

- loss of employment
- financial difficulty
- mental problems
- emotional problems
- spiritual problems

- health problems
- murder
- assaults
- ridicule and mockery
- shame and guilt

Strife and division break relationships, destroy families, disrupt economies, cause financial difficulties, lead to the collapse of nations, and wreck lives. There is no end to the horrible, catastrophic destruction and tragedy caused by strife and division. God warns those who cause strife, dissension, and division:

> "But he, knowing their thoughts, said unto them, Every kingdom divided against itself is brought to desolation; and a house *divided* against a house falleth" (Lu.11:17).

> "For ye are yet carnal: for whereas *there is* among you envying, and strife, and divisions, are ye not carnal, and walk as men" (1 Co.3:3).

> "Now the works of the flesh are manifest, which are *these;* Adultery, fornication, uncleanness, lasciviousness, Idolatry, witchcraft, hatred, variance, emulations, wrath, strife, seditions, heresies, Envyings, murders, drunkenness, revellings, and such like: of the which I tell you before, as I have also told *you* in time past, that they which do such things shall not inherit the kingdom of God" (Ga.5:19-21).

> "*Let* nothing *be done* through strife or vainglory; but in lowliness of mind let each esteem other better than themselves" (Ph.2:3).

> "And the servant of the LORD must not strive; but be gentle unto all *men,* apt to teach, patient" (2 Ti.2:24).

> "Strive not with a man without cause, if he have done thee no harm" (Pr.3:30).

> "A wrathful man stirreth up strife: but *he that is* slow to anger appeaseth strife" (Pr.15:18).

> "He loveth transgression that loveth strife: *and* he that exalteth his gate seeketh destruction" (Pr.17:19).

> "A fool's lips enter into contention, and his mouth calleth for strokes" (Pr.18:6).

> "Go not forth hastily to strive, lest *thou know not* what to do in the end thereof, when thy neighbour hath put thee to shame" (Pr.25:8).

---

4 (19:18-24) **Rebellion, Caused by—Jealousy, Results of—David, Attempts Against His Life—Saul, Attempts to Kill David**: there was the eighth attempt by Saul to kill David, clear evidence of Saul's repeated rebellion against God's Spirit. Starting with these verses, David's days as a fugitive who is forced to flee for his life begin, and they continue on until Saul's death.[1] Never again during Saul's life would David return home. Suspense and drama again reach a climax in the scene described in these verses.

OUTLINE	SCRIPTURE	SCRIPTURE	OUTLINE
4. The eighth attempt to kill David: Repeated rebellion against God's Spirit aroused by jealousy a. David fled & went to seek counsel from Samuel b. Saul heard that David was with Samuel in Naioth at Ramah	18 So David fled, and escaped, and came to Samuel to Ramah, and told him all that Saul had done to him. And he and Samuel went and dwelt in Naioth. 19 And it was told Saul, saying, Behold, David *is* at Naioth in Ramah.	20 And Saul sent messengers to take David: and when they saw the company of the prophets prophesying, and Samuel standing *as* appointed over them, the Spirit of God was upon the messengers of Saul, and they also prophesied.	c. God's Spirit protected David 1) Saul sent men to capture David • They saw a group of prophets prophesying under Samuel's leadership • They themselves were stricken by the Spirit of God & began to prophesy

---

[1] Ronald F. Youngblood. *1 Samuel*, p.716.

OUTLINE	SCRIPTURE	SCRIPTURE	OUTLINE
2) Saul sent a second & third group of men to arrest David: They too were stricken by God's Spirit & began to prophesy 3) Saul himself left for Ramah & discovered that David & Samuel had gone to Naioth	21 And when it was told Saul, he sent other messengers, and they prophesied likewise. And Saul sent messengers again the third time, and they prophesied also. 22 Then went he also to Ramah, and came to a great well that *is* in Sechu: and he asked and said, Where *are* Samuel and David? And *one* said, Behold, *they be* at Naioth in Ramah.	23 And he went thither to Naioth in Ramah: and the Spirit of God was upon him also, and he went on, and prophesied, until he came to Naioth in Ramah. 24 And he stript off his clothes also, and prophesied before Samuel in like manner, and lay down naked all that day and all that night. Wherefore they say, *Is* Saul also among the prophets?	• Saul was overcome by God's Spirit & gripped by a trance of prophesying as he walked along, traveling to Naioth • Saul stripped off his royal robes & prophesied before Samuel, lying that way all day & night: A symbol of God's Spirit stripping Saul of his throne

a. After David had fled from his home and made his escape, he went to seek counsel from Samuel in the city of Ramah (v.18). Obviously, David needed encouragement, but he also needed guidance about what steps to take next. Note that Samuel took him to Naioth, which means *habitations* or *dwellings*. This refers to a complex of buildings, perhaps some religious center in the city of Ramah such as a school for the prophets that had been founded by Samuel (9:22).

b. Not long afterwards, Saul received a report that David was with Samuel in Naioth at Ramah (v.19).

c. But note how God's Spirit miraculously protected David, this dear servant of God, a servant who was now being pursued by the king as a fugitive (vv.20-24).

1) As soon as Saul learned of the whereabouts of David, he sent a platoon of soldiers to capture and arrest him (v.20). But when this platoon of soldiers entered the city, a strange thing happened. They saw a group of prophets prophesying under Samuel's leadership, and immediately, they too were stricken by the Spirit of God and compelled to join the prophets. They began to prophesy, that is, to behave and speak in an ecstatic manner.

2) But Saul's resolve to kill David was set, fixed in concrete; consequently, as soon as he heard about the incident, he sent a second and third group of men to capture and arrest David (v.21). But they too were stricken by God's Spirit and began to prophesy, acting and speaking in the very same ecstatic way.

3) Finally, more determined than ever to kill David, Saul himself left for Ramah, which was usually about a ninety minute journey[2] (v.22). When he reached the outskirts of the city, he stopped at a famous cistern to ask if anyone knew where Samuel and David might be found. Being told that they were still over in Naioth at Ramah, he undoubtedly headed straight for the religious center. But the Spirit of God was protecting David. Before Saul ever reached Naioth, the Spirit of God came upon him. And Saul was overcome and gripped by a trance of prophesying as he walked along, traveling toward David and Samuel (v.23). In an overwhelming show of power, the Spirit of God forced Saul to strip off his robes and to prophesy in Samuel's presence, lying prostrate upon the ground before the prophet all that day and night (v.24).

This was a clear symbol of God's Spirit stripping off Saul's claim to the throne of Israel. God's Spirit gave a powerful picture of God's judgment against Saul: Saul was rejected as king, stripped of his royal power. Never again would Saul be looked upon as the genuine king of Israel, nor would his prophesying be looked upon as a genuine experience as it had been earlier (10:10-12). The former proverb that acknowledged Saul's life-transforming experience—the proverb that asked if Saul was also among the prophets—now underwent an ironic twist. After this humiliating experience of stripping off his clothes by the overwhelming power of God's Spirit, the proverb thereafter questioned the genuineness of Saul's prophesying, his ecstatic speech and behavior.

Thought 1. Rebellion against God is a terrible offense, an evil that will lead to devastating results. If a person repeatedly commits evil and wickedness, God has no choice but to bring His hand of judgment down upon the person. Evil and wickedness doom a person, evil and wickedness such as...

• anger	• greed	• murder
• hostility	• adultery	• vulgarity
• bitterness	• illicit sex	• using God's name in vain
• hatred	• abuse	• idolatry
• covetousness	• assaults	• rejecting Jesus Christ

Man is appointed to die, and after death, appointed to face judgment. All who commit evil and wickedness—rebelling against God, forsaking and rejecting Him—will be doomed to that day of terrible judgment:

"But after thy hardness and impenitent heart treasurest up unto thyself wrath against the day of wrath and revelation of the righteous judgment of God" (Ro.2:5).

"And to you who are troubled rest with us, when the LORD Jesus shall be revealed from heaven with his mighty angels, In flaming fire taking vengeance on them that know not God, and that obey not the gospel of our Lord Jesus Christ" (2 Th.1:7-8).

"The LORD knoweth how to deliver the godly out of temptations, and to reserve the unjust unto the day of judgment to be punished" (2 Pe.2:9).

---

2 Robert D. Bergen. *1, 2 Samuel*, p.210.

"Behold, the Lord cometh with ten thousands of his saints, To execute judgment upon all, and to convince all that are ungodly among them of all their ungodly deeds which they have ungodly committed, and of all their hard *speeches* which ungodly sinners have spoken against him" (Jude 14-15).

"And he went out to meet Asa, and said unto him, Hear ye me, Asa, and all Judah and Benjamin; The Lord *is* with you, while ye be with him; and if ye seek him, he will be found of you; but if ye forsake him, he will forsake you" (2 Chr.15:2).

"He, that being often reproved hardeneth *his* neck, shall suddenly be destroyed, and that without remedy" (Pr.29:1).

"And I will utter my judgments against them touching all their wickedness, who have forsaken me, and have burned incense unto other gods, and worshipped the works of their own hands" (Je.1:16).

"Thou hast forsaken me, saith the Lord, thou art gone backward: therefore will I stretch out my hand against thee, and destroy thee; I am weary with repenting" (Je.15:6).

1. Jonathan's loyalty demanded a willingness to help in times of need

a. David fled to Jonathan: Questioned what wrong had he done against the king? Why was Saul trying to kill him?

b. Jonathan denied any knowledge of his father's breaking his oath of reconciliation with David: Insisted his father always confided in him

c. David swore that Saul was trying to kill him: Suggested that Saul had not confided in Jonathan because of their close friendship

d. Jonathan demonstrated strong loyalty to David: A willingness to help

e. David suggested a plan that would prove his charge against Saul
1) David would not attend a formal dinner engagement with Saul the next day: At the new moon festival
2) Saul would ask about David's absence & Jonathan would make an excuse for him: That David was attending an annual sacrifice for his family

   • If Saul accepted the excuse, David was safe
   • If Saul became angry, then Saul was set on killing him
3) David appealed to Jonathan not to betray him

2. Jonathan's loyalty demanded an unbreakable friendship, a spirit of brotherly love

CHAPTER 20

E. The Story of David & Jonathan's Friendship: A Lesson on Loyalty, 20:1-42

And David fled from Naioth in Ramah, and came and said before Jonathan, What have I done? what *is* mine iniquity? and what *is* my sin before thy father, that he seeketh my life?
2 And he said unto him, God forbid; thou shalt not die: behold, my father will do nothing either great or small, but that he will show it me: and why should my father hide this thing from me? it *is* not *so*.
3 And David sware moreover, and said, Thy father certainly knoweth that I have found grace in thine eyes; and he saith, Let not Jonathan know this, lest he be grieved: but truly *as* the LORD liveth, and *as* thy soul liveth, *there is* but a step between me and death.
4 Then said Jonathan unto David, Whatsoever thy soul desireth, I will even do *it* for thee.
5 And David said unto Jonathan, Behold, to morrow *is* the new moon, and I should not fail to sit with the king at meat: but let me go, that I may hide myself in the field unto the third *day* at even.
6 If thy father at all miss me, then say, David earnestly asked *leave* of me that he might run to Bethlehem his city: for *there is* a yearly sacrifice there for all the family.
7 If he say thus, *It is* well; thy servant shall have peace: but if he be very wroth, *then* be sure that evil is determined by him.
8 Therefore thou shalt deal kindly with thy servant; for thou hast brought thy servant into a covenant of the LORD with thee: notwithstanding, if there be in me iniquity, slay me thyself; for why shouldest thou bring me to thy father?
9 And Jonathan said, Far be it from thee: for if I knew certainly that evil were determined by my father to come upon thee, then would not I tell it thee?
10 Then said David to Jonathan, Who shall tell me? or what *if* thy father answer thee roughly?
11 And Jonathan said unto David, Come, and let us go out into the field. And they went out both of them into the field.
12 And Jonathan said unto David, O LORD God of Israel, when I have sounded my father about to morrow any time, *or* the third *day,* and, behold, *if there be* good toward David, and I then send not unto thee, and show it thee;
13 The LORD do so and much more to Jonathan: but if it please my father *to do* thee evil, then I will show it thee, and send thee away, that thou mayest go in peace: and the LORD be with thee, as he hath been with my father.
14 And thou shalt not only while yet I live show me the kindness of the LORD, that I die not:
15 But *also* thou shalt not cut off thy kindness from my house for ever: no, not when the LORD hath cut off the enemies of David every one from the face of the earth.
16 So Jonathan made *a covenant* with the house of David, *saying,* Let the LORD even require *it* at the hand of David's enemies.
17 And Jonathan caused David to swear again, because he loved him: for he loved him as he loved his own soul.
18 Then Jonathan said to David, To morrow *is* the new moon: and thou shalt be missed, because thy seat will be empty.
19 And *when* thou hast stayed three days, *then* thou shalt go down quickly, and come to the place where thou didst hide thyself when the business was *in hand,* and shalt remain by the stone Ezel.
20 And I will shoot three arrows on the side *thereof,* as though I shot at a mark.
21 And, behold, I will send a lad, *saying,* Go, find out

a. Jonathan strongly affirmed his loyalty

b. David asked exactly who would warn him of Saul's anger & pursuit

c. Jonathan led David over into a field & swore an oath to him: He would find out how Saul felt & get word to David

1) He would send word if Saul spoke favorably about him
2) He would warn him if Saul was angry & determined to kill David

d. Jonathan blessed David: Acknowledged that David, not he, was to become king

e. Jonathan made several requests of David
1) That David not kill him in a purge of Saul's family
2) That David not kill off his personal descendants in any future purge

3) That the LORD judge, condemn David's enemies

4) That David reaffirm the covenant between them: Because of their brotherly love for one another (Le.19:18)

f. Jonathan added details to the plan for notifying David
1) David would not attend the New Moon Festival & be missed
2) David—the day after tomorrow—would go to the place where he hid before & wait by the stone Ezel

3) Jonathan would come with a boy for some target practice: He would shoot three arrows as a signal

- If the arrows were shot short of the boy, this was a signal of safety

- If the arrows were shot beyond the boy, this was a signal of danger

4) Jonathan again challenged David to remember their covenant of commitment & friendship

3. Jonathan's loyalty demanded that he conquer jealousy & envy
a. David hid & did not attend the dinner of the New Moon Festival
b. Saul noticed David's absence at the dinner

1) He said nothing
2) He thought David had become ceremonially unclean: He needed to undergo the cleansing ritual
c. Saul noticed David's absence on the second day
1) He questioned Jonathan

2) Jonathan answered, giving the predetermined excuse

- That David had asked permission to observe a special family sacrifice in Bethlehem

- That he had granted David's request

d. Saul became inflamed, filled with hostility toward Jonathan
1) Called him the son of a perverse & rebellious woman
2) Accused him of siding with David, of bringing shame on himself & his family
3) Warned him that neither he nor his dynasty would

the arrows. If I expressly say unto the lad, Behold, the arrows are on this side of thee, take them; then come thou: for *there is* peace to thee, and no hurt; *as* the LORD liveth.
22 But if I say thus unto the young man, Behold, the arrows *are* beyond thee; go thy way: for the LORD hath sent thee away.
23 And *as touching* the matter which thou and I have spoken of, behold, the LORD *be* between thee and me for ever.
24 So David hid himself in the field: and when the new moon was come, the king sat him down to eat meat.
25 And the king sat upon his seat, as at other times, *even* upon a seat by the wall: and Jonathan arose, and Abner sat by Saul's side, and David's place was empty.
26 Nevertheless Saul spake not any thing that day: for he thought, Something hath befallen him, he is not clean; surely he *is* not clean.
27 And it came to pass on the morrow, *which was* the second *day* of the month, that David's place was empty: and Saul said unto Jonathan his son, Wherefore cometh not the son of Jesse to meat, neither yesterday, nor to day?
28 And Jonathan answered Saul, David earnestly asked *leave* of me *to go* to Bethlehem:
29 And he said, Let me go, I pray thee; for our family hath a sacrifice in the city; and my brother, he hath commanded me *to be there:* and now, if I have found favour in thine eyes, let me get away, I pray thee, and see my brethren. Therefore he cometh not unto the king's table.
30 Then Saul's anger was kindled against Jonathan, and he said unto him, Thou son of the perverse rebellious *woman,* do not I know that thou hast chosen the son of Jesse to thine own confusion, and unto the confusion of thy mother's nakedness?
31 For as long as the son of Jesse liveth upon the ground,

thou shalt not be established, nor thy kingdom. Wherefore now send and fetch him unto me, for he shall surely die.
32 And Jonathan answered Saul his father, and said unto him, Wherefore shall he be slain? what hath he done?
33 And Saul cast a javelin at him to smite him: whereby Jonathan knew that it was determined of his father to slay David.
34 So Jonathan arose from the table in fierce anger, and did eat no meat the second day of the month: for he was grieved for David, because his father had done him shame.
35 And it came to pass in the morning, that Jonathan went out into the field at the time appointed with David, and a little lad with him.
36 And he said unto his lad, Run, find out now the arrows which I shoot. *And* as the lad ran, he shot an arrow beyond him.
37 And when the lad was come to the place of the arrow which Jonathan had shot, Jonathan cried after the lad, and said, *Is* not the arrow beyond thee?
38 And Jonathan cried after the lad, Make speed, haste, stay not. And Jonathan's lad gathered up the arrows, and came to his master.
39 But the lad knew not any thing: only Jonathan and David knew the matter.
40 And Jonathan gave his artillery unto his lad, and said unto him, Go, carry *them* to the city.
41 *And* as soon as the lad was gone, David arose out of *a place* toward the south, and fell on his face to the ground, and bowed himself three times: and they kissed one another, and wept one with another, until David exceeded.
42 And Jonathan said to David, Go in peace, forasmuch as we have sworn both of us in the name of the LORD, saying, The LORD be between me and thee, and between my seed and thy seed for ever. And he arose and departed: and Jonathan went into the city.

ever be established as long as David lived
4) Commanded Jonathan to have David arrested
e. Jonathan responded by asking what crimes David had committed

f. Saul hurled his spear at Jonathan, attempting to kill his very own son

g. Jonathan jumped up & left in fierce anger, knowing the truth
1) Saul was set on killing David
2) Jonathan was so grieved that he could not eat because of Saul's treatment of his friend David

4. Jonathan's loyalty demanded that he keep his oath, his commitment, his promises
a. Jonathan kept his word: Went to the field where David was hiding & charged a young boy to run & find the arrows as he shot them

1) Jonathan shouted out to the boy the prearranged signal with David

- He added three sharp commands that applied to David & that David could not misunderstand

- The boy knew nothing about the prearranged signal

2) Jonathan sent the boy with his weapons back to town

b. David, surprisingly, came out of hiding
1) David humbled himself before Jonathan: Bowed three times, indicating subservience to the crown prince
2) They kissed each other & wept
3) Jonathan assured David of his friendship
- It was a sworn friendship
- It was sworn on the name of the LORD, a *covenant friendship*
- It included both them & their descendants
4) They separated, left the presence of one another

DIVISION III

THE STORY OF SAUL AND DAVID (PART 1): THE LORD GIVES ISRAEL A KING "AFTER HIS OWN HEART," 16:1-20:42

E. The Story of David and Jonathan's Friendship: A Lesson on Loyalty, 20:1-42

(20:1-42) **Introduction—Loyalty, Essential—Loyalty, Duty**: loyalty is an absolute essential in life. No matter the relationship, loyalty is a must. Without loyalty, a relationship crumbles:

⇒ If a husband and wife are not loyal, they face divorce and painful suffering for their children, other family members, friends, and themselves.
⇒ If a worker is not loyal to his employer, the company suffers and the employer loses his job.
⇒ If a company is not loyal to its worker, the worker loses his employment, income, and often retirement.
⇒ If a friend is not loyal, the friendship is severed and all the benefits gained from the friendship are lost.
⇒ If a teacher is not loyal to the student, the student fails to learn and to gain the knowledge he or she should gain.
⇒ If a student is not loyal to the teacher, a sense of alienation and division exists and both the teacher and student suffer.
⇒ If a politician is not loyal to the people he represents, the people suffer weak representation and often corruption in their government.
⇒ If the people are not loyal to their government, the government is weakened and either collapses or is unable to adequately carry out its functions.

Loyalty is the subject of the present passage of Scripture. And seldom in history has such loyalty existed as is described in this Scripture. This is: *The Story of David and Jonathan's Friendship: A Lesson on Loyalty*, 20:1-42.
1. Jonathan's loyalty demanded a willingness to help in times of need (vv.1-8).
2. Jonathan's loyalty demanded an unbreakable friendship, a spirit of brotherly love (vv.9-23).
3. Jonathan's loyalty demanded that he conquer jealousy and envy (vv.24-34).
4. Jonathan's loyalty demanded that he keep his oath, his commitment, his promises (vv.35-42).

1 (20:1-8) **Loyalty, Example of—Service, Example of—Helping, Example of—David, Relationship with Jonathan—Jonathan, Relationship with David—Need, Duty to Meet—Willingness, Essential in Service**: Jonathan's loyalty demanded a willingness to help in times of need. David was desperate: he needed help. In his desperate hour, would Jonathan help him? In the eyes of the public Jonathan was the heir to the throne, and David was a threat to Jonathan's claim to power. But the two young men had pledged, sworn an oath of friendship, that they would always be friends, looking after the welfare and meeting the needs of one another. Now their friendship was to be tested. Jonathan's father, King Saul, was fiercely pursuing David, seeking to kill him. Where would Jonathan stand? With his father? Or would he come to the aid of his close friend in his hour of desperate need? Jonathan had earlier made a commitment of loyalty to David. Now the depth of his commitment and loyalty was to be tested. Would he willingly help David in his hour of need? These questions are dramatically answered throughout this Scripture:

OUTLINE	SCRIPTURE	SCRIPTURE	OUTLINE
1. Jonathan's loyalty demanded a willingness to help in times of need a. David fled to Jonathan: Questioned what wrong had he done against the king? Why was Saul trying to kill him? b. Jonathan denied any knowledge of his father's breaking his oath of reconciliation with David: Insisted his father always confided in him c. David swore that Saul was trying to kill him: Suggested that Saul had not confided in Jonathan because of their close friendship	And David fled from Naioth in Ramah, and came and said before Jonathan, What have I done? what *is* mine iniquity? and what *is* my sin before thy father, that he seeketh my life? 2 And he said unto him, God forbid; thou shalt not die: behold, my father will do nothing either great or small, but that he will show it me: and why should my father hide this thing from me? it *is* not *so*. 3 And David sware moreover, and said, Thy father certainly knoweth that I have found grace in thine eyes; and he saith, Let not Jonathan know this, lest he be grieved: but truly *as* the LORD liveth, and *as* thy soul liveth, *there is* but a step between me and death.	4 Then said Jonathan unto David, Whatsoever thy soul desireth, I will even do *it* for thee. 5 And David said unto Jonathan, Behold, to morrow *is* the new moon, and I should not fail to sit with the king at meat: but let me go, that I may hide myself in the field unto the third *day* at even. 6 If thy father at all miss me, then say, David earnestly asked *leave* of me that he might run to Bethlehem his city: for *there is* a yearly sacrifice there for all the family. 7 If he say thus, *It is* well; thy servant shall have peace: but if he be very wroth, *then* be sure that evil is determined by him. 8 Therefore thou shalt deal	d. Jonathan demonstrated strong loyalty to David: A willingness to help e. David suggested a plan that would prove his charge against Saul 1) David would not attend a formal dinner engagement with Saul the next day: At the new moon festival 2) Saul would ask about David's absence & Jonathan would make an excuse for him: That David was attending an annual sacrifice for his family • If Saul accepted the excuse, David was safe • If Saul became angry, then Saul was set on killing him 3) David appealed to

OUTLINE	SCRIPTURE	SCRIPTURE	OUTLINE
Jonathan not to betray him	kindly with thy servant; for thou hast brought thy servant into a covenant of the LORD with thee: notwithstanding,	if there be in me iniquity, slay me thyself; for why shouldest thou bring me to thy father?	

a. David fled to Jonathan and questioned what wrong he had done against his father, King Saul. Why was Saul trying to kill him (v.1)? Remember that over the last two days Saul had attempted to kill David six times (19:9-24). Imagine six attempts to kill David in just two days! Shocking! Nevertheless, the six assassination attempts had been made, and the last attempt had almost succeeded. Narrowly escaping, David went to the only person he knew who might bring a reconciliation, who might be able to tell him what he had done against the king to arouse his anger so violently. Only Jonathan might know why Saul was trying to kill him. As quickly as he could ride, he fled from Naioth (the religious center or school) at Ramah and went directly to Jonathan, seeking his help and asking these questions.

b. Utterly surprised at David's questions, Jonathan denied knowledge of Saul's latest assassination attempts (v.2). And he gave assurance to David, insisting that his father always confided in him, even in the smallest matters. There was no chance that his father would hide such a serious matter from him. Keep in mind that Jonathan had been forced to intercede on David's behalf once before. On that particular occasion, Saul had sworn a solemn oath to stop his pursuit of David and not to kill him (19:1-7). Now Jonathan felt confident that if David had committed a crime that merited death, his father would have told him. In fact, just as before, his father would have commissioned Jonathan himself to arrest and execute David (19:1).

c. But David knew the truth, for the attempts against his life had occurred. Therefore David took an oath, swore that Saul was trying to kill him (v.3). He suggested that Saul had not confided in Jonathan because of Jonathan's close friendship with David. Saul kept his plan secret from Jonathan to protect Jonathan, to keep him from grieving.

d. Note the strong loyalty demonstrated by Jonathan. He was willing to help his close friend at any price (v.4). Jonathan was in a serious predicament: if his father was truly seeking to kill David, Jonathan was going to be hurt. For Jonathan would become alienated from his dear friend, losing their day-to-day companionship and close association. And neither Jonathan nor David wanted this to happen. They were the very closest of friends, and they were determined to keep their friendship alive and prove their loyalty to one another no matter the cost. For this reason, Jonathan strongly affirmed his loyalty to David. He was willing to help his friend, do whatever David wanted.

e. David suggested a plan that would prove his charge against Saul (vv.5-8). Note that this plan was primarily for the benefit of Jonathan, so that he could learn the truth of his father's intentions to kill David. But no doubt, David was hoping against hope that somehow Jonathan might be able to bring about a permanent reconciliation between the king and David.

David's plan was that he not attend a formal dinner engagement with Saul the next day (v.5). Apparently, the king held a formal dinner each month during the new moon festival. This festival was a religious event held on the first day of the month. It was celebrated by sacrificial offerings, the blowing of trumpets and rest from work especially in the seventh month (Le.23:24-25; Num.10:10; 28:11-15; 29:1-6; 2 Ki.4:23; Ps.81:3; Is.1:13; Amos 8:5).

By not attending the formal dinner, David knew that Saul would notice his absence and ask about it. Jonathan was to make a respectable excuse for David, stating that he was attending an annual sacrifice for his clan. After giving the excuse, Jonathan was to note Saul's reaction:
⇒ If Saul responded favorably, accepting David's absence, it would mean that Saul was at peace with David and that David was safe (v.7).
⇒ If Saul reacted in an outburst of anger, this would mean that Saul was as determined as ever to kill David.

David appealed to Jonathan not to betray him (v.8). He reminded Jonathan of the *covenant friendship* existing between them. And then in an outburst of deep emotion, David declared that he wanted Jonathan himself to kill him if he was guilty of a crime against King Saul. He would rather Jonathan kill him than betray him.

Thought 1. The lesson for us should be clearly understood: loyalty demands a willingness to help in times of need. When we are called upon, we must step forth and lend a helping hand. Friendship demands that we help our friends by being there for them:
⇒ listening to their problems
⇒ relieving their pain
⇒ sharing in their sufferings
⇒ lending a helping hand
⇒ offering provision and aid, whether food, clothing, housing, or finances

A loyal friend sticks closer than a brother. If we are truly loyal, there is a willingness within our hearts to help in times of need. Listen to what God's Holy Word says:

"Let your light so shine before men, that they may see your good works, and glorify your Father which is in heaven" (Mt.5:16).

"And whosoever shall give to drink unto one of these little ones a cup of cold *water* only in the name of a disciple, verily I say unto you, he shall in no wise lose his reward" (Mt.10:42).

"Even as the Son of man came not to be ministered unto, but to minister, and to give his life a ransom for many" (Mt.20:28).

"And went to *him,* and bound up his wounds, pouring in oil and wine, and set him on his own beast, and brought him to an inn, and took care of him. And on the morrow when he departed, he took out two pence, and gave *them* to the host, and said unto him, Take care of him; and whatsoever thou spendest more, when I come again, I will repay thee. Which now of these three, thinkest thou, was neighbour unto him that fell among the thieves? And he said, He that shewed mercy on him. Then said Jesus unto him, Go, and do thou likewise" (Lu.10:34-37).

"If I then, *your* Lord and Master, have washed your feet; ye also ought to wash one another's feet" (Jn.13:14).

"He saith to him again the second time, Simon, *son* of Jonas, lovest thou me? He saith unto him, Yea, Lord; thou knowest that I love thee. He saith unto him, Feed my sheep" (Jn.21:16).

"We then that are strong ought to bear the infirmities of the weak, and not to please ourselves. Let every one of us please *his* neighbour for *his* good to edification" (Ro.15:1-2).

"Bear ye one another's burdens, and so fulfil the law of Christ" (Ga.6:2).

"As we have therefore opportunity, let us do good unto all *men,* especially unto them who are of the household of faith" (Ga.6:10).

"And let us not be weary in well doing: for in due season we shall reap, if we faint not. As we have therefore opportunity, let us do good unto all *men,* especially unto them who are of the household of faith" (Ga.6:9-10).

"That they do good, that they be rich in good works, ready to distribute, willing to communicate [give]" (1 Ti.6:18).

"In all things showing thyself a pattern of good works: in doctrine *showing* uncorruptness, gravity, sincerity" (Tit.2:7).

"And let us consider one another to provoke unto love and to good works" (He.10:24).

"But to do good and to communicate [give] forget not: for with such sacrifices God is well pleased" (He.13:16).

"Even so faith, if it hath not works, is dead, being alone. Yea, a man may say, Thou hast faith, and I have works: show me thy faith without thy works, and I will show thee my faith by my works" (Js.2:17-18).

"Therefore to him that knoweth to do good, and doeth *it* not, to him it is sin" (Js.4:17).

"I was eyes to the blind, and feet *was* I to the lame. I *was* a father to the poor: and the cause *which* I knew not I searched out" (Jb.29:15-16).

"She stretcheth out her hand to the poor; yea, she reacheth forth her hands to the needy" (Pr.31:20).

"If ye be willing and obedient, ye shall eat the good of the land" (Is.1:19).

"The Lord GOD hath given me the tongue of the learned, that I should know how to speak a word in season to *him that is* weary: he wakeneth morning by morning, he wakeneth mine ear to hear as the learned" (Is.50:4).

2 (20:9-23) **Loyalty, Demands of—Friendship, Demands of, Loyalty—Brotherly Love, Example of—Jonathan, Relationship with David—David, Relationship with Jonathan**: Jonathan's loyalty demanded an unbreakable friendship and a spirit of brotherly love. These two demands are dramatically played out in what now takes place:

OUTLINE	SCRIPTURE	SCRIPTURE	OUTLINE
2. Jonathan's loyalty demanded an unbreakable friendship, a spirit of brotherly love a. Jonathan strongly affirmed his loyalty b. David asked exactly who would warn him of Saul's anger & pursuit c. Jonathan led David over into a field & swore an oath to him: He would find out how Saul felt & get word to David 1) He would send word if Saul spoke favorably about him	9 And Jonathan said, Far be it from thee: for if I knew certainly that evil were determined by my father to come upon thee, then would not I tell it thee? 10 Then said David to Jonathan, Who shall tell me? or what *if* thy father answer thee roughly? 11 And Jonathan said unto David, Come, and let us go out into the field. And they went out both of them into the field. 12 And Jonathan said unto David, O LORD God of Israel, when I have sounded my father about to morrow any time, *or* the third *day,* and, behold, *if there be* good toward David, and I then send not unto thee, and show it	thee; 13 The LORD do so and much more to Jonathan: but if it please my father *to do* thee evil, then I will show it thee, and send thee away, that thou mayest go in peace: and the LORD be with thee, as he hath been with my father. 14 And thou shalt not only while yet I live show me the kindness of the LORD, that I die not: 15 But *also* thou shalt not cut off thy kindness from my house for ever: no, not when the LORD hath cut off the enemies of David every one from the face of the earth. 16 So Jonathan made *a covenant* with the house of David, *saying,* Let the LORD	2) He would warn him if Saul was angry & determined to kill David d. Jonathan blessed David: Acknowledged that David, not he, was to become king e. Jonathan made several requests of David 1) That David not kill him in a purge of Saul's family 2) That David not kill off his personal descendants in any future purge 3) That the LORD judge, condemn David's enemies

OUTLINE	SCRIPTURE	SCRIPTURE	OUTLINE
4) That David reaffirm the covenant between them: Because of their brotherly love for one another (Le.19:18) f. Jonathan added details to the plan for notifying David 1) David would not attend the New Moon Festival & be missed 2) David—the day after to-morrow—would go to the place where he hid before & wait by the stone Ezel 3) Jonathan would come	even require *it* at the hand of David's enemies. 17 And Jonathan caused David to swear again, be-cause he loved him: for he loved him as he loved his own soul. 18 Then Jonathan said to David, To morrow *is* the new moon: and thou shalt be missed, because thy seat will be empty. 19 And *when* thou hast stayed three days, *then* thou shalt go down quickly, and come to the place where thou didst hide thyself when the business was *in hand,* and shalt remain by the stone Ezel. 20 And I will shoot three ar-	rows on the side *thereof,* as though I shot at a mark. 21 And, behold, I will send a lad, *saying,* Go, find out the arrows. If I expressly say unto the lad, Behold, the ar-rows are on this side of thee, take them; then come thou: for *there is* peace to thee, and no hurt; *as* the LORD liveth. 22 But if I say thus unto the young man, Behold, the ar-rows *are* beyond thee; go thy way: for the LORD hath sent thee away. 23 And *as touching* the mat-ter which thou and I have spoken of, behold, the LORD *be* between thee and me for ever.	with a boy for some target practice: He would shoot three arrows as a signal • If the arrows were shot short of the boy, this was a signal of safety • If the arrows were shot beyond the boy, this was a signal of danger 4) Jonathan again challenged David to remember their covenant of commitment & friendship

a. Jonathan strongly affirmed his loyalty to David. If he had had any inclination or the slightest notion that his father had broken his reconciliation agreement with David (19:6) and was again planning to kill him, he would have immediately informed David of the plot.

b. Being assured of Jonathan's loyalty, David continued to lay out the details of the plan to prove his charge against Saul (v.10). He asked Jonathan exactly who would warn him if Saul reacted against his absence from the banquet. Note, with this question and from this point on, Jonathan himself laid out all the details of the plan that would uncover Saul's in-tentions toward David.

c. Jonathan led David over into a field and swore an oath to him, promising that he would find out how Saul felt and get word to David (vv.11-13). He promised that he would send word if Saul spoke favorably about David, but that he would warn him if Saul was angry and determined to kill him. Jonathan was declaring that he would be loyal; he would obtain the very information needed and get that information to David. To again affirm his loyalty, Jonathan pronounced a curse upon himself if he betrayed David.

d. Then, amazingly and humbly, Jonathan pronounced a blessing upon David, a blessing that acknowledged David as the future king of Israel (v.13). He asked the LORD to be with David just as He had been with his father the king.

e. Jonathan then made several requests of David, requests that established a permanent covenant between the house of David and the house of Jonathan (vv.14-17). Simply stated, the requests were fourfold:
> ⇒ That David not kill him in a purge of Saul's family (v.14). Jonathan, of course, was looking ahead to the day when David would become king.
> ⇒ That David not kill off his personal descendants in any future purge (v.15).
> ⇒ That the LORD judge and condemn David's enemies (v.16).
> ⇒ That David reaffirm the covenant between them because of their friendship and brotherly love for one another (v.18).

f. Jonathan then added details to the plan for notifying David of his father's intentions (vv.18-23).
> 1) David would not attend the new moon festival that was to be held on the next day (v.18). Thus David would be missed and Saul's reaction would be observed by Jonathan.
> 2) The day after the festival, David would go to the place where he had hid before and wait by the well-known landmark, the stone of Ezel (v.19).
> 3) On the third day, Jonathan and a young boy would come for some target practice (vv.20-22). As a signal, Jona-than would shoot three arrows. If the arrows were shot short of the boy, this was a signal of safety for David. His life was not threatened by Saul. Note that Jonathan again swore a common oath (as the LORD lives) that he would not betray David: he would not tell David he was safe and could return home unless he knew there was no danger.
>
> But if the arrows were shot beyond the boy, this was a signal of danger, and David must flee for his life. They both would know that it was the LORD's sovereign will for David to leave home and flee from Saul. But Jonathan declared that no matter what happened, he and David must remember their covenant of commitment and friendship (v.23).

Thought 1. Loyalty demands an unbreakable friendship, a spirit of brotherly love. Or we might say friendship de-mands an unbreakable loyalty, an unbreakable spirit of brotherly love. True friendship demands loyalty that is shat-terproof and a brotherly love that is unshakable. Tough love and tough loyalty are traits of true friends. A person will not betray his friend when his friend needs help; he will not turn away. If his friend is being ridiculed, mocked, abused, assaulted, or persecuted, he will stand by the side of his friend. He will offer whatever support he can. If his friend has lost his job, home, family, health, a loved one—if his friend is suffering in any way—he will stand by his side, supporting and helping any way he can. This is true friendship and brotherly love, exactly what God demands:

> "And the second *is* like unto it, Thou shalt love thy neighbour as thyself" (Mt.22:39).
>
> "Then said Thomas, which is called Didymus, unto his fellowdisciples, Let us also go, that we may die with him" (Jn.11:16).
>
> "Now before the feast of the passover, when Jesus knew that his hour was come that he should depart out of this world unto the Father, having loved his own which were in the world, he loved them unto the end" (Jn.13:1).
>
> "A new commandment I give unto you, That ye love one another; as I have loved you, that ye also love one another. By this shall all *men* know that ye are my disciples, if ye have love one to another" (Jn.13:34-35).
>
> "Greater love hath no man than this, that a man lay down his life for his friends" (Jn.15:13).
>
> "*Let* love be without dissimulation [hypocrisy]. Abhor that which is evil; cleave to that which is good" (Ro.12:9).
>
> "*Be* kindly affectioned one to another with brotherly love; in honour preferring one another" (Ro.12:10).
>
> "And be ye kind one to another, tenderhearted, forgiving one another, even as God for Christ's sake hath forgiven you" (Ep.4:32).
>
> "The Lord give mercy unto the house of Onesiphorus; for he oft refreshed me, and was not ashamed of my chain" (2 Ti.1:16).
>
> "Seeing ye have purified your souls in obeying the truth through the Spirit unto unfeigned love of the brethren, *see that ye* love one another with a pure heart fervently" (1 Pt.1:22).
>
> "When my father and my mother forsake me, then the LORD will take me up" (Ps.27:10).
>
> "A friend loveth at all times, and a brother is born for adversity" (Pr.17:17).
>
> "Two *are* better than one; because they have a good reward for their labour. For if they fall, the one will lift up his fellow: but woe to him *that is* alone when he falleth; for *he hath* not another to help him up" (Ec.4:9-10).

3 (20:24-34) **Jealousy, Conquering and Overcoming—Envy, Conquering and Overcoming—Loyalty, Demands of—Victory, over Jealousy and Envy—Jonathan, Relationship with David—David, Relationship with Jonathan:** Jonathan's loyalty demanded that he conquer jealousy and envy. And if any person ever had to conquer jealousy and envy, it was Jonathan. For he was the natural heir to the throne of Israel, yet he subjected himself to David. And remember, Jonathan was somewhat older than David (18:1). In addition, Jonathan witnessed David's receiving all the acclaim and fame of the public. But in all of Scripture, there is never an indication that Jonathan allowed jealousy or envy to come between him and David. He was a man who conquered these two terrible evils. And Jonathan conquered jealousy and envy despite the fact that his father constantly warned him about David's threat to Jonathan's claim to the throne. In this passage, Saul is seen once again drilling his perceived threat by David into Jonathan's mind.

OUTLINE	SCRIPTURE	SCRIPTURE	OUTLINE

3. Jonathan's loyalty demanded that he conquer jealousy & envy
a. David hid & did not attend the dinner of the New Moon Festival
b. Saul noticed David's absence at the dinner
 	
  1) He said nothing
  2) He thought David had become ceremonially unclean: He needed to undergo the cleansing ritual
c. Saul noticed David's absence on the second day
  1) He questioned Jonathan
	24 So David hid himself in the field: and when the new moon was come, the king sat him down to eat meat.
	25 And the king sat upon his seat, as at other times, *even* upon a seat by the wall: and Jonathan arose, and Abner sat by Saul's side, and David's place was empty.
	26 Nevertheless Saul spake not any thing that day: for he thought, Something hath befallen him, he is not clean; surely he *is* not clean.
	27 And it came to pass on the morrow, *which was* the second *day* of the month, that David's place was empty: and Saul said unto Jonathan his son, Wherefore cometh not the son of Jesse to meat, neither yesterday, nor to day?
		28 And Jonathan answered Saul, David earnestly asked *leave* of me *to go* to Bethlehem:
		29 And he said, Let me go, I pray thee; for our family hath a sacrifice in the city; and my brother, he hath commanded me *to be there:* and now, if I have found favour in thine eyes, let me get away, I pray thee, and see my brethren. Therefore he cometh not unto the king's table.
		30 Then Saul's anger was kindled against Jonathan, and he said unto him, Thou son of the perverse rebellious *woman,* do not I know that thou hast chosen the son of Jesse to thine own confusion, and unto the confusion of thy mother's nakedness?
			2) Jonathan answered, giving the predetermined excuse
			
			• That David had asked permission to observe a special family sacrifice in Bethlehem
			
			• That he had granted David's request
			
			d. Saul became inflamed, filled with hostility toward Jonathan
			1) Called him the son of a perverse & rebellious woman
			2) Accused him of siding with David, of bringing shame on himself & his family

OUTLINE	SCRIPTURE	SCRIPTURE	OUTLINE
3) Warned him that neither he nor his dynasty would ever be established as long as David lived 4) Commanded Jonathan to have David arrested e. Jonathan responded by asking what crimes David had committed f. Saul hurled his spear at Jon-	31 For as long as the son of Jesse liveth upon the ground, thou shalt not be established, nor thy kingdom. Wherefore now send and fetch him unto me, for he shall surely die. 32 And Jonathan answered Saul his father, and said unto him, Wherefore shall he be slain? what hath he done? 33 And Saul cast a javelin at	him to smite him: whereby Jonathan knew that it was determined of his father to slay David. 34 So Jonathan arose from the table in fierce anger, and did eat no meat the second day of the month: for he was grieved for David, because his father had done him shame.	athan, attempting to kill his very own son g. Jonathan jumped up & left in fierce anger, knowing the truth 1) Saul was set on killing David 2) Jonathan was so grieved that he could not eat because of Saul's treatment of his friend David

a. David did just as he and Jonathan had agreed: he hid and did not attend the dinner of the new moon festival (v.24).

b. On the next day at the dinner, Saul immediately noticed David's absence (vv.24-26). Note that he and Abner, his commander-in-chief, sat on one side of the table while Jonathan, next to David's empty place, sat on the other side. But Saul said nothing. He thought that David had become ceremonially unclean, that he needed to undergo the cleansing ritual before he could attend a religious service.

c. But the next day when Saul again noticed David's absence, he questioned Jonathan (vv.27-29). This was not a holiday and David, who was one of the leading commanders in the armed forces, should have been at his place at the king's table.

Jonathan answered his father by giving him the predetermined excuse that he and David had agreed upon. He replied that David had asked permission to observe a special family sacrifice in Bethlehem, and that he, Jonathan, had granted David's request.

d. All at once Saul became inflamed, filled with hostility toward Jonathan (vv.30-31). No longer referring to Jonathan as his own son, he addressed him as the son of a perverse and rebellious woman. And Saul accused him of siding with David and bringing shame upon himself and his family. Burning with hostility, Saul threw the threat of David in the face of Jonathan, warning that neither he nor his dynasty would ever be established as long as David lived. With flaming anger, Saul commanded Jonathan to have David arrested and brought before him, for David must die.

Just imagine how much easier it would have been for Jonathan to give place to jealousy over David. By right, Jonathan was heir to the throne; and all the power, wealth, and honor of being king belonged to him at his father's death. But not only this, remaining loyal to David meant that he had to go against the wishes of his father. Despite all the obstacles confronting him, Jonathan made a final, climactic decision to conquer the temptation to be jealous and envious of David. He made a determined decision to remain loyal and to honor his covenant of friendship with David.

e. Thus Jonathan responded to his father by asking Saul what crimes David had committed (v.32).

f. In a rage, Saul hurled his spear at Jonathan, attempting to kill his very own son (v.33). Jonathan jumped up and left the table in fierce anger, knowing the truth: Saul was set on killing David (v.34). Note that Jonathan was so grieved that he could not eat. His grief was not because of his father's shameful treatment of him, but because of Saul's shameful treatment of his friend David. If Jonathan followed through with his commitment to warn David, he would prove to be one of the most loyal friends who ever lived.

Thought 1. Jonathan conquered jealousy and envy, but his father did not. What made the difference? The power of God. God has provided a way for jealousy and envy to be conquered, the very same way that all evil is to be overcome: through the power of the cross and the resurrection of the Lord Jesus Christ. Through the cross we receive forgiveness for having committed the sins of jealousy and envy. And through the power of the resurrection, we receive the power of the Holy Spirit who raised Christ from the dead. Through His Spirit, God gives us the power to conquer jealousy and envy and any other evil that harasses us. It is through the power of God, and His power alone, that jealousy and envy can be conquered.

"**And the God of peace shall bruise Satan under your feet shortly. The grace of our Lord Jesus Christ** *be* **with you. Amen" (Ro.16:20).**

"**There hath no temptation taken you but such as is common to man: but God** *is* **faithful, who will not suffer you to be tempted above that ye are able; but will with the temptation also make a way to escape, that ye may be able to bear** *it*" **(1 Co.10:13).**

"**That he would grant you, according to the riches of his glory, to be strengthened with might by his Spirit in the inner man" (Ep.3:16).**

"**Now unto him that is able to do exceeding abundantly above all that we ask or think, according to the power that worketh in us" (Ep.3:20).**

"**Wherefore in all things it behoved him to be made like unto** *his* **brethren, that he might be a merciful and faithful high priest in things** *pertaining* **to God, to make reconciliation for the sins of the people. For in that he himself hath suffered being tempted, he is able to succour them that are tempted" (He.2:17-18).**

"**Submit yourselves therefore to God. Resist the devil, and he will flee from you" (Js.4:7).**

"**My brethren, count it all joy when ye fall into divers temptations; Knowing** *this,* **that the trying of your faith worketh patience. But let patience have** *her* **perfect work, that ye may be perfect and entire, wanting nothing. If any of you lack wisdom, let him ask of God, that giveth to all** *men* **liberally, and upbraideth not; and it shall be given him" (Js.1:2-5).**

"Blessed *is* the man that endureth temptation: for when he is tried, he shall receive the crown of life, which the Lord hath promised to them that love him" (Js.1:12).

"Who his own self bare our sins in his own body on the tree, that we, being dead to sins, should live unto righteousness: by whose stripes ye were healed" (1 Pt.2:24).

"Casting all your care upon him; for he careth for you. Be sober, be vigilant; because your adversary the devil, as a roaring lion, walketh about, seeking whom he may devour: Whom resist stedfast in the faith, knowing that the same afflictions are accomplished in your brethren that are in the world. But the God of all grace, who hath called us unto his eternal glory by Christ Jesus, after that ye have suffered a while, make you perfect, stablish, strengthen, settle *you*" (1 Pt.5:7-10).

"The Lord knoweth how to deliver the godly out of temptations, and to reserve the unjust unto the day of judgment to be punished" (2 Pt.2:9).

"For whatsoever is born of God overcometh the world: and this is the victory that overcometh the world, *even* our faith. Who is he that overcometh the world, but he that believeth that Jesus is the Son of God" (1 Jn.5:4-5).

"Because thou hast kept the word of my patience, I also will keep thee from the hour of temptation, which shall come upon all the world, to try them that dwell upon the earth" (Re.3:10).

"Through thee will we push down our enemies: through thy name will we tread them under that rise up against us" (Ps.44:5).

"Fear thou not; for I *am* with thee: be not dismayed; for I *am* thy God: I will strengthen thee; yea, I will help thee; yea, I will uphold thee with the right hand of my righteousness" (Is.41:10).

4 (20:35-42) **Oath, Duty—Commitment, Duty—Promises of Man, Duty—Loyalty, Demands of—Jonathan, Relationship with David—David, Relationship with Jonathan**: Jonathan's loyalty demanded that he keep his oath, his commitment, his promises. Jonathan was as loyal to David as a friend could be; consequently, he did exactly as he and David had prearranged:

OUTLINE	SCRIPTURE	SCRIPTURE	OUTLINE
4. Jonathan's loyalty demanded that he keep his oath, his commitment, his promises a. Jonathan kept his word: Went to the field where David was hiding & charged a young boy to run & find the arrows as he shot them 1) Jonathan shouted out to the boy the prearranged signal with David • He added three sharp commands that applied to David & that David could not misunderstand • The boy knew nothing about the prearranged	35 And it came to pass in the morning, that Jonathan went out into the field at the time appointed with David, and a little lad with him. 36 And he said unto his lad, Run, find out now the arrows which I shoot. *And* as the lad ran, he shot an arrow beyond him. 37 And when the lad was come to the place of the arrow which Jonathan had shot, Jonathan cried after the lad, and said, *Is* not the arrow beyond thee? 38 And Jonathan cried after the lad, Make speed, haste, stay not. And Jonathan's lad gathered up the arrows, and came to his master. 39 But the lad knew not any thing: only Jonathan and Da-	vid knew the matter. 40 And Jonathan gave his artillery unto his lad, and said unto him, Go, carry *them* to the city. 41 *And* as soon as the lad was gone, David arose out of *a place* toward the south, and fell on his face to the ground, and bowed himself three times: and they kissed one another, and wept one with another, until David exceeded. 42 And Jonathan said to David, Go in peace, forasmuch as we have sworn both of us in the name of the LORD, saying, The LORD be between me and thee, and between my seed and thy seed for ever. And he arose and departed: and Jonathan went into the city.	signal 2) Jonathan sent the boy with his weapons back to town b. David, surprisingly, came out of hiding 1) David humbled himself before Jonathan: Bowed three times, indicating subservience to the crown prince 2) They kissed each other & wept 3) Jonathan assured David of his friendship • It was a sworn friendship • It was sworn on the name of the LORD, a *covenant friendship* • It included both them & their descendants 4) They separated, left the presence of one another

a. Jonathan kept his word and went to the prearranged field where David was hiding (v.36). He charged a young boy to run and find the arrows as he shot them. As the boy was running, Jonathan shot an arrow beyond him and shouted the prearranged signal: the arrow is still out beyond you. Then Jonathan added three commands that applied to David and that David could not misunderstand, "Make haste! Hurry, go quickly! Do not wait or delay!"

The boy knew nothing about the prearranged signal between Jonathan and David. Thus, as soon as the young boy returned the arrows to Jonathan, he sent the young boy back to town with his weapons.

b. Surprisingly, instead of fleeing, David came out of hiding to say good-bye to his dear friend, for he feared that they would never again meet (vv.41-42). To their knowledge, this would be the last time that these two friends, so closely bound together by God's Spirit, would ever see one another face-to-face. Neither knew there would be one more occasion when Jonathan would secretly go to David for the purpose of encouraging him in a moment of intense distress (23:16-18). A loyalty of unsurpassed friendship existed between the two, a friendship rooted in their common faith in the LORD. The emotions of the moment can be felt by anyone picturing the scene. Walking toward each other, David humbled himself before Jonathan: he bowed three times indicating his subservience to the royal prince. Interestingly, in Scripture this is the most anyone ever bowed before another person in one encounter.[1] The two friends kissed each other and wept. But David wept the most. He was the one becoming the fugitive and being forced to leave his family and friends. Hereafter David would become a criminal charged with a capital crime and doomed to be executed if caught. The weight of alienation, being completely cut off from everyone he loved and from all his earthly possessions, all came crashing in upon David. No doubt he wept uncontrollably, sensing that he simply could not bear the pressure of the ordeal. Remember that David had a heart *just like God's*, a heart that was sensitive and tender as well as strong and courageous.

Weeping right along with David, Jonathan assured him of his friendship (v.42). Their relationship was a sworn friendship; it was sworn on the name of the LORD Himself, a covenant friendship that would last until death. And their friendship included both them and their descendants. Having confirmed their commitment, their covenant of friendship, the two separated, leaving each other for what they feared would be the last time.

Thought 1. Jonathan set a dynamic example for us; he kept his oath, his commitment, his promise, his vow made to David. When we make a promise to a person, we are to be faithful to our word. Making a promise to a friend or to anyone else means just as much as taking an oath or making a vow. Our word is to be our bond, guaranteeing exactly what we say. In making promises, we are to mean what we say and say what we mean. No promise is to be made unless we intend to keep it. We are to speak the truth and only the truth, and we are to live by the truth, promising only what we intend to keep. When it comes to promises or oaths or vows, we are to do exactly what we commit ourselves to do. This is the clear teaching of God's Holy Word:

"But let your communication be, Yea, yea; Nay, nay: for whatsoever is more than these cometh of evil" (Mt.5:37).

"Let your speech *be* alway with grace, seasoned with salt, that ye may know how ye ought to answer every man" (Col.4:6).

"Sound speech, that cannot be condemned; that he that is of the contrary part may be ashamed, having no evil thing to say of you" (Tit.2:8).

"For even hereunto were ye called: because Christ also suffered for us, leaving us an example, that ye should follow his steps: Who did no sin, neither was guile put [deceit] found in his mouth" (1 Pe.2:21-22).

"For he that will love life, and see good days, let him refrain his tongue from evil, and his lips that they speak no guile" (1 Pe.3:10).

"*Then* shall an oath of the LORD be between them both, that he hath not put his hand unto his neighbour's goods; and the owner of it shall accept *thereof*, and he shall not make *it* good" (Ex.22:11).

"Thou shalt fear the LORD thy God, and serve him, and shalt swear by his name" (De.6:13).

"When thou shalt vow a vow unto the LORD thy God, thou shalt not slack to pay it: for the LORD thy God will surely require it of thee; and it would be sin in thee. But if thou shalt forbear to vow, it shall be no sin in thee. That which is gone out of thy lips thou shalt keep and perform; *even* a freewill offering, according as thou hast vowed unto the LORD thy God, which thou hast promised with thy mouth" (De.23:21-23).

"If a man vow a vow unto the LORD, or swear an oath to bind his soul with a bond; he shall not break his word, he shall do according to all that proceedeth out of his mouth" (Nu.30:2).

"Thou shalt make thy prayer unto him, and he shall hear thee, and thou shalt pay thy vows" (Jb.22:27).

"*It is* a snare to the man *who* devoureth *that which is* holy, and after vows to make enquiry" (Pr.20:25).

"When thou vowest a vow unto God, defer not to pay it; for *he hath* no pleasure in fools: pay that which thou hast vowed. Better *is it* that thou shouldest not vow, than that thou shouldest vow and not pay. Suffer not thy mouth to cause thy flesh to sin; neither say thou before the angel, that it *was* an error: wherefore should God be angry at thy voice, and destroy the work of thine hands" (Ec.5:4-6).

"The law of truth was in his mouth, and iniquity was not found in his lips: he walked with me in peace and equity, and did turn many away from iniquity" (Mal.2:6).

---

[1] Robert D. Bergen. *1, 2 Samuel*, p.219.

DIVISION IV

THE STORY OF SAUL AND DAVID (PART 2): DAVID THE FUGITIVE, 21:1–31:13

(21:1–31:13) **DIVISION OVERVIEW**: Saul's jealous rage and relentless determination to assassinate David eventually forced David to flee for his life. Most likely David was in his early twenties when he was forced to flee, leaving behind his family, friends, and home. This calculation is based upon the fact that David was younger than the twenty-year old age requirement for military duty when he first began to serve Saul, for he was not yet enlisted in the king's army. And David was thirty years old when he began to reign over Judah right after Saul's death (2 Sam.5:4-5).

Just imagine! Being no more than twenty-two or twenty-three years old and being forced to leave family, friends, and home, fleeing for one's life and living as a fugitive on the run for seven or eight long years. From this point on to the end of First Samuel, David was to live a life of strain, stress, adversity, and affliction—a life of extreme hardship. Until Saul's death, he was to be fiercely pursued by the king as a fugitive with the charge of a capital crime hanging over his head. He was to live one of the most distressful, tension-filled lives imaginable. But through all the strain and stress, the LORD was preparing David to become the *servant* of the LORD's people. Although he was to be the ruler of the nation, he was first of all to be the servant of the people, empathizing with their needs and seeking to help them in every way he could. In order to empathize and feel for the people, David had to go through the experiences of intense, agonizing suffering during the days of his fugitive years. And because of the suffering he had to bear, David became the great psalmist whose life and writings so clearly point us to the LORD Himself as our great Savior, Deliverer, Provider, and Protector (Heb.2:18; 4:15-16).

THE STORY OF SAUL AND DAVID (PART 2): DAVID THE FUGITIVE, 21:1–31:13

A. The Immediate, Desperate Flight of David from Saul: A Picture of Desperation and of God's Deliverance, 21:1–22:5

B. The Insane Murder of the Priests by Saul: A Picture of the Terrible Evil of Certain Sins, 22:6-23

C. The Rescue of Keilah by David and the Insane Pursuit of David by Saul: A Picture of the Believer's Deliverance from All Enemies, 23:1-29

D. The Life of Saul Mercifully Spared by David: Lessons on Honoring God's Anointed, 24:1-22

E. The Encounter of David with Nabal and Abigail: Lessons on Dealing with a Harsh, Selfish Man and a Wise, Courageous Woman, 25:1-44

F. The Life of Saul Again Spared by David: Lessons on Reaping What One Sows, 26:1-25

G. The Desperate Flight of David to Philistia, Seeking a Safe Residence: Giving in to Doubt and Unbelief, to Deception and Lies, 27:1-12

H. The Desperation of Saul Seen in His Seeking a Spirit Medium: A Study of the Occult, 28:1-25

I.   **The Dismissal of David to Keep Him from Fighting against Israel: A Picture of God Working All Things Out for the Believer, 29:1-11**

J.   **The Defeat of the Amalekites by David: A Picture of Christ Setting the Captives (His Loved Ones) Free, 30:1-31**

K. **The Tragic End of Saul and His Sons, Including Jonathan, David's Closest Friend: The Surety of God's Word and of God's Judgment, 31:1-13**

CHAPTER 21

IV. THE STORY OF SAUL & DAVID (PART 2): DAVID THE FUGITIVE, 21:1–31:13

A. The Immediate, Desperate Flight of David from Saul: A Picture of Desperation & of God's Deliverance, 21:1–22:5

1. David fled to the High Priest Ahimelech at Nob: Seeking the help of God's servant

a. The unexpected fear of Ahimelech: Was suspicious of a breach between David & Saul

b. The lie, deception of David: Led to tragic results, 22:6-19
  1) He said he was on a secret mission for the king

  2) He said his men were to meet him at another location

c. The request by David for food
  1) David asked for five loaves of bread

  2) The priest had no ordinary bread, only holy bread
  • David's men could have it if they obeyed a military purity law, abstaining from sex during battle, Ex.19:15; 2 S.11:6-13
  • David assured the priest that his soldiers were holy: He personally required them to maintain an active, holy relationship with the LORD

  3) The priest gave David the holy, consecrated bread— "the bread of the Presence": It had just been removed & replaced with hot bread

d. The uneasy & tragic presence of Saul's servant—his chief shepherd, Doeg the Edomite, 22:9, 22

Then came David to Nob to Ahimelech the priest: and Ahimelech was afraid at the meeting of David, and said unto him, Why *art* thou alone, and no man with thee?
2 And David said unto Ahimelech the priest, The king hath commanded me a business, and hath said unto me, Let no man know any thing of the business whereabout I send thee, and what I have commanded thee: and I have appointed *my* servants to such and such a place.
3 Now therefore what is under thine hand? give *me* five *loaves of* bread in mine hand, or what there is present.
4 And the priest answered David, and said, *There is* no common bread under mine hand, but there is hallowed bread; if the young men have kept themselves at least from women.
5 And David answered the priest, and said unto him, Of a truth women *have been* kept from us about these three days, since I came out, and the vessels of the young men are holy, and *the bread is* in a manner common, yea, though it were sanctified this day in the vessel.
6 So the priest gave him hallowed *bread:* for there was no bread there but the showbread, that was taken from before the LORD, to put hot bread in the day when it was taken away.
7 Now a certain man of the servants of Saul *was* there that day, detained before the LORD; and his name *was* Doeg, an Edomite, the chiefest of the herdmen that *belonged* to Saul.

8 And David said unto Ahimelech, And is there not here under thine hand spear or sword? for I have neither brought my sword nor my weapons with me, because the king's business required haste.
9 And the priest said, The sword of Goliath the Philistine, whom thou slewest in the valley of Elah, behold, it *is here* wrapped in a cloth behind the ephod: if thou wilt take that, take *it:* for *there is* no other save that here. And David said, *There is* none like that; give it me.
10 And David arose, and fled that day for fear of Saul, and went to Achish the king of Gath.
11 And the servants of Achish said unto him, *Is* not this David the king of the land? did they not sing one to another of him in dances, saying, Saul hath slain his thousands, and David his ten thousands?
12 And David laid up these words in his heart, and was sore afraid of Achish the king of Gath.
13 And he changed his behaviour before them, and feigned himself mad in their hands, and scrabbled on the doors of the gate, and let his spittle fall down upon his beard.
14 Then said Achish unto his servants, Lo, ye see the man is mad: wherefore *then* have ye brought him to me?
15 Have I need of mad men, that ye have brought this *fellow* to play the mad man in my presence? shall this *fellow* come into my house?

CHAPTER 22

David therefore departed thence, and escaped to the cave Adullam: and when his brethren and all his father's house heard *it,* they went down thither to him.
2 And every one *that was* in distress, and every one that *was* in debt, and every one *that was* discontented, gathered themselves unto him; and he became a captain over

e. The request by David for a weapon
  1) He stated that he had left without his sword because the king's mission was urgent

  2) The priest informed him that Goliath's sword—the very sword David had earlier dedicated to the LORD—was still there: He could take it

2. David fled to the Philistine king, Achish: Deliverance from life-threatening fear

a. The threat to David by the officials of Achish
  1) They saw David as a defector & a mercenary—an enemy of Saul
  2) They feared & were suspicious that he might turn against them

b. The cautious fear of David & his strategy of escape, Ps.34

  1) David pretended to be insane: Walked around drooling saliva & abusing public property by writing graffiti on the doors of the city gates

  2) Achish strongly objected to a madman's being in his army & presence

  3) Achish had David removed, driven from his presence, Ps.34

3. David escaped to the cave of Adullam: A time of deep anguish & of crying out to the LORD in prayer, Ps.142

a. His family joined him: Feared Saul's reprisal

b. A force of 400 men also joined him: Those distressed, indebted, or discontented— "men of broken fortunes & restless spirits"[1]

---

1 Matthew Henry. *Matthew Henry's Commentary*, Vol.2. (Old Tappan, NJ: Fleming H. Revell Co., n.d.), p.398.

183

4. David sought to take care of his parents: The believer's clear duty a. David moved to Mizpah & asked the king of Moab to grant sanctuary to his parents b. David's parents stayed in	them: and there were with him about four hundred men. 3 And David went thence to Mizpeh of Moab: and he said unto the king of Moab, Let my father and my mother, I pray thee, come forth, *and be* with you, till I know what God will do for me. 4 And he brought them be-	fore the king of Moab: and they dwelt with him all the while that David was in the hold. 5 And the prophet Gad said unto David, Abide not in the hold; depart, and get thee into the land of Judah. Then David departed, and came into the forest of Hareth.	Moab as long as David was hiding out in a stronghold in the land of Moab **5. David was guided by the LORD through the prophet Gad: God's guidance through the trials of life** a. Was to leave Mizpah b. Was to return to Judah

DIVISION IV

THE STORY OF SAUL AND DAVID (PART 2):
DAVID THE FUGITIVE, 21:1–31:13

A. The Immediate, Desperate Flight of David from Saul: A Picture of Desperation and of God's Deliverance, 21:1–22:5

(21:1–22:5) **Introduction—Hardship, Fact of—Adversity, Result of—Hopelessness, Caused by—Helplessness, Caused by**: at some point in life, all human beings face desperate situations. Sometimes the circumstances are so distressful that they cause unbearable pain and agony and there seems to be no way out, no solution or answer. The hardship, the adversity just erupts and we feel helpless and hopeless. Emotionally we may suffer anguish, anxiety, and all kinds of physical and emotional difficulties such as headaches, ulcers, heart attacks, depression, and psychotic disorders. Our lives become dramatically changed and are often left shattered and in ruins.

From this point on to the end of First Samuel, David was to live a life of severe hardship and adversity. He was now a fugitive, fleeing for his life. The king himself was charging David with a capital crime and was fiercely pursuing him, determined to execute David. Remember that David had just been warned by Jonathan to flee, to hurry and not delay in making his escape from Saul. This is the beginning of David's flight as a fugitive, an exile that would last about ten years. This is: *The Immediate, Desperate Flight of David from Saul: A Picture of Desperation and of God's Deliverance, 21:1–22:5.*

1. David fled to the High Priest Ahimelech at Nob: seeking the help of God's servant (vv.1-9).
2. David fled to the Philistine king, Achish: deliverance from life-threatening fear (vv.10-15).
3. David escaped to the cave of Adullam: a time of deep anguish and of crying out to the LORD in prayer, Ps.142 (ch.22:1-2)
4. David sought to take care of his parents: the believer's clear duty (vv.3-4).
5. David was guided by God through the prophet Gad: God's guidance through the trials of life (v.5).

1 (21:1-9) **Seeking, Help from Ministers—Help, Seeking from Ministers—Ministers, Duties—David, Flight from Saul—David, Sins and Weaknesses of—Ahimelech, High Priest of Israel—Showbread or Holy Bread, Use of—Deception, Example of, David**: David fled from Saul to the High Priest Ahimelech at Nob, seeking the help of God's servant. During the prior week, Saul had made several attempts to kill David. Barely escaping the last attempt, David was now fleeing for his life. In desperation he fled to the one person he felt might be able to help him, the High Priest Ahimelech. David was hungry and needed a weapon, but most of all he needed the counsel of the High Priest in seeking the guidance of the LORD (22:10).

Note that the Tabernacle had been relocated to Nob after the destruction of Shiloh (4:2-3; Je.7:12). Nob was a town about two miles northeast of Jerusalem and about three miles southeast of Gibeah, which was the capital of Israel during Saul's kingship. Over eighty-five priests were serving at the Tabernacle during this time (22:17-18). The ephod and the table of the showbread or holy bread are mentioned in connection with the Tabernacle at this time, but not the Ark of God (22:6, 9). Apparently the Ark was still at Abinadab's house at Kirjath-Jearim, where it remained until David brought it to Jerusalem (7:1; 2 Sa.6:2-3). The Tabernacle with the altar and other furnishings had escaped the destruction of Shiloh and were moved to Nob, where Ahimelech was now serving as High Priest.

Samuel could no longer help David; neither could Jonathan. There seemed to be no person who could help him, for it was the king himself who was threatening his life. But perhaps—just perhaps—help could be found from one person and in one place: the High Priest at the house of God. Thus David's flight from Saul's fury led him to seek the help of God's servant:

OUTLINE	SCRIPTURE	SCRIPTURE	OUTLINE
1. David fled to the High Priest Ahimelech at Nob: Seeking the help of God's servant a. The unexpected fear of Ahimelech: Was suspicious	Then came David to Nob to Ahimelech the priest: and Ahimelech was afraid at the meeting of David, and said unto him, Why *art* thou	alone, and no man with thee? 2 And David said unto Ahimelech the priest, The king hath commanded me a	of a breach between David & Saul b. The lie, deception of David: Led to tragic results, 22:6-19 1) He said he was on a secret

OUTLINE	SCRIPTURE	SCRIPTURE	OUTLINE
mission for the king	business, and hath said unto me, Let no man know any thing of the business whereabout I send thee, and what I have commanded thee: and I have appointed *my* servants to such and such a place.	was no bread there but the showbread, that was taken from before the LORD, to put hot bread in the day when it was taken away.	"the bread of the Presence": It had just been removed & replaced with hot bread
2) He said his men were to meet him at another location		7 Now a certain man of the servants of Saul *was* there that day, detained before the LORD; and his name *was* Doeg, an Edomite, the chiefest of the herdmen that *belonged* to Saul.	d. The uneasy & tragic presence of Saul's servant—his chief shepherd, Doeg the Edomite, 22:9, 22
c. The request by David for food	3 Now therefore what is under thine hand? give *me* five *loaves of* bread in mine hand, or what there is present.		
1) David asked for five loaves of bread			
2) The priest had no ordinary bread, only holy bread	4 And the priest answered David, and said, *There is* no common bread under mine hand, but there is hallowed bread; if the young men have kept themselves at least from women.	8 And David said unto Ahimelech, And is there not here under thine hand spear or sword? for I have neither brought my sword nor my weapons with me, because the king's business required haste.	e. The request by David for a weapon
• David's men could have it if they obeyed a military purity law, abstaining from sex during battle, Ex.19:15; 2 S.11:6-13			1) He stated that he had left without his sword because the king's mission was urgent
• David assured the priest that his soldiers were holy: He personally required them to maintain an active, holy relationship with the LORD	5 And David answered the priest, and said unto him, Of a truth women *have been* kept from us about these three days, since I came out, and the vessels of the young men are holy, and *the bread is* in a manner common, yea, though it were sanctified this day in the vessel.	9 And the priest said, The sword of Goliath the Philistine, whom thou slewest in the valley of Elah, behold, it *is here* wrapped in a cloth behind the ephod: if thou wilt take that, take *it:* for *there is* no other save that here. And David said, *There is* none like that; give it	2) The priest informed him that Goliath's sword—the very sword David had earlier dedicated to the LORD—was still there: He could take it
3) The priest gave David the holy, consecrated bread—	6 So the priest gave him hallowed *bread:* for there	me.	

a. The response of Ahimelech to David's arrival was unexpected (v.1). Ahimelech trembled with fear when he saw that David was all alone, that no one else from the king's court was with him. This was most unusual, for David was the commander of the royal guard for King Saul. Ahimelech became suspicious of a breach, a broken relationship between David and Saul. No doubt he had heard about the recent events at the religious center at Naioth where the lives of the young prophets had been endangered by David's presence.[2]

b. Note the lie, the deception of David that was to lead to tragic results (vv.2; 22:9-19). David descriptively gave a reason why he was alone: he said he was on a secret mission for the king and that his men were to meet him at another location. This was a gross deception, a lie born out of desperation and need. David, extremely hungry, felt he could not tell Ahimelech the truth lest the High Priest refuse to help him, fearing reprisal from Saul. But even more than this, David needed the counsel of Ahimelech in seeking the guidance of God (22:10, 15). He felt he could not run the risk of the priest's refusal to help him seek the LORD as to what he should do next. Consequently, David lied and deceived the priest in order to secure his own health. David was failing to cast himself totally upon the care of God, not trusting God to move upon the priest to help him.

But note this possibility as well: perhaps David was attempting to protect Ahimelech by lying to him. If Ahimelech did not know the truth that David was attempting to escape Saul's pursuit, then the priest could claim ignorance. He could not be justly charged with helping David escape, for he would not be aware that David was charged with a capital crime.

c. David requested food of the High Priest, asking for five loaves of bread or for whatever other food he could find. The priest had no ordinary bread, only holy bread, and this posed a problem. Holy bread was to be eaten only by priests (Ex.25:23-30; Le.24:5-9). However, the priest told David that his men could have the bread if they had obeyed the military purity law, that of having abstained from sex during the past three days (Ex.19:15; Le.15:16-18).

David assured the priest that his soldiers were holy, ceremonially clean. He personally required them to maintain an active, holy relationship with the LORD. And although they were not with him at this particular moment, he knew that they were obeying his command to maintain their purity before the LORD. Hearing this, the priest gave David the holy, consecrated bread that had just been removed from the table of God's Presence and replaced with hot bread.

Jesus Christ used this experience of David to teach a wonderful truth: meeting needs and preserving life always take precedence over religious ceremony and ritual. David did not break the law to indulge a lust but to meet a genuine need. God's great concern is always to make sure that human needs are met, not the needs of religion and religious beliefs, nor religious practices, rituals, ceremonies, rules, and regulations. Jesus taught that human need and compassion are always to take precedence over religious rules (Mt.12:2-4; Mk.2:25-26).

d. Note that Saul's chief, supervising shepherd was at the Tabernacle at the same time David was (v.7). David was later to say that he felt uneasy about the chief shepherd's presence, fearing that he would report David's whereabouts to Saul. Tragically, David was correct. Doeg was to be the cause for the murder of all eighty-five priests serving the Tabernacle at that time. This will be seen in the next chapter (22:6-23).

---

[2] Robert D. Bergen. *1, 2 Samuel*, p.221.

e. In addition to his request for food, David asked for a weapon (vv.8-9). He stated that he had left without his sword because the king's mission was urgent. Accepting David's word, the priest informed him that Goliath's sword was there, the very sword that David had earlier dedicated to the LORD and left at the Tabernacle. It was wrapped in a cloth behind the ephod; therefore if David wanted it returned, he could take it. Based upon David's response, he was excited, for apparently among swords, none could compare to the sword of Goliath.

Thought 1. Ministers must always be available to help people, to meet their needs. This is the very purpose for the existence of ministers, the very reason the LORD has called them to serve Him. They are to go forth ministering even as the Son of Man came not to be ministered unto, but to minister and to give His life a ransom for many (Mt.20:28). The minister is to deny himself and take up his cross daily, following the LORD in meeting the needs of people.

But this command to meet the needs of people is not given just to ministers. We are all to serve others, reaching out to help wherever help is needed. If a person has a need, we are to give whatever aid we can and meet that need. In God's eyes, we are all to be ministers, serving one another and meeting the desperate needs of this world.

⇒ When people need food, we are to feed them.
⇒ When people are sick, we are to visit them.
⇒ When people need clothing, we are to provide clothing.
⇒ When people are homeless, we are to shelter them.
⇒ When people are financially destitute, we are to do what we can to provide jobs.
⇒ When people are involved in accidents, we are to rescue them.
⇒ When people are emotionally disturbed, we are to counsel them and encourage them.
⇒ When people are dying, we are to comfort them.
⇒ When children are orphaned, we are to adopt them or provide foster homes or some other means of suitable care and oversight for them.
⇒ When people are widowed, we are to provide friendship for them.
⇒ When people are living in sin and wickedness, we are to share the truth of righteousness and coming judgment with them.
⇒ When people are gripped by unbelief and rejection of God and are doomed to live eternally separated from God, we must share the gospel with them.

When there are so many needs, so many people throughout the world who are living in desperation and fear—we must reach out and minister to them. This is the command of God's Holy Word:

"Blessed *are* the merciful: for they shall obtain mercy" (Mt.5:7).

"Jesus said unto him, If thou wilt be perfect, go *and* sell that thou hast, and give to the poor, and thou shalt have treasure in heaven: and come *and* follow me" (Mt.19:21).

"Be ye therefore merciful, as your Father also is merciful" (Lu.6:36).

"But a certain Samaritan, as he journeyed, came where he was: and when he saw him, he had compassion *on him,* And went to *him,* and bound up his wounds, pouring in oil and wine, and set him on his own beast, and brought him to an inn, and took care of him. And on the morrow when he departed, he took out two pence, and gave *them* to the host, and said unto him, Take care of him; and whatsoever thou spendest more, when I come again, I will repay thee" (Lu.10:33-35).

"I have showed you all things, how that so labouring ye ought to support the weak, and to remember the words of the LORD Jesus, how he said, It is more blessed to give than to receive" (Ac.20:35).

"We then that are strong ought to bear the infirmities of the weak, and not to please ourselves" (Ro.15:1).

"Only *they would* that we should remember the poor; the same which I also was forward to do" (Ga.2:10).

"Bear ye one another's burdens, and so fulfil the law of Christ" (Ga.6:2).

"Now we exhort you, brethren, warn them that are unruly, comfort the feebleminded, support the weak, be patient toward all *men*" (1 Th.5:14).

"Remember them that are in bonds, as bound with them; *and* them which suffer adversity, as being yourselves also in the body" (He.13:3).

"Pure religion and undefiled before God and the Father is this, To visit the fatherless and widows in their affliction, *and* to keep himself unspotted from the world" (Js.1:27).

"If there be among you a poor man of one of thy brethren within any of thy gates in thy land which the LORD thy God giveth thee, thou shalt not harden thine heart, nor shut thine hand from thy poor brother" (De.15:7).

"I was eyes to the blind, and feet *was* I to the lame. I *was* a father to the poor: and the cause *which* I knew not I searched out" (Jb.29:15-16).

"Blessed *is* he that considereth the poor: the LORD will deliver him in time of trouble" (Ps.41:1).

"Defend the poor and fatherless: do justice to the afflicted and needy" (Ps.82:3).

"He that hath pity upon the poor lendeth unto the LORD; and that which he hath given will he pay him again" (Pr.19:17).

"Whoso stoppeth his ears at the cry of the poor, he also shall cry himself, but shall not be heard" (Pr.21:13).

"She stretcheth out her hand to the poor; yea, she reacheth forth her hands to the needy" (Pr.31:20).

"The LORD GOD hath given me the tongue of the learned, that I should know how to speak a word in season to *him that is* weary: he wakeneth morning by morning, he wakeneth mine ear to hear as the learned" (Is.50:4).

"*Is it* [your purpose] not to deal thy bread to the hungry, and that thou bring the poor that are cast out to thy house? when thou seest the naked, that thou cover him; and that thou hide not thyself from thine own flesh" (Is.58:7).

"He hath showed thee, O man, what *is* good; and what doth the LORD require of thee, but to do justly, and to love mercy, and to walk humbly with thy God" (Mi.6:8).

2 (21:10-15) **Fear, Deliverance from, Example of—Deliverance, from What, Fear—David, As a Fugitive**: David fled to King Achish who was the Philistine king ruling from the capital city of Gath. David hoped that King Achish would give him refuge and sanctuary from King Saul. At first, King Achish saw great advantage in David's becoming a mercenary soldier for him; thus he gave David sanctuary. But what happened next gives a glimpse into the fear, distress, and pressure David was constantly under during these days:

OUTLINE	SCRIPTURE	SCRIPTURE	OUTLINE

2. David fled to the Philistine king, Achish: Deliverance from life-threatening fear
 	
a. The threat to David by the officials of Achish
  1) They saw David as a defector & a mercenary—an enemy of Saul
  2) They feared & were suspicious that he might turn against them
b. The cautious fear of David & his strategy of escape, Ps.34
	10 And David arose, and fled that day for fear of Saul, and went to Achish the king of Gath.
	11 And the servants of Achish said unto him, *Is* not this David the king of the land? did they not sing one to another of him in dances, saying, Saul hath slain his thousands, and David his ten thousands?
	12 And David laid up these words in his heart, and was sore afraid of Achish the king of Gath.
		13 And he changed his behaviour before them, and feigned himself mad in their hands, and scrabbled on the doors of the gate, and let his spittle fall down upon his beard.
		14 Then said Achish unto his servants, Lo, ye see the man is mad: wherefore *then* have ye brought him to me?
		15 Have I need of mad men, that ye have brought this *fellow* to play the mad man in my presence? shall this *fellow* come into my house?
			1) David pretended to be insane: Walked around drooling saliva & abusing public property by writing graffiti on the doors of the city gates
			
			2) Achish strongly objected to a madman's being in his army & presence
			
			3) Achish had David removed, driven from his presence, Ps.34

a. The officials of Achish became suspicious of David and felt that he was a threat to the Philistines (v.11). They too saw great advantage in having David on their side as a defector and a mercenary fighting against the Israelites. But the officials were suspicious of David and began to whisper that he might turn against them when fighting with the Israelites broke out. Note that the officials referred to David as the king of Israel and that they were aware the Israelites considered him to be a hero. Of course, this only intensified the Philistines' fear of David.

b. David became aware of the whispering suspicion against him and fear gripped his heart. Convinced that his life was in jeopardy, David planned a unique strategy of escape (vv.12-15). Note that this experience provides the background for Psalm 34 and perhaps Psalm 56. David's strategy was to pretend that he was insane. This he did by walking around drooling saliva and abusing public property by making marks and writing graffiti on the doors of the city gates.

Convinced of David's insanity, King Achish strongly objected to a madman's being in his presence and serving in his army. He had David removed from the royal court and most likely driven from the city. In that day and time an insane person was thought to be under the influence of some powerful spirit or god; consequently, the insane person could not be harmed lest the gods be provoked.

Thought 1. David tells us in Psalm 34 that it was the LORD who delivered him through this crisis. No matter what the crisis is, the LORD will deliver us, providing a way for us to escape the crisis or to overcome and conquer it. The LORD delivers us through all our problems and troubles, and He saves us from the grasp of all enemies who threaten us. The Word of God declares that the LORD will always save and deliver us:

"There hath no temptation taken you but such as is common to man: but God *is* faithful, who will not suffer you to be tempted above that ye are able; but will with the temptation also make a way to escape, that ye may be able to bear *it*" (1 Co.10:13).

"Who delivered us from so great a death, and doth deliver: in whom we trust that he will yet deliver *us*" (2 Co.1:10).

"And the LORD shall deliver me from every evil work, and will preserve *me* unto his heavenly kingdom: to whom *be* glory for ever and ever. Amen" (2 Ti.4:18).

"Forasmuch then as the children are partakers of flesh and blood, he also himself likewise took part of the same; that through death he might destroy him that had the power of death, that is, the devil; And deliver them who through fear of death were all their lifetime subject to bondage" (He.2:14-15).

"The LORD knoweth how to deliver the godly out of temptations, and to reserve the unjust unto the day of judgment to be punished" (2 Pt.2:9).

"The LORD *is* my strength and my shield; my heart trusted in him, and I am helped: therefore my heart greatly rejoiceth; and with my song will I praise him" (Ps.28:7).

"But I *am* poor and needy; *yet* the L ORD thinketh upon me: thou *art* my help and my deliverer; make no tarrying, O my God" (Ps.40:17).

"Surely he shall deliver thee from the snare of the fowler, *and* from the noisome pestilence" (Ps.91:3).

"Fear thou not; for I *am* with thee: be not dismayed; for I *am* thy God: I will strengthen thee; yea, I will help thee; yea, I will uphold thee with the right hand of my righteousness" (Is.41:10).

"Fear not: for I have redeemed thee, I have called *thee* by thy name; thou *art* mine. When thou passest through the waters, I *will be* with thee; and through the rivers, they shall not overflow thee: when thou walkest through the fire, thou shalt not be burned; neither shall the flame kindle upon thee" (Is.43:1-2).

"And *even* to *your* old age I *am* he; and *even* to hoar [gray] hairs will I carry *you:* I have made, and I will bear; even I will carry, and will deliver *you*" (Is.46:4).

"Be not afraid of their faces: for I *am* with thee to deliver thee, saith the L ORD" (Je.1:8).

"He delivereth and rescueth, and he worketh signs and wonders in heaven and in earth, who hath delivered Daniel from the power of the lions" (Da.6:27).

[3] (22:1-2) **Anguish, Deliverance from—Distress, Deliverance from—Fear, Deliverance from—Crying Out to God, Example of—Prayer, Example of**: David escaped to the cave of Adullam after leaving Gath and fleeing from the Philistines. After settling down at the cave, David's brothers and his father's household came to join him at the cave, fearing Saul's reprisal against them. This meant that David's older brothers deserted Saul's army and became fugitives just like David.

Eventually a force of 400 men rallied around David, men who were distressed, indebted, or just disgusted with the way Saul was running the government. As Matthew Henry said, these were "men of broken fortunes and restless spirits."[3] David was now a fugitive, and men in similar circumstances saw in David a great leader who represented the future of the nation. That is why, by the hundreds, they began to flock to him and link up with him, building the power base that was to serve the nation throughout the years of David's reign (2 S.23:8-9; 1 Chr.11:10-41).

OUTLINE	SCRIPTURE	SCRIPTURE	OUTLINE
3. David escaped to the cave of Adullam: A time of deep anguish & of crying out to the L ORD in prayer, Ps.142 a. His family joined him: Feared Saul's reprisal b. A force of 400 men also	David therefore departed thence, and escaped to the cave Adullam: and when his brethren and all his father's house heard it, they went down thither to him. 2 And every one *that was* in	distress, and every one that *was* in debt, and every one *that was* discontented, gathered themselves unto him; and he became a captain over them: and there were with him about four hundred men.	joined him: Those distressed, indebted, or discontented— "men of broken fortunes & restless spirits"[1]

Thought 1. Psalm 142 tells us that an overwhelming sense of loneliness, of being forsaken, of having no man to help him gripped David's spirit during the early days of living in the cave. But he cried unto the L ORD in deep anguish of spirit, and the L ORD heard him.

When we are in distress and trouble, facing trial and temptation, in deep anguish and agony, facing all kinds of afflictions and problems—there is great hope. We can cry out to the L ORD in prayer and He will hear us. The L ORD will answer our prayer and meet our need. No matter our distress or anguish, if we turn to the L ORD and cry out for His help, He promises to meet our need.

"Therefore I say unto you, What things soever ye desire, when ye pray, believe that ye receive *them*, and ye shall have *them*" (Mk.11:24).

"And I say unto you, Ask, and it shall be given you; seek, and ye shall find; knock, and it shall be opened unto you" (Lu.11:9).

"If ye abide in me, and my words abide in you, ye shall ask what ye will, and it shall be done unto you" (Jn.15:7).

"Is any among you afflicted? let him pray. Is any merry? let him sing psalms" (Js.5:13).

"Confess *your* faults one to another, and pray one for another, that ye may be healed. The effectual fervent prayer of a righteous man availeth much" (Js.5:16).

"If my people, which are called by my name, shall humble themselves, and pray, and seek my face, and turn from their wicked ways; then will I hear from heaven, and will forgive their sin, and will heal their land" (2 Chr.7:14).

"This poor man cried, and the L ORD heard *him*, and saved him out of all his troubles" (Ps.34:6).

"From the end of the earth will I cry unto thee, when my heart is overwhelmed: lead me to the rock *that* is higher than I" (Ps.61:2).

"He shall call upon me, and I will answer him: I *will be* with him in trouble; I will deliver him, and honour him" (Ps.91:15).

"Then shalt thou call, and the L ORD shall answer; thou shalt cry, and he shall say, Here I *am*. If thou take away from the midst of thee the yoke, the putting forth of the finger, and speaking vanity" (Is.58:9).

---

3 Matthew Henry. *Matthew Henry's Commentary*, p.398.

"And it shall come to pass, that before they call, I will answer; and while they are yet speaking, I will hear" (Is.65:24).

"And ye shall seek me, and find *me,* when ye shall search for me with all your heart" (Je.29:13).

Thought 2. Psalm 142 gives a graphic description of the deep anguish and agony of soul that David was experiencing while living in the cave of Adullam.

"I cried unto the LORD with my voice; with my voice unto the LORD did I make my supplication. I poured out my complaint before him; I showed before him my trouble. When my spirit was overwhelmed within me, then thou knewest my path. In the way wherein I walked have they privily laid a snare for me. I looked on my right hand, and beheld, but there was no man that would know me: refuge failed me; no man cared for my soul. I cried unto thee, O LORD: I said, Thou art my refuge and my portion in the land of the living. Attend unto my cry; for I am brought very low: deliver me from my persecutors; for they are stronger than I. Bring my soul out of prison, that I may praise thy name: the righteous shall compass me about; for thou shalt deal bountifully with me" (Ps.142).

4 (22:3-4) **Parents, Duty Toward—Believer, Duty to Parents—David, Family of**: David took responsibility for his parents and sought to take care of them, even during his days as a fugitive. This is clearly seen in the events that happened. After some time in the cave at Adullam, David moved to Mizpah and asked the king of Moab to grant sanctuary to his parents. Remember that David's great-grandmother was Ruth who was from Moab (Ruth 4:13-22). Probably for this reason the king of Moab granted the request. Note that the parents stayed in Moab as long as David was hiding out in a stronghold or fortress in the land of Moab. Just where the stronghold or fortress was located is not stated, but it obviously gave David a secure and safe place to hide from the pursuit of Saul.

OUTLINE	SCRIPTURE	SCRIPTURE	OUTLINE
4. David sought to take care of his parents: The believer's clear duty a. David moved to Mizpah & asked the king of Moab to grant sanctuary to his parents	3 And David went thence to Mizpeh of Moab: and he said unto the king of Moab, Let my father and my mother, I pray thee, come forth, *and be* with you, till I know what	God will do for me. 4 And he brought them before the king of Moab: and they dwelt with him all the while that David was in the hold.	b. David's parents stayed in Moab as long as David was hiding out in a stronghold in the land of Moab

Thought 1. The lesson for us is clear: we must take care of our parents. David set a dynamic example for us in the care of his parents. Despite his own distressing circumstances—a time of extreme trouble—David did not forget nor ignore his parents. He made sure they were taken care of and looked after, being protected and provided for.

When our parents are aged and unable to care for themselves, we are to provide for them. We are to make sure they have housing, food, clothing, and whatever medical help is available and needed. No person must ever forsake his parents in their hour of need. This is the clear teaching of God's Holy Word:

"For God commanded, saying, Honour thy father and mother: and, He that curseth father or mother, let him die the death" (Mt.15:4).

"For Moses said, Honour thy father and thy mother; and, Whoso curseth father or mother, let him die the death" (Mk.7:10).

"Children, obey your parents in the LORD: for this is right. Honour thy father and mother; (which is the first commandment with promise;) That it may be well with thee, and thou mayest live long on the earth" (Ep.6:1-3).

"Rebuke not an elder, but intreat *him* as a father; *and* the younger men as brethren" (1 Ti.5:1).

"But if any widow have children or nephews, let them learn first to show piety at home, and to requite their parents: for that is good and acceptable before God" (1 Ti.5:4).

"Honour thy father and thy mother: that thy days may be long upon the land which the LORD thy God giveth thee" (Ex.20:12).

"Ye shall fear every man his mother, and his father, and keep my sabbaths: I *am* the LORD your God" (Le.19:3).

"Thou shalt rise up before the hoary [aged, gray] head, and honour the face of the old man, and fear thy God: I *am* the LORD" (Le.19:32).

"Cursed *be* he that setteth light by his father or his mother. And all the people shall say, Amen" (De.27:16).

"My son, hear the instruction of thy father, and forsake not the law of thy mother" (Pr.1:8).

"Whoso curseth his father or his mother, his lamp shall be put out in obscure darkness" (Pr.20:20).

"Hearken unto thy father that begat thee, and despise not thy mother when she is old" (Pr.23:22).

"The eye *that* mocketh at *his* father, and despiseth to obey *his* mother, the ravens of the valley shall pick it out, and the young eagles shall eat it" (Pr.30:17).

5 (22:5) **Guidance, of God, Example of—God, Guidance of, Example of—David, Guidance by God**: David was guided by God through the prophet Gad. For some reason it was unwise for David to remain in the stronghold or fortress. Just why is not stated, but God wanted David to leave Mizpah and return to Judah. Therefore the LORD sent the prophet Gad to give David these very instructions. As a result, David left the fortress and returned to Judah, setting up camp in the forest of Hereth. Being a military genius, David knew that the forest would provide both an excellent camouflage and many hiding places for protection against any large, mobilized force launched by Saul against him.

Note, this is the first mention of the prophet Gad who was now to join forces with David and become his own personal prophet. Gad was later to provide music for the temple services, write a history of David's kingship, and rebuke David for taking a census of the Israelites (2 S.24:11-25; 1 Chr.29:29; 2 Chr.29:25).

OUTLINE	SCRIPTURE	SCRIPTURE	OUTLINE
5. David was guided by the LORD through the prophet Gad: God's guidance	5 And the prophet Gad said unto David, Abide not in the hold; depart, and get thee into	the land of Judah. Then David departed, and came into the forest of Hareth.	**through the trials of life** a. Was to leave Mizpah b. Was to return to Judah

Thought 1. Just as God guided David, so God will guide us. Day by day, hour by hour, moment by moment—God promises to guide us...
* in making decisions
* in being tested and tried
* in facing difficult circumstances
* in facing trials and problems
* in confronting temptations and seductions
* in combating opposition and abuse
* in suffering disease or accident
* in facing death and the loss of loved ones
* in being perplexed and bewildered and not knowing what to do next
* in learning how to meet the necessities of life—food, housing, and clothing
* in learning how to become secure and gain a sense of fulfillment and purpose

We desperately need the guidance of God. In fact, a moment of time is never experienced when we do not need His guidance. And the wonderful news is just this: God will guide us. This is the wonderful promise of His Holy Word:

"Through the tender mercy of our God; whereby the dayspring from on high hath visited us, To give light to them that sit in darkness and *in* the shadow of death, to guide our feet into the way of peace" (Lu.1:78-79).

"Then spake Jesus again unto them, saying, I am the light of the world: he that followeth me shall not walk in darkness, but shall have the light of life" (Jn.8:12).

"Howbeit when he, the Spirit of truth, is come, he will guide you into all truth: for he shall not speak of himself; but whatsoever he shall hear, *that* shall he speak: and he will show you things to come" (Jn.16:13).

"The LORD *is* my shepherd; I shall not want. He maketh me to lie down in green pastures: he leadeth me beside the still waters. He restoreth my soul: he leadeth me in the paths of righteousness for his name's sake. Yea, though I walk through the valley of the shadow of death, I will fear no evil: for thou *art* with me; thy rod and thy staff they comfort me. Thou preparest a table before me in the presence of mine enemies: thou anointest my head with oil; my cup runneth over. Surely goodness and mercy shall follow me all the days of my life: and I will dwell in the house of the LORD for ever" (Ps.23:1-6).

"The meek will he guide in judgment: and the meek will he teach his way" (Ps.25:9).

"For this God *is* our God for ever and ever: he will be our guide *even* unto death" (Ps.48:14).

"Thou shalt guide me with thy counsel, and afterward receive me *to* glory" (Ps.73:24).

"Unto the upright there ariseth light in the darkness: *he is* gracious, and full of compassion, and righteous" (Ps.112:4).

"But the path of the just *is* as the shining light, that shineth more and more unto the perfect day" (Pr.4:18).

"And thine ears shall hear a word behind thee, saying, This *is* the way, walk ye in it, when ye turn to the right hand, and when ye turn to the left" (Is.30:21).

"And I will bring the blind by a way *that* they knew not; I will lead them in paths *that* they have not known: I will make darkness light before them, and crooked things straight. These things will I do unto them, and not forsake them" (Is.42:16).

1. The suspicion of Saul that a massive conspiracy against him existed: The terrible evil of hostility, anger, wrath

a. Saul heard of David's return to Judea with followers flocking to him: Heard while conducting official business

b. Saul flew into a rage, a half-crazed tirade: Launched a barrage of insane accusations against his officials

1) Suggested they would lose their wealth & leadership positions under David

2) Suggested they were conspiring against him

3) Suggested Jonathan was the ringleader of the conspiracy, that David was merely Jonathan's hired assassin

c. Saul was told immediately that David had fled to the High Priest Ahimelech for help: Disclosed by Doeg the Edomite

1) He witnessed David's visit

2) He saw the priest pray for David & give him food & a sword

2. The arrest & murder of the priests by Saul: The terrible evil of injustice & murder

a. The false charge against the priests & their arrest by a perverted mind: Accused them of joining David's conspiracy

b. The defense of Ahimelech
1) He defended David

B. The Insane Murder of the Priests by Saul: A Picture of the Terrible Evil of Certain Sins, 22:6-23

6 When Saul heard that David was discovered, and the men that *were* with him, (now Saul abode in Gibeah under a tree in Ramah, having his spear in his hand, and all his servants *were* standing about him;)

7 Then Saul said unto his servants that stood about him, Hear now, ye Benjamites; will the son of Jesse give every one of you fields and vineyards, *and* make you all captains of thousands, and captains of hundreds;

8 That all of you have conspired against me, and *there is* none that showeth me that my son hath made a league with the son of Jesse, and *there is* none of you that is sorry for me, or showeth unto me that my son hath stirred up my servant against me, to lie in wait, as at this day?

9 Then answered Doeg the Edomite, which was set over the servants of Saul, and said, I saw the son of Jesse coming to Nob, to Ahimelech the son of Ahitub.

10 And he enquired of the LORD for him, and gave him victuals, and gave him the sword of Goliath the Philistine.

11 Then the king sent to call Ahimelech the priest, the son of Ahitub, and all his father's house, the priests that *were* in Nob: and they came all of them to the king.

12 And Saul said, Hear now, thou son of Ahitub. And he answered, Here I *am*, my lord.

13 And Saul said unto him, Why have ye conspired against me, thou and the son of Jesse, in that thou hast given him bread, and a sword, and hast enquired of God for him, that he should rise against me, to lie in wait, as at this day?

14 Then Ahimelech answered the king, and said,

And who *is so* faithful among all thy servants as David, which is the king's son in law, and goeth at thy bidding, and is honourable in thine house?

15 Did I then begin to enquire of God for him? be it far from me: let not the king impute *any* thing unto his servant, *nor* to all the house of my father: for thy servant knew nothing of all this, less or more.

16 And the king said, Thou shalt surely die, Ahimelech, thou, and all thy father's house.

17 And the king said unto the footmen that stood about him, Turn, and slay the priests of the LORD; because their hand also *is* with David, and because they knew when he fled, and did not show it to me. But the servants of the king would not put forth their hand to fall upon the priests of the LORD.

18 And the king said to Doeg, Turn thou, and fall upon the priests. And Doeg the Edomite turned, and he fell upon the priests, and slew on that day fourscore and five persons that did wear a linen ephod.

19 And Nob, the city of the priests, smote he with the edge of the sword, both men and women, children and sucklings, and oxen, and asses, and sheep, with the edge of the sword.

20 And one of the sons of Ahimelech the son of Ahitub, named Abiathar, escaped, and fled after David.

21 And Abiathar showed David that Saul had slain the LORD's priests.

22 And David said unto Abiathar, I knew *it* that day, when Doeg the Edomite *was* there, that he would surely tell Saul: I have occasioned *the death* of all the persons of thy father's house.

23 Abide thou with me, fear not: for he that seeketh my life seeketh thy life: but with me thou *shalt be* in safeguard.

• Was loyal to Saul
• Was Saul's son-in-law & captain of the bodyguard
• Was highly respected

2) He had done nothing except seek the LORD for David

3) He personally was Saul's loyal servant

4) He knew nothing, was not involved in a plot

c. The disturbing, unjust verdict by Saul: All the priests with their families were to be executed

1) Saul ordered his personal guards to execute the priests: But they refused, would not raise a hand against them

2) Saul then ordered Doeg the Edomite to execute the priests
• He obeyed & killed 85 priests

• He then journeyed to Nob where he carried out a mass execution: Killed all the men, women, children, & animals

3. The escape of the priest Abiathar & David's grief: The terrible results of lying, 21:1-2

a. Abiathar fled to David & told him of the atrocity

b. David grieved for the priests & accepted responsibility for their deaths
1) Due to his failure to kill Doeg
2) Due to his seeking their help by lying, 21:1-2

c. David granted protection to the priest Abiathar

DIVISION IV

THE STORY OF SAUL AND DAVID (PART 2):
DAVID THE FUGITIVE, 21:1–31:13

B. The Insane Murder of the Priests by Saul: A Picture of the Terrible Evil of Certain Sins, 22:6-23

(22:6-23) **Introduction—Perfection, Fact, Short of—Imperfection, Caused by—Corruption, Seed of—Sin, Results—Death, Caused by**: all bad circumstances, behaviors, thoughts, and events—including death—are short of God's glory. And to be short of God's glory is to be short of perfection. This is what is wrong with the world: it is short of perfection. The world—including man—has become corrupted; and because of the *seed of corruption*, we and our world are disintegrating, deteriorating, and decaying. We are ever rushing toward the point of death and the time when we will cease to exist.

What has caused this *seed of corruption*? Sin! The terrible evil of sin. Sinful, evil behavior has planted the seed of corruption, disintegration, deterioration, and decay within the universe. The universe and everything within the universe faces death because of sin. Death is the inevitable consequence of sin.

This present Scripture shows just how terrible the evil of sin can be. Certain sins are exposed in the lives of Saul and David. And the terrible consequences of these sins are painted as a lesson for us. This is: *The Insane Murder of the Priests by Saul: A Picture of the Terrible Evil of Certain Sins,* 22:6-23.

1. The suspicion of Saul that a massive conspiracy against him existed: the terrible evil of hostility, anger, wrath (vv.6-10).
2. The arrest and murder of the priests by Saul: the terrible evil of injustice and murder (vv.11-19).
3. The escape of the priest Abiathar and David's grief: the terrible results of lying, 21:1-2 (vv.20-23).

1 (22:6-10) **Hostility, Example of—Anger, Example of—Wrath, Example of—Saul, Attempts to Kill David—David, Attempts Against His Life—Conspiracy, Suspicion of—Suspicion, of Conspiracy, Example of**: there was the suspicion of Saul that a massive conspiracy against him existed. What happened as a result of his suspicion is a tragic, terrible picture of evil, of just what can happen when a person becomes angry and hostile, full of wrath.

OUTLINE	SCRIPTURE	SCRIPTURE	OUTLINE
1. The suspicion of Saul that a massive conspiracy against him existed: The terrible evil of hostility, anger, wrath	6 When Saul heard that David was discovered, and the men that *were* with him, (now Saul abode in Gibeah under a tree in Ramah, having his spear in his hand, and all his servants *were* standing about him;)	that my son hath made a league with the son of Jesse, and *there is* none of you that is sorry for me, or showeth unto me that my son hath stirred up my servant against me, to lie in wait, as at this day?	the ringleader of the conspiracy, that David was merely Jonathan's hired assassin
a. Saul heard of David's return to Judea with followers flocking to him: Heard while conducting official business			
b. Saul flew into a rage, a half-crazed tirade: Launched a barrage of insane accusations against his officials	7 Then Saul said unto his servants that stood about him, Hear now, ye Benjamites; will the son of Jesse give every one of you fields and vineyards, *and* make you all captains of thousands, and captains of hundreds;	9 Then answered Doeg the Edomite, which was set over the servants of Saul, and said, I saw the son of Jesse coming to Nob, to Ahimelech the son of Ahitub.	c. Saul was told immediately that David had fled to the High Priest Ahimelech for help: Disclosed by Doeg the Edomite
1) Suggested they would lose their wealth & leadership positions under David		10 And he enquired of the LORD for him, and gave him victuals, and gave him the sword of Goliath the Philistine.	1) He witnessed David's visit
2) Suggested they were conspiring against him	8 That all of you have conspired against me, and *there is* none that showeth me		2) He saw the priest pray for David & give him food & a sword
3) Suggested Jonathan was			

a. Saul soon heard of David's return to Judea with followers flocking to him (v.6). Saul received the spy report while conducting some official business out in the open, under a tamarisk tree on the hill of Gibeah.

b. Upon receiving the spy report, Saul immediately flew into a rage, a half-crazed tirade (vv.7-8). He launched a barrage of insane accusations against his officials, suggesting they would lose their wealth and leadership positions if they allowed David to usurp or seize the throne. Feeling that his officers had been complacent in capturing David, he became filled with bitter rage and hostility. By their lethargy and complacency in capturing David, Saul suggested that they—his very own commanders—were conspiring against him. But that was not the only charge of Saul's raging insanity: he suggested that Jonathan was actually the ringleader of the conspiracy, that he had hired David as an assassin, charging him to kill his father, King Saul.

Stunned by Saul's angry, hostile outburst, the commanders stood in stone silence, most likely wondering how best to defend themselves against such outrageous, insane accusations. What happened next was to cause one of the greatest tragedies in David's life.

c. Doeg the Edomite stepped forth and revealed that David had visited the High Priest Ahimelech at the Tabernacle in Nob (vv.9-10). He told Saul that he had personally witnessed David's visit and saw the priest pray for David, giving him provisions and the sword of Goliath.

In Saul's distorted and hostile mind, this was a very serious charge against the High Priest. For it meant that Ahimelech was supporting and giving aid to his archenemy, David.

Thought 1. Anger is a terrible evil, an evil that can give rise to further hostility and wrath. And hostility and wrath can lead to vengeance. In fact, the LORD says that anger is the root of murder. And a person who has anger within his heart stands guilty before God and will face the judgment of God. There is, of course, a justified anger, an anger that is directed against the evil of this world. A person should despise the wicked behavior of lawlessness, violence, and immorality. But all anger that is directed against another human being—all hostility and wrath against others—is a terrible evil, an evil that will face the judgment of God.

"But I say unto you, That whosoever is angry with his brother without a cause shall be in danger of the judgment: and whosoever shall say to his brother, Raca, shall be in danger of the council: but whosoever shall say, Thou fool, shall be in danger of hell fire" (Mt.5:22).

"Now the works of the flesh are manifest, which are *these;* Adultery, fornication, uncleanness, lasciviousness, Idolatry, witchcraft, hatred, variance, emulations, wrath, strife, seditions, heresies, Envyings, murders, drunkenness, revellings, and such like: of the which I tell you before, as I have also told *you* in time past, that they which do such things shall not inherit the kingdom of God" (Ga.5:19-21).

"Whosoever hateth his brother is a murderer: and ye know that no murderer hath eternal life abiding in him" (1 Jn.3:15).

"Cease from anger, and forsake wrath: fret not thyself in any wise to do evil" (Ps.37:8).

"Be not hasty in thy spirit to be angry: for anger resteth in the bosom of fools" (Ec.7:9).

2 (22:11-19) **Murder, Example of—Murder, of Priests and Ministers—Injustice, Example of—Injustice, Against Priests and Ministers—Saul, Unjust Acts of—Ahimelech, the High Priest, Murder of—Doeg, the Edomite, Evil of**: there was the arrest and murder of the priests by Saul, a terrible, horrendous act of injustice. All kinds of wild imaginations were running through Saul's insane, distorted mind. He apparently pictured David securing the support of the priests and amassing a large force of fugitives against him. Tragically, he concluded that he must stamp out the opposition before it grew any more. And this meant the execution of the High Priest—and all the priests. Scripture gives a graphic description:

OUTLINE	SCRIPTURE	SCRIPTURE	OUTLINE
2. The arrest & murder of the priests by Saul: The terrible evil of injustice & murder	11 Then the king sent to call Ahimelech the priest, the son of Ahitub, and all his father's house, the priests that *were* in Nob: and they came all of them to the king.	or more. 16 And the king said, Thou shalt surely die, Ahimelech, thou, and all thy father's house.	not involved in a plot c. The disturbing, unjust verdict by Saul: All the priests with their families were to be executed
a. The false charge against the priests & their arrest by a perverted mind: Accused them of joining David's conspiracy	12 And Saul said, Hear now, thou son of Ahitub. And he answered, Here I *am,* my lord. 13 And Saul said unto him, Why have ye conspired against me, thou and the son of Jesse, in that thou hast given him bread, and a sword, and hast enquired of God for him, that he should rise against me, to lie in wait, as at this day?	17 And the king said unto the footmen that stood about him, Turn, and slay the priests of the LORD; because their hand also *is* with David, and because they knew when he fled, and did not show it to me. But the servants of the king would not put forth their hand to fall upon the priests of the LORD.	1) Saul ordered his personal guards to execute the priests: But they refused, would not raise a hand against them
b. The defense of Ahimelech 1) He defended David • Was loyal to Saul • Was Saul's son-in-law & captain of the body-guard • Was highly respected 2) He had done nothing except seek the LORD for David 3) He personally was Saul's loyal servant 4) He knew nothing, was	14 Then Ahimelech answered the king, and said, And who *is so* faithful among all thy servants as David, which is the king's son in law, and goeth at thy bidding, and is honourable in thine house? 15 Did I then begin to enquire of God for him? be it far from me: let not the king impute *any* thing unto his servant, *nor* to all the house of my father: for thy servant knew nothing of all this, less	18 And the king said to Doeg, Turn thou, and fall upon the priests. And Doeg the Edomite turned, and he fell upon the priests, and slew on that day fourscore and five persons that did wear a linen ephod. 19 And Nob, the city of the priests, smote he with the edge of the sword, both men and women, children and sucklings, and oxen, and asses, and sheep, with the edge of the sword.	2) Saul then ordered Doeg the Edomite to execute the priests • He obeyed & killed 85 priests • He then journeyed to Nob where he carried out a mass execution: Killed all the men, women, children, & animals

a. Saul had the priests arrested and then leveled his false, perverted charges against them (vv.11-13). Saul directed the charge against the High Priest Ahimelech himself, charging him and the other priests with joining the conspiracy of David. Saul charged that by giving David food and a sword and by praying for him, they had aided and encouraged him to revolt against the king. In fact, Saul alleged that David could be secretly lurking anywhere at that very moment, ready to assassinate him at the first opportunity. Thus Saul concluded that all the priests were guilty of a capital crime for giving aid to David, guilty of being traitors to Saul and the nation.

b. Utterly shocked at this barrage of insane accusations, Ahimelech offered what was a simple but truthful and powerful defense (vv.14-15). First, Ahimelech defended David, declaring that David had been loyal to Saul, in fact, more loyal than Saul's other servants. Moreover, David was Saul's son-in-law and the captain of the royal bodyguard. In addition, David was highly respected even by those in Saul's royal household.

Second, Ahimelech declared that his prayer and his seeking of the LORD for David were not unusual. For he had often sought the LORD on David's behalf (v.15). Thus he was carrying out his ministry just as he was charged to do, and in no way could he be charged with showing favoritism nor with joining any conspiracy of David's.

Third, Ahimelech declared that he was personally Saul's servant and was loyal to him (v.15). Note that Ahimelech referred to himself as Saul's servant two different times in this one verse.

Fourth, Ahimelech claimed that he knew absolutely nothing about a conspiracy. At the time of meeting the need of David, he was ignorant of this whole affair.

Note that Ahimelech appealed to Saul not to charge him or the other priests with a capital crime. They were not conspirators against the king, nor had they joined David in any conspiracy against Saul.

c. Determined to eliminate any who stood opposed to him, Saul issued the disturbing, unjust verdict against Ahimelech and the other priests. They were all—they and their families—to be executed (v.16). Immediately, Saul turned and ordered his personal guards to execute the priests (v.17). But a surprising thing happened: they refused, would not raise a hand against the priests. No doubt they feared killing the servants of the Living God and viewed the sentence upon them as an unjust verdict. Murdering the priests would be opposing God Himself.

Under God's sovereign leadership, Saul somehow understood the reluctance of his personal guards to carry out his order. Therefore, Saul immediately turned and ordered Doeg the Edomite to execute the priests (vv.18-19). Tragically, this unbelieving pagan obeyed and killed eighty-five priests who had been appointed by God to serve His people. Once this horrible atrocity had been carried out, Doeg traveled to Nob where he committed an even more horrendous act: the execution of every living thing within the city. He killed all the men, women, children, and animals. He and Saul had obviously twisted the harem principle or law of total destruction to suit their own selfish ends (see DEEPER STUDY # 1—1 Sa.15:3 for more discussion).

> **Thought 1**. Any thinking and honest person knows that murder is a horrible evil. A person may be a sociopath—have no values and no sense of ethics or morality—yet if he thinks and is honest, he knows that taking someone's life is the most terrible thing that can be committed against the victim. For murder wipes out the very existence of a person. Not even one opportunity to look, hear, taste, touch, love, or think will ever again be experienced by the victim of murder.
>
> God created the world, and He created the life of man to be the summit of His creation. Therefore, life is precious to God. Nothing is any more precious or valued than the *sanctity of life*. And no life is ever to be deliberately taken from a person. Premeditated murder—deliberate murder—is not only a capital offense among men, it is a capital offense to God. And such an offense against God will bear the severest judgment.
>
> > "For the wrath of God is revealed from heaven against all ungodliness and unrighteousness of men, who hold the truth in unrighteousness....Being filled with all unrighteousness, fornication, wickedness, covetousness, maliciousness; full of envy, murder, debate, deceit, malignity; whisperers, Backbiters, haters of God, despiteful, proud, boasters, inventors of evil things, disobedient to parents, Without understanding, covenantbreakers, without natural affection, implacable, unmerciful: Who knowing the judgment of God, that they which commit such things are worthy of death, not only do the same, but have pleasure in them that do them" (Ro.1:18, 29-32).
> >
> > "Now the works of the flesh are manifest, which are *these;* Adultery, fornication, uncleanness, lasciviousness, Idolatry, witchcraft, hatred, variance, emulations, wrath, strife, seditions, heresies, Envyings, murders, drunkenness, revellings, and such like: of the which I tell you before, as I have also told *you* in time past, that they which do such things shall not inherit the kingdom of God" (Ga.5:19-21).
> >
> > "Whosoever hateth his brother is a murderer: and ye know that no murderer hath eternal life abiding in him" (1 Jn.3:15).
> >
> > "But the fearful, and unbelieving, and the abominable, and murderers, and whoremongers, and sorcerers, and idolaters, and all liars, shall have their part in the lake which burneth with fire and brimstone: which is the second death" (Re.21:8).
> >
> > "Thou shalt not kill [murder]" (Ex.20:13).

3 (22:20-23) **Lying, Results, Injustice and Murder—Grief, Caused by—Abiathar, the Priest, Escaped Execution**: there was the priest Abiathar's escape and David's crushed spirit and agonizing grief. What happened shows the terrible result of lying:

OUTLINE	SCRIPTURE	SCRIPTURE	OUTLINE
3. The escape of the priest Abiathar & David's grief: The terrible results of lying, 21:1-2 a. Abiathar fled to David & told him of the atrocity b. David grieved for the priests & accepted responsibility	20 And one of the sons of Ahimelech the son of Ahitub, named Abiathar, escaped, and fled after David. 21 And Abiathar showed David that Saul had slain the LORD's priests. 22 And David said unto Abiathar, I knew *it* that day,	when Doeg the Edomite *was* there, that he would surely tell Saul: I have occasioned *the death* of all the persons of thy father's house. 23 Abide thou with me, fear not: for he that seeketh my life seeketh thy life: but with me thou *shalt be* in safeguard.	for their deaths 1) Due to his failure to kill Doeg 2) Due to his seeking their help by lying, 21:1-2 c. David granted protection to the priest Abiathar

a. One of the sons of Ahimelech escaped the slaughter of the priests and fled to join David. Arriving at David's hideout, he reported the horrible atrocity committed against the priests and charged Saul with being the instigator (vv.20-21). Shocked and stunned, David was stricken with an agonizing grief for the priests. And note, he accepted responsibility for their deaths (v.22). There were at least two reasons why David accepted responsibility for the horrible crime:

⇒ He had neglected to kill Doeg when he discovered that Doeg was in the Tabernacle while he was seeking the help of the priest (21:7).

⇒ He had sought the help of the priests by lying to them, claiming that he was on a secret mission for the king (21:2).

b. Knowing that his lie and deception had led to the horrible massacre of the priests was a heavy burden that David had to bear for the rest of his life, for the priests were completely innocent of any crime. They had tragically been slaughtered due to David, and not only due to him personally, but due to the terrible evil of his lying and deception. No doubt, he sought the forgiveness of God. And God forgave him just as He promises to forgive any person who confesses and repents of his sins. But this lie and deception led to such a horrible evil, it is doubtful that David was ever able to forget the atrocity his sin had caused.

c. David granted protection to the priest Abiathar, the only survivor of the massacre (v.23). David invited him to join his band of fugitives, assuring him that he would be safe. From this point on, David had the priest Abiathar accompanying him, as well as the prophet Gad (22:5, 23). However, note that Abiathar did not join David until David moved on to Keilah (23:6).

Thought 1. Lying and deception can cause devastating consequences. Lying and deception can...

• arouse lust, greed, and covetousness
• break hearts
• cause financial difficulty
• lead to false accusations
• cause a person to lose his job
• keep a person from securing employment or a promotion
• lead to unjust verdicts
• lead to imprisonment and even execution

Lies can destroy people and property, causing devastation and the most catastrophic upheavals in life. For this reason, God strongly condemns all liars and deceivers:

"**For the wrath of God is revealed from heaven against all ungodliness and unrighteousness of men, who hold the truth in unrighteousness....Being filled with all unrighteousness, fornication, wickedness, covetousness, maliciousness; full of envy, murder, debate, deceit, malignity; whisperers, Backbiters, haters of God, despiteful, proud, boasters, inventors of evil things, disobedient to parents, Without understanding, covenantbreakers, without natural affection, implacable, unmerciful: Who knowing the judgment of God, that they which commit such things are worthy of death, not only do the same, but have pleasure in them that do them**" (Ro.1:18, 29-32).

"**Lie not one to another, seeing that ye have put off the old man with his deeds**" (Col.3:9).

"**But the fearful, and unbelieving, and the abominable, and murderers, and whoremongers, and sorcerers, and idolaters, and all liars, shall have their part in the lake which burneth with fire and brimstone: which is the second death**" (Re.21:8).

"**Ye shall not steal, neither deal falsely, neither lie one to another**" (Le.19:11).

"**Thou shalt destroy them that speak leasing [lying]: the LORD will abhor the bloody and deceitful man**" (Ps.5:6).

"**But the king shall rejoice in God; every one that sweareth by him shall glory: but the mouth of them that speak lies shall be stopped**" (Ps.63:11).

"**He that worketh deceit shall not dwell within my house: he that telleth lies shall not tarry in my sight**" (Ps.101:7).

"**Lying lips *are* abomination to the LORD: but they that deal truly *are* his delight**" (Pr.12:22).

"**A false witness shall not be unpunished, and *he that* speaketh lies shall not escape**" (Pr.19:5).

"**The getting of treasures by a lying tongue *is* a vanity tossed to and fro of them that seek death**" (Pr.21:6).

CHAPTER 23

C. The Rescue of Keilah by David & the Insane Pursuit of David by Saul: A Picture of the Believer's Deliverance from All Enemies, 23:1-29

1. David saved the city of Keilah: Deliverance through courage
  a. David heard about the Philistine's attack
    1) He prayed: Asked the LORD if he should deliver the city
    2) The LORD answered: Go—save Keilah

  b. David's men opposed the defense of the city: The Philistine army was far superior in number & weapons

  c. David prayed again, seeking assurance of God's will
    1) The LORD's answer: Go
    2) The assurance: Victory was guaranteed—through the LORD
  d. David led his men in battle against the Philistines
    1) Inflicted heavy losses on them
    2) Saved the citizens of Keilah (in Judea)

  e. David was finally joined by the priest Abiathar at Keilah: He now had the ephod (used in prayer to seek God's will)

2. David escaped the fierce pursuit of Saul from place to place: Deliverance through prayer
  a. Saul heard that David was in Keilah, a walled, gated city
    1) He felt David could be trapped
    2) He mobilized his army to attack the city & seize David

  b. David learned about the plot & prayed, consulting the LORD

    1) First, he shared what he had heard with the LORD

    2) Second, he asked the LORD two questions
      • Would Saul attack Keilah in an attempt to

Then they told David, saying, Behold, the Philistines fight against Keilah, and they rob the threshingfloors.

2 Therefore David enquired of the LORD, saying, Shall I go and smite these Philistines? And the LORD said unto David, Go, and smite the Philistines, and save Keilah.

3 And David's men said unto him, Behold, we be afraid here in Judah: how much more then if we come to Keilah against the armies of the Philistines?

4 Then David enquired of the LORD yet again. And the LORD answered him and said, Arise, go down to Keilah; for I will deliver the Philistines into thine hand.

5 So David and his men went to Keilah, and fought with the Philistines, and brought away their cattle, and smote them with a great slaughter. So David saved the inhabitants of Keilah.

6 And it came to pass, when Abiathar the son of Ahimelech fled to David to Keilah, *that* he came down *with* an ephod in his hand.

7 And it was told Saul that David was come to Keilah. And Saul said, God hath delivered him into mine hand; for he is shut in, by entering into a town that hath gates and bars.

8 And Saul called all the people together to war, to go down to Keilah, to besiege David and his men.

9 And David knew that Saul secretly practised mischief against him; and he said to Abiathar the priest, Bring hither the ephod.

10 Then said David, O LORD God of Israel, thy servant hath certainly heard that Saul seeketh to come to Keilah, to destroy the city for my sake.

11 Will the men of Keilah deliver me up into his hand? will Saul come down, as thy servant hath heard? O LORD

God of Israel, I beseech thee, tell thy servant. And the LORD said, He will come down.

12 Then said David, Will the men of Keilah deliver me and my men into the hand of Saul? And the LORD said, They will deliver *thee* up.

13 Then David and his men, *which were* about six hundred, arose and departed out of Keilah, and went whithersoever they could go. And it was told Saul that David was escaped from Keilah; and he forbare to go forth.

14 And David abode in the wilderness in strong holds, and remained in a mountain in the wilderness of Ziph. And Saul sought him every day, but God delivered him not into his hand.

15 And David saw that Saul was come out to seek his life: and David *was* in the wilderness of Ziph in a wood.

16 And Jonathan Saul's son arose, and went to David into the wood, and strengthened his hand in God.

17 And he said unto him, Fear not: for the hand of Saul my father shall not find thee; and thou shalt be king over Israel, and I shall be next unto thee; and that also Saul my father knoweth.

18 And they two made a covenant before the LORD: and David abode in the woo'd, and Jonathan went to his house.

19 Then came up the Ziphites to Saul to Gibeah, saying, Doth not David hide himself with us in strong holds in the wood, in the hill of Hachilah, which *is* on the south of Jeshimon?

20 Now therefore, O king, come down according to all the desire of thy soul to come down; and our part *shall be* to deliver him into the king's hand.

21 And Saul said, Blessed *be* ye of the LORD; for ye have compassion on me.

22 Go, I pray you, prepare yet, and know and see his place where his haunt is, *and* who hath seen him there: for it is told me *that* he dealeth very subtilly.

23 See therefore, and take knowledge of all the lurking places where he hideth

arrest him?

    • Would the citizens of Keilah betray him & his men, give them over to Saul?
    3) Third, the LORD answered "yes" to both questions
  c. David quickly mobilized his men & left Keilah, adopting a two-prong strategy
    1) That of constant relocation, moving from place to place

    2) That of seeking refuge in frontier areas that could be easily defended
  d. Saul turned away from Keilah to pursue David, hunting for him

  e. David heard that Saul was right on his heels, searching nearby—at Horesh in the Desert of Ziph

3. David was warned & encouraged by Jonathan: Deliverance through encouragement
  a. Jonathan strengthened David
  b. Jonathan reminded David of the LORD's promise that David would someday be king: He should not fear Saul

  c. Jonathan & David renewed their covenant before the LORD

4. David narrowly escaped the betrayal by the Ziphites & capture by Saul: Deliverance through God the Protector & Helper of believers, Ps.54
  a. David was betrayed by the Ziphites
    1) Revealed David's location
    2) Committed themselves to personally arrest David & turn him over to Saul

  b. Saul abused the LORD's name: Gave a false blessing, v.7
  c. Saul sent the spies ahead of him to gather more information on David
    1) All the places he went

    2) All his supporters
    3) All his hideouts
  d. Saul promised a fierce

pursuit of David 1) Saul committed to tracking David down throughout all the clans of Judah	himself, and come ye again to me with the certainty, and I will go with you: and it shall come to pass, if he be in the land, that I will search him out throughout all the thousands of Judah.	26 And Saul went on this side of the mountain, and David and his men on that side of the mountain: and David made haste to get away for fear of Saul; for Saul and his men compassed David and his men round about to take them.	2) His forces were scaling or climbing one side of the mountain while David's forces were on the other side, hurrying away

2) The Ziphites set out ahead of Saul
  3) David & his men were hiding out in the Desert of Maon—in a rocky stronghold
	24 And they arose, and went to Ziph before Saul: but David and his men *were* in the wilderness of Maon, in the plain on the south of Jeshimon.	27 But there came a messenger unto Saul, saying, Haste thee, and come; for the Philistines have invaded the land.	3) His forces closed in, ready to capture David
			4) His pursuit was halted: At a crucial moment Saul received an urgent message:
			  • The Philistines had invaded Israel

e. Saul began his fierce pursuit of David
  1) His forces began a cat & mouse pursuit, right on David's heels
	25 Saul also and his men went to seek *him.* And they told David: wherefore he came down into a rock, and abode in the wilderness of Maon. And when Saul heard *that,* he pursued after David in the wilderness of Maon.	28 Wherefore Saul returned from pursuing after David, and went against the Philistines: therefore they called that place Sela-hammahlekoth.
		29 And David went up from thence, and dwelt in strong holds at En-gedi.
			• Saul was forced to break off his pursuit of David
			f. David was saved
			  1) The place was memorialized, named Sela Hammahlekoth, the Rock of Escape
			  2) David moved to the stronghold of En Gedi

DIVISION IV

THE STORY OF SAUL AND DAVID (PART 2):
DAVID THE FUGITIVE, 21:1–31:13

C. The Rescue of Keilah by David and the Insane Pursuit of David by Saul: A Picture of the Believer's Deliverance from All Enemies, 23:1-29

(23:1-29) **Introduction—Deliverance, Need for—Rescue, Need for—Misfortune, Need of Deliverance—Hardship, Need of Deliverance—Trial, Need of Deliverance—Circumstances, Bad, Need of**: many times throughout life we are in need of deliverance. Some misfortune, hardship, or trial has happened, and we need to be rescued. The misfortune may be as serious as almost drowning while swimming or being seriously injured in an accident. It may even be an assault or some other act of violence against us.

Other hardships confront us such as disease, financial difficulties, the loss of a loved one, depression, or any number of other emotional or mental illnesses.

Whatever misfortune, hardship, or trial confronts us, God will protect us and help us through the circumstance if we turn to Him. And nothing is too hard for the LORD to conquer and overcome. If we turn to the LORD in repentance, He will deliver us from all distress and from all enemies who confront us.

God's power to deliver is the subject of the present passage of Scripture. David was being fiercely pursued by King Saul who was attempting to kill him. But in every instance, even when Saul was closing in and the crucial moment of capture was immediately at hand, the LORD delivered David. This passage paints the picture of Saul's fierce, cat-and-mouse pursuit of David. This story is high drama at its best: *The Rescue of Keilah by David and the Insane Pursuit of David by Saul: A Picture of the Believer's Deliverance from All Enemies*, 23:1-29.

1. David saved the city of Keilah: deliverance through courage (vv.1-6).
2. David escaped the fierce pursuit of Saul from place to place: deliverance through prayer (vv.7-15).
3. David was warned and encouraged by Jonathan: deliverance through encouragement (vv.16-18).
4. David narrowly escaped the betrayal of the Ziphites and capture by Saul: deliverance through God the Protector and Helper of believers, Ps.54 (vv.19-29).

1 (23:1-6) **Courage, Example of—Fearlessness, Example of—Prayer, Example of—Deliverance, Source of—David, Courage of**: David saved the citizens of Keilah who had been attacked and were fighting against the Philistines. Keilah was a fortified city about eighteen miles southwest of Jerusalem and about twelve miles southeast of Gath, which was one of the major cities of the Philistines. It was harvest season, the time when Philistine marauders (raiders, bandits) would usually sweep down upon the Israelites, stealing and looting their grain and any other valuable plunder. (See note—Judg.6:33-40 for more discussion.)

At the time of the attack, David was hiding out in the forest of Hereth (22:5), having set up a secret campsite to avoid Saul's pursuit. What happened next shows the depth of David's courage, what a fearless man he was:

OUTLINE	SCRIPTURE	SCRIPTURE	OUTLINE
1. David saved the city of Keilah: Deliverance through courage a. David heard about the Philistine's attack 1) He prayed: Asked the LORD if he should deliver the city 2) The LORD answered: Go—save Keilah b. David's men opposed the defense of the city: The Philistine army was far superior in number & weapons c. David prayed again, seeking	Then they told David, saying, Behold, the Philistines fight against Keilah, and they rob the threshingfloors. 2 Therefore David enquired of the LORD, saying, Shall I go and smite these Philistines? And the LORD said unto David, Go, and smite the Philistines, and save Keilah. 3 And David's men said unto him, Behold, we be afraid here in Judah: how much more then if we come to Keilah against the armies of the Philistines? 4 Then David enquired of	the LORD yet again. And the LORD answered him and said, Arise, go down to Keilah; for I will deliver the Philistines into thine hand. 5 So David and his men went to Keilah, and fought with the Philistines, and brought away their cattle, and smote them with a great slaughter. So David saved the inhabitants of Keilah. 6 And it came to pass, when Abiathar the son of Ahimelech fled to David to Keilah, *that* he came down *with* an ephod in his hand.	assurance of God's will 1) The LORD's answer: Go 2) The assurance: Victory was guaranteed—through the LORD d. David led his men in battle against the Philistines 1) Inflicted heavy losses on them 2) Saved the citizens of Keilah (in Judea) e. David was finally joined by the priest Abiathar at Keilah: He now had the ephod (used in prayer to seek God's will)

a. As soon as the Philistines attacked Keilah, David heard about their attack. No doubt both David and Saul had spies who were active throughout the land; thus David was bound to hear about any major military action by the Philistines. Immediately David went to prayer, asking the LORD if he should attempt to defend and deliver the city. The LORD answered, telling David to go and save Keilah.

b. Shockingly, David's men opposed the defense of the city (v.3). The Philistine army was far superior in both troops and weapons. Moreover, to begin fighting the Philistine army meant that David's small band of 600 men could be caught between two armies, Saul's and the Philistines'.

Note the excuse for not fighting given by David's men: fear. They already lived in constant fear of Saul's army, being fiercely pursued by him and being forced to move from place to place, looking for secret places to hide. Why should they endanger their lives even more by attacking the Philistine forces?

As leader of the fugitive band, David was responsible for the lives of his men, and keeping their loyalty was essential. But David knew that the LORD had given him the command to defend the city of Keilah. What could he do, for the LORD said go, but his men stood opposed. He did the only thing he could do.

c. David again prayed, seeking assurance of God's will (v.4). And again, the LORD said go. But this time, the LORD gave strong assurance, guaranteeing victory over the Philistines.

d. Hearing this confirmation, David and his men attacked the Philistines, inflicting heavy losses on them. Thus the citizens of Keilah were saved from their oppressors (v.5). In addition, David and his men were not only given victory by the LORD, but they were also able to take the livestock and plunder of the Philistines.

e. Note that it was here at Keilah where Abiathar the priest joined David (v.6). Remember that Abiathar had been the only person to escape the slaughter of the priests by Saul (22:6-23, esp. 20). When Abiathar escaped the slaughter, he was able to save the ephod and take it with him. The ephod was a sleeveless, coat-like garment that had a pouch attached to it to carry the Urim and Thummim, thought to be two stones that were cast when seeking God's will. David now had both a priest and a prophet for counsel and advice in helping him seek the LORD's will. Their advice would prove to be most helpful while he was fleeing the fierce pursuit of Saul and later when he would be ruling as king, governing the nation of Israel.

Thought 1. When enemies attack us, we need what David had: courage, bold courage. If David had given in to the fear of his men, the citizens of Keilah would have never been delivered from their Philistine oppressors. So it is with us: if we give in to fear, we will never be delivered from the oppressions and enemies of this life, oppressions and enemies such as...

- people who ridicule, mock, suppress, abuse, assault, persecute, or kill us
- financial difficulty, divorce, disease, accident, injury, depression, distress, loneliness, purposelessness, emptiness, guilt, or the death of a loved one

Any person or any thing that works to defeat us in this life stands as an enemy, an oppressor against us. In facing the enemies and oppressors of this life, we must be courageous. We must develop a spirit of courage, for it is bold courage that will conquer the enemies and oppressors of this life.

"**That he would grant you, according to the riches of his glory, to be strengthened with might by his Spirit in the inner man**" (Ep.3:16).

"**Only let your conversation [behavior, conduct] be as it becometh the gospel of Christ: that whether I come and see you, or else be absent, I may hear of your affairs, that ye stand fast in one spirit, with one mind striving together for the faith of the gospel; And in nothing terrified by your adversaries: which is to them an evident token of perdition, but to you of salvation, and that of God**" (Ph.1:27-28).

"**For God hath not given us the spirit of fear; but of power, and of love, and of a sound mind**" (2 Ti.1:7).

"**Be strong and of a good courage, fear not, nor be afraid of them: for the LORD thy God, he *it is* that doth go with thee; he will not fail thee, nor forsake thee**" (De.31:6).

"Be strong and of a good courage: for unto this people shalt thou divide for an inheritance the land, which I sware unto their fathers to give them" (Jos.1:6).

"For thou hast girded me with strength to battle: them that rose up against me hast thou subdued under me" (2 S.22:40).

"Behold, God *is* my salvation; I will trust, and not be afraid: for the LORD JEHOVAH *is* my strength and *my* song; he also is become my salvation" (Is.12:2).

"But they that wait upon the LORD shall renew *their* strength; they shall mount up with wings as eagles; they shall run, and not be weary; *and* they shall walk, and not faint" (Is.40:31).

"Fear thou not; for I *am* with thee: be not dismayed; for I *am* thy God: I will strengthen thee; yea, I will help thee; yea, I will uphold thee with the right hand of my righteousness" (Is.41:10).

2 (23:7-15) **Deliverance, Source—Prayer, Results—David, Attempts Against His Life—Saul, Attempts to Kill David**: David escaped the fierce pursuit of Saul by staying alert and moving quickly from place to place. This event is a strong lesson on prayer, showing how God delivers His people through prayer.

OUTLINE	SCRIPTURE	SCRIPTURE	OUTLINE
2. David escaped the fierce pursuit of Saul from place to place: Deliverance through prayer	7 And it was told Saul that David was come to Keilah. And Saul said, God hath delivered him into mine hand; for he is shut in, by entering into a town that hath gates and bars.	tell thy servant. And the LORD said, He will come down. 12 Then said David, Will the men of Keilah deliver me and my men into the hand of Saul? And the LORD said, They will deliver *thee* up.	• Would the citizens of Keilah betray him & his men, give them over to Saul?
a. Saul heard that David was in Keilah, a walled, gated city 1) He felt David could be trapped 2) He mobilized his army to attack the city & seize David	8 And Saul called all the people together to war, to go down to Keilah, to besiege David and his men.	13 Then David and his men, *which were* about six hundred, arose and departed out of Keilah, and went whithersoever they could go. And it	3) Third, the LORD answered "yes" to both questions c. David quickly mobilized his men & left Keilah, adopting a two-prong strategy
b. David learned about the plot & prayed, consulting the LORD	9 And David knew that Saul secretly practised mischief against him; and he said to Abiathar the priest, Bring hither the ephod.	was told Saul that David was escaped from Keilah; and he forbare to go forth.	1) That of constant relocation, moving from place to place
1) First, he shared what he had heard with the LORD	10 Then said David, O LORD God of Israel, thy servant hath certainly heard that Saul seeketh to come to Keilah, to destroy the city for my sake.	14 And David abode in the wilderness in strong holds, and remained in a mountain in the wilderness of Ziph. And Saul sought him every day, but God delivered him not into his hand.	2) That of seeking refuge in frontier areas that could be easily defended d. Saul turned away from Keilah to pursue David, hunting for him
2) Second, he asked the LORD two questions • Would Saul attack Keilah in an attempt to arrest him?	11 Will the men of Keilah deliver me up into his hand? will Saul come down, as thy servant hath heard? O LORD God of Israel, I beseech thee,	15 And David saw that Saul was come out to seek his life: and David *was* in the wilderness of Ziph in a wood.	e. David heard that Saul was right on his heels, searching nearby—at Horesh in the Desert of Ziph

a. Through his spy network, Saul heard that David was in Keilah, a gated, walled city (vv.7-8). At long last, Saul felt that David had trapped himself by entering this enclosed city. It would be far easier to capture David within a fortified city than out in the open where he could escape by fleeing in any direction. Receiving this good news from his spies, Saul immediately mobilized his army to attack the city and seize David.

b. But keep in mind that David also had his spy network. Thus David soon learned about Saul's plot and immediately began to cry out to the LORD for guidance (vv.9-12). Note that he instructed the priest Abiathar to bring the ephod so that he could use the Urim and Thummim in seeking the LORD's will. In praying and consulting the LORD, three things happened.

First, David shared with the LORD what he had heard about Saul (v.10). He had definitely heard that Saul was planning to come to Keilah to destroy the city because of him. Note that Saul was willing to destroy his own people in order to capture David.

Second, David asked the LORD two questions (vv.11-12). Would Saul attack Keilah in an attempt to arrest him? And would the citizens of Keilah betray him and his men, giving them over to Saul?

Thirdly, the LORD answered both questions positively. "Yes," Saul would attack in an attempt to arrest David, and "Yes," the citizens would betray David and his men by turning them over to Saul. Being willing to surrender David and his men to the king may seem like the height of ingratitude. But keep this fact in mind: the citizens of Keilah had probably heard about Saul's massacre of the priests at Nob because the priests had helped David (22:6-23). Therefore they were bound to fear the retribution of Saul if they gave sanctuary and support to David.

c. Having received God's instructions, David quickly mobilized his men and left Keilah (vv.13-14). Under no circumstances did David want to be the cause of another city's being destroyed and its citizens slaughtered by Saul. Enough guilt was already weighing down upon his spirit due to the slaughter of the priests. As quickly as he could, he and his men fled from the fierce pursuit of Saul. And from this point on, David adopted a two-pronged strategy:

⇒ that of constantly relocating, moving from place to place.

⇒ that of seeking refuge in frontier areas, in strongholds that could be easily defended.

d. As soon as Saul heard that David had fled from Keilah, he began to search for and seek out David with a fierce determination to hunt him down. But note what Scripture says: God kept Saul from finding David. David was not delivered into the hands of the king.

e. One day David heard that Saul was right on his heels, searching nearby. David was at Horesh in the Desert of Ziph, a dry, barren, destitute area that was close by the Dead Sea (v.15). It was an area where survival would have been almost impossible.[1]

> **Thought 1**. Deliverance comes through prayer. It is God Himself who delivers us, but God works through prayer. When we face the trials and temptations of this life, God expects us to turn to Him, to pray and seek His face for help. God cares for us; therefore He is concerned about what happens to us. Every time a particular trial confronts us, God wants to help us. He wants to empower us to conquer the trial or temptation. He wants us to be triumphant, victorious over all trials and temptations. No greater message of encouragement could be given us than the message of prayer. We can pray, cry out to the LORD, and He will hear us. In our moment of need—whether mild or desperate need—if we will just pray, God will hear us and deliver us. This is the wonderful promise of His Holy Word:
>
> > **"Ask, and it shall be given you; seek, and ye shall find; knock, and it shall be opened unto you"** (Mt.7:7).
> >
> > **"And he spake a parable unto them *to this end,* that men ought always to pray, and not to faint"** (Lu.18:1).
> >
> > **"If ye abide in me, and my words abide in you, ye shall ask what ye will, and it shall be done unto you"** (Jn.15:7).
> >
> > **"Be careful [anxious] for nothing; but in every thing by prayer and supplication with thanksgiving let your requests be made known unto God. And the peace of God, which passeth all understanding, shall keep your hearts and minds through Christ Jesus"** (Ph.4:6-7).
> >
> > **"Pray without ceasing"** (1 Th.5:17).
> >
> > **"But if from thence thou shalt seek the LORD thy God, thou shalt find *him,* if thou seek him with all thy heart and with all thy soul"** (De.4:29).
> >
> > **"Now therefore, O LORD our God, I beseech thee, save thou us out of his hand, that all the kingdoms of the earth may know that thou *art* the LORD God, *even* thou only"** (2 K.19:19).
> >
> > **"He shall call upon me, and I will answer him: I *will be* with him in trouble; I will deliver him, and honour him"** (Ps.91:15).
> >
> > **"Then shalt thou call, and the LORD shall answer; thou shalt cry, and he shall say, Here I *am.* If thou take away from the midst of thee the yoke, the putting forth of the finger, and speaking vanity"** (Is.58:9).
> >
> > **"And it shall come to pass, that before they call, I will answer; and while they are yet speaking, I will hear"** (Is.65:24).

---

3 (23:16-18) **Encouragement, Source, Friends—Encouragement, Example of—Friendship, Duty—Brotherly Love, Duty—David, Encouraged By—Jonathan, Loyalty to David**: David had been warned that Saul was nearby by his close friend Jonathan, and Jonathan was risking his life to visit and warn David. Note that Jonathan not only warned David of his father's fierce pursuit, but he also encouraged David and helped him find strength in the LORD. No doubt the two men prayed together and sought the LORD, requesting that the LORD empower David with the necessary courage and strength to bear the pressure of the stressful circumstances.

Notice how Jonathan encouraged David: he reminded David of the LORD's promise that he would someday be king. Therefore he should not fear his father Saul, for the LORD would keep Saul from capturing and harming David. Because of the LORD's promise, David was assured of becoming king. And note how Jonathan was expecting to be second to David in his government. Moreover, even Jonathan's father Saul knew this.

Before Jonathan left, he and David renewed their covenant of friendship before the LORD. They were committed to remain friends and to guard each other's welfare as long as they lived. Having renewed their *friendship covenant,* each went his way. Jonathan went home, but David remained at Horesh. And this was to be their last meeting. Jonathan is not mentioned again until his death upon the battlefield along with his father (1 S.31:2).

OUTLINE	SCRIPTURE	SCRIPTURE	OUTLINE
3. David was warned & encouraged by Jonathan: Deliverance through encouragement	16 And Jonathan Saul's son arose, and went to David into the wood, and strengthened his hand in God.	Israel, and I shall be next unto thee; and that also Saul my father knoweth.	king: He should not fear Saul
a. Jonathan strengthened David	17 And he said unto him, Fear not: for the hand of Saul my father shall not find thee; and thou shalt be king over	18 And they two made a covenant before the LORD: and David abode in the wood, and Jonathan went to his house.	c. Jonathan & David renewed their covenant before the LORD
b. Jonathan reminded David of the LORD's promise that David would someday be			

---

[1] Warren W. Wiersbe. *Be Successful.* (Wheaton, IL: Victor Books, 2001), p.125.

Thought 1. Tension, anxiety, pressure, stress, strain—the weight of circumstances can create all kinds of problems for us. We can become so physically or mentally pressured that we are gripped by a spirit of agony and affliction. Hardship and misfortune can come upon us and cause all kinds of distressful problems for us.

When we see a person suffer hardship or misfortune, we must go to them in a spirit of encouragement. Encouragement is one of the ways a person can conquer misfortune and hardship. Encouragement will arouse a person, motivate him to get up and tackle whatever circumstances confront him. Our responsibility to encourage one another cannot be overstressed. We are all human beings living upon the same earth, created by the LORD God Himself, made to be neighbors one with the other, and commanded to love one another with a brotherly love. For this reason, God's Holy Word teaches us to encourage and serve one another:

"But a certain Samaritan, as he journeyed, came where he was: and when he saw him, he had compassion *on him,* And went to *him,* and bound up his wounds, pouring in oil and wine, and set him on his own beast, and brought him to an inn, and took care of him. And on the morrow when he departed, he took out two pence, and gave *them* to the host, and said unto him, Take care of him; and whatsoever thou spendest more, when I come again, I will repay thee. Which now of these three, thinkest thou, was neighbour unto him that fell among the thieves? And he said, He that showed mercy on him. Then said Jesus unto him, Go, and do thou likewise" (Lu.10:33-37).

"If I then, *your* LORD and Master, have washed your feet; ye also ought to wash one another's feet" (Jn.13:14).

"He saith to him again the second time, Simon, *son* of Jonas, lovest thou me? He saith unto him, Yea, LORD; thou knowest that I love thee. He saith unto him, Feed my sheep" (Jn.21:16).

"Bear ye one another's burdens, and so fulfil the law of Christ" (Ga.6:2).

"As we have therefore opportunity, let us do good unto all *men,* especially unto them who are of the household of faith" (Ga.6:10).

"And I intreat thee also, true yokefellow, help those women which laboured with me in the gospel, with Clement also, and *with* other my fellowlabourers, whose names *are* in the book of life" (Ph.4:3).

"And the men which were expressed by name rose up, and took the captives, and with the spoil clothed all that were naked among them, and arrayed them, and shod them, and gave them to eat and to drink, and anointed them, and carried all the feeble of them upon asses, and brought them to Jericho, the city of palm trees, to their brethren: then they returned to Samaria" (2 Chr.28:15).

"I was eyes to the blind, and feet *was* I to the lame. I *was* a father to the poor: and the cause *which* I knew not I searched out" (Jb.29:15-16).

"She stretcheth out her hand to the poor; yea, she reacheth forth her hands to the needy" (Pr.31:20).

"The LORD GOD hath given me the tongue of the learned, that I should know how to speak a word in season to *him that is* weary: he wakeneth morning by morning, he wakeneth mine ear to hear as the learned" (Is.50:4).

4 (23:19-29) **Betrayal, Example of—Protection, Source—Help, Source—The LORD Our Helper, Example of—David, Attempts Against His Life—Saul, Attempts to Kill David**: David narrowly escaped the betrayal by the Ziphites and being captured by Saul. This narrow escape of David's is *high drama* at its best, and the experience made such an impact upon David that he wrote Psalm 54 in honor of the occasion, describing what happened.

OUTLINE	SCRIPTURE	SCRIPTURE	OUTLINE

4. David narrowly escaped the betrayal by the Ziphites & capture by Saul: Deliverance through God the Protector & Helper of believers, Ps.54
a. David was betrayed by the Ziphites
  1) Revealed David's location
  2) Committed themselves to personally arrest David & turn him over to Saul
 	
b. Saul abused the LORD's name: Gave a false blessing, v.7
c. Saul sent the spies ahead of him to gather more information on David
  1) All the places he went
	19 Then came up the Ziphites to Saul to Gibeah, saying, Doth not David hide himself with us in strongholds in the wood, in the hill of Hachilah, which *is* on the south of Jeshimon?
	20 Now therefore, O king, come down according to all the desire of thy soul to come down; and our part *shall be* to deliver him into the king's hand.
	21 And Saul said, Blessed *be* ye of the LORD; for ye have compassion on me.
	22 Go, I pray you, prepare yet, and know and see his place where his haunt is, *and* who hath seen him there: for it is told me *that* he dealeth
		very subtilly.
		23 See therefore, and take knowledge of all the lurking places where he hideth himself, and come ye again to me with the certainty, and I will go with you: and it shall come to pass, if he be in the land, that I will search him out throughout all the thousands of Judah.
		24 And they arose, and went to Ziph before Saul: but David and his men *were* in the wilderness of Maon, in the plain on the south of Jeshimon.
		25 Saul also and his men went to seek *him.* And they told David: wherefore he came down into a rock,
			2) All his supporters
			3) All his hideouts
			d. Saul promised a fierce pursuit of David
			  1) Saul committed to tracking David down throughout all the clans of Judah
			
			2) The Ziphites set out ahead of Saul
			3) David & his men were hiding out in the Desert of Maon—in a rocky stronghold
			e. Saul began his fierce pursuit of David
			  1) His forces began a cat & mouse pursuit, right on

OUTLINE	SCRIPTURE	SCRIPTURE	OUTLINE
David's heels	and abode in the wilderness of Maon. And when Saul heard *that,* he pursued after David in the wilderness of Maon.	27 But there came a messenger unto Saul, saying, Haste thee, and come; for the Philistines have invaded the land.	4) His pursuit was halted: At a crucial moment Saul received an urgent message: • The Philistines had invaded Israel
2) His forces were scaling or climbing one side of the mountain while David's forces were on the other side, hurrying away	26 And Saul went on this side of the mountain, and David and his men on that side of the mountain: and David made haste to get away for fear of Saul; for Saul and his men compassed David and his men round about to take them.	28 Wherefore Saul returned from pursuing after David, and went against the Philistines: therefore they called that place Selahammahlekoth.	• Saul was forced to break off his pursuit of David f. David was saved 1) The place was memorialized, named Sela Hammahlekoth, the Rock of Escape
3) His forces closed in, ready to capture David		29 And David went up from thence, and dwelt in strong holds at En-gedi.	2) David moved to the stronghold of En Gedi

a. David was betrayed by the Ziphites, most likely to prevent Saul from destroying their towns and surrounding territory (vv.19-20). Discovering David's location, the Ziphites reported this important information to Saul. In addition, they committed themselves to personally arrest David and to turn him over to the king.

b. Receiving this report pleased Saul so much that he pronounced a blessing upon the Ziphites (v.21). But note that this was a false blessing, an abuse of the LORD's name, for Saul was committing a terrible evil in seeking to kill David. Consequently, the blessing was empty, useless.

c. Saul needed more than just general information about David's whereabouts, so he sent the Ziphite spies on ahead to gather more detailed information on David (vv.22-23). He wanted to know all the places David went, all his supporters, and all his hideouts. Knowing this would almost certainly guarantee David's capture.

d. Saul promised the Ziphites that he would launch a fierce pursuit of David once he had received the information (vv.23-24). Being gripped by a passionate determination to capture and kill David, Saul committed himself to track David down even if he had to pursue the fugitive throughout all the clans of Judah.

Hearing such staunch determination, the Ziphites set out ahead of Saul to spy in order to gather the detailed information requested by the king. But by the time the Ziphites had returned to Ziph, David and his men had fled to a rocky stronghold in the Desert of Maon which was in the Arabah Valley.

e. As soon as Saul could break camp, he began his fierce pursuit of David, a pursuit that proved to be a cat-and-mouse hunt with Saul right on the heels of David. Time and again spies informed David of Saul's whereabouts, and David fled. But as soon as David moved elsewhere, Saul's spies discovered his whereabouts and reported the information to Saul. Then Saul immediately responded to David's movements. Eventually David went down to the rocky stronghold in the Desert of Maon. Receiving this information, Saul continued his mad chase, again right on the heels of David. Saul's forces were actually scaling one side of the rocky stronghold while David's forces were on the other side hurrying and fleeing to escape. Just as Saul's forces were closing in, ready to seize David—at the very crucial moment of capture—Saul received an urgent message from the leaders or elders of Israel. The Philistines had just invaded Israel and were raiding and plundering the land. Reluctantly, Saul was forced to break off his insane pursuit of David and march out to meet the Philistines in battle.

f. David was saved, delivered by the sovereign power of God to move events in order to help His people. To honor God's deliverance of David, the place was memorialized and named Sela Hammahlekoth, which means the Rock of Escape. As soon as Saul had withdrawn, David moved to the strongholds of En Gedi.

Thought 1. Our Protector and Helper is God. It was God who protected and helped David, who delivered him from the hand of Saul. Just as God delivered David, so He will deliver us. No matter what confronts or attacks us—whether another person or some circumstance, trial, or temptation—the LORD will protect and help us.
(1) The LORD is our protector.

"But there shall not an hair of your head perish" (Lu.21:18).

"The LORD shall fight for you, and ye shall hold your peace" (Ex.14:14).

"I will send my fear before thee, and will destroy all the people to whom thou shalt come, and I will make all thine enemies turn their backs unto thee" (Ex.23:27).

"And Elisha prayed, and said, LORD, I pray thee, open his eyes, that he may see. And the LORD opened the eyes of the young man; and he saw: and, behold, the mountain *was* full of horses and chariots of fire round about Elisha" (2 K.6:17).

"For the eyes of the LORD run to and fro throughout the whole earth, to show himself strong in the behalf of *them* whose heart *is* perfect toward him. Herein thou hast done foolishly: therefore from henceforth thou shalt have wars" (2 Chr.16:9).

"With him *is* an arm of flesh; but with us *is* the LORD our God to help us, and to fight our battles. And the people rested themselves upon the words of Hezekiah king of Judah" (2 Chr.32:8).

"The angel of the LORD encampeth round about them that fear him, and delivereth them" (Ps.34:7).

"He shall cover thee with his feathers, and under his wings shalt thou trust: his truth *shall be thy* shield and buckler" (Ps.91:4).

"As the mountains *are* round about Jerusalem, so the LORD *is* round about his people from henceforth even for ever" (Ps.125:2).

"My God hath sent his angel, and hath shut the lions' mouths, that they have not hurt me: forasmuch as before him innocency was found in me; and also before thee, O king, have I done no hurt" (Da.6:22).

"For I, saith the LORD, will be unto her a wall of fire round about, and will be the glory in the midst of her" (Zec.2:5).

(2) The LORD is our helper.

"*Let your* conversation [behavior, conduct] *be* without covetousness; *and be* content with such things as ye have: for he hath said, I will never leave thee, nor forsake thee. So that we may boldly say, The LORD *is* my helper, and I will not fear what man shall do unto me" (He.13:5-6).

"The LORD *is* my strength and my shield; my heart trusted in him, and I am helped: therefore my heart greatly rejoiceth; and with my song will I praise him" (Ps.28:7).

"But I *am* poor and needy; *yet* the LORD thinketh upon me: thou *art* my help and my deliverer; make no tarrying, O my God" (Ps.40:17).

"But thou, O LORD, be merciful unto me, and raise me up, that I may requite them" (Is.41:10).

"...Fear not: for I have redeemed thee, I have called thee by thy name; thou art mine. When thou passest through the waters, I will be with thee; and through the rivers, they shall not overflow thee: when thou walkest through the fire, thou shalt not be burned; neither shall the flame kindle upon thee" (Is.43:1-2).

CHAPTER 24

D. The Life of Saul Mercifully Spared by David: Lessons on Honoring God's Anointed, 24:1-22

1. David's respect for the office of king: A lesson on the need to honor *God's anointed leader*

a. David's hideout was discovered by Saul

  1) He mobilized a force of 3000 soldiers: Began searching near the inaccessible Rocks of the Wild Goats

  2) He entered a cave near the sheep pens to attend to his needs

b. David & his men were hiding far back in the very same cave

c. David's men suggested this was of God: He should seize the moment, kill Saul

d. David crept up & cut off only a corner of Saul's robe

e. David's conscience bothered him

  1) The reason: He had shown disrespect to his master or ruler, the LORD's anointed

  2) The result: David rebuked his men & stopped them from killing Saul

2. David's humility & his loyalty to King Saul: A lesson on the need for humility & loyalty

a. David showed the utmost humility to Saul
  1) Addressed him as king
  2) Bowed to the ground

b. David presented a strong case for reconciliation
  1) The charge of treason by others was false
  2) The proof was fivefold

   • Saul had been in the very cave where David was

And it came to pass, when Saul was returned from following the Philistines, that it was told him, saying, Behold, David is in the wilderness of En-gedi.

2 Then Saul took three thousand chosen men out of all Israel, and went to seek David and his men upon the rocks of the wild goats.

3 And he came to the sheepcotes by the way, where *was* a cave; and Saul went in to cover his feet: and David and his men remained in the sides of the cave.

4 And the men of David said unto him, Behold the day of which the LORD said unto thee, Behold, I will deliver thine enemy into thine hand, that thou mayest do to him as it shall seem good unto thee. Then David arose, and cut off the skirt of Saul's robe privily.

5 And it came to pass afterward, that David's heart smote him, because he had cut off Saul's skirt.

6 And he said unto his men, The LORD forbid that I should do this thing unto my master, the LORD's anointed, to stretch forth mine hand against him, seeing he is the anointed of the LORD.

7 So David stayed his servants with these words, and suffered them not to rise against Saul. But Saul rose up out of the cave, and went on *his* way.

8 David also arose afterward, and went out of the cave, and cried after Saul, saying, My lord the king. And when Saul looked behind him, David stooped with his face to the earth, and bowed himself.

9 And David said to Saul, Wherefore hearest thou men's words, saying, Behold, David seeketh thy hurt?

10 Behold, this day thine eyes have seen how that the LORD had delivered thee to day into mine hand in the cave: and *some* bade *me* kill thee: but *mine eye* spared thee; and I said, I will not put forth mine hand against my lord; for he *is* the LORD's anointed.

11 Moreover, my father, see, yea, see the skirt of thy robe in my hand: for in that I cut off the skirt of thy robe and killed thee not, know thou and see that *there is* neither evil nor transgression in mine hand, and I have not sinned against thee; yet thou huntest my soul to take it.

12 The LORD judge between me and thee, and the LORD avenge me of thee: but mine hand shall not be upon thee.

13 As saith the proverb of the ancients, Wickedness proceedeth from the wicked: but mine hand shall not be upon thee.

14 After whom is the king of Israel come out? after whom dost thou pursue? after a dead dog, after a flea.

15 The LORD therefore be judge, and judge between me and thee, and see, and plead my cause, and deliver me out of thine hand.

16 And it came to pass, when David had made an end of speaking these words unto Saul, that Saul said, *Is* this thy voice, my son David? And Saul lifted up his voice, and wept.

17 And he said to David, Thou *art* more righteous than I: for thou hast rewarded me good, whereas I have rewarded thee evil.

18 And thou hast showed this day how that thou hast dealt well with me: forasmuch as when the LORD had delivered me into thine hand, thou killedst me not.

19 For if a man find his enemy, will he let him go well away? wherefore the LORD reward thee good for that thou hast done unto me this day.

20 And now, behold, I know well that thou shalt surely be king, and that the kingdom of Israel shall be established in thine hand.

21 Swear now therefore unto me by the LORD, that thou

  • Some of David's men had urged him to kill Saul: He refused
  • Saul was God's anointed

  • Saul was David's father-in-law
  • Saul's robe had been cut by David, but David refused to kill him

  3) The verdict: David was innocent

c. David attempted to convince Saul of the injustice being done
  1) By warning Saul of God's judgment
  2) By quoting an ancient proverb
  3) By assuring Saul he would never harm him
  4) By questioning Saul & claiming that he was not a threat: He was as a dead dog or flea to Saul
  5) By calling upon the LORD to decide who was right & to punish the guilty
  6) By calling out for the LORD to vindicate & deliver him from Saul

3. Saul's remorse & confession that David would be king: A lesson on repaying good for evil

a. Saul confessed that David was more righteous than he
  1) David had repaid him good for evil

  2) David had been kind to him
   • By not killing him

   • By defying common sense & human nature to retaliate against one's enemy
  3) Saul pronounced a blessing upon David

b. Saul confessed God's royal plans for David: That David would be king & would establish the kingdom of Israel

c. Saul made two requests
  1) That David not kill off his

| descendants | wilt not cut off my seed after me, and that thou wilt not destroy my name out of my father's house. | 22 And David sware unto Saul. And Saul went home; but David and his men gat them up unto the hold. | 3) The result: David swore an oath |
| 2) That David not wipe out his family's name | | | d. Saul & David ended their encounter |

DIVISION IV

THE STORY OF SAUL AND DAVID (PART 2):
DAVID THE FUGITIVE, 21:1–31:13

D. The Life of Saul Mercifully Spared by David: Lessons on Honoring God's Anointed, 24:1-22

(24:1-22) **Introduction—Good for Evil, Fact—Evil, Duty Toward—Indulgence, Duty—Correction, Duty—Discipline, Duty—License, Duty**: repaying or doing good for evil is not a simple thing to do. For example, how can we love our enemies—those who abuse, assault, or commit some act of violence against us, perhaps even attempting to kill us?

Think for a moment: If someone ridicules, mocks, or curses us—what does it mean to do good to that person? If a person steals from us, causes financial difficulty, or destroys our property—what does it mean to do good to him or her?

To do good for evil does not mean to give license to wickedness nor to indulge evil. To do good would mean to correct and discipline the wicked or evil person. Correction and discipline are good, helpful, and beneficial for the person who lives a life of sinful behavior. But when we seek to correct and discipline the wicked, we do it with a spirit of care and compassion, not out of a spirit gripped by vindictiveness and revenge. We correct and discipline the wicked and evil of this earth by executing the compassionate, righteous laws of God. These laws are spelled out in God's Holy Word.

David was gripped by the compassionate, righteous laws of God. For this reason, when the opportunity came to take revenge upon his enemy, King Saul, he acted instead in compassion, not in vengeance and retaliation. David rendered good for evil. This is the subject of this captivating passage of Scripture: *The Life of Saul Mercifully Spared by David: Lessons on Honoring God's Anointed*, 24:1-22.

1. David's respect for the office of king: a lesson on the need to honor *God's anointed leader* (vv.1-7).
2. David's humility and his loyalty to King Saul: a lesson on the need for humility and loyalty (vv.8-15).
3. Saul's remorse and confession that David would be king: a lesson on repaying good for evil (vv.16-22).

1 (24:1-7) **Respect, Example of—Rulers, Duty to—Ministers, Duty to—Leaders, Duty to—Anointed, Importance of—David, Respect for Saul**: there was David's respect for the office of king, a strong lesson on the need to honor God's anointed leader. Remember, Saul had been right on the verge of capturing David when he received an urgent message that the Philistines had attacked Israel. As a result, he was forced to give up his pursuit, forced to return and defend the nation against the Philistine invaders. After turning back the Philistine aggression, he returned home to Gibeah and reinstated his spy network to find out where David was hiding. Note what happened:

OUTLINE	SCRIPTURE	SCRIPTURE	OUTLINE
1. David's respect for the office of king: A lesson on the need to honor *God's anointed leader* a. David's hideout was discovered by Saul 1) He mobilized a force of 3000 soldiers: Began searching near the inaccessible Rocks of the Wild Goats 2) He entered a cave near the sheep pens to attend to his needs b. David & his men were hiding far back in the very same cave c. David's men suggested this was of God: He should seize the moment, kill Saul	And it came to pass, when Saul was returned from following the Philistines, that it was told him, saying, Behold, David is in the wilderness of En-gedi. 2 Then Saul took three thousand chosen men out of all Israel, and went to seek David and his men upon the rocks of the wild goats. 3 And he came to the sheepcotes by the way, where *was* a cave; and Saul went in to cover his feet: and David and his men remained in the sides of the cave. 4 And the men of David said unto him, Behold the day of which the LORD said unto thee, Behold, I will deliver thine enemy into thine hand,	that thou mayest do to him as it shall seem good unto thee. Then David arose, and cut off the skirt of Saul's robe privily. 5 And it came to pass afterward, that David's heart smote him, because he had cut off Saul's skirt. 6 And he said unto his men, The LORD forbid that I should do this thing unto my master, the LORD's anointed, to stretch forth mine hand against him, seeing he is the anointed of the LORD. 7 So David stayed his servants with these words, and suffered them not to rise against Saul. But Saul rose up out of the cave, and went on *his* way.	d. David crept up & cut off only a corner of Saul's robe e. David's conscience bothered him 1) The reason: He had shown disrespect to his master or ruler, the LORD's anointed 2) The result: David rebuked his men & stopped them from killing Saul

a. David's hideout was soon discovered by the spies who passed on the information to Saul. David was hiding out in the Wilderness or Desert of En Gedi, which was an oasis with plenty of fresh water and fruitful vineyards. En Gedi was located east of Hebron close by the Dead Sea.

As soon as Saul received this information from his spies, he mobilized a *special force* of 3,000 soldiers who set out in search of David. They marched to the inaccessible Rocks of the Wild Goats where they began their search. As evening approached, they came to a very fertile area where a number of sheep pens had been built and decided to make camp there. As the cloak of darkness began to set in, Saul walked out from the camp looking for a place to relieve himself and noticed off in the distance a large cave to which he headed.

b. Unknown to Saul, David and his men were hiding far back in the very same cave (v.4).

c. So remarkable was the coincidence that David's men suggested this was of God (v.4). God had placed David's enemy into his hands: he should therefore seize the moment and kill Saul.

d. But note what David did: quietly tiptoeing, he crept up and cut off only a corner of Saul's robe (v.4). Obviously Saul had taken off his robe and laid it aside some distance away, which enabled David to creep up unnoticed.

e. Afterward, however, David was stricken in conscience for what he had done (vv.5-7). And note, he shared the fact with his men. He stated that he had been disrespectful to his master, their ruler and the LORD's anointed. Since Saul was the LORD's anointed, the men's counsel to kill him could not be carried out. To kill the LORD's anointed would be an act of outright rebellion against the LORD, for the LORD commanded His people not to curse their rulers (Ex.22:28). In fact, the hand of God's judgment had fallen in the past when God's people rebelled against their leaders (Nu.12:2-15; 16:1-35).[1]

With this rebuke, David was able to stop his men from killing Saul. As a result, Saul left the cave and returned to his men at the campsite.

Thought 1. Civil leaders and religious leaders are to be respected. We are to honor our leaders, not curse or ridicule them, certainly not assault or kill them. Even when a leader is wrong, we are to show respect and honor for the position the person holds. If the leader is wrong, acting in some wicked or evil way, we should do everything in our power to correct the leader. But in correcting, God demands that we still show respect and honor for the leader. If we retaliate in some unkind, lawless, or violent way, we stoop to the level of the wicked and corrupt leader. Such disrespectful, dishonoring, and lawless behavior makes us no better than the immoral and unjust leader. God's Holy Word is clear and straightforward: we must honor both our civil and religious leaders.

(1) We must honor our civil leaders.

> "They say unto him, Caesar's. Then saith he unto them, Render therefore unto Caesar the things which are Caesar's; and unto God the things that are God's" (Mt.22:21).
> "Then said Paul, I wist [knew] not, brethren, that he was the high priest: for it is written, Thou shalt not speak evil of the ruler of thy people" (Ac.23:5).
> "Let every soul be subject unto the higher powers. For there is no power but of God: the powers that be are ordained of God" (Ro.13:1).
> "Put them in mind to be subject to principalities and powers, to obey magistrates, to be ready to every good work" (Tit.3:1).
> "Submit yourselves to every ordinance of man for the LORD's sake: whether it be to the king, as supreme; Or unto governors, as unto them that are sent by him for the punishment of evildoers, and for the praise of them that do well" (1 Pe.2:13-14).
> "Honour all *men*. Love the brotherhood. Fear God. Honour the king" (1 Pe.2:17).
> "But the LORD hardened Pharaoh's heart, so that he would not let the children of Israel go" (Ex.10:20).
> "Thou shalt not revile the gods, nor curse the ruler of thy people" (Ex.22:28).
> "By the blessing of the upright the city is exalted: but it is overthrown by the mouth of the wicked" (Pr.11:11).
> "Righteousness exalteth a nation: but sin *is* a reproach to any people" (Pr.14:34).
> "*It is* an abomination to kings to commit wickedness: for the throne is established by righteousness" (Pr.16:12).
> "I *counsel thee* to keep the king's commandment, and *that* in regard of the oath of God" (Ec.8:2).

(2) We must honor our religious leaders.

> "Receive him therefore in the LORD with all gladness; and hold such in reputation" (Ph.2:29).
> "And we beseech you, brethren, to know them which labour among you, and are over you in the LORD, and admonish you; And to esteem them very highly in love for their work's sake. *And* be at peace among yourselves" (1 Th.5:12-13).
> "Let the elders that rule well be counted worthy of double honour, especially they who labour in the word and doctrine" (1 Ti.5:17).
> "Remember them which have the rule over you, who have spoken unto you the word of God: whose faith follow, considering the end of *their* conversation [behavior, conduct]" (He.13:7).

2 (24:8-15) **Humility, Example of—Loyalty, Example of—David, Respect for Saul—Ruler, Respect for, Example of—Leader, Respect for, Example of**: there was David's humility and his loyalty to King Saul. As soon as Saul had left the cave and walked a short distance, but still within earshot, David walked out to the edge of the cave and called out to the king. Standing some distance apart, the two men confronted one another and each in his turn spoke, with David speaking first. The speech of each man is the longest recorded in First Samuel, with David speaking 114 Hebrew words and Saul speaking 67 Hebrew words.[2] Note David's speech:

---

[1] Robert D. Bergen. *1, 2 Samuel*, p.239.

[2] Ibid., p.239.

OUTLINE	SCRIPTURE	SCRIPTURE	OUTLINE

2. David's humility & his loyalty to King Saul: A lesson on the need for humility & loyalty
a. David showed the utmost humility to Saul
  1) Addressed him as king
  2) Bowed to the ground
b. David presented a strong case for reconciliation
  1) The charge of treason by others was false
  2) The proof was fivefold
 	
  • Saul had been in the very cave where David was
  • Some of David's men had urged him to kill Saul: He refused
  • Saul was God's anointed
  • Saul was David's father-in-law
  • Saul's robe had been cut by David, but Da-
	8 David also arose afterward, and went out of the cave, and cried after Saul, saying, My lord the king. And when Saul looked behind him, David stooped with his face to the earth, and bowed himself.
	9 And David said to Saul, Wherefore hearest thou men's words, saying, Behold, David seeketh thy hurt?
	10 Behold, this day thine eyes have seen how that the LORD had delivered thee to day into mine hand in the cave: and *some* bade *me* kill thee: but *mine eye* spared thee; and I said, I will not put forth mine hand against my lord; for he *is* the LORD's anointed.
	11 Moreover, my father, see, yea, see the skirt of thy robe in my hand: for in that I cut off the skirt of thy robe
		and killed thee not, know thou and see that *there is* neither evil nor transgression in mine hand, and I have not sinned against thee; yet thou huntest my soul to take it.
		12 The LORD judge between me and thee, and the LORD avenge me of thee: but mine hand shall not be upon thee.
		13 As saith the proverb of the ancients, Wickedness proceedeth from the wicked: but mine hand shall not be upon thee.
		14 After whom is the king of Israel come out? after whom dost thou pursue? after a dead dog, after a flea.
		15 The LORD therefore be judge, and judge between me and thee, and see, and plead my cause, and deliver me out of thine hand.
			vid refused to kill him
			  3) The verdict: David was innocent
			
			c. David attempted to convince Saul of the injustice being done
			  1) By warning Saul of God's judgment
			  2) By quoting an ancient proverb
			  3) By assuring Saul he would never harm him
			  4) By questioning Saul & claiming that he was not a threat: He was as a dead dog or flea to Saul
			  5) By calling upon the LORD to decide who was right & to punish the guilty
			  6) By calling out for the LORD to vindicate & deliver him from Saul

a. David showed the utmost humility toward Saul by addressing him as king and bowing to the earth (v.8). Note that David actually addressed Saul as "my master" (6); "the LORD's anointed" (6, 10); "my LORD" (8, 10); "the king" (8, 14); and "my father" (11). David was making every effort to convince Saul of his respect and honor.

b. David presented a strong case for reconciliation between himself and Saul (vv.9-11). He declared that the charges of treason being launched by others were absolutely false. The proof was fivefold:
⇒ First, Saul had just been in the very cave where David was, delivered there by the LORD.
⇒ Second, some of David's own men had urged him to kill Saul, but he had refused.
⇒ Third, David had refused because Saul was God's anointed, and David both acknowledged and honored the fact.
⇒ Fourth, Saul was, in fact, David's father-in-law.
⇒ Fifth, Saul's robe had just been cut by David, yet David had refused to kill him.

With the proof and evidence presented, David pronounced the verdict: he was innocent (v.11). Then he cried out for Saul to understand and recognize that he was not guilty of wrongdoing and rebellion against the throne. He had not wronged Saul, and yet Saul was hunting him down like a wild animal to kill him. The evidence was irrefutable, and Saul needed to acknowledge the fact.

c. David attempted to convince Saul of the injustice being done by his pursuing him and seeking to kill him (vv.12-15). Doing all he could to strike and melt the heart of Saul, David shouted out six points:
1) David warned Saul of God's judgment (v.12). The LORD was going to judge between him and Saul, and David cried out to the LORD to avenge the wrongs that had been done to him. But he assured Saul that his own hand would never retaliate nor seek revenge against the king.
2) David then quoted an ancient proverb that teaches an obvious fact: only a wicked person would do evil against another person (v.13).
3) David assured Saul that he was not wicked; he would never harm him (v.13).
4) David asked a series of questions that clearly showed he was not a personal threat to Saul (v.14). In fact, he was nothing more than a dead or lifeless dog or a small flea before Saul. He was totally insignificant and posed no threat whatsoever to Saul.
5) Closing his appeal to the king, David then called upon the LORD to decide who was right and to judge and punish the guilty party (v.15).
6) Finally, with a thundering voice, David called out for the LORD to vindicate and deliver him from the hand of Saul (v.15).

Thought 1. David sets a dynamic example for us of humility and loyalty. Just imagine what was happening. With raging anger and hostility, Saul was fiercely pursuing David, seeking to kill him. But out of respect for God's Holy Word—which states that rulers are to be honored—David humbled himself before King Saul. He humbled himself and declared his loyalty. Saul was wrong, wicked, and evil, and he had even been driven insane by his sinful behavior. Nevertheless, he was the ruler over God's people. For this reason, David humbled himself and declared his loyalty to King Saul.

What a dynamic example for us. God's Holy Word commands us to live lives of humility and to give our loyalty to the leaders who rule over us.
(1) We are to live lives of humility.

"But ye *shall* not *be* so: but he that is greatest among you, let him be as the younger; and he that is chief, as he that doth serve" (Lu.22:26).

"For I say, through the grace given unto me, to every man that is among you, not to think *of himself* more highly than he ought to think; but to think soberly, according as God hath dealt to every man the measure of faith" (Ro.12:3).

"*Let* nothing *be done* through strife or vainglory; but in lowliness of mind let each esteem other better than themselves. Look not every man on his own things, but every man also on the things of others. Let this mind be in you, which was also in Christ Jesus" (Ph.2:3-5).

"Humble yourselves in the sight of the LORD, and he shall lift you up" (Js.4:10).

"Likewise, ye younger, submit yourselves unto the elder. Yea, all *of you* be subject one to another, and be clothed with humility: for God resisteth the proud, and giveth grace to the humble. Humble yourselves therefore under the mighty hand of God, that he may exalt you in due time" (1 Pe.5:5-6).

"He hath showed thee, O man, what *is* good; and what doth the LORD require of thee, but to do justly, and to love mercy, and to walk humbly with thy God?" (Mi.6:8).

(2) We are to honor and be loyal to those who rule over us.

"Let every soul be subject unto the higher powers. For there is no power but of God: the powers that be are ordained of God" (Ro.13:1).

"That ye submit yourselves unto such, and to every one that helpeth with *us*, and laboureth" (1 Co.16:16).

"Receive him therefore in the LORD with all gladness; and hold such in reputation" (Ph.2:29).

"And we beseech you, brethren, to know them which labour among you, and are over you in the LORD, and admonish you; And to esteem them very highly in love for their work's sake. *And* be at peace among yourselves" (1 Th.5:12-13).

"Let the elders that rule well be counted worthy of double honour, especially they who labour in the word and doctrine" (1 Ti.5:17).

"Put them in mind to be subject to principalities and powers, to obey magistrates, to be ready to every good work" (Tit.3:1).

"Remember them which have the rule over you, who have spoken unto you the word of God: whose faith follow, considering the end of *their* conversation [behavior, conduct]" (He.13:7).

"Honour all *men*. Love the brotherhood. Fear God. Honour the king" (1 Pe.2:17).

"Likewise, ye younger, submit yourselves unto the elder. Yea, all *of you* be subject one to another, and be clothed with humility: for God resisteth the proud, and giveth grace to the humble" (1 Pe.5:5).

"Thou shalt not revile the gods, nor curse the ruler of thy people" (Ex.22:28).

3 (24:16-22) **Remorse, Example of—Good for Evil, Example of—Saul, Acknowledged David to Be King—Covenant, Between David and Saul—David, Respect for Saul**: there was Saul's remorse and confession that David truly would be king someday. This is a striking lesson on repaying good for evil. After David had finished speaking, Saul called back, "Is that really you, my son David?" (NLT). Note that Saul addressed David as "my son." Having just called out the question, Saul visibly wept aloud. But this outburst of tears was only an emotional reaction to a convicted heart, for Saul never repented or had a true change of heart. Picture the scene as Saul addressed David at that moment:

OUTLINE	SCRIPTURE	SCRIPTURE	OUTLINE
3. Saul's remorse & confession that David would be king: A lesson on repaying good for evil	16 And it came to pass, when David had made an end of speaking these words unto Saul, that Saul said, *Is* this thy voice, my son David? And Saul lifted up his voice, and wept.	emy, will he let him go well away? wherefore the LORD reward thee good for that thou hast done unto me this day.	• By defying common sense & human nature to retaliate against one's enemy
	17 And he said to David, Thou *art* more righteous than I: for thou hast rewarded me good, whereas I have rewarded thee evil.	20 And now, behold, I know well that thou shalt surely be king, and that the kingdom of Israel shall be established in thine hand.	3) Saul pronounced a blessing upon David b. Saul confessed God's royal plans for David: That David would be king & would establish the kingdom of Israel
a. Saul confessed that David was more righteous than he 1) David had repaid him good for evil			
2) David had been kind to him	18 And thou hast showed this day how that thou hast dealt well with me: forasmuch as when the LORD had delivered me into thine hand, thou killedst me not.	21 Swear now therefore unto me by the LORD, that thou wilt not cut off my seed after me, and that thou wilt not destroy my name out of my father's house.	c. Saul made two requests 1) That David not kill off his descendants 2) That David not wipe out his family's name
• By not killing him	19 For if a man find his en-	22 And David sware unto Saul. And Saul went home; but David and his men gat them up unto the hold.	3) The result: David swore an oath d. Saul & David ended their

a. First, Saul confessed that David was more righteous than he (vv.17-19). Clearing David of all guilt, he shouted out that David had repaid him good for evil. Saul was the one who had been doing evil to David while David was doing good to him. Moreover, David had shown mercy to him by not killing him when he had the chance in the cave. Note that Saul acknowledged that the LORD had delivered him into the hands of David but that David had deliberately chosen to spare his life. This defied common sense and human nature, which seeks to retaliate against one's enemy. Then because of David's repaying Saul good for evil, the king pronounced a blessing upon David. He asked the LORD to reward him for the kindness he had shown to the king that day.

b. Amazingly, Saul confessed God's royal plans for David, that David would someday be king and would establish or reunite the kingdom of Israel that Saul himself had torn apart (vv.20; 15:28; 16:12). In this confession, he confirmed what his very own son had earlier predicted for David (23:17).

c. Tragically, even in the midst of confessing his evil against David, Saul's utter selfishness came out and was exposed. This is seen in the two requests he made (vv.21-22). Note that his major concern was to preserve his name and the lives of his descendants to make sure that his name was always preserved and honored. He requested that David swear to two things:

⇒ that David not kill off his descendants
⇒ that David not wipe out his family's name

Saul was probably unaware that his own son Jonathan had made a similar covenant with David (20:14-17, 42). Then without any hesitation whatsoever, David made the very same covenant with Saul. He swore that he would do what he could to preserve the descendants of Saul and the name of the family. Sometime later David would keep his word, fulfilling the covenant he had just confirmed with Saul: he would save the life of Jonathan's crippled son, Mephibosheth, and actually bring him into the royal palace (2 S.9:1-13; 19:29; 21:7).

d. Having agreed to the covenant, Saul and David ended their encounter. Saul returned home, but David and his men returned to their stronghold in En Gedi (v.22).

Thought 1. Nothing is anymore difficult than doing good for evil. Time and again God's Holy Word teaches that we are to love our enemies. We are not to seek revenge, retaliating against those who have wronged us. As difficult as it may be, we are to be kind to those who ridicule, mock, or even curse us. Even if a person abuses, assaults, or attempts to kill us, we must not be consumed with the spirit of vengeance and seek to retaliate. But of course we must attempt to get away and seek the help of others. A wicked abuser or persecutor must be corrected, must never be indulged nor given the license to commit his evil. But in our correcting this evil behavior, our corrective action is to be carried out in a spirit of regret and compassion, not of revenge and retaliation. We are always to render "good for evil," keeping in mind that the good is correction and discipline, not license and indulgence. God's Holy Word declares that we are to render good for evil.

"But I say unto you, Love your enemies, bless them that curse you, do good to them that hate you, and pray for them which despitefully use you, and persecute you" (Mt.5:44).

"But I say unto you which hear, Love your enemies, do good to them which hate you" (Lu.6:27).

"But love ye your enemies, and do good, and lend, hoping for nothing again; and your reward shall be great, and ye shall be the children of the Highest: for he is kind unto the unthankful and *to* the evil" (Lu.6:35).

"Therefore if thine enemy hunger, feed him; if he thirst, give him drink: for in so doing thou shalt heap coals of fire on his head" (Ro.12:20).

"See that none render evil for evil unto any *man;* but ever follow that which is good, both among yourselves, and to all *men*" (1 Th.5:15).

"If thou see the ass of him that hateth thee lying under his burden, and wouldest forbear to help him, thou shalt surely help with him" (Ex.23:5).

"If thine enemy be hungry, give him bread to eat; and if he be thirsty, give him water to drink" (Pr.25:21).

CHAPTER 25

E. The Encounter of David with Nabal & Abigail: Lessons on Dealing with a Harsh, Selfish Man & a Wise, Courageous Woman, 25:1-44

1. **The death of Samuel: A very special priest & prophet**
   a. All Israel mourned & buried Samuel at his home
   b. David hid out in the wilderness of Paran or Maon

2. **The experience of David with Nabal (husband of Abigail who was later to become David's wife): A selfish man with a cold, hard heart**
   a. Nabal's background
      1) He was very wealthy
      2) He was married to a sensible, intelligent, & beautiful woman named Abigail
      3) He was harsh, mean, dishonest

   b. David's request for supplies
      1) He heard that Nabal was sheering sheep
      2) He sent a delegation to Nabal with a personal message from him

      • He greeted Nabal: By wishing him long life & good health

      • He informed Nabal that he (David) had been protecting his shepherds & flocks from raiders: Nabal's workers could verify this fact, 23:1, 5

      • He requested supplies
      • He appealed as a "son" to Nabal, indicating a close bond in that he had protected Nabal's property just as a son would

   c. Nabal's harsh denial of David's request
      1) He ridiculed & insulted the messengers & David
      2) He charged David with

And Samuel died; and all the Israelites were gathered together, and lamented him, and buried him in his house at Ramah. And David arose, and went down to the wilderness of Paran.

2 And *there was* a man in Maon, whose possessions *were* in Carmel; and the man *was* very great, and he had three thousand sheep, and a thousand goats: and he was shearing his sheep in Carmel.

3 Now the name of the man *was* Nabal; and the name of his wife Abigail: and *she was* a woman of good understanding, and of a beautiful countenance: but the man *was* churlish and evil in his doings; and he *was* of the house of Caleb.

4 And David heard in the wilderness that Nabal did shear his sheep.

5 And David sent out ten young men, and David said unto the young men, Get you up to Carmel, and go to Nabal, and greet him in my name:

6 And thus shall ye say to him that liveth *in prosperity*, Peace *be* both to thee, and peace *be* to thine house, and peace *be* unto all that thou hast.

7 And now I have heard that thou hast shearers: now thy shepherds which were with us, we hurt them not, neither was there ought missing unto them, all the while they were in Carmel.

8 Ask thy young men, and they will show thee. Wherefore let the young men find favour in thine eyes: for we come in a good day: give, I pray thee, whatsoever cometh to thine hand unto thy servants, and to thy son David.

9 And when David's young men came, they spake to Nabal according to all those words in the name of David, and ceased.

10 And Nabal answered David's servants, and said, Who *is* David? and who *is* the son of Jesse? there be many servants now a days that break away every man from his master.

11 Shall I then take my bread, and my water, and my flesh that I have killed for my shearers, and give *it* unto men, whom I know not whence they *be*?

12 So David's young men turned their way, and went again, and came and told him all those sayings.

13 And David said unto his men, Gird ye on every man his sword. And they girded on every man his sword; and David also girded on his sword: and there went up after David about four hundred men; and two hundred abode by the stuff.

14 But one of the young men told Abigail, Nabal's wife, saying, Behold, David sent messengers out of the wilderness to salute our master; and he railed on them.

15 But the men *were* very good unto us, and we were not hurt, neither missed we any thing, as long as we were conversant with them, when we were in the fields:

16 They were a wall unto us both by night and day, all the while we were with them keeping the sheep.

17 Now therefore know and consider what thou wilt do; for evil is determined against our master, and against all his household: for he *is such* a son of Belial, that *a man* cannot speak to him.

18 Then Abigail made haste, and took two hundred loaves, and two bottles of wine, and five sheep ready dressed, and five measures of parched *corn*, and an hundred clusters of raisins, and two hundred cakes of figs, and laid *them* on asses.

19 And she said unto her servants, Go on before me; behold, I come after you. But she told not her husband Nabal.

20 And it was *so, as* she rode on the ass, that she came down by the covert of the hill, and, behold, David and his men came down against her; and she met them.

rebellion, with breaking away from his master, Saul

3) He exposed a cold heart & a greedy spirit: Note that "I" or "my" is used seven times in the Hebrew

4) He gave nothing to David's men: They returned & gave their report to David

d. David's angry reaction to Nabal's greed—his mean, selfish spirit
   1) He mobilized 400 men to take vengeance

   2) He left 200 men to guard their camp

e. A servant's reaction to Nabal's refusal to help David: He went straight to Abigail
   1) He shared Nabal's insults against David's messengers
   2) He shared the reason David's request for supplies should be granted
      • David always treated them well, never mistreated them
      • David protected them from marauders

   3) He urged Abigail to take action & warned her of David's likely retaliation
   4) He expressed frustration: Called Nabal evil, wicked, a scoundrel to his wife

3. **The experience of David with Abigail: A woman of wisdom, courage, humility, & beauty**
   a. Abigail's immediate preparation & quick journey to David
      1) She gathered generous supplies

      2) She sent her servants on ahead

      3) She acted in secrecy: Did not tell her husband

      4) She quickly journeyed to David: Met him as he was marching to retaliate against her husband

b. Abigail's confrontation with David: A man filled with venoumous anger
1) He had just made a serious charge against Nabal: That Nabal had paid or rendered evil for good

2) He had just vowed to retaliate against Nabal, even against all his workers

c. Abigail's humble, courageous approach to David: She showed a desperate humility

1) She bowed
2) She fell at his feet
d. Abigail demonstrated unselfishness, a spirit of self-sacrifice: Requested that David place the blame on her alone

e. Abigail confessed the wicked, foolish behavior of her husband: He had lived up to his nickname, "Fool"

f. Abigail pleaded ignorance: She had not personally seen the men sent by David
g. Abigail boldly announced that she had come on behalf of the LORD: To keep David from becoming guilty of vengeance & bloodshed

h. Abigail presented the supplies to David

i. Abigail asked forgiveness for the offense committed against David
j. Abigail predicted, foretold David's destiny: To establish a lasting dynasty as king
1) He must not, therefore, commit evil
2) He must know that his life was being protected by the LORD & that the LORD would take vengeance on behalf of David, casting away David's enemies

k. Abigail challenged David to consider how much better it would be to turn around &

21 Now David had said, Surely in vain have I kept all that this *fellow* hath in the wilderness, so that nothing was missed of all that *pertained* unto him: and he hath requited me evil for good.
22 So and more also do God unto the enemies of David, if I leave of all that *pertain* to him by the morning light any that pisseth against the wall.
23 And when Abigail saw David, she hasted, and lighted off the ass, and fell before David on her face, and bowed herself to the ground,
24 And fell at his feet, and said, Upon me, my lord, *upon me let this* iniquity *be:* and let thine handmaid, I pray thee, speak in thine audience, and hear the words of thine handmaid.
25 Let not my lord, I pray thee, regard this man of Belial, *even* Nabal: for as his name *is,* so *is* he; Nabal *is* his name, and folly *is* with him: but I thine handmaid saw not the young men of my lord, whom thou didst send.
26 Now therefore, my lord, *as* the LORD liveth, and *as* thy soul liveth, seeing the LORD hath withholden thee from coming to *shed* blood, and from avenging thyself with thine own hand, now let thine enemies, and they that seek evil to my lord, be as Nabal.
27 And now this blessing which thine handmaid hath brought unto my lord, let it even be given unto the young men that follow my lord.
28 I pray thee, forgive the trespass of thine handmaid: for the LORD will certainly make my lord a sure house; because my lord fighteth the battles of the LORD, and evil hath not been found in thee *all* thy days.
29 Yet a man is risen to pursue thee, and to seek thy soul: but the soul of my lord shall be bound in the bundle of life with the LORD thy God; and the souls of thine enemies, them shall he sling out, *as out* of the middle of a sling.
30 And it shall come to pass, when the LORD shall have done to my lord according to

all the good that he hath spoken concerning thee, and shall have appointed thee ruler over Israel;
31 That this shall be no grief unto thee, nor offence of heart unto my lord, either that thou hast shed blood causeless, or that my lord hath avenged himself: but when the LORD shall have dealt well with my lord, then remember thine handmaid.
32 And David said to Abigail, Blessed *be* the LORD God of Israel, which sent thee this day to meet me:
33 And blessed *be* thy advice, and blessed *be* thou, which hast kept me this day from coming to *shed* blood, and from avenging myself with mine own hand.
34 For in very deed, *as* the LORD God of Israel liveth, which hath kept me back from hurting thee, except thou hadst hasted and come to meet me, surely there had not been left unto Nabal by the morning light any that pisseth against the wall.
35 So David received of her hand *that* which she had brought him, and said unto her, Go up in peace to thine house; see, I have hearkened to thy voice, and have accepted thy person.
36 And Abigail came to Nabal; and, behold, he held a feast in his house, like the feast of a king; and Nabal's heart *was* merry within him, for he *was* very drunken: wherefore she told him nothing, less or more, until the morning light.
37 But it came to pass in the morning, when the wine was gone out of Nabal, and his wife had told him these things, that his heart died within him, and he became *as* a stone.
38 And it came to pass about ten days *after,* that the LORD smote Nabal, that he died.
39 And when David heard that Nabal was dead, he said, Blessed *be* the LORD, that hath pleaded the cause of my reproach from the hand of Nabal, and hath kept his servant from evil: for the LORD hath returned the wickedness of Nabal upon

not take vengeance
1) He was to become God's appointed leader

2) He would be far better off not to take *office* with the blood of vengeance upon his conscience
l. Abigail asked David to remember her after he became king

4. The heart of David before God & God's intercessor, Abigail: A heart that forgave & changed
a. David praised God & blessed Abigail
1) For good, sound advice, Pr.25:12
2) For keeping him from the guilt of bloodshed & vengeance, Ps.141:5
b. David confessed the sin of his vengeful heart: That he was set, determined to retaliate, take vengeance against Nabal & all his men, Ps.73:2

c. David accepted the supplies & sent Abigail home in peace: He granted her request, Pr.28:23

5. The marriage of David to Abigail: The judgment of God against Nabal & the vindication of God's servant
a. Abigail's sharing of the event with Nabal & his death
1) Nabal was very drunk, so Abigail could not share the event until morning
2) Nabal (once told) immediately suffered a stroke & was paralyzed

3) Nabal died ten days later: Due to God's judgment

b. David's praise to the LORD
1) Because the LORD had judged his enemy Nabal & vindicated David's cause
2) Because the LORD had kept him from the evil of revenge

c. David's request for marriage with Abigail: He had been deeply impressed with her	his own head. And David sent and communed with Abigail, to take her to him to wife.	servants of my lord.	
		42 And Abigail hasted, and arose, and rode upon an ass, with five damsels of hers that went after her; and she went after the messengers of David, and became his wife.	3) Abigail rushed with her five maids to David & married him
1) David sent his servants to ask &, if Abigail accepted, to bring her to him	40 And when the servants of David were come to Abigail to Carmel, they spake unto her, saying, David sent us unto thee to take thee to him to wife.		
		43 David also took Ahinoam of Jezreel; and they were also both of them his wives.	d. David's other wives 1) Ahinoam of Jezreel
2) Abigail humbly accepted: Offering herself as his maidservant, to do whatever David needed	41 And she arose, and bowed herself on *her* face to the earth, and said, Behold, *let* thine handmaid *be* a servant to wash the feet of the	44 But Saul had given Michal his daughter, David's wife, to Phalti the son of Laish, which *was* of Gallim.	2) Michal, Saul's daughter: Saul had taken her away & given her to Phalti

DIVISION IV

THE STORY OF SAUL AND DAVID (PART 2):
DAVID THE FUGITIVE, 21:1–31:13

E. The Encounter of David with Nabal and Abigail: Lessons on Dealing with a Harsh, Selfish Man and a Wise, Courageous Woman, 25:1-44

(25:1-44) **Introduction—Mean-Spirited, Example of—Hard-hearted, Example of—Women, Courageous—Women, Wise**: a sharp contrast is drawn between a harsh, selfish man and a wise, courageous woman in the present lesson of Scripture. The picture painted of the man is that of a cold, mean person who was selfish and dishonest. Tragically, there are some persons who walk upon this earth who are hard and mean-spirited.

On the other hand the picture painted of the woman is that of a sensible, intelligent, understanding, wise, courageous, humble, and beautiful person. Just imagine such a woman, and thankfully there are courageous and wise women of the highest character who walk among us.

This is a description of the man and woman who encountered David in the present passage of Scripture. This is: *The Encounter of David with Nabal and Abigail: Lessons on Dealing with a Harsh, Selfish Man and a Wise, Courageous Woman*, 25:1-44.

1. The death of Samuel: a very special priest and prophet (v.1).
2. The experience of David with Nabal (husband of Abigail who was later to become David's wife): a selfish man with a cold, hard heart (vv.2-17).
3. The experience of David with Abigail: a woman of wisdom, courage, humility, and beauty (vv.18-31).
4. The heart of David before God and God's intercessor, Abigail: a heart that forgave and changed (vv.32-35).
5. The marriage of David to Abigail: the judgment of God against Nabal and the vindication of God's servant (vv.36-44).

[1] (25:1) **Death, Example of—Samuel, Death of**: there was the death of Samuel, the spiritual leader of Israel who had served as both prophet and judge to the people. Remember, Samuel was the last person to serve as *judge* of Israel. His life and death closed the era of the judges and prepared the way for the monarchy, the rule of the kings. More than anyone else, Samuel's faith and courage had helped the Israelites begin the movement toward a united nation, toward undergoing a transition from twelve disunified tribes to a unified monarchy.

Samuel was a nationwide leader in both politics and religion. For this reason, all Israel mourned his death; and many attended his funeral, including all the tribal leaders. No doubt many thousands were present to pay their last respects to this great servant of God, one of the major national leaders of Israel. Note that he was buried in his home in Ramah, not in an elaborate tomb in some important public place. Warren W. Wiersbe says that this was in stark contrast to King Saul who had built a public monument for himself at Carmel (15:12)—a sharp contrast between pride and humility.[1]

Receiving word of Samuel's death, David retreated deeper into the desert, probably for the purpose of mourning Samuel's death in an area much more protected from Saul's reach. Remember that Samuel had been David's spiritual mentor and counselor ever since he had been a young boy. A deep sense of loss and grief must have gripped his heart, driving him to his face before God. He was bound to be wondering who now would be able to advise and counsel him, especially in these days when Saul was so fiercely pursuing him.

The place to which David retreated was the Wilderness of Paran. This area was more than 100 miles south of the stronghold at En Gedi where David and his men had been hiding out from Saul. However, it should be noted that some texts and translations say that David retreated to Maon which was one of David's favorite hideouts (23:24-25). Note that the event with Nabal and Abigail, which begins in verse two, took place in Maon. Whatever the case, whether the Desert of Paran or Maon, David retreated farther away from Saul's pursuit, most likely to be more free to seek the face of God.

---

[1] Warren W. Wiersbe. *Be Successful*, p.134.

OUTLINE	SCRIPTURE
1. The death of Samuel: A very special priest & prophet	And Samuel died; and all the Israelites were gathered together, and lamented him, and buried him in his house at Ramah. And David arose, and went down to the wilderness of Paran.
a. All Israel mourned & buried Samuel at his home	
b. David hid out in the wilderness of Paran or Maon	

Thought 1. Samuel's death is a reminder that we must all die. The day is coming when we will no longer live upon this earth. Death is universal: every single person born into this world dies and no person can stop death. But some of us do not even reach old age. We are snatched away by the dark tentacles of death much sooner through such tragedies as…

- premature births
- accidents
- diseases
- suicides
- assaults
- murders

No matter how much we may want to remain on this earth and no matter what we do, we simply cannot stop the dark grip of death. Everyone of us *must* die. This is the clear teaching of God's Holy Word:

"Wherefore, as by one man sin entered into the world, and death by sin; and so death passed upon all men, for that all have sinned" (Ro.5:12).

"For we that are in *this* tabernacle do groan, being burdened: not for that we would be unclothed, but clothed upon, that mortality might be swallowed up of life" (2 Co.5:4).

"And as it is appointed unto men once to die, but after this the judgment" (He.9:27).

"But the rich, in that he is made low: because as the flower of the grass he shall pass away" (Jas.1:10).

"For all flesh *is* as grass, and all the glory of man as the flower of grass. The grass withereth, and the flower thereof falleth away" (1 Pe.1:24).

"For we must needs die, and *are* as water spilt on the ground, which cannot be gathered up again; neither doth God respect *any* person: yet doth he devise means, that his banished be not expelled from him" (2 Sa.14:14).

"For I know *that* thou wilt bring me *to* death, and *to* the house appointed for all living" (Jb.30:23).

"For he seeth *that* wise men die, likewise the fool and the brutish person perish, and leave their wealth to others" (Ps.49:10).

"What man *is he that* liveth, and shall not see death? shall he deliver his soul from the hand of the grave? Selah" (Ps.89:48).

"Thou carriest them away as with a flood; they are *as* a sleep: in the morning *they are* like grass *which* groweth up. In the morning it flourisheth, and groweth up; in the evening it is cut down, and withereth" (Ps.90:5-6).

"*As for* man, his days *are* as grass: as a flower of the field, so he flourisheth. For the wind passeth over it, and it is gone; and the place thereof shall know it no more" (Ps.103:15-16).

"All go unto one place; all are of the dust, and all turn to dust again" (Ec.3:20).

"*There is* no man that hath power over the spirit to retain the spirit; neither *hath he* power in the day of death: and *there is* no discharge in *that* war; neither shall wickedness deliver those that are given to it" (Ec.8:8).

"The voice said, Cry. And he said, What shall I cry? All flesh *is* grass, and all the goodliness thereof *is* as the flower of the field: The grass withereth, the flower fadeth: because the spirit of the LORD bloweth upon it: surely the people *is* grass" (Is.40:6-7).

---

2 (25:2-17) **Hard-hearted, Example of—Selfish, Example of—Greed, Example of—Dishonesty, Example of—Cold-hearted, Example of—Meanness, Example of—Nabal, Opposed David—Abigail, Described**: there was David's experience with Nabal, the husband of Abigail who was later to become David's wife. Having just been forced to flee for their lives, David and his 600 men were bound to face hunger and the need for other supplies. Just feeding such a large number of fugitives who were constantly on the run was an awesome responsibility. To provide food and supplies, David had to depend upon wealthy landowners and others who were sympathetic to his cause. Keep in mind that David had been protecting the citizens of Israel from Philistine raiders and marauders who would often sweep down upon the land killing, destroying, and stealing whatever they needed or wanted (23:1-6). Because of David's protection, many citizens and property owners willingly supported David and his fugitive band. But when David approached Nabal, he confronted a man with a cold, hard heart who was rooted in selfishness and greed.

OUTLINE	SCRIPTURE	SCRIPTURE	OUTLINE
2. The experience of David with Nabal (husband of Abigail who was later to become David's wife): A selfish man with a cold, hard heart	2 And *there was* a man in Maon, whose possessions *were* in Carmel; and the man *was* very great, and he had three thousand sheep, and a	thousand goats: and he was shearing his sheep in Carmel. 3 Now the name of the man *was* Nabal; and the name of his wife Abigail: and *she was*	a. Nabal's background 1) He was very wealthy 2) He was married to a sensible, intelligent, & beautiful woman named Abigail

213

OUTLINE	SCRIPTURE	SCRIPTURE	OUTLINE
3) He was harsh, mean, dishonest	a woman of good understanding, and of a beautiful countenance: but the man *was* churlish and evil in his doings; and he *was* of the house of Caleb.	ants now a days that break away every man from his master.	
		11 Shall I then take my bread, and my water, and my flesh that I have killed for my shearers, and give *it* unto men, whom I know not whence they *be?*	3) He exposed a cold heart & a greedy spirit: Note that "I" or "my" is used seven times in the Hebrew
b. David's request for supplies 1) He heard that Nabal was sheering sheep	4 And David heard in the wilderness that Nabal did shear his sheep.		
2) He sent a delegation to Nabal with a personal message from him	5 And David sent out ten young men, and David said unto the young men, Get you up to Carmel, and go to Nabal, and greet him in my name:	12 So David's young men turned their way, and went again, and came and told him all those sayings.	4) He gave nothing to David's men: They returned & gave their report to David
		13 And David said unto his men, Gird ye on every man his sword. And they girded on every man his sword; and David also girded on his sword: and there went up after David about four hundred men; and two hundred abode by the stuff.	d. David's angry reaction to Nabal's greed—his mean, selfish spirit 1) He mobilized 400 men to take vengeance 2) He left 200 men to guard their camp
• He greeted Nabal: By wishing him long life & good health	6 And thus shall ye say to him that liveth *in prosperity,* Peace *be* both to thee, and peace *be* to thine house, and peace *be* unto all that thou hast.		
• He informed Nabal that he (David) had been protecting his shepherds & flocks from raiders: Nabal's workers could verify this fact, 23:1, 5 • He requested supplies • He appealed as a "son" to Nabal, indicating a close bond in that he had protected Nabal's property just as a son would	7 And now I have heard that thou hast shearers: now thy shepherds which were with us, we hurt them not, neither was there ought missing unto them, all the while they were in Carmel. 8 Ask thy young men, and they will show thee. Wherefore let the young men find favour in thine eyes: for we come in a good day: give, I pray thee, whatsoever cometh to thine hand unto thy servants, and to thy son David.	14 But one of the young men told Abigail, Nabal's wife, saying, Behold, David sent messengers out of the wilderness to salute our master; and he railed on them. 15 But the men *were* very good unto us, and we were not hurt, neither missed we any thing, as long as we were conversant with them, when we were in the fields: 16 They were a wall unto us both by night and day, all the while we were with them keeping the sheep.	e. A servant's reaction to Nabal's refusal to help David: He went straight to Abigail 1) He shared Nabal's insults against David's messengers 2) He shared the reason David's request for supplies should be granted • David always treated them well, never mistreated them • David protected them from marauders
c. Nabal's harsh denial of David's request 1) He ridiculed & insulted the messengers & David	9 And when David's young men came, they spake to Nabal according to all those words in the name of David, and ceased.	17 Now therefore know and consider what thou wilt do; for evil is determined against our master, and against all his household: for he *is such* a son of Belial, that *a man* cannot speak to him.	3) He urged Abigail to take action & warned her of David's likely retaliation 4) He expressed frustration: Called Nabal evil, wicked, a scoundrel to his wife
2) He charged David with rebellion, with breaking away from his master, Saul	10 And Nabal answered David's servants, and said, Who *is* David? and who *is* the son of Jesse? there be many serv-		

a. Note Nabal's background: he was very wealthy, owning over 1,000 goats and 3,000 sheep (vv.2-3). He was married to Abigail, a sensible and intelligent woman who was also very beautiful. Nabal was a descendant of Caleb, a distinguished and highly esteemed clan. But note what else Scripture says about him: he was harsh and evil in his dealings. His heart was cold and mean. He was greedy and dishonest in dealing with people.

b. While hiding out in the Wilderness of Maon, some dire circumstance arose and David had to approach Nabal for food and supplies. He heard that Nabal was sheering sheep, so he sent a delegation to the very successful farmer with a personal message (vv.5-8). The message included four points:
  ⇒ David greeted Nabal by wishing him a long life and good health (v.6).
  ⇒ David informed Nabal that he had been protecting his shepherds and flocks from bandits and marauders and that Nabal's workers could verify this fact (7; 23:1, 5).
  ⇒ David requested supplies (v.7).
  ⇒ David appealed as a "son" to Nabal, indicating a close bond between them in that David had protected Nabal's property just as a son would.

In light of his wealth and the protection David had provided, Nabal should have provided generous supplies for David and his men. But the response of Nabal to the request was a strong indictment against his character, an indictment that would soon lead to the hand of God's judgment falling upon him.

c. In a spirit of bitter contempt, Nabal denied David's request (vv.9-12). He rebuffed the messengers, ridiculing, demeaning, and insulting both them and David. In addition, he charged David with rebellion, with being nothing but a slave who had broken away from his master, King Saul.

Nabal demonstrated a cold and greedy spirit. He asked why he should take his bread and water and the meat he had killed for his shearers and give it to men he did not know. Note this fact: within this one verse, the word "I" or "my" is used seven times in the original Hebrew. This hard and selfish man gave nothing to David and his men. Turning around, David's messengers returned to David and shared with him the humiliating, contemptible behavior of Nabal toward them.

d. David's reaction was immediate, spontaneous: anger boiled up in him and he became increasingly incensed. He ordered his men to mobilize immediately to take vengeance against this selfish, ungrateful scoundrel. Mobilizing 400 men, David began the march to take vengeance against Nabal. Two hundred men were left behind to guard their camp.

e. While the above events were taking place, one of Nabal's servants who had heard the conversation reacted to Nabal's refusal to help David (vv.14-17). As a result, he went straight to Abigail and relayed his master's insults against David's messengers. Note that he justified David's request for supplies, stating that the request should have been granted. For David had always been very good to all the shepherds and servants of Nabal, never mistreating them. Night and day David had been a wall around them, protecting them from bandits and marauders.

The servant urged Abigail to take immediate action and warned her of David's likely retaliation (v.17). He expressed personal frustration, calling Nabal "a son of Belial" which means an evil, wicked, worthless person who is a scoundrel. Later in history, the word "Belial" was used to refer to Satan himself.

Thought 1. In a world with such desperate needs, God warns us against having cold, hard hearts. He warns us against being selfish and greedy, against covetousness. We must not hoard wealth, refusing to extend a helping hand to those in need. When there are so many people who are in such desperate need, we must help them. We must give to help the hungry, homeless, unclothed, diseased, poverty-stricken, destitute, impoverished, orphaned, widowed, imprisoned, and the person seeking refuge.

When a person needs the very basic necessities of life, we must give to meet those needs. In addition, when people are suffering under the bondages of sin and darkness, we must give by sharing the wonderful news of the gospel with them. The gospel of Christ must be taken to the desperate of this world who are held in the grip of despair and hopelessness. We must not allow our hearts to become cold, hard, selfish, and covetous.

"I was a stranger, and ye took me not in: naked, and ye clothed me not: sick, and in prison, and ye visited me not. Then shall they also answer him, saying, LORD, when saw we thee an hungred, or athirst, or a stranger, or naked, or sick, or in prison, and did not minister unto thee? Then shall he answer them, saying, Verily I say unto you, Inasmuch as ye did *it* not to one of the least of these, ye did *it* not to me. And these shall go away into everlasting punishment: but the righteous into life eternal" (Mt.25:43-46).

"And he said unto them, Take heed, and beware of covetousness: for a man's life consisteth not in the abundance of the things which he possesseth" (Lu.12:15).

"But after thy hardness and impenitent heart treasurest up unto thyself wrath against the day of wrath and revelation of the righteous judgment of God" (Ro.2:5).

"Mortify therefore your members which are upon the earth; fornication, uncleanness, inordinate affection, evil concupiscence, and covetousness, which is idolatry: For which things' sake the wrath of God cometh on the children of disobedience" (Col.3:5-6).

"For the love of money is the root of all evil: which while some coveted after, they have erred from the faith, and pierced themselves through with many sorrows" (1 Ti.6:10).

"But exhort one another daily, while it is called To day; lest any of you be hardened through the deceitfulness of sin" (He.3:13).

"He that withholdeth corn, the people shall curse him: but blessing *shall be* upon the head of him that selleth *it*" (Pr.11:26).

"He that is greedy of gain troubleth his own house; but he that hateth gifts shall live" (Pr.15:27).

"Happy *is* the man that feareth alway: but he that hardeneth his heart shall fall into mischief" (Pr.28:14).

"He, that being often reproved hardeneth *his* neck, shall suddenly be destroyed, and that without remedy" (Pr.29:1).

"Woe unto them that join house to house, *that* lay field to field, till *there be* no place, that they may be placed alone in the midst of the earth" (Is.5:8).

---

3 (25:18-31) **Sensible, Example of—Courage, Example of—Understanding, Example of—Humility, Example of—Beauty, Example of—Abigail, David's Wife, First Meeting**: there was David's experience with Abigail, his very first meeting with a woman who was later to become his wife. A beautiful and brave woman, Abigail demonstrated unusual intelligence, understanding, and wisdom. Her courage is seen in what she was about to do: go against the decision of her husband not to help David. She made the courageous decision to go out alone to attempt a reconciliation with the fugitive David, a fugitive whom she was almost certain would be seeking vengeance against her husband, herself, and their household. What bravery! She understood the crisis, and she had the inner boldness and the courage necessary to meet the crisis head-on. And this she did:

OUTLINE	SCRIPTURE	SCRIPTURE	OUTLINE
3. The experience of David with Abigail: A woman of wisdom, courage, humility, & beauty	18 Then Abigail made haste, and took two hundred loaves, and two bottles of wine, and	five sheep ready dressed, and five measures of parched *corn,* and an hundred clusters	a. Abigail's immediate preparation & quick journey to David

OUTLINE	SCRIPTURE	SCRIPTURE	OUTLINE
1) She gathered generous supplies 2) She sent her servants on ahead 3) She acted in secrecy: Did not tell her husband 4) She quickly journeyed to David: Met him as he was marching to retaliate against her husband b. Abigail's confrontation with David: A man filled with venomous anger 1) He had just made a serious charge against Nabal: That Nabal had paid or rendered evil for good 2) He had just vowed to retaliate against Nabal, even against all his workers c. Abigail's humble, courageous approach to David: She showed a desperate humility 1) She bowed 2) She fell at his feet d. Abigail demonstrated unselfishness, a spirit of self-sacrifice: Requested that David place the blame on her alone e. Abigail confessed the wicked, foolish behavior of her husband: He had lived up to his nickname, "Fool" f. Abigail pleaded ignorance: She had not personally seen the men sent by David	of raisins, and two hundred cakes of figs, and laid *them* on asses. 19 And she said unto her servants, Go on before me; behold, I come after you. But she told not her husband Nabal. 20 And it was *so, as* she rode on the ass, that she came down by the covert of the hill, and, behold, David and his men came down against her; and she met them. 21 Now David had said, Surely in vain have I kept all that this *fellow* hath in the wilderness, so that nothing was missed of all that *pertained* unto him: and he hath requited me evil for good. 22 So and more also do God unto the enemies of David, if I leave of all that *pertain* to him by the morning light any that pisseth against the wall. 23 And when Abigail saw David, she hasted, and lighted off the ass, and fell before David on her face, and bowed herself to the ground, 24 And fell at his feet, and said, Upon me, my lord, *upon* me *let this* iniquity *be:* and let thine handmaid, I pray thee, speak in thine audience, and hear the words of thine handmaid. 25 Let not my lord, I pray thee, regard this man of Belial, *even* Nabal: for as his name *is,* so *is* he; Nabal *is* his name, and folly *is* with him: but I thine handmaid saw not the young men of my lord, whom thou didst send.	26 Now therefore, my lord, *as* the LORD liveth, and *as* thy soul liveth, seeing the LORD hath withholden thee from coming to *shed* blood, and from avenging thyself with thine own hand, now let thine enemies, and they that seek evil to my lord, be as Nabal. 27 And now this blessing which thine handmaid hath brought unto my lord, let it even be given unto the young men that follow my lord. 28 I pray thee, forgive the trespass of thine handmaid: for the LORD will certainly make my lord a sure house; because my lord fighteth the battles of the LORD, and evil hath not been found in thee *all* thy days. 29 Yet a man is risen to pursue thee, and to seek thy soul: but the soul of my lord shall be bound in the bundle of life with the LORD thy God; and the souls of thine enemies, them shall he sling out, *as out* of the middle of a sling. 30 And it shall come to pass, when the LORD shall have done to my lord according to all the good that he hath spoken concerning thee, and shall have appointed thee ruler over Israel; 31 That this shall be no grief unto thee, nor offence of heart unto my lord, either that thou hast shed blood causeless, or that my lord hath avenged himself: but when the LORD shall have dealt well with my lord, then remember thine handmaid.	g. Abigail boldly announced that she had come on behalf of the LORD: To keep David from becoming guilty of vengeance & bloodshed h. Abigail presented the supplies to David i. Abigail asked forgiveness for the offense committed against David j. Abigail predicted, foretold David's destiny: To establish a lasting dynasty as king 1) He must not, therefore, commit evil 2) He must know that his life was being protected by the LORD & that the LORD would take vengeance on behalf of David, casting away David's enemies k. Abigail challenged David to consider how much better it would be to turn around & not take vengeance 1) He was to become God's appointed leader 2) He would be far better off not to take *office* with the blood of vengeance upon his conscience l. Abigail asked David to remember her after he became king

a. Losing no time, Abigail immediately made preparations and took a quick journey to meet David (vv.18-20). She had a generous supply of provisions packed and loaded on donkeys. Wisely, she then sent her servants on ahead of her so that the first thing David saw would be the provisions. She hoped that by seeing the provisions, this might soften his anger and make reconciliation easier to achieve. Note that she acted in secrecy, not telling her husband what she was doing.

As quickly as Abigail could, she traveled to meet David. Just as she was riding into a mountain ravine, she saw David and his 400 men descending down the mountain toward her, marching to retaliate, to take vengeance against her husband and his household.

b. Drawing closer and closer to the moment of confrontation, Abigail could tell that she was about to confront a man filled with venomous anger (vv.21-22). In fact, David had become so furious, so inflamed with anger, that he had not yet settled down. He was still venting his anger against Nabal and had just made a serious charge against him: that Nabal had paid or rendered evil for good. David had been protecting and watching over Nabal's property, making sure that nothing was stolen, and now Nabal was repaying David's goodness and kindness with evil. For this reason, David vowed to retaliate against Nabal and against all the male workers who served him.

c. At first sight of David and his men, Abigail quickly got off her donkey and made a humble, courageous approach to the fugitive (v.23). She showed a desperate humility by bowing and falling at his feet.

d. Then she demonstrated unselfishness, a spirit of self-sacrifice (v.24). She requested that David place the blame on her for the injustice done him. In contrast to the selfishness of her husband, she demonstrated a spirit of unselfishness by accepting responsibility for the evil done against David and his men.

e. Abigail then confessed that her husband's behavior had been wicked, foolish. She stated that his name, Nabal, meaning *fool*, was an appropriate name for him; for he had done a foolish thing (v.25).

f. As for herself, Abigail pleaded ignorance of David's requests for supplies. She had not personally seen the messengers sent by him (v.25).

g. After making her initial plea, Abigail boldly announced that she had actually come on behalf of the LORD (v.26). The LORD had sent her to keep David from becoming guilty of vengeance and bloodshed. This was a very bold statement to make, for it showed that Abigail was expecting David to back off and not continue his pursuit of vengeance against her husband.

h. Apparently at this point, Abigail pointed to the supplies, encouraging David to take them and give them to the men who were following him (v.27).

i. Abigail then asked David to forgive her offense, implying that she and she alone was the guilty party who had committed the terrible evil against David (v.28).

j. Expressing her personal belief in the LORD's promise to David, she predicted that the LORD would place David upon the throne and use him to establish a permanent dynasty for the nation (vv.28-29). He must not, therefore, act rashly in seeking vengeance and shedding innocent blood. He must guard against wrongdoing as long as he lived, for his life was being protected by the LORD. Therefore, it must be the LORD who casts away David's enemies and not David himself. Painting a descriptive picture, Abigail told David that his life was bound securely in the *bundle of the living* by the LORD his God. But the lives of his enemies would be slung away just like stones shot from a sling.

k. Abigail then challenged David to consider how much better it would be to turn around and not take vengeance against her husband (vv.30-31). Saying no to vengeance would be far better because David was to become God's appointed leader. It would be far better for David to take office and become king without the blood of vengeance upon his conscience.

l. In closing her appeal, Abigail asked David to remember her after he became king (v.31). Obviously she was requesting that David never react against her or her family in the future, but rather that he show favor, especially to her children.

Thought 1. If there has ever been a need for women of courage and character, it is today. Of course the same could be said of men. But this particular point of Holy Scripture deals with a woman, a woman of unusual courage and character. Brave women of strong moral integrity must permeate every generation, for it is primarily the mothers of the world who nurture the character of their children. For the most part, all of us are a product of our mothers. Consequently, the character of our mothers essentially becomes the character of society. This is an awesome responsibility; nevertheless, it is a fact. We are reared primarily by our mothers, which means that we take on their character, becoming much like them. The women of this world, in particular the mothers, determine what most little boys and girls become. And when these little boys and girls grow, they become us, the adults of the world. And it is us, the adults, who take responsibility for society, the communities and states and nations of this world.

The importance of women of courage and character cannot be overstressed. Listen to what the Word of God says:

> **"I commend unto you Phebe our sister, which is a servant of the church which is at Cenchrea: That ye receive her in the LORD, as becometh saints, and that ye assist her in whatsoever business she hath need of you: for she hath been a succourer of many, and of myself also" (Ro.16:1-2).**
>
> **"Greet Priscilla and Aquila my helpers in Christ Jesus....Greet Mary, who bestowed much labour on us....Salute Tryphena and Tryphosa, who labour in the LORD. Salute the beloved Persis, which laboured much in the LORD" (Ro.16:3, 6, 12).**
>
> **"In like manner also, that women adorn themselves in modest apparel, with shamefacedness and sobriety; not with broided hair, or gold, or pearls, or costly array; But (which becometh women professing godliness) with good works" (1 Ti.2:9-10).**
>
> **"Likewise, ye wives, *be* in subjection to your own husbands; that, if any obey not the word, they also may without the word be won by the conversation of the wives; While they behold your chaste conversation *coupled* with fear" (1 Pt.3:1-2).**
>
> **"A gracious woman retaineth honour..." (Pr.11:16).**
>
> **"A virtuous woman *is* a crown to her husband: but she that maketh ashamed *is* as rottenness in his bones" (Pr.12:4).**
>
> **"Every wise woman buildeth her house: but the foolish plucketh it down with her hands" (Pr.14:1).**
>
> **"Who can find a virtuous woman? for her price *is* far above rubies....Strength and honour *are* her clothing; and she shall rejoice in time to come. She openeth her mouth with wisdom; and in her tongue *is* the law of kindness. She looketh well to the ways of her household, and eateth not the bread of idleness. Her children arise up, and call her blessed; her husband *also,* and he praiseth her. Many daughters have done virtuously, but thou excellest them all. Favour *is* deceitful, and beauty *is* vain: *but* a woman *that* feareth the LORD, she shall be praised. Give her of the fruit of her hands; and let her own works praise her in the gates" (Pr.31:10, 25-31).**

4 (25:32-35) **Forgiveness, Human, Example of—Heart, a Forgiving, Example of—David, Heart of:** there was David's heart exposed before God and before Abigail, the dear lady who had just become an intercessor for the LORD. Boldly, Abigail had presented several logical arguments for David to forgive and not take vengeance against her husband Nabal. Her pleas for forgiveness were persuasive and touched David's heart. His heart was changed and he forgave the terrible evil of injustice done against him. He burst out with a statement of praise to God and pronounced a blessing upon Abigail for her good, sound advice. He also praised her for keeping him from the guilt of bloodshed and vengeance (Ps.25:12; 141:5). And then David confessed the sin of his vengeful heart, that he had been determined to retaliate and to take revenge on Nabal and all his male servants (Ps.73:2).

Finally David accepted the supplies and sent Abigail home in peace (v.35). He had heard her persuasive arguments and plea and he granted her request (Pr.28:23).

OUTLINE	SCRIPTURE	SCRIPTURE	OUTLINE

4. The heart of David before God & God's intercessor, Abigail: A heart that forgave & changed
a. David praised God & blessed Abigail
  1) For good, sound advice, Pr.25:12
  2) For keeping him from the guilt of bloodshed & vengeance, Ps.141:5
b. David confessed the sin of his vengeful heart: That he was set, determined to retal-
	32 And David said to Abigail, Blessed *be* the LORD God of Israel, which sent thee this day to meet me:
	33 And blessed *be* thy advice, and blessed *be* thou, which hast kept me this day from coming to *shed* blood, and from avenging myself with mine own hand.
	34 For in very deed, *as* the LORD God of Israel liveth, which hath kept me
		back from hurting thee, except thou hadst hasted and come to meet me, surely there had not been left unto Nabal by the morning light any that pisseth against the wall.
		35 So David received of her hand *that* which she had brought him, and said unto her, Go up in peace to thine house; see, I have hearkened to thy voice, and have accepted thy person.
			iate, take vengeance against Nabal & all his men, Ps.73:2
			
			c. David accepted the supplies & sent Abigail home in peace: He granted her request, Pr.28:23

Thought 1. Forgiving others is a serious matter. It is serious because if we refuse to forgive others, God will not forgive us. Then we will be doomed to an eternity separated from God. Just think for a moment: What if God did not forgive us? What kind of predicament would we be in, for we have all committed evil and wickedness against God? God tells us that our sins are as repulsive as stinking, filthy rags (Is.64:6). Yet there is wonderful news: God does forgive. He has mercy upon us and forgives all the evil and wickedness we have done against Him. He forgives us and washes away all our sins.

But on the other hand, God turns around and says to us: if you are to receive my forgiveness, you too must forgive others. Just as I have forgiven your offenses, so you must forgive the offenses of others. This is the clear teaching of God's Holy Word.

> "Blessed *are* the merciful: for they shall obtain mercy" (Mt.5:7).
>
> "For if ye forgive men their trespasses, your heavenly Father will also forgive you: But if ye forgive not men their trespasses, neither will your Father forgive your trespasses" (Mt.6:14-15).
>
> "And when ye stand praying, forgive, if ye have ought against any: that your Father also which is in heaven may forgive you your trespasses" (Mk.11:25).
>
> "Be ye therefore merciful, as your Father also is merciful" (Lu.6:36).
>
> "And forgive us our sins; for we also forgive every one that is indebted to us. And lead us not into temptation; but deliver us from evil" (Lu.11:4).
>
> "And if he trespass against thee seven times in a day, and seven times in a day turn again to thee, saying, I repent; thou shalt forgive him" (Lu.17:4).
>
> "And be ye kind one to another, tenderhearted, forgiving one another, even as God for Christ's sake hath forgiven you" (Ep.4:32).
>
> "Forbearing one another, and forgiving one another, if any man have a quarrel against any: even as Christ forgave you, so also *do* ye" (Col.3:13).
>
> "Let not mercy and truth forsake thee: bind them about thy neck; write them upon the table of thine heart" (Pr.3:3).
>
> "The merciful man doeth good to his own soul: but *he that is* cruel troubleth his own flesh" (Pr.11:17).
>
> "He hath showed thee, O man, what *is* good; and what doth the LORD require of thee, but to do justly, and to love mercy, and to walk humbly with thy God" (Mi.6:8).

Thought 2. God warns us against anger and retaliation, against taking revenge upon people.

> "But I say unto you, That ye resist not evil: but whosoever shall smite thee on thy right cheek, turn to him the other also" (Mt.5:39).
>
> "For the wrath of God is revealed from heaven against all ungodliness and unrighteousness of men, who hold the truth in unrighteousness….Being filled with all unrighteousness, fornication, wickedness, covetousness, maliciousness; full of envy, murder, debate, deceit, malignity; whisperers, Backbiters, haters of God, despiteful, proud, boasters, inventors of evil things, disobedient to parents, Without understanding, covenantbreakers, without natural affection, implacable, unmerciful: Who knowing the judgment of God, that they which commit such things are worthy of death, not only do the same, but have pleasure in them that do them" (Ro.1:18, 29-32).
>
> "Recompense to no man evil for evil. Provide things honest in the sight of all men" (Ro.12:17).
>
> "Now the works of the flesh are manifest, which are *these*; Adultery, fornication, uncleanness, lasciviousness, Idolatry, witchcraft, hatred, variance, emulations, wrath, strife, seditions, heresies, Envyings, murders, drunkenness, revellings, and such like: of the which I tell you before, as I have also told *you* in time past, that they which do such things shall not inherit the kingdom of God" (Ga.5:19-21).

"See that none render evil for evil unto any *man;* but ever follow that which is good, both among yourselves, and to all *men*" (1 Th.5:15).

"Not rendering evil for evil, or railing for railing: but contrariwise blessing; knowing that ye are thereunto called, that ye should inherit a blessing" (1 Pe.3:9).

"He that saith he is in the light, and hateth his brother, is in darkness even until now" (1 Jn.2:9).

"Whosoever hateth his brother is a murderer: and ye know that no murderer hath eternal life abiding in him" (1 Jn.3:15).

"But the fearful, and unbelieving, and the abominable, and murderers, and whoremongers, and sorcerers, and idolaters, and all liars, shall have their part in the lake which burneth with fire and brimstone: which is the second death" (Re.21:8).

"Thou shalt not avenge, nor bear any grudge against the children of thy people, but thou shalt love thy neighbour as thyself: I *am* the LORD" (Le.19:18).

"Say not thou, I will recompense evil; *but* wait on the LORD, and he shall save thee" (Pr.20:22).

"Say not, I will do so to him as he hath done to me: I will render to the man according to his work" (Pr.24:29).

---

5 (25:36-44) **Judgment, Example of—Vindication, of God's Servant, Example of—Marriage, of David—David, Wives of—Abigail, Wife of David**: there was God's judgment against Nabal and David's marriage to Abigail. What happened next is a clear picture of God's judgment and the vindication of His servant David.

OUTLINE	SCRIPTURE	SCRIPTURE	OUTLINE

5. The marriage of David to Abigail: The judgment of God against Nabal & the vindication of God's servant
 a. Abigail's sharing of the event with Nabal & his death
   1) Nabal was very drunk, so Abigail could not share the event until morning
   2) Nabal (once told) immediately suffered a stroke & was paralyzed
 	
   3) Nabal died ten days later: Due to God's judgment
 	
 b. David's praise to the LORD
   1) Because the LORD had judged his enemy Nabal & vindicated David's cause
 	
   2) Because the LORD had kept him from the evil of revenge
	36 And Abigail came to Nabal; and, behold, he held a feast in his house, like the feast of a king; and Nabal's heart *was* merry within him, for he *was* very drunken: wherefore she told him nothing, less or more, until the morning light.
	 37 But it came to pass in the morning, when the wine was gone out of Nabal, and his wife had told him these things, that his heart died within him, and he became *as* a stone.
	 38 And it came to pass about ten days *after,* that the LORD smote Nabal, that he died.
	 39 And when David heard that Nabal was dead, he said, Blessed *be* the LORD, that hath pleaded the cause of my reproach from the hand of Nabal, and hath kept his servant from evil: for the LORD hath returned the wickedness of Nabal upon his
		own head. And David sent and communed with Abigail, to take her to him to wife.
		 40 And when the servants of David were come to Abigail to Carmel, they spake unto her, saying, David sent us unto thee to take thee to him to wife.
		 41 And she arose, and bowed herself on *her* face to the earth, and said, Behold, *let* thine handmaid *be* a servant to wash the feet of the servants of my lord.
		 42 And Abigail hasted, and arose, and rode upon an ass, with five damsels of hers that went after her; and she went after the messengers of David, and became his wife.
		 43 David also took Ahinoam of Jezreel; and they were also both of them his wives.
		 44 But Saul had given Michal his daughter, David's wife, to Phalti the son of Laish, which *was* of Gallim.
			c. David's request for marriage with Abigail: He had been deeply impressed with her
			   1) David sent his servants to ask &, if Abigail accepted, to bring her to him
			
			   2) Abigail humbly accepted: Offering herself as his maidservant, to do whatever David needed
			
			   3) Abigail rushed with her five maids to David & married him
			
			 d. David's other wives
			   1) Ahinoam of Jezreel
			
			   2) Michal, Saul's daughter: Saul had taken her away & given her to Phalti

a. Note what happened when Abigail met with her husband and shared with him her encounter with David (vv.36-38). When she first arrived home, her husband was having a large banquet in celebration of the annual sheep-shearing that had just been completed. The banquet was as large as one that a king would hold. Nabal was so drunk that Abigail could not share about her encounter with David until morning. When morning arrived, she met with her husband and shared the events that had taken place. Suddenly, without warning, Nabal became like a stone. That is, he most likely suffered a stroke and became paralyzed. About ten days later he died. But note what Scripture says: his death was due to the hand of God's judgment.

b. Note David's response when he heard the news of Nabal's death: he offered up praise to the LORD (v.39). But David was not praising the LORD in the sense of rejoicing and taking delight in the death of Nabal. On the contrary, he was praising the LORD for two very specific reasons:

⇒ Because the LORD had judged and vindicated his cause over the contempt and injustice of Nabal.

⇒ Because the LORD had kept him from the evil of revenge and bloodshed. As Robert D. Bergen points out, David blessed the LORD as judge and pastor. As the Chief Judge, He had vindicated David and punished the wealthy rancher. As the Chief Pastor, the LORD had watched over David's soul and kept him from doing wrong.[2]

c. Note David's request that Abigail marry him (v.39-42). Several weeks had passed since David and Abigail's confrontation, but the beauty and character of Abigail had obviously captivated David's thoughts and heart—so much so that he decided to request her hand in marriage. He sent his servants to ask and, if she accepted, to bring her to him. With the same decisiveness and humility she had already demonstrated, she quickly and humbly accepted. She actually bowed down with her face to the ground before David's servants, and she offered herself as David's maidservant to do whatever David needed, even if it meant washing the feet of his servants. Imagine such a spirit of humility! As quickly as she could, she made preparation and rushed with her five maids to David. Soon afterward, they were married. Observe this fact: by marrying Abigail, David immediately became a very wealthy property owner, for he was able to lay claim to Nabal's estate (2 S.12:8; 16:21-22).

d. Note that David now had three wives (vv.43-44). There was Abigail, and Ahinoam of Jezreel, and Michal, who was Saul's daughter. However, Saul had taken Michal away from David and given her to Phalti. Just why Michal divorced David is never stated by Scripture. But the divorce could have been forced by Saul after he discovered that Michal had helped David escape his pursuit, or perhaps Michal herself requested the divorce due to the fact that David had been a fugitive for some years now. Whatever the case, she had divorced her husband and married another man.

Thought 1. God's judgment is the major lesson for us in this point. If a person has a cold, hard heart and is selfish and greedy, the hand of God's judgment will fall upon the person.

⇒ If our hearts are cold and hard against people or against God—God will not accept us. He will reject a cold, hard heart.

⇒ If our hearts are selfish and greedy, coveting more and more—God will not accept us. He will reject all selfish, greedy, and covetous hearts.

⇒ If we are mean and harsh and dishonest toward people—God will not accept us. He will reject every mean and harsh and dishonest person.

The hand of God's judgment is set against such people as Nabal. A cold, greedy, and dishonest person is not worthy of the kingdom of God. And none of us would want such a person living with us, certainly not for eternity. Imagine what the environment, the very atmosphere would be like living around such a person. God warns all hard-hearted, mean-spirited and dishonest persons: you will not inherit the kingdom of God.

"But after thy hardness and impenitent heart treasurest up unto thyself wrath against the day of wrath and revelation of the righteous judgment of God" (Ro.2:5).

"For the wrath of God is revealed from heaven against all ungodliness and unrighteousness of men, who hold the truth in unrighteousness....Being filled with all unrighteousness, fornication, wickedness, covetousness, maliciousness; full of envy, murder, debate, deceit, malignity; whisperers, Backbiters, haters of God, despiteful, proud, boasters, inventors of evil things, disobedient to parents, Without understanding, covenantbreakers, without natural affection, implacable, unmerciful: Who knowing the judgment of God, that they which commit such things are worthy of death, not only do the same, but have pleasure in them that do them" (Ro.1:18, 29-32).

"Nay, ye do wrong, and defraud, and that *your* brethren. Know ye not that the unrighteous shall not inherit the kingdom of God? Be not deceived: neither fornicators, nor idolaters, nor adulterers, nor effeminate, nor abusers of themselves with mankind, Nor thieves, nor covetous, nor drunkards, nor revilers, nor extortioners, shall inherit the kingdom of God" (1 Co.6:8-10).

"Now the works of the flesh are manifest, which are *these;* Adultery, fornication, uncleanness, lasciviousness, Idolatry, witchcraft, hatred, variance, emulations, wrath, strife, seditions, heresies, Envyings, murders, drunkenness, revellings, and such like: of the which I tell you before, as I have also told *you* in time past, that they which do such things shall not inherit the kingdom of God" (Ga.5:19-21).

"Take heed, brethren, lest there be in any of you an evil heart of unbelief, in departing from the living God. But exhort one another daily, while it is called To day; lest any of you be hardened through the deceitfulness of sin" (He.3:12-13).

"But the fearful, and unbelieving, and the abominable, and murderers, and whoremongers, and sorcerers, and idolaters, and all liars, shall have their part in the lake which burneth with fire and brimstone: which is the second death" (Re.21:8).

"He, that being often reproved hardeneth *his* neck, shall suddenly be destroyed, and that without remedy" (Pr.29:1).

---

2 Robert D. Bergen. *1, 2 Samuel*, p.252.

CHAPTER 26

F. The Life of Saul Again Spared by David: Lessons on Reaping What One Sows, 26:1-25

1. **The betrayal of David & Saul's renewal of his pursuit: A heart filled with anger & murder**
   a. David was betrayed by the Ziphites
   b. Saul set out to pursue David: In the Desert of Ziph
      1) Took 3,000 crack troops

      2) Camped on the hill of Hakilah
   c. David stayed hidden in the desert

      1) He sent out scouts
      2) He learned where Saul had camped
2. **The bold, secret venture of David into Saul's camp— under the cloak of darkness: A heart set on never harming God's anointed**
   a. David sneaked up to Saul's camp: Noted where Saul & Abner were sleeping

   b. David asked for a volunteer to sneak into Saul's camp with him
      1) The two soldiers asked
         • Ahimelech the Hittite
         • Abishai, David's nephew
      2) Abishai volunteered

   c. David & Abishai sneaked right up to where Saul was sleeping
      1) His spear was by his head
      2) His soldiers & Abner were in a deep sleep

      3) Abishai whispered that this was a God-given opportunity: He requested the right to kill Saul with his own spear

   d. David refused to harm Saul, the LORD's anointed
      1) Because David would become guilty before God

      2) Because vengeance is the LORD's & the LORD would judge Saul in His own time & way

And the Ziphites came unto Saul to Gibeah, saying, Doth not David hide himself in the hill of Hachilah, *which is* before Jeshimon?
2 Then Saul arose, and went down to the wilderness of Ziph, having three thousand chosen men of Israel with him, to seek David in the wilderness of Ziph.
3 And Saul pitched in the hill of Hachilah, which *is* before Jeshimon, by the way. But David abode in the wilderness, and he saw that Saul came after him into the wilderness.
4 David therefore sent out spies, and understood that Saul was come in very deed.
5 And David arose, and came to the place where Saul had pitched: and David beheld the place where Saul lay, and Abner the son of Ner, the captain of his host: and Saul lay in the trench, and the people pitched round about him.
6 Then answered David and said to Ahimelech the Hittite, and to Abishai the son of Zeruiah, brother to Joab, saying, Who will go down with me to Saul to the camp? And Abishai said, I will go down with thee.
7 So David and Abishai came to the people by night: and, behold, Saul lay sleeping within the trench, and his spear stuck in the ground at his bolster: but Abner and the people lay round about him.
8 Then said Abishai to David, God hath delivered thine enemy into thine hand this day: now therefore let me smite him, I pray thee, with the spear even to the earth at once, and I will not *smite* him the second time.
9 And David said to Abishai, Destroy him not: for who can stretch forth his hand against the LORD's anointed, and be guiltless?
10 David said furthermore, *As* the LORD liveth, the LORD shall smite him; or his day shall come to die; or he shall descend into battle, and perish.
11 The LORD forbid that I should stretch forth mine hand against the LORD's anointed: but, I pray thee, take thou now the spear that *is* at his bolster, and the cruse of water, and let us go.
12 So David took the spear and the cruse of water from Saul's bolster; and they gat them away, and no man saw *it*, nor knew *it*, neither awaked: for they *were* all asleep; because a deep sleep from the LORD was fallen upon them.
13 Then David went over to the other side, and stood on the top of an hill afar off; a great space *being* between them:
14 And David cried to the people, and to Abner the son of Ner, saying, Answerest thou not, Abner? Then Abner answered and said, Who *art* thou *that* criest to the king?
15 And David said to Abner, *Art* not thou a *valiant* man? and who *is* like to thee in Israel? wherefore then hast thou not kept thy lord the king? for there came one of the people in to destroy the king thy lord.
16 This thing *is* not good that thou hast done. *As* the LORD liveth, ye *are* worthy to die, because ye have not kept your master, the LORD's anointed. And now see where the king's spear is, and the cruse of water that *was* at his bolster.
17 And Saul knew David's voice, and said, *Is* this thy voice, my son David? And David said, *It is* my voice, my lord, O king.
18 And he said, Wherefore doth my lord thus pursue after his servant? for what have I done? or what evil *is* in mine hand?
19 Now therefore, I pray thee, let my lord the king hear the words of his servant. If the LORD have stirred thee up against me, let him accept an offering: but if *they be* the children of men, cursed *be* they before the LORD; for they have driven me out this day from abiding in the inheritance of the LORD, saying, Go, serve other gods.
20 Now therefore, let not my

      3) Because David feared the LORD

   e. David and Abishai sneaked back out of Saul's camp
      1) They took Saul's spear (a symbol of authority) & water jug (a symbol of life)
      2) They were not detected: The LORD had sent a deep sleep upon Saul & his troops

      3) They crossed over to the other side & stood on top of a hill, a safe distance away

3. **The charge of David against Abner—failing to protect God's anointed & deserving to die: A lesson on neglect, unfaithfulness**
   a. David called out & awoke Abner & the troops
   b. David challenged Abner
      1) His manhood
      2) His position in Israel
      3) His irresponsibility & neglect

   c. David charged Abner with terrible failure & issued the legal verdict
      1) The verdict: Death—he deserved to die
      2) The reason: He failed to protect God's anointed
      3) The evidence: The king's spear & water jug
4. **The attempt of David to resolve the conflict with Saul: Seeking peace with one's brother**
   a. Saul recognized David's voice

   b. David presented a strong case for reconciliation
      1) If he had done any wrong, deserved any guilt—where was the evidence?
      2) If the LORD was chastising him for sin through Saul, then he would present an offering of peace to God
      3) If others had turned Saul against him, they deserved to be cursed:
         • For they kept him from his inheritance
         • For they tried to force him to other nations & their false gods
   c. David pleaded with Saul

1) Not to let him die in exile, on foreign soil 2) To consider the true facts: He (David) was nothing more than a flea or partridge **5. The confession of Saul: A lesson on reaping what one sows** a. Saul confessed his sin & asked David to return: A short-lived, temporary confession—acted not out of repentance, but because David had spared his life b. David offered to return Saul's symbol of authority, his spear c. David proclaimed God's law	blood fall to the earth before the face of the LORD: for the king of Israel is come out to seek a flea, as when one doth hunt a partridge in the mountains. 21 Then said Saul, I have sinned: return, my son David: for I will no more do thee harm, because my soul was precious in thine eyes this day: behold, I have played the fool, and have erred exceedingly. 22 And David answered and said, Behold the king's spear! and let one of the young men come over and fetch it. 23 The LORD render to every	man his righteousness and his faithfulness: for the LORD delivered thee into *my* hand to day, but I would not stretch forth mine hand against the LORD'S anointed. 24 And, behold, as thy life was much set by this day in mine eyes, so let my life be much set by in the eyes of the LORD, and let him deliver me out of all tribulation. 25 Then Saul said to David, Blessed *be* thou, my son David: thou shalt both do great things, and also shalt still prevail. So David went on his way, and Saul returned to his place.	of sowing & reaping: God rewards a person for righteousness & faithfulness 1) David proved righteous by sparing Saul's life 2) David cried out for the LORD to reward him accordingly: To rescue & deliver him d. Saul spoke the last words he would ever speak to David: A blessing & a prediction of a glorious future—David would do great things & be triumphant

DIVISION IV

THE STORY OF SAUL AND DAVID (PART 2):
DAVID THE FUGITIVE, 21:1–31:13

F.   The Life of Saul Again Spared by David: Lessons on Reaping What One Sows, 26:1-25

(26:1-25) **Introduction—Reaping and Sowing, Spiritual—Reaping, Spiritual, Fact—Sowing, Spiritual, Results**: sowing and reaping—this is one of the truest laws in all the universe. What we sow, we will reap, and there is no escaping the fact. Consider our attitudes, for example: if we sow love and kindness, we will reap friends and good relationships. Consider our behavior and conduct: if we sow diligence in whatever we do, we will reap far more production and fruitfulness. As we walk throughout life, if we will sow as we should, we will reap a sense of purpose, fulfillment, and satisfaction—living a conquering, victorious life.

The events of this chapter show the truth of *sowing and reaping*. This is: *The Life of Saul Again Spared by David: Lessons on Reaping What One Sows*, 26:1-25.

1. The betrayal of David and Saul's renewal of his pursuit: a heart filled with anger and murder (vv.1-4).
2. The bold, secret venture of David into Saul's camp—under the cloak of darkness: a heart set on never harming God's anointed (vv.5-13).
3. The charge of David against Abner—failing to protect God's anointed and deserving to die: a lesson on neglect, unfaithfulness (vv.14-16).
4. The attempt of David to resolve the conflict with Saul: seeking peace with one's brother (vv.17-20).
5. The confession of Saul: a lesson on reaping what one sows (vv.21-25).

1 (26:1-4) **Betrayal, Example of—Anger, Example of—Murder, Escaped or Prevented—David, Attempts Against His Life—Saul, Attempts to Kill David**: there was the betrayal of David and Saul's renewal of his pursuit to capture and kill him. Unknown to Saul, this was to be his final pursuit of David. And in this account, Saul is the tragic picture of a man whose heart was filled with anger and murder, so much so that David finally accepted that reconciliation with the king was impossible. The first scene opens with the betrayal of David:

OUTLINE	SCRIPTURE	SCRIPTURE	OUTLINE
1. The betrayal of David & Saul's renewal of his pursuit: A heart filled with anger & murder a. David was betrayed by the Ziphites b. Saul set out to pursue David: In the Desert of Ziph 1) Took 3,000 crack troops	And the Ziphites came unto Saul to Gibeah, saying, Doth not David hide himself in the hill of Hachilah, *which is* before Jeshimon? 2 Then Saul arose, and went down to the wilderness of Ziph, having three thousand chosen men of Israel with him, to seek David in	the wilderness of Ziph. 3 And Saul pitched in the hill of Hachilah, which *is* before Jeshimon, by the way. But David abode in the wilderness, and he saw that Saul came after him into the wilderness. 4 David therefore sent out spies, and understood that Saul was come in very deed.	2) Camped on the hill of Hakilah c. David stayed hidden in the desert 1) He sent out scouts 2) He learned where Saul had camped

a. For the second time the Ziphites betrayed David (23:19-29). Apparently they had a permanent spy network that was continually seeking intelligence on any opposition that might arise against Saul. For some time they had been seeking information on David and discovered that he was hiding out on the hill of Hakilah, which faced Jeshimon, a desert or wasteland. Because of the strongholds or fortifications scattered throughout the area, this particular hideout provided security for David and his men, giving them a significant advantage over any approaching enemy. As soon as the Ziphites discovered David's hideout, they reported the important information to Saul, who was presently at his capital in Gibeah.

b. Losing no time, Saul mobilized 3,000 crack troops and set out on a fierce pursuit of David, traveling down to the Desert of Ziph as quickly as he could. Reaching the general area of David's reported hideout, Saul set up camp beside the road that led up to the hill of Hakilah near the desert Jeshimon.

c. Note that David's hideout was nearby, someplace out in the desert. When he received information that Saul was once again pursuing him and was actually camping nearby, David sent out scouts to locate Saul's camp.

Thought 1. Hearts filled with anger and violence descend into the depths of depravity. Consuming anger and the violent act of murder are two of the worst evils that can be committed, for anger and murder are directed against other people. The angry person and the murderer attack, assault, and abuse people both verbally and physically. A person consumed with anger usually commits some irresponsible act or lawless, violent behavior. And the murderer ends up taking a human life, exposing an ignorant and evil heart that disregards the *sanctity of life*.

God hates anger and hates murder. God hates any wicked, evil act committed against another person. And God warns us, His hand of judgment will fall upon any of us who become consumed with anger or commit murder:

"But I say unto you, That whosoever is angry with his brother without a cause shall be in danger of the judgment: and whosoever shall say to his brother, Raca, shall be in danger of the council: but whosoever shall say, Thou fool, shall be in danger of hell fire" (Mt.5:22).

"For the wrath of God is revealed from heaven against all ungodliness and unrighteousness of men, who hold the truth in unrighteousness....Being filled with all unrighteousness, fornication, wickedness, covetousness, maliciousness; full of envy, murder, debate, deceit, malignity; whisperers, Backbiters, haters of God, despiteful, proud, boasters, inventors of evil things, disobedient to parents, Without understanding, covenantbreakers, without natural affection, implacable, unmerciful: Who knowing the judgment of God, that they which commit such things are worthy of death, not only do the same, but have pleasure in them that do them" (Ro.1:18, 29-32).

"Now the works of the flesh are manifest, which are *these;* Adultery, fornication, uncleanness, lasciviousness, Idolatry, witchcraft, hatred, variance, emulations, wrath, strife, seditions, heresies, Envyings, murders, drunkenness, revellings, and such like: of the which I tell you before, as I have also told *you* in time past, that they which do such things shall not inherit the kingdom of God" (Ga.5:19-21).

"Whosoever hateth his brother is a murderer: and ye know that no murderer hath eternal life abiding in him" (1 Jn.3:15).

"But the fearful, and unbelieving, and the abominable, and murderers, and whoremongers, and sorcerers, and idolaters, and all liars, shall have their part in the lake which burneth with fire and brimstone: which is the second death" (Re.21:8).

---

2 (26:5-13) **Rulers, Duty to—Leaders, Duty to—Ministers, Duty to—Anointed, the, Duty to—David, Respect for Saul**: there was the bold, secret venture of David into Saul's camp under the cloak of darkness. For the second time, David crept up on the king without the king's being aware of his presence (24:1-22). Without question, David's heart was set on never harming God's anointed leader:

OUTLINE	SCRIPTURE	SCRIPTURE	OUTLINE
2. The bold, secret venture of David into Saul's camp—under the cloak of darkness: A heart set on never harming God's anointed a. David sneaked up to Saul's camp: Noted where Saul & Abner were sleeping	5 And David arose, and came to the place where Saul had pitched: and David beheld the place where Saul lay, and Abner the son of Ner, the captain of his host: and Saul lay in the trench, and the people pitched round about him.	people lay round about him. 8 Then said Abishai to David, God hath delivered thine enemy into thine hand this day: now therefore let me smite him, I pray thee, with the spear even to the earth at once, and I will not *smite* him the second time.	3) Abishai whispered that this was a God-given opportunity: He requested the right to kill Saul with his own spear
b. David asked for a volunteer to sneak into Saul's camp with him 1) The two soldiers asked • Abimelech the Hittite • Abishai, David's nephew 2) Abishai volunteered	6 Then answered David and said to Ahimelech the Hittite, and to Abishai the son of Zeruiah, brother to Joab, saying, Who will go down with me to Saul to the camp? And Abishai said, I will go down with thee.	9 And David said to Abishai, Destroy him not: for who can stretch forth his hand against the LORD's anointed, and be guiltless? 10 David said furthermore, *As* the LORD liveth, the LORD shall smite him; or his day shall come to die; or he shall descend into battle, and perish.	d. David refused to harm Saul, the LORD's anointed 1) Because David would become guilty before God 2) Because vengeance is the LORD's & the LORD would judge Saul in His own time & way
c. David & Abishai sneaked right up to where Saul was sleeping 1) His spear was by his head 2) His soldiers & Abner were in a deep sleep	7 So David and Abishai came to the people by night: and, behold, Saul lay sleeping within the trench, and his spear stuck in the ground at his bolster: but Abner and the	11 The LORD forbid that I should stretch forth mine hand against the LORD's	3) Because David feared the LORD

OUTLINE	SCRIPTURE	SCRIPTURE	OUTLINE
e. David and Abishai sneaked back out of Saul's camp 1) They took Saul's spear (a symbol of authority) & water jug (a symbol of	anointed: but, I pray thee, take thou now the spear that *is* at his bolster, and the cruse of water, and let us go. 12 So David took the spear and the cruse of water from Saul's bolster; and they gat them away, and no man saw *it,* nor knew *it,* neither	awaked: for they *were* all asleep; because a deep sleep from the LORD was fallen upon them. 13 Then David went over to the other side, and stood on the top of an hill afar off; a great space *being* between them:	life) 2) They were not detected: The LORD had sent a deep sleep upon Saul & his troops 3) They crossed over to the other side & stood on top of a hill, a safe distance away

a. Knowing Saul's location, David sneaked up to the king's camp to gather intelligence information, noting how many soldiers were pursuing him, who the commanders were, and the weapons they had at their disposal. One thing David noticed was that Saul and his commander-in-chief were lying in the middle of the camp, with the troops encircling them. And they were all sound asleep.

b. David turned to the two men and courageously asked for a volunteer to sneak into Saul's camp with him (v.6). The two soldiers asked were Ahimelech the Hittite and Abishai, David's nephew. Without hesitation, Abishai volunteered.

c. Together David and Abishai crept right up to where Saul was sleeping, noticing that all the soldiers were in a deep sleep (vv.7-8). When they reached Saul, they noticed his spear stuck in the ground right beside his head. Immediately, Abishai whispered that this was a God-given opportunity, and he requested the right to kill Saul with his own spear.

d. But David refused to harm Saul, for Saul was the LORD's anointed (vv.9-11). Once before when David and his men had the opportunity to kill Saul, David's conscience had stricken him and he had learned from that experience that he was not to harm any man anointed by the LORD (24:5-7; Ex.22:28). Note that David whispered three reasons why they must not harm the king:

⇒ Because Saul was the LORD's anointed and David would become guilty before God if he killed the LORD's anointed ruler (v.9).

⇒ Because vengeance was the LORD's and the LORD Himself would judge Saul in His own time and way.

⇒ Because David himself feared the LORD, what the LORD would do to him if he laid a hand on the LORD's anointed (v.11).

e. Quietly and quickly, David and Abishai sneaked back out of Saul's camp, taking Saul's spear and his water jug. Keep in mind that the spear was a symbol of authority and the water jug a symbol of life (the water of life).

No one detected the two men, and note why: the LORD had sent a deep sleep upon Saul and his troops (v.12). Something extraordinary happened that night, a miracle worked by the hand of God to demonstrate His sovereign power over the affairs of men, even the armies of the world.

Having completed his reconnaissance mission, David and Abishai crossed over to the other side and stood on top of a hill, a safe distance away (v.13). Once again David had confronted his fierce enemy with the opportunity to kill him. But because Saul was the anointed ruler, David had demonstrated the utmost respect in allowing God's anointed to live.

Thought 1. Respect is to be shown to leaders, whether rulers of nations, ministers of the gospel, supervisors at work, officials of social organizations or clubs, or teachers or leaders of any other position. Leaders are to be honored. If a leader is corrupt, his corruption is to be opposed, but the office of the leader must be honored. It is the office of leadership that is to be respected and honored. And if the person filling that office is responsible, moral, and just, the person is to be honored as well as the office. But if the person in the leadership position is irresponsible, immoral, and unjust, the corrupted person is to be opposed. His corruption is not to be licensed and indulged. Indulging and giving license to a corrupt official only endorses his corruption and encourages him to continue in his irresponsible, immoral, and unjust ways. Such a person is to be opposed. But his office, the leadership position itself, is to be respected and honored. Leadership offices and positions are necessary to carry on life, society, and governments. For this reason, the office of leadership must be respected and honored. This is the clear teaching of God's Holy Word:

"And he saith unto them, Whose is this image and superscription? They say unto him, Caesar's. Then saith he unto them, Render therefore unto Caesar the things which are Caesar's; and unto God the things that are God's" (Mt.22:20-21).

"Then said Paul, I wist [knew] not, brethren, that he was the high priest: for it is written, Thou shalt not speak evil of the ruler of thy people" (Ac.23:5).

"Let every soul be subject unto the higher powers. For there is no power but of God: the powers that be are ordained of God" (Ro.13:1).

"Receive him therefore in the LORD with all gladness; and hold such in reputation" (Ph.2:29).

"And we beseech you, brethren, to know them which labour among you, and are over you in the LORD, and admonish you; And to esteem them very highly in love for their work's sake. *And* be at peace among yourselves" (1 Th.5:12-13).

"Let the elders that rule well be counted worthy of double honour, especially they who labour in the word and doctrine" (1 Ti.5:17).

"Put them in mind to be subject to principalities and powers, to obey magistrates, to be ready to every good work" (Tit.3:1).

"Remember them which have the rule over you, who have spoken unto you the word of God: whose faith follow, considering the end of *their* conversation [behavior, conduct]" (He.13:7).

"Submit yourselves to every ordinance of man for the LORD's sake: whether it be to the king, as supreme; Or unto governors, as unto them that are sent by him for the punishment of evildoers, and for the praise of them that do well" (1 Pe.2:13-14).

"Honour all *men*. Love the brotherhood. Fear God. Honour the king" (1 Pe.2:17).

"But the LORD hardened Pharaoh's heart, so that he would not let the children of Israel go" (Ex.10:20).

"Thou shalt not...curse the ruler of thy people" (Ex.22:28).

"By the blessing of the upright the city is exalted: but it is overthrown by the mouth of the wicked" (Pr.11:11).

"Righteousness exalteth a nation: but sin *is* a reproach to any people" (Pr.14:34).

"*It is* an abomination to kings to commit wickedness: for the throne is established by righteousness" (Pr.16:12).

"I *counsel thee* to keep the king's commandment, and *that* in regard of the oath of God" (Ec.8:2).

---

3 (26:14-16) **Neglect, Example of—Unfaithfulness, Example of—Failure, Example of—Irresponsibility, Example of—Abner, Failure of**: there was the charge of David against Abner, the commander of Saul's army: he had failed to protect God's anointed and deserved to die. Having climbed a safe distance up the hill, David shouted out across the canyon and awoke Abner and his troops from their deep slumber. Note the series of questions in the Scripture that David shouted out, challenging...

- Abner's manhood
- Abner's position in Israel
- Abner's irresponsibility and neglect of his duty in guarding King Saul (v.15)

After shouting out the questions that demonstrated Abner's irresponsible neglect, David charged Abner with terrible failure and shouted out the legal verdict (v.16). He deserved to die. Abner had failed to protect God's anointed. And there was clear evidence: the king's spear and water jug were missing.

OUTLINE	SCRIPTURE	SCRIPTURE	OUTLINE
3. The charge of David against Abner—failing to protect God's anointed & deserving to die: A lesson on neglect, unfaithfulness a. David called out & awoke Abner & the troops b. David challenged Abner 1) His manhood 2) His position in Israel 3) His irresponsibility & neglect	14 And David cried to the people, and to Abner the son of Ner, saying, Answerest thou not, Abner? Then Abner answered and said, Who *art* thou *that* criest to the king? 15 And David said to Abner, *Art* not thou a *valiant* man? and who *is* like to thee in Israel? wherefore then hast thou not kept thy lord the	king? for there came one of the people in to destroy the king thy lord. 16 This thing *is* not good that thou hast done. *As* the LORD liveth, ye *are* worthy to die, because ye have not kept your master, the LORD'S anointed. And now see where the king's spear is, and the cruse of water that *was* at his bolster.	c. David charged Abner with terrible failure & issued the legal verdict 1) The verdict: Death—he deserved to die 2) The reason: He failed to protect God's anointed 3) The evidence: The king's spear & water jug

Thought 1. Abner neglected his duty of protecting the king. He had been unfaithful, giving only half-hearted service to Saul. For he had allowed David and Abishai to sneak into camp and become a threat to the king. And there was evidence, the spear and the water jug. This is a striking lesson for us on neglect, unfaithfulness, and half-hearted service.

Far too many of us are neglectful, serving only half-heartedly. How many of us give only half-hearted service at our employment? How many of us are unfaithful to our commitments:

⟹ to our spouses and children?
⟹ to our employment?
⟹ to social and community clubs?
⟹ to our government?
⟹ to our friends and neighbors?
⟹ to our studies and securing an education?
⟹ to the Lord and His church?

Neglect, unfaithfulness, half-hearted service—this is irresponsible behavior. And it weakens our families, our societies, our nations, and our churches. Furthermore, if we are often neglectful and prove unfaithful, we can irreparably harm those whom we fail.

Neglect and unfaithfulness are serious matters to God. Listen to what God's Holy Word says, much of which is a warning:

"Then he which had received the one talent came and said, LORD, I knew thee that thou art an hard man, reaping where thou hast not sown, and gathering where thou hast not strawed: And I was afraid, and went and hid thy talent in the earth: lo, *there* thou hast *that is* thine. His lord answered and said unto him, *Thou* wicked and slothful servant, thou knewest that I reap where I sowed not, and gather where I have not strawed: Thou oughtest therefore to have put my money to the exchangers, and *then* at my coming I should have received mine own with usury. Take therefore the talent from him, and give *it* unto him which hath ten talents. For unto every one that hath shall be given, and he shall have abundance: but from him that hath not shall be taken away even that which he hath. And cast ye the unprofitable servant into outer darkness: there shall be weeping and gnashing of teeth" (Mt.25:24-30).

"And every one that heareth these sayings of mine, and doeth them not, shall be likened unto a foolish man, which built his house upon the sand: And the rain descended, and the floods came, and the winds blew, and beat upon that house; and it fell: and great was the fall of it" (Mt.7:26-27).

"And that servant, which knew his lord's will, and prepared not *himself,* neither did according to his will, shall be beaten with many *stripes*" (Lu.12:47).

"And if ye have not been faithful in that which is another man's, who shall give you that which is your own" (Lu.16:12).

"What *doth it* profit, my brethren, though a man say he hath faith, and have not works? can faith save him" (Js.2:14).

"Therefore to him that knoweth to do good, and doeth *it* not, to him it is sin" (Js.4:17).

"And he did *that which was* right in the sight of the LORD, but not with a perfect heart" (2 Chr.25:2).

"Their heart is divided; now shall they be found faulty" (Ho.10:2).

4 (26:17-20) **Peace, Social, Seeking, Example of—Reconciliation, Brotherly, Seeking, Example of—David, Relationship with Saul**: there was David's attempt to resolve the conflict with Saul, seeking peace and reconciliation with him. Naturally, David's loud taunting of Abner had awakened Saul.

OUTLINE	SCRIPTURE	SCRIPTURE	OUTLINE
4. The attempt of David to resolve the conflict with Saul: Seeking peace with one's brother a. Saul recognized David's voice b. David presented a strong case for reconciliation 1) If he had done any wrong, deserved any guilt—where was the evidence? 2) If the LORD was chastising him for sin through Saul, then he would present an offering of peace	17 And Saul knew David's voice, and said, *Is* this thy voice, my son David? And David said, *It is* my voice, my lord, O king. 18 And he said, Wherefore doth my lord thus pursue after his servant? for what have I done? or what evil *is* in mine hand? 19 Now therefore, I pray thee, let my lord the king hear the words of his servant. If the LORD have stirred thee up against me, let him accept	an offering: but if *they be* the children of men, cursed *be* they before the LORD; for they have driven me out this day from abiding in the inheritance of the LORD, saying, Go, serve other gods. 20 Now therefore, let not my blood fall to the earth before the face of the LORD: for the king of Israel is come out to seek a flea, as when one doth hunt a partridge in the mountains.	to God 3) If others had turned Saul against him, they deserved to be cursed: • For they kept him from his inheritance • For they tried to force him to other nations & their false gods c. David pleaded with Saul 1) Not to let him die in exile, on foreign soil 2) To consider the true facts: He (David) was nothing more than a flea or par-

a. As soon as Saul recognized David's voice, he immediately called out to him, asking David to confirm his identity (v.1). Note that Saul addressed David as "my son." But in replying, David does not address Saul as his father, but rather as "my lord the king." Remember that David was no longer related to Saul as his son-in-law. Saul's daughter Michal had divorced him and married another man (25:44). By now, David probably knew deep within his heart that reconciliation and reestablishment of the relationship with Saul was impossible.

b. Nevertheless, David presented a strong case for reconciliation, a strong case for peace between two brothers. Three strong arguments were presented point by point:

1) If David had done any wrong, deserved any guilt—where was the evidence? Note that David asked Saul for the proof (v.18).

2) If the LORD was chastising David for sin through Saul, then he would readily present an offering of peace to God, and the LORD could remove His hand of chastisement from David (v.19).

3) But if others had turned Saul against him, they deserved to be cursed (v.19). Note that David gave two reasons why the troublemakers should be cursed: because they had kept him from his inheritance and because they were trying to force him to serve other nations. And by being in other nations, they hoped that David would be influenced to serve their false gods (v.19).

c. Having completed his arguments, David pleaded with Saul to reconcile and bring peace between them (v.20). He pleaded with Saul not to let him die in exile, on foreign soil. And he pleaded for Saul to consider the true facts: David was nothing more than a flea or a partridge before the mighty King Saul.

Thought 1. God wants people reconciled, living together in peace. Conflict, fighting, violence, and war are not of God. God never intended people to be attacking, assaulting, maiming, and killing one another. Neither should we be verbally fighting, bickering, complaining, murmuring, squabbling, or causing all kinds of dissension and division. A couple living in dissension will separate; a group of people divided against themselves will disintegrate. A nation divided against itself cannot stand.

When there is trouble between two of us, we must seek reconciliation or we will be split asunder, damaging and harming our relationship and potentially destroying it. Whether individuals or nations, reconciliation and peace should always be given a chance. Listen to what God's Holy Word says:

"Blessed *are* the peacemakers: for they shall be called the children of God" (Mt.5:9).

"And suddenly there was with the angel a multitude of the heavenly host praising God, and saying, Glory to God in the highest, and on earth peace, good will toward men" (Lu.2:13-14).

"For God is not *the author* of confusion, but of peace, as in all churches of the saints" (1 Co.14:33).

"Finally, brethren, farewell. Be perfect, be of good comfort, be of one mind, live in peace; and the God of love and peace shall be with you" (2 Co.13:11).

"For he is our peace, who hath made both one, and hath broken down the middle wall of partition *between us*" (Ep.2:14).

"And, having made peace through the blood of his cross, by him to reconcile all things unto himself; by him, *I say,* whether *they be* things in earth, or things in heaven" (Col.1:20).

"And let the peace of God rule in your hearts, to the which also ye are called in one body; and be ye thankful" (Col.3:15).

"*Let* nothing *be done* through strife or vainglory; but in lowliness of mind let each esteem other better than themselves. Look not every man on his own things, but every man also on the things of others" (Ph.2:3-4).

"Of these things put *them* in remembrance, charging *them* before the LORD that they strive not about words to no profit, *but* to the subverting of the hearers" (2 Ti.2:14).

"And the servant of the LORD must not strive; but be gentle unto all *men,* apt to teach, patient" (2 Ti.2:24).

"Follow peace with all *men,* and holiness, without which no man shall see the LORD" (He.12:14).

"But the wisdom that is from above is first pure, then peaceable, gentle, *and* easy to be intreated, full of mercy and good fruits, without partiality, and without hypocrisy. And the fruit of righteousness is sown in peace of them that make peace" (Js.3:17-18).

"Depart from evil, and do good; seek peace, and pursue it" (Ps.34:14).

"Deceit *is* in the heart of them that imagine evil: but to the counsellors of peace *is* joy" (Pr.12:20).

"*It is* an honour for a man to cease from strife: but every fool will be meddling" (Pr.20:3).

"Acquaint now thyself with him, and be at peace: thereby good shall come unto thee" (Jb.22:21).

"Or let him take hold of my strength, *that* he may make peace with me; *and* he shall make peace with me" (Is.27:5).

5 (26:21-25) **Reaping, What One Sows—Confession, False—Saul, False Confession of**: there was the confession of Saul, a striking lesson on reaping what one sows. Just as before, Saul was emotionally touched and aroused, and he offered up another false confession (24:16-22).

OUTLINE	SCRIPTURE	SCRIPTURE	OUTLINE
5. The confession of Saul: A lesson on reaping what one sows a. Saul confessed his sin & asked David to return: A short-lived, temporary confession—acted not out of repentance, but because David had spared his life b. David offered to return Saul's symbol of authority, his spear c. David proclaimed God's law of sowing & reaping: God rewards a person for righteousness & faithfulness	21 Then said Saul, I have sinned: return, my son David: for I will no more do thee harm, because my soul was precious in thine eyes this day: behold, I have played the fool, and have erred exceedingly. 22 And David answered and said, Behold the king's spear! and let one of the young men come over and fetch it. 23 The LORD render to every man his righteousness and his faithfulness: for the LORD delivered thee into *my* hand to	day, but I would not stretch forth mine hand against the LORD'S anointed. 24 And, behold, as thy life was much set by this day in mine eyes, so let my life be much set by in the eyes of the LORD, and let him deliver me out of all tribulation. 25 Then Saul said to David, Blessed *be* thou, my son David: thou shalt both do great things, and also shalt still prevail. So David went on his way, and Saul returned to his place.	1) David proved righteous by sparing Saul's life 2) David cried out for the LORD to reward him accordingly: To rescue & deliver him d. Saul spoke the last words he would ever speak to David: A blessing & a prediction of a glorious future—David would do great things & be triumphant

a. Convicted and emotionally moved by David's appeal for peace, Saul confessed his sin and asked David to return (v.21). But note: Saul's confession was false, based entirely upon his emotions. His confession was short-lived, temporary, and never led to repentance. He was emotionally moved because David had spared his life, not because he was making a decision to stop pursuing David. He did confess his sin, that he had acted like a fool and committed evil against David. But he was making a decision to confess out of emotion, not out of a conviction and willingness to repent.

When Saul asked David to come back and rejoin him, David knew better. He knew that Saul could not be trusted, that his deceptive heart was lying and would soon turn against him. By returning he would be endangering his life, so he rejected Saul's appeal for him to return.

b. Instead, David offered to return Saul's symbol of authority, his spear. He instructed Saul to send one of his young men over to get it (v.22).

c. While the young man was making his way toward David, David shouted out a truth that he wanted Saul to remember: the law of God concerning sowing and reaping (vv.23-24). God rewards a person for righteousness and faithfulness. If a man is faithful and sows righteousness, he will reap righteousness. But the implication for unfaithfulness is just as clear: if a man sows unrighteousness, he will reap unrighteousness. At this point, David shouted out that he had proven righteous by sparing Saul's life. The LORD had actually delivered Saul into his hands that very day, but David had not laid a hand on Saul because Saul was the LORD's anointed. Then David cried out for the LORD to reward him just as he had rewarded Saul, for the LORD to rescue and deliver him from all trouble (v.24).

d. Saul, unaware that these would be the last words he would ever speak to David, pronounced a blessing upon his former commander and predicted a glorious future for David, who was to be the future king. He declared David would do great things and be triumphant throughout his life (v.25). Having spoken these last words, Saul and David went their separate ways.

Thought 1. One of the major laws of life is the law of *sowing and reaping*. If a farmer sows good seed on fertile soil, he will reap a good harvest. If a laborer sows responsible, diligent work, he will be productive. If an employer sows just wages and good working relationships, the company will reap increased production. If a student sows focused concentration and diligent study, the student will reap an excellent education and be far better prepared to secure gainful employment. If a neighbor sows kindness and helpfulness, the neighbor will reap good relationships and many friends. If a husband and wife sow peace and love, they will reap a loving, peaceful family. If a lost, unsaved person sows faith in Christ, this person will reap salvation and eternal life, the glorious privilege of living forever in the presence of God.

But the converse of the positive results of *sowing and reaping* is also true. If we sow the negative, we will reap negative, unfavorable results.

⇒ If a farmer sows bad seed, he will reap a poor harvest.

⇒ If a laborer sows irresponsible, slothful work, he will be unproductive and perhaps lose his job.

⇒ If an employer sows unfair wages and bad working relationships, the company reaps less production and profit and loses capable workers.

⇒ If a student sows inattention and disinterest, failing to study, the student reaps a poor education and is less prepared to secure a good job.

⇒ If a neighbor sows ill feelings, the neighbor will reap bad relationships and few friends.

⇒ If a husband and wife sow strife and discord, they reap a disturbed family, and perhaps end up separated or divorced.

⇒ If a lost, unsaved person continues to sow unbelief in Christ, this person will reap judgment and the terrible fact of hell and eternal separation from God.

No greater lesson can be learned than the lesson of *sowing and reaping*. As we walk throughout life, if we sow what we should, we will reap a fruitful, productive life. This is the clear teaching of God's Holy Word:

"**A sower went out to sow his seed: and as he sowed, some fell by the way side; and it was trodden down, and the fowls of the air devoured it. And some fell upon a rock; and as soon as it was sprung up, it withered away, because it lacked moisture. And some fell among thorns; and the thorns sprang up with it, and choked it. And other fell on good ground, and sprang up, and bare fruit an hundredfold. And when he had said these things, he cried, He that hath ears to hear, let him hear**" (Lu.8:5-8).

"**Be not deceived; God is not mocked: for whatsoever a man soweth, that shall he also reap. For he that soweth to his flesh shall of the flesh reap corruption; but he that soweth to the Spirit shall of the Spirit reap life everlasting**" (Ga.6:7-8).

"**And let us not be weary in well doing: for in due season we shall reap, if we faint not**" (Ga.6:9).

"**Even as I have seen, they that plow iniquity, and sow wickedness, reap the same**" (Jb.4:8).

"**They that sow in tears shall reap in joy. He that goeth forth and weepeth, bearing precious seed, shall doubtless come again with rejoicing, bringing his sheaves *with him***" (Ps.126:5-6).

"**He that soweth iniquity shall reap vanity: and the rod of his anger shall fail**" (Pr.22:8).

"**For they have sown the wind, and they shall reap the whirlwind: it hath no stalk: the bud shall yield no meal: if so be it yield, the strangers shall swallow it up**" (Ho.8:7).

"**Sow to yourselves in righteousness, reap in mercy; break up your fallow ground: for *it is* time to seek the LORD, till he come and rain righteousness upon you**" (Ho.10:12).

CHAPTER 27

G. The Desperate Flight of David to Philistia, Seeking a Safe Residence: Giving in to Doubt & Unbelief, to Deception & Lies, 27:1-12

1. **David's move to Philistia: Giving in to doubt & unbelief—not trusting God's promises**
   a. David came to two desperate conclusions (of unbelief)
      1) That Saul's relentless pursuit would succeed, kill him
      2) That he must flee the promised land, live in the land of the enemy, the Philistines
   b. David & his 600 men left the promised land & went to King Achish of Gath, the capital of Philistia
      1) They were welcomed as mercenary soldiers by Achish
      2) They & their families settled in Gath, including David's two wives
   c. David was no longer pursued by Saul
   d. David eventually & wisely requested the right to leave the royal city of Gath to settle in a country town
      1) The reason: To prevent any sense of a threat to King Achish

And David said in his heart, I shall now perish one day by the hand of Saul: *there is* nothing better for me than that I should speedily escape into the land of the Philistines; and Saul shall despair of me, to seek me any more in any coast of Israel: so shall I escape out of his hand.
2 And David arose, and he passed over with the six hundred men that *were* with him unto Achish, the son of Maoch, king of Gath.
3 And David dwelt with Achish at Gath, he and his men, every man with his household, *even* David with his two wives, Ahinoam the Jezreelitess, and Abigail the Carmelitess, Nabal's wife.
4 And it was told Saul that David was fled to Gath: and he sought no more again for him.
5 And David said unto Achish, If I have now found grace in thine eyes, let them give me a place in some town in the country, that I may dwell there: for why should thy servant dwell in the royal city with thee?
6 Then Achish gave him Ziklag that day: wherefore Ziklag pertaineth unto the kings of Judah unto this day.
7 And the time that David dwelt in the country of the Philistines was a full year and four months.
8 And David and his men went up, and invaded the Geshurites, and the Gezrites, and the Amalekites: for those *nations were* of old the inhabitants of the land, as thou goest to Shur, even unto the land of Egypt.
9 And David smote the land, and left neither man nor woman alive, and took away the sheep, and the oxen, and the asses, and the camels, and the apparel, and returned, and came to Achish.
10 And Achish said, Whither have ye made a road to day? And David said, Against the south of Judah, and against the south of the Jerahmeelites, and against the south of the Kenites.
11 And David saved neither man nor woman alive, to bring *tidings* to Gath, saying, Lest they should tell on us, saying, So did David, and so *will be* his manner all the while he dwelleth in the country of the Philistines.
12 And Achish believed David, saying, He hath made his people Israel utterly to abhor him; therefore he shall be my servant for ever.

2) The request granted: King Achish gave the town of Ziklag to David

e. David lived in Philistia for one year & four months

2. **David's military operations while living in Philistia: Giving in to lies & deception**
   a. David used this time wisely to conquer more of the promised land
      1) The nations attacked
      2) The policy pursued
         • To follow God's decree of judgment against the brutal, evil nations of Canaan: Total extermination, Dt.20:16-18
         • To save the spoils
   b. David reported his activities & paid tribute to Achish
      1) He lied to & deceived Achish: Suggested he was raiding areas under Israel's control
      2) He was successful in deceiving King Achish: David's policy of extermination left no informant surviving who could tell the King the truth
      3) Achish was totally deceived by David's lies: Trusted David fully

DIVISION IV

THE STORY OF SAUL AND DAVID (PART 2): DAVID THE FUGITIVE, 21:1–31:13

G. The Desperate Flight of David to Philistia, Seeking a Safe Residence: Giving in to Doubt and Unbelief, to Deception and Lies, 27:1-12

(27:1-12) **Introduction**: doubt, unbelief, deception, lies—how many people give in to these negative emotions or behaviors every day? Doubting, disbelieving, deceiving, lying? These weaknesses of human character cause all kinds of problems, problems that will be seen in the discussion of this passage. For the moment, the point to see is that David himself, shockingly, was about to give in to doubt and unbelief and to live a life of deception and lies. For about seven years David had been living under the most distressing circumstances imaginable: being a fugitive who was hunted down by a king determined to kill him. David never knew when the king would be coming around the next bend or hill with a battalion of soldiers to attack him. This pressure and all the distressing circumstances discussed below had been weighing ever so heavily upon David, resulting in one of the most distressful, tension-filled lives imaginable. Finally the strain took its toll and David became despondent and discouraged. He began to doubt the promises of God and was gripped by a spirit of unbelief. And this distrust was to lead him into a year and a half of deceptive living. David slipped into a period of critical weakness, a period when he failed to trust God's promises. He should have walked in faith and patience, waiting long enough for God to strengthen and encourage his heart. But instead he fled the circumstances that were causing so much strain and stress for him. And in his failure of doubt and unbelief, David teaches us to guard ever so diligently against failing to trust God's promises. This is: *The Desperate Flight of David to Philistia, Seeking a Safe Residence: Giving in to Doubt and Unbelief, to Deception and Lies,* 27:1-12.

1. David's move to Philistia: giving in to doubt and unbelief—not trusting God's promises (vv.1-7).
2. David's military operations while living in Philistia: giving in to lies and deception (vv.8-12).

1 (27:1-7) **Doubt, Example of, David—Unbelief, Example of, David—Distrust, Example of, David—Promises, of God, Doubting—David, Doubting and Distrusting God's Promises**: David left the promised land and moved into the territory of the Philistines. After so many years of being on the run as a fugitive, David gave in to doubt and unbelief. He failed to continue trusting God's promises. God's Holy Word paints a descriptive picture of what happened:

OUTLINE	SCRIPTURE	SCRIPTURE	OUTLINE

1. David's move to Philistia: Giving in to doubt & unbelief— not trusting God's promises
a. David came to two desperate conclusions (of unbelief)
  1) That Saul's relentless pursuit would succeed, kill him
  2) That he must flee the promised land, live in the land of the enemy, the Philistines
b. David & his 600 men left the promised land & went to King Achish of Gath, the capital of Philistia
 	
  1) They were welcomed as mercenary soldiers by Achish
  2) They & their families settled in Gath, including David's two wives
	And David said in his heart, I shall now perish one day by the hand of Saul: *there is* nothing better for me than that I should speedily escape into the land of the Philistines; and Saul shall despair of me, to seek me any more in any coast of Israel: so shall I escape out of his hand. 2 And David arose, and he passed over with the six hundred men that *were* with him unto Achish, the son of Maoch, king of Gath. 3 And David dwelt with Achish at Gath, he and his men, every man with his household, *even* David with his two wives, Ahinoam the Jezreelitess, and Abigail the	Carmelitess, Nabal's wife. 4 And it was told Saul that David was fled to Gath: and he sought no more again for him. 5 And David said unto Achish, If I have now found grace in thine eyes, let them give me a place in some town in the country, that I may dwell there: for why should thy servant dwell in the royal city with thee? 6 Then Achish gave him Ziklag that day: wherefore Ziklag pertaineth unto the kings of Judah unto this day. 7 And the time that David dwelt in the country of the Philistines was a full year and four months.	c. David was no longer pursued by Saul
			
			d. David eventually & wisely requested the right to leave the royal city of Gath to settle in a country town
			  1) The reason: To prevent any sense of a threat to King Achish
			
			  2) The request granted: King Achish gave the town of Ziklag to David
			
			e. David lived in Philistia for one year & four months

a. After his latest confrontation with Saul, David came to two desperate conclusions (v.1). And note that these were conclusions of unbelief:
⇒ that Saul's relentless pursuit would succeed and he would be killed by the hand of Saul
⇒ that he must flee for his life, flee the promised land, and live in the land of the enemy, the Philistines

Keep in mind God's promises to David, that he was the anointed king of Israel and would eventually be given the power of the throne. His wife Abigail had declared the fact (25:27-31) and so had his close friend Jonathan (20:13-15). Even Saul himself had admitted that David would someday secure the throne (24:20-31; 26:25).[1]

But despite all the assurances David had, the pressure of being fiercely pursued for seven long years weighed heavily upon his shoulders. Just imagine what David had to bear day by day:
⇒ He was a fugitive, being hunted down like a wild animal.
⇒ He was forced to live in the desert wilderness, having no settled home.
⇒ He faced the threat of death every day, never knowing when Saul and his army would show up to attack, attempting to capture and kill him.
⇒ He was constantly having to break camp in order to escape the fierce pursuit of his enemy, King Saul.
⇒ He had been under constant pressure to provide food and supplies for over 600 men and their families, which totaled over 2,000 people.
⇒ Most likely he was under the constant strain of warfare, protecting Israelite cities and farmers from marauders who swept down upon the people, plundering their crops, livestock, and other valuables.
⇒ He no doubt suffered intense guilt and anxiety over the fact that his two wives had to live under such hardship with their own lives being continually threatened.

For over seven years David had borne the weight, pressure, strain, and stress of the constant warfare and responsibility for such a large group of people and the possibility of imminent danger from either Saul or the Philistines. Finally, the burden and distress of the circumstances became too much to bear. In his own words:[2]

> **"How long wilt thou forget me, O LORD? for ever? how long wilt thou hide thy face from me? How long shall I take counsel in my soul, *having* sorrow in my heart daily? how long shall mine enemy be exalted over me?" (Ps.13:1-2).**

b. Lacking the faith and patience to wait upon God, David instructed his 600 men and their families to break camp and prepare to leave the promised land. They would go to King Achish and seek the right to live among the Philistines (vv.2-3). Remember that David had attempted to live among the Philistines right after becoming a fugitive. But at that time King Achish and his officials felt that they could not trust David, not being aware that he had become a fugitive from Saul. Consequently, David had been forced to flee for his life. But this time David was a well-known fugitive, known to

---
[1] Warren W. Wiersbe. *Be Successful,* p.145-146.
[2] *Ibid.,* p.146.

be a threat to the throne of Saul. Being aware that David was a fugitive on the run, King Achish welcomed David and his men as mercenary soldiers. They and their families were allowed to settle in Gath, the Philistine capital.

c. Hearing of David's flight into Philistine territory, Saul backed off and no longer pursued David (v.4). He could not risk facing the entire Philistine army, not even to capture his archenemy.

d. David eventually and wisely requested the right to leave the royal city in order to settle in a country town (v.5). His reason for making the request was to prevent any sense of a threat to King Achish. Obviously, the 2,000 followers of David were a heavy burden upon the city of Gath, consuming the city's resources and causing a disturbing disruption in the life of its citizens. An influx of so many strangers would have caused grumbling, dissension, and division among the citizens. Thus David's request to move elsewhere was a wise move. Sensing the wisdom of the request, King Achish granted David's wish and gave the town of Ziklag to him and his followers (v.6). Note the reference to the fact that David lived in Philistine territory for one year and four months (v.7).

Thought 1. Breaking under the pressure of his circumstances, David began to doubt God's promises. His faith wavered and he became despondent and discouraged, failing to trust the promises of God.

So it is with us. Far too often we allow circumstances to defeat us. Some problem or difficulty, misfortune or hardship, trial or temptation, bad or perplexing circumstance happens to us, and we become stressed out. We become pressured, strained, distressed, or grief-stricken; and we begin to doubt the promises of God. We begin to question the validity of God's promises and unbelief sets in. Unbelief grabs our heart, and we fail to rely on God's Word to us. We turn away from the LORD and take things into our own hands. We fail to trust God, fail to be patient, not waiting long enough for the LORD to work the circumstance out. Or we lack the faith in God's power, the belief that God will give us the power to overcome and conquer the pressuring, distressing trial. If there is any one lesson we need to learn, it is the lesson of trust and patience, believing in the promises of God enough to wait upon God to meet our needs. We must learn not to give in to doubt and unbelief, failing to trust God's promises.

Doubt and unbelief will keep us from entering the *spiritual rest* promised by God. God's *spiritual rest* means purpose, fulfillment, satisfaction, assurance, and confidence as we walk throughout life. To have God's spiritual rest means to have the wonderful, productive, and fruitful life that only God can provide. It means to be victorious over all the enemies of life, conquering all that opposes us and attempts to defeat us in life. To have *spiritual rest* means to have the power to overcome any and all distressing circumstances of life and to know that we will live eternally, conquering even death itself. For these reasons, we must never give in to doubt and unbelief, never fail to believe God's promises. Doubt, unbelief, and distrust stand against all the promises of God.

"And immediately Jesus stretched forth *his* hand, and caught him, and said unto him, O thou of little faith, wherefore didst thou doubt" (Mt.14:31).

"And he said unto them, Why are ye so fearful? how is it that ye have no faith" (Mk.4:40).

"Then he said unto them, O fools, and slow of heart to believe all that the prophets have spoken" (Lu.24:25).

"The other disciples therefore said unto him, We have seen the LORD. But he said unto them, Except I shall see in his hands the print of the nails, and put my finger into the print of the nails, and thrust my hand into his side, I will not believe" (Jn.20:25).

"Take heed, brethren, lest there be in any of you an evil heart of unbelief, in departing from the living God. But exhort one another daily, while it is called To day; lest any of you be hardened through the deceitfulness of sin. For we are made partakers of Christ, if we hold the beginning of our confidence stedfast unto the end" (He.3:12-14).

"And to whom sware he that they should not enter into his rest, but to them that believed not? So we see that they could not enter in because of unbelief" (He.3:18-19).

"Let us therefore fear, lest, a promise being left *us* of entering into his rest, any of you should seem to come short of it. For unto us was the gospel preached, as well as unto them: but the word preached did not profit them, not being mixed with faith in them that heard *it*. For we which have believed do enter into rest, as he said, As I have sworn in my wrath, if they shall enter into my rest: although the works were finished from the foundation of the world" (He.4:1-3).

"Let us labour therefore to enter into that rest, lest any man fall after the same example of unbelief" (He.4:11).

---

2 (27:8-12) **Lying, Example of—Deception, Example of—David, Weaknesses and Sins of**: David carried out some major military operations while living in Philistine territory, in the city of Ziklag. But keep in mind that during these years David was living a life of doubt and unbelief, not trusting God's promises. As a result, he was living outside the *promised land*. Consequently, we now find him living a life of deception and lies:

OUTLINE	SCRIPTURE	SCRIPTURE	OUTLINE
2. David's military operations while living in Philistia: Giving in to lies & deception a. David used this time wisely to conquer more of the promised land	8 And David and his men went up, and invaded the Geshurites, and the Gezrites, and the Amalekites: for those *nations were* of old the inhabitants of the land, as thou	goest to Shur, even unto the land of Egypt. 9 And David smote the land, and left neither man nor woman alive, and took away the sheep, and the oxen, and	1) The nations attacked 2) The policy pursued • To follow God's decree of judgment against the brutal, evil nations of

OUTLINE	SCRIPTURE	SCRIPTURE	OUTLINE
Canaan: Total extermination, Dt.20:16-18 • To save the spoils	the asses, and the camels, and the apparel, and returned, and came to Achish.	bring *tidings* to Gath, saying, Lest they should tell on us, saying, So did David, and so	David's policy of extermination left no informant surviving who could tell the King the truth
b. David reported his activities & paid tribute to Achish	10 And Achish said, Whither have ye made a road to day?	*will be* his manner all the while he dwelleth in the country of the Philistines.	
1) He lied to & deceived Achish: Suggested he was raiding areas under Israel's control	And David said, Against the south of Judah, and against the south of the Jerahmeelites, and against the south of the Kenites.	12 And Achish believed David, saying, He hath made his people Israel utterly to abhor him; therefore he	3) Achish was totally deceived by David's lies: Trusted David fully
2) He was successful in deceiving King Achish:	11 And David saved neither man nor woman alive, to	shall be my servant for ever.	

a. David wisely used his time in Ziklag to conquer more of the *promised land* (vv.8-9). Under Joshua, Ziklag had been assigned to the tribe of Simeon and Judah, but the city and its surrounding territory had never been conquered by the Israelites (Jos.15:31; 19:5). For decades it had been under Philistine control, but with one stroke of genius, David was able to secure the city and its surrounding area with a simple request from King Achish. Hereafter the city would belong to the kings of Judah as long as they ruled upon the throne of Israel. Because Ziklag was so isolated, David was able to conquer surrounding territory that was controlled by several Canaanite nations: the Geshurites, the Girzites, and the Amalekites. Note that these three nations of people had lived in this land from ancient times. Also note the policy pursued by David when he attacked one of the surrounding areas: he followed the *harem principle* pronounced against the evil and brutal nations of Canaan. This was the principle of judgment pronounced by God, a judgment of total extermination because a people had reached the point of never changing, of never repenting and turning from their brutal savagery. (See DEEPER STUDY # 1—1 Sa.15:3 for more discussion.) However when destroying theses nations, David did plunder the cities and their territories, saving the animals and spoils to give to King Achish as a reward.

b. When David visited and reported his activities to King Achish, he gave much of the plunder as a tribute to the king just as any common warlord would do. But when King Achish would ask what areas he had raided, note what happened: David lied to and deceived the king. He suggested that he was raiding areas under Israel's control (vv.10-12). And David was successful in deceiving King Achish, because his policy of extermination left no informant surviving who could tell the king the truth—that David was actually attacking territory or nations that were friendly with King Achish. He was totally deceived by David's lies, trusting David fully (v.12). In fact, the king was so convinced of David's loyalty that he felt David would be a mercenary in his service forever.

Despite David's awful deception and lies, God was still working out events to fulfill His promises to David, just as He does for so many of us when we slip back and begin to doubt and distrust God's promises. During all this time, word was trickling back to the Israelites that David was conquering some of their enemies. Of course, this was good news to the Israelites, and David's popularity among the Israelite leaders and people grew even more.[3]

> **Thought 1**. Lying to or deceiving a person is one of the worst evils that can be committed. Lies and deception always do damage, for the offended person acts upon what he has been told. If a man lies and tells a woman that he loves her, what happens? If an employee or employer lies to the other, what happens? If one business deceives another business, what happens? If a student or teacher lies to the another, what happens? If a nation lies to another nation, what happens?
>
> Marriage cannot survive lies—not without major damage and distrust or else a total turning away from the lies by the guilty party and a very forgiving spirit by the other. Likewise, employers and employees cannot survive in an environment of mistrust and deception, with lies being told by one or both parties. Companies may succeed temporarily if they deceive one another, but in the end they will be found out and their lies will be their downfall. If nations lie to one another, the outcome can be catastrophic for the entire world. If young people lie by cheating on tests, it adversely affects their education and ability to achieve future employment.
>
> And if a lie or some deception is not immediately exposed, it still causes all kinds of problems for the liar and deceiver: a constant pressure that the lie will be discovered; a nagging conscience and guilt; an eating away at inner peace; a fear of embarrassment and shame and the potential for disturbed relationships. Or, a liar's heart can become so hard that he deceives himself, thinking his lie is justified and not harmful. He becomes enslaved to lying, telling one lie after another, deceiving his loved ones, friends, and fellow workers time and again. Example after example could be given of the devastating effects caused by lies and deception. Lies and deception arouse God to issue His most severe warnings, warnings that we must heed:
>
> **"For the wrath of God is revealed from heaven against all ungodliness and unrighteousness of men, who hold the truth in unrighteousness....Being filled with all unrighteousness, fornication, wickedness, covetousness, maliciousness; full of envy, murder, debate, deceit, malignity; whisperers, Backbiters, haters of God, despiteful, proud, boasters, inventors of evil things, disobedient to parents, Without understanding, covenantbreakers, without natural affection, implacable, unmerciful: Who knowing the judgment of God, that they which commit such things are worthy of death, not only do the same, but have pleasure in them that do them" (Ro.1:18, 29-32).**
>
> **"Now the works of the flesh are manifest, which are *these;* Adultery, fornication, uncleanness, lasciviousness, Idolatry, witchcraft, hatred, variance, emulations, wrath, strife, seditions, heresies,**

---

3 Warren W. Wiersbe. *Be Successful*, p.148.

Envyings, murders, drunkenness, revellings, and such like: of the which I tell you before, as I have also told *you* in time past, that they which do such things shall not inherit the kingdom of God" (Ga.5:19-21).

"But the fearful, and unbelieving, and the abominable, and murderers, and whoremongers, and sorcerers, and idolaters, and all liars, shall have their part in the lake which burneth with fire and brimstone: which is the second death" (Re.21:8).

"Thou shalt destroy them that speak leasing [lying]: the LORD will abhor the bloody and deceitful man" (Ps.5:6).

"But the king shall rejoice in God; every one that sweareth by him shall glory: but the mouth of them that speak lies shall be stopped" (Ps.63:11).

"He that worketh deceit shall not dwell within my house: he that telleth lies shall not tarry in my sight" (Ps.101:7).

"Lying lips *are* abomination to the LORD: but they that deal truly *are* his delight" (Pr.12:22).

"A false witness shall not be unpunished, and *he that* speaketh lies shall not escape" (Pr.19:5).

"The getting of treasures by a lying tongue *is* a vanity tossed to and fro of them that seek death" (Pr.21:6).

CHAPTER 28

H. The Desperation of Saul Seen in His Seeking a Spirit Medium: A Study of the Occult, 28:1-25

1. Saul's desperate situation: The reasons why a person seeks a spirit medium
 a. There was a serious problem, a tragic situation
  1) The Philistines had invaded Israel
  2) The Philistine king demanded that David fight
   • David promised to serve bravely
   • David was promoted as the king's bodyguard
 b. There was no spiritual leader available for counsel
  1) Samuel was dead
  2) False prophets—spiritists & mediums—had been expelled from Israel by Saul
 c. There was a terrifying fear
  1) The Philistines invaded & camped at Shunem
  2) The Israelites camped at Gilboa
  3) The enemy struck terror in Saul
 d. There was no answer to prayer, no guidance when seeking the LORD: Due to sin, lack of repentance

2. Saul's tragic decision to seek a spirit medium: The disobedience of turning to the occult
 a. Saul's order obeyed by his attendants: A spirit medium was found in Endor
 b. Saul's disguise & quick trip to the medium—under the cover of darkness
 c. Saul's request of the spirit medium: For her to consult a spirit for him, the spirit he named

3. Saul's terrible evil: The results of consulting a spirit medium (or false prophet)
 a. The spirit medium was deceived even more: Encouraged to think that God's command could be broken,

And it came to pass in those days, that the Philistines gathered their armies together for warfare, to fight with Israel. And Achish said unto David, Know thou assuredly, that thou shalt go out with me to battle, thou and thy men. 2 And David said to Achish, Surely thou shalt know what thy servant can do. And Achish said to David, Therefore will I make thee keeper of mine head for ever. 3 Now Samuel was dead, and all Israel had lamented him, and buried him in Ramah, even in his own city. And Saul had put away those that had familiar spirits, and the wizards, out of the land. 4 And the Philistines gathered themselves together, and came and pitched in Shunem: and Saul gathered all Israel together, and they pitched in Gilboa. 5 And when Saul saw the host of the Philistines, he was afraid, and his heart greatly trembled. 6 And when Saul enquired of the LORD, the LORD answered him not, neither by dreams nor by Urim, nor by prophets. 7 Then said Saul unto his servants, Seek me a woman that hath a familiar spirit, that I may go to her, and enquire of her. And his servants said to him, Behold, *there is* a woman that hath a familiar spirit at Endor. 8 And Saul disguised himself, and put on other raiment, and he went, and two men with him, and they came to the woman by night: and he said, I pray thee, divine unto me by the familiar spirit, and bring me *him* up, whom I shall name unto thee. 9 And the woman said unto him, Behold, thou knowest what Saul hath done, how he hath cut off those that have familiar spirits, and the wizards, out of the land: wherefore then layest thou a snare

for my life, to cause me to die? 10 And Saul sware to her by the LORD, saying, *As* the LORD liveth, there shall no punishment happen to thee for this thing. 11 Then said the woman, Whom shall I bring up unto thee? And he said, Bring me up Samuel. 12 And when the woman saw Samuel, she cried with a loud voice: and the woman spake to Saul, saying, Why hast thou deceived me? for thou *art* Saul. 13 And the king said unto her, Be not afraid: for what sawest thou? And the woman said unto Saul, I saw gods ascending out of the earth. 14 And he said unto her, What form *is* he of? And she said, An old man cometh up; and he *is* covered with a mantle. And Saul perceived that it *was* Samuel, and he stooped with *his* face to the ground, and bowed himself. 15 And Samuel said to Saul, Why hast thou disquieted me, to bring me up? And Saul answered, I am sore distressed; for the Philistines make war against me, and God is departed from me, and answereth me no more, neither by prophets, nor by dreams: therefore I have called thee, that thou mayest make known unto me what I shall do. 16 Then said Samuel, Wherefore then dost thou ask of me, seeing the LORD is departed from thee, and is become thine enemy? 17 And the LORD hath done to him, as he spake by me: for the LORD hath rent the kingdom out of thine hand, and given it to thy neighbour, *even* to David: 18 Because thou obeyedst not the voice of the LORD, nor executedst his fierce wrath upon Amalek, therefore hath the LORD done this thing unto thee this day. 19 Moreover the LORD will also deliver Israel with thee into the hand of the Philistines: and to morrow *shalt* thou and thy sons *be* with me: the LORD also shall deliver the host of Israel into the hand of the Philistines.

that there was no condemnation for practicing the occult, Ex.22:18; Le.19:31; 20:6, 27; De.18:9-13

 b. Saul (the seeker) was deceived: Thought peace & security could come from the medium instead of from the LORD
  1) Saul's request for Samuel
  2) The medium's encounter with Samuel: Shock, surprise, & then she suddenly recognized Saul
  3) Saul's easing of her fear & asking what she saw
  4) The medium's description
   • A spirit coming out of the ground
   • An old man wearing a robe
  5) Saul's conviction that she saw Samuel
 c. Saul bowed—worshipped, paid homage—to the dead, not to the LORD
 d. Saul felt distress, danger, & alienation—that his prayers were not answered
  1) Samuel's question: Why had he been brought up?
  2) Saul's explanation
   • His personal distress
   • The Philistine invasion
   • Unanswered prayer
 e. Saul was to suffer the LORD's judgment, be rejected: Predicted by Samuel
  1) The LORD had turned away & become Saul's enemy—just as predicted
   • Had torn the kingdom out of Saul's hand
   • Had given it to David
  2) The reason for the LORD's judgment: A life of disobedience, ch.13, 15; 28:7-8
  3) The judgment foretold: The death of Saul & his sons, & the utter defeat of Israel in the coming battle

4. Saul's utter despair: The hopelessness of a person who continually disobeys God a. The effect of hopelessness 1) Fear 2) Sapped energy—weakness—no appetite b. The assistance of the medium & of Saul's men 1) The medium strongly urged Saul to eat • She stressed that she had obeyed him • She pleaded with him to listen to her & eat	20 Then Saul fell straightway all along on the earth, and was sore afraid, because of the words of Samuel: and there was no strength in him; for he had eaten no bread all the day, nor all the night. 21 And the woman came unto Saul, and saw that he was sore troubled, and said unto him, Behold, thine handmaid hath obeyed thy voice, and I have put my life in my hand, and have hearkened unto thy words which thou spakest unto me. 22 Now therefore, I pray thee, hearken thou also unto the voice of thine handmaid, and let me set a morsel of bread before thee; and eat,	that thou mayest have strength, when thou goest on thy way. 23 But he refused, and said, I will not eat. But his servants, together with the woman, compelled him; and he hearkened unto their voice. So he arose from the earth, and sat upon the bed. 24 And the woman had a fat calf in the house; and she hasted, and killed it, and took flour, and kneaded *it,* and did bake unleavened bread thereof: 25 And she brought *it* before Saul, and before his servants; and they did eat. Then they rose up, and went away that night.	2) Saul refused 3) The medium & Saul's men kept on urging him to eat • Saul finally listened • Saul got up & sat on the couch 4) The medium prepared a complete meal • Saul & his men ate the meal • Saul & his men then got up & left

DIVISION IV

THE STORY OF SAUL AND DAVID (PART 2):
DAVID THE FUGITIVE, 21:1–31:13

H. The Desperation of Saul Seen in His Seeking a Spirit Medium: A Study of the Occult, 28:1-25

(28:1-25) **Introduction—Occult, World of, Dangers and Failure of—Sorcery, Dangers and Failure of—Spiritists, Dangers and Failure of—Psychics, Dangers and Failure of—Astrology, Dangers and Failure of—Fortune-tellers, Dangers and Failure of—Prophets, False, Dangers and Failure of**: the world of the occult is a dark, strange, and dangerous world. It is dangerous because it seduces people to put their trust in false prophets instead of in God. Mediums, spiritists, sorcerers, psychics, palm-readers, fortune-tellers, astrologers—all these and a host of other false prophets claim to have the power to predict the future and change the destiny of a person. The world of the occult promises to look into the future and to change the future for a person, causing good things to happen that will benefit the person. But the tragic truth is, no one sees the future but God Himself, and no one can bring permanent deliverance and peace to the human soul but God Himself. No person can snatch or free any of us from the bondages that enslave us in this life and doom us to death—no one except God Himself. In the end, down the road, the world of the occult will lead a person into despair and hopelessness.

This present Scripture carries the reader into the dark world of the occult. Facing the most desperate situation of his life, King Saul sought the advice and counsel of a spirit medium. When he should have repented of his evil and turned back to God, he sought help from the dark world of witchcraft and sorcery. And when he did, he received word that the hand of God's judgment would fall upon him and he would die within twenty-four hours. This is: *The Desperation of Saul Seen in His Seeking a Spirit Medium: A Study of the Occult*, 28:1-25.

1. Saul's desperate situation: the reasons why a person seeks a spirit medium (vv.1-6).
2. Saul's tragic decision to seek a spirit medium: the disobedience of turning to the occult (vv.7-8).
3. Saul's terrible evil: the results of consulting a spirit medium (or false prophet) (vv.9-19).
4. Saul's utter despair: the hopelessness of a person who continually disobeys God (vv.20-25).

1 (28:1-6) **Witchcraft, Reasons Why a Person Seeks—Medium, Spirit, Reasons Why a Person Seeks—Necromancers, Reasons Why a Person Seeks—Spiritists, Reasons Why a Person Seeks—Psychics, Reasons Why a Person Seeks—Desperation, Results of—Crisis, Results of—Philistines, Invasion of Israel—Prayer, Unanswered**: there was Saul's desperate situation, an invasion by the massive army of the Philistines against Israel. As soon as the Philistines struck, Saul began to seek the LORD, asking for His guidance and help. But because of his disobedience and rebellion against God, the LORD could not hear or answer him. As a result, Saul began to seek for a medium, a spiritist, or a psychic. And in his desperate, frantic search for divine help, we can see how a person might come to seek help from witchcraft and sorcery. Four basic reasons why a person turns to the world of the occult can be gleaned from this passage:

OUTLINE	SCRIPTURE	SCRIPTURE	OUTLINE
1. Saul's desperate situation: The reasons why a person seeks a spirit medium a. There was a serious prob-	And it came to pass in those days, that the Philistines gathered their armies together for warfare, to fight with Is-	rael. And Achish said unto David, Know thou assuredly, that thou shalt go out with me to battle, thou and thy men.	lem, a tragic situation 1) The Philistines had invaded Israel

OUTLINE	SCRIPTURE	SCRIPTURE	OUTLINE
2) The Philistine king demanded that David fight • David promised to serve bravely • David was promoted as the king's bodyguard b. There was no spiritual leader available for counsel 1) Samuel was dead 2) False prophets—spiritists & mediums—had been expelled from Israel by Saul	2 And David said to Achish, Surely thou shalt know what thy servant can do. And Achish said to David, Therefore will I make thee keeper of mine head for ever. 3 Now Samuel was dead, and all Israel had lamented him, and buried him in Ramah, even in his own city. And Saul had put away those that had familiar spirits, and the wizards, out of the land.	4 And the Philistines gathered themselves together, and came and pitched in Shunem: and Saul gathered all Israel together, and they pitched in Gilboa. 5 And when Saul saw the host of the Philistines, he was afraid, and his heart greatly trembled. 6 And when Saul enquired of the LORD, the LORD answered him not, neither by dreams nor by Urim, nor by prophets.	c. There was a terrifying fear 1) The Philistines invaded & camped at Shunem 2) The Israelites camped at Gilboa 3) The enemy struck terror in Saul d. There was no answer to prayer, no guidance when seeking the LORD: Due to sin, lack of repentance

a. There was a serious problem, a tragic situation that arose (vv.1-2). The Philistine army launched a massive invasion against the nation of Israel. And in Saul's mind, he not only had to face the Philistines, he had to face David as well. Remember, David had fled Israel to escape the fierce pursuit of Saul (27:1-12). Perhaps Saul even thought that the invasion was an attempt to overthrow his government so that David could rule Israel on behalf of the Philistines. Whatever the case, Saul was facing a very critical situation.

Note that King Achish of the Philistines expected David to fight right by his side. This posed a very serious dilemma for David, for it meant that he would be fighting against his own people, the very people whom he had been appointed to serve as king by God. To squelch any doubt in King Achish's mind, David promised to serve courageously, assuring the king that he would witness just how bravely he and his men could fight (v.2).

Note how ambiguous David's response was: Did David mean that he and his men would fight bravely against the Israelites or against the Philistines? There is no doubt what King Achish understood the response to mean, for he immediately promoted David and his men to be the king's own personal bodyguard. As will be seen below, the LORD intervened and worked out the events so that David did not have to fight against the Israelites. But the question arises, would he have fought against his own people? He had already jeopardized the LORD's blessing upon his life by deserting the promised land and by living among the unbelieving Philistines for the last year. Was David about to rebel even more against the LORD by fighting against the LORD's people? If he refused to stand by the side of King Achish and fight for the Philistines, David would have been risking immediate execution by the king. As a result of leaving the promised land and going to live among the Philistines, David had gotten himself into a predicament that was humanly impossible to escape. Only the sovereign power and working of God could deliver him.

But for the present, the point to see is the serious problem, the tragic situation confronting King Saul. Not only was he facing the Philistine invasion, to his mind he was having to face David who had joined forces with the Philistines. Seldom had he ever faced such a dark, desperate moment.

b. There was no spiritual leader available to Saul for counsel (v.3). Samuel was now dead, no longer at hand for Saul to seek his guidance. Saul did not even have false prophets to whom he could turn. For sometime earlier, in an attempt to obey the commandment of the LORD, Saul had expelled all the spiritists and mediums from the land of Israel. The term *medium* refers to necromancers, persons who claim that they can communicate with the dead. And the term *spiritist* is a general term referring to any person who claims to have contact with spirits (Ex.22:18; Le.19:31; 20:6-7; De.18:9-14).

c. There was Saul's terrifying, gripping fear that left little hope for escape (vv.4-5). The Philistines had set up camp at Shunem, which strategically sat on a hill next to the Via Maris, the major trade route running through Israel.[1] Saul had mobilized the Israelite forces and had camped at Gilboa. But note what Scripture says: looking out over the massive Philistine force, Saul was stricken with terror and became frantic.

d. There was no answer to prayer for Saul, no direction when seeking the guidance and help of the LORD (v.6). The doors of heaven seemed to be closed to him, all because of his sin and lack of repentance before the LORD. For years he had been guilty of disobeying the commandments of the LORD, rebelling against Him. As a result, the LORD was not able to hear Saul. Remember, Saul was guilty of many crimes: he had allowed his heart to be filled with a spirit of anger, hostility, and murder, fiercely seeking to take the life of David. He had also slaughtered many of the Aaronic priests at Nob (22:18-20). Saul had chosen to follow his own way in life, doing his own thing, instead of following the LORD and His commandments. Saul refused to repent. For this reason, the LORD could not answer Saul's prayer.

Thought 1. When we face desperate situations, seeking the help of the LORD is the answer. But if we continue living with sin and iniquity in our hearts, the LORD will not hear us (Ps.66:18). It is sin that separates us from the LORD. If we rebel and disobey the commandments of God, we turn away from Him. We walk our own way in life, having nothing to do with God. And if we are living and having nothing to do with God, how can we expect the LORD to hear us?

When we come before the LORD, we must make sure that our hearts and lives have been cleansed from sin. A heart that is repentant—confessing its sin and turning back to the LORD—is the heart the LORD receives. A person with a pure heart will never be turned away from, not by the LORD. The prayer of a righteous man, a person who is following after the LORD, will avail much. When we face desperate situations, God will hear our prayer if we have repented of our sins and are living an obedient life before him. And the LORD will never fail to hear our prayers.

---

[1] Robert D. Bergen. *1, 2 Samuel*, p.265.

"Blessed *are* they that mourn: for they shall be comforted" (Mt.5:4).

"Then Peter said unto them, Repent, and be baptized every one of you in the name of Jesus Christ for the remission of sins, and ye shall receive the gift of the Holy Ghost" (Ac.2:38).

"Repent ye therefore, and be converted, that your sins may be blotted out, when the times of refreshing shall come from the presence of the LORD" (Ac.3:19).

"Repent therefore of this thy wickedness, and pray God, if perhaps the thought of thine heart may be forgiven thee" (Ac.8:22).

"If my people, which are called by my name, shall humble themselves, and pray, and seek my face, and turn from their wicked ways; then will I hear from heaven, and will forgive their sin, and will heal their land" (2 Chr.7:14).

"He shall call upon me, and I will answer him: I *will be* with him in trouble; I will deliver him, and honour him" (Ps.91:15).

"Let the wicked forsake his way, and the unrighteous man his thoughts: and let him return unto the LORD, and he will have mercy upon him; and to our God, for he will abundantly pardon" (Is.55:7).

"Then shalt thou call, and the LORD shall answer; thou shalt cry, and he shall say, Here I *am.* If thou take away from the midst of thee the yoke, the putting forth of the finger, and speaking vanity" (Is.58:9).

"But if the wicked will turn from all his sins that he hath committed, and keep all my statutes, and do that which is lawful and right, he shall surely live, he shall not die" (Eze.18:21).

"Therefore also now, saith the LORD, turn ye *even* to me with all your heart, and with fasting, and with weeping, and with mourning" (Joel 2:12).

---

2 (28:7-8) **Witchcraft, Seeking—Medium, Spirit, Seeking—Spiritist, Seeking—Sorcery, Seeking—Saul, Sins and Weaknesses of**: there was Saul's tragic, shocking decision to seek a spirit medium. His decision was shocking because he had earlier attempted to expel all spiritists from the promised land. But here he was giving an order for his personal attendants to find a spirit medium who might be able to counsel and advise him. Saul was a leader who was gripped by a spirit of despair, helplessness, and hopelessness. For this reason he was seeking help from a spiritist, from the dark, strange world of the occult.

When Saul gave the order for a spirit medium to be found, some of his attendants knew exactly where one was located, in Endor. She had apparently escaped the earlier purge by Saul, or else some of the spiritists had secretly been allowed to remain in Israel by officers who had not agreed with Saul's expulsion. Whatever the case, Saul was desperate for some kind of spiritual help, so he immediately disguised himself and, with two attendants, made a quick trip to the medium under the cover of darkness (v.8). A disguise was necessary in order to protect him from Philistine patrols and in order to keep anyone from knowing that he, the king, was seeking counsel from a spiritist, as this was strictly forbidden by the LORD's commandments. Arriving at the medium's house in Endor, Saul immediately asked the woman to consult a spirit for him, the spirit of the person he himself would name.

OUTLINE	SCRIPTURE	SCRIPTURE	OUTLINE
2. Saul's tragic decision to seek a spirit medium: The disobedience of turning to the occult a. Saul's order obeyed by his attendants: A spirit medium was found in Endor b. Saul's disguise & quick trip	7 Then said Saul unto his servants, Seek me a woman that hath a familiar spirit, that I may go to her, and enquire of her. And his servants said to him, Behold, *there is* a woman that hath a familiar spirit at Endor. 8 And Saul disguised him-	self, and put on other raiment, and he went, and two men with him, and they came to the woman by night: and he said, I pray thee, divine unto me by the familiar spirit, and bring me *him* up, whom I shall name unto thee.	to the medium—under the cover of darkness c. Saul's request of the spirit medium: For her to consult a spirit for him, the spirit he named

Thought 1. Saul was committing a very serious offense against the LORD, one of the worst evils that can be done against God. When a person turns to the world of the occult, he turns completely away from God. The person is putting his trust in spirits, and the spirits are not of God. They are spirits of the evil one (Satan), deceptive spirits who seek to cut the heart of God by turning people away from God. When a person places his trust in an evil spirit of sorcery, God's heart is cut and hurt, suffering deep, intense pain. The LORD knows that He and He alone can help and save a person. So when a person seeks help from a false spirit, a false trust, the person is dooming himself. The false spirit cannot help, cannot deliver the person from the bondage of sin and death. The person will continue in sin and eventually die, to be eternally separated from God. There is no hope in trusting the world of the occult, in witchcraft or sorcery, spiritism or mediums. For this reason, God issues a severe warning to all who turn away from him and place their hope in spiritism and sorcery:

"Now the works of the flesh are manifest, which are *these;* Adultery, fornication, uncleanness, lasciviousness, Idolatry, witchcraft, hatred, variance, emulations, wrath, strife, seditions, heresies, Envyings, murders, drunkenness, revellings, and such like: of the which I tell you before, as I have also told *you* in time past, that they which do such things shall not inherit the kingdom of God" (Ga.5:19-21).

"But the fearful, and unbelieving, and the abominable, and murderers, and whoremongers, and sorcerers, and idolaters, and all liars, shall have their part in the lake which burneth with fire and brimstone: which is the second death" (Re.21:8).

"And the soul that turneth after such as have familiar spirits, and after wizards, to go a whoring after them, I will even set my face against that soul, and will cut him off from among his people" (Le.20:6).

"So Saul died for his transgression which he committed against the LORD, *even* against the word of the LORD, which he kept not, and also for asking *counsel* of *one that had* a familiar spirit, to enquire *of it*" (1 Chr.10:13).

"And I will cut off witchcrafts out of thine hand; and thou shalt have no *more* soothsayers" (Mic.5:12).

3 (28:9-19) **Spiritism, Results of Seeking—Medium, Spirit, Results of Seeking—Occult, Results of Seeking—Witchcraft, Results of Seeking—Sorcery, Results of Seeking**: In Saul's experience seeking the counsel and advice of the spirit medium, five sad results occurred, results that take place when any person consults the world of the occult.

a. First, the spirit medium was deceived more and more, encouraged to think that there was no condemnation for practicing the occult (vv.9-10). When the disguised Saul asked the medium to bring up from the dead the person he would name, the woman refused. She was afraid Saul and his attendants were agents who had been sent by Saul to complete the purge of sorcery throughout the nation. But note how Saul encouraged her, taking an oath that she would not be punished for helping him seek advice from the dead.

By placing his confidence in the realm of spiritism, Saul was encouraging the woman to continue in the evil of the occult. He was leading her more and more into the world of deception, into believing that the dark world of sorcery could actually help the desperate seeker. But God's Word is clear:

OUTLINE	SCRIPTURE	SCRIPTURE	OUTLINE
3. Saul's terrible evil: The results of consulting a spirit medium (or false prophet) a. The spirit medium was deceived even more: Encouraged to think that God's command could be broken, hat there was no condemnation for practicing the occult, Ex.22:18; Le.19:31; 20:6, 27; De.18:9-13	9 And the woman said unto him, Behold, thou knowest what Saul hath done, how he hath cut off those that have familiar spirits, and the wizards, out of the land: wherefore then layest thou a snare for my life, to cause me to die? 10 And Saul sware to her by the LORD, saying, *As* the LORD liveth, there shall no punishment happen to thee for this thing.	15 And Samuel said to Saul, Why hast thou disquieted me, to bring me up? And Saul answered, I am sore distressed; for the Philistines make war against me, and God is departed from me, and answereth me no more, neither by prophets, nor by dreams: therefore I have called thee, that thou mayest make known unto me what I shall do.	d. Saul felt distress, danger, & alienation—that his prayers were not answered 1) Samuel's question: Why had he been brought up? 2) Saul's explanation • His personal distress • The Philistine invasion • Unanswered prayer
b. Saul (the seeker) was deceived: Thought peace & security could come from the medium instead of from the LORD 1) Saul's request for Samuel 2) The medium's encounter with Samuel: Shock, surprise, & then she suddenly recognized Saul	11 Then said the woman, Whom shall I bring up unto thee? And he said, Bring me up Samuel. 12 And when the woman saw Samuel, she cried with a loud voice: and the woman spake to Saul, saying, Why hast thou deceived me? for thou *art* Saul.	16 Then said Samuel, Wherefore then dost thou ask of me, seeing the LORD is departed from thee, and is become thine enemy? 17 And the LORD hath done to him, as he spake by me: for the LORD hath rent the kingdom out of thine hand, and given it to thy neighbour, *even* to David:	e. Saul was to suffer the LORD's judgment, be rejected: Predicted by Samuel 1) The LORD had turned away & become Saul's enemy—just as predicted • Had torn the kingdom out of Saul's hand • Had given it to David
3) Saul's easing of her fear & asking what she saw 4) The medium's description • A spirit coming out of the ground • An old man wearing a robe 5) Saul's conviction that she saw Samuel c. Saul bowed—worshipped, paid homage—to the dead, not to the LORD	13 And the king said unto her, Be not afraid: for what sawest thou? And the woman said unto Saul, I saw gods ascending out of the earth. 14 And he said unto her, What form *is* he of? And she said, An old man cometh up; and he *is* covered with a mantle. And Saul perceived that it *was* Samuel, and he stooped with *his* face to the ground, and bowed himself.	18 Because thou obeyedst not the voice of the LORD, nor executedst his fierce wrath upon Amalek, therefore hath the LORD done this thing unto thee this day. 19 Moreover the LORD will also deliver Israel with thee into the hand of the Philistines: and to morrow *shalt* thou and thy sons *be* with me: the LORD also shall deliver the host of Israel into the hand of the Philistines.	2) The reason for the LORD's judgment: A life of disobedience, ch.13, 15; 28:7-8 3) The judgment foretold: The death of Saul & his sons, & the utter defeat of Israel in the coming battle

"Thou shalt not suffer a witch to live" (Ex.22:18).

"Regard not them that have familiar spirits, neither seek after wizards, to be defiled by them: I *am* the LORD your God" (Le.19:31).

"And the soul that turneth after such as have familiar spirits, and after wizards, to go a whoring after them, I will even set my face against that soul, and will cut him off from among his people.... A man also or woman that hath a familiar spirit, or that is a wizard, shall surely be put to death: they shall stone them with stones: their blood *shall be* upon them" (Le.20:6, 27).

"When thou art come into the land which the LORD thy God giveth thee, thou shalt not learn to do after the abominations of those nations. There shall not be found among you *any one* that maketh his son or his daughter to pass through the fire, or that useth divination, *or* an observer of times, or an enchanter, or a witch, Or a charmer, or a consulter with familiar spirits, or a wizard, or a necromancer. For all that do these things *are* an abomination unto the LORD: and because of these abominations the LORD thy God doth drive them out from before thee. Thou shalt be perfect with the LORD thy God" (De.18:9-13).

"And when they shall say unto you, Seek unto them that have familiar spirits, and unto wizards that peep, and that mutter: should not a people seek unto their God? for the living to the dead? To the law and to the testimony: if they speak not according to this word, it is because there is no light in them" (Is.8:19-20).

b. Second, Saul (the seeker) was deceived (vv.11-14). Saul thought that he could secure help—deliverance, peace, and security—from the medium instead of from the LORD. Sitting there before the medium, Saul requested that she bring up Samuel for consultation (v.11). Note that Samuel seemed to appear without the woman's having done anything. Suddenly, immediately, the medium saw Samuel and cried out in utter shock and surprise at Samuel's appearance. Simultaneously, she recognized Saul. The implication is that the actual appearance of a dead person was a new experience for her. She never expected the event to happen, yet Samuel had actually appeared. It *seemed* or *appeared* that the LORD had miraculously sent the prophet at Saul's request.

Knowing from her reaction that she was seeing something, Saul attempted to ease her fear and asked what she saw. By his question, it is evident that Saul himself did not see Samuel. To the best of her ability the medium described that she saw a spirit coming up out of the ground, an old man wearing a robe. Saul was convinced that it was Samuel.

Saul was seeking deliverance, peace, and security from a spirit medium, but he was going to be woefully disappointed. For deliverance, peace, and security come only from the LORD. It is the LORD and the LORD alone who could have helped Saul and who can help us in our desperate situations.

"Peace I leave with you, my peace I give unto you: not as the world giveth, give I unto you. Let not your heart be troubled, neither let it be afraid" (Jn.14:27).

"These things I have spoken unto you, that in me ye might have peace. In the world ye shall have tribulation: but be of good cheer; I have overcome the world" (Jn.16:33).

"The LORD will give strength unto his people; the LORD will bless his people with peace" (Ps.29:11).

"Great peace have they which love thy law: and nothing shall offend them" (Ps.119:165).

"Thou wilt keep *him* in perfect peace, *whose* mind *is* stayed *on thee:* because he trusteth in thee" (Is.26:3).

c. Third, Saul bowed—worshipped and paid homage—to the dead, not to the LORD (v.14). Being told that Samuel had appeared, Saul immediately prostrated himself upon the ground. He was paying homage to the spirit of a dead man, not to the LORD—an act that is strictly forbidden.

"Then saith Jesus unto him, Get thee hence, Satan: for it is written, Thou shalt worship the LORD thy God, and him only shalt thou serve" (Mt.4:10).

"O come, let us worship and bow down: let us kneel before the LORD our maker" (Ps.95:6).

"O worship the LORD in the beauty of holiness: fear before him, all the earth" (Ps.96:9).

d. Fourth, Saul felt distress, danger, and alienation because his prayers were not answered by the LORD (v.15). Either directly or through the medium, Samuel asked Saul why he had disturbed him by bringing him up from the dead? Thinking that Samuel was unaware of the events that were happening, Saul explained his personal distress, the Philistine invasion and the fact that his prayers were not being answered by the LORD. As a result, he was calling upon Samuel for assistance and guidance.

But Saul's answer for help was not to be found in the world of the occult. False prophets were not the answer to the unbearable anxiety, strain, and pressure he was experiencing. Only the LORD could deliver him from his distress.

"Be careful for nothing; but in every thing by prayer and supplication with thanksgiving let your requests be made known unto God. And the peace of God, which passeth all understanding, shall keep your hearts and minds through Christ Jesus" (Ph.4:6-7).

"Casting all your care upon him; for he careth for you" (1 Pe.5:7).

e. Fifth, Saul was to suffer the LORD's judgment and be rejected by him (vv.16-19). Note that Samuel had been sent by the LORD to appear before Saul with a very specific message, a message of judgment:

⇒ The LORD had turned away and become Saul's enemy, just as Samuel had predicted when he was living upon the earth. The kingdom had been torn away from Saul and given to David (v.17).

⇒ The reason for the LORD's judgment was that Saul had lived a life of disobedience and had refused to execute the judgment of God against the brutal, savage Amalekites (vv.7-8, 18; ch.13, 15).

⇒ Then the shocking news of God's immediate judgment was pronounced upon Saul. The next day Saul and his sons would die, and the Israelites would be utterly defeated in battle (v.19). Saul had lived a life of disobedience and rebellion against God. Consequently, the hand of God's judgment was to fall upon him.

"**For we must all appear before the judgment seat of Christ; that every one may receive the things** *done* **in** *his* **body, according to that he hath done, whether** *it be* **good or bad" (2 Co.5:10).**

"**And as it is appointed unto men once to die, but after this the judgment" (He.9:27).**

"**The LORD knoweth how to deliver the godly out of temptations, and to reserve the unjust unto the day of judgment to be punished" (2 Pe.2:9).**

Thought 1. In attempting to understand the above passage, it is helpful to read what several commentators say. Five different quotes follow:

(1) Warren W. Wiersbe says this:

> *Taking the plain meaning of the text, it seems clear that Samuel did appear to the woman* but she was shocked when it happened. *Samuel didn't come up from the realm of the dead because she was a good medium but because the Lord willed it to happen. This was not a demon imitating Samuel, or the medium using clever tricks, otherwise the woman wouldn't have been shocked. Her surprised loud cry was evidence that Samuel's sudden appearing was something she didn't expect to happen. She saw the prophet but Saul didn't (vv. 13-14), but Samuel spoke directly to Saul and not through the medium. Samuel was a prophet of God and needed no "mouthpiece" to convey the Lord's message. In fact, verse 21 suggests that the woman was not close to Saul during the time Samuel delivered his message to the king.*
>
> *Saul had only one question for Samuel: "What shall I do?" The Philistines were ready to attack, Saul was a weak and worried man, and everything he did to ascertain the Lord's will didn't work. "God is departed from me." Seven times in his brief message Samuel used the word "Lord" as he reminded Saul that God had departed from him because he refused to obey God's will. God tore the kingdom from Saul because he hadn't obeyed in the matter of slaying the Amalekites (15:28), and for the first time, Samuel announced that David was the "neighbor" who would inherit the kingdom (28:17). But the direst news of all was that the next day Saul and his sons would be slain in battle and join Samuel in the realm of the dead.[2]*

(2) Robert D. Bergen says this:

> *Questions naturally arise at this point: Did the medium actually make contact with a living spirit-being, and if so, was it really the prophet Samuel? While this matter is not likely to be settled to everyone's satisfaction, the following observations can be made. First, the plain statement of the Hebrew text is that she did in fact see Samuel. Second, the medium reacted to Samuel's appearance as though it was a genuine—and terrifying—experience: she "cried out at the top of her voice." Her strong reaction also suggests that Samuel's appearance was unexpected; perhaps this was the first time she had ever actually succeeded in contacting the dead. Third, the speeches attributed to Samuel contained allusions to a prior interchange between the two, allusions that would have been appropriate only for the real Samuel to have made. Fourth, Samuel's role and message as a prophet, so much a part of his ministry in life, was unchanged in his encounter with Saul here.*
>
> *Indeed, a straightforward reading of the biblical account suggests the possibility that mediums may possess the capacity to contact dead persons and establish lines of communication between the living and the dead. This view is not explicitly rejected elsewhere in Scripture; the Torah prohibits necromancy not because it is a hoax but because it promotes reliance on supernatural guidance from some source other than the Lord.*
>
> *An alternative reading of this passage suggests that it was not the skill of the medium but rather a unique act of God that brought Saul into contact with Samuel. The medium did not possess the capacity to disturb a dead saint; but God, as "a sign of his grace,"[3] permitted Saul to have one last encounter with the prophet who had played such a determinative role in the king's career.[4]*

(3) *The Nelson Study Bible* New King James Version says this:

> *The appearance of Samuel has been interpreted in various ways. It has been suggested that the appearance took place in Saul's mind, as part of his psychological breakdown. The church fathers believed that a demon impersonated Samuel and appeared to Saul. Others have thought that the medium was a fraud who tricked Saul into thinking that he saw Samuel. It seems best to follow the early view that this was a genuine appearance of Samuel which God Himself brought about. Several points favor this interpretation: (1) The medium was surprised (v. 12); (2) Saul identified the figure as Samuel (v. 14); (3) the message Samuel spoke was clearly from God (vv. 16-19); (4) the text says that the figure was Samuel (vv. 12, 15, 16). There is no inherent difficulty with God bringing back the spirit of Samuel from heaven and allowing him to appear to Saul—in spite of the woman's evil profession.[5]*

---

2 Warren W. Wiersbe. *Be Successful*, p.157-158.

3 D.F. Payne. *I and II Samuel*, DSB. (Philadelphia, PA: Westminster Press, 1982), p.145.

4 Robert D. Bergen. *1, 2 Samuel*, p.266-267.

5 *The Nelson Study Bible*, NKJV, 28:12.

(4) *The NIV Study Bible* says this:

> *The episode has been understood in many different ways, among them the following: 1. God permitted the spirit of Samuel to appear to the woman. 2. The woman had contact with an evil or devilish spirit in the form of Samuel by whom she was deceived and controlled. 3. By using parapsychological powers such as telepathy or clairvoyance, the woman was able to discern Saul's thoughts and picture Samuel in her own mind. Whatever the explanation of this mysterious affair, the medium was used in some way to convey to Saul that the impending battle would bring death, would dash his hopes for a dynasty and would conclude his reign with a devastating defeat of Israel that would leave the nation at the mercy of the Philistines, the very people against whom he had struggled all his years as king. And this would come, as Samuel had previously announced (15:26,28), because of his unfaithfulness to the Lord.* [6]

(5) Matthew Henry says this in several scattered paragraphs:

(a) *Saul seeks for a witch, v. 7. When God* answered him not, *if he had humbled himself by repentance and perse-vered in seeking God, who knows but that at length he might have been entreated for him? but, since he can discern no comfort either from heaven or earth (Isa. viii. 21, 22), he resolves to knock at the gates of hell, and to see if any there will befriend him and give him advice:* Seek me a *woman that has a familiar spirit (v.7).*

(b) *But to think that any good souls would come up at the beck of an evil spirit, or that God, who had denied a man the benefit of his own institutions, would suffer him to reap any real advantage by a cursed, diabolical invention, was very absurd.*

(c) *God permitted the devil, to answer the design, to put on Samuel's shape, that those who would not* receive the love of the truth *might be* given up to strong delusions and believe a lie. *That it could not be the soul of Samuel himself they might easily apprehend when it* ascended out of the earth, *for the* spirit of a man, *much more of a good man*, goes upward, *Eccl. iii. 21. But if people will be deceived, it is just with God to say, "Let them be de-ceived." That the devil, by the divine permission, should be able to personate Samuel is not strange, since he can* transform himself into an angel of light! *nor is it strange that he should be permitted to do it upon this oc-casion, that Saul might be driven to despair, by enquiring of the devil, since he would not, in a right manner, enquire of the Lord, by which he might have had comfort. Saul, being told of gods ascending, was eager to know what was the form of this deity, and in what shape he appeared, so far was he from conceiving any horror at it, his heart being wretchedly* hardened by the deceitfulness of sin. *Saul, it seems, was not permitted to see any manner of similitude himself, but he must take the woman's word for it, that she saw* an old man covered with a mantle, or robe, *the habit of a judge, which Samuel had sometimes worn.*

(d) *The spectre, or apparition, personating Samuel, asks why he is sent for (v.15):* Why hast thou disquieted me to bring me up? *To us this discovers that it was an evil spirit that personated Samuel; for (as bishop Patrick ob-serves) it is not in the power of witches to disturb the rest of good men and to bring them back into the world when they please; nor would the true Samuel have acknowledged such a power in magical arts: but to Saul this was a proper device of Satan's, to draw veneration from him, to possess him with an opinion of the power of divination, and so to rivet him in the devil's interests.*

(e) *It is cold comfort which this evil spirit in Samuel's mantle gives to Saul, and is manifestly intended to drive him to despair and self-murder. Had it been the true Samuel, when Saul desired to be told what he should do he would have told him to repent and make his peace with God, and recall David from his banishment, and would then have told him that he might hope in this way to find mercy with God; but, instead of that, he represents his case as helpless and hopeless, serving him as he did Judas, to whom he was first a tempter and then a tormen-tor, persuading him first to sell his master and then to hang himself. 1. He upbraids him with his present dis-tress (v.16), tells him, not only that God had departed from him, but that he had become his enemy, and there-fore he must expect no comfortable answer from him:* "Wherefore dost thou ask me? How can I be thy friend when God is thy enemy, or thy counsellor when he has left thee?" *2. He upbraids him with the anointing of David to the kingdom, v.17. He could not have touched upon a string that sounded more unpleasant in the ear of Saul than this. Nothing is said to reconcile him to David, but all tends rather to exasperate him against Da-vid and widen the breach. Yet, to make him believe that he was Samuel, the apparition affirmed that it was God who spoke by him. The devil knows how to speak with an air of religion, and can teach* false apostles to trans-form themselves into the apostles of Christ *and imitate their language. Those who use spells and charms, and plead, in defence of them, that they find nothing in them but what is good, may remember what good words the devil here spoke, and yet with what a malicious design. 3. He upbraids him with his disobedience to the com-mand of God in not destroying the Amalekites, v.18. Satan had helped him to palliate and excuse that sin when Samuel was dealing with him to bring him to repentance, but now he aggravates it, to make him despair of God's mercy. See what those get that hearken to Satan's temptations. He himself will be their accuser, and in-sult over them.* [7]

---

4 (28:20-25) **Despair, Example of—Hopelessness, Example of—Disobedience, Results of—Saul, Despair and Hope-lessness of**: Hearing that he and his sons were to die the next day was more than Saul could bear: he collapsed prostrate on the floor in utter despair, stricken with fear and a sense of hopelessness. In addition, his strength was completely gone, for he had eaten nothing in over twenty-four hours. The stress and pressure of everything was weighing ever so heavily upon

---

6 *The NIV Study Bible*, 28:12.
7 Matthew Henry. *Matthew Henry's Commentary*, p.430-432. Set in outline points by us for clarity.

him. Seeing Saul collapsed, the medium and Saul's attendants immediately rushed to him, urging him to eat (vv.21-25). Using a psychological argument, the medium stressed that she had obeyed him; therefore now he needed to listen and to obey her by eating. But Saul refused. However, she and Saul's men kept on urging him to eat until finally he listened. He then got up and sat on the couch while she prepared a complete meal (vv.23-24). After eating the meal, Saul and his men left to return to camp.

OUTLINE	SCRIPTURE	SCRIPTURE	OUTLINE
4. Saul's utter despair: The hopelessness of a person who continually disobeys God a. The effect of hopelessness 　1) Fear 　2) Sapped energy—weakness—no appetite b. The assistance of the medium & of Saul's men 　1) The medium strongly urged Saul to eat 　　• She stressed that she had obeyed him 　　• She pleaded with him to listen to her & eat	20 Then Saul fell straightway all along on the earth, and was sore afraid, because of the words of Samuel: and there was no strength in him; for he had eaten no bread all the day, nor all the night. 21 And the woman came unto Saul, and saw that he was sore troubled, and said unto him, Behold, thine handmaid hath obeyed thy voice, and I have put my life in my hand, and have hearkened unto thy words which thou spakest unto me. 22 Now therefore, I pray thee, hearken thou also unto the voice of thine handmaid, and let me set a morsel of bread before thee; and eat,	that thou mayest have strength, when thou goest on thy way. 23 But he refused, and said, I will not eat. But his servants, together with the woman, compelled him; and he hearkened unto their voice. So he arose from the earth, and sat upon the bed. 24 And the woman had a fat calf in the house; and she hasted, and killed it, and took flour, and kneaded *it,* and did bake unleavened bread thereof: 25 And she brought *it* before Saul, and before his servants; and they did eat. Then they rose up, and went away that night.	2) Saul refused 3) The medium & Saul's men kept on urging him to eat 　• Saul finally listened 　• Saul got up & sat on the couch 4) The medium prepared a complete meal 　• Saul & his men ate the meal 　• Saul & his men then got up & left

Thought 1. The fate of the disobedient person is that of utter despair and hopelessness. There is no hope for the person who lives a life of disobedience. If a person walks through life rebelling against or ignoring God's holy commandments, that person will end up in a hopeless, helpless predicament. After having rejected God, he will stand face-to-face with God and have to hear God's judgment pronounced upon him. Hopelessness and utter despair will be the fate, the destiny, of all who reject the LORD.

> "That at that time ye were without Christ, being aliens from the commonwealth of Israel, and strangers from the covenants of promise, having no hope, and without God in the world" (Ep.2:12).
> "My days are swifter than a weaver's shuttle, and are spent without hope" (Jb.7:6).
> "My soul is weary of my life; I will leave my complaint upon myself; I will speak in the bitterness of my soul" (Jb.10:1).
> "And where *is* now my hope? as for my hope, who shall see it" (Jb.17:15).
> "O my God, my soul is cast down within me: therefore will I remember thee from the land of Jordan, and of the Hermonites, from the hill Mizar" (Ps.42:6).
> "But Zion said, The LORD hath forsaken me, and my LORD hath forgotten me" (Is.49:14).
> "And I said, My strength and my hope is perished from the LORD" (Lam.3:18).

CHAPTER 29

1. The predicament of David: A lesson on evil associations
a. The Philistines marched to invade Israel—the promised land of God: Their army was massive
b. The difficulty of David's situation: He had been ordered to march & fight against Israel

2. The solution to David's predicament: A picture of God's power to deliver His people
a. The surprise of the Philistine commanders to see Hebrews in the ranks: They questioned Achish
b. The answer of Achish: He had confidence in David's loyalty

c. The anger of the commanders & their demand that David be discharged, dismissed—sent back
1) Because he might betray, turn against them
2) Because he might use the battle as an opportunity to join the Israelites & gain Saul's favor

3) Because David had been a famous enemy of the Philistines: His exploits

I. The Dismissal of David to Keep Him from Fighting Against Israel: A Picture of God's Working All Things Out for the Believer, 29:1-11

Now the Philistines gathered together all their armies to Aphek: and the Israelites pitched by a fountain which *is* in Jezreel.
2 And the lords of the Philistines passed on by hundreds, and by thousands: but David and his men passed on in the rereward with Achish.
3 Then said the princes of the Philistines, What *do* these Hebrews *here?* And Achish said unto the princes of the Philistines, *Is* not this David, the servant of Saul the king of Israel, which hath been with me these days, or these years, and I have found no fault in him since he fell *unto me* unto this day?
4 And the princes of the Philistines were wroth with him; and the princes of the Philistines said unto him, Make this fellow return, that he may go again to his place which thou hast appointed him, and let him not go down with us to battle, lest in the battle he be an adversary to us: for wherewith should he reconcile himself unto his master? *should it* not *be* with the heads of these men?
5 *Is* not this David, of whom they sang one to another in dances, saying, Saul slew his thousands, and David his ten thousands?
6 Then Achish called David, and said unto him, Surely, *as* the LORD liveth, thou hast been upright, and thy going out and thy coming in with me in the host *is* good in my sight: for I have not found evil in thee since the day of thy coming unto me unto this day: nevertheless the lords favour thee not.
7 Wherefore now return, and go in peace, that thou displease not the lords of the Philistines.
8 And David said unto Achish, But what have I done? and what hast thou found in thy servant so long as I have been with thee unto this day, that I may not go fight against the enemies of my lord the king?
9 And Achish answered and said to David, I know that thou *art* good in my sight, as an angel of God: notwithstanding the princes of the Philistines have said, He shall not go up with us to the battle.
10 Wherefore now rise up early in the morning with thy master's servants that are come with thee: and as soon as ye be up early in the morning, and have light, depart.
11 So David and his men rose up early to depart in the morning, to return into the land of the Philistines. And the Philistines went up to Jezreel.

had even been celebrated in song
3. The dismissal or discharge of David from this battle: A picture of God's power to keep the believer from terrible evil
a. The dismissal by Achish
1) He commended David
2) He gave the reason for the dismissal: The commanders opposed him

3) He gave three brief orders: Turn back— go—do nothing

b. The objections of David
1) He asked why the complaints, suspicion
2) He wanted to fight
• Against Israel (or pretended he did)
• For his "lord the king" (Achish or Saul or God?)

c. The vindication of David by King Achish
1) David had been as an "angel of God" (blessed the king)
2) David was dismissed only because of the commanders' insistence

d. The urgency of David's arising & leaving early—lest he anger the commanders

e. The deliverance of David from his predicament: He left
1) Avoided fighting against Israel
2) Avoided helping an enemy conquer the promised land

DIVISION IV

THE STORY OF SAUL AND DAVID (PART 2): DAVID THE FUGITIVE, 21:1–31:13

I. The Dismissal of David to Keep Him from Fighting Against Israel: A Picture of God's Working All Things Out for the Believer, 29:1-11

(29:1-11) Introduction—Hopelessness, Caused by—Circumstances, Bad, Results of—Predicaments, Results of—Problems, Deliverance from—Difficulties, Deliverance from: we sometimes get ourselves into awkward, unpleasant, or even perilous predicaments, situations that cause all kinds of problems and difficulties. And sometimes the problems and difficulties become critical, boxing us in, appearing to have no answer or solution. There seems to be no way out and serious consequences loom over the horizon. The critical circumstance may be anything ranging from divorce to bankruptcy to a deep trauma suffered as a result of a robbery or assault, or intense grief over a serious accident or even the death of a loved one.

There is no end to the list of circumstances that seem hopeless, impossible to solve. But the wonderful message of God's Holy Word is this: there is no circumstance beyond solution, no problem or difficulty beyond the power of God to control or work out, even working the circumstance our for our good. An amazing promise! Yet it is the teaching of God's Holy Word. God loves us and cares for us, and He particularly begins to work for us when we face crises. No matter what the trial or temptation is, God has the power to hold us in the palm of His hand and to work all things out for the believer.

This is the wonderful message, the practical lesson learned from the predicament that David found himself facing. In the present Scripture, David faced a hopeless, impossible situation. And it was a situation that was caused by his own shameful shortcomings. Nevertheless, the LORD held David in the palm of His hand and worked all events out for good. This is: *The Dismissal of David to Keep Him from Fighting Against Israel: A Picture of God's Working All Things Out for the Believer, 29:1-11.*

1. The predicament of David: a lesson on evil associations (vv.1-2).
2. The solution to David's predicament: a picture of God's power to deliver His people (vv.3-5).
3. The dismissal or discharge of David from this battle: a picture of God's power to keep the believer from terrible evil (vv.6-11).

1 (29:1-2) **Evil Associations, Example of, David—Worldliness, Example of, David—Spiritual Separation, Failure to Live, David**: there was the predicament of David, a very serious predicament. David had forsaken the promised land and fled to the unbelieving Philistines, seeking security from them. He had failed to trust the LORD for security and protection from Saul, doubting the promises of God. For about seven years he had been fiercely pursued by Saul, hunted down like a wild animal. The pressure, strain, and stress of having to live as a fugitive and having to provide food and supplies for his six hundred followers and their families—all this became too much for David to bear. For these seven years he had been living like a political criminal on the run, never feeling safe and secure, never knowing when Saul or some other marauding enemy might attack. The pressure simply became too much, and David made the tragic decision to forsake the promised land and to seek the security of the unbelieving, worldly Philistines. (See outline and notes—1 Sa.27:1-12 for more discussion.)

As was seen in the last chapter, the Philistines had invaded Israel with a massive army. And David's forces were enlisted to fight for the Philistines by the side of King Achish. Because of his evil association with the Philistines, David was caught in the middle of a most difficult situation, that of having to fight against his own people, the Israelites. He was being forced to march against the very people over whom God had chosen him to serve as king. Note that he and his men were marching at the rear of the Philistine army, serving as the personal bodyguard of King Achish (v.2).

OUTLINE	SCRIPTURE	SCRIPTURE	OUTLINE
1. The predicament of David: A lesson on evil associations a. The Philistines marched to invade Israel—the promised land of God: Their army	Now the Philistines gathered together all their armies to Aphek: and the Israelites pitched by a fountain which *is* in Jezreel.	2 And the lords of the Philistines passed on by hundreds, and by thousands: but David and his men passed on in the rereward with Achish.	was massive b. The difficulty of David's situation: He had been ordered to march & fight against Israel

Thought 1. Evil associations will always create problems for us. For if we become friends with the immoral, lawless, and unjust of this world, they will influence us. And before we know it, we will be participating in their worldly behavior. It is impossible to walk in the footsteps of the wicked and live a righteous life.

⇒ If we follow the worldly, we will become contaminated with worldliness.
⇒ If we follow the immoral, we will commit immorality.
⇒ If we follow the lawless, we will commit lawless deeds.
⇒ If we follow the unjust, we will commit acts of injustice.
⇒ If we follow unbelievers, we will begin to question and doubt God.
⇒ If we follow those who distrust God, we will begin to distrust the promises of God.
⇒ If we follow carnal, fleshly believers, we will become carnal and fleshly, feeding the appetites and lusts of our bodies.

Evil associations will contaminate, pollute, and corrupt us. And being closely tied to the worldly will lead us down the path of destruction and death. Listen to what the Word of God says about evil associations:

"**For where your treasure is, there will your heart be also**" (Lu.21:34).

"**If ye were of the world, the world would love his own: but because ye are not of the world, but I have chosen you out of the world, therefore the world hateth you**" (Jn.15:19).

"**And with many other words did he testify and exhort, saying, Save yourselves from this untoward generation**" (Ac.2:40).

"**And be not conformed to this world: but be ye transformed by the renewing of your mind, that ye may prove what is that good, and acceptable, and perfect, will of God**" (Ro.12:2).

"**But now I have written unto you not to keep company, if any man that is called a brother be a fornicator, or covetous, or an idolater, or a railer, or a drunkard, or an extortioner; with such an one no not to eat**" (1 Co.5:11).

"**Be ye not unequally yoked together with unbelievers: for what fellowship hath righteousness with unrighteousness? and what communion hath light with darkness? And what concord hath Christ with Belial? or what part hath he that believeth with an infidel? And what agreement hath the temple of God with idols? for ye are the temple of the living God; as God hath said, I will dwell in them, and walk in *them;* and I will be their God, and they shall be my people**" (2 Co.6:14-16).

"Wherefore come out from among them, and be ye separate, saith the LORD, and touch not the unclean *thing;* and I will receive you, And will be a Father unto you, and ye shall be my sons and daughters, saith the LORD Almighty" (2 Co.6:17-18).

"And have no fellowship with the unfruitful works of darkness, but rather reprove *them*" (Ep.5:11).

"Now we command you, brethren, in the name of our Lord Jesus Christ, that ye withdraw yourselves from every brother that walketh disorderly, and not after the tradition which he received of us" (2 Th.3:6).

"Love not the world, neither the things *that are* in the world. If any man love the world, the love of the Father is not in him. For all that *is* in the world, the lust of the flesh, and the lust of the eyes, and the pride of life, is not of the Father, but is of the world" (1 Jn.2:15-16).

"Thou shalt not follow a multitude to *do* evil; neither shalt thou speak in a cause to decline after many to wrest *judgment*" (Ex.23:2).

"Take heed to thyself, lest thou make a covenant with the inhabitants of the land whither thou goest, lest it be for a snare in the midst of thee" (Ex.34:12).

"Blessed *is* the man that walketh not in the counsel of the ungodly, nor standeth in the way of sinners, nor sitteth in the seat of the scornful" (Ps.1:1).

"Enter not into the path of the wicked, and go not in the way of evil *men*" (Pr.4:14).

"Be not thou envious against evil men, neither desire to be with them" (Pr.24:1).

"Depart ye, depart ye, go ye out from thence, touch no unclean *thing;* go ye out of the midst of her; be ye clean, that bear the vessels of the LORD" (Is.52:11).

2 (29:3-5) **Deliverance, of God, Example of—Rescue, Source—David, Delivered and Rescued, by God's Sovereignty**: there was the solution to David's predicament, God Himself. Only the LORD had the power to maneuver events so that David would not have to fight against the Israelites. Note what happened:

OUTLINE	SCRIPTURE	SCRIPTURE	OUTLINE
2. The solution to David's predicament: A picture of God's power to deliver His people a. The surprise of the Philistine commanders to see Hebrews in the ranks: They questioned Achish b. The answer of Achish: He had confidence in David's loyalty c. The anger of the commanders & their demand that David be discharged, dismissed—sent back	3 Then said the princes of the Philistines, What *do* these Hebrews *here?* And Achish said unto the princes of the Philistines, *Is* not this David, the servant of Saul the king of Israel, which hath been with me these days, or these years, and I have found no fault in him since he fell *unto me* unto this day? 4 And the princes of the Philistines were wroth with him; and the princes of the Philistines said unto him,	Make this fellow return, that he may go again to his place which thou hast appointed him, and let him not go down with us to battle, lest in the battle he be an adversary to us: for wherewith should he reconcile himself unto his master? *should it* not *be* with the heads of these men? 5 *Is* not this David, of whom they sang one to another in dances, saying, Saul slew his thousands, and David his ten thousands?	1) Because he might betray, turn against them 2) Because he might use the battle as an opportunity to join the Israelites & gain Saul's favor 3) Because David had been a famous enemy of the Philistines: His exploits

As the massive army of the Philistines began to march in units of hundreds and divisions of thousands, David and his 600 men were marching at the rear with King Achish. Surprised at seeing David and his men marching with the army, the Philistine commanders protested, questioning what the Hebrews were doing there (v.3). King Achish assured his commanders that he had confidence in David's loyalty, for David had served him for over a year now, and David had never failed in his service to the king.

But the Philistine commanders became adamant, even angry, with the king and demanded that David be discharged and sent back to Ziklag, the city that the king had assigned to David (27:6). Note that the commanders gave three reasons for this demand:

⇒ because David might betray, turn against the Philistines
⇒ because David might use the battle as an opportunity to gain Saul's favor by joining in with the Israelites (v.4)
⇒ because David had been a famous enemy of the Philistines whose exploits had even been celebrated in song

After all, in a former war some Hebrew mercenaries had actually turned against the Philistines in the heat of battle and helped Israel defeat their army (14:21). Preventing a repeat of this betrayal, the commanders insisted that David be sent back.

Thought 1. God has the power to deliver His people. He had the sovereign power to move events to save David, and He has the power to save us. Just like David, we sometimes get ourselves into predicaments that we cannot handle. The situation becomes desperate and hopeless, and there is no way out. No helping hand is available, not with the power to save and deliver us out of the distressing situation. It may be some critical disease, accident, financial strain, deteriorating relationship, loss of employment, broken marriage, or death of a loved one. Whatever the circumstance, God has the power to deliver us. He even has the power to maneuver events, working all things out for our good in order to rescue and deliver us.

"There hath no temptation taken you but such as is common to man: but God *is* faithful, who will not suffer you to be tempted above that ye are able; but will with the temptation also make a way to escape, that ye may be able to bear *it*" (1 Co.10:13).

"Who delivered us from so great a death, and doth deliver: in whom we trust that he will yet deliver *us*" (2 Co.1:10).

"And the LORD shall deliver me from every evil work, and will preserve *me* unto his heavenly kingdom: to whom *be* glory for ever and ever. Amen" (2 Ti.4:18).

"The LORD knoweth how to deliver the godly out of temptations, and to reserve the unjust unto the day of judgment to be punished" (2 Pe.2:9).

"Forasmuch then as the children are partakers of flesh and blood, he also himself likewise took part of the same; that through death he might destroy him that had the power of death, that is, the devil; And deliver them who through fear of death were all their lifetime subject to bondage" (He.2:14-15).

"And he said, The LORD *is* my rock, and my fortress, and my deliverer" (2 S.22:2).

"Surely he shall deliver thee from the snare of the fowler, *and* from the noisome pestilence" (Ps.91:3).

"And *even* to *your* old age I *am* he; and *even* to hoar [gray] hairs will I carry *you:* I have made, and I will bear; even I will carry, and will deliver *you*" (Is.46:4).

"Be not afraid of their faces: for I *am* with thee to deliver thee, saith the LORD" (Je.1:8).

---

3 (29:6-11) **Power, of God, to Keep the Believer—Keeper, Divine—God, Power to Keep—Keeping Power of God, Example of—Working All Things Out, Example of—God, Sovereignty, Example of—Sustaining Providence—Divine Keeper**: there was the dismissal or discharge of David from this battle, from fighting on the side of the Philistines. Scripture paints a clear picture of God's sovereign power to keep the believer from terrible evil:

OUTLINE	SCRIPTURE	SCRIPTURE	OUTLINE

3. The dismissal or discharge of David from this battle: A picture of God's power to keep the believer from terrible evil
a. The dismissal by Achish
  1) He commended David
  2) He gave the reason for the dismissal: The commanders opposed him
 	
  3) He gave three brief orders: Turn back—go—do nothing
 	
b. The objections of David
  1) He asked why the complaints, suspicion
  2) He wanted to fight
    • Against Israel (or pretended he did)
    • For his "lord the king"
	6 Then Achish called David, and said unto him, Surely, *as* the LORD liveth, thou hast been upright, and thy going out and thy coming in with me in the host *is* good in my sight: for I have not found evil in thee since the day of thy coming unto me unto this day: nevertheless the lords favour thee not. 7 Wherefore now return, and go in peace, that thou displease not the lords of the Philistines. 8 And David said unto Achish, But what have I done? and what hast thou found in thy servant so long as I have been with thee unto this day, that I may not go fight against the enemies of	my lord the king? 9 And Achish answered and said to David, I know that thou *art* good in my sight, as an angel of God: notwithstanding the princes of the Philistines have said, He shall not go up with us to the battle. 10 Wherefore now rise up early in the morning with thy master's servants that are come with thee: and as soon as ye be up early in the morning, and have light, depart. 11 So David and his men rose up early to depart in the morning, to return into the land of the Philistines. And the Philistines went up to Jezreel.	(Achish or Saul or God?)
			c. The vindication of David by King Achish
			  1) David had been as an "angel of God" (blessed the king)
			  2) David was dismissed only because of the commanders' insistence
			d. The urgency of David's arising & leaving early—lest he anger the commanders
			
			e. The deliverance of David from his predicament: He left
			  1) Avoided fighting against Israel
			  2) Avoided helping an enemy conquer the promised land

a. After hearing the reasonable arguments of his commanders, King Achish agreed to dismiss David and send him back to Ziklag (vv.6-7). But King Achish did not want to lose the permanent service of David, for he had benefited greatly from the plunder David had been bringing him from his conquests (27:9-12). For this reason, the king tactfully approached David and commended him for the loyal service he had given over the past year. Then he informed David of the commanders' opposition and the decision to dismiss him and his men from the Philistine army. Giving three brief orders, the king commanded David to *turn back, go, do nothing* to oppose the decision, lest the commanders become even more suspicious and displeased with David's presence.

b. But note what David did: he objected to his dismissal (v.8). He asked why the commanders were suspicious and complaining. He wanted to fight against Israel, or at least pretended he did. He wanted to fight for his "lord the king." What did David mean by his "lord the king?" Did he mean King Achish, or King Saul, or his supreme King, the LORD Himself?

Note how ambiguous David's objection was, not naming just whom he considered his enemy to be, and not identifying just whom he considered his "lord the king" to be. The author of *First Samuel* leaves it up to the reader to determine what David meant and against whom he would have fought had he been forced to enter battle against the Israelites. That David had definitely been called by God to serve as the future king of Israel and that he had a heart "after God's own heart" is unquestionable. But so is the fact that David had been gripped by a spirit of doubt in the promises of God and had left the promised land to live among the unbelieving, worldly Philistines. Moreover, David had not only forsaken the promised land to live in the world of unbelievers, he was continually lying to and deceiving King Achish (27:10-12).

How far had David backslid, slipped away from the LORD? Far enough to have fought with the Philistines against his own people, the Israelites? It is as though the author has left it up to each reader to draw his own conclusion—perhaps for the purpose of allowing different lessons to be drawn from this experience of David (1 Co.10:6).

c. Sensing tension in David, King Achish began to vindicate David's service to the Philistines (v.9). In the eyes of King Achish, David had been as an "angel of God"; that is, David had been a blessing to the king, enriching him significantly through the plunder he had paid as a vessel or mercenary commander under his service. Nevertheless, David had to be dismissed because of the commanders' insistence. But he must know that it was only because of their demand, not due to King Achish himself.

d. The decision was made: David had to arise early in the morning and leave with his men lest he further anger the commanders (v.10).

e. Thus David was delivered from his predicament by the sovereign working of God in moving events (v.11). Early in the morning David left with his men. He avoided having to fight against his own people, the people of Israel whom God had appointed him to serve. And he avoided having to help an enemy in their conquest of the promised land.

David had been in a predicament from which he could not escape. If he had refused to stand with the Philistines in their fight against the Israelites, he and his men would have been executed on the spot. As a result of his having forsaken the promised land and having gone out to join the unbelieving, worldly Philistines, he had placed himself in an impossible, hopeless situation. There was no escape, except through the power of God. And God stepped forth to rescue, deliver His chosen servant: moving events through His sovereign power, God worked all things out for David's good. It was as though the LORD were holding David in the palm of His hand, keeping him from destroying himself. The *keeping power* of God was holding David up, keeping him from going too far, from reaching the point of no return, beyond the point of repentance. God's *keeping power* kept David from slaughtering the people of God and from destroying the promised land and placing it into the hands of the enemy.

Thought 1. God's keeping power protects us and prevents us from falling, from going too far, from reaching the point of never returning, of never repenting. If we are genuine believers, sincerely seeking the LORD with our whole hearts, God holds us in the palm of His hand and does not let us go. He keeps us, securing us and assuring us of living with Him eternally. God is able to present us faultless before His presence with eternal joy.

"But even the very hairs of your head are all numbered. Fear not therefore: ye are of more value than many sparrows" (Lu.12:7).

"And now I am no more in the world, but these are in the world, and I come to thee. Holy Father, keep through thine own name those whom thou hast given me, that they may be one, as we *are*" (Jn.17:11).

"Now unto him that is able to do exceeding abundantly above all that we ask or think, according to the power that worketh in us" (Ep.3:20).

"For the which cause I also suffer these things: nevertheless I am not ashamed: for I know whom I have believed, and am persuaded that he is able to keep that which I have committed unto him against that day" (2 Ti.1:12).

"Who are kept by the power of God through faith unto salvation ready to be revealed in the last time" (1 Pe.1:5).

"Now unto him that is able to keep you from falling, and to present you faultless before the presence of his glory with exceeding joy, To the only wise God our Saviour, be glory and majesty, dominion and power, both now and ever. Amen. " (Jude 24-25).

"And, behold, I *am* with thee, and will keep thee in all *places* whither thou goest, and will bring thee again into this land; for I will not leave thee, until I have done *that* which I have spoken to thee of" (Ge.28:15).

"The eternal God *is thy* refuge, and underneath *are* the everlasting arms: and he shall thrust out the enemy from before thee; and shall say, Destroy *them*" (De.33:27).

"Thou hast also given me the shield of thy salvation: and thy right hand hath holden me up, and thy gentleness hath made me great" (Ps.18:35).

"*They* [angels] shall bear thee up in *their* hands, lest thou dash thy foot against a stone" (Ps.91:12).

"Fear thou not; for I *am* with thee: be not dismayed; for I *am* thy God: I will strengthen thee; yea, I will help thee; yea, I will uphold thee with the right hand of my righteousness" (Is.41:10).

CHAPTER 30

J. The Defeat of the Amalekites by David: A Picture of Christ's Setting the Captives (His Loved Ones) Free, 30:1-31

1. **David & his men discovered their city burned & their families taken captive by the Amalekites: A lesson on prayer—seeking the LORD during bitter, painful trials**
   a. The Amalekites' raid on David's city, Ziklag
      1) They took everyone captive: Women, children, & elderly
      2) They killed no one, but enslaved them
   b. The shocking discovery of David & his men
      1) Their city burned
      2) Their families taken captive
   c. The overwhelming emotions of the men: They wept to the point of utter exhaustion
   d. The capture of David's two wives
   e. The hostility & threat by David's men to stone David: Were flooded with thoughts of their families' being abused
   f. The distress of David & his source of strength
      1) He sought the LORD for strength
      2) He sought the LORD for guidance

   • David's question: Should he pursue & would he catch the raiding party?
   • The LORD's answer: *Yes*

2. **David & his men pursued the Amalekites: A lesson on compassion**
   a. The utter exhaustion of David & his men
      1) Two hundred were so worn out they could not cross Besor Ravine

And it came to pass, when David and his men were come to Ziklag on the third day, that the Amalekites had invaded the south, and Ziklag, and smitten Ziklag, and burned it with fire;

2 And had taken the women captives, that *were* therein: they slew not any, either great or small, but carried *them* away, and went on their way.

3 So David and his men came to the city, and, behold, it was burned with fire; and their wives, and their sons, and their daughters, were taken captives.

4 Then David and the people that *were* with him lifted up their voice and wept, until they had no more power to weep.

5 And David's two wives were taken captives, Ahinoam the Jezreelitess, and Abigail the wife of Nabal the Carmelite.

6 And David was greatly distressed; for the people spake of stoning him, because the soul of all the people was grieved, every man for his sons and for his daughters: but David encouraged himself in the LORD his God.

7 And David said to Abiathar the priest, Ahimelech's son, I pray thee, bring me hither the ephod. And Abiathar brought thither the ephod to David.

8 And David enquired at the LORD, saying, Shall I pursue after this troop? shall I overtake them? And he answered him, Pursue: for thou shalt surely overtake *them,* and without fail recover *all.*

9 So David went, he and the six hundred men that *were* with him, and came to the brook Besor, where those that were left behind stayed.

10 But David pursued, he and four hundred men: for two hundred abode behind, which were so faint that they

could not go over the brook Besor.

11 And they found an Egyptian in the field, and brought him to David, and gave him bread, and he did eat; and they made him drink water;

12 And they gave him a piece of a cake of figs, and two clusters of raisins: and when he had eaten, his spirit came again to him: for he had eaten no bread, nor drunk *any* water, three days and three nights.

13 And David said unto him, To whom *belongest* thou? and whence *art* thou? And he said, I *am* a young man of Egypt, servant to an Amalekite; and my master left me, because three days agone I fell sick.

14 We made an invasion *upon* the south of the Cherethites, and upon *the coast* which *belongeth* to Judah, and upon the south of Caleb; and we burned Ziklag with fire.

15 And David said to him, Canst thou bring me down to this company? And he said, Swear unto me by God, that thou wilt neither kill me, nor deliver me into the hands of my master, and I will bring thee down to this company.

16 And when he had brought him down, behold, *they were* spread abroad upon all the earth, eating and drinking, and dancing, because of all the great spoil that they had taken out of the land of the Philistines, and out of the land of Judah.

17 And David smote them from the twilight even unto the evening of the next day: and there escaped not a man of them, save four hundred young men, which rode upon camels, and fled.

18 And David recovered all that the Amalekites had carried away: and David rescued his two wives.

19 And there was nothing lacking to them, neither small nor great, neither sons nor daughters, neither spoil, nor any *thing* that they had taken to them: David recovered all.

20 And David took all the flocks and the herds, *which* they drave before those *other* cattle, and said,

2) David & 400 men continued the pursuit
b. The discovery of a half-dead Egyptian in a field & David's compassion
   1) They gave him water & food

   2) They revived him: He had not eaten or drunk for three days or three nights

c. The interrogation by David & his discovery that the man was one of the enemy
   1) He was an Egyptian slave of an Amalekite
   2) He had become ill on the march & had been abandoned
   3) He had taken part in the raiding & burning of Ziklag

d. The request by David: Would the Egyptian lead them to the camp of the raiding party?
   1) A dangerous risk: The man could betray them
   2) The man negotiated for his life & freedom

3. **David & his men defeated the Amalekites, setting free their families & recovering their possessions: A picture of Christ's setting the captives free (from Satan & sin)**
   a. David found the Amalekites partying, drinking

   b. David attacked & killed all the enemy except 400 who escaped on camels

   c. David recovered everything
      1) Freed his two wives who had been taken captive

      2) Freed every person who had been taken captive
      3) Recovered the plunder
         • All possessions
         • All the flocks & herds

      4) Received the largest portion of the plunder—as the leader

4. David demonstrated a spirit of justice & generosity: A picture of covetousness, & of justice & generosity
a. The return to the 200 men who had been too exhausted to fight
  1) They came out to meet the conquerors
  2) David greeted them: Did not rebuke them
b. The opposition & covetousness of some wicked troublemakers among David's men
  1) They opposed the exhausted men's receiving a share of the plunder
  2) They suggested the laggards could, however, have their families
 	
c. The wisdom & justice of David's decision
  1) The victory was the LORD's & the plunder was a gift from Him
 	
  2) The task of the supply soldier was as vital & important as that of the combat warrior
  3) The decision: Justice demanded that all share &
	This *is* David's spoil.
	21 And David came to the two hundred men, which were so faint that they could not follow David, whom they had made also to abide at the brook Besor: and they went forth to meet David, and to meet the people that *were* with him: and when David came near to the people, he saluted them.
	22 Then answered all the wicked men and *men* of Belial, of those that went with David, and said, Because they went not with us, we will not give them *ought* of the spoil that we have recovered, save to every man his wife and his children, that they may lead *them* away, and depart.
	23 Then said David, Ye shall not do so, my brethren, with that which the LORD hath given us, who hath preserved us, and delivered the company that came against us into our hand.
	24 For who will hearken unto you in this matter? but as his part *is* that goeth down to the battle, so *shall* his part *be* that tarrieth by the stuff: they shall part alike.
		25 And it was *so* from that day forward, that he made it a statute and an ordinance for Israel unto this day.
		26 And when David came to Ziklag, he sent of the spoil unto the elders of Judah, *even* to his friends, saying, Behold a present for you of the spoil of the enemies of the LORD;
		27 To *them* which *were* in Bethel, and to *them* which *were* in south Ramoth, and to *them* which *were* in Jattir,
		28 And to *them* which *were* in Aroer, and to *them* which *were* in Siphmoth, and to *them* which *were* in Eshtemoa,
		29 And to *them* which *were* in Rachal, and to *them* which *were* in the cities of the Jerahmeelites, and to *them* which *were* in the cities of the Kenites,
		30 And to *them* which *were* in Hormah, and to *them* which *were* in Chor-ashan, and to *them* which *were* in Athach,
		31 And to *them* which *were* in Hebron, and to all the places where David himself and his men were wont to haunt.
			share alike
			4) The principle of equal distribution was made a permanent law
			d. The generosity of David: He sent gifts (some plunder) to the leaders of various cities throughout Judah, leaders who had provided supplies for him during his years as a fugitive from Saul
			  1) Bethel & Ramoth
			  2) Negev & Jattir
			
			  3) Aroer
			  4) Siphmoth & Eshtemoa
			
			  5) Racal & the cities ruled by the Jerahmeelites & the Kenites
			
			  6) Hormah & Bor
			  7) Ashan & Athach
			
			  8) Hebron
			  9) All the cities & districts where David & his men had moved about

DIVISION IV

THE STORY OF SAUL AND DAVID (PART 2):
DAVID THE FUGITIVE, 21:1–31:13

J. The Defeat of the Amalekites by David: A Picture of Christ's Setting the Captives (His Loved Ones) Free, 30:1-31

(30:1-31) **Introduction—Slavery, Evil of—Bondage, Spiritual, Deliverance from—Prostitution, Deliverance from—Sex, Bondage of, Deliverance from**: enslavement, being held in bondage, is one of the most terrible evils on the face of the earth. And yet multitudes of people are in bondage, some being enslaved by men and others being enslaved by substances. Tragically, people are held in bondage to secure cheap labor or to work in the sex trade or to serve the will of some master or wealthy person. But in addition to the human slave market, there are many who are enslaved to drugs, alcohol, tobacco, food, sex, and a host of other worldly vices.

But there is wonderful news: we can be set free from the slavery and bondages of this world. Jesus Christ can set us free. This is the practical lesson of this present passage of Scripture, the glorious truth that Jesus Christ sets the captives free. This is: *The Defeat of the Amalekites by David: A Picture of Christ's Setting the Captives (His Loved Ones) Free*, 30:1-31.

1. David and his men discovered their city burned and their families taken captive by the Amalekites: a lesson on prayer—seeking the LORD during bitter, painful trials (vv.1-8).
2. David and his men pursued the Amalekites: a lesson on compassion (vv.9-15).
3. David and his men defeated the Amalekites, setting free their families and recovering their possessions: a picture of Christ setting the captives free (from Satan and sin) (vv.16-20).
4. David demonstrated a spirit of justice and generosity: a picture of covetousness and of justice and generosity (vv.21-31).

1 (30:1-8) **Prayer, When to Pray—Trials, Answer to—Distress, Answer to—David, Prayer Life of—David, Source of Strength—Amalekites, Invasion of Israel—David, Opposition to**: when David and his men returned home from the battlefield, they discovered their city burned and their families taken captive by the Amalekites. Remember, David had forsaken the promised land and sought refuge among the unbelieving, worldly Philistines. For over a year now he had been living among the Philistines and had even joined their armed forces who were poised and ready to strike against Israel. He had been ready to commit two terrible evils: the evil of fighting against his own people over whom God had appointed him to serve as king, and the evil of helping the enemy attack the promised land. But in His sovereign power, God had stepped in to prevent David from engaging in the battle. He had aroused the Philistine commanders to oppose David's presence lest he turn against them to fight for the Israelites. As a result of the commanders' opposition, King Achish had discharged David. He and his men were sent back home to Ziklag, the city the king had given to David in the land of the Philistines. Ziklag was about fifty miles from the battlefield, so it took David and his men about three days to reach their home. But shockingly, when they arrived they found their city burned to the ground and their families missing. Warren W. Wiersbe says this:

> *Perhaps the LORD permitted this raid on Ziklag to encourage David to get out of enemy territory and go back to Judah where he belonged....[The Amalekites] burned the city, an act of vengeance on their part but perhaps a message from the Lord that it was time for David to think about returning to Judah.* [1]

OUTLINE	SCRIPTURE	SCRIPTURE	OUTLINE
1. David & his men discovered their city burned & their families taken captive by the Amalekites: A lesson on prayer—seeking the LORD during bitter, painful trials a. The Amalekites' raid on David's city, Ziklag 1) They took everyone captive: Women, children, & elderly 2) They killed no one, but enslaved them b. The shocking discovery of David & his men 1) Their city burned 2) Their families taken captive c. The overwhelming emotions of the men: They wept to the point of utter exhaustion d. The capture of David's two wives	And it came to pass, when David and his men were come to Ziklag on the third day, that the Amalekites had invaded the south, and Ziklag, and smitten Ziklag, and burned it with fire; 2 And had taken the women captives, that *were* therein: they slew not any, either great or small, but carried *them* away, and went on their way. 3 So David and his men came to the city, and, behold, it was burned with fire; and their wives, and their sons, and their daughters, were taken captives. 4 Then David and the people that *were* with him lifted up their voice and wept, until they had no more power to weep. 5 And David's two wives were taken captives, Ahino-	am the Jezreelitess, and Abigail the wife of Nabal the Carmelite. 6 And David was greatly distressed; for the people spake of stoning him, because the soul of all the people was grieved, every man for his sons and for his daughters: but David encouraged himself in the LORD his God. 7 And David said to Abiathar the priest, Ahimelech's son, I pray thee, bring me hither the ephod. And Abiathar brought thither the ephod to David. 8 And David enquired at the LORD, saying, Shall I pursue after this troop? shall I overtake them? And he answered him, Pursue: for thou shalt surely overtake *them,* and without fail recover *all.*	e. The hostility & threat by David's men to stone David: Were flooded with thoughts of their families' being abused f. The distress of David & his source of strength 1) He sought the LORD for strength 2) He sought the LORD for guidance • David's question: Should he pursue & would he catch the raiding party? • The LORD's answer: "Yes"

a. The Amalekites' raid on David's city, Ziklag, was unopposed because David and his men had been off preparing to join the Philistine army in their attack against Israel. It had been an ideal time for the Amalekites to attack, for all the men were away. As a result, the Amalekites were able to capture everyone alive and enslave them either for their own use or else to be sold at the slave markets (Amos 1:6, 9). All the women, children, and elderly were carried off as captives.

b. The discovery was an utter shock to David and his men. Seeing their city burned and realizing that their families had been taken captive shook them. They were stunned, in a state of shock.

c. Overwhelming emotions struck the men, and they wept to the point of utter exhaustion until they could weep no more.

d. Even the two wives of David had been taken captive, both Abigail and Jezreel (v.5).

e. Standing there grieving, David's men were flooded with thoughts of their families' being abused. They became hostile and began to direct their hostility toward David, threatening to stone him (v.6).

f. Once again David was under terrible strain. He had to bear not only the distress of losing his wives, but he also had to bear the pressure of the present crisis, the threat of his own men against his life (vv.6-8). In this situation David had only one choice: he had to seek the face of the LORD for strength and for guidance about what to do. Taking immediate action, David called for Abiathar the priest to bring the ephod so they could seek the LORD. As soon as the priest arrived, David prayed and asked the LORD if he should pursue the raiding party and if he would catch them. Immediately the LORD responded, answering both questions, "Yes."

Thought 1. This is a strong lesson for us on prayer, on seeking the LORD during bitter, painful trials. With the loss of his family and then having his closest friends turn against him, David faced the most bitter trial a person can face. Imagine losing your entire family and then later, for whatever reason, having all your friends turn against you.

Bitter trials confront us all, and most of us will suffer trials just as David did. A loved one will die, and a deep, intense grief will strike our hearts. We will feel the pain, emptiness, and loneliness of no longer having the loved

---

[1] Warren W. Wiersbe. *Be Successful*, p.150.

one with us. And many of us have already suffered the grief of losing a parent, child, brother, sister, or close friend.

Moreover, as we walk throughout life, most of us will experience a time when a friend or neighbor or co-worker or even a relative will become upset with us and turn against us, opposing us. Then the breach or divisiveness will cause great anxiety or distress. Sometimes even physical and emotional problems result, such as headaches, depression, or any number of other problems.

The answer to bitter, painful trials is the LORD, praying and seeking His face for strength to bear the trials, to overcome and conquer them. If we ask, God gives us strength. If we seek, we will find. If we knock, it will be opened unto us. This is the promise of the LORD.

"Ask, and it shall be given you; seek, and ye shall find; knock, and it shall be opened unto you" (Mt.7:7).

"If ye abide in me, and my words abide in you, ye shall ask what ye will, and it shall be done unto you" (Jn.15:7).

"Hitherto have ye asked nothing in my name: ask, and ye shall receive, that your joy may be full" (Jn.16:24).

"Is any among you afflicted? let him pray. Is any merry? let him sing psalms" (Js.5:13).

"Seek the LORD and his strength, seek his face continually" (1 Chr.16:11).

"He shall call upon me, and I will answer him: I will be with him in trouble; I will deliver him, and honour him" (Ps.91:15).

"And it shall come to pass, that before they call, I will answer; and while they are yet speaking, I will hear" (Is.65:24).

"And ye shall seek me, and find me, when ye shall search for me with all your heart" (Je.29:13).

2 (30:9-15) **Compassion, Example of—Service, Example of—Ministering, Example of—David, Heart of, Filled with Compassion**: assured by the LORD, David and his men immediately began pursuing the Amalekites. Just imagine the emotions of David and his men as they were vigorously pursuing their savage foe: stricken with grief over the loss of their families, picturing their wives and children being raped and in chains and driven along like a herd of animals. Such images were bound to cause intense grief, but also arouse a spirit of bitter hostility toward the Amalekites. Note how Scripture describes their pursuit of this brutal enemy:

OUTLINE	SCRIPTURE	SCRIPTURE	OUTLINE
2. David & his men pursued the Amalekites: A lesson on compassion a. The utter exhaustion of David & his men 　1) Two hundred were so worn out they could not cross Besor Ravine 　2) David & 400 men continued the pursuit b. The discovery of a half-dead Egyptian in a field & David's compassion 1) They gave him water & food 2) They revived him: He had not eaten or drunk for three days or three nights	9 So David went, he and the six hundred men that *were* with him, and came to the brook Besor, where those that were left behind stayed. 10 But David pursued, he and four hundred men: for two hundred abode behind, which were so faint that they could not go over the brook Besor. 11 And they found an Egyptian in the field, and brought him to David, and gave him bread, and he did eat; and they made him drink water; 12 And they gave him a piece of a cake of figs, and two clusters of raisins: and when he had eaten, his spirit came again to him: for he had eaten no bread, nor drunk *any* water, three days and three nights.	13 And David said unto him, To whom *belongest* thou? and whence art thou? And he said, I *am* a young man of Egypt, servant to an Amalekite; and my master left me, because three days agone I fell sick. 14 We made an invasion *upon* the south of the Cherethites, and upon *the coast* which *belongeth* to Judah, and upon the south of Caleb; and we burned Ziklag with fire. 15 And David said to him, Canst thou bring me down to this company? And he said, Swear unto me by God, that thou wilt neither kill me, nor deliver me into the hands of my master, and I will bring thee down to this company.	c. The interrogation by David & his discovery that the man was one of the enemy 　1) He was an Egyptian slave of an Amalekite 　2) He had become ill on the march & had been abandoned 　3) He had taken part in the raiding & burning of Ziklag d. The request by David: Would the Egyptian lead them to the camp of the raiding party? 　1) A dangerous risk: The man could betray them 　2) The man negotiated for his life & freedom

a. David and his men were utterly exhausted, for they had already spent the last three days traveling from the battlefield to their home at Ziklag, a journey of over fifty miles (vv.9-10). In addition, experiencing the destruction of their homes and the loss of their families drained the strength out of their bodies. A state of total exhaustion, of being bone-weary and completely worn out had overtaken some of the men. When they had traveled about another sixteen miles in their pursuit of the Amalekites, they came to a deep and wide ravine known as the Besor Ravine. Being thoroughly exhausted, 200 of the men could not cross the ravine. They simply could go no further. So leaving these 200 men behind, David and the remaining 400 men continued their fierce pursuit.

b. While racing as rapidly as they could to catch the Amalekites, suddenly some of the men spotted a half-dead Egyptian lying in a field. They brought him to David and gave him drink and food, for he had not eaten or drunk for three days and nights.

c. Once revived, David began an interrogation of the Egyptian and discovered that he was one of the enemy (vv.13-14). He was an Egyptian slave of an Amalekite who had become ill on the march and been abandoned by his master. He informed David that the Amalekites had raided three different areas:

⇒ The Negev of the Kerethites, which was a coastal area inhabited by a clan of people closely connected to the Philistines.
⇒ The territory belonging to Judah, which was David's own home tribe.
⇒ The Negev of Caleb, which was the territory surrounding Hebron, which was also in the tribe of Judah and had been formerly given to Caleb by Joshua (Jos.14:13-14; 15:13-15).

d. Learning that the Egyptian knew so much about the plans of the Amalekites, David immediately asked if he would lead them to the camp of the raiding party (v.15). By making this request, David was running a dangerous risk, for the Egyptian could betray them. But having been assured by the LORD that he was to pursue the Amalekites, David trusted the LORD to protect him and his men. Sensing an opportunity to save his life, the Egyptian agreed on one condition: that David spare his life and swear that he would not kill him or hand him back over to his master.

Thought 1: This is a striking lesson on compassion. Rushing to save their families, David and his men did not have to stop to help this Egyptian. Spotting the man, it was visibly evident that he was half-dead, and it would take some time to revive and refresh him. Stopping to help him meant a delay in their pursuit to save their families. Nevertheless, compassion reached out to help the man. And because David was filled with compassion, he was rewarded with additional information about the Amalekites.

Our hearts are always to be filled with compassion, reaching out to help any person who is in need. And there are needs all around us. Within every community, some people are in pain and suffering from...

- disease
- old age
- rejection
- depression
- discouragement
- abuse
- lack of finances
- inadequate housing
- loneliness
- purposelessness
- emptiness
- grief and sorrow
- unemployment

There are a host of hardships and misfortunes all around us and people who are suffering and need our help. For this reason we must reach out in compassion. When we know of a person who needs help, we must arouse our hearts and we must act in compassion. Listen to what the Word of God says about compassion:

> "Blessed are the merciful: for they shall obtain mercy" (Mt.5:7).
> "Be ye therefore merciful, as your Father also is merciful" (Lu.6:36).
> "But a certain Samaritan, as he journeyed, came where he was: and when he saw him, he had compassion on him, And went to him, and bound up his wounds, pouring in oil and wine, and set him on his own beast, and brought him to an inn, and took care of him" (Lu.10:33-34).
> "I have showed you all things, how that so labouring ye ought to support the weak, and to remember the words of the Lord Jesus, how he said, It is more blessed to give than to receive" (Ac.20:35).
> "We then that are strong ought to bear the infirmities of the weak, and not to please ourselves" (Ro.15:1).
> "Bear ye one another's burdens, and so fulfil the law of Christ" (Ga.6:2).
> "Put on therefore, as the elect of God, holy and beloved, bowels of mercies, kindness, humbleness of mind, meekness, longsuffering" (Col.3:12).
> "Remember them that are in bonds, as bound with them; and them which suffer adversity, as being yourselves also in the body" (He.13:3).
> "Pure religion and undefiled before God and the Father is this, To visit the fatherless and widows in their affliction, and to keep himself unspotted from the world" (Js.1:27).
> "The merciful man doeth good to his own soul: but he that is cruel troubleth his own flesh" (Pr.11:17).
> "Is not this the fast that I have chosen? to loose the bands of wickedness, to undo the heavy burdens, and to let the oppressed go free, and that ye break every yoke? Is it not to deal thy bread to the hungry, and that thou bring the poor that are cast out to thy house? when thou seest the naked, that thou cover him; and that thou hide not thyself from thine own flesh" (Is.58:6-7).

3 (30:16-20) **Captives, Set Free—Type, of Christ—Christ, Types of—David, Type of Christ—Rescue, Types of, Christ—Salvation, Types of, Christ**: David and his men defeated the Amalekites, setting free their families and recovering their possessions. In setting their loved ones free, David became a clear picture of Christ, who sets the captives free. A clear picture of the wonderful deliverance is described by the Scripture:

OUTLINE	SCRIPTURE	SCRIPTURE	OUTLINE
3. David & his men defeated the Amalekites, setting free their families & recovering their possessions: A picture of Christ setting the captives	16 And when he had brought him down, behold, *they were* spread abroad upon all the earth, eating and drinking, and dancing, because of all	the great spoil that they had taken out of the land of the Philistines, and out of the land of Judah. 17 And David smote them	**free (from Satan & sin)** a. David found the Amalekites partying, drinking b. David attacked & killed all

OUTLINE	SCRIPTURE	SCRIPTURE	OUTLINE
the enemy except 400 who escaped on camels	from the twilight even unto the evening of the next day: and there escaped not a man of them, save four hundred young men, which rode upon camels, and fled.	lacking to them, neither small nor great, neither sons nor daughters, neither spoil, nor any *thing* that they had taken to them: David recovered all.	had been taken captive 3) Recovered the plunder • All possessions • All the flocks & herds
c. David recovered everything 1) Freed his two wives who had been taken captive	18 And David recovered all that the Amalekites had carried away: and David rescued his two wives.	20 And David took all the flocks and the herds, *which* they drave before those *other* cattle, and said, This *is* David's spoil.	4) Received the largest portion of the plunder—as the leader
2) Freed every person who	19 And there was nothing		

a. Being led by the Egyptian, David and his men soon spotted the Amalekites. To their amazement, the enemy was scattered out across the countryside partying. They were dancing and drinking, celebrating over the great amount of spoils they had been able to plunder.

b. Despite their exhaustion, David and his men immediately attacked the Amalekites and fought them from dusk until evening of the next day. All the enemy were killed except 400, who escaped fleeing on camels (v.17).

c. David recovered everything, freeing his own two wives and every other person who had been taken captive. In addition, he recovered all the plunder, all the possessions that had been stolen including all the flocks and herds. As a reward for having led his men in the recovery of their families and possessions, his men gave David all the livestock the Amalekites had stolen in their raids on the other territories.

Thought 1. Just as David rescued the captives, those whom he loved, so Christ has rescued the captives, those whom He loves. We are held captive by three forces. First, we are held captive by sin. We sin and we cannot help but sin. No matter how much we may try, we disobey and come short of God's glory. Sin has captivated us, and we cannot break free from its grasp.

Second, death has captured us, holding us in its grasp and refusing to let us go. We die, every one of us, and there is nothing we can do to keep from dying. From dust we came and to dust we will return. We are captivated by death.

Third, we are held captive by hell. As unpleasant as it may be, we are doomed to hell and cannot escape its grasp. Being doomed to hell is the result of our unbelief, disobedience, and rejection of Jesus Christ, God's very own Son.

But here is the wonderful news: we can be set free, delivered from our enslavement to these three forces. We no longer have to be captive to sin, death, or hell. Why? Because the Lord Jesus Christ came to earth for the very purpose of setting the captives free. And we are the captives. We can be set free by the death of the Lord Jesus Christ. Christ died to set us free, died upon the cross bearing our sins. And if we believe this wonderful truth, that Christ bore our sins to make us acceptable to God, the most wonderful thing happens: God truly accepts us. He sets us free from sin, death, and hell. This is exactly what Scripture declares:

"Much more then, being now justified by his blood, we shall be saved from wrath through him" (Ro.5:9).

"Who gave himself for our sins, that he might deliver us from this present evil world, according to the will of God and our Father" (Ga.1:4).

"Christ hath redeemed us from the curse of the law, being made a curse for us: for it is written, Cursed is every one that hangeth on a tree" (Ga.3:13).

"Who gave himself for us, that he might redeem us from all iniquity, and purify unto himself a peculiar people, zealous of good works" (Tit.2:14).

"Forasmuch then as the children are partakers of flesh and blood, he also himself likewise took part of the same; that through death he might destroy him that had the power of death, that is, the devil; And deliver them who through fear of death were all their lifetime subject to bondage" (He.2:14-15).

"Wherefore he is able also to save them to the uttermost that come unto God by him, seeing he ever liveth to make intercession for them" (He.7:25).

4 (30:21-31) **Justice, Example of—Generosity, Example of—Covetousness, Example of—David, Justice of—David, Generosity of**: David demonstrated a strong spirit of justice and generosity. What happened next gives a glimpse into the heart of David, who was soon to become the future ruler of Israel:

OUTLINE	SCRIPTURE	SCRIPTURE	OUTLINE
4. David demonstrated a spirit of justice & generosity: A picture of covetousness, & of justice & generosity a. The return to the 200 men who had been too exhausted to fight	21 And David came to the two hundred men, which were so faint that they could not follow David, whom they had made also to abide at the brook Besor: and they went forth to meet David, and to	meet the people that *were* with him: and when David came near to the people, he saluted them. 22 Then answered all the wicked men and *men* of Belial, of those that went with	1) They came out to meet the conquerors 2) David greeted them: Did not rebuke them b. The opposition & covetousness of some wicked troublemakers among David's men

OUTLINE	SCRIPTURE	SCRIPTURE	OUTLINE
1) They opposed the exhausted men's receiving a share of the plunder 2) They suggested the laggards could, however, have their families	David, and said, Because they went not with us, we will not give them *ought* of the spoil that we have recovered, save to every man his wife and his children, that they may lead *them* away, and depart.	*even* to his friends, saying, Behold a present for you of the spoil of the enemies of the LORD; 27 To *them* which *were* in Bethel, and to *them* which *were* in south Ramoth, and to *them* which *were* in Jattir,	throughout Judah, leaders who had provided supplies for him during his years as a fugitive from Saul 1) Bethel & Ramoth 2) Negev & Jattir
c. The wisdom & justice of David's decision 1) The victory was the LORD's & the plunder was a gift from Him	23 Then said David, Ye shall not do so, my brethren, with that which the LORD hath given us, who hath preserved us, and delivered the company that came against us into our hand.	28 And to *them* which *were* in Aroer, and to *them* which *were* in Siphmoth, and to *them* which *were* in Eshtemoa,	3) Aroer 4) Siphmoth & Eshtemoa
2) The task of the supply soldier was as vital & important as that of the combat warrior 3) The decision: Justice demanded that all share & share alike 4) The principle of equal distribution was made a permanent law	24 For who will hearken unto you in this matter? but as his part *is* that goeth down to the battle, so *shall* his part *be* that tarrieth by the stuff: they shall part alike. 25 And it was *so* from that day forward, that he made it a statute and an ordinance for Israel unto this day.	29 And to *them* which *were* in Rachal, and to *them* which *were* in the cities of the Jerahmeelites, and to *them* which *were* in the cities of the Kenites, 30 And to *them* which *were* in Hormah, and to *them* which *were* in Chor-ashan, and to *them* which *were* in Athach,	5) Racal & the cities ruled by the Jerahmeelites & the Kenites 6) Hormah & Bor 7) Ashan & Athach
d. The generosity of David: He sent gifts (some plunder) to the leaders of various cities	26 And when David came to Ziklag, he sent of the spoil unto the elders of Judah,	31 And to *them* which *were* in Hebron, and to all the places where David himself and his men were wont to haunt.	8) Hebron 9) All the cities & districts where David & his men had moved about

a. Joying and rejoicing over the recovery of their families and possessions, David and his men made their way back to the 200 men who had been too exhausted to pursue the Amalekites (v.21). As soon as the 200 men spotted David and the others returning, they rushed out to meet the conquerors. Note David's attitude toward them: he did not rebuke nor scorn, but rather greeted them with a joyful heart, for the LORD had given them a wonderful victory that day.

b. But David's spirit of acceptance did not exist in the hearts of all the men. There was opposition and covetousness within the hearts of some wicked troublemakers among David's men (v.22). They opposed the exhausted men's receiving a share of the plunder, suggesting that they were laggards. However, the troublemakers yielded to the laggards' having their families returned.

c. Nevertheless, David intervened and demonstrated a strong spirit of wisdom and justice in dealing with people (vv.23-25). He declared two facts: first, the victory was the LORD's; therefore the plunder was a gift from Him. It was the LORD and the LORD alone who had protected them and helped them defeat the enemy. Second, the task of the supply soldier was just as vital and important as that of the combat warrior.

Having established these two facts, David made his decision: justice demanded that all share and share alike. Note that this principle of equal distribution was made a permanent law from that day to the day that the author was writing the book of *First Samuel*.

d. When David arrived back in Ziklag, his spirit of generosity continued to shine brightly (vv.25-31). He sent some plunder as gifts to a large number of city leaders scattered throughout Judah, leaders who had provided supplies for him during his distressing years as a fugitive from Saul. For years David had been building relationships with leaders of various territories, relationships that were going to help him in unifying and consolidating the nation once he became king. And soon—in just three days—David was going to receive word about the death of King Saul and the defeat of the Israelite army by the Philistines. As a result, events would move rapidly and David would be crowned king, just as the LORD had promised (2 Sa.1-2).

Thought 1. We must not be greedy or treat others unfairly. If we are greedy, we seek more and more, banking and hoarding what we have. A greedy heart is consumed by lust, the lust for more pleasure, comfort, possessions, wealth, recognition, fame, position, and power. A greedy heart also mistreats others by blinding a person to the desperate needs of the world. A greedy person seldom reaches out with a helping hand, to give to and meet the needs of people. And sometimes a greedy person is aroused to cheat and steal in order to get more and more, treating others unfairly and unjustly. But God's Word is clear: we must always be just in all dealings, never cheating or stealing from anyone.
(1) Covetousness is condemned by God. God's Holy Word says this:

"And he said unto them, Take heed, and beware of covetousness: for a man's life consisteth not in the abundance of the things which he possesseth" (Lu.12:15).
"For the wrath of God is revealed from heaven against all ungodliness and unrighteousness of men, who hold the truth in unrighteousness....Being filled with all unrighteousness, fornication, wickedness, covetousness, maliciousness; full of envy, murder, debate, deceit, malignity; whisperers....Who

knowing the judgment of God, that they which commit such things are worthy of death, not only do the same, but have pleasure in them that do them" (Ro.1:18, 29, 32).

"But fornication, and all uncleanness, or covetousness, let it not be once named among you, as becometh saints; Neither filthiness, nor foolish talking, nor jesting, which are not convenient: but rather giving of thanks. For this ye know, that no whoremonger, nor unclean person, nor covetous man, who is an idolater, hath any inheritance in the kingdom of Christ and of God" (Ep.5:3-5).

"Mortify therefore your members which are upon the earth; fornication, uncleanness, inordinate affection, evil concupiscence, and covetousness, which is idolatry: For which things' sake the wrath of God cometh on the children of disobedience" (Col.3:5-6).

"Thou shalt not covet thy neighbour's house, thou shalt not covet thy neighbour's wife, nor his manservant, nor his maidservant, nor his ox, nor his ass, nor any thing that is thy neighbour's" (Ex.20:17).

"For from the least of them even unto the greatest of them every one is given to covetousness; and from the prophet even unto the priest every one dealeth falsely" (Je.6:13).

"And they come unto thee as the people cometh, and they sit before thee as my people, and they hear thy words, but they will not do them: for with their mouth they show much love, but their heart goeth after their covetousness" (Eze.33:31).

"And they covet fields, and take them by violence; and houses, and take them away: so they oppress a man and his house, even a man and his heritage" (Mic.2:2).

"Woe to him that coveteth an evil covetousness to his house, that he may set his nest on high, that he may be delivered from the power of evil" (Hab.2:9).

(2) God demands that we treat people justly, fairly. He even demands that we be generous in dealing with people. This is exactly what Holy Scripture says:

"And as ye would that men should do to you, do ye also to them likewise. For if ye love them which love you, what thank have ye? for sinners also love those that love them. And if ye do good to them which do good to you, what thank have ye? for sinners also do even the same. And if ye lend to them of whom ye hope to receive, what thank have ye? for sinners also lend to sinners, to receive as much again. But love ye your enemies, and do good, and lend, hoping for nothing again; and your reward shall be great, and ye shall be the children of the Highest: for he is kind unto the unthankful and to the evil" (Lu.6:31-35).

"Neither was there any among them that lacked: for as many as were possessors of lands or houses sold them, and brought the prices of the things that were sold, And laid them down at the apostles' feet: and distribution was made unto every man according as he had need. And Joses, who by the apostles was surnamed Barnabas, (which is, being interpreted, The son of consolation,) a Levite, and of the country of Cyprus" (Ac.4:34-35).

"Recompense to no man evil for evil. Provide things honest in the sight of all men" (Ro.12:17).

"Render therefore to all their dues: tribute to whom tribute is due; custom to whom custom; fear to whom fear; honour to whom honour" (Ro.13:7).

"Owe no man any thing, but to love one another: for he that loveth another hath fulfilled the law" (Ro.13:8).

"How that in a great trial of affliction the abundance of their joy and their deep poverty abounded unto the riches of their liberality" (2 Co.8:2).

"But this I say, He which soweth sparingly shall reap also sparingly; and he which soweth bountifully shall reap also bountifully" (2 Co.9:6).

"For even in Thessalonica ye sent once and again unto my necessity" (Ph.4:16).

"Masters, give unto your servants that which is just and equal; knowing that ye also have a Master in heaven" (Col.4:1).

"That which is altogether just shalt thou follow, that thou mayest live, and inherit the land which the LORD thy God giveth thee" (De.16:20).

"Defend the poor and fatherless: do justice to the afflicted and needy" (Ps.82:3).

"A false balance is abomination to the LORD: but a just weight is his delight" (Pr.11:1).

"The liberal soul shall be made fat: and he that watereth shall be watered also himself" (Pr.11:25).

"To do justice and judgment is more acceptable to the LORD than sacrifice" (Pr.21:3).

"He that hath a bountiful eye shall be blessed; for he giveth of his bread to the poor" (Pr.22:9).

"Thus saith the LORD, Keep ye judgment, and do justice: for my salvation is near to come, and my righteousness to be revealed" (Is.56:1).

"And if thou draw out thy soul to the hungry, and satisfy the afflicted soul; then shall thy light rise in obscurity, and thy darkness be as the noonday" (Is.58:10).

"Bring ye all the tithes into the storehouse, that there may be meat in mine house, and prove me now herewith, saith the LORD of hosts, if I will not open you the windows of heaven, and pour you out a blessing, that there shall not be room enough to receive it" (Mal.3:10).

CHAPTER 31

K. The Tragic End of Saul & His Sons, Including Jonathan, David's Closest Friend: The Surety of God's Word & of God's Judgment, 31:1-13

1. **The painful tragedy & death of Saul: The surety of God's judgment**
   a. Saul witnessed his army routed & many slain
   b. Saul witnessed his sons, including Jonathan, killed

   c. Saul himself was critically wounded in the midst of fierce fighting

   d. Saul chose to commit suicide: To keep from being tortured & mutilated (a Near Eastern custom), Judg.16:25
      1) Saul first asked his armor-bearer to strike the final blow of death: He refused
      2) Saul was shamefully forced to commit suicide

      3) The armor-bearer himself then committed suicide

   e. Saul & his sons & his army shamefully fell that very day: Saul's dynasty, his kingdom, collapsed

Now the Philistines fought against Israel: and the men of Israel fled from before the Philistines, and fell down slain in mount Gilboa.
2 And the Philistines followed hard upon Saul and upon his sons; and the Philistines slew Jonathan, and Abinadab, and Melchi-shua, Saul's sons.
3 And the battle went sore against Saul, and the archers hit him; and he was sore wounded of the archers.
4 Then said Saul unto his armourbearer, Draw thy sword, and thrust me through therewith; lest these uncircumcised come and thrust me through, and abuse me. But his armourbearer would not; for he was sore afraid. Therefore Saul took a sword, and fell upon it.
5 And when his armourbearer saw that Saul was dead, he fell likewise upon his sword, and died with him.
6 So Saul died, and his three sons, and his armourbearer, and all his men, that same day together.

7 And when the men of Israel that were on the other side of the valley, and they that were on the other side Jordan, saw that the men of Israel fled, and that Saul and his sons were dead, they forsook the cities, and fled; and the Philistines came and dwelt in them.
8 And it came to pass on the morrow, when the Philistines came to strip the slain, that they found Saul and his three sons fallen in mount Gilboa.
9 And they cut off his head, and stripped off his armour, and sent into the land of the Philistines round about, to publish it in the house of their idols, and among the people.
10 And they put his armour in the house of Ashtaroth: and they fastened his body to the wall of Beth-shan.
11 And when the inhabitants of Jabesh-gilead heard of that which the Philistines had done to Saul;
12 All the valiant men arose, and went all night, and took the body of Saul and the bodies of his sons from the wall of Beth-shan, and came to Jabesh, and burnt them there.
13 And they took their bones, and buried them under a tree at Jabesh, and fasted seven days.

   f. Saul's death & the army's defeat tragically impacted the nation
      1) The Israelites of northern Israel abandoned their cities & fled to remote regions, becoming refugees
      2) The Philistines occupied their cities

2. **The abuse of Saul's body & the celebration of victory by the Philistines: A picture of false gods & false religion**
   a. They found the bodies of Saul & his sons: Cut off Saul's head & stripped off his armor
   b. They announced & celebrated the victory in their temples throughout the land

      1) Gave Saul's armor to their god of war, Ashtoreth
      2) Fastened his body to the wall of Beth Shan

3. **The respect of Jabesh-Gilead for Saul: A lesson on respecting "God's anointed"**

   a. They heard about the abuse of Saul's body & rescued it
      1) Sent a squadron out under the cover of darkness
      2) Recovered the bodies of Saul & his sons & burned them
   b. They buried their bones at Jabesh
   c. They fasted for seven days

DIVISION IV

THE STORY OF SAUL AND DAVID (PART 2): DAVID THE FUGITIVE, 21:1–31:13

K. The Tragic End of Saul and His Sons, Including Jonathan, David's Closest Friend: The Surety of God's Word and of God's Judgment, 31:1-13

(31:1-13) **Introduction—Judgment, Surety of—Word of God, Surety of**: nothing is any more certain than God's Word. Whatever God says will come to pass. Heaven and earth will pass away, but the words of the LORD will not. They will endure forever. So it is with judgment. When God says that judgment is coming, it will come. Nothing will stop the judgment, for it was pronounced by the LORD Himself. And when He gives a pronouncement, it is inevitable. It must take place.

Years before the event of this Scripture, God had pronounced judgment upon Saul. And just the day before this event, God had repeated His prediction: Saul and his three sons would die on the battlefield. And now the event was about to take place. The day had finally come. Just as God had predicted, Saul and his sons were about to die. This is: *The Tragic End of Saul and His Sons, Including Jonathan, David's Closest Friend: The Surety of God's Word and of God's Judgment,* 31:1-13.

1. The painful tragedy and death of Saul: the surety of God's judgment (vv.1-7).
2. The abuse of Saul's body and the celebration of victory by the Philistines: a picture of false gods and false religion (vv.8-10).
3. The respect of Jabesh-Gilead for Saul: a lesson on respecting "God's anointed" (vv.11-13).

1 (31:1-7) **Tragedy, of Death, Example of—Death, Tragic, of Saul—Judgment, Surety of**: there was the painful tragedy and death of King Saul, just hours after he had consulted with the spirit medium (28:1-25). Remember, the Philistines had already invaded Israel with a massive army. Their objective was to kill Saul and to put an end to his dynasty because of the trouble he had caused the Philistines for the past forty years of his rule (Acts 13:21).[1] Saul had been stricken with utter terror when he saw the massive army, knowing what their objective was. For this reason he had gone to the spirit medium for counsel. Shockingly, the medium claimed to see Samuel in her séance and the message Samuel gave was a message of God's judgment. Saul and his sons were to die in the battle that was about to take place with the Philistines. Scripture dramatically paints the scene of Saul's death:

OUTLINE	SCRIPTURE	SCRIPTURE	OUTLINE
1. The painful tragedy & death of Saul: The surety of God's judgment a. Saul witnessed his army routed & many slain b. Saul witnessed his sons, including Jonathan, killed c. Saul himself was critically wounded in the midst of fierce fighting d. Saul chose to commit suicide: To keep from being tortured & mutilated (a Near Eastern custom), Judg.16:25 1) Saul first asked his armor-bearer to strike the final	Now the Philistines fought against Israel: and the men of Israel fled from before the Philistines, and fell down slain in mount Gilboa. 2 And the Philistines followed hard upon Saul and upon his sons; and the Philistines slew Jonathan, and Abinadab, and Melchi-shua, Saul's sons. 3 And the battle went sore against Saul, and the archers hit him; and he was sore wounded of the archers. 4 Then said Saul unto his armourbearer, Draw thy sword, and thrust me through therewith; lest these uncircumcised come and thrust me through, and abuse me. But	his armourbearer would not; for he was sore afraid. Therefore Saul took a sword, and fell upon it. 5 And when his armourbearer saw that Saul was dead, he fell likewise upon his sword, and died with him. 6 So Saul died, and his three sons, and his armourbearer, and all his men, that same day together. 7 And when the men of Israel that *were* on the other side of the valley, and *they* that *were* on the other side Jordan, saw that the men of Israel fled, and that Saul and his sons were dead, they forsook the cities, and fled; and the Philistines came and dwelt in them.	blow of death: He refused 2) Saul was shamefully forced to commit suicide 3) The armor-bearer himself then committed suicide e. Saul & his sons & his army shamefully fell that very day: Saul's dynasty, his kingdom, collapsed f. Saul's death & the army's defeat tragically impacted the nation 1) The Israelites of northern Israel abandoned their cities & fled to remote regions, becoming refugees 2) The Philistines occupied their cities

Saul's troops stood no chance against the massive Philistine army with its hundreds, perhaps thousands, of chariots. And Saul witnessed many of his soldiers slaughtered on Mount Gilboa. A dramatic battle was fought with the Philistines pressing hard and closing in on Saul and his sons. Before Saul's very eyes his three sons were killed: Jonathan, Abinadab, and Melchai-Shua.

In the midst of fierce fighting Saul himself was critically wounded. An arrow from one of the archers struck him in a crucial spot and he collapsed to the earth severely wounded, knowing that he would gradually die. Instead of being caught by the enemy, tortured, and mutilated, which was a Near Eastern custom, Saul chose to commit suicide. He first asked his armor-bearer to strike the final blow of death, but the armor-bearer refused. Shamefully, Saul ended his own life by taking his sword and falling upon it (v.4). When his armor-bearer saw that Saul was dead, he too committed suicide by falling upon his sword and dying with his king.

Samuel's prediction had been fulfilled: the hand of God's judgment had fallen upon Saul. Both he and his sons died on the battlefield and his army shamefully fell that very day. Saul's dynasty—his kingdom—had collapsed. The result of Israel's defeat and of Saul's death was twofold: the Israelites of northern Israel abandoned their cities and fled to remote regions, becoming refugees, and the Philistines came right behind occupying their cities.

> **Thought 1**. When God pronounces judgment, it will take place. The LORD warned Saul that if he continued to live a wicked and disobedient life, he would face the judgment of God. The hand of God's judgment would fall upon him. But Saul refused to heed the warning of the LORD. As is seen throughout his life, he refused to repent of his evil, self-centered ways. He refused to trust the LORD to help him govern the nation and lead the people in the path of righteousness and justice. Consequently, God had no choice but to pronounce judgment upon Saul. And once that judgment was pronounced, it was to take place. Judgment was certain.
>
> The surety of God's judgment is the lesson to learn from Saul's death. God forewarns us: if we continue in the way of wickedness and disobedience, we will face the judgment of God. His hand of condemnation will fall upon us. This is exactly what the Holy Word of God teaches:
>
> **"For the Son of man shall come in the glory of his Father with his angels; and then he shall reward every man according to his works" (Mt.16:27).**
>
> **"For we must all appear before the judgment seat of Christ; that every one may receive the things *done* in *his* body, according to that he hath done, whether *it be* good or bad" (2 Co.5:10).**
>
> **"And to you who are troubled rest with us, when the Lord Jesus shall be revealed from heaven with his mighty angels, In flaming fire taking vengeance on them that know not God, and that obey not the gospel of our Lord Jesus Christ" (2 Th.1:7-8).**

---

1 Robert D. Bergen. *1, 2 Samuel*, p.282.

"And as it is appointed unto men once to die, but after this the judgment" (He.9:27).

"But the heavens and the earth, which are now, by the same word are kept in store, reserved unto fire against the day of judgment and perdition of ungodly men" (2 Pe.3:7).

"And Enoch also, the seventh from Adam, prophesied of these, saying, Behold, the Lord cometh with ten thousands of his saints, To execute judgment upon all, and to convince all that are ungodly among them of all their ungodly deeds which they have ungodly committed, and of all their hard *speeches* which ungodly sinners have spoken against him" (Jude 14-15).

"And, behold, I come quickly; and my reward *is* with me, to give every man according as his work shall be" (Re.22:12).

2 (31:8-10) **False Gods, Worshipping—Religion, False, Worshipping—Philistines, Victory over Israel—Saul, Death of**: there was the abuse of Saul's body and the celebration of victory by the Philistines. A huge celebration took place all across the Philistine nation, a celebration that shows just how steeped the Philistines were in idolatry and false religion. The day after their resounding victory over the Israelite forces, the Philistines arose and returned to follow the battlefield custom of stripping the dead of their valuables. While stripping soldier after soldier, suddenly several of the Philistines came across the bodies of Saul and his three sons. Following the custom of the victor, the Philistines cut off Saul's head and removed his armor. They then sent messengers throughout the land proclaiming the news of the glorious victory over their arch-enemy, King Saul and the Israelites.

Note where the victory was announced and celebrated: in the temples of their idols where the people had assembled to worship their false gods in celebration of their great victory over the Israelites. Most likely the armor of Saul was paraded through the streets of the major Philistine cities as part of the festivities. But eventually the armor was placed as a permanent symbol of their victory in the temple of Ashtoreth, the goddess of war and fertility. The decapitated bodies of Saul and his sons were taken just a few miles to the city of Beth Shan, a city in the Jezreel valley that was under the control of the Philistines. After being paraded through the streets of the Philistine cities, Saul's head was placed on permanent display in the temple of Dagon (1 Chr.10:10).

OUTLINE	SCRIPTURE	SCRIPTURE	OUTLINE
2. The abuse of Saul's body & the celebration of victory by the Philistines: A picture of false gods & false religion a. They found the bodies of Saul & his sons: Cut off Saul's head & stripped off his armor	8 And it came to pass on the morrow, when the Philistines came to strip the slain, that they found Saul and his three sons fallen in mount Gilboa. 9 And they cut off his head, and stripped off his armour,	and sent into the land of the Philistines round about, to publish *it in* the house of their idols, and among the people. 10 And they put his armour in the house of Ashtaroth: and they fastened his body to the wall of Beth-shan.	b. They announced & celebrated the victory in their temples throughout the land 1) Gave Saul's armor to their god of war, Ashtoreth 2) Fastened his body to the wall of Beth Shan

Thought 1. In ancient history religion played a significant role in people's lives. Many, if not most, of their major functions took place in their temples or worship centers. But we must always remember, their religion was corrupt, the worship of idols and gods created by their own imaginations. They did not worship the LORD [Jehovah, Yahweh], the great Creator and Sovereign Majesty of the universe, the only living and true God. Ever since the fall of Adam and Eve, man's worship had become more and more corrupted, generation by generation, until man began to create his own idea of God. Man molded and made God to fit his own wild imaginations and lusts. Man wanted a god that would allow him to live as he wished, doing his own thing. The result was catastrophic: man began to take wood, stone, and metal to make idols. And in looking at the world, they took the most enjoyable, frightening, or hopeful experiences and ascribed those very names to their gods. Some gods were worshipped as goddesses of sex and fertility in honor of the fruitfulness in bearing both children and the harvest of the earth. Other gods were worshipped as the gods of war and storms.

On and on the list could go, but the point to see is the corruption of idolatry and false worship. For God warns us against engaging in false worship and idolatry, and His warning is severe:

"For the wrath of God is revealed from heaven against all ungodliness and unrighteousness of men, who hold the truth in unrighteousness; Because that which may be known of God is manifest in them; for God hath showed *it* unto them. For the invisible things of him from the creation of the world are clearly seen, being understood by the things that are made, *even* his eternal power and Godhead; so that they are without excuse: Because that, when they knew God, they glorified *him* not as God, neither were thankful; but became vain in their imaginations, and their foolish heart was darkened. Professing themselves to be wise, they became fools, And changed the glory of the uncorruptible God into an image made like to corruptible man, and to birds, and fourfooted beasts, and creeping things....Who knowing the judgment of God, that they which commit such things are worthy of death, not only do the same, but have pleasure in them that do them" (Ro.1:18-23, 32).

"Now the works of the flesh are manifest, which are *these;* Adultery, fornication, uncleanness, lasciviousness, Idolatry, witchcraft, hatred, variance, emulations, wrath, strife, seditions, heresies, Envyings, murders, drunkenness, revellings, and such like: of the which I tell you before, as I have also told *you* in time past, that they which do such things shall not inherit the kingdom of God" (Ga.5:19-21).

"But fornication, and all uncleanness, or covetousness, let it not be once named among you, as becometh saints; Neither filthiness, nor foolish talking, nor jesting, which are not convenient: but rather giving of thanks. For this ye know, that no whoremonger, nor unclean person, nor covetous man, who is an idolater, hath any inheritance in the kingdom of Christ and of God" (Ep.5:3-5).

"Little children, keep yourselves from idols. Amen" (1 Jn.5:21).

"But the fearful, and unbelieving, and the abominable, and murderers, and whoremongers, and sorcerers, and idolaters, and all liars, shall have their part in the lake which burneth with fire and brimstone: which is the second death" (Re.21:8).

"Thou shalt not make unto thee any graven image, or any likeness *of any thing* that *is* in heaven above, or that *is* in the earth beneath, or that *is* in the water under the earth" (Ex.20:4).

"Ye shall make you no idols nor graven image, neither rear you up a standing image, neither shall ye set up *any* image of stone in your land, to bow down unto it: for I *am* the LORD your God" (Le.26:1).

"Take heed to yourselves, that your heart be not deceived, and ye turn aside, and serve other gods, and worship them" (De.11:16).

"I *am* the LORD: that *is* my name: and my glory will I not give to another, neither my praise to graven images" (Is.42:8).

---

3 (31:11-13) **Ruler, Respect for—Ministers, Respect for—Anointed, the, Respect for—Leader, Respect for—Saul, Respect for—Jabesh-Gilead, Testimony of**: there was the respect by the people of Jabesh-Gilead for Saul, respect for *God's anointed ruler*. Right after Saul had been crowned king, his very first military campaign was to rescue the territory of Jabesh-Gilead from the Ammonites (11:1-11). Although that particular military action had happened forty years earlier, the people of Jabesh-Gilead had never forgotten what Saul had done for them. As soon as they heard about the abuse of Saul's body, they felt a deep sense of obligation to rescue it. Quickly organizing a squadron of courageous men, they sent them out on the extremely dangerous and difficult mission. Traveling some fifteen to twenty miles under the cover of darkness to Beth Shan, the squadron was able to recover the bodies of Saul and his sons without being detected. After returning to Jabesh-Gilead, they burned the smelly, decaying bodies that had been dead for days now. In honor of their king, God's anointed leader, they buried the bones of Saul and his sons at Jabesh under a tamarisk tree, and they then fasted for seven days.

OUTLINE	SCRIPTURE	SCRIPTURE	OUTLINE
3. The respect of Jabesh-Gilead for Saul: A lesson on respecting "God's anointed"	11 And when the inhabitants of Jabesh-gilead heard of that which the Philistines had done to Saul;	ies of his sons from the wall of Beth-shan, and came to Jabesh, and burnt them there.	2) Recovered the bodies of Saul & his sons & burned them
a. They heard about the abuse of Saul's body & rescued it	12 All the valiant men arose, and went all night, and took the body of Saul and the bod-	13 And they took their bones, and buried *them* under a tree at Jabesh, and fasted seven days.	b. They buried their bones at Jabesh
1) Sent a squadron out under the cover of darkness			c. They fasted for seven days

Thought 1. No leader ever deserved to be disrespected or dishonored any more than Saul. Given every opportunity possible to succeed, he failed and failed miserably. He became a jealous, angry man filled with so much hostility that he became mentally insane, extremely paranoid. Murdering anyone he could who stood in his way, even priests, he dedicated his life not to governing God's people but to destroying a young man whom God had appointed to succeed Saul as king. Despite knowing this fact and despite being loved and courageously supported by the young man David, Saul was fiercely determined to destroy him. And the intense pursuit continued for years.

Nevertheless, Saul was the appointed ruler, *God's anointed*. For that reason he was to be respected. And Jabesh-Gilead demonstrated this respect, setting a dynamic example for us. We must respect our leaders, no matter who they are. Even when a leader is wrong, we are to respect the office. Of course, we are not to indulge or give license to evil behavior and unjust decisions. But when we oppose, our opposition is to be carried out in righteousness and honor. The official position of *God's anointed* is always to be honored and respected.

"Let every soul be subject unto the higher powers. For there is no power but of God: the powers that be are ordained of God" (Ro.13:1).

"That ye submit yourselves unto such, and to every one that helpeth with *us*, and laboureth" (1 Co.16:16).

"Receive him therefore in the Lord with all gladness; and hold such in reputation" (Ph.2:29).

"And we beseech you, brethren, to know them which labour among you, and are over you in the Lord, and admonish you; And to esteem them very highly in love for their work's sake. *And* be at peace among yourselves" (1 Th.5:12-13).

"Let the elders that rule well be counted worthy of double honour, especially they who labour in the word and doctrine" (1 Ti.5:17).

"Put them in mind to be subject to principalities and powers, to obey magistrates, to be ready to every good work" (Tit.3:1).

"Remember them which have the rule over you, who have spoken unto you the word of God: whose faith follow, considering the end of *their* conversation" (He.13:7).

"Honour all *men*. Love the brotherhood. Fear God. Honour the king" (1 Pe.2:17).

"Likewise, ye younger, submit yourselves unto the elder. Yea, all *of you* be subject one to another, and be clothed with humility: for God resisteth the proud, and giveth grace to the humble" (1 Pe.5:5).

"Thou shalt not...curse the ruler of thy people" (Ex.22:28).

Thought 2. In closing this great book of *First Samuel*, Joyce D. Baldwin, an Old Testament scholar, says this:

> *In assessing the tragedy of King Saul, Christian writers have usually thought of him as a foil to David. Whereas Saul's life was a failure in terms of his calling to kingship, David succeeded in defeating Israel's enemies, in organizing the kingdom and in setting up a dynasty; in short, he became a model for future generations, who were taught to look for an ideal society led by another David [Christ]. Saul, by contrast, is a study in failure. But was this altogether his fault?...*
>
> *The evidence suggests that Saul had a brooding temperament, and was given to melancholy; it was easy for him to retreat from the limelight and become intensely jealous of a rival. But was his inherited temperament part of his "fate"? It was a potent factor in Saul's life; but the text indicates that Saul was responsible for his deliberate, stubborn refusal to admit when he had done wrong, and humble himself in repentance. This stubborn streak in Saul brought about a rift in relationship with Samuel, which left the king without the spiritual support he needed, and this increased his isolation, depression, and fits of mania. Saul calls forth our sympathy because his human frailty reminds us of our own, but his failure was not inevitable: he was responsible for his rejection of instructions from the one who had appointed him king, and he paid the penalty.*
>
> *Another aspect of Saul's experience is "the deterioration of charismatic gifts into madness," in which "we plumb to the depths of a human psyche."[2] We know that "the spirit of God came mightily upon him, and he prophesied" (1 Sa. 10:10), so fulfilling the prophecy of Samuel that he would "be turned into another man" (1 Sa. 10:6). This sign of divine equipment for his future task of ruling over the Lord's heritage stood for the strength on which he was to depend when he was in office, a strength far exceeding his own. But later, after the rift with David, when the Spirit of God came upon Saul he was thereby prevented from harming David. The gifts of the Spirit were not permitted to be used to oppose the work of God. It may be that here lies the key to the disintegration of Saul's powers that so characterized his last years...there can scarcely be a more dangerous plight than to be found in opposition to God. This was where Saul's disobedience landed him.[3]*

Thought 3. In closing his comments on the great book of *First Samuel*, Kenneth Chafin says this:

> *At this point it's impossible to make a balanced assessment of Saul and his reign. While at his death all looks bleak for the country, the people of God are moving slowly from their past tribal organization toward a united nation. The Second Book of Samuel is but a continuation of the story, and after pausing to interpret the death of Saul and Jonathan it moves on to continue the story of how God deals with people. The Book of 2 Samuel is one of my favorite books in the Old Testament because each of its stories sheds more light upon God's nature and His purpose and how He wants us to respond to His revelation. Sometimes these ancient events come alive with frightening application to our lives and our world today. David captures the stage completely in 2 Samuel and in his growth, his failures, and his triumphs we find our own journey of faith made richer.[4]*

Thought 4. Perhaps the best transition from *First Samuel* to *Second Samuel* is a statement made by the biblical writer himself:

> **"So Saul died for his transgression which he committed against the LORD, *even* against the word of the LORD, which he kept not, and also for asking *counsel* of *one that had* a familiar spirit, to enquire *of it;* And enquired not of the LORD: therefore he slew him, and turned the kingdom unto David the son of Jesse" (1 Chr.10:13-14).**

---

2 A point made, but not developed, by W. Lee Humphreys. *The Tragedy of King Saul: A Study of the Structure of 1 Samuel 9 – 31.* (Sheffield: JSOT Press 6, 1978), p.25.

3 Joyce G. Baldwin. *1 & 2 Samuel.* "The Tyndale Old Testament Commentaries." (Downers Grove, IL: Inter-Varsity Press, 1988), pp.172, 174-175.

4 Kenneth Chafin. *The Preacher's Commentary on 1, 2 Samuel.* (Nashville, TN: Word Publishing, 1989, 2003), p.234.

RESOURCES

MAP 1
THE MINISTRY OF SAMUEL
(1 SAMUEL 7:15-17)

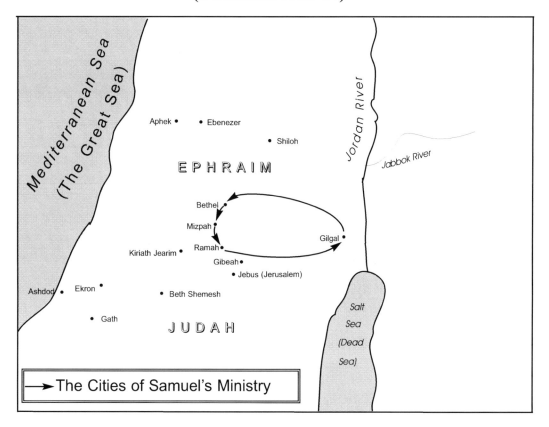

Mediterranean Sea (The Great Sea)

Aphek • • Ebenezer

• Shiloh

E P H R A I M

Jordan River

Jabbok River

Bethel •

Mizpah •

Kiriath Jearim • Ramah •

Gibeah •

• Jebus (Jerusalem)

Gilgal •

Ashdod • Ekron •

• Beth Shemesh

Salt Sea (Dead Sea)

• Gath

J U D A H

→ The Cities of Samuel's Ministry

MAP 2
SAUL'S MILITARY CAMPAIGNS

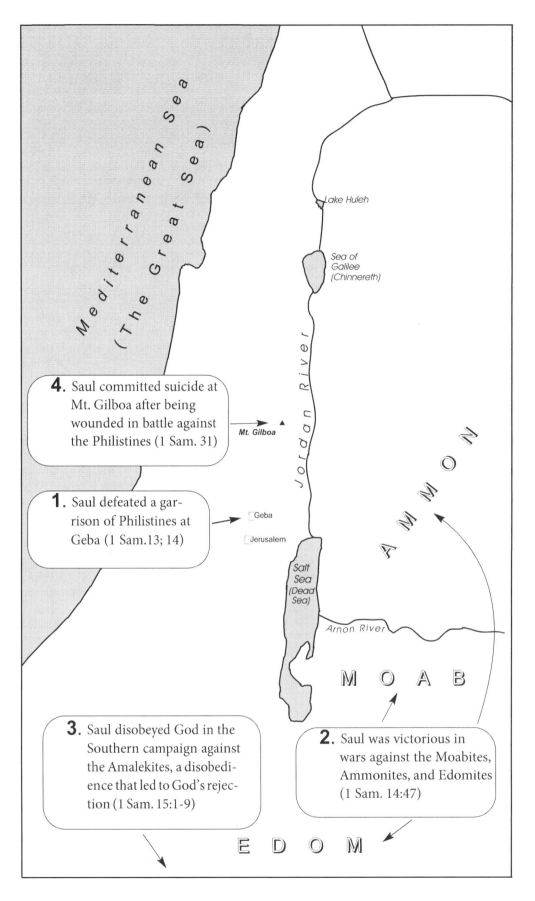

4. Saul committed suicide at Mt. Gilboa after being wounded in battle against the Philistines (1 Sam. 31)

Mt. Gilboa

1. Saul defeated a garrison of Philistines at Geba (1 Sam.13; 14)

Geba

Jerusalem

Mediterranean Sea (The Great Sea)

Lake Huleh

Sea of Galilee (Chinnereth)

Jordan River

AMMON

Salt Sea (Dead Sea)

Arnon River

M O A B

3. Saul disobeyed God in the Southern campaign against the Amalekites, a disobedience that led to God's rejection (1 Sam. 15:1-9)

2. Saul was victorious in wars against the Moabites, Ammonites, and Edomites (1 Sam. 14:47)

E D O M

---

1   The idea for this map was stirred by *Nelson's Complete Book of Bible Maps and Charts* © 1993 by Thomas Nelson, Inc., p.100.

MAP 3
DAVID'S FLIGHT FROM SAUL

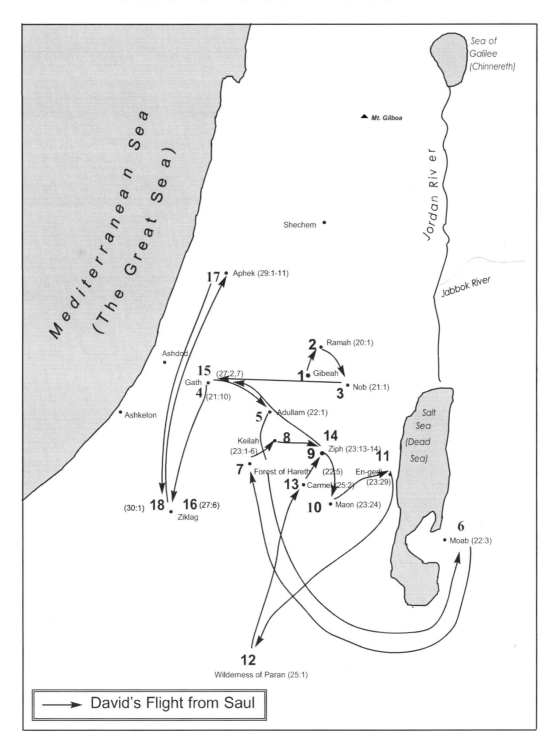

Sea of Galilee (Chinnereth)

Mediterranean Sea (The Great Sea)

▲ Mt. Gilboa

Jordan River

Jabbok River

Shechem •

17 • Aphek (29:1-11)

Ashdod •

2 Ramah (20:1) •

15 (27:2,7)
Gath •

1 • Gibeah

3 • Nob (21:1)

4 (21:10)

Ashkelon •

5 • Adullam (22:1)

Salt Sea (Dead Sea)

Keilah **8**
(23:1-6) **14**

9 • Ziph (23:13-14)

11

7 • Forest of Hareth (22:5) En-gedi (23:29)

13 • Carmel (25:2)

(30:1) **18** **16** (27:6)
Ziklag

10 • Maon (23:24)

6 • Moab (22:3)

12
Wilderness of Paran (25:1)

⟶ David's Flight from Saul

265

THE FAMILY LINE OF SAUL

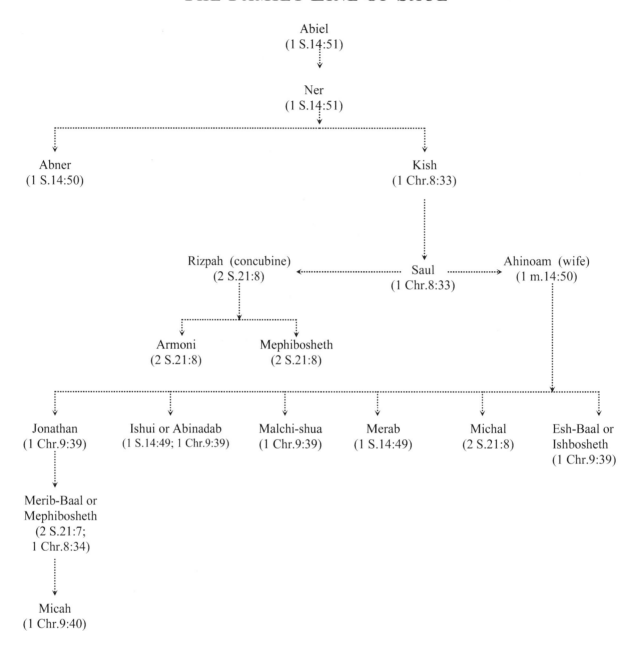

Abiel
(1 S.14:51)

Ner
(1 S.14:51)

Abner
(1 S.14:50)

Kish
(1 Chr.8:33)

Rizpah (concubine)
(2 S.21:8)

Saul
(1 Chr.8:33)

Ahinoam (wife)
(1 m.14:50)

Armoni
(2 S.21:8)

Mephibosheth
(2 S.21:8)

Jonathan
(1 Chr.9:39)

Ishui or Abinadab
(1 S.14:49; 1 Chr.9:39)

Malchi-shua
(1 Chr.9:39)

Merab
(1 S.14:49)

Michal
(2 S.21:8)

Esh-Baal or
Ishbosheth
(1 Chr.9:39)

Merib-Baal or
Mephibosheth
(2 S.21:7;
1 Chr.8:34)

Micah
(1 Chr.9:40)

Types, Symbols, and Pictures
The Book of 1 Samuel

What is a biblical type or symbol? Simply put, a *biblical type* is a *foreshadowing* of what was to come at a later time in history. Through a person, place or thing a biblical type points toward a New Testament fulfillment.

In addition to biblical types, there are what we may call *biblical pictures*. A biblical picture is a lesson that we can see in the Scriptures *without distorting the truth*. The study of biblical types and pictures is a valuable study in that it helps us apply the truth of the Scriptures in our lives. Scripture itself tells us this:

These things happened to them as examples and were written down as warnings for us, on whom the fulfillment of the ages has come (1 Co.10:11).
For everything that was written in the past was written to teach us, so that through endurance and the encouragement of the Scriptures we might have hope (Ro.15:4).

Alphabetical Outline

PERSON/PLACE/THING	SCRIPTURE, OUTLINE AND DISCUSSION
Anointing Oil: *A Symbol of Being Set Apart and Empowered by God's Spirit*	1 S.10:1-8
David Defeated the Amalekites: *A Picture of Christ's Setting the Captives Free*	1 S.11:1-15
David Dismissed by Achish: *A Picture of God's Working All Things Out for the Believer*	1 S.29:1-11
Samuel: *A Very Special Priest Seen in Prophecy*	1 S.2:35-36
Zadok: *A Very Special Priest Seen in Prophecy*	1 S.2:35-36; 2 S.8:17; 15:24

TYPES, SYMBOLS, AND PICTURES
THE BOOK OF 1 SAMUEL

What is a biblical type or symbol? Simply put, a *biblical type* is a "foreshadowing" of what was to come at a later time in history. Through a person, place or thing a biblical type points toward a New Testament fulfillment.

In addition to biblical types, there are what we may call *biblical pictures*. A biblical picture is a lesson that we can see in the Scriptures *without distorting the truth*. The study of biblical types and pictures is a valuable study in that it helps us apply the truth of the Scriptures in our lives. Scripture itself tells us this:

"Now all these things happened unto them for examples: and they are written for our admonition, upon whom the ends of the world are come" (1 Co.10:11).
"For whatsoever things were written aforetime were written for our learning, that we through patience and comfort of the scriptures might have hope" (Ro.15:4).

CHRONOLOGICAL OUTLINE

PERSON/PLACE/THING	SCRIPTURE, OUTLINE AND DISCUSSION
Samuel: *A Very Special Priest Seen in Prophecy*	(1 S.2:35-36)
Zadok: *A Very Special Priest Seen in Prophecy*	(1 S.2:35-36; 2 S.8:17; 15:24)
Anointing Oil: *A Symbol of Being Set Apart and Empowered by God's Spirit*	(1 S.10:1-8)
David Defeated the Amalekites: *A Picture of Christ Setting the Captives Free*	(1 S.11:1-15)
David Dismissed by Achish: *A Picture of God Working All Things Out for the Believer*	(1 S.29:1-11)

INDEX

REMEMBER: When you look up a subject and turn to the Scripture reference, you have not just the Scripture but also an outline and a discussion (commentary) of the Scripture and subject.

This is one of the GREAT FEATURES of *The Preacher's Outline & Sermon Bible®*. Once you have all the volumes, you will have not only what all other Bible indexes give you, that is, a list of all the subjects and their Scripture references, but in addition you will have...

- an outline of every Scripture and subject in the Bible
- a discussion (commentary) on every Scripture and subject
- every subject supported by other Scripture, already written out or cross referenced

DISCOVER THE UNIQUE VALUE for yourself. Quickly glance below to the first subject of the Index. It is:

ABIATHAR
Escaped execution. 22:20
Priest of Nob. 22:20
Son of Ahitub. 22:20

Turn to the first reference. Glance at the Scripture and the outline, then read the commentary. You will immediately see the TREMENDOUS BENEFIT of the INDEX of *The Preacher's Outline & Sermon Bible®*.

OUTLINE AND SUBJECT INDEX

ABIATHAR
Escaped execution. 22:20
Priest of Nob. 22:20
Son of Ahitub. 22:20

ABIGAIL
Character of. Wise, courageous, humble. 25:18-31
Described. 25:3
Wife. Of David. 25:42

ABNER
Bodyguard of Saul. 26:14-16
Failed in his duty. 26:14-16

ABUSE
Of position. Eli's sons a. their position for worldly gain. 2:12-17

ACCEPTANCE
Conditions of, requirements for. A person must turn away from sin to be accepted by God. 12:20-25

ACCESS
Duty. To seek a. with God just as He dictates. 6:13-21

ACCUSERS, FALSE
Example of. Eli falsely accused Hannah of drunkenness. 1:14

ACHISH
Harbored David. 21:10-13
King of the Philistines. 21:10
Sent David away, thinking him insane. 21:14-15

ADULLAM
Place of hiding. David hid from Saul. 22:1-2

ADVERSITY
Result of. Can drive a person to call out for help. 21:1-22:5

AHIMELECH
Helped David. A. gave David food & a sword. 21:1-9

High Priest of Israel. 21:1-9
Lived at Nob. 21:1
Murder of. By Doeg the Edomite. 22:11-19

AHINOAM
Wife of David. 25:43

AMALEKITES
Destruction – Judgment of. A nation under God's judgment. 15:1-35
Relation with Israel.
Invaded Israel. 30:1-8
Were defeated by Israel. 15:1-9
Were enemies. 15:1-9
Were preserved by Saul. 15:1-9

AMMONITES
Defeat of. 11:4-11
Nahash. King of the A. 11:1-3
Wars against Israel. 11:1-3

ANGER
Example of. Saul.
Had intense a. toward David. 26:1-4
Was angry with Ahimelech for helping David. 22:6-10
Justified. When against evil. 11:4-11, Thgt.1; 17:16-30
Result of. Descends into the depths of depravity. 26:1-4, Thgt.1
Righteous a. Example of. King Saul's anger burned against the Ammonites. 11:4-11

ANGUISH
Deliverance from. David. 22:1-2
Example of. Hannah was in deep anguish because she was persecuted. 1:3-8

ANOINTING
Example of. David. 16:6-13
Honor of. 24:1-22
Persons anointed. King Saul. 10:1-8
Private – Secret a.
David's a. was done secretly. 16:1-13
Saul's a. was done secretly. 10:1-8
Respect for. 31:11-13

Results. Holy Spirit empowers. 10:1-8, Thgt.1
Source of. The Lord. 10:1-8; 24:5-7
Symbol of.
God's choosing. 10:1-8
God's enabling power. 10:1-8, Thgt.1

APPEARANCE
Deceitful. 9:1-2
Outward.
Glorying in. 9:1-2
Judging by. 9:1-2
Pride in. 9:1-2

APPOINTMENT
To leadership. 9:15-17

APPROACH
Duty. To a. God through the substitute sacrifice. 6:15

ARK OF THE COVENANT
Captured by the Philistines.
A. recovered. 7:1-6
A. returned by the Philistines. 5:1–6:21
A. was captured in battle. 4:1-22
Aroused God to afflict the Philistines severely. 6:1-12
Aroused God to defeat the false god Dagon. 5:1-5
Location of. Shiloh. 7:1-6
Misuse of.
Believed to have magical powers. 4:3-11
Idolized. 4:3-11

ASHDOD
Ark of God taken there. 5:1
Capital city of Philistines. 5:1-2
Location of the temple of Dagon. 5:2

ASHTORETH
Fertility goddess. Female counterpart to Baal. 7:1-6
Worship of. By Canaanites. 7:1-6

ASSAULT
Caused by. Jealousy. 19:8-10

269

ASSOCIATIONS
Evil.
Example of. David. 29:1-2
Results of. Listed. 29:1-2, Thgt.1

ASSURANCE
Minister's duty.
Eli gave **a**. to Hannah. 1:17
Samuel gave **a**. to the people
12:20-25
Source of. God.
God gave **a**. to Hannah. 1:18
God gave **a**. to Samuel. 8:6-9

ASTROLOGY
Dangers of. 28:1-25

BAAL
Male fertility god. Paired with Ashto-
reth. 7:1-6
Name, Meaning of. Lord, master. 7:1-6

BARREN
Example of. Hannah. 1:2

BEAUTY
Example of. Abigail. 25:18-31

BELIAL
Meaning of. Corrupt, wicked. 2:12

BELIEVER(S)
Danger. Facing of. 13:15-23
Duty - Requirements.
Not to neglect. 26:14-16, Thgt.1
Repentance & true commitment.
7:1-6, Thgt.1
To answer God's call to serve. 3:3-
10, Thgt.1
To approach God.
In the prescribed manner. 6:13-21
With a substitute sacrifice. 6:15
To avoid carnality. 8:1-5, Thgt.1
To be faithful. 7:15-17
To be separate from the world.
18:20-30, Thgt.1
To desire God first. 8:1-5, Thgt.1
To do good for evil. 24:16-22,
Thgt.1
To encourage others. 23:16-18,
Thgt.1
To forgive. 15:32-35, Thgt.1
To meet needs. 3:1-4:1; 7:15-17,
Thgt.1; 25:2-17, Thgt.1
To parents. To care for when old
22:3-4
To support leaders. 11:12-15
Empowered. By the Holy Spirit. 16:6-
13, Thgt.1
Guidance of. By God. 22:5, Thgt.1
Persecuted. By unbelievers. Pictured
by the Ammonite siege. 11:1-3

BETHEL
Army post of Israel. 13:1-7

BETH-SHAN
Philistine city. 31:8-10
Religions in city.
Ashtoreth worshipped there. 31:8-10
Dagon worshipped there. 31:8-10
Saul & Jonathan's dead bodies dese-
crated there. 31:8-10

BETRAYAL
Example of. Ziphites betrayed David.
23:19-29; 26:1-4

BIGAMY
Example of.
A priest. 1:2
David had three wives. 25:42-44

BONDAGE
Spiritual. Deliverance from, through
prayer. 7:7-14; 30:1-31

BRIBE
Accepting of. By judges. 8:1-5

BROTHERLY LOVE
Counteracts. Jealousy & envy. 19:1-7,
Thgt.1
Duty. To encourage. 23:16-18
Example of. David & Jonathan. 19:1-
7; 20:9-23

CALL, OF GOD
Anointing for. Holy Spirit helps us to
carry out our call. 10:1-8, Thgt.1
Fleeing from. 10:17-27
Message of. 3:11-14
Need for. 3:1-2
Proof of.
Continuing fellowship with God.
3:21
LORD's presence & power. 3:19
Obedience. 4:1
Recognition of God's hand by peo-
ple. 3:20
Purpose of.
To fight, to go to war. Saul sum-
moned troops against Ammonites
with a graphic picture of injustice.
11:7
To lead to repent. Demanded by
God. 12:20-25
To meet needs. 3:1-4:1
To serve people. 3:3-10, Thgt.1;
9:15-17
Response to. Demands a positive re-
sponse. 3:3-10, Thgt.1

CALLOUSNESS
Spiritual. Example of. Saul. 14:16-23

CANAANITES
Destruction of. 15:3, D.S. #1

CAPTIVES
Set free. 30:16-20

CARNAL(ITY)
Example of. Elkanah followed culture
of the day. 1:2
Zeal. 14:24-46

CHARISMA
Dependence upon. 9:1-2

CHILDREN
Godly.
Contrasted with wickedness. 2:18-21
Example of. Samuel as a boy. 2:18-21
Wicked. Example of. The sons of Eli.
2:12-17

CHOSEN
Who the **c**. are. Leaders. 9:15-17,
Thgt.1

CHRIST (See **JESUS CHRIST**)

CIRCUMSTANCES
Bad **c**. Results of. 29:1-11

COMMITMENT
Duty. God's people must have a total
c. 7:1-6; 35-42
Evidence of.
Keeping the LORD's command-
ments. 1:1-28
Loving the LORD. 1:1-28
Obeying the LORD. 1:1-28
Observing the feasts. 1:3-8
Example of.
Elkanah showed a strong **c**. 1:3-8
Samuel showed a strong **c**. 2:18-21

COMPASSION
Example of. David. For family. 30:9-15

CONDONING
Of evil. Eli **c**. the evil behavior of his
sons. 4:12-18

CONFESS - CONFESSION
Duty. God's people must **c**. their sins.
7:1-6
Example. Saul. 15:22-25
Kinds of **c**.
False. Of Saul. 26:21-25
Weak & inadequate. Saul's **c**.
15:22-25

CONFIDENCE
Example of. David ran to the battle.
17:48

CONQUERING - CONQUEST
Assurance of. 17:1-58
Who or what must be **c**.
Enemies. 17:40-58
Envy. How to. 19:1-7; 20:24-34
Jealousy. How to. 19:1-7; 20:24-34

CONSPIRACY
Suspicion of. By Saul. 22:6-10

CONVERSION
Example of. Saul. Given a new heart.
10:1-8, 9-16

CORRUPTION
Seed of. Explained. 22:6-23

COURAGE
Example of.
Abigail. 25:18-31
David.
Had **c**. to fight Goliath. 17:16-30
Rescued Keilah. 23:1-6
Needed. By David. 17:16-30, Thgt.1;
23:1-6, Thgt.1

COVENANT
Of enemies. Between David & Saul.
David promised not to eliminate
Saul's family. 24:16-22

Motive, focus of. Seeking the world. Desired to be like the other nations. 8:1-22

Renewal - Revival. After the Ark was returned. 7:1-6

Victory.
Over Goliath. 17:1-58
Over the Ammonites. 11:4-11
Over the Philistines. 7:7-14

Weapons of. Unrefined. 13:19-21

JABESH-GILEAD
Siege of. By the Ammonites. 11:1-3
Testimony of. Burial place of Saul & Jonathan. 31:11-13

JEALOUSY
Conquering. How to c. 19:1-7; 20:24-34
Evil of. Saul had rages of j. 18:1-30
Example of.
David's brothers. J. of David. 17:16-30
Eli. J. of Samuel. 3:17
Saul. J. of David. 18:1-9
Problems caused by. Listed. 18:1-9, Thgt.1
Result of. J. causes lack of control, fear, rage, plotting, lies, deception. 18:10-30; 19:8-10, 11-17, 18-24

JESUS CHRIST
Approach to. Must a. through the sacrifice of Christ. 6:13-21, Thgt.1
Lordship. Universal. 2:35-36
Priesthood of.
Predicted. 2:35-36
Priest forever. 2:35-36
Types of. David. 30:16-20

JONATHAN
End of. Tragic. 31:1-13
Example. Of commitment. 20:35-42, Thgt.1
Friend. Of David.
Had an unbreakable relationship. 20:1-23
Helped David escape. 20:35-42
Loyalty of. To David. 23:16-18
Made a strong covenant. 18:1-9; 19:2
Man of faith. 14:6
Mighty warrior. 14:1-14
Son of Saul. 13:16; 14:1

JUDGES
Corrupt. Samuel's sons were corrupt j. 8:1-5
Era closed by Samuel. 1:1-7:17

JUDGMENT
By appearance. 9:1-2
Caused by.
Being devoted to the ban. 15:3, D.S. #1
Condoning sin. 3:13
Corruption. 4:3-11
Hardening of one's heart. 3:14
Idolatry. 4:3-11
Sinful behavior. 4:1-3, Thgt.1
Wickedness. 4:19-22
Worldliness. 8:10-18, Thgt.1
Duty. Must be taught by ministers. 3:11-14, Thgt.1
Example of. Nabal. 25:36-44
Fact. Day reserved for j. 2:10

How God judges. By reversing circumstances. 2:3-7
Of death & life. 2:6
Of the barren & the fruitful. 2:6
Of the full & the hungry. 2:5
Of the humble & the exalted. 2:7-8
Of the poor & the rich. 2:7-8
Of the strong & the weak. 2:4
Judicial j. of God. Discussed. 15:3, D.S. #1
Truth of. 5:1–6:21
Warning against. 12:12-15
Who is to be judged.
Every person. 4:1-22
False worshippers. 5:1–6:21
Liars. 27:8-12, Thgt.1
Murderers. 19:8-10, Thgt.1; 22:11-19, Thgt.1
Opposers of God. 5:6-12
Sinners. 15:26-29, Thgt.1
The angry. 22:6-10, Thgt.1
The cold-hearted. 25:36-44, Thgt.1
The disobedient. 15:26-29
The greedy. 25:36-44, Thgt.1
The harsh. 25:36-44, Thgt.1
The mean. 25:36-44, Thgt.1
The priesthood. Eli & his family were judged. 2:27-34; 3:11-14
The unrepentant. 31:1-13
The wicked. 2:9-10; 4:12-22
Unbelievers. 5:1–6:21; 5:6-12

JUSTICE
Demanded. By God. 30:21-31, Thgt.1
Example of. David divided spoils equally among all. 30:21-31
Executed. By God. Without partiality or favoritism. 15:3, D.S. #1, pt.4, Thgt.1
Perverted. By priests, ministers. 8:1-5

KEILAH, CITY OF
Attacked by Philistines. 23:1
Disloyal to David. 23:9-12
Saved by David. 23:1-6

KING(S)
Anointing of. Secretly.
Of David. 16:13
Of Saul. 10:1
Desire for. By Israel.
Demanded. 8:1-5
Desired a king "like all the nations" had. 12:1-25
Installation of. 10:17-27
Of Israel. Saul.
Disqualification of. 13:8-14
First king. 10:1
Reasons for the rule of a king. Three reasons. 8:1-22
Rights of. 8:10-18
Rule of. Prepared for the r. of the kings—by Samuel. 1:1-7:17

KISS
Of respect. Meaning. 10:1

LEADERS - LEADERSHIP
Character of. Good character needed. 8:1-5
Corrupt l. 8:1-22
Duty of.
To be an example. 12:1-5, Thgt.1
To listen to the people. 12:1-5
To serve. 9:15-17

Duty to.
To respect. 24:1-7, Thgt.1; 26:5-13
To support. 11:12-15
Need for. 3:1-2, Thgt.1; 8:1-22
Respect for. Example of. David toward Saul. 24:8-15; 31:11-13

LIES - LYING
Caused by. Jealousy. 18:17-19
Consequences of. Listed. 22:20-23, Thgt.1
Giving in to. David. 27:1-12
Results of. Injustice & murder. 22:20-23

LIFE
Kinds of.
Compromising l. 1:1-28
Immoral l. 1:1-28
Lawless l. 1:1-28
Permissive l. 1:1-28
Violent l. 1:1-28
Victorious living.
Example of. Samuel. 7:1-17
Yearning of mankind. 7:1-17

LOTS
Use of. To choose a king. 10:21

LOYALTY
Demands of. 20:9-23, 35-42
Duty. To be l. to friends. 20:1-24
Example of.
David. A dynamic example of l. 24:1-7
Jonathan & David. 20:1-42
Military troops. To Saul. 14:24-46

MAON
Hiding place of David. 23:24

MARRIAGE
Of David.
To Abigail. 25:42
To Ahinoam. 25:43
To Michal. 18:27

MEDIUM(S)
Spirit.
Reasons people seek. 28:1-6
Results of Seeking. 28:9-19

MESSAGE(S)
Of God's call. 3:11-14
Of Samuel.
At coronation of Saul. 12:1-25
First m. 3:11-14
Rejected. Meant rejecting God Himself. 8:6-9
Renewal. A twenty-year sermon. 7:1-6

MESSIAH
Meaning of. Anointed One. 2:10
Messiah is the promised seed. 2:10
Mission of. 2:10
Prophesied about. By Hannah. 2:8-10

MICHAL
Daughter of Saul. 18:20
Wife of David. 18:27

MICMASH
Army post of Israel. 13:1-7

INDEX

LEADERSHIP MINISTRIES WORLDWIDE

PURPOSE STATEMENT

LEADERSHIP MINISTRIES WORLDWIDE exists to equip ministers, teachers, and laypersons in their understanding, preaching, and teaching of God's Word by publishing and distributing worldwide *The Preacher's Outline & Sermon Bible®* and derivative works to reach & disciple all people for Jesus Christ.

MISSION STATEMENT

1. To make the Bible so understandable – its truth so clear and plain – that men and women everywhere, whether teacher or student, preacher or hearer, can grasp its message and receive Jesus Christ as Savior, and…

2. To place the Bible in the hands of all who will preach and teach God's Holy Word, verse by verse, precept by precept, regardless of the individual's ability to purchase it.

The Preacher's Outline & Sermon Bible and derivative works been given to LMW as LMW Resources for printing and distribution worldwide at/below cost, by those who remain anonymous. One fact, however, is as true today as it was in the time of Christ:

THE GOSPEL IS FREE, BUT THE COST OF TAKING IT IS NOT

LMW depends on the generous gifts of believers with a heart for Him and a love for the lost. They help pay for the printing, translating, and distributing of LMW Resources into the hands of God's servants worldwide, who will present the Gospel message with clarity, authority, and understanding beyond their own.

LMW was incorporated in the state of Tennessee in July 1992 and received IRS 501 (c)(3) non-profit status in March 1994. LMW is an international, nondenominational mission organization. All proceeds from USA sales, along with donations from donor partners, go directly to underwrite translation and distribution projects of LMW Resources to preachers, church and lay leaders, and Bible students around the world.

LMW Resources

This material, like similar works, has come from imperfect man and is thus susceptible to human error. We are nevertheless grateful to God for both calling us and empowering us through His Holy Spirit to undertake this task. Because of His goodness and grace, *The Preacher's Outline & Sermon Bible®* New Testament and the Old Testament volumes have been completed.

LMW Resources include *The Minister's Personal Handbook, The Believer's Personal Handbook,* and other helpful resources available in printed form as well as electronically on various digital platforms.

God has given the strength and stamina to bring us this far. Our confidence is that as we keep our eyes on Him and remain grounded in the undeniable truths of the Word, we will continue to produce other helpful resources for God's dear servants to use in their Bible study and discipleship.

We offer this material, first, to Him in whose name we labor and serve and for whose glory it has been produced and, second, to everyone everywhere who studies, preaches, and teaches the Word.

Our daily prayer is that each volume will lead thousands, millions, yes even billions, into a better understanding of the Holy Scriptures and a fuller knowledge of Jesus Christ the Incarnate Word, of whom the Scriptures so faithfully testify.

You will be pleased to know that Leadership Ministries Worldwide partners with Christian organizations, printers, and mission groups around the world to make LMW Resources available and affordable in many countries and foreign languages. It is our goal that *every* leader around the world, both clergy and lay, will be able to understand God's holy Word and present God's message with more clarity, authority, and understanding—all beyond his or her own power.

Leadership Ministries Worldwide
1928 Central Avenue • Chattanooga, TN 37408
1(800) 987-8790
Email: info@lmw.org
lmw.org

LEADERSHIP MINISTRIES WORLDWIDE

Product Listing

THE PREACHER'S OUTLINE & SERMON BIBLE® (POSB)

Available in KJV (44 vols) & NIV (40 vols)

OLD TESTAMENT

- Genesis I: Chs. 1–11
- Genesis II: Chs. 12–50
- Exodus I: Chs. 1–18
- Exodus II: Chs. 19–40
- Leviticus
- Numbers
- Deuteronomy
- Joshua
- Judges, Ruth
- 1 Samuel
- 2 Samuel
- 1 Kings
- 2 Kings
- 1 Chronicles
- 2 Chronicles
- Ezra, Nehemiah, Esther
- Job

- Psalms I: Chs. 1-41
- Psalms II: Chs. 42-106
- Psalms III: Chs. 107-150
- Proverbs
- Ecclesiastes, Song of Solomon
- Isaiah I: Chs. 1-35
- Isaiah II: Chs. 36-66
- Jeremiah I: Chs. 1-29
- Jeremiah II: Chs. 30-52, Lamentations
- Ezekiel
- Daniel, Hosea
  Joel, Amos, Obadiah, Jonah, Micah, Nahum
- Habakkuk, Zephaniah, Haggai, Zechariah, Malachi

NEW TESTAMENT

- Matthew I: Chs. 1–15
- Matthew II: Chs. 16–28
- Mark
- Luke
- John
- Acts
- Romans
- 1 & 2 Corinthians
- Galatians, Ephesians, Philippians, Colossians
- 1 & 2 Thessalonians, 1 & 2 Timothy, Titus, Philemon
- Hebrews, James
- 1 & 2 Peter, 1, 2, & 3 John, Jude
- Revelation
- Master Outline & Subject Index

Handbooks

- **What the Bible Says to the Believer** —
  The Believer's Personal Handbook
  11 Chapters. – Over 500 Subjects, 300 Promises, & 400 Verses Expounded - Gift leatherette or paperback options

- **What the Bible Says to the Minister** —
  The Minister's Personal Handbook
  12 Chapters. - 127 Subjects - 400 Verses Expounded - Gift leatherette or paperback options

- **What the Bible Says to the Business Leader**—The
  Business Leader's Personal Handbook
  12 Chapters – Over 100 topics plus hundreds of scriptural values for conducting business in a 21st-century world — Paperback

- **What the Bible Says About Series** —
  Various Subjects

everyWORD

Scripture, Outline, Commentary of the Gospels with ESV Scripture

- everyWORD: Matthew 1–16:12
- everyWORD: Matthew 16:13–28:20
- everyWORD: Mark
- everyWORD: Luke 1–13:21
- everyWORD: Luke 13:22–24:53
- everyWORD: John

- **The Teacher's Outline & Study Bible™** - Various New Testament Books
  Complete 30 - 45 minute lessons – with illustrations and discussion questions
- *Practical Illustrations — Companion to the POSB Arranged by topic and Scripture reference*
- *LMW Resources on various digital platforms Learn more on our website at lmw.org*
- *Contact for resources in other languages*

Contact Us

LEADERSHIP MINISTRIES WORLDWIDE
1928 Central Avenue • Chattanooga, TN 37408
1(800) 987-8790 • E-mail - info@lmw.org
Order online at lmw.org

Made in the USA
Columbia, SC
31 January 2025

52864676R00165